THE
CAMBRIDGE EDITION OF
THE WORKS OF
JOSEPH CONRAD

LAST ESSAYS

Frontispiece to the 1926 Dent edition of *Last Essays*:
facsimile of the last leaf of 'Legends'

THE CAMBRIDGE EDITION OF THE WORKS OF JOSEPH CONRAD

JOSEPH CONRAD

LAST ESSAYS

EDITED BY
Harold Ray Stevens and J. H. Stape

WITH THE ASSISTANCE OF
Mary Burgoyne and Alexandre Fachard

THE CONGO DIARY
CO-EDITED AND WITH EXPLANATORY NOTES BY
Owen Knowles and Harold Ray Stevens

CAMBRIDGE
UNIVERSITY PRESS

CAMBRIDGE
UNIVERSITY PRESS

University Printing House, Cambridge CB2 8BS, United Kingdom

One Liberty Plaza, 20th Floor, New York, NY 10006, USA

477 Williamstown Road, Port Melbourne, VIC 3207, Australia

314-321, 3rd Floor, Plot 3, Splendor Forum, Jasola District Centre, New Delhi - 110025, India

79 Anson Road, #06-04/06, Singapore 079906

Cambridge University Press is part of the University of Cambridge.

It furthers the University's mission by disseminating knowledge in the pursuit of education, learning and research at the highest international levels of excellence.

www.cambridge.org
Information on this title: www.cambridge.org/9780521190596

This, the Cambridge Edition text of *Last Essays*, the 'Up-river Book', 'Uncollected Essays' and 'Geography' now correctly established from the original sources and first published in 2010 © the Estate of Joseph Conrad 2010. Introduction, textual essay, apparatus, appendices, notes and glossary © Cambridge University Press 2010. Permission to reproduce these texts entire or in part, or to quote from them, or to reproduce the introduction, textual essay, apparatus, appendices, notes and glossary entire or in part should be requested from Cambridge University Press.

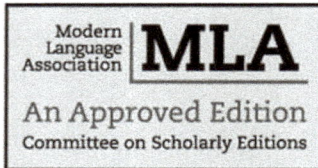

First published 2010

Modern Language Association **MLA**

An Approved Edition
Committee on Scholarly Editions

A catalogue record for this publication is available from the British Library

Library of Congress Cataloging in Publication data
Conrad, Joseph, 1857-1924.
Last essays / Joseph Conrad ; edited by Harold Ray Stevens and J. H. Stape with the assistance of Mary Burgoyne and Alexandre Fachard. The Congo diary / co-edited and with explanatory notes by Owen Knowles and Harold Ray Stevens.
p. cm. – (The Cambridge edition of the works of Joseph Conrad)
Includes bibliographical references.
ISBN 978-0-521-19059-6 (hardback)
I. Stevens, H. Ray (Harold Ray), 1936– II. Stape, J. H. (John Henry) III. Knowles, Owen.
IV. Conrad, Joseph, 1857-1924. Congo diary. V. Title.
PR6005.04L27 2010
824'.912 – dc22 2010031631

ISBN 978-0-521-19059-6 Hardback

Published in association with

THE CENTRE FOR JOSEPH CONRAD STUDIES
ST MARY'S UNIVERSITY COLLEGE
TWICKENHAM, LONDON

CENTER FOR CONRAD STUDIES
INSTITUTE FOR BIBLIOGRAPHY AND EDITING
KENT STATE UNIVERSITY

Preparation of this volume has been supported by

THE JOSEPH CONRAD SOCIETY (UK)

THE KENT STATE UNIVERSITY FOUNDATION

MCDANIEL COLLEGE, WESTMINSTER, MARYLAND

NATIONAL ENDOWMENT FOR THE HUMANITIES

RESEARCH AND GRADUATE STUDIES, KENT STATE UNIVERSITY

CONTENTS

ix

ILLUSTRATIONS

GENERAL EDITORS' PREFACE

JOSEPH CONRAD'S place in twentieth-century literature is now firmly established. Although his novels, stories and other writings have become integral to modern thought and culture, the need for an accurate and authoritative edition of his works remains. Owing to successive rounds of authorial revision, transmissional errors and deliberate editorial intervention, Conrad's texts exist in various unsatisfactory and sometimes even confused forms.

During the last years of his life he attempted to have his works published in a uniform edition that would fix and preserve them for posterity. But although trusted by scholars, students and the general reader alike, the received texts published in the British and American collected editions, and in various reprintings of them since 1921, have proved to be at least as defective as their predecessors. Grounded in thorough research in the surviving original documents, the Cambridge Edition is designed to reverse this trend by presenting Conrad's novels, stories and other prose in texts that are as trustworthy as modern scholarship can make them.

The present volume contains critical texts of Conrad's posthumously published volume *Last Essays*, compiled and edited by his friend Richard Curle acting as his literary executor. Curle's contents and arrangements are respected; however, Conrad's 'Up-river Book' has been added as an integral element of the volume. Also reprinted here are uncollected pieces by Conrad that Curle did not include in the volume he produced. The Cambridge texts of the essays are based on various copy-texts – the manuscripts, typescripts and early printings that have survived – and incorporate readings drawn from later authoritative documents as well as editorial emendations. The 'Appendices' reprint Curle's introductions to *Last Essays* and 'The Congo Diary', offer supplementary material for appreciating Conrad's letter on the loss of the *Dalgonar* and publish the following items for the first time: two rejected draft openings to the 'Preface to *The Shorter Tales of Joseph Conrad*'; a draft of Conrad's prefatory note to his essay on the

Torrens; draft material for 'Travel'; and 'Geography', the *Ur*-version of 'Geography and Some Explorers'.

The 'Introduction' provides a literary history of the work focussed on its genesis, sources and reception, including its place in Conrad's life and art. The essay on 'The Texts' traces the textual history of the volume, examines the origins of its individual texts and explains the policies followed in editing them. The 'Apparatus' records basic textual evidence, documenting the discussion of genealogy and authority in 'The Texts: An Essay' as well as other editorial decisions, and the 'Textual Notes' deal with cruxes and textual issues. The 'Explanatory Notes' comment on specific readings that require glosses, dealing with sources, identifying real-life place-names and related matters, as well as explaining nautical terms and foreign words and phrases. Supplementing this material are maps and illustrations.

Although they may interest the great variety of readers, the 'Introduction' and 'Explanatory Notes' are intended primarily for a nonspecialist audience, whereas the textual essay and 'Apparatus' are designed with the textual scholar and specialist in mind.

The support of the institutions listed on p. vii has been essential to the success of this series and is gratefully acknowledged. In addition to those, and the individuals and institutions listed in the 'Acknowledgements', the General Editors and the Editorial Board also wish to thank the Trustees and beneficiaries of the Estate of Joseph Conrad, Doubleday and Company and J. M. Dent and Company for permission to publish these new texts of Conrad's works.

THE GENERAL EDITORS

ACKNOWLEDGEMENTS

THANKS ARE DUE to the following institutions and individuals for facilitating access to manuscripts and unpublished materials: the Alderman Library, University of Virginia; the Baker Library, Dartmouth College and Phillip H. Cronenwett; the Beinecke Rare Book and Manuscript Library, Yale University; the Henry W. and Albert A. Berg Collection, and Philip Milito, Anne Garner and Isaac Gewirtz (Curator), and the Manuscripts Division, New York Public Library, Astor, Lenox and Tilden Foundations; Boston Public Library, Rare Books Department, and Kimberly Reynolds and Elizabeth Prindle; the British Library, Manuscripts Department; Bryn Mawr College; the Everett Needham Case Library, Colgate University and former curator Bruce M. Brown; the Fales Library and Special Collections, New York University; R. A. Gekoski, Bookseller; the Harry Ransom Center, University of Texas at Austin; the Houghton Library, Harvard University; the Huntington Library; the Lilly Library, Indiana University; the National Geographic Society Archives and Carolyn Clewell; Deborah Oppenheimer; the Pierpont Morgan Library; the Rosenbach Museum and Library, Philadelphia; Special Collections Library, Texas Tech University and Donald W. Rude; Mariuccia G. R. Sprenger; the Sterling Memorial Library, Yale University; and Andrea White.

Special thanks are due to the late S. W. Reid, former Chief Executive Editor of the Cambridge Edition of the Works of Joseph Conrad, under whose ægis this project began and whose encouragement, advice and wisdom were so unstintingly available to Conrad textual scholars for more than two decades; and to Robert W. Trogdon, Director of the Institute for Bibliography and Editing at Kent State University, whose advice and sharing of textual knowledge have been invaluable and who has also assisted with the on-site verification of the texts. We are also grateful to Nancy Birk, Raymond T. Brebach and Ruth Ann Stevens for on-site verifications. Thanks for assistance with support tasks are due to Catherine L. Tisch and, at an early stage of this project, to Gale Graham.

The editors are grateful to Laurence Davies and Allan H. Simmons, who made valuable suggestions on the 'Introduction' and 'Explanatory Notes' and otherwise helped to guide this edition towards completion; to Helen Baron and Paul Eggert for commenting on textual matters; to Captain Alston Kennerley, who kindly reviewed the 'Glossary of Nautical Terms'; and to Donald J. Shewan for his work on the maps. Thanks are also due to Stephen Donovan, who generously shared content for *Conrad First: The Joseph Conrad Periodical Archive* (www.conradfirst.net) prior to its public availability; to Anne Arnold, who shared the results of her work on the Société Anonyme Belge pour le Commerce du Haut-Congo in the Archives Æquatoria, Leuven, and to Honoré Vinck; and to James Lutzweiler and Peter L. Schillingsburg, who replied to calls for information.

Special gratitude is due to Owen Knowles, who unstintingly made available his knowledge of Conrad's African context. It is likewise a pleasure to acknowledge the advice and assistance of colleagues associated with the Cambridge Edition as well as others who have answered queries posed throughout the lengthy evolution of this project: the late Bruce Harkness, the late Hans van Marle, Gene M. Moore, Gerald Morgan, Zdzisław Najder, Donald W. Rude and Jean Szczypien. Lastly, at Cambridge University Press, we should like to acknowledge the help and cooperation of Linda Bree and Maartje Scheltens, and, for useful comments during copy-editing, Leigh Mueller.

We join with Mary Burgoyne, who gathered the materials for the uncollected essays and arranged for reproduction of the *Punch* cartoon, in duly thanking the following individuals: Amanda Corp, Head of the Issue Desk, the London Library; André Gailani, Picture Research and Permissions, Punch Limited; Marianne Hansen, Special Collections Librarian, Mariam Coffin Canaday Library, Bryn Mawr College; Mike Kelly, Curator of Books, Fales Library and Special Collections, New York University; Laurie Klein, Public Services Assistant, the Beinecke Rare Book and Manuscript Library, Yale University; and Aaron Zacks, Technology and Digital Services Intern, the Harry Ransom Center, University of Texas at Austin.

For assistance with research into maps and charts of the Congo Free State, Harold Ray Stevens is indebted to David McNeill of the Royal Geographic Society, to Mathilde Leduc-Grimaldi of the Royal Museum for Central Africa and to Habte M. Teclemariam of the Library of Congress, and, for searching the archives of the Ministry of Defence, London, for a still missing typescript, to the staff of R. H. Searle of the

Whitehall Library and to the Public Records Office (now the National Archives). Gratitude is also due to David W. Tutein for answering queries. He is grateful to Donald W. Rude and to Allan H. Simmons, the editors, respectively, of *Conradiana: A Journal of Joseph Conrad Studies* and *The Conradian: The Journal of the Joseph Conrad Society (UK)*; to Wiesław Krajka, general editor of the 'Conrad: Eastern and Western Perspectives' series; and to Robert Langenfeld, editor of *English Literature in Transition, 1880–1920*, for permission to use material that appeared in earlier versions of work adapted here. His gratitude is likewise expressed to Suzanne Paris of Greenwood Press for permission to adapt materials from his essay in *A Joseph Conrad Companion* (1999), edited by Leonard Orr and Ted Billy.

Harold Ray Stevens also wishes to express thanks to the office of the Dean of Academic Affairs of McDaniel College for a sabbatical leave and a travel grant for work on this edition. He is especially grateful to Ruth Ann Stevens, who not only has served as second reader and fellow-traveller in Conrad studies for four decades, but also for more than fifty years has provided support and encouragement in ways too numerous to record here.

J. H. Stape is indebted to the Harry Ransom Center, the University of Texas at Austin, for an Alfred A. and Blanche W. Knopf Fellowship during the 2008–9 award period.

For their support of the Edition we also wish to express gratitude to present and former administrators of Kent State University, including, in alphabetical order, Rudolph O. Buttlar, Carol A. Cartwright, Cheryl A. Casper, Ronald J. Corthell, Joseph H. Danks, Susanna G. Fein, Robert G. Frank, Paul L. Gaston, Alex Gildzen, Charlee Heimlich, Dean H. Keller, Lester A. Lefton, Sanford E. Marovitz, Timothy S. Moerland, Thomas D. Moore, Terry P. Roark, Michael Schwartz, F. S. Schwarzbach, Jeanne Somers, Carol M. Toncar and Eugene P. Wenninger. Acknowledgement of support goes to the staff of Kent State University's Libraries and Media Services, to Mark Weber and Cara L. Gilgenbach, and the Systems staff, including Thomas E. Klinger, Todd M. Ryan and Richard A. Wiggins.

The facsimiles and illustrations that precede the textual essay are reproduced by courtesy of the Beinecke Rare Book and Manuscript Library, Yale University; Punch Limited; the Rare Books Department, Boston Public Library; and the Houghton Library, Harvard University.

CHRONOLOGY

J OSEPH CONRAD'S life may be seen as having several distinct stages: in the Ukraine, in Russian exile and in Austrian Poland before his father's death (1857–69); in Austrian Poland and the south of France as the ward of his maternal uncle (1870–78); in the British merchant service, mainly as a junior officer sailing in the Far East and Australia (1878–early 1890s); after a transitional period (early 1890s), as a writer of critical esteem (1895–1914); as an acclaimed writer, although perhaps with his greatest work achieved (1914–24). After 1895 the history of his life is essentially the history of his works.

Publication dates given below are those of the English book editions, unless otherwise specified. Only the first serial appearance of essays is noted.

1857 December 3	Józef Teodor Konrad Korzeniowski (Nałęcz coat-of-arms) born in Berdyczów in the Ukraine, part of the Russian Empire, to Apollo Korzeniowski and Ewelina (or Ewa), née Bobrowska, Korzeniowska
1862 May	Apollo Korzeniowski, his wife and son forced into exile in Russia
1865 April	Ewa Korzeniowska dies of tuberculosis
1867	Conrad visits Odessa with his maternal uncle Tadeusz Bobrowski; perhaps his first view of the sea
1868	Korzeniowski permitted to leave Russia
1869 February	Korzeniowski and Conrad move to Cracow
May	Korzeniowski dies
1870	Conrad, ward of Bobrowski, begins study with tutor, Adam Pulman
1873 May	Visits Switzerland and northern Italy

xviii

1874 October	Takes position in Marseilles with Delestang et Fils, wholesalers and shippers
1875	Apprentice in *Mont-Blanc* (to Caribbean)
1876–7	In *Saint-Antoine* (to Caribbean)
1878 late February or early March	Attempts suicide
April	Leaves Marseilles in British steamer *Mavis* (Mediterranean waters)
June	Lands at Lowestoft, Suffolk; first time in England
July–September	Sails as ordinary seaman in *Skimmer of the Sea* (North Sea)
1878–80	In *Duke of Sutherland* (to Sydney), *Europa* (Mediterranean waters)
1880	Meets G. F. W. Hope and Adolf Krieger
June	Passes examination for second mate
1880–81	Third mate in *Loch Etive* (to Sydney)
1881–4	Second mate in *Palestine, Riversdale, Narcissus* (Eastern seas)
1884 December	Passes examination for first mate
1885–6	Second mate in *Tilkhurst* (to Singapore and India)
1886	Submits 'The Black Mate', perhaps his first story, to *Tit-Bits* competition
August	Becomes a British subject
November	Passes examination for master and receives 'Certificate of Competency'
1886–7	Second mate in *Falconhurst* (British waters)
1887–8	First mate in *Highland Forest, Vidar* (Eastern seas)
1888–9	Captain of barque *Otago* (Bangkok to Australia and Mauritius)
1889 autumn	Begins *Almayer's Folly* in London
1890 February–April	In Poland for first time since 1874
May–December	In the Congo. Second-in-command, then temporarily captain, of *Roi des Belges*
June 13	Arrives at Matadi. Begins 'The Congo Diary'
August 3	Leaves Kinshasa in *Roi des Belges*. Begins 'Up-river Book'

1891	Manages warehouse of Barr, Moering in London
1891–3	First mate in *Torrens* (London and Plymouth to Adelaide)
1893	Meets John Galsworthy and Edward L. ('Ted') Sanderson (passengers on *Torrens*)
autumn	Visits Bobrowski in the Ukraine
November	Signs on as second mate in *Adowa*, which sails only to Rouen and back
1894 January	Signs off *Adowa*, ending his career as a seaman
February	Bobrowski dies. Meets Edward Garnett and Jessie George
1895 April	*Almayer's Folly*
1896 March	*An Outcast of the Islands*. Marries Jessie George
September	Settles in Stanford-le-Hope, Essex, after six-month honeymoon in Brittany
1897	Begins friendship with R. B. Cunninghame Graham; meets Henry James and Stephen Crane
December	*The Nigger of the 'Narcissus'*
1898	Meets Ford Madox (Hueffer) Ford and H. G. Wells
January	Alfred Borys Leo Conrad born
April	*Tales of Unrest*
October	Moves to Pent Farm, Postling, near Hythe, Kent, sub-let from Ford
1899 February–April	'The Heart of Darkness' in thousandth number of *Blackwood's Edinburgh Magazine*
1900 September	Begins association with literary agent J. B. Pinker
October	*Lord Jim*
1901 June	*The Inheritors* (with Ford)
1902 November	*Youth: A Narrative and Two Other Stories*
1903 April	*Typhoon and Other Stories*
October	*Romance* (with Ford)
1904 March	Writes 'A Glance at Two Books' (published August 1925)
October	*Nostromo*

1905 June	*One Day More* staged in London
1906 March	'A Middle Class Family' (later 'John Galsworthy') in *Outlook*
August	John Alexander Conrad born
October	*The Mirror of the Sea*
1907 January	Writes 'Cookery', preface to *A Handbook of Cookery for a Small House* by Jessie Conrad (published as a pamphlet September 1921)
September	*The Secret Agent.* Moves to Someries, Luton, Bedfordshire
1908 August	*A Set of Six*
1909	Moves to Aldington, Kent
September	'The Silence of the Sea' in *Daily Mail*
1910	Moves to Capel House, Orlestone, Kent
1911 October	*Under Western Eyes*
1912 January	*Some Reminiscences* (as *A Personal Record* in America)
October	*'Twixt Land and Sea*
November	'The Future of Constantinople' in *The Times.* Writes comment responding to criticism. Begins friendship with Richard Curle
1913 September	*Chance*, with 'main' publication date of January 1914
1914 July–November	Visits Austrian Poland with family; delayed by outbreak of First World War; returns via Vienna and Genoa
1915 February	*Within the Tides*
September	*Victory*
1916 September–November	Observes First World War naval activity aboard Q-ship *Ready*; writes 'Admiralty Paper' (later 'The Unlighted Coast')
1917 March	*The Shadow-Line*
1919 March	Moves to Spring Grove, near Wye, Kent. Dramatic version of *Victory* opens in London
August	*The Arrow of Gold*
October	Moves to Oswalds, Bishopsbourne, near Canterbury, Kent

1920 May	Writes on 'Gaspar Ruiz' for Dent's school edition *Youth and Gaspar Ruiz*
June	*The Rescue*
July	Writes 'Memorandum' on Liverpool training-ship
1921 January	'Introductory Note to *A Hugh Walpole Anthology*' requested by Hugh Walpole
January–April	Visits Corsica. Collected editions begin publication in England (Heinemann) and in America (Doubleday)
February	*Notes on Life and Letters*
July	'Heroes of the Straits' (later 'The Dover Patrol') in *The Times*
October	Writes foreword to *Landscapes of Corsica and Ireland* by A. S. Kinkead
December	'The Loss of the *Dalgonar*' in *London Mercury*
1922 July–August	Writes preface (later 'Travel') to Richard Curle's *Into the East: Notes on Burma and Malaya* (published March 1923)
October	Preface to *A Handbook of Cookery for a Small House* by Jessie Conrad opens serialization of extracts from her book in *Woman's Pictorial Magazine*
November	*The Secret Agent* staged in London
December	'Notices to Mariners' (later 'Outside Literature') in *Manchester Guardian*
1923 February	*A Handbook of Cookery for a Small House* by Jessie Conrad with preface by Conrad
March	Writes introduction to Thomas Beer's *Stephen Crane: A Study in American Letters*
May	'My Hotel in Mid-Atlantic' (later 'Ocean Travel') in *Evening News*
May–June	Visits America, guest of F. N. Doubleday
October	'The *Torrens*: A Personal Tribute' in *Blue Peter*. Writes 'His War-book', introduction to Stephen Crane's *The Red Badge of Courage* (March 1925)
November	Foreword to *Britain's Life-boats: The Story of a Century of Heroic Service* by A. J. Dawson

December	*The Rover.* 'Christmas-day at Sea' in *Daily Mail*
1924 February	'The Romance of Travel' (later 'Geography and Some Explorers') in *Countries of the World.* Begins 'Preface to *The Shorter Tales of Joseph Conrad*'
May	Declines knighthood
August 3	Dies at Oswalds. Roman Catholic funeral and burial, Canterbury
August 15	'Legends' in *Daily Mail*
September	*The Nature of a Crime* (with Ford)
October	*The Shorter Tales of Joseph Conrad* (30 October in America)
1925 January	*Tales of Hearsay*
August	'The Enterprise of Writing a Book' (later 'A Glance at Two Books') in *T. P.'s & Cassell's Weekly.* 'The Unlighted Coast' in *The Times*
September	*Suspense* (unfinished)
October	'The Congo Diary' in *Blue Peter*
October 3–9	Curle drafts introduction to *Last Essays* on the *Mauretania*, on voyage to New York
October 9	Curle arrives in New York City to discuss volume with Doubleday; during trip consults 'The Congo Diary' at Harvard University
November 3	Curle returns to England; preparations of book typescript and attending to proofs occur over next few months
1926 February 12	Dent's receive first print order of *Last Essays*
March 3	*Last Essays* published in England (26 March in America)
1928 June	*The Sisters*

ABBREVIATIONS AND NOTE ON EDITIONS

ABBREVIATIONS

[London is the place of publication unless otherwise specified.]

Bibliography	William R. Cagle and Robert W. Trogdon, 'A Bibliography of Joseph Conrad'. Typescript, unpublished
CDP	*Congo Diary and Other Uncollected Pieces*, ed. Zdzisław Najder. Garden City, NY: Doubleday, 1978
Chronology	Owen Knowles, *A Conrad Chronology*. Macmillan, 1989
CWW	Norman Sherry, *Conrad's Western World*. Cambridge University Press, 1971
Documents	*Conrad between the Lines: Documents in a Life*, ed. Gene M. Moore, Allan H. Simmons and J. H. Stape. Amsterdam: Rodopi, 2000
Knowles and Stape	Owen Knowles and J. H. Stape, 'Conrad, Galsworthy's "The Doldrums", and the *Torrens*'. *The Conradian*, 34, no. 1 (2009), 38–57
Letters	*The Collected Letters of Joseph Conrad*. General Editors Frederick R. Karl and Laurence Davies, with Owen Knowles, Gene M. Moore and J. H. Stape. 9 vols. Cambridge University Press, 1983–2007
Miłobędzki	Józef Miłobędzki, ed. 'Joseph Conrad's Congo Diary', *Nautologia* (Gydinia), 7, no. 1 (1972), 7–53
Najder	Zdzisław Najder, *Joseph Conrad: A Chronicle*. New Brunswick, NJ: Rutgers University Press, 1983

Portrait in Letters	*A Portrait in Letters: Correspondence to and about Conrad*, ed. J. H. Stape and Owen Knowles. Amsterdam: Rodopi, 1996
Register	Gene M. Moore, comp. 'A Descriptive Location Register of Joseph Conrad's Literary Manuscripts'. *The Conradian*, 27, no. 2 (2002), 1–93

LOCATIONS OF UNPUBLISHED DOCUMENTS

Berg	Berg Collection, New York Public Library, Astor, Lenox and Tilden Foundations
BL	British Library
Bodleian	Bodleian Library, Oxford University
Boston	Boston Public Library
Bryn Mawr	Mariam Coffin Canaday Library, Bryn Mawr College, Bryn Mawr, Pennsylvania
Colgate	Everett Needham Case Library, Colgate University, Hamilton, New York
Dartmouth	Baker Library, Dartmouth College, Hanover, New Hampshire
Harvard	Houghton Library, Harvard University, Cambridge, Massachusetts
HRC	Harry Ransom Center, University of Texas at Austin
Indiana	Lilly Library, Indiana University, Bloomington
Morgan	Pierpont Morgan Library, New York
National Archives	National Archives of the United Kingdom
NGS	Archives of the National Geographic Society, Washington, DC
NYU	Fales Library and Special Collections, New York University, New York
Rosenbach	Rosenbach Museum and Library, Philadelphia
TTU	Special Collections Library, Texas Tech University, Lubbock
Virginia	Alderman Library, University of Virginia, Charlottesville

Yale	Beinecke Rare Book and Manuscript Library, Yale University, New Haven, Connecticut
Yale-S	Sterling Memorial Library, Yale University

NOTE ON EDITIONS

REFERENCES TO Conrad's works are to the Cambridge Edition of the Works of Joseph Conrad where these have been published. Otherwise, references are, for the sake of convenience, to Dent's Collected Edition, 1946–55, whose pagination is identical with that of the various 'editions' published by Doubleday throughout the 1920s. References to the Cambridge Edition take the following form: title (year of publication), whereas publication dates are not provided for citations from Dent's Collected Edition.

Citations from critical and other works are to author, title and date of publication.

INTRODUCTION

PUBLISHED IN March 1926, less than two years after Conrad's death, *Last Essays* is both an unlikely and rather predictable posthumous volume. Its unlikelihood stems from its heterogeneity and scope: it brings together pieces written during the last thirty-four of Joseph Conrad's sixty-six years, encompassing facets of his literary and maritime careers as well as his personal life. The book's functional title and arrangement are the work of a close friend, the journalist Richard Curle, his literary executor. An act of homage to a writer of preeminent significance, it was also published to benefit the writer's widow and sons, taking advantage of the fame and genuine popularity Conrad had achieved by the end of his life.

The 'essays' – a title of convenience for a medley of genres including reviews, diaries, introductions to books and reminiscences – range from an abridged version of a notebook that records events during and observations about Conrad's life-transforming experience in the Congo Free State in 1890 to 'Legends', an essay left unfinished on his desk when he died near Canterbury on 3 August 1924.[1] The earliest piece, 'The Congo Diary', pencilled into one of two notebooks that record Conrad's initiation into life along the Congo river, provides the raw material for understanding why he rejected colonial exploitation while participating in it, a stance that would lead him to write 'An Outpost of Progress' and 'Heart of Darkness'. In 'Legends', a fragment that ends (and closes Conrad's career) with the word 'yarn', he was exploring ways in which memory, personal interests and the passage of time can transform the facts of life into legend, a theme present in critical reactions to his work: 'The facts of a legend need not be literally true. But they ought to be credible and they must be in a sort of fundamental accord with the nature of the life it records that is with the character of its subject-matter.'[2]

---

[1] For details of the writing, revision and original printing of the texts collected in this volume, as well as for a history of its production and publication, see 'The Texts', pp. 189–272.

[2] See pp. 36.5–9. Subsequent references to the texts of this edition appear in round brackets.

Last Essays illustrates the range of Conrad's thought on diverse topics, and its 'subject-matter' is almost bewilderingly diverse, yet, like *Notes on Life and Letters* (1921), which Conrad himself saw into print, it serves, as it were, as an instalment in autobiography, showing the wide range of the writer's interests. These include the transition from militant geographers in ships under sail to merchant seamen in steamships; the rigging of sailing ships and attention to the technical aspects of international travel and to the training of merchant seamen; reminiscences of experiences both on land and at sea; the human element in travel and the progress of the *Roi des Belges* up the Congo river. The First World War, which continued to dominate the life of England long after 1918, is also inevitably present in this volume, in Conrad's first-hand observations of the exploits of men aboard the Q-ship *HMS Ready*. He also pays tribute to the men of the Cinque Ports and to the heroism of the Dover Patrol, which kept enemy forces off the coast.

The volume includes literary criticism: introductions to works by Curle and Stephen Crane and reviews of books by John Galsworthy and W. H. Hudson. Its diversity ranges from the domestic subject of cookery to advice about the future of Constantinople and control of the Dardanelles and the Bosporus Straits. Across the volume are insights into the human condition, most particularly perhaps in the threadbare observations about his experience in the Congo Free State, where he witnessed the ivory trade, slavery and exploitation, 'horrors' that altered his view of life and later turned into fiction. Unsurprisingly for a writer whose canon includes a trio of political novels (*Nostromo*, *The Secret Agent*, *Under Western Eyes*) Conrad also meditates on geopolitics, concentrating on the force that shaped his early life – Russian hegemony over Central and Eastern Europe – and on the Eastern Question that had bedevilled European affairs from before his birth.

Complementing excursions into impressionism and experiments with irony and point of view, the essays illustrate Conrad's wide narrative range, from the functional prose of 'The Congo Diary', the 'Up-river Book' and the 'Memorandum' to a record of his thoughts on the need to differentiate between æsthetic and utilitarian writing in 'Outside Literature'. These forays are balanced by an attempt to discuss the manipulation of fact in the shaping of reputations and biography in 'Legends' and an unsuccessful struggle to combine the two in 'The Unlighted Coast'.

ORIGINS

LAST ESSAYS brings together the nine essays Conrad wrote after the publication of *Notes on Life and Letters* (1921);[1] six that Curle arranged to have published separately with Jessie Conrad's concurrence after her husband's death;[2] one that Conrad overlooked when compiling the previous volume; one ('Cookery') written originally in 1907 as the 'Preface to Jessie Conrad's *A Handbook of Cookery for a Small House*', but which was not published until 1921; and two pieces printed for the first time (the 'Memorandum' and the second part of 'The Future of Constantinople'). The forgotten essay, 'John Galsworthy: An Appreciation' (1906), was a matter of embarrassment to the writer. A similar fate might have befallen 'The Future of Constantinople', a letter to *The Times* of November 1912, with a previously unpublished draft of a second document responding to criticism of, and elaborating upon, comments in the letter.

Richard Henry Parnell Curle (1883–1968), a journalist whom Conrad had met in 1912, had been instrumental in tracking down Conrad's scattered writings for *Notes on Life and Letters*,[3] and was the logical person in the writer's circle to deal with his literary remains, also seeing into print *Suspense* (1925), a novel left unfinished on Conrad's death.[4] Curle's energies extended to abridging 'The Congo Diary', but he omitted the 'Up-river Book', the second of Conrad's surviving documents from the Congo.[5] Despite its title and apparent completeness, the collection neither is exhaustive nor gathers every piece of writing by Conrad then uncollected. Curle's task in assembling the material was formidable, because preliminary discussions with Conrad about an additional volume similar to *Notes on Life and Letters* were general at best. Curle recalls Conrad's wish to publish a 'pendent volume' to *The Mirror of the Sea* that would include 'Legends', 'The Torrens', 'Christmas-day at Sea', 'Ocean Travel', 'Outside Literature' and,

---

[1] That is, 'Geography and Some Explorers', 'The *Torrens*: A Personal Tribute', 'Christmas-day at Sea', 'Ocean Travel', 'Outside Literature', 'The Dover Patrol', 'The Loss of the *Dalgonar*', 'Travel' and 'Stephen Crane'.

[2] These include 'Legends', 'The Unlighted Coast', 'His War-book', 'A Glance at Two Books', 'Preface to *The Shorter Tales of Joseph Conrad*' and 'The Congo Diary'.

[3] On Curle's involvement in that volume, see *Notes on Life and Letters*, ed. J. H. Stape (2004), pp. xxxvi–xxxviii, 213.

[4] The task of collecting his letters fell to Jean Aubry (who wrote under the pen name G. Jean-Aubry), a French friend also engaged in overseeing the translation of Conrad's work into French, a project he had taken over from André Gide.

[5] First published in 1972 (Miłobędzki) 'Up-river Book' was reprinted in *CDP*, pp. 17–38.

so Curle says, part of 'Geography and Some Explorers'.[1] That volume would have emphasized the men Conrad had sailed with rather than the sea itself, extending his desire to be remembered as more than simply a spinner of sea-tales, a concern expressed as late as the spring of 1924 in his 'Preface' to *The Shorter Tales of Joseph Conrad*: 'As a matter of fact I have written of the sea very little if the pages were counted. It has been the scene but very seldom the aim of my endeavour ... I aimed at an element as restless, as dangerous, as changeable as the sea, and even more vast:– the unappeasable ocean of human life' (109.26–32). Seventeen months before his death, he requested that his agent obtain permission from the owner of the copyright of 'Stephen Crane' to include it in 'a posthumous vol: of coll[ect]^{ed} pieces', a '"suite" to the Personal Record, which I have had long in my mind'.[2] Conrad thus anticipated that a final volume of reminiscences, memoirs and essays would complement *The Mirror of the Sea* and *A Personal Record*. The volume that emerged, however, is much closer to *Notes on Life and Letters* in both subject matter and form.

Curle acknowledged, in his Introduction to the volume he edited as well as in a letter to Conrad's literary agent, Eric S. Pinker, that 'additional matter' might be collected for a later printing of *Last Essays* because it did not, in fact, include all of Conrad's uncollected writings.[3] Curle chose not to print everything 'to avoid any aspect of absolute completeness, as though a dead author's desk had been ransacked for every fragment', and asserted that 'Nothing has been printed merely for the purpose of adding to the bulk' (362). Most of the essays chosen were selected from his personal library;[4] those not readily available to him, such as the text of the 'Memorandum' written for Lawrence Holt, he ferreted out. Despite his efforts, at least one piece seems to have been overlooked. Had Curle known of – or remembered – 'The Silence of the Sea', published in the *Daily Mail* on 18 September 1909, he would almost certainly have included it. The essay refers to 'Overdue and Missing' (collected in *The Mirror of the Sea*), and complements other writings that demonstrate Conrad's interest in lost and missing ships, such as those on the *Titanic* disaster (collected in *Notes on Life and Letters*), and it discusses disasters at sea as do 'The

[1] Curle's 'Introduction' (Appendix A).
[2] Conrad to Eric S. Pinker, 21 March 1923 (*Letters*, VIII, 58–9).
[3] Richard Curle to Pinker, 15 June 1926 (Berg).
[4] Note on the fly-leaf of George T. Keating's copy of *Last Essays* (Yale).

Loss of the *Dalgonar* and the 'Memorandum'. Curle also omitted the 'Foreword' to Alec John Dawson's *Britain's Life-boats* (1923) which, like 'The Dover Patrol' and 'The Unlighted Coast', commemorates the war-time service of seamen in the English Channel and North Sea. Other omitted items show the diversity of Conrad's interests and bear witness to friendships: the 'Foreword' to Alice S. Kinkead's *Landscapes of Corsica and Ireland* (1921), and the 'Introductory Note to *A Hugh Walpole Anthology*' (1921). Finally, Curle omitted the 'Author's Note to *Youth and Gaspar Ruiz*' (1920), which complements Conrad's prefaces to his collected edition.[1]

WRITING TO THE MARKET

CONRAD'S OCCASIONAL ESSAYS were well suited to a reading public that by the latter part of the nineteenth century had both expanded and become increasingly diverse.[2] Writers of fiction variously took advantage of this shift, diversifying their output to suit demand. Once he had established himself as an author with *Almayer's Folly* and *An Outcast of the Islands*, and with his contacts in literary London made, Conrad could count on literary journalism to increase his income. He none the less expressed an ambivalent attitude to writing articles for serial publication, remarking to his friend Edward Sanderson in 1898 that the 'degradation of daily journalism has been spared to me so far' (*Letters*, II, 34).[3] Despite such disdain, Conrad was not reluctant to turn out occasional prose, although he did so mainly when commissioned, and, by his late career, as a recourse for meeting immediate financial needs. For example, in 1918 he wrote three

---

[1] In 1978, *CDP* brought these pieces together, with a more comprehensive transcription of 'The Congo Diary' than Curle's and a transcription of 'Up-river Book' and various additional essays. Critical texts of the essays mentioned are offered in the present volume, following 'Up-river Book'.

[2] For authoritative discussions of this topic, see John Gross, *The Rise and Fall of the Man of Letters: Aspects of English Literary Life since 1800* (1969), pp. 199–232, and David Vincent, *Literacy and Popular Culture: England 1750–1914* (1989).

[3] For a comprehensive discussion of Conrad's attitudes towards publishing occasional work and his evolution as a profitable essayist, see 'Introduction', *Notes on Life and Letters* (2004), pp. xxvi–xxxii. Cedric Watts's *Joseph Conrad: A Literary Life* (1989) discusses Conrad's financial matters within the context of the early twentieth-century marketplace; see also his 'Marketing Modernism: How Conrad Prospered', *Modernist Writers and the Marketplace*, ed. Ian R. Willison, Warwick Gould and Warren Chernaik (1996), pp. 81–8.

articles on the British Merchant Service to pay for his wife's hospital bills,[1] and, before travelling to America in the spring of 1923, he proposed writing three pieces to pay for his travel expenses.[2]

Conrad routinely complained to his literary agent about his financial situation, but considering that the average annual income for an English family in 1924 was £210,[3] he was well paid for essays published in newspapers and periodicals: he received £400 for 'Stephen Crane', £50 for 'Ocean Travel', £60 for 'Christmas-day at Sea' and another $500 for its reprinting in America. By 1916 he was financially secure, earning more than £10,000 in a single year.[4] His income from writing allowed him to live quite comfortably, and *The Times* reported the value of his estate on his death at £20,045.[5] Realizing that the end of his productive life was approaching, Conrad worked under increasing, if self-imposed, pressure from about 1920 onwards to complete *The Rover* and *Suspense*, to guide Mrs Conrad's *A Handbook of Cookery for a Small House* through press and to write the preface and organize the contents of *The Shorter Tales*.[6]

The occasional pieces he wrote after the publication of *Notes on Life and Letters* were mainly by request – a pattern long established – or in response to events reported in the press. The origins are quite varied. Thomas Beer, an American journalist and short-story writer, commissioned the introduction to his biography of Stephen Crane, and Heinemann accepted 'His War-book' for an edition of Crane's *Red Badge of Courage*. Curle solicited 'Travel' as the introduction to *Into the East*; Conrad's friend and owner of *The Times*, Lord Northcliffe, asked for 'The Dover Patrol'; and the ship-builder Lawrence Durning Holt requested the 'Memorandum' for his scheme of establishing a training-ship. Curle encouraged Conrad to write reminiscences of his experience in the *Torrens*, and Curle's friend, the publisher J. A. Hammerton, commissioned 'Geography and Some Explorers' for *Countries of the World*. David Bone, a friend, and captain of the *Tuscania* on which Conrad sailed to America, suggested that he write 'Notices to Mariners' (later 'Outside Literature'). Finally, the Admiralty had

---

[1] *Notes on Life and Letters* (2004), p. xxxi.
[2] Conrad to Eric S. Pinker, 9 April 1923 (*Letters*, VIII, 74).
[3] *Notes on Life and Letters* (2004), p. xxxii.
[4] Richard Curle, *The Last Twelve Years of Joseph Conrad* (1928), p. 136.
[5] J. H. Stape, *The Several Lives of Joseph Conrad* (2007), p. 265.
[6] See 'Chronology' for publication details.

requested 'The Unlighted Coast', as a contribution to the war-effort. As in the past, Conrad was also moved to comment on matters of public interest, writing on the loss of the *Dalgonar* in response to an article in the *London Mercury*, and on the future of Constantinople in the form of a letter to *The Times*. There were only three exceptions to the general pattern of commissioned journalism and responses to requests from friends: 'Ocean Travel' and 'Christmas-day at Sea' were written to help offset the costs of his trip to America, and Conrad decided to write the 'Preface' to *The Shorter Tales* himself rather than to allow Muirhead Bone to do so, as F. N. Doubleday, his American publisher, had suggested.[1]

Curle became increasingly involved in Conrad's business affairs when Eric S. Pinker became Conrad's literary agent following the death of his father, J. B. Pinker, in early 1922. Curle had already played a role in the private printing and sale and distribution of Conrad pamphlets begun at Clement K. Shorter's suggestion and continued by the collector and bibliographer Thomas J. Wise.[2] Conrad and Curle issued as pamphlets six essays that were subsequently reprinted in *Last Essays*, beginning in September 1921 with 'Cookery', a preface written for Jessie Conrad's as yet unpublished *Simple Cooking Precepts for a Little House* (as it was then titled) which appeared two years later under the title *A Handbook of Cookery for a Small House*.[3] Skills that Conrad honed in his early career when he was acting as his own agent continued to be profitable to him, and he negotiated publication rights and the private sale of manuscripts and typescripts with firmness and a certain canniness. Negotiations for two essays, 'Cookery' and 'Geography and Some Explorers', as well as his dealings with Thomas Beer for the writing of 'Stephen Crane', vividly demonstrate his business acumen.

From the beginning, Conrad's name and the prominence given to his short preface attracted interest to his wife's *Handbook of Cookery*, a volume ready in 1907 but remaining unpublished until 1923.

---

[1] For additional information on this topic, see 'The Texts'.

[2] On this topic, see J. H. Stape, '"Conrad Privately Printed": The Shorter and Wise Limited Edition Pamphlets', *The Ugo Mursia Memorial Lectures: Papers from the International Conference, University of Pisa, September 7th–11th, 1983*, ed. Mario Curreli (1988), pp. 91–107.

[3] Others were *The Dover Patrol* and *John Galsworthy* (August 1922), *Travel. A Preface to Into the East* (December 1922), *The 'Torrens'* (October 1923) and *Geography and Some Explorers* (January 1924). Curle also printed *The Congo Diary* as a pamphlet in January 1926.

A publisher's advance of £25 from the firm of Alston Rivers,[1] which did not exercise its option to publish, came in 1907.[2] Fourteen years later, Samuel A. Everitt of Doubleday, Page & Company asked Pinker if rumours that Mrs Conrad had written a cookery book were true.[3] Conrad's interest in this project was now rekindled, and he hastened to bring out his preface in pamphlet form, while he and Eric Pinker negotiated over the book with Doubleday, Page & Company and with Heinemann (a firm now largely owned by F. N. Doubleday), and with the New York journal the *Delineator* and the London *Woman's Pictorial Magazine* for the serial. One hundred copies of the pamphlet were printed, ninety 'signed by the author' for sale and ten for distribution by Conrad.[4] The pamphlet complicated negotiations with Doubleday for publication rights,[5] but problems were resolved through the intervention of Conrad's longstanding friend and supporter S. S. Pawling of Heinemann.[6] The cookery book duly appeared first in serial form, in the *Delineator* and the *Woman's Pictorial*, and then in the British and American volumes. Thus the Conrads' profits came from six sources: Alston Rivers, the sale of the pamphlets (perhaps bringing in 180 guineas), two magazines and the Doubleday and Heinemann volumes.

Negotiations for 'Geography and Some Explorers' are no less relevant to understanding how Conrad was marketing himself and being handled by his agent during his late career. J. A. Hammerton had asked Curle to write a series of articles for the multi-volume *Countries of the World*, and, ever ready to do Conrad a favour, Curle suggested to Hammerton that Conrad write the general introduction to the series for a fee of £200. Eric Pinker subsequently offered the piece to

---

[1] Rivers was Ford Madox Hueffer's publisher, and initial negotiations were through him (*Letters*, III, 410 n. 2).
[2] Conrad to Ernest Dawson, 3 January 1907 (*Letters*, III, 399).
[3] Everitt to J. B. Pinker, 4 March 1921 (Berg).
[4] Note filed with Wise's bibliographical description (BL Ashley 2945).
[5] Mary M. Meloney, an editor at the *Delineator*, questioned whether the pamphlet's appearance might cause cancellation of the printing of the serial, which in turn might impact upon the book rights (Memorandum of 8 December 1921 accompanying Meloney to J. B. Pinker, 9 December 1921 (Berg)). For the serial publication of extracts, including Conrad's preface, in the *Woman's Pictorial Magazine*, starting 14 October 1922, see *Letters*, VII, 530. This serial was lavishly illustrated with photographs of the Conrads, their house and samples of the recipes themselves, as served in a London tea-room.
[6] Conrad to Eric S. Pinker, 16 May 1922 (*Letters*, VII, 469).

Gilbert Grosvenor of *National Geographic Magazine* for $500,[1] and in due course the essay appeared in both publications. To maximize Conrad's profits, Curle rushed a copy of the essay to the London printers Strangeways & Sons for publication as a limited-edition pamphlet.[2]

Finally, in his occasionally complex and sometimes almost whimsical financial negotiations over his introduction to Beer's *Stephen Crane: A Study in American Letters*, Conrad revealed some of his rationale for disrupting work on his fiction to write essays.[3] After Beer invited him to write the introduction, Conrad agreed to write 3,000–4,500 words, later expanding his contribution to nearly double this number. Pleased that his name was 'worth something with the American public', he explained to his agent that Beer seemed to be a 'man of means' able to pay the £400 offered, despite the opinion of Alfred A. Knopf, the biography's publisher, that the figure was excessive for a piece that, in essence, merely expanded 'Stephen Crane: A Note without Dates' (1919). Ultimately, Conrad felt that the fee for what he called 'mostly twaddle' was nevertheless 'good weight of paper to Beer for his money' (*Letters*, VIII, 56). Conrad also asked Pinker to secure rights to print twenty-five copies as a pamphlet and to include the essay in a future volume.[4] In the event, Conrad wrote out the introduction in longhand with an eye to selling the manuscript (more valuable than typescript) to Wise, receiving £110 for that.[5] Conrad's rationale for payment is central to understanding why he occasionally turned to journalism late in life. Illustrative is his comment to Eric Pinker on 23 March 1923. Assessing the value of his words – counted in the margins of the 'Stephen Crane' manuscript – Conrad wrote:

I am giving him 8300 words . . . his plain request having been for 3 or 4 pages . . . 8,000 w., for £400 that is £50 per thousand. I have been paid as much as £250 for 2400 words. (Tradition). . . . I have repeatedly been paid £100 for 12–1300 words

---

[1] For a detailed discussion of this transaction, see Ray Stevens, 'Conrad, Gilbert Grosvenor, *The National Geographic Magazine*, and "Geography and Some Explorers"', *Conradiana*, 23 (1991), 197–202.

[2] James Bain of Strangeways, who purchased twenty-five of the thirty copies for £75, quickly put the pamphlets up for sale at 6 guineas each; see Curle to Bain, 13 January 1924; Bain to Mr Campbell, 13 February 1924 (Berg).

[3] See Conrad to Eric S. Pinker, 9 March 1923 (*Letters*, VIII, 43–5).

[4] Conrad to Pinker, 21 March 1923 (*Letters*, VIII, 55); Alfred A. Knopf to Pinker, 19 May 1923 (Berg). In the end, Knopf's forcefully expressed objections led to the plan's cancellation.

[5] Conrad to Thomas J. Wise, 26 March 1923 (*Letters*, VIII, 63). The original letter is accompanied by the cancelled cheque.

by The Times; and several times £50 per column by the D[ai]ly Mail (1100–1200 words) *as a matter of course.*   (*Letters*, VIII, 58)

THE ESSAYS

C O N R A D   H A D several compelling reasons for writing short pieces for serial publication in the late stages of his career. For one thing, serial publication kept his name before the public. Typically, he accepted shorter projects in the interstices of longer works, and he seems particularly to have welcomed respites from the tussle with *Suspense*, a long-contemplated novel finally begun in June 1920. Finding it problematic, he repeatedly laid it aside, writing introductory 'Notes' for his collected edition, readying *Notes on Life and Letters* for print and composing *The Rover*. Despite a healthy bank balance as he neared the end of his life, Conrad was increasingly concerned about his family's future, an anxiety he addressed by spinning journalism out of his experience at sea – a perennial topic of public interest in England – and his wide knowledge of geopolitics. Some of these essays indulge a reminiscent vein, glancing backwards on friends and experiences, a congenial activity for a man in his sixth decade.

THE CONGO

T W O   N O T E B O O K S, written in pencil between 13 June and 19 August 1890, are all that survive, apart from a handful of letters and the early stages of *Almayer's Folly*, of whatever Conrad wrote in the Congo, where the 32-year-old master mariner who had recently resigned his only command went to fulfil a boyhood dream of exploring unknown Africa. 'The Congo Diary' and 'Up-river Book' provide both a fragmentary biographical record of and insight into this major transitional period as he reacted to colonial life and employment in the Congo Free State.[1] They also demonstrate that Conrad was in command of written English by 1890 and aware of the requirements of differing styles and linguistic registers. 'Up-river Book' testifies to his powers of observation, often in alienating circumstances that later became the

---

[1] 'The Congo Diary' is the title Curle gave to the overland portion of Conrad's journey. No title appears in Conrad's notebook.

crucible for fiction. Perhaps nowhere in Conrad is the interrelation-
ship of personal experience and literature more intriguing than in
the role that his Congo experience played in shaping 'An Outpost of
Progress' (1896) and 'Heart of Darkness' (1899), the two works he
acknowledges as having brought out of the 'centre of Africa'.[1] Hired
by the Société Anonyme Belge pour le Commerce du Haut-Congo
to command a river steamer on the Congo, Conrad's experience not
only led him to leave the country before his contract ran out, but also,
partly as a result of the serious illness contracted there, influenced his
decision to leave the sea.

'Up-river Book' records approximately half of the 985-mile (1,576-
km) voyage of the *Roi des Belges* from Kinshasa on Stanley Pool to
Kisangani at Stanley Falls. Conrad stopped charting the Congo river,
the purpose of this record, near Bangala. The precision, accuracy and
factual observation are focussed on the Congo's bends, bights, bores,
islands and currents and on landmarks and settlements along the river,
a necessary record if he were to fulfil his contract to command ships.
Frequently ill, usually rushed, harried by both his European colleagues
and Congo natives, Conrad recorded his observations in functional
and fluent English, one of the three languages he used while in Africa.
He wrote letters in idiomatic (if occasionally misspelled) French, the
language of his daily life, to Marguerite Poradowska, a recently wid-
owed relation by marriage and writer living in Brussels.[2] He also wrote
letters in business French to Albert Thys, l'Administrateur-Délégué
of the Société Anonyme Belge and *aide-de-camp* to King Leopold II
of Belgium. He spoke with the overseer of railway operations Roger
Casement and various missionaries in English, the language he used
for the two notebooks he kept. His correspondence to his maternal
uncle, Tadeusz Bobrowski, was in Polish. And he picked up at least
a few words and phrases in the local language, Kikongo, in order to
communicate, however minimally, with the indigenous populations.

The prose in this document is of the same rough-and-ready sort used
to make short entries in ships' logs, a duty in his spells as first mate and
testimony to twelve years he had then spent in the British Merchant

---

[1] 'Author's Note', *Youth, Heart of Darkness, The End of the Tether*, ed. Owen Knowles
(2010), p. 6.23.
[2] On Poradowska, see 123.24n. References to the 'Explanatory Notes' in this volume
take this form.

Service. The account of the voyage in the *Roi des Belges*, then, is a professional document, almost rigorously devoid of subjectivity, and by the time Conrad left the Congo, he had confirmed English as his language of literary record.[1]

A more subjective document, 'The Congo Diary' records his observations on the 230-mile (368-km) overland trek from Matadi to Stanley Pool. A creative voice is present, although there is little evidence of the incipient skill required of a novelist. He usually wrote when he was exhausted, lonely, dispirited, beset by mosquitoes or frogs, dropped unceremoniously by his carriers into a muddy puddle, debilitated by fever or annoyed by the unpleasantness of fellow travellers. Random passages suggest an increasing awareness of his ability to write about the human condition in extreme circumstances. 'The Congo Diary' also records his misgivings about his decision to become involved in these: he comments with increasing awareness on the interaction of landscape, mood, sensory observations, impressions and health, combined with sketches of the terrain of his overland journey.

These negotiations with daily realities occasionally occur in highly idiomatic English: 'Getting jolly well sick of this fun' (5 July). Observations about the dead along the way become increasingly personal (3–5 July). He explains with intriguing detail the path of a bullet through a young boy's head (1 August), and records the ominous symbolism that can arise from physical description by commenting with irony and understatement on a brief encounter with the approaching night, the rising of the moon, eerie sounds emanating from the jungle and a grotesquely pigmented African albino emerging from the shadows (4 July). The well-known entry of 24 June referring to the 'Idiotic employment' of packing ivory is followed later (in leaves not printed before) by two that record his initials 'J. C. K.' and the date 'Matadi. 23^d. 6th. 90.' Three references are made to the 'SAB' (Société Anonyme Belge) and 'GK' (Georges-Antoine Klein), the agent who died on board the *Roi des Belges* on Conrad's return from Stanley Falls, a possible model for Kurtz in 'Heart of Darkness'. Figures on the first page record weights of casks packed with ivory, a major export to Europe in 1890, while the second records enumerations jotted down when

---

[1] More critical comment has been offered about Conrad's infrequent use of Polish and French phrases than his remarkable command of English. Najder comments, for example, on the Polonism 'much more trees' (28 July), '*wiele wiecej drzew*' (*CDP*, p. 13 n. 23), and Curle notes that 'Route very accidented' is an 'odd Gallicism' (*Last Essays* (1926), p. 246 n. 1).

packing them. Pencilled comments remind one of Kayerts's actions in 'An Outpost of Progress', when large ivory tusks were being weighed: he put 'his hand in his pocket found there a dirty bit of paper and the stump of a pencil. He . . . noted stealthily the weights' (*Tales of Unrest*, p. 106). Required to perform menial tasks, Conrad was, however much against the grain, actively engaged in the work of exploitation, the major purpose of the enterprise employing him being to generate profits for investors, primarily Leopold II of Belgium.

Before leaving Matadi, Conrad sets the tone for most encounters with people he actually met in the Congo and who are later reworked in his fiction: doubt, alienation, irritability and ill-will. On 24 June, he was moved to note that the 'Prominent characteristic of the social life' was 'People speaking ill of each other.' Roger Casement and the missionaries he met along the way proved to be notable exceptions. Finally, themes that Conrad will develop in his later fiction are evident: absurdity; morality, religion and death; camaraderie or the lack of it; dissension and inscrutable contrasts. The commentary becomes increasingly figurative and is occasionally impressionistic, especially when recording weather and atmospheric conditions. Conrad's descriptions convey images of broad expanses of terrain, and his myth-making ability allows him to create oxymoronically an almost epic context to contrast with the duress of his feeling 'seedy' during what he judged to be a 'stupid tramp' through difficult terrain.

THE SEA

'OUTSIDE LITERATURE' contrasts factual and imaginative writing, selecting 'Notices to Mariners' – the essay's original title – as Conrad's medium. The Admiralty regularly sent notices to ships at sea that contained information necessary for safe navigation. One of the duties of a ship's first mate was to record in her log each day's activities, which would include any notices from the Admiralty received during the preceding twenty-four hours. 'Notices to Mariners' extols the need for the kind of factual accuracy that served Conrad well in his first profession; however, Conradian irony and impressionism demonstrate the incompatibility of a devotion to precision and the creative impulse,[1]

---

[1] For a discussion of Conrad's various narrative techniques in *Last Essays*, see Ray Stevens, 'A Milch-Cow's Overview of Sailing Ships, and Other Conradian Narrative Perspectives in the Lighter Later Essays', *Conrad's Literary Career*, ed. Keith Carabine, Owen Knowles and Wiesław Krajka (1992), pp. 263–78.

a discussion reminiscent of meditations in *The Mirror of the Sea* and *A Personal Record*. The factual accuracy of the Admiralty's notices conflicts with bantering irony when Conrad refers to an examination he had taken years before, and failed. He 'remembered' his illustration inaccurately, because he failed that examination.[1] Faulty memory or erroneous reporting led Conrad to impressionistic frivolity rather than factual accuracy: 'I looked at the face of the clock; it was round like the moon, white as a ghost, unfeeling, idiotic' (32.9–11).

This literary interest continues variously in other essays that explore Conrad's lifelong concern with the sea, seamanship, sailors and disasters at sea – including a letter to the editor of the *London Mercury* (December 1921) in response to a query raised about the wreck of a ship off the coast of Chile some eight years before that involved heroic efforts by the seamen of a French ship in saving her crew. 'The Loss of the *Dalgonar*' illustrates continuing interest in the need for precise and unambiguous reporting to reflect the human drama of the sea, as the men of the French vessel *Loire* worked to save those of the disabled merchant vessel in tumultuous seas. Conrad's interest in documenting life and death at sea continues in 'The Silence of the Sea', reminiscent of his two essays on the *Titanic* (*Notes on Life and Letters*) and reflections in 'Overdue and Missing' (*The Mirror of the Sea*). Interest in lost ships also frames his passage through the Torres Strait in 'Geography and Some Explorers' where references to two shipwrecks open and close the high point of his career, as commander of a sailing ship. Further, in the 'Memorandum' he suggests that the number of sea-cadets on a new sailing ship be kept below the sixty proposed by the builder: 'What I have in my mind is the possibility of some accident . . . and its effect on the public mind. Regard ought to be paid also to the facility of getting a lesser number of people out of a sinking ship or saving them all in case of a shipwreck' (60.15–19).[2]

---

[1] Hans van Marle, '"Plucked and Passed on Tower Hill": Conrad's Examination Ordeals', *Conradiana*, 8 (1976), 84.

[2] Such interest recalls Conrad's testimony before the Board of Trade's Departmental Committee on the Manning of Merchant Ships on 3 July 1894, one of the purposes of which was to 'inquire and determine whether any amendment of the law is necessary in order to secure as regards British ships 1) The proper manning of such ships 2) The detention of such ships if proceeding or about to proceed to sea undermanned from ports in the United Kingdom'. Conrad's testimony is reprinted in Edmund Bojarski, 'Conrad at the Crossroads: From Navigator to Novelist with Some New Biographical Mysteries', *Texas Quarterly*, 10 (Winter 1968), 15–29.

The 'Memorandum' was written to comment on the proposed building of a barque to train sixty to eighty cadets. Conrad's consciousness of style and audience continues when he notes that he was 'not
speaking as a literary person indulging his fancy but as the usual
sort of merchant officer who . . . draws upon his ordinary experience'
(51.35–37). He compares the development of respect for maritime
traditions in apprentices who would spend twelve to eighteen months
on a cadet-ship to an education in Classics. His unacknowledged point
of reference, in addition to his years as mariner – especially when he
supervised apprentices aboard the *Torrens* – was the merchant sailors'
training-ship, the *Conway*. The practical tone required for the 'Memorandum' prevented Conrad from developing the reminiscent quality
of 'The *Torrens*', written for the *Blue Peter* and its more general audience, even though his experience in the ship, to which he refers several
times in the 'Memorandum', is central to his argument.

Conrad indulged literary fancy in 'The Unlighted Coast', commissioned by the Admiralty in 1916, when it invited him to join writers
such as Rudyard Kipling to promote the work of the Navy during the
First World War. Asked to report on the Royal Naval Reserve, Conrad
visited various northern naval installations and recorded his observations during a ten-day voyage in the HMS *Ready*, a Q-ship, an armed
merchant vessel disguised (in the case of the *Ready*, as a Norwegian
timber-freighter) to lure and destroy German submarines. The Admiralty wanted propaganda 'outside literature', not the impressionistic
reminiscence that Conrad submitted: his decision to 'talk around the
war' rather than to develop 'war talk' led to the essay's rejection. Whatever its inadequacy for official purposes, 'The Unlighted Coast' offers
insight into literary technique. Twenty years of the writer's sea-life
are reduced to a moment in the life of a young gunner, as his prose
becomes notably purple. Conrad concludes paradoxically, continuing
his contrast of factual and imaginative writing: 'It's very likely that my
impressions set down truthfully are altogether untrue' (40.31–32).

Five years later he returned to the North Sea to commemorate
the contributions of merchant seamen who had guarded the country
during the Great War, blending factual record with reminiscence. His
praise for the contributions of the Merchant Service, begun earlier in
'Tradition' (1918), continues in 'The Dover Patrol', published in *The
Times* in July 1921, on the day the Prince of Wales unveiled the Dover
Patrol Memorial. As in 'The Unlighted Coast', where Conrad recalls
Cæsar's galleys and the Danish rovers, the moments of the war broaden

as he reflects on similar service by British sailors during the Napoleonic war. Individual hours expand into generations, and facts become a legendary record for the men who defended the North Sea's southern exit. The perspectival shift here, a familiar one in his work, recalls the opening of 'Heart of Darkness' where Britain's Roman colonizers and Africa's modern European ones collide. Even more fundamental, perhaps, is the sense of human continuity in communities established to accomplish a particular endeavour.

Although Conrad's greatest sense of achievement at sea might have come when he commanded the *Otago, Last Essays* suggests that his most enjoyable service was that in the *Torrens* (November 1891 – October 1893), in which, as first mate, he enjoyed his longest unbroken period of service at sea. His reminiscence praises the days of sail in a famed clipper ship engaged in the passenger trade to Australia. For Conrad, this service proved transitional, 'marking the end of my sea-life with . . . pleasant memories and precious friendships' (18.19–20). Even in this commemorative and nostalgic narrative, concerned with contrasting types of people who go to sea, Conrad discusses an 'outside literature' item, insisting upon accuracy. He praises Basil Lubbock's *The Colonial Clippers* (1921), which mentions his service in the ship, but corrects Lubbock by pointing out that he completed two voyages, not one, in her.

The reminiscent mood dominates the pot-boiling 'My Hotel in Mid-Atlantic' (later 'Ocean Travel'), written on the *Tuscania* and rushed into print in May 1923. The essay contrasts the passing days of the clipper with modern steamships, the latter having all the amenities of Ritz hotels and leaving passengers little more to do than to enjoy strolling on the promenade-deck. The narrative voice shifts from contrast to reminiscence, with the crew loading a milch-cow on a clipper thirty years earlier, an event viewed with ironic whimsy – from the milch-cow's perspective. Reminiscence, faulty memory and the creation of legend converge in 'Christmas-day at Sea', in which Conrad 'recalls' a chance meeting in 1879 between an English wool clipper and an American whaler and the transfer of a gift of two boxes of figs and dated Sydney newspapers.[1] In an essay devoted to the trans-national camaraderie of the sea, Conrad remembers, or purports to remember, forty-four years after the fact, details about the weather, the conditions of the sea and

---

[1] Curle incorrectly identified the clipper as the *Duke of Sutherland* in which Conrad had served in 1879 (see Appendix A).

conversations with the captain, carpenter and steward. He fails, however, to recall a significant detail: on Christmas-day 1879, he was not part of a crew outbound from Australia but in the Mediterranean on the steamship *Europa*. His focus, however, is reminiscence, not precise memory: the bond of lonesome seamen rejoicing in a keg of figs and newspapers bobbing on the Southern Ocean acts as a contrast with the sterile impersonality of modern Ritz Hotel-style steamships.[1] Thus, he emphasizes his theme of solidarity over the mechanical efficiency that was making the world a safer but less intimately human place.

This theme undergoes a significant transformation in 'Geography and Some Explorers', an essay contrasting the exploitative early explorers, whose goal was 'loot', to later ones like Captain Cook, whose voyages and scientific records were free from 'taint of that sort' (9.17–18). The omniscient narration about 'militant geography' shifts to personal experience – first literarily, then intellectually and, finally, actively. Conrad's map-gazing is revealed in the marginalia of a leaf of the manuscript: he sketched a rough map of the Western hemisphere to assist in visualizing the scenes he recalls. The great names merge with his own sea-faring adventures, as the gunner did in 'The Unlighted Coast'. Conrad thus wanders from Europe to America with Columbus and to Mexico, Peru and what is now the south-western United States with the Conquistadors and to Panama with Balboa. Then he sweeps across the Pacific with Tasman, along the Australian coast with Cook, back to New Zealand, to the Arctic with Franklin and McLintock, to Poland, into the heart of Africa in the *Roi des Belges* and, finally, through the Torres Strait in command of the *Otago*.

Verbal play and literary allusion dominate an essay framed by two events central to Conrad's life: his childhood encounter (possibly a mythical and certainly a mythologized event) with the blank spaces on the map of Africa, and the voyage in the *Otago*. Marlow in 'Heart of Darkness' records the map-pointing incident graphically, where a (possibly) biographical fact becomes a metaphor in fiction.[2] Likewise, in *A Personal Record* (2008, pp. 13–15), Conrad refers to his boast

[1] See also 'Some Reflexions on the Loss of the *Titanic*', *Notes on Life and Letters* (2004), pp. 167–78. For further discussion of 'Christmas-day at Sea', see Ray Stevens and Robert W. Trogdon, '"Christmas Day at Sea": A Whaler, Bundle of Papers, Two Boxes of Figs, Bibliographical Completeness, and Biographical and Textual Inaccuracies of Hemispheric Proportions', *Conradiana*, 33 (2001), 251–63.
[2] Doubt has been cast on the episode as authentic biography. See the 'Explanatory Notes' for passages paralleling Conrad's.

that he would explore the Congo. 'Geography and Some Explorers' returns to the theme of exploitation in the Congo, referring to Reshid and his Arab slave-traders as Conrad at Stanley Falls smokes a 'pipe of peace' (14.17) and recalls the fulfilment of his boyhood dream.

He concludes his last completed sea-essay, intended for the 'pendent volume' to *The Mirror of the Sea*, by referring to his 36-hour trip through the Torres Strait following the path blazed by the great explorers. As he left the high-point of his sea-adventure, he spotted the small island to which Cook had rowed in 1762, leaving the *Endeavour* to be alone with his thoughts when his explorations were over. Identifying with Cook's triumph, and with echoing images of an explorer's camp early in the essay and his own camp in the Congo, Conrad becomes one with 'the famous seaman navigator . . . thanks to the books of travel and discovery which have peopled it [the sea] with unforgettable shades of the masters in the calling which in a humble way was to be mine too' (17.21–29). Here, as in *A Personal Record*, Conrad's maritime and writing experiences conjoin.

His self-identification with 'legendary' figures perhaps lies behind the background of his final work. In any event, he may have anticipated a sequel in 'Legends', destined for the *National Geographic*. Curle estimated that Conrad had completed three-quarters of the essay when he died, but this estimate is problematic, given that Conrad had commented that the essay would be about 'Sailors Saints University Dons etc. Subjects of Legend'.[1]

GEOPOLITICS: CONSTANTINOPLE

CONRAD'S THOUGHTS about the geopolitics of his childhood that continued with unremitting persistence throughout his life were not legendary but all too real. His concern is reflected in two forays into the world of diplomacy and geopolitics: a letter to *The Times* in November 1912, written during the First Balkan War of 1912–13, which was followed by an unpublished document elaborating on the letter. The essays collected in *Notes on Life and Letters* vividly testify to Conrad's alertness to political questions, and various pieces brought together in *Last Essays* likewise suggest, although they do not take up in detail, topics of international concern.

---

[1] Conrad to Curle, 8 July 1924 (*Letters*, VIII, 400).

The two comments on the future political configuration of the Balkans and Turkey see Conrad discussing geopolitics and international affairs in perceptive detail. His interest in geopolitical forces affecting Eastern Europe, Poland and, consequently, himself dated almost from childhood. His comment to Austin Harrison, editor of the *English Review*, made while he was writing his letter to *The Times*, illustrates a lifelong interest: 'Is it really possible that I should have lived long enough to see the end of the Eastern Question which has dogged my footsteps I may say from my very craddle [*sic*]?' (*Letters*, V, 124). The resolution of the Eastern Question, the fate of the European possessions of the Ottoman Empire when it was finally expelled from Eastern Europe, had been central to European politics since the Treaty of Karlowitz (1699),[1] and foreshadowed the Ottoman Empire's eventual demise. Conrad's letter discusses his multi-ethnic, multi-cultural and idealistic solution to the centuries-old problem of the fate of Constantinople as the army of the Ottoman Empire faced defeat at Tchataldja, east of Constantinople.[2]

PREFACES AND REVIEWS

CONRAD'S 'Preface' to his *Shorter Tales* evolves from principles of selection to concerns about his legacy. The preface suggests how some of his collections evolved: they often 'just happened', because the creative process commonly shapes a volume in a way its author had not originally intended. As the discussion of the financial negotiations for publishing his preface to Mrs Conrad's *A Handbook of Cookery for a Small House* has suggested, Conrad's role in preparing the text of his wife's cookery book was significant. Whereas Jessie Conrad had expanded her book by 1921, Conrad did not revise his preface, 'a mock serious thing into which I dragged Red Indians and other incongruities', written fourteen years previously.[3]

Having declined Curle's earlier request to write an introduction for *Wanderings: A Book of Travel and Reminiscence* (1920), Conrad did

---

[1] The Treaty ended a war (1683–97) in which the Ottoman Empire was defeated by Austria, Poland and Venice.
[2] For an extended discussion of Conrad's interest in the Eastern Question and the resolution of the conflict on the Balkan Peninsula, see Harold Ray Stevens, 'Conrad, Geopolitics, and "The Future of Constantinople"', *The Conradian*, 31, no. 2 (2006), 15–27.
[3] Conrad to Ford Madox Ford, 25 January 1907 (*Letters*, III, 410).

write, at Curle's request, a preface to *Into the East: Notes on Burma and Malaya* (1923). Conrad criticized the proliferation of repetitive books of travel, in the paramnesiac tone and manner of one resigned to a modern world over-supplied with travel books and steamships, bewailing the loss of vibrancy that corresponds to laments in other essays on changes in sea-travel. Curle's book is a noteworthy exception, however, because its author captures the spirit of modern travel over well-travelled roads as 'he looks on, sensitive, meditative . . . alive to the saving grace of human and historical associations' (70.20–22).

Conrad reviewed two early volumes of fiction, *The Island Pharisees* (1904) and *The Man of Property* (1906), by his friend John Galsworthy. The first review included comments on *Green Mansions* by W. H. Hudson, whom he had met in 1899 as part of Edward Garnett's Mont Blanc Restaurant circle, a luncheon club that facilitated the mingling of established writers and fledgling ones. Conrad, who had read the manuscript of *The Island Pharisees* more than a year before he wrote his review, had encouraged Heinemann to publish it after its rejection by Duckworth and Constable, and complimented Galsworthy on the terms he negotiated.[1] The novel was published in January 1904, but Conrad's review was not written until two months later. It did not appear in his lifetime for reasons that remain uncertain: the review seems peculiarly incomplete because it stops rather than concludes, and devotes more time to discussing the state of the generic English novel than to examining the qualities of Galsworthy and Hudson. Conrad's review of *The Man of Property*, however, was published within two weeks of the novel's appearance. Even though he wrote it hastily, he had followed the book's development from its inception in 1903,[2] and expressed satisfaction when Galsworthy completed it. Even though Conrad wrote to Galsworthy that the volume was 'undubitably [*sic*] a piece of art' (*Letters*, III, 314), the review was less than enthusiastic, and Conrad was uncomfortable and defensive when he tried to explain why: the essay was 'inept and benighted' (*Letters*, III, 322). He later added that he wanted to present a 'literary tribute', but that he feared being misinterpreted: 'So I simply endeavoured to send people to the book by a sort of allusive *compte-rendu*, a mere

---

[1] Conrad to John Galsworthy, 2 January 1903, [7?] July 1903, 1 November 1903 (*Letters*, III, 4, 44, 71).
[2] Conrad to Galsworthy, 4 June 1903 (*Letters*, III, 40).

"notice" in fact' (*Letters*, III, 327). In addition, he was concerned that literary London might believe his review to be simply praise from a friend, a concern he would later express when refusing to write a review of Curle's *Wanderings*. Various biographers have speculated about other motives for writing as he did: jealousy; frustration that Galsworthy seemed so much more successful with much less effort; envy of Galsworthy's speed of composition; discontent with the conclusion of *The Man of Property* and with Bosinney's fortuitous death; belief that the novel could not be probed deeply lest its flaws become too obvious; perhaps even aggravation with Galsworthy's 'disconcerting honesty' (95.20). The candour and honesty of Conrad's eleven specific comments testify to his critical skills, however, for a century of literary criticism has confirmed his judgement,[1] despite the fact that Galsworthy was awarded the Nobel Prize for Literature in 1932.

'Stephen Crane' presented no such problems, because Conrad discusses this friendship anecdotally, merely hinting at his reservations about the limits of Crane's talent and achievements. While defending Crane against charges of intemperate behaviour and commenting sympathetically on his friend's relationship with his companion, the journalist and once-and-future brothel-keeper Cora Howarth, Conrad comments on Crane's work ethic, financial concerns, horsemanship, fiction, friendships and health, and on their unconsummated plans for collaboration on a play. Encapsulated in an incident in *A Personal Record* are the main ideas of Conrad's essays on Crane: among other topics broached there is a stream-of-consciousness meditation on time, on the writing of *Nostromo*, followed by a meditation on Crane's short life, all reworked in the introduction to Beer's biography, a book, for all its unreliability, marking the turning-point in the recovery of Crane's reputation. An introduction to the 1925 Heinemann edition of *The Red Badge of Courage*, written a week after 'Stephen Crane' was drafted, 'His War-book' moves beyond reminiscence to somewhat generalized but generous appreciation. Conrad, along with Edward Garnett, continued to admire and even champion Crane's work at a time when the American writer had almost been forgotten. The introduction emphasizes flight – a central event in both Henry Fleming's and Lord Jim's

---

[1] For a more complete discussion of this, see Ray Stevens, 'The Muddle of Minutiæ, or What Text Should We Read: The Case of an Omitted Paragraph in a Forgotten Conrad Book Review', *English Literature in Transition, 1880–1920*, 36 (1993), 305–21.

lives – impressionistic detail and the relative unimportance in fiction of chronological time.

Despite the variety of the pieces brought together in *Last Essays*, Conrad's voice is remarkably consistent. Even though some biographers and critics fault him for not being completely truthful in his memoirs, reminiscences and essays on his life and letters, his rationales seem plausible. Perhaps nothing is more human than to attempt to conceal unpleasant incidents in one's life. 'A Familiar Preface' to *A Personal Record* affirms the artist's need to be selective in his personal writings, and, certainly, Conrad foresaw the problems that critics have raised, addressing these not only in this volume but also in *A Personal Record*, *The Mirror of the Sea*, *Notes on Life and Letters* and in his correspondence, which he no doubt knew would eventually become public. In an often-quoted letter to Richard Curle, Conrad objected to the explicit naming of a location in 'Youth':

> Didn't it ever occur to you... that I knew what I was doing in leaving the facts of my life and even my tales in the background. Explicitness... is fatal to the glamour of all artistic work, robbing it of all suggestiveness, destroying all illusion.... Yet nothing is more clear than the utter insignificance of explicit statement and also its power to call attention away from things that matter in the region of art.
>
> (*Letters*, VII, 457)

His similar sentiment in 'Legends', that the facts of one's life that lead to the creation of legend need to be more credible than literally true 'in a sort of fundamental accord with the nature of the life it records' (36.7–8), continued to intrigue him a few days before his death in the way that his philosophy of composition continues to challenge readers a century later.

RECEPTION

THE REVIEWS OF Conrad's four volumes of essays and memoirs – *The Mirror of the Sea* (1906), *A Personal Record* (1912), *Notes on Life and Letters* (1921) and *Last Essays* (1926) – question Conrad's candour about certain events in his life. He invited such speculation not only in his published work but also in interviews and letters, writing, for example, in the 'Author's Note' to *Notes on Life and Letters*: 'Conrad literary, Conrad political, Conrad reminiscent, Conrad controversial. Well, yes! A one-man show – or is it merely the show of one man?'

(2004: 3.23–25). On arriving in New York in 1923, Conrad told a reporter that he 'wrote in retrospect of what he saw and learned during the first 35 years of his life',[1] and had earlier commented to a journalist who had asked about aspects of his life that had become a part of his literary record – specifically about incidents in 'A Smile of Fortune' and 'The Secret Sharer' purported to have happened when he was in command of the *Otago*:

> I had to *make* material from my own life's incidents arranged, combined, coloured for artistic purposes. I don't think there's anything reprehensible in that. After all I *am* a writer of fiction; and it is not what actually happened, but the manner of presenting it that settles the literary and even the moral value of my work. My little vol: of autobiography [*A Personal Record*] of course is absolutely genuine. The rest is a more or less close approximation to facts and suggestions. What I claim as true are my mental and emotional reactions to life, to men, to their affairs and their passions as I have seen them. I have in that sense kept always true to myself.[2]

Conrad anticipated, encouraged and addressed critical commentary about the life he recorded in his essays and memoirs, and responded to critics of *The Mirror of the Sea* who thought he was not forthright, calling the book 'a very intimate revelation' that attempted 'to lay bare with the unreserve of a last hour's confession the terms of my relation with the sea', making a 'full confession not of my sins but of my emotions' (pp. vii–x). Further, in 'A Familiar Preface' to *A Personal Record*, he promised 'truth of a modest sort' while asserting that fiction as human history is often nearer truth than history. Quoting Thomas à Kempis in the *Imitation of Christ*, he elaborated: '"there are persons esteemed on their reputation who by showing themselves destroy the opinion one had of them." This is the danger incurred by an author of fiction who sets out to talk about himself without disguise.'[3] Conrad also addressed those who object to his lack of factual precision: 'I haven't lived through wonderful adventures to be related seriatim.'[4]

Last Essays variously addresses these concerns. 'Outside Literature' and 'Legends' differentiate between factual accuracy and literary licence, while 'The Congo Diary' records personal experiences that

---

[1] 'Americans Kind, So Why Lecture?' *Joseph Conrad: Interviews and Recollections*, ed. Martin Ray (1990), p. 189. The query came from a reporter for Boston's *Christian Science Monitor*.
[2] Conrad to A. T. Saunders, 14 June 1917 (*Letters*, VI, 100).
[3] *A Personal Record*, ed. Zdzisław Najder and J. H. Stape (2008), pp. 12.39–13.1.
[4] Ibid., p. 18.2–3.

find æsthetic treatment in 'An Outpost of Progress' and 'Heart of Darkness'.[1] The 'Memorandum' gives objective reality to Conrad's experience at sea and is also, in a sense, an act of reminiscence drawing on hard-won professional expertise. 'Geography and Some Explorers', 'The *Torrens*', 'Ocean Travel', 'The Unlighted Coast', 'The Loss of the *Dalgonar*' and other essays confirm the interplay of personal experience and its creative development. The prefaces and reviews reflect Conrad's friendships with Galsworthy, Curle and Crane, which determined the contexts within which Conrad wrote, fostering a backward glance at such technical issues as literary impressionism and realism. The reviews of Galsworthy's *The Island Pharisees* and *The Man of Property* are conditioned by the fact that Conrad read the manuscripts at various stages, and 'His War-book', an introduction to *The Red Badge of Courage*, reflects observations recorded twelve years previously in *A Personal Record* and revisited in the reminiscent 'Stephen Crane', finished only days before he wrote this piece. Finally, in 'Legends', Conrad might well have had in mind the story of his life in letters, essays and fiction: 'The facts of a legend need not be literally true. But they ought to be credible and they must be in a sort of fundamental accord with the nature of the life it records that is with the character of its subject-matter' (36.5–9).

Critical reaction to the three volumes that preceded *Last Essays* places the posthumous volume in context as the planned 'pendent volume' to *The Mirror of the Sea* or *A Personal Record* anticipated by both Conrad and Curle. In the end, however, the volume more closely resembles *Notes on Life and Letters* in its variety and in its engagements with literature, geopolitics and the personal past. As Captain Felix Riesenberg wrote in the *Saturday Review of Literature* about *Last Essays*: 'This book abounds in a wealth of interesting information about Conrad, largely because he had no intention whatever of engaging in explanations . . . Conrad is now subject to a sort of perpetual Board of Inquiry. What its findings will be remains to be seen, but books will be written about him, books he would probably be unable to understand' (24 April 1926, p. 736).

This 'Board of Inquiry' had actually begun with *The Mirror of the Sea*. For example, the *Athenæum*'s reviewer commented that the volume

---

[1] Ray Stevens, 'Conrad, Slavery and the African Ivory Trade in the 1890s', *Approaches to Teaching Conrad's 'Heart of Darkness' and 'The Secret Sharer'*, ed. Hunt Hawkins and Brian W. Shaffer (2002), pp. 22–30.

had 'seductive diction', 'intimate charm' and a poet's brilliant impressionist vision (27 October 1906, p. 513). The drumbeat continued in the reception of *A Personal Record*: in 'the whole fascinating library of confession, we suppose there was never a volume so wild in its disorder', wrote the reviewer for the *Nation*, concluding that one needed to read it with Conradian irony (24 February 1912, pp. 857–8). *Current Literature* discovered that Conrad answered critics of earlier works by expressing an artistic profession of faith with a 'circuitousness almost mischievous' (April 1912, 471–2). E. M. Forster in reviewing *Notes on Life and Letters* noted in Conrad a 'dread of intimacy', intentionally throwing up 'smoke screens with a reticence to confession' that comes from 'the central chasm of his tremendous genius'.[1] The *New Statesman*'s Robert Lynd, long a commentator on Conrad's work, complained: 'Glimpses we get – amazing glimpses – but never the close and detailed spectacle we desire',[2] and the *New Republic* recorded that Conrad was unable 'to satisfy the reader with a clear sense of design and purpose' (1 June 1921, p. 25).

Similar themes, praise and reservations dominate the no less than sixty-five recorded reviews of *Last Essays*.[3] English reviews focus, among other things, on Conrad's lack of facility in the essay in contrast to his stature as a writer of fiction. John Shand, writing in the *New Criterion*, for example, began: 'Joseph Conrad is not at his best in an essay.' Unlike William Hazlitt and Charles Lamb, for whom the essay 'was just big enough', the essay was 'too small for Conrad', where 'the impersonal style of the anonymous reviewer' rears its head, and Conrad seems to strain for the next thought rather than just letting it fall into place, as he does in the novels: even though there is enough of 'information, interest, amusement' in the volume, Conrad remains 'primarily a teller of tales' and *Last Essays* is ultimately 'irrelevant to his fame' (5 October 1926, pp. 782–5).

J. F. Muirhead of the *Landmark* wrote that *Last Essays* deepens 'the impression I have always had of the essentially foreign note in Conrad's

---

[1] 'The Pride of Mr. Conrad', *Nation and Athenæum*, 19 March 1921, pp. 881–2; rpt as 'Joseph Conrad: A Note', *Abinger Harvest* (1936), pp. 136–41.

[2] 'Mr. Conrad At Home', 12 March 1921, p. 674; rpt *Books and Authors* (1923), pp. 196–205. On Lynd's Conrad criticism, see Richard Niland, '"Who's that fellow Lynn?": Conrad and Robert Lynd', *The Conradian*, 33, no. 1 (2008), 130–44.

[3] Allan H. Simmons, John G. Peters and J. H. Stape, general eds., *Conrad: The Contemporary Reviews*, vol. IV: *The Rescue to Last Essays*, ed. Mary Burgoyne and Katherine Isobel Baxter (forthcoming).

writing'. While he writes English 'better than most Englishmen', it is not 'in the manner of a native', expressing 'a foreign psychology and temperament' (May 1926, 352). Various themes relate to this foreignness in the essays, among them the reliance on reminiscences of childhood. This is most evident in 'Geography and Some Explorers', argued Dudley Carew in the *London Mercury*, who further claimed that the essay illustrates that in Conrad the 'child is father of the man'. He declared that the reason the writer had left such an impression on his time was because of 'his loyalty to the ideals and purposes of his childhood' and the 'steadfastness with which they were upheld' (August 1926, 440).

The *Cambridge Review*, on the other hand, marvelled at the extent of Conrad's knowledge of British seamen and adventurers, concluding that the essays about the sea demonstrate that Conrad's life as a mariner was central to his art even though he could with grace and ease contribute an introduction to a volume on cookery in this 'miscellaneous' but 'notable book' (7 May 1926, p. 389). On the volume's reprinting by Penguin Books, a similar observation was made in the *Irish Times*: 'There is, as always in Conrad's work, a smack of the sea', although the reviewer also noticed in some of the shorter essays a 'delightful vein of humour' (2 September 1944, p. 2). The *Times Literary Supplement* praised a 'half dozen' essays, singling out 'Geography and Some Explorers' and 'The *Torrens*' that 'have the full measure of the nobility of Conrad's prose and the additional virtue given by a flavour of intimacy' (4 March 1926, p. 159). H. C. Minchin in the *Sunday Times* concluded that, when reading Conrad, one feels 'never far inland' because the 'modulation of his grave ... gentle periods resembles the rhythmical fall of waves upon a neighbouring shore' (14 March 1926, p. 9). Resorting to a belletristic catch-phrase, the anonymous reviewer of the *English Review* found 'the essential Conrad' in 'Geography and Some Explorers' and 'The *Torrens*', essays that, he thought, possessed 'something of the quality of our highest odes' (May 1926, 714–15). And, finally, *Punch's* 'Staff of Learned Clerks' concluded that the sea-essays were 'invaluable', but that it was even 'worth while [*sic*] re-reading a long and rather desultory article on Stephen Crane to recapture the memorable paragraph about Stephen Crane's three dogs' (31 March 1926, p. 362).

In America, the most extensive and appreciative review was by Percy A. Hutchison, a staff writer for the *New York Times Book Review*, who, perhaps predictably given the way in which Conrad had been marketed by

Doubleday, concentrated on the sea-essays. Hutchison found the 'clue to Conrad' missing in *The Mirror* and *A Personal Record* but revealed in 'Geography and Some Explorers': 'Spiritually he belonged to "the company of the great navigators"' whose memory accompanied him on his own travels. 'The *Torrens*', he claimed, came closest to *The Mirror of the Sea* in its reliance on remembrance, whereas 'The Unlighted Coast' was a vintage example of Conradian impressionism and 'The Dover Patrol' illustrated his struggle with æsthetics when writing a commemorative essay (28 March 1926, pp. 3, 14).

Lawrence S. Morris, a literary journalist and translator, likewise singled out 'Geography and Some Explorers' in his comments in the *New Republic*: Conrad, who died 'in ignorance of his actual self', wrote two dozen volumes about his 'unusually clear, simple and consistent' dream world, polarized by his childhood experience with a map that led to 'perseverance in the face of the unknown' (12 May 1926, p. 383). Other essays, continued Morris in typically belletristic fashion, focus on 'delightful charm and disarming humility'. He found that Conrad incorporated reminiscence in 'The *Torrens*' and other sea-essays; faithfulness, impressionism and friendship in 'Stephen Crane'; the 'silent endurance' of men in war-time in 'The Unlighted Coast' and 'The Dover Patrol'; and the need to continue the tradition of duty and loyalty in the 'Memorandum'. Psychologically significant incidents of youth, Morris concluded, shape significant adult experiences. And Yale's Sterling Professor of English, Wilbur Cross, citing 'Geography and Some Explorers' and 'Stephen Crane', argued in the *Yale Review* that Conrad knew both himself and Crane well (September 1926, 161–3).

As was to be expected, some reviewers were less generous. The anonymous critic for the New York *Nation* commented that, with the exception of the 'sensitive memoir' of Crane, the essays 'betray a vapidity rather surprising': the 'atmospheric magic . . . fidelity . . . [and] stoicism in the face of disaster' central to Conrad's novels are irrelevant here (October 1926, 381–2). In the *New York Tribune*, a commentator on Thomas Beer's biography of Stephen Crane found Conrad's preface 'dull and patronizing'.[1] The poet, literary critic and philosopher of modern art, Herbert Read, writing for London's *Nation and Athenæum*, concluded that Conrad lacked a creative imagination but used his 'amazing visual memory' successfully in 'Geography and Some

---

[1] Thomas Beer to Edward Garnett, 4 March 1924 (HRC).

Explorers', a 'simple and clear expression of the romantic traditions of the sea and its sailors', and in the 'Memorandum', which embodies 'the last instinctive pride of the authentic sailors' (3 April 1926, p. 30). He preferred the two essays on Crane to much in the volume because they revealed Conrad's 'temperament', a word much used in criticism of Conrad's occasional writing, and concluded that the writer's inadequacy as an essayist was illustrated in the desire 'to render the truth of a phase of life' through the external details of natural objects. Conversely, the anonymous reviewer for the *Living Age* dismissed the bulk of the essays, finding acceptable only the 'formal impressiveness' of 'Geography and Some Explorers' and the 'delicately worded' accounts of Crane (June 1926, 255).

The American humorist and writer of detective stories, Will Cuppy, donning a different, more serious hat for the New York *Bookman*, contrasted Conrad's 'imaginative sympathy' and love for the excitement and humanity of the passing days of ships under sail in the *Torrens* with the mechanical and boring ease of the modern liner in 'Ocean Travel'. Understanding the development of 'personal relationships' on sailing ships, he claimed, was central to understanding the writer's belief that 'truth in life comes only from personal contacts' (July 1926, 598–9).

Reaction to the publication of the fragmentary 'Congo Diary', given wide circulation for the first time, was mixed. Cuppy dismissed it, wondering whom it could possibly interest. The *Bookman*'s R. Ellis Roberts, however, devoted much of his review to it, commenting that the Congo experience was central to Conrad's development as a novelist (June 1926, 172–3), and the reviewer for *The Times* drew attention to Curle's notes drawing parallels to 'Heart of Darkness'. That the two reviews most sympathetic to 'The Congo Diary' took their cue from Curle's anodyne introduction indicates that Conrad's contemporary reviewers were uncertain about how to approach the transmutation of the raw materials of life into fiction.

THE WRITINGS COLLECTED in *Last Essays* variously discuss two topics that are central to Conrad criticism: the nature of his artistry in English reflected in his understanding of the literature of his adopted country, and the ways in which his personal experience influenced and underwrote his writings. Viewed through this lens, *Last Essays* becomes a primer for exploring the contours of Conrad's literary career and the varieties of his style. How did someone brought up in Polish and who subsequently spent nineteen years at sea evolve into one of the most original writers of English, his third language? Conrad is hardly alone among twentieth-century writers who struggled to find a distinctive voice, and he is also allied to his contemporaries who wrestled more explicitly with Freudian and Jungian psychology and the evolution of introspection as a major literary force. D. H. Lawrence fought to free himself through studying psychology, writing poetry and highly autobiographical fiction. James Joyce worked in the 'smithy of his soul' to arrive at *A Portrait of the Artist as a Young Man* (1916) and *Ulysses* (1922), both derived from the autobiographical record, and Virginia Woolf would likewise tussle with narratives drawing from life. In the very informality and assumed casualness of *Last Essays* from 'The Congo Diary' to 'Legends' Conrad no less explores and experiments with ways to address his audience and the problem of the self, or rather, as modern views of consciousness have taught us, selves.

LAST ESSAYS

GEOGRAPHY AND SOME
EXPLORERS
1924

I T I S S A F E to say that for the majority of mankind the superiority of Geography over Geometry lies in the appeal of its figures. 5
It may be an effect of the incorrigible frivolity inherent in human
nature, but most of us will agree that a map is more fascinating to
look at than a figure in a treatise on conic sections – at any rate
for the simple minds which are the equipment of the majority of
the dwellers on this earth.   10
   No doubt a trigonometrical survey may be a romantic undertaking, striding over deserts and leaping over valleys never before
trodden by the foot of civilised man; but its accurate operations
can never have for us the fascination of the first hazardous steps
of a venturesome, often lonely explorer jotting down by the light 15
of his campfire the thoughts, the impressions and the toil of his
day. For a long time yet a few suggestive words grappling with
things seen will have the advantage over a long array of precise no
doubt interesting, and even profitable figures. The earth is a stage
and though it may be an advantage, even to the right comprehen- 20
sion of the play, to know its exact configuration, it is always the
drama of human endeavour that will be the thing, with a ruling
passion expressed by outward action marching perhaps blindly to
success or failure, which themselves are often undistinguishable
from each other at first. Of all the sciences Geography finds its 25
origin in action, and what is more, in adventurous action of the
kind that appeals to sedentary people who like to dream of arduous adventure in the manner of prisoners dreaming behind their
bars of all the hardships and hazards of liberty dear to the heart
of man.   30
   Descriptive Geography like any other kind of science has
been built on the experience of certain phenomena and on
experiments prompted by that unappeasable curiosity of men
which their intelligence has elevated into a quite respectable passion for acquiring knowledge. Like other sciences it has fought its 35

way to truth through a long series of errors. It has suffered from
the love of the marvellous, from our credulity, from rash and
unwarrantable assumptions, from the play of unbridled fancy.
Geography had its phase of circumstantially extravagant speculation which had nothing to do with the pursuit of truth but has
given us a curious glimpse of the mediæval mind playing in its
ponderous childish way with the problems of our earth's shape,
its size, its character, its products, its inhabitants. Cartography was
almost as pictorial then, as some modern newspapers. It crowded
its maps with pictures of strange pageants, strange trees, strange
beasts, drawn with amazing precision in the midst of theoreti-
cally conceived continents. It delineated imaginary Kingdoms of
Monomotapa and of Prester John, the regions infested by lions,
haunted by unicorns, inhabited by men with reversed feet, or eyes
in the middle of their breasts. All this might have been amusing if
the mediæval gravity in the absurd had not been in itself a wearisome thing. But what of that! Has not the key science of modern
chemistry passed through its dishonest phase of Alchemy (a por-
tentous development of the confidence-trick) and our knowledge
of the starry sky been arrived at through the superstitious idealism
of Astrology looking for men's fate in the depths of the infinite!
Mere megalomania on a colossal scale. Yet, for solemn fooling of
the scientific order, I prefer the kind that does not lay itself out
to thrive on the fears and the cupidities of men. From that point
of view Geography is the most blameless of sciences. Its fabulous
phase never aimed at cheating simple mortals (who are a multitude) out of their peace of mind or their money. At the most it has
enticed some of them away from their homes, to death may be,
now and then to a little disputed glory, not seldom to contumely,
never to high fortune. The greatest of them all who has presented
modern geography with a new world to work upon, was at one time
loaded with chains and thrown into prison. Columbus remains a
pathetic figure, not a sufferer in the cause of geography but a
victim of the imperfections of jealous human hearts, accepting
his fate with resignation. Among explorers he appears lofty in his
troubles and like a man of a kingly nature. His contribution to the
knowledge of the earth was certainly royal. And if the discovery
of America was the occasion of the greatest outburst of reckless
cruelty and greed known to history we may say this, at least, for it
that the gold of Mexico and Peru unlike the gold of Alchemists

was really there, palpable yet, as ever, the most elusive of the Fata
Morgana that lure the men away from their homes, as a moment
of reflexion will convince anyone. For nothing is more certain
than that there will never be enough gold to go round, as the
Conquistadors found out by experience.

I suppose it is not very charitable of me but I must say that to
this day I feel a malicious pleasure at the many disappointments
of those pertinacious searchers for Eldorado, who climbed mountains, pushed through forests, swam rivers, floundered in bogs,
without giving a single thought to the science of geography. Not
for them the serene joys of scientific research but infinite toil
in hunger, thirst, sickness, battle; with broken heads, unseemly
squabbles, and empty pockets in the end. I cannot help thinking
it served them right. It is an ugly tale which has not much to do
with the service of geography. The geographical knowledge of our
day is of the kind that would have been beyond the conception
of the hardy followers of Cortez and Pizarro; and of that most
estimable of Conquerors who was called Cabeza de Vaca, who
was high-minded and dealt humanely with the heathen nations
whose territories he traversed in search of one more Eldorado. It
is said they loved him greatly; but now the very memory of those
nations is gone from the earth, while their territories, which they
could not take with them, are being traversed many times every
twenty-four hours by the trains of the Southern Pacific Railroad.

The discovery of the New World marks the end of the fabulous
geography, and it must be owned that the history of the Conquest
contains at least one great moment – I mean a geographical great
moment – when Vasco Núñez de Balboa, while crossing the Isthmus of Panama, set his eyes for the first time on the ocean the
immensity of which he did not suspect, and which in his elation
he named the Pacific. It is anything but that; but the privileged
Conquistador can not be blamed, for surrendering to his first
impression. The Gulf of Panama which is what he really saw with
that first glance is one of the calmest spots on the waters of the
globe. Too calm. The old navigators dreaded it as a dangerous
region where one might be caught and lie becalmed for weeks
with one's crew dying slowly of thirst under a cloudless sky. The
worst of fates, this, to feel yourself die in a long and helpless agony.
How much preferable a region of storms where man and ship can
at least put up a fight and remain defiant almost to the last. I must

not be understood to mean that a tempest at sea is a delightful
experience, but I would rather face the fiercest tempest than a gulf
pacific even to deadliness, a prison-house for incautious caravels
and a place of torture for their crews. But Balboa was charmed
5   with its serene aspect. He did not know where he was. He probably
thought himself within a stone's throw, as it were, of the Indies
and Cathay. Or did he perhaps like a man touched with grace,
have a moment of exalted vision, the awed feeling that what he
was looking at was an abyss of waters, comparable in its extent to
10 the view of the unfathomable firmament, and sown all over with
groups of islands resembling the constellations of the sky?

But whatever spiritual glimpse of the truth he might have had,
Balboa could not possibly know that this great moment of his life
had added suddenly thousands of miles to the circumference of
15 the globe, had opened an immense theatre for the human drama
of adventure and exploration, a field for the missionary labours
of, mainly, Protestant churches, and spread an enormous canvas
on which arm-chair geographers could paint the most fanciful
variants of their pet theory of a great southern continent. I will
20 not quarrel with the old post-Columbian cartographers for their
wild but on the whole interesting inventions. The provocation to
let oneself go was considerable. Geography militant, which had
succeeded geography fabulous, did not seem able to accept the
idea that there was much more water than land on this globe.
25 Nothing would satisfy their sense of the fitness of things but an
enormous extent of solid earth which they placed in that region of
the South, where, as a matter of fact, the great white-crested seas of
stormy latitudes will be free to chase each other all round the globe
to the end of time. I suppose, their landsmen's temperament stood
30 in the way of their recognition that the world of geography, so far
as the apportioning of space goes, seems to have been planned
mostly for the convenience of fishes.

What is surprising to me is that the seamen of the time should
have really believed that the large continents to the north of
35 the equator, demanded as a matter of good art or else of sound
science, to be balanced by corresponding masses of land in the
southern hemisphere. They were simple souls. The chorus of arm
chair people all singing the same tune made them blind to the
many plain signs of a great open sea. Every bit of coast line dis-
40 covered, every mountain top glimpsed in the distance, had to be

dragged loyally into the scheme of the Terra Australis Incognita. Even Tasman, the best seaman of them all before James Cook, the most accomplished of seventeenth century explorers and navigators, that went forth to settle the geography of the Pacific – even Tasman after coming unexpectedly upon the North Island of New Zealand, and lingering long enough there to chart roughly a bit of the coast line and lose a boat's crew in a sudden affray with the Maoris, seemed to take it for granted that this was the western limit of an enormous continent extending away towards the point of South America. Mighty is the power of a theory, especially if based on such a commonsense notion as the balance of continents. And it must be remembered that it is difficult for us now to realize not only the navigational dangers of unknown seas but the awful geographical incertitudes of the first explorers in that new world of waters.

Tasman's journal (which was published not a very long time ago) gives us some idea of their perplexing difficulties. The early navigators had had no means of ascertaining their exact position on the globe. They could calculate their latitudes but the problem of longitude was a matter which bewildered their minds and often falsified their judgment. It had to be a matter of pure guess work. Tasman and his officers when they met on board the *Heemskerck* anchored in Murderers' Bay, to consider their further course in the light of their instructions, did not know where any of the problematic places named in their instructions were, neither did they know where they themselves were. Tasman might have sailed north or east, but in the end he decided to sail between the two, and, circling about, returned to Batavia where he was received coldly by his employers the Honorable Governor General and the Council in Batavia. Their final judgment was that Abel Tasman was a skilful navigator but that he had shown himself "remiss" in his investigations, and that he had been guilty of leaving certain problems unsolved.

We are told that Tasman did not expect this arm-chair criticism; and indeed, even now, it seems surprising to an unprejudiced mind. It was the voyage during which, amongst other things, Tasman discovered the island by which his name lives on the charts, took first contact with New Zealand (which was not seen again till 130 years afterwards), sailed over many thousands of miles of uncharted seas bringing with him a journal which was of

much value afterwards for his exploring successors. It may be he
was hurt by the verdict of the Honorable Council but he does not
seem to have been cast down by it, for it appears that shortly afterward he asked for a rise of salary – and, what is still more significant,
5   he got it. He was obviously a valuable servant but I am sorry to say
that his character as a man was not of the kind to cause Governors
and Councils to treat him with particular consideration. Except in
professional achievement he is not comparable to Captain Cook,
a humble son of the soil, like himself but a modest man of genius,
10   the familiar associate of the most learned in the land, medallist of
the Royal Society and a captain in the Royal Navy. But there was a
taint of an unscrupulous adventurer in Tasman. It is certain that
at various times his patron the governor Anthony van Diemen
and the Honourable Council in Batavia had employed him in
15   some shady transactions connected with the Japan trade. There
is also no doubt that, once, he had on his own responsibility, kidnapped an influential Chinaman who stood in the way of some
business negotiation Tasman was conducting with the Sultan of
Acheen. The Chinaman may have been a worthless person but
20   one wonders what happened to him in the end, and, in any case,
the proceeding is open to criticism. Then in his old age he got
into some disreputable scrape which caused the congregation with
which he worshipped to ask him to resign his membership. Even
the Honourable Council was startled, and dismissed him from his
25   employment though characteristically enough not actually from
their service. The action of the Council fixes the character of the
man better than any scandalous story. He was valuable but com-
promising. All these regrettable details came to my knowledge
quite recently in a very amusing and interesting book, but I must
30   confess that my early admiration for Tasman as one of the early
fathers of militant geography has not been affected very much
by it. Remiss or not he had in the course of his voyages mapped
8000 miles of an island which by common consent is called now
a continent – a, geologically, very old continent indeed, but now
35   the home of a very young Commonwealth with all the possibilities
of material and intellectual splendour still hidden in its future. I
like to think that in that portion of the Elysian Fields set apart for
great navigators James Cook would not refuse to acknowledge the
civilities of Abel Tasman, a fellow seaman who had first reported
40   the existence of New Zealand in the perplexed bewildered way of

those times, 130 years before Captain Cook on his second voyage
laid for ever the ghost of Terra Australis Incognita and added New
Zealand to the scientific domain of the geography triumphant of
our day.

No shadow of remissness or doubtful motive rests upon the
achievement of Captain Cook who came out of a labourer's cottage to take his place at the head of the masters of maritime
exploration, who worked at the great geographical problem of
the Pacific. *Endeavour* was the name of the ship of his first voyage,
and it was also the watchword of his professional life. *Resolution*
was the name of the ship he commanded himself on his second
expedition; and it was the determining quality of his soul. I will
not say that it was the greatest, because he had all the other manly
qualities of a great man. The voyages of the early explorers were
prompted by an acquisitive spirit, the idea of lucre in some form,
the desire of trade, or the desire of loot, disguised in more or
less fine words. But Cook's three voyages were free from any taint
of that sort. His aims needed no disguise; they were scientific.
His deeds speak for themselves with the masterly simplicity of a
hard-won success. In that respect he seems to belong to the single-
minded explorers of the nineteenth century, the late Fathers of
Militant Geography whose only object was the search for truth.
Geography is a science of facts and they devoted themselves to the
discovery of facts in the configuration and features of the main
continents.

It was a century of landsmen investigators. In saying this I do not
forget the Polar Explorers whose aims were certainly as pure as the
air of those high latitudes where not a few of them laid down their
lives for the advancement of Geography. Seamen, men of science,
it is difficult to speak of them without admirative emotion. The
dominating figure amongst the seamen explorers of the first half
of the nineteenth century is that of another good man Sir John
Franklin whose fame rests not only on the extent of his discoveries
but on professional prestige and high personal character. This
great navigator, who never returned home, served geography even
in his death. The persistent efforts extending over ten years to
ascertain his fate advanced greatly our knowledge of the Polar
Regions.

As gradually revealed to the world his fate appeared the more
tragic in this, that for the first two years the way of the *Erebus*

and *Terror* expedition seemed to be the way to the desired and
important success, while in truth it was all the time the way of
death, the end of the darkest drama perhaps played behind the
curtain of Arctic mystery. The last words unveiling the mystery of
5   the *Erebus* and *Terror* expedition were brought home and disclosed
to the world by Sir Leopold M'Clintock in his book *The Voyage
of the Fox in the Arctic Seas*. It is a little book but it records with
manly simplicity the tragic ending of a great tale. It so happened
that I was born in the year of its publication. Therefore, I may
10 be excused for not getting hold of it till ten years afterwards.
I can only account for it falling into my hands by the fact that
the fate of Sir John Franklin was a matter of European interest,
and that Sir Leopold M'Clintock's book was translated I believe
into every language of the white races. My copy was probably
15 in French. But I have read the work many times since. I have
now on my shelves a copy of a popular edition got up exactly as
I remember my first one. It contains the touching facsimile of
a printed form filled in with a summary record of the two ships,
with the name of "Sir John Franklin commanding the expedition"
20 and written in ink, and the pathetic underlined entry "*All well.*"
It was found by Sir Leopold M'Clintock under a cairn and it is
dated just a year before the two ships had to be abandoned in
their deadly ice-trap and their crews' long and desperate struggle
for life began. There could hardly have been imagined a better
25 book to let in the breath of the stern romance of Polar exploration
into the existence of a boy whose knowledge of the Poles of the
earth had been till then of an abstract formal kind as the mere
imaginary ends of the imaginary axis upon which the earth turns.
The great spirit of the realities of the story sent me off on romantic
30 explorations of my inner self; to the discovery of the taste for
poring over maps; revealed to me the existence of a latent devotion
to geography which interfered with my devotion, such as it was, to
my other school-work. Unfortunately the marks awarded for that
subject were almost as few as the hours apportioned to it in the
35 school curriculum by persons of no romantic sense for the real,
ignorant of the great possibilities of active life; with no desire for
struggle, no notion of the wide spaces of the world – mere bored
professors in fact, who were not only middle-aged but looked to
me as if they had never been young. And their geography was very
40 much like themselves, a bloodless thing with a dry skin covering

a repulsive armature of uninteresting bones. I would be ashamed of my warmth in digging up a hatchet which has been buried now for nearly fifty years if those fellows had not tried so often to take my scalp at the yearly exams. There are things that one does not forget. And besides the geography which I had discovered for myself was the Geography of open spaces and wide horizons built up on men's devoted work in the open air, the old Geography, still militant but already conscious of its approaching end with the death of the last great explorer. The antagonism was radical. Thus it happened that I got no marks at all for my first and only paper on Arctic geography, which I wrote at the age of thirteen. I still think that for my tender years it was an erudite performance. I certainly did know something of Arctic geography, but what I was after really, I suppose, was the history of Arctic exploration. My knowledge had considerable gaps, but I had managed to compress my enthusiasm into just two pages, which in itself was a sort of merit. Yet I got no marks. For one thing it was not a "set subject". I believe the only comment made about it to my private tutor was that I seemed to have been wasting my time on reading books of travel instead of attending to my studies. I tell you those fellows were always trying to take my scalp. On another occasion I just saved it by proficiency in map-drawing. It must have been good, I suppose; but all I remember about it is that it was done in a loving spirit.

I have no doubt that star-gazing is a fine occupation, for it leads you within the borders of the unattainable. But map-gazing, to which I became addicted so early, brings the problems of the great spaces of the earth into stimulating and directive contact with sane curiosity and gives an honest precision to one's imaginative faculty. And the honest maps of the nineteenth century nourished in me a passionate interest in the truth of geographical facts and the desire for precise knowledge which was extended later to other subjects.

For a change had come over the spirit of cartographers. From the middle of the eighteenth century on, the business of map-making had been growing into an honest occupation registering the hard won knowledge but also in a scientific spirit recording the geographical ignorance of its time. And it was Africa, the continent out of which the Romans used to say "some new thing was always coming" that got cleared of the dull imaginary wonders

of the dark ages which were replaced by exciting spaces of white paper. Regions unknown! My imagination could depict to itself there worthy adventurers and devoted men, nibbling at the edges, attacking from north and south and east and west, conquering a
5 bit of truth here and a bit of truth there and sometimes swallowed up by the mystery their hearts were so persistently set on unveiling.

Amongst them Mungo Park of western Sudan and Bruce of Abyssinia were I believe the first friends I made when I began to take notice – I mean geographical notice – of the continents of the
10 world into which I was born. The fame of these two had already been for a long time European and their figures had become historical by then. But their story was a very novel thing to me, for the very latest geographical news that could have been whispered to me in my cradle was that of the expedition of Burton and Speke,
15 the news of the existence of Tanganyika and of Victoria Nyanza.

I stand here confessed as a contemporary of the Great Lakes. Yes, I could have heard of their discovery in my cradle and it was only right that grown to a boy's estate I should have in the later sixties done my first bit of map-drawing, and paid my first homage
20 to the prestige of their first explorers. It consisted in entering laboriously in pencil the outline of Tanganyika on my beloved old atlas which having been published in about 1852 knew nothing of course of the Great Lakes.

The heart of its Africa was white and big. Surely it could have
25 been nothing but a romantic impulse which prompted the idea of bringing it up to date with all the accuracy of which I was capable. Thus I could imagine myself stepping in the very footprints of geographical discovery. And it was not all wasted time. As a bit of prophetic practice it was not bad for me. Many years afterwards
30 as second officer in the Merchant Service it has been my duty to correct and bring up to date charts of more than one ship, according to Admiralty notices. I did this work conscientiously and with a sense of responsibility; but it was not in the nature of things that I should ever recapture the excitement of that entry
35 of Tanganyika on the blank of my old atlas.

It must not be supposed that I gave up my interest in the Polar regions. My heart and my warm participation swung from the frigid to the torrid zone, fascinated by the problems, no doubt, but more yet by the men who like masters of a great art worked
40 each according to his temperament to complete the picture of the

earth. Almost each day of my schoolboy life had its hour given up to their company. And to this day I think that it was a very good company.

Not the least interesting part in the study of geographical discovery lies in the insight it gives one into the characters of that special kind of men who devoted the best part of their lives to the exploration of land and sea. In the world of mentality and imagination which I was entering, it was they and not the characters of famous fiction who were my first friends. Of some of them I had soon formed for myself an image indissolubly connected with certain parts of the world. For instance Western Sudan of which I could draw the rivers and principal features from memory even now, means for me an episode in Mungo Park's life. It means for me the vision of a young, emaciated, fair-haired man, clad simply in a tattered shirt and worn out breeches, gasping for breath and lying on the ground in the shade of an enormous African tree (species unknown) while from a neighboring village of grass huts a charitable black-skinned woman is approaching him with a calabash full of pure cold water, a simple draught of which, according to himself, seems to have effected a miraculous cure. The Central Sudan on the other hand is represented to me by a very different picture: that of a self-confident and keen-eyed person in a long cloak and wearing a turban on his head, riding slowly towards a gate in the mud walls of an African city, from which an excited population is streaming out to behold the wonder: Dr Barth, the protégé of Lord Palmerston subsidised by the British Foreign Office, approaching Kano which no European eye has seen till then but where forty years later my friend Sir Hugh Clifford the Governor of Nigeria had travelled in state in order to open a College! I must confess that I read that bit of news and inspected the many pictures in the illustrated papers without any particular elation. Education is a great thing but Dr Barth gets in the way. Neither will the monuments left by all sorts of empire-builders suppress for me the memory of David Livingstone. The words central Africa bring before my eyes an old man with a rugged kind face and a clipped grey moustache, pacing wearily at the head of a few black followers along the reed-fringed lakes towards the dark native hut on the Congo headwaters in which he died clinging in his very last hour to his heart's unappeased desire for the sources of the Nile. That passion had changed him in his last days from a great explorer

into a restless wanderer refusing to go home any more. From his
exalted place among the blessed of militant geography and with
his memory enshrined in Westminster Abbey he can well afford
to smile without bitterness at the fatal delusion of his exploring
5 days, a notable European figure and the most venerated perhaps
of all objects of my early geographical enthusiasm.

Only once did that enthusiasm expose me to the derision of
my school-boy chums. One day, putting my finger on a blank spot
in the very middle of the, then white, heart of Africa I declared
10 that some day I would go there. My chums' chaffing was perfectly
justifiable. I myself was ashamed of having been betrayed into
mere vapouring. Nothing was further from my wildest hopes. Yet
it is a fact that about eighteen years afterwards a wretched little
stern wheel steamboat I commanded lay moored to the bank of
15 an African river. Everything was dark under the stars. Every other
white man on board was asleep. I was glad to be alone on deck
smoking the pipe of peace after an anxious day. The subdued
thundering mutter of Stanley Falls hung in the heavy night air
of the last navigable reach of the Upper Congo, while no more
20 than ten miles away in Reshid's camp just above the Falls the yet
unbroken power of the Congo Arabs slumbered uneasily. Their
day was over. Away in the middle of the stream, on a little island
nestling all black in the foam of the broken water a solitary little
light glimmered feebly, and I said to myself with awe "this is the
25 very spot of my boyish boast." A great melancholy descended on
me. Yes, this was the very spot. But there was no shadowy friend
to stand by my side in the night of the enormous wilderness,
no great haunting memory but only the unholy recollection of
a prosaic newspaper stunt and the distasteful knowledge of the
30 vilest scramble for loot that ever disfigured the history of human
conscience and geographical exploration. What an end to the
idealised realities of a boy's day-dreams! I wondered what I was
doing there, for indeed it was only an unforeseen episode hard
to believe in now, in my seaman's life. Still the fact remains that
35 I have smoked the pipe of peace at midnight in the very heart of
the African continent, and felt very lonely there.

But never so at sea. There I never felt lonely because I never
lacked company. The company of great navigators, the first grown-
up friends of my early boyhood. The unchangeable sea preserves
40 for one the sense of its past, the memory of things accomplished

by wisdom and daring amongst its restless waves. It was those things that commanded my profound loyalty; and perhaps it is by the professional favour of the great navigators ever present to my memory that, neither explorer nor scientific navigator, I have been permitted to sail through the very heart of the old Pacific mystery; a region which even in my time remained imperfectly charted and still remote from the knowledge of men.

It was in 1888 when in command of a ship loading in Sydney a mixed cargo for Mauritius that, one day, all of a sudden, all the deep-lying historic sense of the exploring adventures in the Pacific surged up to the surface of my being. Almost without reflection I sat down and wrote a letter to my owners, suggesting, that instead of the usual southern route, I should take the ship to Mauritius by way of Torres Straits. I ought to have received a severe rap on the knuckles, if only for wasting their time in submitting such an unheard of proposition. I must say I awaited the reply with some trepidation. It came in due course but instead of beginning with chiding words, "We fail to understand etc etc" it simply called my attention in the first paragraph to the fact that "there would be an additional insurance premium to pay for that route" and so on. And it ended like this: "Upon the whole however we have no objection to your taking the ship through Torres Straits if you are certain that the season is not too far advanced to endanger the success of your passage by the calms which as you know, prevail at times in the Arafura Sea." I read and in my heart I felt compunctious. The season was somewhat advanced and I had not been scrupulously honest in my argumentation. Perhaps it was because I never expected it to be effective. And here it was all left to my responsibility. My letter must have struck a lucky day in Messrs H. Simpson & Sons' offices – a romantic day! I won't pretend that I regret my lapse from strict honesty, for what would the memory of my sea life have been for me if it had not included a passage through Torres Straits in their fullest extent, from the mouth of the Great Fly River right on along the track of the early navigators.

The season being advanced I was insistent on leaving Sydney during a heavy south-east gale. Both the pilot and the tug-master were scandalized by my obstinacy and they hastened to leave me to my own devices while still inside Sydney Heads. The fierce Southeaster caught me up on its wings and no later than the ninth day I was outside the entrance of Torres Straits named after

the undaunted and reticent Spaniard who in the seventeenth century first sailed that way without knowing where he was, without suspecting he had New Guinea on one side of him and the whole of the solid Australian continent on the other (he thought he was
5 passing through an archipelago); the Straits whose existence for a century and a half had been doubted, argued about, squabbled over by geographers and even denied by the disreputable and skilful navigator Abel Tasman (who thought it was a large bay) – and whose true contours were first laid down on the map by
10 James Cook, the navigator without fear and without reproach, the greatest in achievement and character of the later seamen-fathers of militant geography. If the dead haunt the scenes of their earthly exploits then I must have been attended benevolently by those three shades: the inflexible Spaniard, of such lofty spirit that in
15 his report he disdains to say a single word about the appalling hardships and dangers of his passage; the pig-headed Hollander who having made up his mind that there was no passage there, missed the truth by only fifty miles or so; and the great Englishman, a son of the soil, a great commander and a great professional
20 seaman who solved that question among many others, and left no doubtful problems of the Pacific behind him. Great shades! All friends of my youth!

It was not without a certain emotion that commanding very likely the first and certainly the last merchant ship that carried a
25 cargo that way from Sydney to Mauritius I put her head at daybreak for Bligh's Entrance and packed on her every bit of canvas she could carry. Windswept, sunlit empty waters were all around me half-veiled by a brilliant haze. The first thing that caught my eye upon the play of green, white-capped waves was a black speck
30 marking conveniently the end of a low sandbank. It looked like the wreck of some small vessel. I altered the course slightly in order to pass close by in the hope of being able to read the letters on her stern. They were already faded. Her name was *Honolulu.* The name of the port I could not make out. The story of her life is
35 known by now to God alone, and the winds must have drifted long ago round her remains a quiet grave of the very sand on which she had died. Thirty-six hours afterwards, of which about nine were spent at anchor, approaching the other end of the Straits, I sighted a gaunt, grey wreck of a big American ship lying high
40 and dry on the southernmost of the Warrior Reefs. I had heard of

her. She had been there for years. She was legendary. She loomed up sinister, an enormous *memento mori* raised by refraction on this serene afternoon above the far away line of the far horizon drawn under the sinking sun.

And thus I passed out of Torres Straits before dusk settled on its waters. Just as a clear sun sank ahead of my ship I took a bearing of a little island for a fresh departure, an insignificant crumb of dark earth lonely like an advanced sentinel of that mass of broken land and water to watch the approaches from the side of the Arafura Sea. But to me it was a hallowed spot for I knew that the *Endeavour* had been hove to off it in the year 1762 for her captain, whose name was James Cook, to go ashore for half an hour. What he could possibly want to do I can not imagine. Perhaps only to be alone with his thoughts for a moment. The dangers and triumphs of exploration and discovery were over for that voyage. All that remained to do was to go home. And perhaps his great and equable soul, tempered in the incessant perils of a long exploration, wanted to commune with itself at the end of its task. It may be that on this dry crumb of the earth's crust which I was setting by compass he had tasted a moment of perfect peace. I could depict to myself the famous seaman navigator a lonely figure in a three cornered red hat and square skirted laced coat pacing to and fro slowly on the rocky shore, while in the ship's boat, lying off on her oars, the coxswain kept his eyes open for the slightest sign of the captain's hand.

Thus the sea has been for me a hallowed ground, thanks to the books of travel and discovery which have peopled it with unforgettable shades of the masters in the calling which in a humble way was to be mine too, men great in their endeavour and in hard won successes of militant geography; men who went forth each according to his lights and with varied motives, laudable or sinful but each bearing in his breast a spark of the sacred fire.

THE *TORRENS*
A PERSONAL TRIBUTE
1923

I T I S O N E of the pleasant surprises of my accumulated years
5   to be still here when the shade of that beautiful ship is being
evoked for a moment by a sea-travel magazine before the eyes of
a public which does its sea-travelling under very different conditions. Personally I cannot help thinking them so much improved
as needlessly sophisticated. However that opinion of mine may be
10   wildly wrong. I am not familiar with the demands of the spirit of
the age. And, besides, I know next to nothing of sea-travel. Even
of people who do that thing I know but few. My two years in the
Torrens is my only professional experience of passengers; and
though we – officers brought up in strenuous Indiamen and
15   famous wool-clippers – did not think much of passengers regard-
ing them as derogatory nuisances with delicate feelings which
prevented one driving one's ship till all was blue, I will confess that this experience was most fortunate from every point of
view marking the end of my sea-life with new impressions, pleas-
20   ant memories and precious friendships. The pleasant memories
include the excellent ship's companies it was my luck to work with
on each of my two voyages. But the *Torrens* had a fame which
attracted the right kind of sailor, and when engaging her crew
her chief officer had always a large and promising crowd to pick
25   and choose from. There was in it always a certain proportion of
men who had served in her before and were anxious to join again;
apart from her more brilliant qualities, such as her speed and her
celebrated good looks (which by themselves go a long way with
a sailor) she was regarded as a "comfortable ship," in a strictly
30   professional sense: which means that she was known to handle
easily and to be a good sea-boat in heavy weather. I cannot say that
during my time in her we ever experienced really heavy weather;
but we had the usual assortment of winds up to "very strong gales"
(logbook style) from various directions; and I can testify that, on

every point of sailing, the way that ship had of letting big seas slip under her did one's heart good to watch. It resembled so much an exhibition of intelligent grace and unerring skill that it could fascinate even the least seamanlike of our passengers. A passage under sail brings out in the course of days whatever there may   5
be of sea-love and sea-sense in any individual whose soul is not indissolubly wedded to the pedestrian shore.

There are of course degrees of landsmanism, even to the incurable. A gentleman whom we had on board on my first voyage presented an extreme instance of it. It, however, trenched upon   10
the morbid in its excessive sea fright which had its pathetic as well as comic moments. We had not been more than ten days out from Plymouth when he took it into his head that his shattered constitution could not stand the voyage. Note that he had not as much as an hour of seasickness. He maintained however that a few more   15
days at sea would certainly kill him. He was absolutely certain of it and he pleaded day after day with a persistent agonized earnestness to be put ashore on the first convenient bit of land which in this case would have been Teneriffe. But it is not so easy for a sailing ship to make an unexpected call without losing much time.   20
Any deviation from a direct course of the voyage (unless in case of actual distress) would have invalidated the ship's insurance. It was not to be thought of, especially as the man looked fit enough and the doctor had reported that he could not find the slightest evidence of organic disease of any sort. I was sorry for my captain.   25
He could not refuse to listen to the man. Neither could he accede to his request. It was absurd. And yet! . . . who could tell? It became worse when he began to offer progressive bribes up to £300 or more. I don't know why I was called to one of those awful conferences. The even, low flow of argument from those trembling lips   30
impressed me. He exhibited to us his bank pass-book to prove that he had the means to buy his life from us. Our doctor stood by in grim silence. The Captain looked dead tired but kept his temper wonderfully under the implication of callous heartlessness. It was I who could not stand the inconclusive anguish of the situation. It   35
was not so long since I had been neurasthenic myself. At the very next pause I remarked in a loud and cheery tone "I suppose I had better get the anchors ready first thing to-morrow." The Captain glared at me speechlessly, as well he might. But the effect of the

hopeful word "anchors" had an instantaneous soothing effect on our passenger. As if satisfied that there was at last somebody on his side he was willing to leave it at that. He went out.

I need not say that next day the anchors were not touched. But we sighted Teneriffe at thirty miles off, to windward – a towering and majestic shadow against the sky. Our passenger spent the day leaning over the rail watching it till it melted away in the dusk. It was the confirmation of a death-sentence for him I suppose. He took it very well.

He gave me the opportunity to admire for many days an exhibition of consistent stoicism. He never repined. He withdrew within himself. Though civil enough when addressed directly he had very few words to give to anybody – as though his fund of speech had been expended while pleading in vain for his life. But his heart was burning with indignant anger. He went ashore unreadable but unforgiving without taking notice of anyone in the ship. I was the only exception. Poor, futile creature as I was he remembered that I at least had seemed to be "on his side". If I may take an Irishman's privilege I will say that if he had really died he could not have abhorred the ship and everyone in her, more. To have been exposed to live for seventy days under a sentence of death was a soul-searing outrage, and he very properly resented it to the last.

I must say that, in general, our passengers would begin very soon to look thoroughly at home in the ship. Its life was homely enough, and far removed from the ideals of Ritz hotels. The monotony of the sea is easier to bear than the boredom of the shore if only because there is no visible remedy and no contrasts at hand to keep discontent alive. The world contains, or contained then, some people who could put up with a sense of peace for three months. The feeling of close confinement in a sailing ship with her propelling power working in the open air and with her daily life going on in public sight, and presenting the varied interests of human character and individual exertion, is always less oppressive than in a steamer even many times her size. Besides in a sailing ship there are neither vibration nor mechanical noises to grow actively wearisome. Another advantage was that the sailing passenger ships at that epoch were never crowded. The cabins of the *Torrens* had two berths each, but they were roomy and not overfurnished with all sorts of inadequate contrivances for comfort so called. I have seen the cabins of a modern passenger steamship with three or

four berths in them (their very couches being numbered) which
were not half as big as ours. Not half as big – in fact some of our
passengers who seized the opportunity of learning to dance the
hornpipe from our boatswain (an agile professor) could pursue
their studies in their own rooms. And that art requires for its   5
practice more space than the proverbial swinging of a cat, I can
assure you. Much more.

The *Torrens* was launched in 1875, only a few months after I
had managed, after lots of trouble, to launch myself on the waters
of the Mediterranean. Thus we began our careers about the same   10
time. From the professional point of view hers was by far the
greater success. It began early and went on growing for fifteen
years under the command of Captain H. R. Angel, whose own
long career as a shipmaster was the greatest success of the three.
He left her in 1890 and people said that he took his ship's luck   15
away with him. The *Torrens* certainly lost some of her masts the
very next voyage, by one of those sudden accidents for which no
man can be made responsible. I joined her a year afterwards on
the 2nd of November 1891, in London, and I ceased to "belong
to her," as the saying is (it was a wrench), on the 15th of October,   20
1893, when in London Dock I took a long look from the quay
at that ship I once had under my care, and stepping round the
corner of a tall warehouse parted from her forever and at the same
time stepped, in merciful ignorance, out of my sea life altogether.

I owed the opportunity of my close association with my famous   25
contemporary to my acquaintance with Captain W. H. Cope who
succeeded Captain H. R. Angel. I had known him some years
before but only slightly, in a social way. I knew that he had been
a Conway boy, that he had had much varied service in mail boats,
and in the Hooghly pilot steamer service before the command of   30
the *Torrens* came in his way. But I had no reason to believe that
he remembered me particularly. However on hearing from his
brother that I was ashore he sent me word that the *Torrens* wanted
a chief officer, as a matter that might interest me. I was then
recovering slowly from a bad break-down after a most unpleasant   35
and persistent tropical disease which I had caught in Africa while
commanding a steamer on the river Congo. Yet the temptation
was great. I confessed to him my doubts of my fitness for the post
from the point of view of health. But he said that moping ashore
never did any one any good and was very encouraging. It was clear   40

that, as the saying goes, my looks did not pity me for he argued
that so far as appearance went there did not seem to be anything
the matter with me. And I suppose I could never have been half as
neurasthenic as our poor passenger who wanted to be put ashore,
for I lasted out two voyages, as my discharges prove though Mr
Basil Lubbock, in his book, *The Colonial Clippers*, credits me with
only one.

But in the end I had to go (and even stay) ashore. Thus my
famous contemporary outlived me at sea by many years and if she
had perhaps a harder life of it than I it was at least untinged with
unavailing regrets, and she escaped the ignominious fate of being
laid up as a coal hulk which so many of her sisters had to suffer.

Mr Lubbock who can put so much interesting knowledge and
right feeling into his studies of our merchant ships calls her: "The
Wonderful *Torrens*". She was! Her fascinations and virtues have
made their marks on the hearts of men. Only last year I received
a letter from a young able seaman whom I remembered having
in my watch, invoking confidently her unforgotten name. "I feel
sure you must be Mr Conrad the chief officer in whose watch I
was when serving in the *Torrens* in 1891 and so I venture to write
to you . . ." A friendly, quiet, middle-aged seaman's letter which
gave me the greatest pleasure. And I know of a retired sailor, a
Britisher, I suppose, in Massachusetts, who is making a model in
loving memory of her who all her life was so worthy of men's loyal
service. I am sorry I had no time to go and see him and to gaze at
the pious work of his hands.

It is touching to read in Mr Lubbock's book that after her
transfer to the Italian flag when she was taken to Genoa to be
broken up, the Genoese shipwrights were so moved by the beauty
of her lines and the perfections of her build that they had no heart
to break her up. They went to work instead to preserve her life for
a few more years, a true labour of love if ever there was one!

But in the end her body of iron and wood so fair to look upon
had to be broken up, I hope with fitting reverence. And as I sit
here thirty years almost to a day since I last set eyes on her, I love to
think that her perfect form found a merciful end on the shores of
the sunlit sea of my boyhood's dreams, and that her fine spirit has
returned to dwell in the regions of the great winds, the inspirers
and the companions of her swift, renowned, sea tossed life which
I too have been permitted to share for a little while.

CHRISTMAS-DAY AT SEA
1923

T HEOLOGICALLY Christmas-day is the greatest occasion for
rejoicing offered to sinful mankind; but this aspect of it is so
august and so great that the human mind fails to contemplate it   5
steadily. Perhaps because it is simply unable to face it because of
its own littleness (for which of course it is in no way to blame).
It prefers to concentrate its attention on ceremonial observances,
expressive generally of good-will and festivity, such, for instance
as giving presents and eating plum puddings. It may be said at   10
once here that from that conventional point of view the spirit of
Christmas-day at sea appears weak, distinctly weak. The opportunities, the materials too, are lacking. Of course a ship's company
got a plum pudding of some sort, and when the captain appears
on deck for the first time the officer of the morning watch greets   15
him with a "Merry Christmas, sir" in a tone only moderately effu-
sive. Anything more would owing to the difference of station not
have been correct. Normally he may expect a return for this in
the shape of a "The same to you" of a nicely graduated heartiness.
He does not get it always however.   20
    One Christmas morning, many years ago (I was young then
and anxious to do the correct thing) my conventional greeting
was met by a grimly scathing "Looks like it, doesn't it?" from my
captain. Nothing more. A three days' more or less "thick" weather
had turned frankly into a dense fog and I had him called up   25
according to orders. We were in the chops of the Channel, with
the Scilly islands on a vague bearing within thirty miles of us and
not a breath of wind anywhere. There the ship remained wrapped
in a damp blanket, and as motionless as a post stuck right in the
way of the wretched steamboats groping blindly in and out of the   30
Channel. I felt I had behaved tactlessly; yet how rude it would have
been to have withheld the Season's Greetings from my captain!
    It is very difficult to know what is the right thing to do, when one
is young. I suffered exceedingly from my gaucherie, but imagine
my disgust when in less than half an hour we had the narrowest   35

possible escape from a collision with a steamer which without
the slightest warning sound appeared like a vague dark blot in
the fog on our bow. She only took on the shape of a ship as she
passed within twenty yards of the end of our jibboom, terrifying us
5 with the furious screeching of her whistle. Her form melted into
nothing long before the end of the beastly noise. But I hope that
her people heard the simultaneous yell of execration from thirty-
six throats which we sent after them by way of a Christmas greeting.
Nothing more at variance with the spirit of peace and good-will
10 could be imagined; and I must add that I never saw a whole
ship's company get so much affected by one of the "close calls"
of the sea. We remained jumpy all the morning; and consumed
our Christmas puddings at noon with restless eyes and straining
ears as if under the shadow of some impending marine calamity
15 or other.

On shore, of course, a calamity at Christmas time would hardly
take any other shape than that of an avalanche – avalanche of
unpaid bills. I think that it is the absence of that kind of danger
which makes Christmas at sea rather agreeable upon the whole. An
20 additional charm consists in there being no worry about presents
at sea. Presents ought to be unexpected things. The giving and
receiving of presents at appointed times seems to me a hypocritical
ceremony, like exchanging gifts of Dead-Sea fruit in proof of sham
good fellowship. But the sea of which I write here is a live sea; the
25 fruits one chances to gather on it may be as salt as tears or as bitter
as death, but they never taste like ashes in the mouth.

In all my twenty years of wandering over the restless waters of
the globe I can only remember one Christmas Day celebrated by a
present given and received. It was in my view a proper live-sea trans-
30 action, no offering of Dead-Sea fruit, and in its unexpectedness
perhaps worth recording. Let me tell you first that it happened in
the year 1879 long before there was any thought of wireless telег-
raphy and when an inspired person trying to prophesy broadcasting would have been regarded as a particularly offensive nuisance
35 and probably sent to a Rest-cure Home. We used to call them
madhouses then in our rude, cave-man, way.

The day break of Christmas Day in the year '79 was fine. The
sun began to shine sometime about four o'clock over the sombre
expanse of the Southern Ocean in Lat. 51, and shortly afterwards

a sail was sighted ahead. The wind was light but a heavy swell was running. Presently I wished "Merry Christmas" to my captain. He looked still sleepy but amiable. I reported the distant sail to him and ventured the opinion that there was something wrong with her. He said "Wrong?" in an incredulous tone. I pointed out that she had all her upper sails furled and that she was brought to the wind, which in that region of the world could not be accounted for on any other theory. He took the glasses from me, directed them towards her stripped masts resembling three Swedish safety matches flying up and down and waggling to and fro ridiculously in that heaving and austere wilderness of countless water-hills and returned them to me without a word. He only yawned. This marked display of callousness gave me a shock. In those days I was generally inexperienced and still a comparative stranger in that particular region of the world of waters.

The captain as is a captain's way disappeared from the deck and after a time our carpenter came up the poop-ladder carrying an empty, small wooden keg, of the sort in which certain ship's provisions are packed. I said surprised, "What do you mean by lugging this thing up here, Chips?" "Captain's orders, sir," he explained shortly. I did not like to question him further and so we only exchanged Christmas greetings and he went away. The next person to speak to me was the steward. He came running up the companion stairs. "Have you any old newspapers in your room, sir?"

We had left Sydney N.S.W. eighteen days before. There were several old Sydney *Heralds*, *Telegraphs*, *Bulletins* in my cabin, besides a few home papers received by the last mail. "Why do you ask, steward?" I inquired naturally. "The captain would like to have them," he said.

And even then I did not understand. The inwardness of these eccentricities. I was only lost in astonishment at them. It was eight o'clock before we had closed with that ship which under her short canvas and heading nowhere in particular seemed to be loafing aimlessly on the very threshold of the gloomy home of storms. But long before that hour I had learned from the number of the boats she carried that this nonchalant ship was a whaler. She was the first whaler I had ever seen. She had hoisted the Stars and Stripes at her peak and her signal flags had told us already that her name was: *Alaska* – two years out from New Bedford – last from Honolulu – two hundred and fifteen days on the cruising ground.

We passed, sailing slowly, within a hundred yards of her; and
5 just as our steward started ringing the breakfast bell, the captain and I held up aloft, in good view of the three figures watching us over her stern, the keg properly headed up and containing, besides an enormous bundle of old newspapers, two boxes of figs in honour of the day. We flung it far over the rail. Instantly our
10 ship sliding down the slope of a high swell left it far behind in our wake. On board the *Alaska* a man in a fur cap flourished an arm; another, a much bewhiskered person, ran forward suddenly. I never saw anything so ready and smart as the way that whaler, rolling desperately all the time lowered one of her boats. The
15 southern ocean went on tossing the two ships like a juggler his gilt balls and the microscopic white speck of the boat seemed to come into the game instantly, as if shot out from a catapult, on the enormous and lonely stage. That Yankee whaler lost not a moment in picking up her Christmas present from the English
20 wool-clipper. Before we had increased the distance very much she dipped her ensign in thanks and asked to be reported all well, with a catch of three "fish". I suppose it paid them for two hundred and fifteen days away from the sounds and sights of the inhabited world like outcasts devoted beyond the confines of mankind's life
25 to some enchanted lonely penance.

Christmas Days at sea are of varied character fair to middling and down to plainly atrocious. In this statement I do not include Christmas Days on board the passenger ships. A passenger is of course a brother (or sister) and quite a nice person in his way, but
30 his days are what I suppose he wants them to be – the conventional festivities of an expensive hotel included in the price of his ticket.

OCEAN TRAVEL
1923

THE ONE STATEMENT that can be safely advanced about travelling at sea is that it is not what it used to be. It is different now elementally. It is not so much a matter of changed propelling 5 power; it is something more. In the old days, under the machinery of sails the distinguished and the undistinguished travellers (of whom there were not so very many) were wafted to distant parts of the world by the movement of variable air currents. Now the travelling multitudes are taken to their destination because of 10 the invariable resistance of water to the screwing motion of the propeller with which fire (that other element) has a lot to do. The whole affair of progress across the seas has become much more complicated and much more precise on its physical side. This has grown also into a marvel. But a marvellous achievement 15 is not necessarily interesting. It may render life more tame than perhaps it should be. I do not mean that any marvel of applied science can tame the wild spirit that lurks in all men and of which the proofs are not far to seek. It only makes the conditions of our pilgrimage less exciting. 20

The whole psychology of sea-travel is changed. Formerly a man setting out on a sea-voyage broke away from shore conditions and found in the ship a new kind of home. This applies even to such comparatively short passages as across the Atlantic. But now a man (especially if setting out for the United States) brings the 25 conditions of shore-life with him on board and finds in his ship the usual sort of a hotel with its attempts at all kinds of sham comforts, all the disadvantages of gregarious life, with the added worry of not being able to get away from it for a certain number of days. The only comfort is to be found in the assurance that the 30 number of days is not great and that, barring accidents, it is fixed. There is a definite date to look forward to – the date of release from that more or less luxurious prison any ship must be to any passenger.

That every passenger (even in the biggest and most hotel-like Atlantic ferry with their territorial names) wishes to escape there can be not the slightest doubt. He may say what he likes but it is a fact of human nature. He looks forward to his release as much
5 as any prisoner. The modern traveller has never the time to get into an acquiescent mood. The sham shore conditions which the shipping companies try to create for him stand in the way too. The hold of the land (which is his natural element) is on him all through the passage and he suffers from a subtle disharmony
10 between his natural tastes and his surroundings.

It was otherwise with the old-time traveller under sail: He had to become acclimatised to that moral atmosphere of ship-life which he was fated to breathe for so many days. He was no dweller in an unpleasantly unsteady imitation of a Ritz hotel. He would
15 before long begin to feel himself a citizen of a small community in special conditions and with special interests which gradually ceased to be secret to him, and in the end secured his sympathies. The machinery of his propulsion, the picturesque activities of the men of the sea lay open to his sight and appealed to his sympathies.
20 In the course of my sea-life, a time when it never occurred to me that I myself might be a passenger some day, I was for a couple of years officer of a sailing passenger ship out of the port of London. This gave me the opportunity to watch that process of acclimatisation of which I have spoken, in a group of about
25 sixty persons of various ages and temperaments, some travelling for their health and others only for rest – which they indubitably secured in our passages which averaged about 80 days. Part of our passengers, those from the Midlands generally, used to come on board in London Dock, while others, those from the South and
30 from London itself, preferred to join the ship in Plymouth where we used to call in order to embark the live stock for the voyage. Of that feathered and four-footed company the most important item was the milch-cow which joined the ship mainly "for the benefit of the children," as the advertisements had it. It was the last
35 living thing that came on board already boxed up in its travelling stall and displaying a most praiseworthy composure even while spinning in mid-air at the fore-yard-arm before being landed on the foredeck against the mast to which its straitened habitation was secured for the passage with lashings of chain and rope fit to
40 withstand the heaviest weather we were likely to encounter.

There, on fine mornings (and there are more fine mornings at sea than have ever been dreamt of in a landsman's philosophy) the ship's children, some controlled by nurse-maids, others running loose, trooped forward to pay a visit to *their* cow which looked with mild big eyes at the small citizens of our sea community with the air of knowing all there was to know about them.

All this may sound very primitive but it had a charm and an intimacy of a settled existence no modern steamship with its long barren alleyways swept by the wind and decorated with the name of promenade decks can give. The modern passenger may be able to walk a good many miles in his ship in the course of the day but this is the only thing which differentiates him from the bales of goods – carried in the hold – that and the power of swallowing the food which is presented to him at frequent intervals. He is carried along swiftly and fed delicately but the other lived the life of his ship, that sort of life which is not sustained on bread (and *suprême de volaille*) alone but depends for its interest on enlarged sympathies and awakened perceptions of nature and men.

I have seen old maiden ladies develop during a passage a nice discrimination in the matter of steering. They had their favourite helmsmen. Elderly business men would become good judges of the set of the sails and acquire a seaman's eye for the aspects of the weather – and almost all, men and women, become reconciled to the vast solitude of the sea untroubled by the sound of the world's mechanical contrivances and the noise of its endless controversies. The silence of the universe would lay very close to the sailing ship with her freight of lives from which the daily stresses and anxieties had been removed as if the circle of the horizon had been a magic ring laid on the sea. No doubt the days thus enchanted were empty, but they were not so tedious as people may imagine. They passed quickly and if they brought no profit or excitement, I can not help thinking they were not wasted. No! They were not wasted.

OUTSIDE LITERATURE
1922

H AVING BEEN PROMPTED by a certain literary suggestion
to reflect upon the nature of Notices to Mariners I fell to
5 examining some of my old feelings and impressions which strictly
professional as they were have yet contributed in the end towards
the existence of a certain amount of literature; or at any rate of
pages of prose. The Notices to Mariners are good prose but I think
no critic would admit them into the body of literature. And it is
10 only as compositions in prose that I believe myself competent to
speak of them. And first let me thank God that they don't belong
to imaginative literature. It would be dreadful if they did. An
imaginatively written Notice to Mariners would be a deadly thing. I
mean it literally. It would be sure to kill a number of people before
15 its imaginative quality had been appreciated – and suppressed.
That their style must be clear and concise and the punctuation
of the ordinary kind would not necessarily militate against their
being regarded as literature. The Maxims of La Rochefoucauld are
concise enough. But they open horizons; they plumb the depths;
20 they make us squirm, shudder, smile in turn and even sigh –
at times; whereas the prose of the Notices to Mariners must do
nothing of the kind.

And it doesn't. A mariner detected shuddering or sighing over a
Notice to Mariners would simply (to speak in unliterary language)
25 be not fit for his job. All means of acting on man's spiritual side are
forbidden to that prose. In those compositions which are read as
earnestly as anything that ever came from a printing-press all suggestion of Love, of Adventure, of Romance, of Speculation, of all
that decorates and ennobles life, except Responsibility, is barred.
30 What we expect from them is not suggestion but information of
ideal accuracy such as you do not find in the prose of the works on
science which is mainly imaginative and often solemnly mystify-
ing. That is why some quite decent men are moved to smile as they
read it. But there is no mystification in the language expounding
35 the truth contained in the Notices to Mariners. You would not

want to smile at them. No decent man would. Even Mr Punch to whom as a great burlesque poet nothing is supposed to be sacred and who has been seen lately taking liberties with the explosive atom would not dream of making fun out of Notices to Mariners. Mr Punch knows better. He knows that for an inspired poet who 5
sees the mystic relations of sublunary matters Notices to Mariners are things to be read reverently. They are like declarations of a minutely careful Providence. They can be imagined as dictated in a quiet voice by the angel who, in the words of the song, sits aloft to watch over poor Jack. They belong to a prose which if certainly 10
not immortal is revelatory to its own generation.

Addressed to a special public, limited to a very definite special subject, having no connection with the intellectual culture of mankind, and yet of some importance to civilisation, which is founded on the protection of life and property, that prose has 15
only one ideal to attain, to hold on to: the ideal of perfect accuracy. You would say that such an ideal may easily be captured by a steady prosaic mind devoting itself for a few minutes (the Notices to Mariners are short) every day to the task of composition. Why, yes! But what about misprints – the bane of authors? 20

And then the absences. I mean the absences of mind. It is a fact that the most pedestrian mind will sometimes take a flight from the office where it works (I suppose Notices to Mariners are written in some sort of office) towards subjects of poetic fancy, its children, its lady-love, its glass of beer, and such other things interesting to 25
its mortal envelope. I often wondered what the author of Notices to Mariners looks like. I have tried to represent him to myself as a monk, a man who has renounced the vanities of the world, and for preference belonging to the order of Trappists who are bidden to remember death – *memento mori* – and nothing else. A sobering 30
thought! Just suppose the author of Notices to Mariners acquiring convivial habits and sitting down to write a Notice in that happy frame of mind when nothing matters much and one letter of the alphabet is as good as another. For myself – who am not convivial in that sense and have written a varied lot of prose with a quite 35
ridiculous scrupulosity and an absurd seriousness, I don't mind confessing that if I were told to write a Notice to Mariners I would not pray perhaps – for I have my own convictions about the abuse of prayer – but I would certainly fast. I would fast in the evening and get up to write my Notice to Mariners at four o'clock in the 40

morning for fear of accidents. One letter is so soon written for
another, with fatal results.

It has happened to me many years ago to endanger the course
of my humble career at sea simply by writing the letter W instead
5   of the letter E at the bottom of a page full of figures. It was an
examination and I ought to have been plucked mercilessly. But
in consideration, I believe, of all my other answers being correct I
was handed that azimuth paper back by the examiner's assistant,
with the calm remark "You have fourteen minutes yet." I looked
10 at the face of the clock; it was round like the moon, white as a
ghost, unfeeling, idiotic. I sat down under it with the conviction
of the crushing materiality of Time, and calling, in my mind, the
assistant examiner a sarcastic brute. For no man could have gone
over all those figures in fourteen minutes. I hope my exasperated
15 consternation at this check could not be detected. It was funny
even to myself. Then just at the moment when my sinking heart
had touched bottom I saw the error staring at me, enormous,
gross, palpable. I traced hastily a capital E over the W and went
back to the desk with my sheet of blue paper in a still shaky
20 hand. The assistant hardly glanced at it before he let it drop, and
I saw then that in my lack of comprehension it was I who had
been an unqualified brute. For in his remark about the fourteen
minutes he had clearly tried to give me a hint. He was a charming
young man, obviously poor, with an intelligent as if suffering face.
25 Not exactly sickly but delicate. A sea voyage would have done
him good . . . But it was I who went to sea – this time bound to
Calcutta.

And it was in Calcutta a few months afterwards that my captain
one morning on going ashore saw me busy about the decks and
30 beckoned to me in that way ship masters have, or used to have.
I mean ship-masters who commanded their ships from truck to
keelson as it were, technically and spiritually, in motion and at
rest, and through every moment of their life, when the seaman's
calling was by the mere force of its conditions more vocational
35 than it can be at the present day. My shipmaster had that way of
beckoning. What way? Well, – all I can say of it is that one dropped
everything. I can't describe it better. So I dropped whatever I was
doing, and he said: "You will find a Notice on the cabin table. Go
in and enter it on the proper Admiralty sheet. Do it now." Which
40 I hastened to do.

That examination the issue of which had hung on a capital letter had caused me to be officially certified as fit to undertake that particular duty; and ever since then my familiarity with Notices to Mariners, which are not literature, went on growing through a course of years up to the moment when stepping ashore for the 5 very last time, I lost all touch with the most trusted kind of printed prose. Henceforth I had to begin, while totally unprovided with Notices to Authors to write prose myself; and the pains I took with it only my Maker knows! And yet I could never learn to trust it. I can't trust it to this day. We who write prose which is 10 not that of the Notices to Mariners are forgotten by Providence. No Angel watches us at our toil. A dreadful doubt hangs over the whole achievement of literature, I mean that of its greatest and its humblest men. Wasn't it papa Augier who being given a copy of *Hamlet* as a remarkable play glanced through it expertly 15 and then dropped it with the dry remark: "*Vous appelez ça une pièce, vous?*" The whole tragedy of art lies in the nutshell of this terrifying anecdote. But it never will occur to anybody to doubt the prosaic force of the author of Notices to Mariners, which are not literature, and his fidelity to his honourable ideal – the ideal 20 of Perfect Accuracy.

LEGENDS

1924

To watch the growth of a legend is a sad occupation. It is not so much because legends deal with people and things finished and done with; that they spring as it were from amongst the bones of dead men. Flowers (as I have seen myself) will do that too. That's all in the order of nature and both flowers and legends are upon the whole decorative, which is all to the good. I have nothing against a legend twining its tendrils fancifully about the facts of history or the tables of statistics (which can be fanciful too, though they can never be made very decorative). They spring up from noble soil, they are a form of memory which we all like to leave behind us, that lingers about the achievement of men who had their day and the vanished forms of things which have served the needs of their time. One could welcome that fine form of imaginative recognition of the past with nothing worse than gentle melancholy which the passage of time brings in its train, if it were not disfigured by touches of fatuity of which no legend is wholly free, because I suspect that those who record its tales as picked out on the lips of men are doing it in a spirit of love. And that is only right and proper. But love is uncritical. It is an enthusiastic state seeing romance in what may be not true to the spirit of its subject, so to speak. And thus the false which is often fatuous also creeps into a worthy or even noble story.

Or even into a holy story. *The Golden Legend* itself, the legend of saints and their miracles, is an awful example of that danger – as any one who turns over a few pages of it may see. Saintliness is made absurd by the presentation of the miraculous facts themselves. It lacks spirituality in a surprising way.

Yes, fatuity lurks in all legends fatally by the effect of our common credulity. However the legend I have in my mind has nothing to do with saints – but with beings at first sight infinitely different, but whose lives were hard (no saint I take it ever slept on a bed of roses) if not exactly ascetic, and if not hermit like yet as far removed from the commonest amenities and the simplest affections which make life sweet, and as much removed from the material interests of this world as the most complete spiritual renunciation could make it. Perhaps nobody would guess from what precedes that I have sailors in my mind. I do not mean to be irreverent if I insist that in a temporal sense there was much that 5 was edifying in their lives. They did not work miracles to be sure but I have seen them repeatedly do all that men can do for their faith – if it was only the faith in their own manhood. And that is something surely. But there was something more in it, something larger – a fidelity to the demands of their calling which I verily 10 believe was for all of them I knew both afloat and ashore vocational quite as much in its way as any spiritual call a man's nature has ever responded to. And all that for no perceptible reward in the praise of men and the favour of gods. I mean the sea-gods, an indigent pitiless lot who had nothing to offer to servants at their 15 shrine but a ward in some hospital on shore or a sudden wedding with death in a great uproar, but with no gilding of fine words about it. *La mort sans phrases.*

In all this there is material for a fine legend if not of saintly virtues then of a consistent display of manhood. And the leg- 20 end will not be long for the last days of sailing ships were short if one thinks of countless ages since the first sail of leather or rudely woven rushes was displayed to the wind. Stretching the period both ways to the utmost it lasted from 1850 to 1910. Just sixty years. Two generations. The winking of an eye. Hardly 25 the time to drop a prophetic tear. For the pathos of that era lies in the fact that when the sailing ships and the art of sailing them reached their perfection they were already doomed. It was a swift doom, but it is consoling to know that there was no decadence. 30

That era has however had its historians such as Mr Basil Lubbock for instance whose devotion to the glory of the ships and the merits of the men has the character of one of those romantic passions that last a life-time. He if not of the brotherhood initiated with all the awful ceremonies of a Cape Horn passage speaks with inner 35 knowledge. And there is Miss C. Fox-Smith in whom I verily believe the quintessence of the collective soul of the latter-day seaman has found its last resting place and a poignant voice before taking its flight forever from the earth. Truth itself speaks in her verse – I can safely say since I (surprising thought) have one foot at least in 40

that irrecoverable phase of old sea life for which their piety and their talents have done so much.

It is on that ground that I would remonstrate with Mr Lubbock against the admission into one of his Books of Sea Chronicles of a tale which would degrade the character of any legend. The facts of a legend need not be literally true. But they ought to be credible and they must be in a sort of fundamental accord with the nature of the life it records that is with the character of its subject-matter. The subject of the Golden Legend is in fact the celebration of a miracle-working holiness and the subject of any sea legend must be the celebration of the era of fair ships sailed with consummate seamanship – an era that seems as distant now as the age of miracles.

The history of the latter days of clipper ships and their men may be said to begin with the *Marco-Polo* and the man who commanded her. His name was Forbes, and he is not a figure to stand at the head of a sea-legend. He lacked balance in his character. Luck alone made him and at the first sign of adversity he collapsed. But without going into the details of his short career I am sure I am doing good service to his memory by trying to purge his record of the most fatuous tale that ever cropped up in any legend of the sea.

As adopted alas! (but the best of us may err) by Mr Basil Lubbock it runs that Forbes used to padlock the sheets of *Marco-Polo*'s sails, one reviewer of Miss C. Fox-Smith's book explaining kindly: "to guard against the timid members of a crew" – a priceless phrase, whatever it may mean. What is a "timid member" and how do you recognise him? Anyhow I am sure he is a fitting person to play his part in that padlock story.

I wonder who was the man to tell it? He must have been an ironmonger trying for a new outlet for his wares. And to what sort of audience. Personally I would have been afraid to tell it to the Horse-Marines that mysterious corps which is famed for its capacity to swallow anything in the way of a yarn.

THE UNLIGHTED COAST
1917

I CAME ASHORE bringing with me strongest of all, and the most persistent, the impression of a great darkness. I do not mean darkness in a symbolic or spiritual sense. Indeed one couldn't 5 come from the contact with the watchers of that darkness, and the workers therein, otherwise than spiritually strengthened. What I mean is the fact itself, the fact of darkness spread over the land and water of old civilisation such as wrapped up early mariners' landfalls on their voyages of exploration. 10

To him who had been accustomed to behold after long sea-passages the shadowy contours of the English coast illuminated festally, interminably, unfailingly as if for sleepless feast or for sleepless toil, the impression was very powerful – like a revelation of some deeper truth. Fires in the night are the sign of mankind's 15 life to an eye at sea. There were no such signs anywhere. Not a gleam. And yet life had never before perhaps in the history of that unlighted island known such an intense consciousness of itself. No! Life had not departed from that sombre shore. It was only its old sense of security that was no longer there. 20

It had a strange air of finality. The land had turned to a shadow. Of all scourges and visitations against which mankind prays to heaven, it was not pestilence that had smitten that shore dark; it was war; with sudden death, another of that dreaded company, full of purpose, in the air, on the water and under the water. 25 Breathing the calm air of the night, looking at this placid sea gleaming faintly, here and there, as still water will do in the dark, it was as hard to believe in the existence of this prowling death as in the dauntless, tense life of that obscured land. That mere shadow – big with fate. 30

One seemed to have one's being in the very centre of illusory appearances. The very silence, so profound around us as to seem boundless, and harmonising marvellously with the spirit of the hour, was not true to the usual meaning it conveys to a human mind, that of being cut off from communication with its kind. 35

37

For, just as I was remarking to the officer by my side that surely neither Cæsar's galleys nor the ships of the Danish rovers had ever found on their approach this land so absolutely and scrupulously lightless as this – just then a voice behind us was

5   heard:

"I've here two messages I have just picked up."

It was our wireless man. That shadow emitting no sound waves, no waves of light, was talking to its watchers at sea; filling the silence with words pregnant with the truth, the naked, ugly truth

10   of the situation.

And the man with two white pieces of paper very noticeable in his hand said:

"It's our station at X speaking."

For reasons which had nothing to do with its efficiency we could

15   not use our wireless installation very often, and he was immensely pleased at having picked up something for the first time in two days. We went below to de-code the messages. The little cabin in contrast with the variously shaded and toned darkness we had left seemed scandalously overlighted.

20   Although I helped to decode these messages I don't remember the exact words of their concise phrases; but the first was an inquiry, apparently directed at large into space, relating to an enemy submarine seen off the coast not many hours before. The other was a request addressed by name to a ship at sea for a report

25   on some floating mines discovered in a certain position within the last twenty-four hours. The great motionless shadow was talking to its watchers, small shadows flitting here and there on the obscure gleams of the smooth sea veiled in the unmoral night that from its very nature favours aggression rather than vigilance, without

30   regard to the merits of the case.

These were good samples of the talk that flows on unheard in sunshine, in starlight, under the clouds. War-talk. But how different from the war-talk we hear on the lips of men (and even great men) which often seems but talk around the war, obscuring the

35   one and only question: To be or not to be – the great alternative of an appeal to arms. The other, the grouped-letters war-talk, almost without sound and altogether without fury, is full of sense, of meaning and single-minded purpose: inquiries, information, orders, reports. Words too. But words in direct relation to things

and facts, with the feeling at the back of it all of the correct foresight that planned and of the determination which carries on the
protective work.

We all know that the true defence is at the point of the sword;
but the shield has its part to play too in defensive work. This work   5
had been planned by the Navy in anticipation of the conditions
that would arise. I know that praise often is but more or less conscious impertinence. But, after all, this is seamen's work, and half
a life-time at sea may perhaps justify me in expressing the highest
possible sense of the Navy's clear-eyed foresight in planning, and   10
the judgment, resolution, tact and knowledge of men in getting
the planned system to work, from the first critical days to its full
development of to-day, steadily, without haste, yet with that speed
which is inherent in the force, unswerving purpose and in the
resolute handling of any problem under the sun.   15

It is mainly the officers and men of the various branches of
RNR who under the high command of naval officers have been
entrusted with the manifold duties of that simple work of protection and watchfulness. It was the Navy who trained them to it, and
as the period had in each case to be short, the general efficiency   20
with which the work is done speaks well for the Naval method.
But it is also a high testimony to the capacity, adaptability and the
whole souled earnestness of the officers of the Merchant Service
who hastened to join, some called up, others volunteering without hesitation from all the points of the compass and from the   25
uttermost ends of the Empire.

Much has been said already of these men and of their activities;
of the circumstances, the conditions, the incidents of the task I
may perhaps later say something too, more in the nature of a
personal impression than of detailed description. As to the work   30
itself all I want to point out now is that seen from outside it presents
in its various branches the aspect of a nerve-straining drudgery.
And in that outward aspect there is a proportion of truth. From its
very nature it must be work without glamour. No great moments
can be expected in it. Yet rare as drops of rain in a desert such   35
moments have been vouchsafed to some of the faithful. As I trace
these words I have in my mind the most unexpected, the most
unforeseen instance of the kind. An enormous drop in a parched
and stressful monotony of duty.

On the morning I heard the tale, the pier at one of our "bases"
with its central line of neat shedlike buildings and the great signal-
bridge at the end (recalling the superstructure of a battle-ship)
had been for a moment swept clean of all life by a rain squall as
5 effectually as by a point blank broadside of shrapnel shell.

My companion and I took cover in the wardroom; a good sized
apartment lined with varnished matchboarding. A heavy table
occupied the middle. The officer of the watch, a silent, detached
figure, sat at a writing desk reading a note while a young blue-
10 jacket, cap in hand, waited for the answer. Two R. N. R. officers
smoking by the fire greeted us. Another sat at some distance on a
chair placed against the wall near a window. He took no notice of
our arrival.

But the officer with me murmured with a nod in his direction.
15 "This is our Zeppelin-strafer."

I said: "No! Have you *that* too in your lot?"

"Yes. He'll tell you all about it."

I was introduced with a word or two of comment to "our
Zeppelin-strafer". There was no halo round his head. He was
20 young, so young that he must have belonged to the third generation of those who had gone to sea since my time, one of those
who began that life after 1900. A seaman of the twentieth century!
And yet he was no stranger to me. The memories of my twenty
sea-years crowded upon me, memories of faces, of temperaments,
25 of expressions. And looking at him all I could say to myself was:–
How like! We sat down side by side near the window. He was in no
haste to begin. He belonged to the shy silent type – and, how like!

It's an odious thing to have to write in "descriptive" fashion of
men with whom one talked like a friend, and had found accep-
30 tance as one of themselves. If he sees these lines I hope he will
forgive me. It's very likely that my impressions set down truthfully
are altogether untrue. We were but half an hour together and
when we parted and he closed the door of that room behind him,
I felt that he was as utterly gone from me as though he had stepped
35 out in the middle of the Pacific.

He began to talk to me with a sort of reluctance, hesitatingly
till I mentioned to him that I had been to sea much longer than
himself if not so recently. He knew I was some sort of writing
man and was ready to be civil, but after that remark of mine his
40 articulation became easier. Not much though. He looked down

on the ground, glancing at me only now and again, and spoke in a low tone with unexpected pauses. The best way in which I can characterise that narrative is by saying that he delivered it to me with the aspect, the bearing, of a man who broods over the event in silence.

He was making his way on a foggy day back to his base after a spell of duty outside. His craft mounted one gun; and without going into unnecessary description I may best give an idea of the size of his command by saying that, when he was reposing, the breech of the gun was within four feet of his head as it lay on his pillow.

For reasons that need not be stated, his vessel did not move then more than about three knots through the water – which was smooth. There's seldom much wind with thick weather. On that occasion there was a very light breeze enough to help the fog at its usual pranks of thinning and thickening, opening and shutting, lifting in patches and closing down suddenly – quicker than a wink sometimes.

He was walking up and down his vast deck when turning aft he saw the fore-end of a Zeppelin emerge into misty view out of an apparently thicker layer of fog. From then on for succeeding minutes he moved no more than a ship's timber. The apparition took him completely unawares because he had not heard any noise in the air before. Directly however he caught sight of the Zeppelin he heard the noise of the engines very plainly.

As soon as he regained the power of speech he uttered the words Action – Zeppelin – Astern, in a cautious whisper. An unnecessary precaution. But, he told me, that at first the "enormous thing seemed right on top of us". In fact it was not anything so near as that. It was coming up astern but a little on one side and, he noticed, steering a course which would cross obliquely his wake and bring the monster very close indeed – within five hundred yards perhaps.

For whatever reason it was flying low, so low that he did not need to throw his head up much to watch its steady progress. And there followed for him some moments of unforgettable anguish, something like the anguish of a man whose eternal salvation would depend on the soundness of his judgment.

The problem was how to deal with this gigantic piece of luck. For if he opened fire too soon the chances were that the German

would swerve and get away, or climbing overhead would descend
on him as low as he pleased and bomb him out of existence. His
gun was a very good weapon of its kind but it was not an anti-
aircraft gun and had only a limited amount of elevation. And
5 there was also the possibility that utterly unconscious of the tiny
speck lost in the shimmer of the thin fog-layer below the Zeppelin
would alter his course at any moment for some purpose of its own.

What worried and discomposed him was the insistent whispering of his skipper who had crept up to his elbow and was entreating
10 hoarsely not to waste a moment, "to let the beggar have it now,
sir. Let him have it." The German meantime held on. Ordering
the skipper away he had the fortitude though his heart was in his
mouth all the time, to hold out till the Zeppelin crossed his wake
and exposed the greater part of its side.

15 "And then," he said, "we started to plug it into him as fast as we
could load. And every shot was a hit."

He looked at me with strangely troubled eyes. "It was impossible
to miss – you know," he added in a lowered voice.

Whether conscious or unconscious before of the microscopic
20 strafer below, Fritz must have had the surprise of his life. The
record shock of Zeppelin history. His dismay was boundless. Something very much like panic up there became visible to the eyes
below.

"I could see three or four of them running along" went on the
25 low voice. "I saw them quite plainly. If I had had half a dozen
men with rifles on my deck we could have got every single one of
them."

The Zeppelin swung off wide and with her engines working
noisily made off without more ado. Her own speed or the drift of
30 denser fog blowing over turned her into a mere dark blur swiftly.
As long as the faintest shadow of it remained visible the fire was
kept up. Then it ceased. A profound silence ensued. It was all over.
He was gone.

It was however possible that he might return overhead and
35 take his revenge. But before the strafers on deck had the time to
exchange glances of wonder, apprehension or inquiry, while they
were still in fact staring into the upper fog the shadow re-appeared
nearer than before aslant in the white space, sliding downwards
stern first, its nose tilted up at a perilous angle.

"Of course we opened on him instantly," he went on. "And do you know what he did then?"

At this point he looked at me again and after a little gasp went on as if unwillingly. "He dumped all his bombs overboard. The whole lot of them at once." 5

The resulting explosion was something terrific. He felt as if his little craft were blown clean out of the water and at the same time hit by a tidal wave. And in awful commotion, uproar and black smoke the Zeppelin shot up and vanished for good.

"You must have made him very sick," I said. 10

"He *looked* very sick indeed," said the young strafer quietly.

"I wonder what became of him."

"Hard to say. There was a report, in the papers, some time afterwards . . . Damaged Zeppelin coming to the ground in Norway . . . I sometimes think . . . " 15

He did not finish the sentence. He had been eighteen months of long days and longer nights at his protecting work, out and in, fair or foul, never seeing anything to reward his strained, hopeful vigilance, and sometimes for days seeing nothing at all. For the North Sea is a big place, as our coasters say. So big that there may 20 be half a dozen ships out looking for you because you are a little late in returning (as it happened to a man) and you will come in innocently, having seen no one, unseen by anybody – which is vexing for the anxious searchers.

Eighteen patient, unfaltering months and then this ten glori- 25 ously crowded minutes – if that much? The whole affair probably did not last so long. Rare like drops of water in a desert are such opportunities for the watchers of the lightless shore. And to this one Fortune had not been fickle but simply outrageous. The drop had merely brushed past his lips so unskilled in speech. He had 30 talked to me in all friendliness for which I am only grateful; yet he left me with the impression that had he been permitted to taste the full flavour, his official report would have remained, of his own choice, his first and last utterance. I fancy somehow that rather than talk of luck so immense that there could be no fit words for it 35 in the world he would have preferred to brood over it in adequate silence.

THE DOVER PATROL
1921

THE WORTH of a sentiment lies in the sacrifices men will make for its sake. All ideals are built on the ground of solid
5　achievement which in a given profession creates in the course of time a certain tradition or in other words a standard of conduct. The existence of a standard of conduct in its turn makes the most improbable achievement possible, by augmenting the power of endurance and of self-sacrifice amongst men who look to the past
10　for their lessons and for their inspiration.

The story of the achievement of the Dover Patrol is merged in the greater proud record of the Navy's protective part played with simplicity and self-sacrifice in the great war of the twentieth century, yet that story has its own features, its own particular
15　atmosphere and its own importance.

The opening years of the nineteenth century had their great war too. Longer in its duration it was carried on with less animosity. It was less in the nature of a struggle for dear life, and, except in its spirit it was less intensely national. It did not involve in its toils
20　the whole population. The issues at stake were as great perhaps but did not appear in such definite shapes to the great mass of the people which suffered its hardships and gave up its sons to its struggles. In its most obvious aspect that war like the one of our day was waged against an attempt at universal dominion. But it must
25　be admitted that it was also a war against the revolt of new born ideas represented by a great and dominant figure issued from a revolution and taking its own fatally conquering way amongst the imperfectly awakened nations of Europe. It was a struggle of the old certitudes against a man embodying the new force of
30　subversive beliefs. It ran its course, as momentous if less ruthless than the deadly struggle in which the Dover Patrol has played its part. When it ended it left the world as weary indeed as it is today but much less unsettled in its thoughts and emotions about the spiritual value of its monstrous experience. Men's ideas were
35　simpler then, their sentiments less complex. Their desires and

44

hopes as poignant perhaps remained still obscure. The instinctive
reaction against all the cruel negations a war imposes on humanity
had a less resentful character, and men's judgement of the attained
issue was less embittered by the effort they had been called upon
to make. Yet their personal feelings were much like our own.   5

When the hour of peace struck in 1815 there must have been
on board the King's ships anchored in the Downs and patrolling
in the Channel, in the squadrons on distant stations and in others
cruising off nearly every port of northern Europe, there must
have been the feeling that there never would be such a war again; a   10
feeling of relief mingled no doubt with a half-acknowledged sense
of regret for the occupation that was gone. The great question
arising at the end of every prolonged effort made by mankind –
and now what next? asked without misgivings in the consciousness
of an accomplished duty, was not free from a certain uneasiness as   15
to the days that would follow in other and unknown conditions.
For a whole generation had grown from boyhood to maturity with
no knowledge of peace conditions and unperturbed by moral
doubts of its warlike achievement.

Amongst the men of the Dover Patrol assembled to see the   20
unveiling of the memorial to their own unforgettable dead there
will be also a feeling of regret for those days that are past, regret of
the strenuous life with its earnest purpose, its continuity of risk, its
sense of professional efficiency, its community of desperate toil;
regret even of those moments of extreme bodily fatigue associated   25
with that feeling of spiritual exaltation which enabled them each
in his station from the Admiral commanding to the youngest
member of a small drifter's crew to defy the enmity of nature and
the hostility of men.

Nobody would dream of apportioning shares of importance   30
in the great task of the Navy, so varied in its unity, so diverse
in its singleness of aim and its invariable purpose. But it is a
fact that amongst all those activities directed to the same end,
exposed to the same risk, making the same appeal and entered
upon with the same courage, the work of the Dover Patrol was   35
very special work. The Dover Patrol held the Southern exit of
the North Sea in the same way in which the Grand Fleet may
be said to have held its Northern entrance and the greatness of
its responsibility may be appreciated from the one dominant fact
that on that Patrol rested the safety of our communications with   40

the Army in France and that one of its achievements was the safe
passage across the Channel of about seven million men without
a single instance of failure in the presence of a superior enemy
established in force within easy striking distance on the flank of
5   the line; an enemy superior in numbers and materiel, holding
in his hands every element of successful attack except just for
a portion, an ever so small portion, of that sea-spirit animating
the officers and men of the Dover command who stood in his
way – including the very workers on shore in repair workshops
10 and fitting-out sheds. There was never a greater accord of fearless
executive energy and hard skilled work than in the Dover Patrol.
From the point of view of its spiritual harmony it was worthy to hold
the extreme right wing of the great sea defence. Of its material
success we all know by now; we have all heard of the millions of
15 men transported to and fro across the Straits, of miles of nets
laid along the coasts and kept in repair in defiance of heavy seas
and long range batteries, of mines swept along routes equalling in
length twelve times the circumference of the globe, of merchant
fleets of a hundred ships and more shepherded every day through
20 the Downs. The eloquence of arithmetical figures as applied to
the merits of the Dover Patrol is overwhelming indeed; but no
figure of rhetoric can render justice to the quiet resolution of the
men making up for the inadequacy of the means, the unavoidable
inadequacy of the means for which only the force of circumstances
25 was responsible, for which no past government can be blamed,
since no one could have guessed the enormous scale of material
requirements. The means were inadequate, woefully inadequate,
and thus the only trumps the Admiral of the Dover Patrol held
in his hand at every turn of the dreadful game were the physical
30 endurance, the inborn seamanship, the matter-of-fact, industrious
indefatigable enthusiasm with which every one under his orders
threw his very soul into his appointed task. Threw it in and kept
it there. It was no momentary effort. For the anxious days of
the Dover Patrol were to be many, its nights full of dangers, its
35 problems exacting, its duty-calls incessant, and its men after all
but the flesh and blood of our common humanity. Their souls
were the only trumps in the desperate game, as he who was in
command must have felt at every moment of night and day. It was
a great and successful game but it must be confessed that for more
40 than half the time it was a game of bluff. It came off at every deal.

England's usual luck that this time too has not failed her at the hour of need! And England may well be proud of her traditional luck in the character of her children serving her at sea, on shore, and in the air.

The activities of the Dover Patrol were of many kinds, but there were three imperative duties to which all its energies had to be devoted: the safety of the troop-transport service, the protection of merchant shipping, the closing of the Channel exit against the German submarines. One need not insist on their vital importance for the army and the nation or on the deadly danger of even a temporary failure. The work had to be carried out with the slenderest conceivable means, with obsolete torpedo destroyers and with unarmed drifters in the presence of an enemy of superior force and possessing an infinite advantage in his power to choose his own time for an attack of the most deadly kind. Those three purely naval problems required incessant hard work, incessant risk and incessant vigilance. The routine of the Dover Patrol included the boarding of ships, the regulation of traffic along the cleared war lane, the laying of net and mine barrages on the Belgian coast and across the Channel, their guard and maintenance in all weathers and in all circumstances, with always present in all minds the sense of numerical inferiority in a mission the failure of which might have well brought about something not very far from a national disaster. In such conditions the stress put upon the fortitude of every individual was bound to be very great. The Dover Patrol was equal to it. Its devotion, expressed in a plodding dogged perseverance, stood the test of frequent severe losses in men and ships and of continuous severe strain on its mental and physical faculties as a whole. The tale of the Dover Patrol is the tale of a small nucleus of ships and crews of the Royal Navy and round it of a great number of other men and other vessels mostly fisher folk and fisher craft with the addition of Merchant Service men and of R.N.R. and R.N.V.R. officers and ratings. Though properly speaking not belonging to the fighting service all those men lived up to their own tradition and were found sufficient for the trust reposed in them.

They were found sufficient. No praise could be more adequately expressed, when one looks at the magnitude of the trust and the arduous character of the operations it imposed upon the men and the ships of the Dover Command. Originating in the simple

Downs Boarding Flotilla under the orders of the naval officer commanding at Harwich, the Dover Patrol developed an independent
existence and by the establishment of fortified German naval bases
on the coast of Flanders acquired an importance in the scheme
5 of naval defence which can not well be exaggerated. The rein-
forcements and supplies for the army, the food for the country,
demanded the safety of the Straits. Had the enemy probed the
weakness of the Dover Patrol and broken with his overwhelming
force through that thin defence to invade the waters of the Chan-
10 nel it would have been a disaster of which the fatal consequences
imagination even now shrinks from contemplating.

    The great sailor-like qualities of the Dover Patrol, the consum-
mate seamanship displayed in the planning and execution of its
incessant operations, its steady manner of meeting deadly emer-
15 gencies, its cool vigilance in the presence of an ever menacing
situation may well compel the admiration of any man who knows
something however little of the demands of sea-service. To the
risks of actual warfare the crews of the drifters watching over the
barrage nets were often helplessly exposed. But nothing could
20 dismay either the naval or the auxiliary branches of the Dover
Patrol. These men were concerned about the perfection of their
work, but the sudden flash of German guns in the night troubled
them not at all. As indeed why should it? In their early days some
of them had but a single rifle on board, to meet the three 4-inch
25 guns of German destroyers. Unable to put up a fight and without
speed to get away they made a sacrifice of their lives every time
they went out for a turn of duty; they concentrated their valour on
the calm seamanlike execution of their work amongst exploding
mines and bursting shells. It was their conception of their honour,
30 and they carried it out of this war unblemished by a single display
of weakness, by the slightest moment of hesitation in the long tale
of dangerous service.

    In this simple way these seamen, professional and unprofes-
sional, naval and civilian, have earned for themselves the Memo-
35 rial erected to their faithful labours. The record of the Dover
Patrol's work contains a great moral and a good many professional lessons for their children and their successors: the incal-
culable value of a steady front, the perfecting of nets, the exact
process of laying barrages in a tideway, the evolving of an in-
40 genious method for night bombardments and of a system of long

range firing – a whole great store of new ideas and new practice laid up for future use; but in truth that which in the last instance kept the German forces from breaking disastrously on any dark night into the Channel and jeopardising the very foundations of our resisting power were not the wonderfully planned and exe- 5 cuted defences of nets and mines but the indomitable hearts of the men of the Dover Patrol.

MEMORANDUM

on the scheme for fitting out a sailing-ship for the purpose
of *perfecting* the training of Merchant Service officers belonging
to the Port of Liverpool

5

1920

A SSUMING THAT the generous public spirit of the Liverpool
shipowners will find the capital necessary for the building and
equipping of a southern-going sailing ship to *perfect* the training
of the officers of the Mercantile Marine I conceive that the cost
10 of running such a ship – that is: wages, upkeep, repairs, general
surveys and insurance – ought to be covered by what she may earn
as a cargo carrier on the training voyages which will be planned
for her.

Here I will submit to the originators of the scheme that a voyage
15 to an Australian port (including New Zealand), out by the Cape
and round by the Horn, would be the best for such a purpose.
My reasons are: the healthy climate of that part of the world,
the number of the meteorological regions traversed which will
develop sound judgment as to weather, the comparative facility
20 of the voyage, combined with a great variety of general experience which a round trip of that sort will offer. The length of
passages need not be an objection; the complete training of a
young seaman ought to include the experience of many days
together at sea between water and sky. It would have a spiri-
25 tual and practical value for him even if he is destined never to
be out of sight of land for more than a few days in his future
professional life.

I

Assuming then that the ship would be expected to be self-
30 supporting (and no more) it is my deliberate opinion that her
size should be limited strictly to the tonnage which will enable her

under modern conditions to pay her expenses. I venture to suggest (however shocking it may appear to the minds of men who own and manage fleets of large steamships) 14 to 1500 tons, or as near thereto as is consistent with the earning of her expenses as the proper tonnage for the ship. I admit that I don't know what the best freight carrying capacity of a ship is at the present time; but I beg the committee charged with the elaboration of the scheme to allow me to expose my reasons for what I advance in support of the above opinion. I must premise here that in all what I am going to say I will be drawing on my own experience as a seaman trained to his duties under the British flag and, in regard to the performance of such duties, having a good record for more than sixteen years of sea life, both in sail and steam.

My contention is that for sea-going qualities, ease of handling, quickness in manœuvring, and even in point of actual safety, if caught in a bad position, nothing can beat a, say, 1400 ton ship, designed so as to have a dead weight carrying capacity of about once and a half her registered tonnage. The same remark may be applied to the comfort in bad weather when, it must be remembered, the men managing her propelling machinery must remain exposed on the deck instead of being sheltered under it. The latest big sailing ship (in so far as she still exists) is generally in that respect what the sailors graphically describe as a mere "bathing-machine," her enormous main deck, especially when running before a heavy sea, being always full of water and extremely uncomfortable, besides being dangerous for that very reason. Also, the great length necessarily given to those big ships of three thousand tons and over makes them clumsy to handle, anything but quick in manoeuvre, and renders them rather helpless, from their very size, in case of any serious damage either aloft or about the rudder. It is also to be remarked that a ship's quick response in manœuvring develops a corresponding activity and smartness in her crew. I beg the gentlemen concerned with this scheme to understand that I am not speaking as a literary person indulging his fancy but as the usual sort of merchant officer who has served in all sorts of ships and draws upon his ordinary experience; with this advantage, only, that he had time to think about it and meditate over its lessons. Pursuing the matter further I wish also to touch on the question of the ship's appearance. In a steamship the increase of size certainly makes for good looks, adding to the inherent beauty of the lines an expression of power and dignity which arouses one's admiration. It is not so with a sailing vessel. Hardly any ship of over 2000 tons I have ever seen escaped giving an impression which may be best defined by the word "overgrown"; and I have a good many in my memory to whom nothing but the sailor's graphic phrase "a big, clumsy brute" could in justice be applied. Now in view of the end which the Liverpool shipowners have in equipping a sailing ship, that is: To "*perfect* the training of officers for their fleets," certain ideal elements must be taken into consideration. It is very necessary that those boys should grow attached to their ship (an easy thing for a sailor to do), be proud of her individual appearance, of her sea qualities, of their association with her; and that they should remember their period of training not as a horrible grind in discomfort and without personal gratification of any kind, but as a great time in their lives; an experience it has been their privilege as seamen of the Port of Liverpool to go through; a time to be remembered with pleasure and pride, somewhat as an old public school boy looks back at his old school, the beauty of its old buildings and the prestige of its traditions. The greatest achievements of Merchant Service seamen have been performed in ships of between 900 to 1600 tons, in the way of record passages (which were then the exclusive merit of seamen), of feats in clever handling and in the bringing in of disabled ships to port by their own seamanship and determination without any outside assistance. And if the objection is made that I am advocating things hopelessly out of date, then my answer will be that in this scheme of *perfected* training, associated so closely with men's *morale* and with old traditions, the out-of-datedness argument does not apply. On the practical side that objection may be met by pointing out that those boys are not to be trained for officers of modern sailing ships, but to be *perfected* as future officers of the finest modern steamships. Therefore what is important is to give them for their training not the most modern sailing ship (which in any case is doomed and need not be taken into consideration at all) but to select for them the *best* period of sailing ship practice and service.

One more consideration I want to present to the originators of the scheme, which is this: that in a very large sailing ship there is always a tendency to supply her (on account of the difficulty of manning her effectively) with a lot of labour-saving appliances. This brings me to the second postulate which after the size of 5 the ship I am most anxious to submit for consideration. And it is this:

II

That there should be no labour-saving appliances in the shape of steam winches and so on; and that the hoisting of the sails, the 10 working of the boats, and the general physical work of the sailor's calling should be done by man power, of which of course the cadets on board would be the principal part. A vertical boiler, mainly for the purpose of heaving up the anchors, may be advisable; but the windlass should be of the kind which can be also worked by the 15 crew by means of a capstan on the forecastle-head.

My reasons for this insistence on the use of man-power are as follows: First of all, there is no necessity for anything else. With forty boys out of any given batch on board (Mr Holt mentions eighty as the number and on that point I will offer a remark 20 later) of an advanced physical development and certain weight of body, together with a ship's crew of, say, twelve A.B.s, four petty officers, and some other ratings, the officers ought to be able to handle a ship, of the size and rig I am thinking of, like a plaything. Secondly, it may be laid down as an axiom that 25 no labour done on board ship in the way of duty is either too hard or in any way unworthy of the best effort and attention or so to speak beneath the dignity of any youngster wishing to fit himself to be a good officer. Thirdly, there is undoubtedly something elevating in physical work into which one puts all 30 one's heart in association with others and for a clearly under-stood purpose. Apart from that it will bring these youths into a more intimate contact with the propelling machinery of the ship and they will, so to speak, learn the feel of it. It mustn't be forgotten that seamen's work was never looked upon or had the 35 character of mere slavish toil, as some branches of labour on

shore tend to become. In its essence life at sea has been always a
healthy life, and part of that was owing to the very nature of the
physical exertions required. I affirm with profound conviction
that sailing ship life is an excellent physical developer. I have
repeatedly seen a delicate youngster brought on board by an
anxious relative change out of all knowledge into a stout youth,
during a twelve-months' voyage. I have never seen an apparently delicate boy break down under the conditions of the sea
life of my time. They *all* improved. Moreover any physical work
intelligently done develops a special mentality; in this case it
would be the sailor-mentality; surely a valuable acquisition for a
sea officer either in sail or steam.

III

The sailing ship then I have in my eye (something very much
like the Liverpool *Sierras* which were afloat between '80 and '90)
would be a hull of between 14–15 hundred tons reg. with a d.w.
capacity of over 2000 tons, in which case it would be sufficient
for her to have three square-rigged masts. If the tonnage of the
ship is raised to 2000 tons reg. then there must be four masts, of
which the aftermost one would be rigged fore and aft. In any case I
would advocate for the training ship a long poop and a very roomy
forecastle head; the poop, if the vessel is three-masted, extending
as far as the main rigging; and the object being to reduce the area
of the main deck as much as possible. This would tend to make the
ship much more comfortable. Ships with long poops are always
the driest in all weathers and safest for the individuals having to
move about the decks in heavy weather. The main deck would
have on it a deck-house in the space between the fore coaming of
the main hatch and the foremast; leaving a clear passage across at
each end and having wide alleyways on each side. The house would
contain the vertical boiler for raising steam for the windlass, the
accommodation for the ship's crew, and the berths of the ship's
petty officers. Under the forecastle head there would be space
at the sides for various store-rooms, or the electric light plant, if
carried, could be installed on one side and the store-rooms on the
other. All that however may be left to the skill and ingenuity of
the designer, once the actual size of the ship and the number of
people she has to carry, all told, has been decided upon.

In this matter I have a certain competence because I was (for
3 years) a chief officer of a sailing passenger ship running
between London and Adelaide and I believe the very last of its
kind with the exception perhaps of the *Macquarie* (later training
ship for New Zealand merchant cadets) where the experience of 5
a comparatively large number of persons on board ship could be
obtained by the sailing ship officer. She was only 1270 tons reg.
and the greatest number of people I had on board of her was
113 all told. She had room for 50 passengers when full and we
had perforce to carry a lot of live-stock, a milk cow for the chil- 10
dren and so on, yet her space was not inconveniently crowded
and no passenger ever complained of cramped accommodation and generally they made the round trip in her. She carried
outwards a general cargo and in Adelaide loaded the usual Australian cargo, for the most part wool. Her poop was 78 feet long 15
over all; under that we carried 11 double passenger cabins on
each side, two cabins for the mates, a large pantry amidships and
a doctor's berth and surgery. The accommodation for the captain consisted of two stern cabins, both very roomy, of which one
was his stateroom and the other was planned and furnished as a 20
sitting-room, which he never used at sea, sharing the saloon with
the passengers. This saloon contained two long tables at which
all the people berthed under the poop deck could sit down
to meals. I think that this arrangement could be adopted with
advantage in the cadet ship under contemplation. The artificial 25
lighting of the *Torrens*, being oil and candles, required extreme
vigilance, but assuming the Liverpool cadets being berthed in
cabins as above, if electric light is to be introduced the lamps
could be set in the partitions between them, so that each lamp
would light two cabins. The long saloon would be the common 30
room for navigational studies and meals, the electric lighting
of that space, however economically applied would be always
better than the lamp-lighting of that ship which was sufficient
for the passengers to read, write, or play their games in the
evening. There were never any complaints on that score. The 35
captain of a training ship would probably use all his accommodation at sea too, messing by himself. Apart from that it seems
to me that the man entrusted with the responsible position of
commanding such a training ship would wish to keep in as close
touch with the boys as is conformable with the preservation of 40

proper merchant ship discipline; and that he would not find the
nearness of his cabin to the bulk of them either inconvenient
or irksome.

The accommodation on the poop being sufficient only for
about 42 cadets could be duplicated to a certain extent below,
aft, on the twin deck and be made accessible by means of the
after hatch, fitted with a proper companion-way. There may be
some difficulty with the supply of daylight down there and in
that respect the berths below would be inferior, but as there
would be no doubt different grades among the boys in the way
of seniority and ratings, a boy would be moved by seniority or
on promotion from below to above at some time or other in
the course of his training. This would be something to look
forward to; and in this connection I would remark that the
comfort of the boys should be cared for strictly within the
limits of due regard for their health, physical development
and opportunity for study, and no more. The greatest simplicity in such arrangements compatible with health and self-
respect should be the note; and I believe that no boy properly constituted and wishing to be a seaman will resent such a
system.

I suppose that as regards the boys, at least, a three watch system will be introduced; though I must confess that I have never
seen a boy hurt by the watch and watch duty which in my time
all of them had to go through during the four years of their
apprenticeship. In that case however the utmost vigilance and
alertness in the time of duty should be exacted by the officer
of the watch from the cadets at their various stations, whether
at the lee helm with the helmsman, or on the lookout with
an A.B. of the ship's crew, or about the decks at the different
sheets, tacks and braces they may be specially told off to. The
disadvantage of the three watch system is that the cadet will be
always on duty at the same hours. Some system of shifts should
be introduced if only to change the boys in rotation from one
watch to another; for the habit of wakefulness is also a matter of
training, and the boys should be accustomed to keep their alertness at all periods of the night. I should suggest that the senior
cadets (especially those who had obtained the rating of cadet
petty-officer) should be employed as assistants to the officer of
the watch to the fullest possible extent; and when sufficiently

advanced be entrusted with the trimming of the yards, the taking in or setting of light sails in manageable weather and so
on. The progression of stations will be, I imagine, from waist-
cadets to mizzen-topmen, main through fore to forecastlemen,
which last would be selected from the strongest and the most 5
advanced, during the training course of 18 months. I imagine
that the training ship with some luck in her weather and with
quick dispatch at either end, could do two round voyages in
that time. The *Torrens*, a fast ship, could have done it with ease,
though as a matter of fact she made one voyage every eleven 10
months, but then she would lie for weeks on the berth, both in
London and Port Adelaide.

That ship carried four anchors, that is, three bowers and one
stream, besides one big and one small kedge, and this is the
number that would be sufficient for the training ship. Of course 15
the anchors would be stock anchors. In this connection I wish
to remark that if the anchor is hove up by steam the catting
and fishing should be done by hand under all circumstances
with the help of the forecastle-head capstan. As to the sails I
assume that she would carry (unless she is to be really a very 20
big ship) six topsails, *three* top-gallantsails, three royals, four or
three headsails, the usual number of staysails; and, I suggest, two
courses. The crossjack course may be done away with. In my first
year on board the *Torrens* we abolished that sail mainly out of
regard for the feelings of the passengers who had their chairs 25
placed all about the mizzenmast; and it made no difference
whatever to the speed of the ship. The fair weather mizzen
staysail which was a particularly big sail replaced it perfectly at
all trims from sharp up to two points abaft the beam. With the
wind aft the cross-jack was merely a nuisance. 30

I advocate the ship carrying single topgallantsails as a matter of traditional practice and training. For the same reason
I would suggest that the clew-lines of the upper sails and the
clew-garnets of the courses should be led to the quarters of the
yard and not to the yard-arm. The proper furling of a sail with a 35
smooth bunt and tightly rolled yard-arms, is a great point in the
habits of smartness and proper merchant-ship discipline. It was
also a matter of correct seamanship because a sail that was not
properly furled in bad weather was likely to free itself and blow
away from the yard. The shifting of clew-lines to the yard-arms 40

was really a dodge of under-manning since it is obvious that
with no bunt to the sail less men are required to make some
sort of furl of it. The training ship however will be anything but
under-manned and unless she is very big there would be plenty
of hands in her to furl the three topgallantsails together. I have
repeatedly seen the four boys of the *Torrens* with the addition
of one able seaman furl the main topgallantsail of that ship
in a stiff breeze. In a ship of 1600 tons six boys and two able
seamen ought to master a topgallantsail in almost any weather.
When I joined the *Torrens* the then master of her, Capt. Cope
(an old Conway boy) fell in at once with my suggestion to shift
the clew-lines back to the quarters of the yard, on the ground
that the ship was manned well enough to do things properly.

In regard to boats I will again refer to my experience of
the *Torrens* (a sailing ship with a hundred souls on board). We
carried in her, aft, two quarter-boats on davits abreast the mizzen
rigging. They were well above water, toggled-in against a spar so
as to be disengaged by one single jerk on a lanyard (their tackle-
falls being always coiled clear on deck) and in other respects
were ready for lowering instantly. Owing to the shortness of a
merchantman's crew the orders as to these boats were that in an
emergency the nearest men (up to four) were to get into her at
once, the officer of the watch and the midshipman of the watch
attending to the falls. The only real test of quickness we had,
happened in the daytime and in light weather, when the ship
was luffed up till the sails lifted and one of the quarter-boats was
lowered to pick up a parrot which had flown overboard. Not
having been on deck at the time I don't know how long all this
took, but the parrot survived the experience; so we must have
been quick enough to have saved a child, for instance, of which
we always had several on board.

On the skids abaft the mainmast we carried two bigger spare
boats bottom up and not ready for lowering. But the principal
boats of the ship were two very roomy life-boats, carried on skids
forward, just abaft the fore rigging. They stood in chocks and
their davits were fore-and-afted at sea, but the lowering tackles
were always hooked and the falls coiled in tubs secured on the
top of the deck-house of which I have spoken before. Those life-
boats were fitted out ready to "abandon ship," with sea anchors,
oil-bags, oars, mast and sail, blue lights, water breakers and

ship's bread in tins. Their chocks were held in position by a bolt in the usual way, and the ship's carpenter was instructed when making his report to me in the morning to report: "Davits and bolts free." When the bolt was knocked out a lift of three inches was all that was necessary to swing out those life-boats. Now and again I had a test, generally at eight o'clock in the morning at the change of watches, and I managed to bring things to a point when the whole operation took seven minutes from the time of the order: "Both watches. Out lifeboats," to the moment when they were swung back and landed again in their chocks; the second mate taking charge of the starboard and the senior apprentice (acting third) of the port side. This for a merchant ship was quite as good as could be expected and would have met almost any emergency short of sudden disaster. In the Channel and between the chops of the Channel and the Western Islands (either homeward or outward bound), on the first appearance of thick weather with a moderate sea it was a standing order that the officer of the watch immediately after calling the captain was to swing these boats outboard ready for lowering. In that position they remained weather permitting till the fog cleared. I have entered into those details because from the nature of things there can be very few sailing ship officers left now who have had the experience of the care of upwards of a hundred people on board a 1300 ton ship.

How far the boys should be given an insight into the stowage of a large single hold I am not prepared to say. The proper stowage of a sailing ship was an extremely important part of her preparation for sea, affecting sailing powers, the comfort of everybody on board and even her absolute safety. The stowage of a subdivided hold of a large steamship is from the very nature of things a much less nice matter. It is also different in its nature since the order of the ports of call is a paramount consideration in the disposition of a steamship's cargo. But an insight into the old conditions cannot do any harm and may be found useful on occasion.

Next I venture to offer the suggestion that the ship should have no auxiliary propulsion of any kind. Let her *be* a sailing ship. I don't exactly know how this may affect the rate of insurance, but I assure you that a very few years ago, well within the life of the man

who is addressing you now, nobody thought a sailing ship less safe
than a steamship. A ship's safety apart from the "Act of God" rests
in the hands of the men who are aboard her, from the highest to
the lowest in their different degrees. Machinery, per se, will not
5   make a ship more safe and the saved space would be useful for
other purposes.

The ship will have of course to make use of tugs at the end of
her passages. This will afford to the cadets the opportunity to
get an insight into the various points of seamanship connected
10   with the operations of towage. The mere handling of steel and
other kinds of hawsers will by itself give them valuable practice.

General Remarks. Finally I beg leave to touch upon the actual number of people on board. Mr Lawrence Holt's letter speaks of 60–80
cadets. I should suggest that the lesser number should be adopted.
15   And even less than 60 if possible. What I have in my mind is the
possibility of some accident (which may happen to the best ship
afloat) and its effect on the public mind. Regard ought to be paid
also to the facility of getting a lesser number of people out of a
sinking ship or saving them all in case of a shipwreck.
20   I have assumed that the period of training would be 18 months.
This in the case of a Conway boy would work out his apprenticeship
as follows: One year sea service allowed for Conway training; one
year and a half in the sailing ship; the last year and a half as
apprentice or cadet in a steamship.
25   In case of boys joining straight from a school on shore I suppose
they would be kept for $2\frac{1}{2}$ years on board the sailing vessel and
finish their time in steam.
I don't touch on the point of navigational studies, for which
no doubt a provision will be made. I will only remark that the
30   greatest care and accuracy should be required from the cadets
acting as assistant officers of the watch (and generally from all
senior boys) in keeping the ship's dead reckoning. This is a point
of seamanship rather than navigation.
The ship whether at anchor or alongside the quay ought to offer
35   that aspect of finished smartness alow and aloft that a training ship
should have. It must be remembered that wherever she goes she
will be representing the entire maritime community of the Port
of Liverpool, employers and employed, shipowners and seamen.

The cadets going ashore on leave should always wear the ship's uniform, unless specifically invited to play games. The ship will no doubt have a football team and a cricket eleven.

A harbour watch (as distinguished from anchor watch) composed of one senior and two junior cadets should be kept. And, 5 generally, a proper amount of formality should be observed in the ship's routine both at sea and in port. It is conducive to self-respect in all ranks.

THE LOSS OF THE *DALGONAR*
1921

(*To the Editor of* THE LONDON MERCURY)

SIR,
5 Since you have invited comments from nautical readers on a certain obscure passage in the "True Story" printed in your September number, I will refer here to the point raised by Mr L. C. Gane and to some other mistakes of minor importance. Not that I think they matter in the least for your readers, who, in any
10 case, would have perceived the great quality of the narrative.

The passage queried by Mr L. C. Gane, quite justifiably, runs as follows:

"At noon wore ship . . . 7 p.m. wind and sea increasing, took in the *mizzen fore upper topsail.* 11 p.m. wind and sea still increasing,
15 took in the *mizzen and main upper topsails.*"

The italicized words have, nautically speaking, no sense; the first four absolutely, the second five in relation to the first statement; since it is obvious that the mizzen upper topsail could not have been taken in twice.
20 These are obviously slips of the pen or errors of transcription. The first statement evidently was meant for:

"Took in the mizzen and fore upper topsails,"

the word missing in your text being the "and" after the word "mizzen". The ship then was carrying her fore-sail, lower fore-
25 topsail, lower and upper main-topsail and lower mizzen-topsail. At 11 p.m., the gale still increasing, the sails taken in were the "mizzen *lower* and main upper topsails"; the word missing in the phrase as it stands in the text being the word "lower" after the word "mizzen". Thus, at 11 p.m., the ship was reduced down to her foresail and the
30 fore and main lower topsails, which was a possible and seamanlike canvas for her to carry in the then state of the weather. I can not however defend myself from the impression conveyed by the narrative and also from what happened afterwards that the foresail

was carried on her too long. That large piece of canvas must have had the effect (at least at times) of forcing the ship $1\frac{1}{2}$ or perhaps 2 knots through the water – for no object that I can see. And *there* was the danger. But it is easy to be wise after the event!

The paragraph queried by Mr Gane contains also a printing 5
error: the plural "s" should come out of the word "foresails". A ship has got only one foresail.

As to other minor corrections, the words "*main draft*" in the opening paragraph of the story should be "*mean draft*," as is obvious from the inspection of the figures. The draught of water is a 10
formal log-book entry in any ship about to proceed to sea. Another misprint (on page 483) consists in a superfluous letter. The line runs:

"and *web* squared-in the main and crossjack yards, etc., etc."

The "b" got in there by mistake. It should, of course, run: 15

"and *we* squared-in the main, etc. etc.,"

in what is a correct description of wearing ship, which was the last manœuvre attempted before the *Dalgonar* became unmanageable.

On the next page the meaningless word printed as "nil" should, of course, be "rail". 20

I agree with all my heart with the editorial note heading the story. There can be nothing finer or more simple. The crew of the *Dalgonar* behaved as well as I have ever seen the crew of a British merchant ship behave in a critical situation, and they deserve fully the encomiums and blessings Mr Mull, the Chief Officer, 25
gives to them in his report written on board the *Loire*. A tribute of admiration is due, too, to the captain of the French ship for his humane determination to save those men, and for the display of seamanlike resolution and skill in maintaining his ship in position for so long in such desperate weather. Nobody but a seaman can 30
appreciate the risks and the difficulty of the task, and the severe strain put on the endurance of the crew and officers of the *Loire* in sheer physical exertions, in unremitting vigilance and plucky seamanship, which enabled them to remain by and finally to take off the crew of the *Dalgonar*. 35

I am etc etc
J. CONRAD.

TRAVEL
PREFACE TO RICHARD
CURLE'S *INTO THE EAST*
1922

5   THERE IS NO FATE so uncertain as the fate of books of
travel. They are the most assailable of all men's literary productions. The man who writes a travel book delivers himself more
than any other into the hands of his enemies. The popularising
scientific writer's position is much more secure. His very subject
10 is, properly speaking, marvellous in itself and for that reason the
intelligent multitude swallows it eagerly, or at least receives it with
open mouth and forms its own amazing conclusions. A writer
of fiction – well! He romances all the time, and the truth he
has in him being disguised in various garments, from gold man-
15 tles to rags, is almost beyond the reach of criticism. All really he
has got to attend to is grammar and punctuation. Metaphysics of
course are simply intoxicating for those who like that way of killing
our appointed time in this valley of tears. But as to those whose
fancy leads them to investigate more or less profoundly that same
20 valley...!

  But after all a traveller is very much to be envied. He is to be
envied for the instinct that prompts him, for the courage that
sustains him. He is to be admired for enduring a spectacle almost
intolerably gorgeous and varied, but with only hints, here and
25 there, of dramatic scenes, with, practically, no star actors in it,
with the knowledge that the curtain will not fall for months and
months to come; and that he must play the exacting part of a
spectator of those human characteristics and activities, in their
picturesque, ugly, or savage settings, without, so to speak, the
30 prospect of going home, to bed presently. Imagine a lover of
drama and of stage effects forced to sleep in his very stall, and,
every day, opening his eyes upon a never-ceasing performance.
The taste for that sort of thing may well be envied as evidence
of the capacity for mental and physical resistance not only against
35 the strain of all the "things that seem to be," but against one's

own weakness. Perhaps that's the reason why the Arabs, racially great travellers and great lovers of wonders, invented the proverb, "travelling is victory," which stands as the motto of this book. It expresses indeed a romantic conception. But there is a soberness of temperament in the Arab race which has prevented it from 5 rushing exultingly into the writing of travel books. Of course I am an ignorant person, from circumstances which it would not be to my advantage to disclose, but I can only call to mind one Arab traveller who had written a book; and surely if there had been shoals of them I would have heard of another. 10

Those people did much of their travelling sword in hand and with the name of the One God on their lips. But theirs were personally conducted parties as destructive to the peace and the spiritual character of places they visited as any crowd from a tourist agency invading the shades of Vallombrosa. Let us forget the Arabs 15 as well as their successors who are achieving victory every year at the price of so many pounds per head for a certain number of days. They demand neither our admiration nor our pity.

Nowadays many people encompass the globe. That kind of victory became to a certain extent fashionable for some years after 20 the piercing of the Isthmus of Suez. Multitudes rushed through that short cut with blank minds and, alas, also blank note books where the megalomania from which we all more or less suffer, got recorded in the shape of "Impressions". The inanity of the mass of travel books the Suez Canal is responsible for took the proportions 25 of an enormous and melancholy joke. For it was a mournful sight to see so many people giving themselves away. Their books covered private shelves and the tables of *cabinets de lecture* in a swarm more devastating to the world's freshness of impression than a swarm of locusts in a field of young corn. When that visitation began I was 30 quite a boy and in my innocence I read them all, or, at least, all I could lay my hands on. Women, single or in pairs, fashionable couples, professors of intense gravity, facetious business men – I read all their travel books including even Baron Hübner's *Voyage Round the World*, which I should think remains unequalled to this 35 day.

That category of travellers with their parrot-like remarks, their strange attempts at being funny and their lamentable essays in seriousness, has apparently passed away. Or perhaps they only print their books for circulation amongst friends. I suspect 40

however they have ceased to write simply because there are too
many of them. They do not appear as travellers even to the most
naive minds and perhaps even to their own minds. They are simply an enormous company of people who go round the world for
5   a change and rest, either suffering from overwork (whatever that
may mean) or from neurasthenia. And I am sure my best wishes go
with them for an easy and radical recovery. Steamship companies
love them.

Sporting travellers form a class by themselves. They mostly write
10   for other sportsmen, though I must confess that their books
hold for me even now some fascination. They are apt to grow
monotonous in the descriptive statistics of slaughter and as to the
shortcomings of their "boys". Also in their admiration for their
trackers who seem all to have been made from the same pattern.
15   I have noticed them adopting of late years a half-apologetic tone
about their exploits; whereas the men of twenty-five years ago with
their much less perfect weapons and their big records were frankly
exulting. Frankness is a virtue I like. I would respect the modern
attitude more if I were sure of its absolute genuineness. Modera-
20   tion in game-killing is enforced now by many regulations; but on
considering how easy it is not to shoot an antelope one becomes
slightly doubtful of the perfect candour of men who travel thousands of miles in dreary steamboats and uncomfortable, primitive
trains for mere sport. On the other hand I admit that a sportsman
25   who would consistently miss every antelope would be an extremely
uninteresting person. The world of explorers and discoverers, the
heroes of my boyhood, has vanished almost to nothing in the
nineteenth century. Some of them wrote the classics of travel, but
no passage of years can dim my admiration for their selfless spirit
30   and manly faithfulness to their task pursued in solitude or with a
few devoted henchmen, persevered in through numberless days
with death only a pace behind, but with a calm mind and a steady
heart.

What about mere wanderers? – those individuals that one meets
35   in various fairly well-known localities but who come upon one
round unexpected corners, often shabby and depressed, sometimes haggard and jaunty; with tales in their mouths of the flattest
description or of a comic quality bordering on tears; with, now
and then, a story that would frighten you to death if you were
40   one of those men that don't know how to smile in time. I would

class them as an outcast tribe if it did not sound so rude. And I would not be rude for anything to people capable of starting on their travels with their hands, and very little else besides, in their pockets. I have known amongst them men of ruffianly mental complexion, cultivating a truculent manner and a cold steady stare, who if it were possible to bluff one's own destiny might have been sitting in high places. And I ask myself, in my half-reluctant partiality for the class, whether some of them have not achieved it. But success disguises them at once and contemporary history gives them other names.

In my review of the categories of men who move about the earth I come now to the real travellers who wrote books, the protagonists of the modern travellers, in the same way, I may say, in which Hannon may be looked upon as a protagonist of the discoverers and the circumnavigators of the globe. Only the *Periplus* was probably a dreary official report. At any rate it has not come down to us. The outstanding figure amongst those men who dedicated their books of travel to popes and emperors is Marco Polo with his meticulous descriptive gift, his cautious credulity, his eye for splendour and his historian's rather than a traveller's temperament. He gave his readers what the readers of that day wanted, historical facts in a foreign and gorgeous atmosphere. But the time for such books of travel is past on this earth girt about with cables, with an atmosphere made restless by the waves of ether, lighted by that sun of the twentieth century under which there is nothing new left now and but very little of what may still be called obscure.

The day of many volumed "Journeys, through or to," of "Relations of this or that" (and much charm and ability some of them had), the days of heroic travel are gone; unless, of course, in the newspaper sense in which heroism like everything else in the world becomes as common if not as nourishing as our daily bread. There would be always a lady or a gentleman ready to discover with considerable fuss a bit of territory of, say, ten square miles, resembling exactly the surrounding and already explored lands, or interview some new ruler, like a reflection in a dim and tarnished mirror of some real chieftain in the books of a hundred years ago, or marvel at a disagreeable fish of ferocious habits which had been described already in some old-time, simply-worded, unsensational "Relation". But even this is a game which is losing its interest and

in a very little time will have come to an end. Presently there will
be no backyard left in the heart of Central Africa that has not
been peeped into by some person more or less commissioned for
the purpose. The Nigeria of Barth, of Denham, of Clapperton, of
5   Mungo Park, of other infinitely curious and profoundly inspired
men, will be bristling with police posts, Colleges, tramway poles,
and all those improving things triumphantly recorded, and always
with the romantic addition that, within twenty miles, the hills, or
the forests, or the holes in the sand, or the depths of the jungle
10 (that blessed word) were swarming with cannibal-tribes miracu-
lously restrained by one white man with two black soldiers and his
native cook for all company. And the great cloud of fatuous daily
photographs and even more fatuous descriptive chatter, under
whose shadow no traveller could live, will brood over those sel-
15 dom visited places of the world that, despoiled of their old black
soul of mystery, have not yet acquired its substitute, which will be
marvellously piebald when it comes.

      THIS MOMENT of ill-humour with "things as they are becom-
ing," is of course perfectly unreasonable or even perverse, which is
20 worse. It would not deserve to be tolerated except for its inherent
piety. As a matter of fact I have been thinking for a moment of
the dead, of the great and good travellers loved in my boyhood,
as I laid aside the MS. of this modern traveller who by publishing
it has delivered himself to his enemies. He is very modern, for he
25 is fashioned by the conditions of an explored earth in which the
latitudes and longitudes having been recorded once for all have
become things of no importance, in the sense that they can no
longer appeal to the spirit of adventure, inflame no imagination,
lead no one up to the very gates of mortal danger.
30   These basic facts of geography having been ascertained by the
observations of heavenly bodies, the glance of the modern traveller contemplating the much surveyed earth beholds in fact a
world in a state of transition; very different in this from the writers
of travel books of Marco Polo's time who in their conscientious
35 narratives seem to progress amongst immutable wonders, to feed
their curiosity on a consistency of the splendid and the bizarre,
presented to their eyes to stare at, to their minds to moralise upon.
      And these things which stand as if imperishable in the pages of
old books of travel, are all blown away, have vanished as utterly

as the smoke of the travellers' camp fires in the icy night-air of
the Gobi Desert, as the smell of incense burned in the temples of
strange gods, as the voices of Asiatic statesmen speculating with
the cruel wisdom of past ages on matters of peace and war.

Nothing obviously strange remains for our eyes now. The Khan 5
of Tartary's court ceremonies were certainly marvellous in quite
a different sense from the procedure followed at Kuala Kangsar
two years ago when the Sultan of Perak was invested with the
K.C.M.G. by the Governor of the Straits Settlements. This modern
traveller describes it all in less words than Marco Polo would have 10
used paragraphs on such a striking occasion. It was curious for
him to watch under the formal routine of official compliments
the Malay princes play up to British etiquette while grafting it on
their own ideas of politeness, and wearing, he thought, a slightly
ironical smile on their dark faces. And to think that only fifty 15
years ago, after a certain amount of jungle and stockade fighting,
the Sultan of Perak, or perhaps his brother ruler next door in
Selangor, having listened attentively to a lecture from a British
Admiral on the heinousness of a certain notable case of piracy,
turned round quickly to his attending chiefs and to the silent 20
throng of his Malay subjects, exclaiming: "Hear now, my people!
Don't let us have any more of this little game." Those words ought
to have been engraved in letters of gold on a marble monument
at the mouth of the Jugra river; for from the moment they were
pronounced dates the era of security for the poor folks of the 25
coast, for the fishermen and traders in the Straits of Malacca. The
downfall of local piracy in fact. The world in transition!

Our very curiosities have changed, growing more subtle
amongst the vanishing mysteries of the earth. Very appropriately
this modern traveller reclining on the verandah of the State Rest- 30
house after having watched the ceremonies of installation in the
blaring of trumpets and the gorgeous bright colours of the throng,
recalls the strong impression of, one might say, indifferent and
rather contemptuous good-will between brown and white, and
gives himself up to the vain (as he himself observes) occupation 35
of speculating on the future of countries. But he does it not in
the spirit of a statesman looking for political truth but in the
doubting mood of a traveller of our day who on the very threshold of the East has questioned himself as to the ultimate truth of
travel: whether perchance it was no more than the mastery of first 40

impressions; and whether the sanity of our outlook on the world, consists in secret revolt against its fact but in the final acceptance of the whole, or in the conformity with all the multiple forms and the mental rejection of life's inscrutable purpose? It is this mood which makes him so responsive to the inner promptings suggested by travel, which informs the felicitous rendering of his visual impressions. This it is that forces him, while looking out into the night from the deck on an Irrawaddy flotilla steamer, to admit to himself man's secret antagonism to the wilderness; or during his few hours' stay in Bhamo, a town on the very frontier of the Chinese enigma, where caravans incessantly come and go through mysterious valleys, and where people live on rumours from day to day, to absorb its spirit of secrecy and waiting and hear suddenly around him "the whisper of innumerable hills passing on one to another the restless murmur of men's hearts". Very modern in impressions, in appreciations, in curiosities, and in his very love of the mother earth, of whose children he has written subtly and tenderly in some three volumes of characteristic tales; a traveller of our day, condemned to make his discoveries on beaten tracks, he looks on, sensitive, meditative, with delicate perceptions and a gift for expression, alive to the saving grace of human and histor-ical associations, and while pursuing amongst the men busy with ascertained facts the riddles presented by a world in transition, he seems to have captured for us the spirit of modern travel itself.

STEPHEN CRANE
INTRODUCTION TO THOMAS
BEER'S *STEPHEN CRANE*
1923

O N A R A I N Y D A Y of March of the year 1923, listening to the author of this biography telling me of his earnest labours for the memory of a man who was certainly unique in his gener-ation I exclaimed to myself with wonder: And so it has come to pass after all – this thing which I did not expect to see! In truth I had never expected the biography of Stephen Crane to appear in my lifetime. My immense pleasure was affected by the devastating touch of time which like a muddy flood covers under a mass of daily trivialities things of value: moments of affectionate commu-nion with kindred spirits, words spoken with the careless freedom of perfect confidence, the deepest emotions of joy and sorrow – together with such things of merely historical importance as the recollection of dates, for instance. After hearing from Mr Beer of his difficulties in fixing certain dates in the history of Stephen Crane's life I discovered that I was unable to remember with any kind of precision the initial date of our friendship. Indeed life is but a dream – especially for those of us who have never kept a diary or possessed a note-book in our lives.

In this extremity I had recourse to another friend of Stephen Crane, who had appreciated him intuitively almost as soon as I did myself and who is a woman of excellent memory. My wife's recollection is that Crane and I met in London in October 1897, and that he came to see us for the first time in our Essex home in the following November.

I have mentioned in a short paper written two years ago that it was Mr S. S. Pawling, partner in the publishing firm of Mr Heinemann, who brought us together. It was done at Stephen Crane's own desire. I was told by Mr Pawling that when asked whom he wanted to meet Crane mentioned two names, of which one was of a notable journalist (who had written some novels) whom Crane knew in America, I believe, and the other was mine.

71

At that time the only facts we knew about each other were that we both had the same publisher in England. The only other fact I knew about Stephen Crane was that he was quite a young man. I had of course read his *Red Badge of Courage* of which people were writing and talking at that time. I certainly did not know that he had the slightest notion of my existence, or that he had seen a single line (there were not many of them then) of my writing. I can safely say that I earned this precious friendship by something like ten months of strenuous work with my pen. It took me just that time to write *The Nigger of the Narcissus* working at what I always considered a very high pressure. It was on the ground of the authorship of that book that Crane wanted to meet me. Nothing could have been more flattering, than to discover that the author of *The Red Badge of Courage* appreciated my effort to present a group of men held together by a common loyalty and a common perplexity in a struggle not with human enemies but with the hostile conditions testing their faithfulness to the conditions of their own calling. Apart from the imaginative analysis of his own temperament tried by the emotions of a battlefield Stephen Crane dealt in his book with the psychology of the mass – the army; while I – in mine – had been dealing with the same subject on a much smaller scale and in more specialized conditions – the crew of a merchant ship, brought to the test of what I may venture to call the moral problem of conduct. This may be thought a very remote connection between these two works and the idea may seem too far-fetched to be mentioned here; but that was my undoubted feeling at the time. It is a fact that I considered Crane, by virtue of his creative experience with *The Red Badge of Courage*, as eminently fit to pronounce a judgment on my first consciously planned attempt to render the truth of a phase of life in the terms of my own temperament with all the sincerity of which I was capable. I had, of course, my own opinion as to what I had done; but I doubted whether anything of my ambitiously comprehensive aim would be understood. I was wrong there; but my doubt was excusable since I myself would have been hard put to it if requested to give my complex intentions the form of a concise and definite statement. In that period of misgivings which so often follows an accomplished task I would often ask myself: who in the world could be interested in such a thing?

It was after reading *The Red Badge* which came into my hands directly after its publication in England that I said to myself: "Here's a man who may understand – if he ever sees the book; though of course that would not mean that he would like it." I do not mean to say that I looked towards the author of *The Red Badge* as the only man in the world. It would have been stupid and ungrateful. I had the moral support of one or two intimate friends and the solid fact of Mr W. E. Henley's acceptance of my tale for serial publication in the *New Review* to give me confidence, while I awaited the larger verdict. It seems to me that in trying to recall my memories of Stephen Crane I have been talking so far only about myself; but that is unavoidable, since this introduction, which I am privileged to write, can only trace what is left on earth of our personal intercourse which was even more short and fleeting than it may appear from the record of dates: October 1897–May 1900. And out of that beggarly tale of months must be deducted the time of his absence from England during the Spanish-American war, and of his visit to the United States shortly before the beginning of his last illness. Even when he was in England our intercourse was not so close and frequent as the warmth of our friendship would have wished it to be. We both lived in the country and, though not very far from each other, in different counties. I had my work to do, always in conditions which made it a matter of urgency. He had his own tasks and his own visions to attend to. I do not think that he had more friendships to claim him than I, but he certainly had more acquaintances and more calls on his time.

This was only natural. It must be remembered that as an author he was my senior, as I used to remind him now and then with affected humility which always provoked his smiles. He had a quiet smile that charmed and frightened one. It made you pause by something revelatory it cast over his whole physiognomy, not like a ray but like a shadow. I often asked myself what it could be, that quality that checked one's care-free mood; and now I think I have had my answer. It was the smile of a man who knows that his time will not be long on this earth.

I would not for a moment wish to convey the impression of melancholy in connection with my memories of Stephen Crane. I saw his smile first over the table-cloth in a restaurant. We shook hands with intense gravity and a direct stare at each other, after

the manner of two children told to make friends. It was under
the encouraging gaze of Sydney Pawling who, a much bigger man
than either of us and possessed of a deep voice, looked like a
grown-up person entertaining two strange small boys – protecting
5   and slightly anxious as to the experiment. He knew very little of
either of us. I was a new author and Crane was a new arrival. It was
the meeting of *The Red Badge* and *The Nigger* in the presence of
their publisher; but as far as our personalities went we were three
strangers breaking bread together for the first time. Yet it was as
10 pleasantly easy a meal as any I can remember. Crane talked in
his characteristic deliberate manner about Greece, at war. I had
already sensed the man's intense earnestness underlying his quiet
surface. Every time he raised his eyes that secret quality (for his
voice was careless) of his soul was betrayed in a clear flash. Most
15 of the true Stephen Crane was in his eyes, most of his strength at
any rate, though it was apparent also in his other features, as for
instance in the structure of his forehead, in the deep solid arches
under the fair eyebrows.

Some people saw traces of weakness in the lower part of his face.
20 What I could see there was a hint of the delicacy of sentiment,
of the inborn fineness of nature which this man, whose life had
been anything but a stroll through a rose-garden, had managed to
preserve like a sacred heritage. I say heritage, not acquisition, for
it was not and could not have been acquired. One could depend
25 on it on all occasions; whereas the cultivated kind is apt to show
ugly gaps under very slight provocation. The coarseness of the
professedly delicate must be very amusing to the misanthrope.
But Crane was no enemy of his kind. That sort of thing did not
amuse him. As to his own temper it was proof against anger and
30 scorn, as I can testify, having seen him both angry and scornful,
always quietly, on fitting occasions. Contempt and indignation
never broke the surface of his moderation simply because he had
no surface. He was all through of the same material, incapable
of affectation of any kind, of any pitiful failure of generosity for
35 the sake of personal advantage, or even from sheer exasperation
which must find its relief.

Many people imagined him a fiery individuality. Certainly he
was not cold-blooded. But his was an equable glow, morally and
temperamentally. I would have said the same of his creative power
40 (I have seen him sit down before a blank sheet of paper, dip his

pen, write the first line at once and go on without haste and without pause for a couple of hours), had he not confided to me that
his mentality did flag at times. I do not think it was anything more
than every writer is familiar with at times. Another man would
have talked of his "failing inspiration". It is very characteristic of 5
Crane that I have never heard him use that word when talking
about his work.

His phraseology was generally of a very modest cast. That
"unique and exquisite faculty," which Edward Garnett, another
of his friends, found in his writing – "of disclosing an individual 10
scene by an odd simile" was not apparent in his conversation. It
was interesting of course, but its charm consisted mainly in the
freshness of his impressions set off by an acute simplicity of view
and expressed with an amusing deliberation. Superabundance of
words was not his failing when communing with those whom he 15
liked and felt he could trust. With the other kind of "friends" he
followed the method of a sort of suspended silence. On a certain
occasion (it was at Brede Place) after two amazingly conceited
idiots had gone away I said to him, "Stevie, you brood like a distant thunder-cloud." He had retired early to the other end of the 20
room, and from there had sent out, now and then, a few words,
more like the heavy drops of rain that precede the storm than
growls of thunder. Poor Crane if he could look black enough at
times, never thundered; though I have no doubt he could have
been dangerous if he had liked. There always seemed to be some- 25
thing (not timidity) which restrained him, not from within but, I
could not help fancying, from outside, with an effect as of a whispered *memento mori* in the ear of a reveller not lost to the sense of
grace.

That of course was a later impression. It must be stated clearly 30
that I know very little of Stephen Crane's life. We did not feel the
need to tell each other formally the story of our lives. That did not
prevent us from being very intimate and also very open with each
other from the first. Our affection would have been "everlasting"
as he himself qualified it, had not the jealous death intervened 35
with her cruel capriciousness by striking down the younger man.
Our intimacy was really too close to admit of indiscretions; not that
he did not speak amusingly of his experiences and of his hardships,
and warmly of the men that helped him in his early days, like Mr
Hamlin Garland for instance, or men kindly encouraging to him, 40

like Mr Howells. Many other names he used to utter lovingly have
been forgotten by me after so many years.

It is a fact that I heard more of his adventures than of his trials,
privations and difficulties. I know he had many. He was the least
5 recriminatory of men (though one of the most sensitive, I should
say), but, in any case, nothing I could have learned would have
shaken the independent judgment I had formed for myself of his
trustworthiness as a man and a friend. Though the word is discredited now and may sound pretentious, I will say that there was in
10 Crane a strain of chivalry which made him safe to trust with one's
life. To be recognisably a man of honour carries no immunity
against human weaknesses, but comports more rigid limitations
in personal relations than the status of an "honourable man," however recognizable that too may be. Some men are "honourable"
15 by courtesy, others by the office they hold, or simply by belonging
to some popular assembly, the election to which is not generally secured by a dignified accuracy of statement and a scrupulous regard for the feelings of others. Many remain honourable
(because of their great circumspection in the conduct of their
20 affairs) without holding within themselves any of these restraints
which are inherent in the character of a man of honour, however
weak or luckless he may be.

I do not know everything about the strength of Crane's circumspection, but I am not afraid of what the biography which follows
25 may disclose to us; though I am convinced that it will be free
from hypocritical reservations. I think I have understood Stephen
Crane, and from my too short acquaintance with his biographer
I am confident he will receive the most humane and sympathetic
treatment. What I discovered very early in our acquaintance was
30 that Crane had not the face of a lucky man. That certitude came
to me at our first meeting while I sat opposite him listening to
his simple tales of Greece, while S. S. Pawling presided at the
initiatory feast – friendly and debonair, looking solidly anchored
in the stream of life, and very reassuring, like a big, prosperous
35 ship to the sides of which we two in our tossing little barks could
hook on for safety. He was interested in the tales too; and the
best proof of it is that when he looked at his watch and jumped
up, saying, "I must leave you two now." It was very near four
o'clock. Nearly a whole afternoon wasted, for an English business
40 man.

No such consideration of waste or duty agitated Crane and myself. The sympathy that, even in regard of the very few years allotted to our friendship, may be said to have sprung up instantaneously between us, was the most undemonstrative case of that sort in the last century. We not only did not tell each other of it (which would have been missish) but even without entering formally into a previous agreement to remain together we went out and began to walk side by side in the manner of two tramps without home, occupation, or care for the next night's shelter. We certainly paid no heed to direction. The first thing I noticed were the Green Park railings, when to my remark that he had seen no war before he went to Greece Crane made answer: "No. But *The Red Badge* is all right." I assured him that I had never doubted it; and, since the title of the work had been pronounced for the first time, feeling I must do something to show I had read it, I said shyly: "I like your general." He knew at once what I was alluding to but said not a word. Nothing could have been more tramp-like than our silent pacing, elbow to elbow, till, after we had left Hyde Park Corner behind us, Crane uttered with his quiet earnestness, the words: "I like your young man – I can just see him." Nothing could have been more characteristic of the depth of our three-hour-old intimacy than that each of us should have selected for praise the merest by-the-way vignette of a minor character.

This was positively the only allusion we made that afternoon to our immortal works. Indeed we talked very little of them at any time, and then always selecting some minor point for particular mention; which, after all, is not a bad way of showing an affectionate appreciation of a piece of work done by a friend. A stranger would have expected more, but, in a manner of speaking, Crane and I had never been strangers. We took each other's work for granted from the very first, I mean from the moment we had exchanged those laudatory remarks alongside the Green Park railings. Henceforth mutual recognition kept to that standard. It consisted often of an approving grunt, sometimes of the mention of some picked out paragraph, or of a line or only of a few words that had caught our fancy and would, for a time, be applied more or less aptly to the turns of our careless, or even serious, talks.

Thus, for instance, there was a time when I persecuted poor Crane with the words "barbarously abrupt". They occur in that marvellous story "The Open Boat" and are applied by him to

the waves of the sea (as seen by men tossing in a small dinghy)
with an inspired audacity of epithet which was one of Crane's
gifts that gave me most delight. How amazingly apt these words
are where they stand, anybody can see by looking at that story,
5   which is altogether a big thing, and has remained an object of my
confirmed admiration. I was always telling Crane that this or that
was "barbarously abrupt," or begging him not to be so "barbarously
abrupt" himself, with a keen enjoyment of the incongruity; for no
human being could be less abrupt than Crane. As to his humanity
10   (in contradistinction to barbarity) it was a shining thing without
a flaw.

It is possible that he may have grown at length weary of my little
joke but he invariably received it with a smile, thus proving his
consistent humanity towards his kind. But, after all, he too liked
15   that story of his, of four men in a very small boat, which by the deep
and simple humanity of presentation seems somehow to illustrate
the essentials of life itself, like a symbolic tale. It opens with a
phrase that anybody could have uttered but which, in relation
to what is to follow, acquires the poignancy of a meaning almost
20   universal. Once, much later in our acquaintance, I made use of
it to him. He came on a flying visit to Pent Farm where we were
living then. I noticed that he looked harassed. I, too, was feeling
for the moment as if things were getting too much for me. He
lay on the couch and I sat on a chair opposite. After a longish
25   silence in which we both could have felt how uncertain was the
issue of life envisaged as a deadly adventure in which we were both
engaged like two men trying to keep afloat in a small boat, I said
suddenly across the width of the mantelpiece:

"None of them knew the colour of the sky."
30   He raised himself sharply. The words had struck him as familiar,
though I believe he failed to place them at first. "Don't you know
that quotation?" I asked. (These words form the opening sentence
of his tale.) The startled expression passed off his face. "Oh, yes,"
he said quietly, and lay down again. Truth to say it was a time when
35   neither he nor I had the leisure to look up idly at the sky. The
waves just then were too "barbarously abrupt".

I do not mean to say that it was always so. Now and then we
were permitted to snatch a glance at the colour of the sky. But
it is a fact that in the history of our essentially undemonstrative
40   friendship (which is nearly as difficult to recapture as a dream)

that first long afternoon is the most care-free instant, and the only
one that had a character of enchantment about it. It was spread
out over a large portion of central London. After the Green Park
the next thing I remember are the Kensington Gardens where
under the lofty and historical trees I was vouchsafed a glimpse of 5
the low mesquite bush overspreading the plum-coloured infinities
of the great Texas plains. Then after a long tramp amongst an
orderly multitude of grimy brick houses – from which the only
things I carried off were the impressions of the coloured rocks
of New Mexico (or was it Arizona?), and my first knowledge of a 10
locality called the Painted Desert – there came suddenly Oxford
Street. I don't know whether the inhabitants of London were
keeping indoors or had gone into the country that afternoon, but
I don't remember seeing any people in the streets except for a
figure, now and then, unreal, flitting by, obviously negligible. The 15
wheeled traffic too was stopped; yet, it seems, not entirely, because
I remember Crane seizing my arm and jerking me back on the
pavement with the calm remark: "You will get run over." I love to
think that the dear fellow had saved my life and that it seemed
to amuse him. As to London's enormous volume of business all 20
I know is that one A.B.C. shop had remained open. We went
through the depressing ceremony of having tea there; but our
interest in each other mitigated its inherent horrors and gave me
a good idea of Crane's stoicism. At least I suppose we had tea,
otherwise they would not have let us sit there so long. To be left 25
alone was all we wanted. Neither of us had then a club to entertain
the other in. It will give a good notion of our indomitable optimism
(on that afternoon) when I say that it was there, in those dismal
surroundings, we reached the conclusion that though the world
had grown old and weary, yet the scheme of creation remained 30
as obscure as ever, and (from our own particular point of view)
there was still much that was interesting to expect from gods and
men.

    As if intoxicated by this draught of hope we rolled out of that
A.B.C. shop, but I kept my head sufficiently to guess what was com- 35
ing and to send a warning telegram to my wife in our Essex home.
Crane then was, I believe, staying temporarily in London. But he
seemed to have no care in the world; and so we resumed our tramp-
ing – east and north and south again, steering through uncharted
streets, forgetting to think of dinner but taking a rest here and 40

there, till we found ourselves, standing in the middle of Piccadilly
Circus, blinking at the lights like two authentic night-birds. By that
time we had been (in Tottenham Court Road) joined by Balzac.
How he came in I have no idea. Crane was not given to literary
5   curiosities of that kind. Somebody he knew, or something he had
read, must have attracted lately his attention to Balzac. And now
suddenly at ten o'clock in the evening he demanded insistently
to be told in particular detail all about the *Comédie Humaine*, its
contents, its scope, its plan, and its general significance, together
10 with a critical description of Balzac's style. I told him hastily that
it was just black on white; and for the rest, I said, he would have
to wait till we got across to Monico's and had eaten some supper.
I hoped he would forget Balzac and his *Comédie*. But not a bit of
it; and I had no option but to hold forth over the remnants of a
15 meal, in the rush of hundreds of waiters and the clatter of tons of
crockery, caring not what I said (for what could Stephen want with
Balzac), in the comfortable assurance that the Monstrous Shade,
even if led by some strange caprice to haunt the long room of
Monico's, did not know enough English to understand a single
20 word I said. I wonder what Crane made of it all. He did not look
bored, and it was eleven o'clock before we parted at the foot of
that monumentally heavy abode of frivolity, the Pavilion, with just
a hand-shake and a good-night – no more – without making any
arrangements for meeting again, as though we had lived in the
25 same town from childhood and were sure to run across each other
next day.

It struck me directly I left him that we had not even exchanged
addresses; but I was not uneasy. Sure enough, before the month
was out there arrived a post-card (from Ravensbrook) asking
30 whether he might come to see us. He came, was received as an old
friend, and before the end of the day conquered my wife's sympathy, as undemonstrative and sincere as his own quiet friendliness.
The friendship that sprang up between them was confirmed by
the interest Crane displayed in our first child, a boy who came
35 on the scene not quite two months afterwards. How strong was
that interest on the part of Stephen Crane and his wife in the
boy is evidenced by the fact that at the age of six weeks he was
invited to come for a long visit to Ravensbrook. He was in fact
impatiently expected there. He arrived in state bringing with him
40 not only his parents but also a young aunt, and was welcomed like

a prince. This visit, during which I suffered from a sense of temporary extinction, is commemorated by a group photograph taken
by an artist summoned with his engine (regardless of expense) to
Ravensbrook. Though the likenesses are not bad it is a very awful
thing. Nobody looks like him or herself in it. The best yet are the   5
Crane dogs, a very important part of the establishment and quite
conscious of it, belonging apparently to some order of outlandish
poodles, amazingly sedate and yet the most restless animals I have
ever met. They pervaded, populated and filled the whole house.
Whichever way one looked at any time, down the passage, up the   10
stairs, into the drawing-room, there was always a dog in sight. Had
I been asked on the first day how many there were I would have
guessed about thirty. As a matter of fact there were only three, but
I think they never sat down, except in Crane's study, where they
had their entrée at all hours.   15
    A scratching would be heard at the door, Crane would drop
his pen with alacrity to throw it open – and the dogs would enter
sedately in single file, taking a lot of time about it, too. Then the
room would resound for a while with grunts, sniffs, yawns, heavy
flops, followed by as much perhaps as three whole minutes of   20
silence. Then the dogs would get up, one after another, never
all together, and direct their footsteps to the door in an impressive and ominous manner. The first arrival waited considerately for
the others before trying to attract attention by means of scratching
on the bottom panel. Then, never before, Crane would raise his   25
head, go meekly to the door – and the procession would file out
at the slowest possible pace. The recurrent sedateness of the proceedings, the utter unconsciousness of the dogs, dear Stephen's
absurd gravity while playing his part in those ceremonies, without
ever a muscle of his face moving, were irresistibly, exasperatingly   30
funny. I tried to preserve my gravity (or at least to keep calm) with
fair success. Only one afternoon on the fifth or sixth repetition I
could not help bursting into a loud interminable laugh and then
the dear fellow asked me in all innocence what was the matter. I
managed to conceal my nervous irritation from him and he never   35
learned the secret of that laugh in which there was a beginning of
hysteria.
    If the definition that man is a laughing animal be true then
Crane was neither one nor the other; indeed he was but a hurried
visitor on this earth on which he had so little reason to be joyous.   40

I might say that I never heard him laugh, except in connection
with the baby. He loved children; but his friendship with our child
was of the kind that put our mutual sentiment, by comparison,
somewhere within the Arctic region. The two could not be com-
5 pared; at least I have never detected Crane stretched full length
and sustained on his elbows on a grass plot, in order to gaze at
me; on the other hand this was his usual attitude of communion
with the small child – with him who was called *the Boy*, and whose
destiny it was to see more war before he came of age than the
10 author of *The Red Badge* had time to see in all the allotted days of
his life. In the gravity of its disposition the baby came quite up to
Crane; yet those two would sometimes find something to laugh at
in each other. Then there would be silence, and glancing out of
the low window of my room I would see them, very still, staring at
15 each other with a solemn understanding that needed no words or
perhaps was beyond words altogether. I could not object on any
ground to their profound intimacy but I do not see why Crane
should have developed such an unreasonable suspicion as to my
paternal efficiency. He seemed to be everlastingly taking the boy's
20 part. I could not see that the baby was being oppressed, hectored
over, or in any way deprived of its rights, or ever wounded in its
feelings by me; but Crane seemed always to nurse some vague
unexpressed grievance as to my conduct. I was inconsiderate. For
instance – why could I not get a dog for the boy? One day he
25 made quite a scene about it. He seemed to imply I should drop
everything to go and look for a dog. I sat under the storm and
said nothing. At last he cried "Hang it all, a boy ought to have
a dog." It was an appeal to first principles but for an answer I
pointed at the window and said: "Behold the boy." . . . He was sit-
30 ting on a rug spread on the grass, with his little red stocking-cap
very much over one eye (a fact of which he seemed unaware); and
propped round with many pillows on account of his propensity to
roll over on his side helplessly. My answer was irresistible. This is
one of the few occasions on which I heard Stephen Crane laugh
35 outright. He dropped his preaching on the dog theme and went
out to the boy while I went on with my work. But he was strangely
incorrigible. When he came back after an hour or so, his first
words were, "Joseph, I will teach your boy to ride." I closed with
the offer at once – but it was not to be. He was not given the
40 time.

The happiest mental picture my wife and I preserve of Crane is on the occasion of our first visit to Brede Place when he rode to meet us at the park gate. He looked at his best on horseback. On that day he must have been feeling well. As usual, he was happy in the saddle. As he went on trotting by the side of the 5 open trap I said to him: "If you give the boy your seat I will be perfectly satisfied." I knew this would please him; and indeed his face remained wreathed in smiles all the way to the front door. He looked about him at that bit of the world, down the green slopes and up the brown fields, with an appreciative serenity and the 10 confident bearing of a man who is feeling very sure of the present and of the future. All because he was looking at life from the saddle, with a good morning's work behind him. Nothing more is needed to give a man a blessed moment of illusion. The more I think of that morning the more I believe it was just that; that it had 15 really been given me to see Crane perfectly happy for a couple of hours; and that it was under this spell that directly we arrived he led me impatiently to the room in which he worked when at Brede. After we got there he said to me, "Joseph, I will give you something." I had no idea what it would be, till I saw him sit down 20 to write an inscription in a very slim volume. He presented it to me with averted head. It was *The Black Riders*. He had never spoken to me of his verse before. It was while holding the book in my hand that I learned that they were written years before in America. I expressed my appreciation of them that afternoon in the usual 25 half a dozen, or dozen, words which we allowed ourselves when completely pleased with each other's work. When the pleasure was not so complete the words would be many. And that was a great waste of breath and time. I must confess that we were no critics, I mean temperamentally. Crane was even less of a critic than myself. 30 Criticism is very much a matter of a vocabulary, very consciously used; with us it was the intonation that mattered. The tone of a grunt could convey an infinity of meaning between us.

The articulate literary conscience at our elbow was Edward Garnett. He, of course, was worth listening to. His analytical appre- 35 ciation (or appreciative analysis) of Crane's art, in the London *Academy* of 17th December 1898,[1] goes to the root of the matter

---

[1] Extended and re-published in the volume *Friday Nights*. Alfred A. Knopf. 1922. New York.

with Edward's almost uncanny insight, and well balanced sympathy with the blind, pathetic striving of the artist towards a complete realization of his individual gift. How highly Edward Garnett
rated Crane's gift is recorded in the conclusions of that admirable
5   and, within the limits of its space, masterly article of some two
columns, where at the end are set down such affirmative phrases
as: "The chief impressionist of the age."... "Mr Crane's talent
is unique"... and where he hails him as "the creator of fresh
rhythms and phrases," while the very last words state confidently
10 that: "Undoubtedly, of the young school it is Mr Crane who is the
genius – the others have their talents."
    My part here being not that of critic but of private friend all I
will say is that I agreed warmly at the time with that article which
from the quoted phrases might be supposed a merely enthusiastic
15 pronouncement, but on reading will be found to be based on
that calm sagacity which Edward Garnett, for all his fiery zeal in
the cause of letters, could always summon for the judgment of
matters emotional – as all response to the various forms of art
must be in the main. I had occasion to re-read it last year in
20 its expanded form in a collection of literary essays of great, now
almost historical, interest in the record of American and English
imaginative literature. I found there a passage or two, not bearing
precisely on Crane's work but giving a view of his temperament, on
which of course his art was based; and of the conditions moral and
25 material under which he had to put forth his creative faculties and
his power of steady composition. On those matters, as a man who
had the opportunity to look at Crane's life in England I wish to
offer a few remarks before closing my contribution to the memory
of my friend.
30   I do not know that he was ever dunned for money and had to
work under a threat of legal proceedings. I don't think he was
ever "dunned" in the sense in which such a phrase is used about
a spendthrift unscrupulous in incurring debts. No doubt he was
sometimes pressed for money. He lived by his pen and the prices
35 he obtained were not great. Personally he was not extravagant; and
I will not quarrel with him for not choosing to live in a garret. The
tenancy of Brede Place was held by him at a nominal rent. That
glorious old place was not restored then, and the greatest part of it
was uninhabitable. The Cranes had furnished in a modest way six
40 or seven of the least dilapidated rooms, which even then looked

bare and half empty. Certainly there was a horse, and at one time
even two, but that luxury was not so very expensive at that time.
One man looked after them. Riding was the only exercise open to
Crane; and if he did work so hard surely he was entitled to some
relaxation, if only for the preservation of his unique talent.   5

His greatest extravagance was hospitality of which I too had my
share; often in the company, I am sorry to say, of men who after
sitting at his board chose to speak of him and of his wife slight-
ingly. Having some rudimentary sense of decency their behaviour
while actually under the Cranes' roof often produced on me a   10
disagreeable impression. Once I ventured to say to him, "You are
too good-natured, Stephen." He gave me one of his quiet smiles
that seemed to hint so poignantly at the vanity of all things, and
after a period of silence remarked: "I am glad those Indians are
gone." He was surrounded by men who secretly envious, hostile to   15
the real quality of his genius (and a little afraid of it), were also in
antagonism with the essential fineness of his nature. But enough
of them. *Pulvis et umbra sunt.* I mean even those that may be alive
yet. They were ever hardly anything else; one would have forgotten
them if it were not for the legend (if one may dignify perfidious   20
and contemptible gossip by that name) they created in order to
satisfy that same obscure instinct of base humanity, which in the
past would often bring against any exceptional man the charge
of consorting with the devil. It was just as vague, just as senseless
and in its implications just as lying as the mediæval kind. I have   25
heard one of these "friends" hint before several other Philistines
that Crane could not write his tales without getting drunk!

Putting aside the gross palpable stupidity of such a statement –
which the creature gave out as an instance of the artistic temperament – I am in a position to disclose what may have been the   30
foundation of this piece of gossip. I have seen repeatedly Crane
at work. A small jug of still smaller ale would be brought into the
study at about ten o'clock; Crane would pour out some of it into a
glass and settle himself at the long table at which he used to write
in Brede Place. I would take a book and settle myself at the other   35
end of the same table, with my back to him; and for two hours or so
not a sound would be heard in that room. At the end of that time
Crane would say suddenly: "I won't do any more now, Joseph." He
would have covered three of his large sheets with his regular, legible, perfectly controlled, handwriting, with no more than half a   40

dozen erasures – mostly single words – in the whole lot. It seemed
to me always a perfect miracle in the way of mastery over material
and expression. Most of the ale would be still in the glass, and
how flat by that time I don't like to think! The most amusing part
5 was to see Crane, as if moved by some obscure sense of duty, drain
the last drop of that untempting remnant before we left the room
to stroll to and fro in front of the house while waiting for lunch.
Such is the origin of some of these gleeful whispers making up
the Crane legend of "unrestrained temperament". I have known
10 various sorts of temperaments – some perfidious and some lying –
but "unrestrained temperament" is mere parrot talk. It has no
meaning. But it was suggestive. It was founded on Crane's visits
to town during which I more than once met him there. We used
to spend afternoons and evenings together and I did not see any
15 of his supposed revels in progress; nor yet have I ever detected
any after effects of them on any occasion. Neither have I ever
seen anybody who would own to having been a partner in those
excesses – if only to the extent of standing by charitably – which
would have been a noble part to play. I daresay all those "excesses"
20 amounted to very little more than the one in which he asked me
to join him in the following letter. It is the only note I have kept
from the very few which we exchanged. The reader will see why it
is one of my most carefully preserved possessions.

Ravensbrook.

25   Oxted.

17 March (1899)

My dear Conrad: I am enclosing you a bit of MS under the suppo-
sition that you might like to keep it in remembrance of my warm
and endless friendship for you. I am still hoping that you will
30 consent to Stokes' invitation to come to the Savage on Saturday
night. Cannot you endure it? Give my affectionate remembrances
to Mrs. Conrad and my love to the boy.

Yours always,

Stephen Crane

35   P.S. You *must* accept says Cora – and I – our invitation to come
home with me on Sat. night.

I joined him. We had a very amusing time with the Savages.
Afterwards Crane refused to go home till the last train. Evidence

of what somebody has called his "unrestrained temperament," no doubt. So we went and sat at Gatti's, I believe; unless it was in a Bodega which existed then in that neighbourhood, and talked. I have a vivid memory of this awful debauch because it was on that evening that Crane told me of a subject for a story – a very 5 exceptional thing for him to do. He called it *The Predecessor*. I could not recall now by what capricious turns and odd associations of thought he reached the enthusiastic conclusion that it would make a good play, and that we must do it together. He wanted me to share in a certain success – "a dead sure thing," he said. His was an 10 unrestrainedly generous temperament. But let that pass. I must have been specially predisposed, because I caught the infection at once. There and then we began to build up the masterpiece, interrupting each other eagerly, for, I don't know how it was, the air around us had suddenly grown thick with felicitous suggestions. 15 We carried on this collaboration as far as the railway time-table would let us, and then made a break for the last train. Afterwards we did talk of our collaboration now and then, but no attempt at it was ever made. Crane had other stories to write; I was immersed deeply in *Lord Jim*, of which I had to keep up the instalments in 20 *Blackwood*; difficulties in presenting the subject on the stage rose one after another before our experience. The general subject consisted in a man personating his "predecessor" (who had died) in the hope of winning a girl's heart. The scenes were to include a ranch at the foot of the Rocky Mountains, I remember, and 25 the action I fear would have been frankly melodramatic. Crane insisted that one of the situations should present the man and the girl on a boundless plain standing by their dead ponies after a furious ride. (A truly Crane touch.) I made some objections. A boundless plain in the light of a sunset could be got into a back- 30 cloth, I admitted; but I doubted whether we could induce the management of any London theatre to deposit two stuffed horses on its stage.

Recalling now those earnestly fantastic discussions it occurs to me that Crane and I must have been unconsciously penetrated by 35 a prophetic sense of the technique and of the very spirit of film-plays of which even the name was unknown then to the world. But if gifted with prophetic sense we must have been strangely ignorant of ourselves, since it must be obvious to any one who has read a page of our writings that a collaboration between us 40

two could never come to anything in the end – could never even have been begun. The project was merely the expression of our affection for each other. We were fascinated for a moment by the will-of-the-wisp of close artistic communion. It would in no case
5 have led us into a bog. I flatter myself we both had too much regard for each other's gifts not to be clear-eyed about them. We would not have followed the lure very far. At the same time it can not be denied that there were profound, if not extensive, similitudes in our temperaments which could create for a moment
10 that fascinating illusion. It is not to be regretted, for it had, at any rate, given us some of the most light-hearted moments in the clear but sober atmosphere of our intimacy. From the force of circumstances there could not be much sunshine in it. "None of them saw the colour of the sky!"
15 And alas! it stood already written that it was the younger man who would fail to make a landing through the surf. So I am glad to have that episode to remember, a brotherly serio-comic interlude, played under the shadow of coming events. But I would not have alluded to it at all if it had not come out in the course of my
20 most interesting talk with the author of this biography, that Crane had thought it worth while to mention it in his correspondence, whether seriously or humorously, I know not. So here it is, without the charm which it had for me but which can not be reproduced in the mere relation of its outward characteristics: a clear gleam
25 on us two, succeeded by the Spanish-American war into which Crane disappeared like a wilful man walking away into the depths of an ominous twilight.

The cloudy afternoon when we two went rushing all over London together, was for him the beginning of the end. The
30 problem was to find £60 that day, before the sun set, before dinner, before the 6.40 train to Oxted, at once, that instant – lest peace should be declared and the opportunity of seeing a war be missed. I had not £60 to lend him. Sixty shillings was nearer my mark. We tried various offices but had no luck, or rather we
35 had the usual luck of money hunting enterprises. The man was either gone out to see about a dog, or would take no interest in the Spanish-American war. In one place the man wanted to know what was the hurry? He would have liked to have forty-eight hours to think the matter over. As we came downstairs Crane's white-
40 faced excitement frightened me. Finally it occurred to me to take

him to Messrs. William Blackwood & Sons' London office. There
he was received in a most friendly way. Presently I escorted him to
Charing Cross where he took the train for home with the assurance that he would have the means to start "for the war" next day.
That is the reason I can not to this day read his tale "The Price 5
of the Harness" without a pang. It has done nothing more deadly
than pay his debt to Messrs. Blackwood; yet now and then I feel
as though that afternoon I had led him by the hand to his doom.
But, indeed, I was only the blind agent of the fate that had him
in her grip! Nothing could have held him back. He was ready to 10
swim the ocean.

Thirteen years afterwards I made use, half consciously, of the
shadow of the primary idea of *The Predecessor* in one of my short
tales which was serialized in the *Metropolitan Magazine*. But in that
tale the dead man in the background is not a predecessor but 15
merely an assistant on a lonely plantation; and instead of the
ranch, the mountains and the plains, there is a cloud-capped
island, a bird-haunted reef and the sea. All this the mere distorted
shadow of what we two used to talk about in a fantastic mood; but
now and then, as I wrote, I had the feeling that he had the right to 20
come and look over my shoulder. But he never came. I received
no suggestions from him, subtly conveyed without words. There
will never be any collaboration for us now. But I wonder, were
he alive whether he would be pleased with the tale. I don't know.
Perhaps not. Or, perhaps, after picking up the volume with that 25
detached air I remember so well, and turning over page after page
in silence, he would suddenly read aloud a line or two and then
looking straight into my eyes as was his wont on such occasions,
say with all the intense earnestness of affection that was in him:
"I – like – that, Joseph." 30

HIS WAR-BOOK
INTRODUCTION TO STEPHEN
CRANE'S *THE RED BADGE*
OF COURAGE
1923

O N E   O F   T H E   M O S T enduring memories of my literary life
is the sensation produced by the appearance in 1895 of
Crane's *Red Badge of Courage* in a small volume belonging to Mr
Heinemann's Pioneer Series of Modern Fiction – very modern
fiction at that time, and upon the whole not devoid of merit. I
have an idea the series was meant to give us shocks and as far as
my recollection goes there were, to use a term made familiar to all
by another war, no "duds" in that small and lively bombardment.
But Crane's work detonated on the mild din of that attack on our
literary sensibilities with the impact and force of a twelve-inch shell
charged with a very high explosive. Unexpected it fell amongst
us – and its fall was followed by a great outcry.

Not of consternation however. The energy of that projectile hurt
nothing and no one (such was its good fortune) and delighted a
good many. It delighted soldiers, men of letters, men in the street;
it was welcomed by all lovers of personal expression as a genuine
revelation satisfying the curiosity of a world in which war and love
have been the subjects of song and story ever since the beginning
of articulate speech.

Here we had an artist, a man not of experience but a man
inspired, a seer with a gift for rendering the significant on the
surface of things and with an incomparable insight into primitive emotions, who, in order to give us the image of war, had
looked profoundly into his own breast. We welcomed him. As if
the whole vocabulary of praise had been blown up sky-high by
this missile from across the Atlantic, a rain of words descended on
our heads, words well or ill chosen, chunks of pedantic praise and
warm appreciation, clever words and words of real understanding, platitudes and felicities of criticism but all as sincere in their

response as the striking piece of work which set so many critical pens scurrying over the paper.

One of the most interesting if not the most valuable of printed criticisms was perhaps that of Mr George Wyndham – soldier, man of the world, and in a sense a man of letters. He went into the whole 5 question of war literature, at any rate during the nineteenth century, evoking comparisons with the *Mémoires* of General Marbot and the famous *Diary of a Cavalry Officer* as records of personal experience. He rendered justice to the interest of what soldiers themselves could tell us but confessed that to gratify the curiosity 10 of the potential combatant who lurks in most men as to the picturesque aspects and emotional reactions of a battle, we must go to the artist with his heaven given faculty of words at the service of his divination as to what the truth of things is and must be. He comes to the conclusion that, 15

"Mr Crane has contrived a masterpiece."

"Contrived," that word of disparaging sound, is the last word I would have used in connection with any piece of work by Stephen Crane who in his art (as indeed in his private life) was the least "contriving" of men. But as to "masterpiece" there is no doubt that 20 the *Red Badge of Courage* is that if only because of the marvellous accord of the vivid impressionistic description of action on that woodland battlefield and the imaged style of the analysis of the emotions in the inward moral struggle going on in the breast of one individual – the Young Soldier of the book, the protagonist 25 of the monodrama presented to us in an effortless succession of graphic and coloured phrases.

Stephen Crane places his Young Soldier in an untried regiment. And this is well contrived – if any contrivance there be in a spontaneous piece of work which seems to spurt and flow like a tapped 30 stream from the depths of the writer's being. In order that the revelation should be complete the Young Soldier has to be deprived of the moral support which he would have found in a tried body of men matured in achievement to the consciousness of its worth. His regiment had been tried by nothing but days of waiting for 35 the order to move; so many days that it, and the Youth within it, have come to think of themselves as merely a part of a "vast blue demonstration". The army had been lying camped near a river idle and fretting till the moment when Stephen Crane lays hold of it at dawn with masterly simplicity: "The cold passed reluctantly 40 from the earth..." These are the first words of the war-book, which was to give him his crumb of fame.

The whole of that opening paragraph is wonderful in the homely dignity of the indicated lines of the landscape, and the
5 shivering awakening of the army at the break of the day before the battle. In the next with a most effective change to racy colloquialism of narrative the action which motivates, sustains and feeds the inner drama forming the subject of the book, begins with the Tall Soldier going down to the river to wash his shirt. He
10 returns waving his garment above his head. He had heard at fifth hand from somebody that the army is going to move to-morrow.

The only immediate effect of this piece of news is that a negro teamster who had been dancing a jig on a wooden box in a ring of laughing soldiers finds himself suddenly deserted. He sits down
15 mournfully. For the rest the Tall Soldier's excitement is met by blank unbelief, profane grumbling, an invincible incredulity. But the regiment is somehow sobered. One feels it though no symptoms can be noticed. It does not know what a battle is. Neither does the Young Soldier. He retires from the babbling throng into
20 what seems a rather comfortable dugout and lies down to think. Thus the drama begins.

He perceives suddenly that he had looked on wars as historical phenomenons of the past. He had never believed in war in his own country. It had been a play affair. He had been drilled, inspected,
25 marched for months till he has despaired of ever seeing "a Greek-like struggle. Such were no more. Men were better or more timid. Secular and religious education had effaced the throat-grappling instinct, or else firm finance held in check the passions."

Very modern this touch. We can remember thoughts like these
30 round about the year 1914. That young soldier is representative of mankind in more ways than one, and first of all in his ignorance. His regiment had listened to the tales of veterans, "tales of grey bewhiskered hordes chewing tobacco with unspeakable valour and sweeping along like the Huns". Still he can not put his faith
35 in veterans' tales. Recruits were their prey. They talked of blood, fire and sudden death but much of it might have been lies. They were in no wise to be trusted. And the question arises before him whether he will or will not run from a battle. And he does not know. He can not know: "A little panic-fear enters his mind." He

jumps up and asks himself aloud "Good Lord! What's the matter with me?"

This is the first time his very words are quoted, on this day before the battle. He dreads not danger but fear itself. He stands before the unknown. He would like to prove to himself by some reasoning process that he will not run from the battle, and in his unblooded regiment he can find no help. He is alone with the problem of courage. In this he stands for the symbol of all untried men.

Some critics have estimated him a morbid case. I can not agree to that. The abnormal cases are at the two extremes: of those who crumple up at the first sight of danger and of those of whom their fellows say "He doesn't know what fear is." Neither will I forget the rare favourites of the gods whose fiery spirit is only soothed by the fury and clamour of a battle. Of such was General Picton of Peninsular fame. But the lot of the mass of mankind is to know fear, the decent fear of disgrace. Of such is the young soldier of the *Red Badge of Courage*. He only seems exceptional because he has got inside of him Stephen Crane's imagination and is presented to us with the insight and the power of expression of an artist, whom a just and severe critic on a review of all his work has called the chief impressionist of his time as Sterne was the greatest impressionist but in a different way of his age.

This is a fundamental judgment. More superficially both Zola's *La Débâcle* and Tolstoy's *War and Peace* were mentioned by critics in connection with Crane's war-book. But Zola's main concern was with the downfall of the Imperial regime he fancied he was portraying; and in Tolstoy's book the subtle presentation of Rostov's squadron under fire for the first time is a mere episode – lost in a mass of other matter – like a handful of pebbles in a heap of sand. I could not see the relevancy. Crane was concerned with elemental truth only; and in any case I think that as an artist he is non-comparable. He dealt with what is enduring and was the most detached of men.

That is why his book is short. Not quite two hundred pages. Gems are small. This monodrama which a happy inspiration or unerring instinct had led him to put before us in narrative form is contained between the opening words I have already quoted and a phrase on p. 194 of the English edition which runs: "He had been to touch the great death, and found that, after all, it was but the great death. He was a man."

On these words the action ends. We are only given one glimpse of the victorious army at dusk, under the falling rain, a "procession of weary soldiers became a bedraggled train, despondent and muttering, marching with churning effort in a trough of liquid brown mud under a low wretched sky . . . " while the last ray of the sun falls upon the river through a break in the leaden clouds.

This war-book so virile and so full of gentle sympathy in which not a single declamatory sentiment defaces the genuine verbal felicity welding analysis and description in a continuous fascination of individual style had been hailed by the critics as the herald of a brilliant career. Crane himself very seldom alluded to it, and always with a wistful smile. Perhaps he was conscious that like the mortally wounded Tall Soldier of his book – who snatching at the air staggers out into a field to meet his appointed death on the first day of battle while the terrified Youth and the kind Tattered Soldier stand by, silent, watching with awe "those ceremonies at the place of meeting" – it was his fate, too, to fall early in the fray.

JOHN GALSWORTHY
AN APPRECIATION
1906

WHEN IN THE FAMILY'S assembly at Timothy Forsyte's house there arose a discussion of Francie Forsyte's verses, Aunt Hester expressed her preference for the poetry of Shelley, Byron and Wordsworth, on the ground that, after reading the works of these poets, "one felt that one had read a book." And the reader of Mr Galsworthy's latest volume of fiction, whether in accord or in difference with the author's view of his subject, would feel that he had read a book.

Beyond that impression one perceives how difficult it is to get critical hold of Mr Galsworthy's work. He gives you no opening. Defending no obvious thesis, setting up no theory, offering no cheap panacea, appealing to no naked sentiment, the author of *The Man of Property* disdains also the effective device of attacking insidiously the actors of his own drama, or rather of his dramatic comedy. This is because he does not write for effect, though his writing will be found effective enough for all that. This book is of a disconcerting honesty, backed by a discouraging skill. There is not a single phrase in it written for the sake of its cleverness. Not one. Light of touch, though weighty in feeling, it gives the impression of verbal austerity, of a *willed* moderation of thought. The passages of high literary merit, so uniformly sustained as to escape the notice of the reader, expose the natural and logical development of the story with a purposeful progression which is primarily satisfying to the intelligence, and ends by stirring the emotions. In the essentials of matter and treatment it is a book of to-day. Its critical spirit and its impartial method are meant for a humanity which has outgrown the stage of fairy tales, realistic, romantic or even epic.

For the fairy tale, be it not ungratefully said, has walked the earth in many unchallenged disguises, and lingers amongst us to this day wearing, sometimes, amazingly heavy clothes. It lingers; and even it lingers with some assurance. Mankind has come of

95

age, but the successive generations still demand artlessly to be
amazed, moved and amused. Certain forms of innocent fun will
never grow old, I suppose. But the secret of the long life of the
fairy tale consists mainly in this, I suspect: that it is amusing to the
5 writer thereof. Whatever public want it supplies, it ministers first
of all to his vanity in an intimate and delightful way. The pride
of fanciful invention; the pride of that invention which soars (on
goose's wings) into the empty blue is like the intoxication of an
elixir sent by the gods above. And whether it is that the gods
10 are unduly generous, or simply because the sight of human folly
amuses their idle malice, that sort of felicity is easier attained pen
in hand than the sober pride, always mingled with misgivings, of
a single-minded observer and conscientious interpreter of reality.
This is why the fairy tale, in its various disguises of optimism,
15 pessimism, romanticism, naturalism and what not, shall always be
with us. And, indeed, that is very comprehensible; the seduction
of irresponsible freedom is very great; and to be tied to the earth
(even as the hewers of wood and drawers of water are tied to the
earth) in the exercise of one's imagination, by every scruple of
20 conscience and honour, may be considered a lot hard enough
not to be lightly embraced. This is why novelists are comparatively
rare. But we must not exaggerate. This world, even if one is tied
fast to its earthly foundation by the subtle and tyrannical bonds
of artistic conviction, is not such a bad place to write fiction in. At
25 any rate, we can know of no other: an excellent reason for us to
try to think as well as possible of the world we do know.
    In this world, whose realities are discovered, interpreted, com-
mented on, criticised and exposed in works of fiction, Mr Galsworthy selects for the subject-matter of his book the Family, an insti-
30 tution which has been with us as long I should think as the oldest
and the least venerable pattern of fairy tale. As Mr Galsworthy,
however, is no theorist but an observer, it is a definite kind of family that falls under his observation. It is the middle-class family;
and even, with more precision, as we are warned in the sub-title,
35 an upper middle-class family; and not an upper middle-class family anywhere at large in space and time, but a family, if not exactly
of to-day, then of only last evening, so to say. Thus at the outset
we are far removed from the vagueness of the traditional "once
upon a time in a far country there was a king," which somehow
40 always manages to peep through the solemn disguises of fairy tales

masquerading as novels with and without purpose. The Forsytes
walk the pavement of London and own some of London's houses.
They wish to own more; they wish to own them all. And maybe
they shall. Time is on their side. The Forsytes never die – so Mr
Galsworthy tells us, while we watch them assembling in old Jolyon   5
Forsyte's drawing-room on the occasion of June Forsyte's engagement to Mr Bosinney, incidentally an architect and an artist, but,
by the only definition that matters, a man of no property whatever.

Irene, the wife of Soames Forsyte, is there also; an exquisite creation of Mr Galsworthy's art, delicate in her charm, fascinatingly   10
passive and a little mysterious in her weakness of a woman formed
for love alone; but still clearly unfortunate in this that she, too,
has no property whatever.

A family is not at first sight an alarming phenomenon. But Mr
Galsworthy looks at the Forsytes with the individual vision of a   15
novelist seeking his inspiration amongst the realities of this earth.
He points out to us this family's formidable character as a unit of
society, as a reproduction in miniature of society itself. It is made
formidable, he says, by the cohesion of its members (between
whom there need not exist either affection or even sympathy)   20
upon a concrete point, the possession of property.

The solidity of the foundation laid by Mr Galsworthy for his
fine piece of imaginative work becomes at once apparent. For
whichever came first, family or property, in the beginnings of
social organisation, or whether they came together and were   25
indeed at first scarcely distinguishable from each other, it is clear
that in the close alliance of these two institutions society has found
the way of its development and nurses the hope of its security.
In their sense of property the Forsytes establish the consciousness
of their right and the promise of their duration. It is an instinct, a   30
primitive instinct. The practical faculty of the Forsytes has erected
it into a principle; their idealism has expanded it into a sort of
religion which has shaped their notions of happiness and decency,
their prejudices, their piety, such thoughts as they happen to have
and the very course of their passions. Life as a whole has come   35
to be perceptible to them exclusively in terms of property. Preservation, acquisition – acquisition, preservation. Their laws, their
morality, their art and their science appear to them, justifiably
enough, consecrated to that double and unique end. It is the
formula of their virtue.   40

In this world of Forsytes (who never die) organised in view
of acquiring and preserving property, Mr Galsworthy (who is no
inventor of didactic fairy tales) places with the sure instinct of a
novelist a man and a woman who are no Forsytes, it is true, but
5   whom he presents as in no sense the declared adversaries of the
great principle of property. They only happen to disregard it. And
this is a crime. They are simply two people to whom life speaks
imperatively in terms of love. And this is enough to establish their
irreconcilable antagonism and to precipitate their unavoidable
10 fate. Deprived naturally and suddenly of the support of laws and
morality, of all human countenance, and even, in a manner of
speaking, of the consolations of religion, they find themselves
miserably crushed, both the woman and the man. And the principle of property is vindicated. The woman being the weaker, it
15 is in her case vindicated with consummate cruelty. For a peculiar cowardice is one of the characteristics of this great and living
principle. Strong in the worship of so many thousands and in the
possession of so many millions, it starts with affright at the slightest challenge, it trembles before mere indifference, it directs its
20 heaviest blows at the disinherited who should appear weakest in
its sight. Irene's fate is made unspeakably atrocious, no less –
but nothing more. Mr Galsworthy's instinct and observation serve
him well here. In Soames Forsyte's town house, whose front door
stands wide open for half an hour or so on a certain foggy night,
25 there is no room for tragedy. It is one of the temples of property,
of a sort of unholy religion whose fundamental dogma, public
ceremonies and awful secret rites, forming the subject-matter of
this remarkable novel, take no account of human dignity. Irene,
as last seen crushed and alive within the hopeless portals, remains
30 for us a poignantly pitiful figure, and nothing more.
    This then, roughly and summarily, is the book in its general
suggestion. Going on to particulars which make up the intrinsic
value of a work of art, it rests upon the subtle and interdependent
relation of Mr Galsworthy's intellect and feelings which forms his
35 temperament, and reveals Mr Galsworthy's very considerable talent as a writer – a talent so considerable that it commands at once
our respectful attention. The foundation of this talent, it seems
to me, lies in a remarkable power of ironic insight combined with
an extremely keen and faithful eye for all the phenomena on the
40 surface of the life he observes. These are the purveyors of his

imagination, whose servant is a style clear, direct, sane, illumined
by a perfectly unaffected sincerity. It is the style of a man whose
sympathy with mankind is too genuine to allow him the smallest
gratification of his vanity at the cost of his fellow creatures. In
its moderation it is a style sufficiently pointed to carry deep his   5
remorseless irony and grave enough to be the dignified vehicle
of his profound compassion. Its sustained harmony is never interrupted by those bursts of cymbals and fifes which some deaf people
acclaim for brilliance. Before all, it is a style well under control,
and therefore it never betrays this tender and ironic writer into   10
an odious cynicism of laughter or tears. For there are two kinds
of cynicism, the cynicism of the hyena and the cynicism of the
crocodile, which last, by the way, commands all sorts of respects
from the inhabitants of these Isles. Mr Galsworthy remains always
a man, whether he is amused or moved.   15

I am afraid that my unavowed intention in writing about this
book (of which I have talked so much and said so little) has been
discovered by now. Therefore I confess. Confession – public, I
mean – is good for one's conscience. Such *is* my intention. And it
would be easier to carry out if I only knew exactly the motives which   20
prompt people to read novels. But I do not know them all. Some of
us, I understand, take up a novel to gratify a natural malevolence,
the author being supposed to hold the mirror up to the odiously
ridiculous nature of our next-door neighbour. From laboriously
collected information I am, however, led to believe that most   25
people read novels for amusement. This is as it should be. But,
whatever be their motives, I entertain towards all novel-readers
(for reasons which must remain concealed from the readers of
this paper) the feelings of warm and respectful affection. I would
not try to deceive them for worlds. Never! This being understood,   30
I go on to declare, in the peace of my heart and the serenity
of my conscience, that if they want amusement they shall find it
between the covers of this book. They shall find plenty of it in this
episode in the history of the Forsytes, where the reconciliation of
a father and son, the dramatic and poignant comedy of Soames   35
Forsyte's marital relations, and the tragedy of Bosinney's failure
are exposed to our gaze with the remorseless yet sympathetic
irony of Mr Galsworthy's art, in the light of the unquenchable fire
burning on the altar of property. They shall find amusement, and
perhaps also something more lasting – if they care for it. I say this   40

with all the reserves and qualifications which strict truth requires around every statement of opinion. Mr Galsworthy may possibly be found disappointing by some, but he will never be found futile by anyone, and never uninteresting by the most exacting. I myself, for
5 instance, am not so sure of Bosinney's tragedy. But this hesitation of my mind, for which the author may not be wholly responsible after all, need only be mentioned, and no more, in the face of his considerable achievement.

A GLANCE AT TWO BOOKS
1904

I

THE NATIONAL ENGLISH NOVELIST seldom regards his
work – the exercise of his Art – as an achievement of active life 5
by which he will produce certain definite effects upon the emotions of his readers but simply as an instinctive, often unreasoned,
outpouring of his own emotions. He does not go about building
up his book with a precise intention and a steady mind. It never
occurs to him that a book is a deed, that the writing of it is an 10
enterprise as much as the conquest of a colony. He has no such
clear conception of his craft. Writing from a full heart, he liber-
ates his soul for the satisfaction of his own sentiment; and when
he has finished the scene he is at liberty to strike his forehead and
exclaim: "This is genius!" 15

Thackeray is reported to have done this, and there is no reason
why any novelist of his type should not. He is, as a matter of
fact, writing lyrically (a lyric is the expression of a mood); he is
expressing his own moods: I take what the Gods give me – he
says in all humility, and when the godhead inspires him with what 20
seems good to his heart, to his imagination, to his tenderness or
to his indignation, he may say, and use the words literally, "This is
genius!"

It is. And it is probably the reason why the distinctively English
novelist is always at his best in denunciations of institutions, of 25
types or of conventionalised society.

It is comparatively easy for us when we are really moved by the
clearness of our own vision to convince an audience that Messrs
A. B. & C. are callous, ferocious or cowardly. We should have to
use much more conscious art to give a permanent impression of 30
those gentlemen as purely altruistic.

Thus Mr Osborne the hard merchant, father of Captain
Osborne, is more definite and flawless, than many of Thackeray's
so-called good characters; and thus Mr Pecksniff is, through scorn

and dislike, rendered more memorable than the brothers Cheeryble. It is not, perhaps, so much that these distinguished writers
were completely incapable of loving their fellow men simply as
men, exposed to suffering, temptation, and affliction, as that,
5 neglecting the one indispensable thing, neglecting to use their
powers of selection and observation, they emotionally excelled in
rendering the disagreeable. And that is easy. To find beauty, grace,
charm, in the bitterness of truth is a graver task.

Thackeray, we imagine, did not love his gentle heroines. He
10 did not love them. He was in love with the sentiments they represented. He was, in fact, in love with what does not exist – and that
is why Amelia Osborne does not exist, either in colour, in shape,
in grace, in goodness. Turgenieff probably did not love his Lisa, a
most pathetic, pure, charming, and profound creation, for what
15 she was, in her creator's mind. He loved her disinterestedly, as it
were, out of pure warmth of heart, as a human being in the tumult
and hazard of life. And that is why we must feel, suffer, and live
with that wonderful creation. That is why she is as real to us as her
stupid mother, as the men of the story, as the sombre Varvara, and
20 all the others that may be called the unpleasant characters in the
House of Gentlefolk.

II

I HAVE BEEN READING two books in English, which have
attracted a good deal of intelligent attention, but neither seems
25 to have been considered as attentively as they might have been
from this point of view. The one, *The Island Pharisees,* by Mr John
Galsworthy is a very good example of the national novel; the other,
Green Mansions, by Mr W. H. Hudson is a proof that love, the pure
love of rendering the external aspects of things, can exist side by
30 side with the national novel in English letters.

Mr Galsworthy's hero in *The Island Pharisees,* during his pilgrimage right across the English social system, asks himself: "Why? Why
is not the world better? Why are we all humbugs? Why is the social
system so out of order?" And he gets no answer to his questions,
35 for indeed in his mood no answer is possible, neither is an answer
needed for the absolute value of the book. Shelton is dissatisfied
with his own people, who are good people, with artists, whose
"at-homes" he drops into, with marriage settlements and wedding

services, with cosmopolitan vagabonds, with Oxford dons, with
policemen – with himself, and his love.

The exposition of all the characters in the book is done with
an almost unerring touch, with a touch indeed that recalls the
sureness and delicacy of Turgeniev's handling. They all live – and   5
Mr Galsworthy – or rather his hero, John Shelton – finds them
all Pharisaic. It is as if he were championing against all these
"good" people, some intangible lost cause, some altruism, some
higher truth that for ever seems to soar out of his grasp. It is not
exactly that Shelton is made to uphold the bitter morality of the   10
cosmopolitan vagabond; for Mr Galsworthy is too good an artist
and too good a philosopher to make his Louis Ferrand impossibly
attractive or even possibly cynical. Shelton does uphold, not so
much the fact, as the ideal of honest revolt; he is the knight
errant of a general idea. Therein he ceases to resemble the other   15
heroes of English fiction, who are the champions of particular
ideas, tilting sometimes at windmills (for the human power of self-
deception is great) but with a particular foe always in their eye.
Shelton, distinctly, does not couch his lance against a windmill.
He is a knight errant, disarmed and faithful, riding forlorn to an   20
inevitable defeat; his adversary is a giant of a thousand heads and a
thousand arms, a monster at once perfectly human and altogether
soulless. Though nobody dies in the book, it is really the record of
a long and tragic adventure whose tragedy is not so much in the
event as in the very atmosphere, in the cold moral dusk in which   25
the hero moves as if impelled by some fatal whisper, without a
sword, corselet or helmet.

Amadis de Gaul would have struck a head off and counted it a
doughty deed; Dickens would have flung himself upon pen and
paper and made a caricature of the monster; would have flung at   30
him an enormous joke vibrating with the stress of cheap emotions;
Shelton no legendary knight and being no humorist (but like
many simpler men, impelled by the destiny he carries within his
breast) goes forth to be delivered, bound hand and foot, to the
monster by his charming and limited Antonia. He is classed as an   35
outsider by the men in the best clubs, and his prospective mother-
in-law tells him not to talk about things. He comes to grief socially
because in a world, which everyone is interested to go on calling
the best of all possible worlds, he has insisted upon touching in
challenge all the shields hung before all the comfortable tents: 40

the immaculate shield of his fiancée, of his mother-in-law, of the
best men in the best clubs. He gets himself called and thought of
as Unsound; and there in his social world the monster has made
an end of him.

5   This is the end of the book; and with it there comes into the
world of letters the beginning of Mr Galsworthy as a novelist. For,
paradoxically, a society that could not stand a Hamlet in the flesh
at any price will read about him and welcome him on the stage to
the end of its own incorrigible existence. This book where each
10   page lives with an interest of its own has for its only serious artistic
defect that of not being long enough, and for its greatest quality
that of a sincere feeling of compassionate regard for mankind
expressed nationally through a fine indignation. Of the promise
of its method, of the accomplished felicity of its phrasing, I have
15   left myself no room to speak.

      The innermost heart of *Green Mansions*, which are the forests of
Mr Hudson's book, is tender, is tranquil, is steeped in that pure
love of the external beauty of things that seems to breathe upon
us from the pages of Turgeniev's work. The charming quietness
20   of the style soothes the hard irritation of our daily life in the
presence of a fine and sincere, of a deep and pellucid personality.
If the other book's gift is lyric, *Green Mansions* come to us with the
tone of the elegy. There are the voices of the birds, the shadows
of the forest leaves, the Indians gliding through them armed with
25   their blow-pipes, the monkeys peering sadly from above, the very
spiders! The birds search for insects; spiders hunt their prey.

"Now, as I sat looking down on the leaves and the small dancing shadow,
scarcely thinking of what I was looking at, I noticed a small spider, with a flat
body and short legs, creep cautiously out on to the upper surface of a leaf.
30   Its pale red colour barred with velvet black first drew my attention to it, for it
was beautiful to the eye."

      "It was beautiful to the eye," so it drew the attention of Mr
Hudson's hero. In that phrase dwells the very soul of the book
whose voice is soothing like a soft voice speaking steadily amongst
35   the vivid changes of a dream. Only you must note that the spider
had come to hunt its prey having mistaken the small dancing
shadow for a fly, because it is there in the fundamental difference
of vision lies the difference between book and book. The other
type of novelist might say: "It attracted my attention because it was

savage and cruel and beautiful only to the eye. And I have written of it here so that it may be hated and laughed at for ever. For of course being greedy and rapacious it was stupid also, mistaking a shadow for substance, like certain evil men we have heard of, that go about crying up the excellence of the world."

5

PREFACE TO
THE SHORTER TALES OF JOSEPH CONRAD
1924

5   THE IDEA OF PUBLISHING a volume of selected stories has
not been received without a good deal of hesitation on my
part. So much in fact as to drive me into the dangerous attempt
to disclose the state of the feelings with which I approach this
explanatory Preface. My hesitation was, I may say, of a private
10 character; private in the sense of being rooted deep in my personality, and not easily explainable even to such good friends as
it has been my fortune to find in the American public. The deep,
complex (and at times even contradictory) feelings which make
up the very essence of an author's attitude to his own creation are
15 real enough, yet they may be, often are, but shapes of cherished
illusions. Frail plants you will admit and fit only for the shade of
solitary thought. Precious – perhaps? Yes. But by their very nature
precious to only one man, to him in whose mind – or is it the
heart? – they are rooted.
20   That consideration would seem to me conclusive against anyone
writing any preface whatever, if it were not for my ineradicable suspicion that in this world, which some philosophers have defined
merely as a series of "vain appearances," our very illusions must
have a practical meaning. Are they not as characteristic of an indi-
25 vidual as his opinions, for instance, or the features of his face? In
fact, being less controllable they must be even more dangerously
revelatory. This is an alarming consideration. But whether because
of a strain of native impudence, acquired callousness, or inborn
trust in the goodness of human nature, it has not prevented me
30 during the last few years from writing a good many revelatory prefaces, for which I have not been, so far, called to account. At any
rate no incensed man with a shot-gun has yet called here to invite
me to desist. Thus encouraged, here I am again volunteering yet
one more of these sincere confessions.

To begin with I may venture to affirm that, however spontaneous the initial impulse, not one of the stories from which those
included in this volume have been selected was achieved without
much conscious thought bearing not only on the problems of
their style but upon their relation to life as I have known it, and   5
on the nature of my reactions to the particular instances as well as
to the general tenor of my personal experience. This gave to each
of the successive sets of tales composed at various times and in
varied mental conditions, a characteristic tone of its own. At least
I thought so. Later, when I had to consider my past work in detail,   10
in order to write the Author's Notes for my first collected edition, I was confirmed in my impression that each of my short-story
volumes had a consistent unity of outlook covering the mingled
subjects of civilisation and wilderness, of land life and life on the
sea.   15

It would not be too much to say that this trait would be apparent
to the least critical of readers, in, for instance, the *Tales of Unrest*.
No story from that volume is included in this collection for a
reason which will become apparent later to the patient reader
of this preface. It is the very first collection of short stories I ever   20
published, with a range of scene including the Malay Archipelago,
rustic Brittany, Central Africa, and the interior of an upper middle-
class house in a residential street of London. It also seems to me
perfectly clear, on the face of it, that the volume called *A Set
of Six* – from which one story has been selected for this book –   25
is very different in its consistent mood of clear and detached
presentation from any other volume of short stories which I have
published before or after. Yet, in Time, it covers almost the whole
of the nineteenth century; and in Space it moves from South
America through England and Russia to end in the South of Italy.   30
A benevolent critic has remarked to me privately that it was the
least atmospheric of all my works, and from my point of view I
accepted this as a tribute to that inner consistency which I would
claim for every set of my shorter tales. In the same way in the case
of the volume *Within the Tides* I take the opinion expressed by one   35
of the reviewers: "that the whole of the book seemed to produce
the impression of being greater than its component parts" as a
confirmation of my sentiment of having welded the diversities
of subject and treatment into a consistency characteristic, in its
nature, of a certain period of my literary production.   40

The friendly reader will understand how, holding that belief
on the subject of my shorter productions, I would recoil at first
from taking any of my stories out of their appointed places in
the group to which they originally belonged. And this the more
5   because their grouping was never the result of a preconceived
plan. It "just happened". And things that "just happen" in one's
work seem impressive and valuable because they spring from
sources profounder than the logic of a deliberate theory suggested by acquired learning, let us say, or by lessons drawn from
10 analysed practice. And no one need quarrel for such a view with
an artist for whom self-expression must, by definition, be the principal object, if not the only *raison d'être*, of his existence. He will
naturally take for his own, for better or worse, all the characteristics of his work; since all of them, intended or not intended, make
15 up the individuality of his self-expression.

I suspect there are moments when what a man most values
in his work – I mean even a man of action – is precisely the
part the general mystery of things plays in its shaping: the discovery of those qualities that have "just happened" in that obscure
20 region where honest success or honourable failure are unconsciously elaborated. But there are moments too when one's idealism (for idealism is practical and sane and the enemy of things
that "just happen" and suchlike mysteries) prompts one to take
up a different, more precise view of one's achievement – whatever
25 it may be.

It must have been in one of those moments that the suggestion
of a selected volume of my shorter stories came before me from
my old friend and publisher, Mr F. N. Doubleday, who is an idealist
and who would simply hate to let anything "just happen" in his
30 business. His business, to my mind, consists, mainly, in being the
intermediary between certain men's reveries and the wide-awake
brain of the rest of the world. Stated like this it seems a strangely
fantastic occupation; yet his ways of carrying it on are always of a
practical sort. I have learned to trust his conclusions implicitly on
35 that ground. Also, for reasons of a deeper, personal kind, having
nothing to do with business, his words have great weight with
me. But in order to reconcile my own idealism to the notion of
taking the stories out of their natural surroundings, out of their
native atmosphere as it were, some principle of selection had to be
40 found. The only one that offered itself with any chance of being

acceptable was the principle of classification by subject; one that, whatever its disadvantages, has at least the advantage of being immune from the infection of illusions.

But I soon found that for a writer whose simple purpose has ever been the sincere rendering of his own deeper and more 5 sympathetic emotions in the face of his belief in men and things – the philosopher's "Vain Appearances" which yet have endured, poignant or amusing, for so many ages, moving processionally towards the End of the World, which when it comes will be the vainest thing of all – the principle was not so easy in its application 10 as it seemed to be at first sight. Though I have been often classed as a writer of the sea I have always felt that I had no speciality in that or any other specific subject. It is true that I have found a full text of life on the sea, long before I thought of writing a line or even felt the faintest stirring towards self-expression by means of 15 the printed word. Sea life had been my life. It had been my own self-sufficient, self-satisfying possession. When the change came over the spirit of my dream (Calderón said that "Life is a Dream") my past had, by the very force of things, to enter for a considerable part into the body of my work, become one of the sources of what 20 I may call, for want of a better word, my inspiration – of the inner force which set the pen in motion. I would add here "for better or worse," if those words did not sound horribly ungrateful after so many proofs of sympathy from the public for which this particular Preface is destined. 25

As a matter of fact I have written of the sea very little if the pages were counted. It has been the scene but very seldom the aim of my endeavour. It is too late after all those years to try to keep back the truth, so I will confess here that when I launched my first paper-boats in the days of my literary childhood I aimed 30 at an element as restless, as dangerous, as changeable as the sea, and even more vast:– the unappeasable ocean of human life. I trust this grandiloquent image will be accepted with an indulgent smile of the kind that is accorded to the lofty ambitions of well-meaning beginners. Much time has passed since, and I can assure 35 my readers that I have never felt more humble than I do to-day while I sit tracing these words, and that I see now more clearly than ever before, that indeed those were but paper-boats, freighted with a grown-up child's dreams and launched innocently upon that terrible sea that, unlike the honest salt water of my early life, 40

knows no hope of changing horizons but lies within the circle of
an Eternal Shadow.

Approaching the problem of selection for this book in the full
consciousness of my feelings, my concern was to give it some sort of
5 unity, or in other words, its own character. Character is not a thing
of shreds and patches. Looking over the directive impulses of my
writing life I discovered my guide in the one that had prompted
me so often to deal with men whose existence was, so to speak, cast
early upon the waters. Thus the characteristic trait of the stories
10 included in this volume consists in the central figure of each being
a seaman presented either in the relations of his professional life
with his own kind, or in contact with lands men and women, and
embroiled in the affairs of that larger part of mankind which
dwells on solid earth.

15   It would have been misleading to label those productions as sea
tales. They deal with feelings of universal import, such for instance
as the sustaining and inspiring sense of youth, or the support given
by a stolid courage which confronts the unmeasurable force of an
elemental fury simply as a thing that has got to be met and lived
20 through with professional constancy. Of course there is something
more than mere ideas in those stories. I modestly hope that there
are human beings in them, and also the articulate appeal of their
humanity so strangely constructed from inertia and restlessness,
from weakness and from strength and many other interesting
25 contradictions which affect their conduct, and in a certain sense
are meant to give a colouring to the actual events of the tale, and
even to the response which is expected from the reader. To call
them "studies of seamen" would have been pretentious and even
misleading, in view of the obscurity of the individuals and the
30 private character of the incidents. *Shorter Tales* is yet the best title
I can think of for this collection. It commends itself to me by its
non-committal character which will neither raise false hopes nor
awaken blind antagonisms.

Why a volume aiming at unity should be wilfully divided into
35 two parts is explained by my desire to give prominence to the
stories which begin them: "Youth," which is certainly a piece
of autobiography ("emotions remembered in tranquillity"), and
Typhoon, which defined from a purely descriptive point of view is
the shorter of the two storm-pieces which I have written at differ-
40 ent times.

From another point of view, the "guiding" point of view (that is of each story being concerned with a man who is also a seaman), the first part deals with younger and the second with older men. I hardly need say that in the arrangement of those two parts there has been no attempt at chronological order.

Therefore let neither friend nor enemy look for the development of the writer's literary faculty in this collection. As far as that is concerned the book is a jumble. The unity of purpose lies elsewhere. In Part First, "Youth" speaks for itself, both in its triumphant feeling and in its wistful regrets. The second story deals with what may be called the "*esprit de corps*," the deep fellowship of two young seamen meeting for the first time. Those two tales may be regarded as purely professional. Of the other two in Part First, one, it must be confessed, is written round a ship rather than round a seaman. The last, trying to render the effect of the fascination of a roving life, has the hard lot of a woman for its principal interest.

Part Two deals with men of a more mature age. There is no denying that in the typhoon which is being wrestled with by Captain MacWhirr, it is the typhoon that takes on almost a symbolic figure. The next story is the story of a married seaman, badly married I admit, whose humanity to a pathetic waif spoils his life for him. The third is the story of a swindle, to be frank, planned on shore, but the sympathetic person is a seaman all right. The last may be looked upon as a story of a seaman's love for a very silent girl, but what I tried partly to suggest there was the existence of certain straightforward characters combining a natural ruthlessness with an unexpected depth of moral delicacy. Falk obeys the law of self-preservation pitilessly; but at the crucial moment of his bizarre love-story he will not condescend to dodge the truth – the horrid truth! Finally let me say that with the exception of "Youth" none of these stories are records of experience in the absolute sense of the word. As I have said before in another preface they are all authentic because they are the product of twenty years of life – my own life. Deliberate invention had little to do with their existence – if they do exist. In each there lurks more than one intention. The facts gleaned from hearsay or experience in various parts of the globe were but opportunities offered to the writer. What he has done with them is matter for a verdict which must be left to the individual consciences of the readers.

COOKERY
PREFACE TO JESSIE CONRAD'S
A HANDBOOK OF COOKERY FOR
A SMALL HOUSE
5   1907

O F ALL the books produced since the most remote ages by
human talents and industry those only that treat of cooking
are, from a moral point of view, above suspicion. The intention of
every other piece of prose may be discussed and even mistrusted;
10 but the purpose of a cookery book is one and unmistakable. Its
object can conceivably be no other than to increase the happiness
of mankind.

This general consideration, and also a feeling of affectionate
interest with which I am accustomed to view all the actions of the
15 writer, prompt me to set down these few words of introduction
for her book. Without making myself responsible for her teaching
(I own that I find it impossible to read through a cookery book)
I come forward modestly but gratefully as a Living Example of
her practice. That practice I dare pronounce most successful. It
20 has been for many priceless years adding to the sum of my daily
happiness.

Good cooking is a moral agent. By good cooking I mean the
conscientious preparation of the simple food of every-day life, not
the more or less skilful concoction of idle feasts and rare dishes.
25 Conscientious cooking is an enemy to gluttony. The trained delicacy of the palate like a cultivated delicacy of sentiment stands
in the way of unseemly excesses. The decency of our life is for a
great part a matter of good taste, of the correct appreciation of
what is fine in simplicity. The intimate influence of conscientious
30 cooking by rendering easy the processes of digestion promotes the
serenity of mind, the graciousness of thought, and that indulgent
view of our neighbours' failings which is the only genuine form of
optimism. Those are its titles to our reverence.

A great authority upon North American Indians accounted for the sombre and excessive ferocity characteristic of these savages by the theory that as a race they suffered from perpetual indigestion. The Noble Red Man was a mighty hunter but his wives had not mastered the art of conscientious cookery. And the consequences were deplorable. The Seven Nations around the Great Lakes and the Horse-tribes of the Plains were but one vast prey to raging dyspepsia. The Noble Red Men were great warriors, great orators, great masters of outdoor pursuits; but the domestic life of their wigwams was clouded by the morose irritability which follows the consumption of ill-cooked food. The gluttony of their indigestible feasts was a direct incentive to counsels of unreasonable violence. Victims of gloomy imaginings, they lived in abject submission to the wiles of a multitude of fraudulent medicine men – quacks – who haunted their existence with vain promises and false nostrums from the cradle to the grave.

It is to be remarked that the quack of modern civilisation, the vendor of patent medicine, preys mainly upon the races of Anglo-Saxon stock who are also great warriors, great orators, mighty hunters, great masters of outdoor pursuits. No virtues apparently will avail for happiness if the righteous art of cooking be neglected by the national conscience. We owe much to the fruitful meditations of our sages, but a sane view of life is, after all, elaborated mainly in the kitchen – the kitchen of the small house, the abode of the preponderant majority of the people. And a sane view of life excludes the belief in patent medicine. The conscientious cook is the natural enemy of the quack without a conscience; and thus his labours make for the honesty and favour the amenity of our existence. For a sane view of life can be no other than kindly and joyous, but a believer in patent medicine is steeped in the gloom of vague fears, the sombre attendants of disordered digestion.

Strong in this conviction I introduce this little book to the inhabitants of the little houses who are the arbiters of the nation's destiny. Ignorant of the value of its methods I have no doubt whatever as to its intention. It is highly moral. There cannot be the slightest question as to that; for is it not a cookery book? – the only product of the human mind altogether above suspicion.

In that respect no more need, or indeed can, be said. As regards the practical intention I gather that no more than the clear and

concise exposition of elementary principles has been the author's aim. And this too is laudable, because modesty is a becoming virtue in an artist. It remains for me only to express the hope that by correctness of practice and soundness of precept this little
5 book will be able to add to the cheerfulness of nations.

THE FUTURE OF
CONSTANTINOPLE
1912

(*To the Editor of* THE TIMES)

SIR,   5
How long the last, Asiatic, phase of the history of the Turks –
Sultanate of Damascus or Caliphate of Baghdad – may last no one
can say. That its European chapter is closed few only can doubt.
But nobody will deny that a fierce scramble for Constantinople
amongst the victors would be a most unseemly and disturbing   10
complication.

The Serbs and Bulgars have no definite historical claim to
advance. Greece has that, of course. But it must go very far back, to
Byzantium – the old and obscure colony. And really I cannot imagine this most democratic of kingdoms desiring a capital other than   15
Athens – the very cradle of democracy, matchless in the wonders
of its life and the vicissitudes of its history.

The Constantinople of which I think is not the Greek colony. It
is the Imperial and symbolic city, one of the refuges of European
civilization and the fit object of Europe's care. It should rest at   20
last under the joint guarantee of all the Powers, after its infinitely
varied, stormy, and tragic existence of august dominion, desperate wars, and abject slavery. It should find a dignified peace as an
independent city, with a small territory, governed by an elected
Senate (in which all the races of its population would be repre-   25
sented) and by – I won't call him its Burgomaster – let us say
its Patrician, as the executive head. The Balkan Powers might be
co-jointly entrusted with his nomination. This would to a certain
extent secure the share of Slavonic influence, since in the Senate
the Greeks, I imagine, would predominate.   30

The independent Constantinople of my vision would be the
splendid spiritual capital of the Balkan Peninsula naturally; its
intellectual capital almost certainly. Commercially, too, as a free
port, it would have all the chances, though Salonika may turn out

a serious competitor. The various capitals of the Balkan States, res-
idences of Courts and centres of political life, need not be jealous
of the unique city which has done so much for the organization
of mankind.

5   From its geographical position the Powers could easily give
effective protection to that small municipal State. This plan, of
course, implies free Dardanelles (but that seems already certain)
and a neutralized Bosporus.

I am, Sir, your obedient servant,

10   J. Conrad

P ERHAPS YOU WILL allow me to expand a little the idea thrown
out in my letter to *The Times*. Of its reception at large I know
nothing – and perhaps it does not merit any sort of reception. Of
course, when one puts down anything in the shape of a proposal
15   one does think over the objections. I am not inclined to believe a
notion right and feasible simply because it has occurred to me. I
am not of that happy temperament. Still, when the first man who
read my letter turned upon me with the words, "So you too, I see,
have joined the ideologues," I believe my cheek blanched.

20   This was a pretty heavy charge to bring against a man conscious
of being guilty of no worse crime than a little imagination. But
it was not the severity of the indictment nor yet the knowledge
that "ideologue" was the term of utmost scorn in the mouth of
Napoleon I which disturbed me. I was not frightened or angry.
25   I was extremely surprised. Ideologue! And I had meant my suggestion to be eminently practical. Practical – that is, strictly in
accordance with the fitness of things.

For to any one with a little historical sense it is not in the fitness
of things that Constantinople should become the capital of a
30   Bulgarian kingdom. I do not wish to hurt youthful susceptibilities
but frankly the city of the Bosporus is too great, too illustrious for
that fate. The crash of its fall reëchoed ominously from one end
of Christendom to the other. Its liberation will send a mournful
whisper of angry dismay through the Mussulman world. And the
35   event at which we look is historically too momentous for anything
but the indestructible city itself, the jewel of the Balkans and once
the only luminous spot through nearly five centuries of European
night, to be its commemorative monument.

If this be mere ideology then I am safe to say it has its incit-
ing cause in a perfectly clear view of possible eventualities. Let us
piously hope that the dawn of peace for the peninsula will succeed this lurid conflagration. The waned Crescent is setting for
ever; but to a calm observer the dawn seems a long way yet below   5
the horizon. There will be many questions to be settled between
themselves by the Balkan Children of the Cross – not to speak of
some other outside Christians with views of their own. And what
if amongst other things we were to see before many years a war
between Greece and Bulgaria for the possession of Constantino-   10
ple?

For in fact, historically and racially, Greece alone has a claim to
Constantinople. But who is going to hand it over to her now? The
Bulgarians are nearer, and, we are given to understand, intoxi-
cated with their success.   15

But in this success they are not alone; and you cannot cut the
crown of victory into four pieces and present each combatant
with one fourth of immortal glory. The only sane way is to leave
the Imperial City outside the field of dispute by a guaranteed
agreement. There will be spoil enough – whether cut and dried   20
already or likely to turn out an awkward morsel to carve – to repay
the blood and treasure. For as to risks taken, there were none to
be proud of in this enterprise.

As to the difficulty of staying the conquering army, that is only
the lofty verbiage of elation. A disciplined army can always be   25
stayed. The Russian army was stayed at San Stefano, and its victory, if not so swift and more dearly bought, was quite as complete. And indeed I would not deny to any of the combatants
the satisfaction of triumphal entry. It is what comes after that will
count.   30

Let us be sincere in this matter. This game was played for
unequal stakes. For Turkey was staking her very head, while the
Allies risked no more than a more or less severe blood-letting. We
know that if the fortune of war had gone the other way, unani-
mous Europe would have stopped it with the *status quo* declara-   35
tion and the hand of Turkey would have been stayed. This fact,
of which not a single Balkanian of them all ever had the slightest doubt, should make them amenable to reason in the final
settlement.

Nobody wishes to rob them of what is won. Constantinople would remain a joint possession, but with a life and dignity of its own, till – till another Eastern Empire comes into being. And I think it would be a rational arrangement. The same objector, while
5 I was trying to parry the charge of being an ideologue, lunged at me with the affirmation that this was "working for Russia". I confess that I don't understand that thrust. I think that for some time the possession of Constantinople has ceased to be one of the immediate aims of Russian policy. But even so, I don't see how I am
10 serving any such dark purpose. It would be certainly easier to make war on Bulgaria and take Constantinople from it than to lay violent hands on a defenceless free town under a European guarantee, to which Russia herself would be a party. Not to mention the fact that such an aggression would be considered a *casus belli* not only
15 by one but by all the Balkan powers (including Greece), the joint guardians of the city under Europe's sanction.

But as far as Russia's desire of an open Black Sea is concerned, the plan should certainly meet with her approval. I don't think that Russia would like to see numerous batteries of Bul-
20 garian guns on the heights behind the town, sealing up the Bosporus most effectually even without the help of the Turks on the other side. Indeed, I don't believe Russia would contemplate such a possibility for a moment. And how would Bulgaria (or Greece for that matter) like the obligation of an unarmed cap-
25 ital and the limitations of her sovereign rights in the matter of defence?

A neutralized Bosporus and a free Constantinople would arouse no envy, no jealousies, and give no offence. Constantinople, a religious and intellectual capital – a common possession, giving no
30 umbrage to any one – a holy city of infinite prestige and incomparable beauty. And I am even thinking here of the Mohammedans. There will be, no doubt, many Muslims left in the peninsula, industrious and peaceable citizens of the Christian states. To them also Constantinople shall be a holy city; for the religious
35 head of Mohammedans in Europe would be residing there, nominated by the Caliph in Asia, subject to confirmation by the Balkan powers.

It seems to me too that such a solution of the Constantinople problem would soothe to a certain extent the grief and unrest of
40 Mussulmans all the world over. A consideration worth the notice

of the European States which have become by conquest masters of Mohammedan territories.

The details of organization, in which all the races of the peninsula would be justly represented, cannot be a matter of insuperable difficulty. Every Bulgarian, Greek, Serb, or Montenegrin entering 5 Constantinople should be able to say: "I am at home here. This ground on which I stand has been liberated by me and my brothers and this Imperial City, free to us all and subject to no one, is the splendid monument of our victory."

THE CONGO NOTEBOOKS

THE CONGO DIARY
1890

[1]

Arrived at Matadi on the 13th of June 1890. –
Mr Gosse chief of the station (O.K.) retaining us for some reason 5
of his own.

Made the acquaintance of Mr Roger Casement, which I should
consider as a great pleasure under any circumstances and now it
becomes a positive piece of luck –

Thinks, speaks well, most intelligent and very sympathetic. – 10
Feel considerably in doubt about the future. Think just now that
my life amongst the people (white) around here can not be very
comfortable. Intend avoid acquaintances as much as possible.

[2]

Through Mr R. C. Have made the acquaint[tan]$^{\underline{ce}}$ of M^r 15
Underwood the manager of the English factory (Hatton & Cook-
son in Kalla Kalla) – av[era]$^{\underline{ge}}$ com[merci]$^{\underline{al}}$ – Hearty and kind.
Lunched there on the 21st. –

24th Gosse and R. C. gone with a large lot of ivory down to
Boma. On G. return intend to start to up the river. Have been 20
myself busy packing ivory in casks. Idiotic employment. Health
good up to now.

Wrote to Simpson, to Gov. B. to Purd to Hope, to Cap Froud,
and to Mar. Prominent characteristic of the social life here: People
speaking ill of each other. – 25

[3]

Saturday 28th June left Matadi with Mr Harou and a caravan
of 31 men. Parted with Casement in a very friendly manner. M^r
Gosse saw us off as far as the State Station. –

First halt. M'poso. 2 Danes in Comp[a]ny. 30

Sund: 29th. Ascent of Palaballa. Sufficiently fatiguing – Camped at 11$\underline{h}$ am at Nsoke-River. Mosquitos –

Monday. 30th – to Congo da Lemba after passing black rocks long ascent. Harou giving up. Bother. Camp bad. Water far. Dirty.
5   At night Harou better.

[4]

1st July.
Tuesday. 1$^{\underline{st}}$ Left early in a heavy mist marching towards Lufu River. – Part route through forest on the sharp slope of a high
10 mountain. Very long descent. Then, market place, from where short walk to the bridge (good) and Camp. V[ery] G[ood]. Bath – Clear river – Feel well Harou all right – 1st chicken. $\underline{2p}$.[m.] No sunshine today –

Wednesday 2^{d} July –
15 Started at 5^{h}30 after a sleepless night – Country more open – Gently andulating [sic] hills. Road good in perfect order – (District of Lukungu). Great market at 9.30. Bought eggs & chickens – Feel not well today. Heavy

[5]

20 cold in the head. Arrived at 11^{h} at Banza Manteka – Camped on the market place. Not well enough to call on the missionary. Water scarce and bad – Camp[in]^{g} place dirty. –
2 Danes still in company.

Thursday 3^{d} July.
25 Left at 6 am. after a good night's rest. Crossed a low range of hills and entered a broad valley or rather plain with a break in the middle – Met an off[ic]^{er} of the State inspecting; a few minutes afterwards saw at a camp[in]^{g} place the dead body of a Backongo – Shot? Horrid smell. – Crossed a

30 ## [6]

range of mountains running NW – SE. by a low pass. Another broad flat valley with a deep ravine through the centre. – Clay

and gravel – Another range parallel to the first-mentioned with a chain of low foothills running close to it – Between the two came to camp on the banks of Luinzono River. Camp[in]ᵍ place clean. River clear. Gov[ernmen]ᵗ Zanzibari with register. Canoe. 2 Danes camp[in]ᵍ on the other bank. – Health good –   5
General tone of landscape grey yellowish, (Dry grass) with

[7]

reddish patches (soil) and clumps of dark green vegetation scattered sparsely about – Mostly in steep gorges between the higher mountains or in ravines cutting the plain – Noticed Palma Christi –   10
Oil palm. Very straight tall and thick trees in some places. Name not known to me – Villages quite invisible. Infer their existence from cal[a]bashes suspended to palm trees for the "malafu". –
Good many caravans and travellers – No women unless on the market place. –   15
Bird notes charming – One especially a flute-like note. Another kind of "boom" ressembling [*sic*]

[8]

the very distant baying of a hound. – Saw only pigeons and a few green parroquets; very small and not many. No birds of prey seen   20
by me. Up to 9 am – Sky clouded and calm – Afterwards gentle breeze from the N$\underline{\text{th}}$ generally and sky clearing – Nights damp and cool. – White mists on the hills up about half way. Water effects, very beautiful this morning. Mists generally raising before sky clears.   25

> [*Sketch: 'Section of today's road.' Marked on the sketch: 'Luinzono River', '3 hills', 'Banza Manteka'. Beneath the sketch: 'Distance 15 miles. General direction NNE ← SSW'.*]

[9]

Friday – 4th July. –   30
Left camp at 6^{h} am – after a very unpleasant night – Marching across a chain of hills and then in a maze of hills – at 8.15 opened out into an andulating [*sic*] plain. Took bearings of a break in the

chain of mountains on the other side. Bearing <u>NNE</u> – Road passes
through that. Sharp ascents up very steep hills not very high. The
higher mountains recede sharply and show a low hilly country –
at 9.30 market place.

5   At 10$^{\underline{h}}$ passed R. Lukanga and at 10.30 Camped on the
Mpwe R.

[10]

[*Sketch: 'To day's march – Direction <u>NNE'/₂N</u>. ← Dist[an]$^{\underline{ce}}$ 13 miles'.
Marked on sketch: 'Camp', '<u>Luinzono</u>'.*]

10   Saw another dead body lying by the path in an attitude of meditative repose. –
        In the evening 3 women of which one albino passed our camp –
Horrid chalky white with pink blotches. Red eyes. Red hair. Features very negroid and ugly. –
15   Mosquitos. At night when the moon rose heard shouts and
drumming in distant villages. Passed a bad night.

[11]

Saturday 5th July. 90.
        Left at 6.15. Morning cool, even cold and very damp – Sky
20 densely overcast. Gentle breeze from NE. Road through a narrow plain up to R. <u>Kwilu</u>. Swift flowing and deep 50 y[ar]ds
wide – Passed in canoes – After[war]$^{\underline{ds}}$ up and down very steep
hills intersected by deep ravines – Main chain of heights running
mostly NW—SE, or W and E (at times[)]. Stopped at Manyamba –
25 Camp[in]$^{\underline{g}}$ place bad – in a hollow – Water very indifferent. Tent
set at 10$^{\underline{h}}$ 15$^{\underline{m}}$

[*Sketch: 'Section of today's road NNE' ← Dist[an]$^{\underline{ce}}$ 12$^{mi[les]}$'. Marked
on sketch: 'Camp', 'Manyamba', 'Kwilu River'.*]

[12]

30   To day fell into a muddy puddle – Beastly. The fault of the man
that carried me. After camp[in]$^{\underline{g}}$ went to a small stream bathed
and washed clothes. – Getting jolly well sick of this fun. –

Tomorrow expect a long march to get to Nsona. 2 days from
Manyanga. –
No sunshine to-day

[13]

Sunday 6th July –   5
Started at 5.40. – The route at first hilly then after a sharp
descent traversing a broad plain. At the end of it a large market
place.
At 10ʰ Sun came out. –
After leaving the market passed another plain then walking on   10
the crest of a chain of hills passed 2 villages and at 11ʰ arrived at
Nsona. – Village invisible –

[*Sketch: 'Section of day's march'. Marked on sketch: 'Camp Nsona',
'Market'. Beneath sketch: 'Direction about NNE ← Distance – 18
miles'.*]   15

[14]

In this camp (Nsona –) there is a good camp[in]ᵍ place. Shady.
Water far and not very good. – This night no mosquitos owing to
large fires lit all round our tent. –
Afternoon very close   20
Night clear and starry.

[15]

Monday – 7th July –
Left at 6ʰ after a good night's rest on the road to Inkandu which
is some distance past Lukungu gov[ernmen]ᵗ station. –   25
Route very accidented. Succession of round steep hills. At times
walking along the crest of a chain of hills. –
Just before Lukunga our carriers took a wide sweep to the southward till the station bore Nᵗʰ. – Walking through long grass for
1½ hours. – Crossed a broad river about 100 feet wide and 4   30
deep. – After another ½ hours walk through manioc plantations
in good order

[16]

rejoined our route to the E[astwar]$^{\underline{d}}$ of the Lukunga Sta[ti]$^{\underline{on}}$
walking along an undulating plain towards the Inkandu market
on a hill. – Hot, thirsty and tired. At 11^h arrived on the M[ar]ket
5 place – About 200 people. – Business brisk. No water. No
camp[in]^g place – After remaining for one hour left in search
of a resting place. –
     Row with carriers – No water. At last about 1$^1/_2$ p.m. camped on
an exposed hill side near a muddy

10   [17]

creek. No shade. Tent on a slope. Sun heavy. Wretched.

[Untitled sketch of day's journey. Marked on sketch: 'Camp', 'Inkandu',
'River bearing N[or]th', 'Lukunga', 'Nsona'. Beneath sketch: 'Direction
NE by N. ← Distance 22 miles'.]

15 Night miserably cold. –
No sleep. Mosquitos –

[18]

Tuesday 8th July
Left at 6$^{\underline{h}}$ am
20 About ten minutes from camp left main gov[ernmen]^t path
for the Manyanga track. Sky overcast. Road up and down all the
time – Passing a couple of villages.
     The country presents a confused wilderness of hills, land slips
on their sides showing red. Fine effect of red hill covered in places
25 by dark green vegetation.
     $^1/_2$ hour before beginning the descent got a glimpse of the
Congo. – Sky clouded.

[19]

[Sketch: 'Today's march – 3$^{\underline{h}}$'. Marked on sketch: 'Manyanga', 'Congo',
30 *'Hill', 'River', 'Camp'. Beneath sketch: 'NbyE ← SbyW| General direc-*
tion NbyE – Dist[an]$^{\underline{ce}}$ 9$^1/_2$ miles.']

Arrived at Manyanga at 9ʰ a.m.
Received most kindly by Messr[s] Heyn & Jaeger. –
Most comfortable and pleasant halt. –

Stayed here till the 25. Both have been sick. – Most kindly care
taken of us. Leave with sincere regret.   5

[20]

(Mafiela)			
Frid^y 25th	–	Nkenghe	–	left
Sat. 26		Nsona		Nkendo.k
Sund. 27		Nkandu		Luasi	10
Mond 28		Nkonzo		Nzungi (Ngoma)
Tues. 29		Nkenghe		Inkissi
Wedn: 30		Nsona		mercredi = Stream
Thurs: 31.		Nkandu		Luila
Frid^y 1st Aug.		Nkonzo		Nselemba	15
Sat^y 2^d		Nkenghe		
Sund. 3^d		Nsona		
Mond. 4th		Nkandu		
Tues^d: 5th		Nkonzo.		
Wedn^y 6th		Nkenghe.		20

[21]

Friday the 25th July 1890. –
Left Manyanga at 2½ p.m – with plenty of hammock carriers.
H[arou] lame and not in very good form. Myself ditto but not
lame. Walked as far as Mafiela and camped – 2ʰ   25

Saturday – 26th
Left very early. – Road ascending all the time. – Passed villages.
Country seems thickly inhabited. At 11ʰ arrived at large Market
place. Left at noon and camped at 1ʰ pm.

[Untitled sketch of the day's journey. Marked: [flag], '†', 'Camp',   30
'a white man died here –', 'market', 'gov[ernmen]t path', 'mount',
'Crocodile pond', 'Mafiela'. 'General direction E¹/₂N ← W¹/₂S'. Sun
visible at 8 am. Very hot | distance – 18 miles'.]

[22]

Sunday, 27th –
Left at 8^h am – Sent luggage carriers straight on to Luasi and
went ourselves round by the Mission of Sutili.
5   Hospitable reception by Mrs Comber – All the missio[naries]
absent. –
The looks of the whole establishment eminently civilized and
very refreshing to see after the lot of tumble down hovels in which
the state & Company agents are content to live – fine buildings.
10   Position on a hill. Rather breezy. –
Left at 3^h pm. At the first heavy ascent met Mr Davis Miss[ionary]
returning

[23]

from a preaching trip. Rev. Bentley away in the South with his
15   wife. –
This being off the road no section given – Distance traversed
about 15 miles – Gen[eral] direction ENE. –
At Luasi we get on again on to the gov[ernmen]ᵗ road. –
Camped at 4¹/₂ pm. With Mr Heche in company. –
20   To day no sunshine –
Wind remarkably cold –
Gloomy day. –

[24]

Monday. 28th
25   Left camp at 6.30 after breakfasting with Heche –
Road at first hilly. Then walking along the ridges of hill chains
with valleys on both sides. – The country more open and there is
much more trees growing in large clumps in the ravines. –
Passed Nzungi and camped 11^h on the right bank of Ngoma. A
30   rapid little river with rocky bed. Village on a hill to the right. –

[*Untitled sketch. Marked: 'Camp', 'Ngoma River', 'Nzungi', [flag],
'Wooded valleys', 'Ridge –', 'River', 'Luasi', 'Camp'. 'General direction
ENE ← Distance – 14 miles'.*]

No sunshine. Gloomy cold day. Squalls.

[25]

Tuesday – 29th
Left camp at 7ʰ after a good night's rest. Continuous ascent;
rather easy at first. – Crossed wooded ravines and the river Lunzadi
by a very decent bridge –   5
At 9ʰ Met Mʳ Louette escorting a sick agent of the Comp[an]ʸ
back to Matadi – Looking very well – Bad news from up the river –
All the steamers disabled. One wrecked. – Country wooded – at
10.30 camped at Inkissi.

[*Untitled sketch. Marked:* 'Camp', *[flag]*, 'Inkissi River', 'Met Mr Lou-   10
ette', 'Lunzadi River', 'Ngoma'. 'General direction ENE ← Dist[an]ce
15 miles'.]

Sun visible at 6.30. Very warm day. –

[26]

29th   15
Inkissi River very rapid, is about 100 yards broad – Passage in
canoes. – Banks wooded very densely and valley of the river rather
deep but very narrow. –
To day did not set the tent but put up in gov[ernmen]ᵗ shimbek.
Zanzibari in charge – Very obliging. – Met ripe pineapple for the   20
first time. –
On the road to day passed a skeleton tied-up to a post. Also
white man's grave – No name. Heap of stones in the form of a
cross.
Health good now –   25

[27]

Wednesday – 30th.
Left at 6 am intending to camp at Kinfumu – Two hours sharp
walk brought me to Nsona na Nsefe – Market – ½ hour after
Harou arrived very ill with bilious attack and fever. – Laid him   30
down in gov[ernmen]ᵗ shimbek – Dose of Ipeca. Vomiting bile in
enormous quantities. At 11ʰ gave him 1 gramme of quinine and
lots of hot tea. Hot fit ending in heavy perspiration. At 2ʰ p.m.

put him in hammock and started for Kinfumu – Row with carriers
all the way. Harou suffering much

[28]

through the jerks of the hammock. Camped at a small stream. –
5   At 4ʰ Harou better. Fever gone. –

[*Untitled sketch. Marked: 'Wooded', 'Camp / grass', [flag], 'Nsona
[n]a Nsefe', 'Wood', 'Stream', 'Open', 'A remarkable conical mountain
bearing NE visible from here', 'Wood', 'Lulufu River', 'Inkissi', 'Sward'.
'General direction NEbyE¹/₂E – Distance 13 miles –'.*]

10   Up till noon, sky clouded and strong NW wind very chilling.
From 1ʰpm to 4ʰ pm sky clear and a very hot day. Expect lots
of bother with carriers to-morrow – Had them all called and
made a speech which they did not understand. They promise
good behaviour.

15   ## [29]

Thursday – 31ˢᵗ
Left at 6ʰ. – Sent Harou ahead and followed in ¹/₂ an hour. –
Road presents several sharp ascents and a few others easier but
rather long – Notice in places sandy surface soil instead of hard
20   clay as heretofore; think however that the layer of sand is not very
thick and that the clay would be found under it. Great difficulty
in carrying Harou. – Too heavy. Bother! Made two long halts to
rest the carriers. Country wooded in valleys and on many of the
ridges.

25   ## [30]

31ˢᵗ

[*Sketch: 'Section of to-day's road'. Marked: 'Luila River', 'Kinzilu
River', 'Kinfumu River', [flag], 'Nkenghe', 'Camp'. Below 'Kinzilu
River' is 'Congo [River]' and 'NE ¹/₂ E ←'.*]

30   At 2.30 pm reached Luila at last and camped on right bank. –
Breeze from SW

General direction of march about NE$^1/_2$E
Distance est[imate]$^{\underline{d}}$ 16 miles
Congo very narrow and rapid. Kinzilu rushing in. A short dis-
tance up from the mouth fine waterfall. –
– Sun rose red – from 9^h a.m. infernally hot day. –   5
Harou very little better.
Self rather seedy. Bathed.
Luila about 60 feet wide. Shallow

[31]

Friday– 1st of August 1890   10
Left at 6.30 am after a very indifferently passed night – Cold,
Heavy mists – Road in long ascents and sharp dips all the way to
Mfumu Mbé –
After leaving there a long and painful climb up a very steep hill;
then a long descent to Mfumu Koko where a long halt was made.   15
Left at 12.30 pm – towards Nselemba. – Many ascents – The
aspect of the country entirely changed – Wooded hills with open-
ings. – Path almost all the afternoon thro' a forest of light trees
with

[32]   20

dense undergrowth. –
After a halt on a wooded hillside reached Nselemba at 4^h 10^m
p.m.

[*Untitled sketch of the day's march. Marked: 'Camp', 'Nselemba', [flag],
'Stream', 'Mostly Wooded', 'Stream', 'Stream', 'Koko', 'Grass', 'Woods',   25
'Mfumu Mbé', 'Camp'.*]

Put up at gov[ernmen]^t shanty. –
Row between the carriers and a man stating himself in
gov[ernmen]^t employ, about a mat. – Blows with sticks raining
hard – Stopped it – Chief came with a youth about 13 suffering   30
from gunshot wound in the head. Bullet entered about an inch
above the right eyebrow and came out

[33]

a little inside the roots of the hair, fairly in the middle of the
brow in a line with the bridge of the nose – Bone not damaged
apparently. Gave him a little glycerine to put on the wound made
5 by the bullet on coming out.

Harou not very well. Mosquitos – Frogs – Beastly. Glad to see
the end of this stupid tramp.

Feel rather seedy –

Sun rose red – Very hot day – wind S$\underline{\text{th}}$

10   General direction of march – NEbyN
Distance about 17 miles

[34]

[*There is an undefinable sketch of four conic-shaped figures under-
pinned by three circles – a doodle lacking a context for interpretation.*
15 *This is followed by a blank leaf.*]

[35]

[*A small sketch of one large and two small hills appears at the top of the
page, with a column of fourteen numbers, of unknown context, adding
up to 702. The following three leaves have been torn out.*]

20 ## [36]

[*A crossed-out list of oil cans, drums and paint tins, followed by
another list with a different enumeration, indicating a corrected count as
follows:*]

Oil Cans –	29 –
25 Oil Drums	12
flattening (?)	3 [*perhaps from 'flattening', 'a paint with a matt finish' (OED); or 'flattened' (i.e. 'squeezed or beaten out' – OED) drums or cans*]
30 Mar[ke]^{t} [?] color – tins	4
Paint tins	28

[*Four blank leaves follow.*]

[37–38]

[Figures and calculations, most likely relating to dead reckoning, and probably of the location of the Torrens. *Among the various figures are readings of latitude and longitude, such as a series of calculations leading to the conclusion: 79° 33′; and 122° 17′ E. / 40° 51′ S, a* 5 *position south of Australia. The abbreviation 'DR' on the first of the two pages most likely stands for 'Dead Reckoning'.]*

[39]

Naturalist amongst
the head hunters –   10
by C. M. Woodford

by Clement[s] Markham.
John Davis –

J. Grant
History of Newspaper   15
Press. (1871)

19 Century for March –
(Tel-el-Kebir). Serg^t Palmer

[40]

Tell	jingula	20
Very early	una nswe	
dawn	kuma	
noon	ntangwalungu	
aftern[oon]	ntangwa wengele	
evening	masika	25
me my	mono. ame	

[41]

Ju leka kuna
Nous dormirons à
(We will sleep at)   30
– Aprésant – wau– (now)

Kana	nzila	Kwenda	kuna
Quand	chemin	aller	à

nkenge

nsona

5 nkandu

nkonzo

Mercredi [Wednesday]

(nkenge –

Kwilu

Muembe nkenghe

Nsona – ntombo [?]

Inkandu

Manyanga

[*At the bottom is a sketch of bananas and a slice of seeded fruit, perhaps*
10 *of the melon family.*]

[42]

Mueni – <u>Sun</u>	[diagram representing the sun]
Ngonda – <u>Moon</u>. –	[diagram of first-quarter moon]
Mbuetete – star(s).	[diagram of a star]
15 Ambno –	bottle.
Day.	Lumbu
after to-morrow	kiamene.
to-day	unu
morrow	mbaji mene
20 Do –	wanga
urgent.	watu (/wenta/go)
Walk	Diata
Reach	Luaka
He	yandi
25 this man	oyu
which is he	nkia muntu
Road	njila
Walk slow.	womboka
Take.	bonga = ma

30 [43]

Sam:	nsona
Dim	nkandu
Lundi 30.	nkonzo
Mardi	nkenge

Mercredi	nsona
Jeudi 3 –	nkandu
Vendre 4.	nkonzo
Samedi 5	nkenge
Dim 6	nsona	5
Lundi 7	nkandu
Mardi 8	nkonzo 11 days
Mercr 9.	Nkenge

[44]

Kodak Camera –   10
The Eastman Dry Plate & Film C$\underline{o}$
115 Oxford Street – £7.

Lukunga – M^r. Hoste. –
Banza Manteka Mr Ingham

Lankonzo   15

G. Stern. Gray's Inn 6$\underline{2}$
vepsalia salt
    Nkenghe

[*Written vertically:*]
Hierarchy   20
Anarchy

[45–46]

*[The last two pages of the notebook, dated 'Matadi. 23^d 6th 90' record
calculations made as Conrad counted, weighed and packed ivory into
casks. The following initials also appear: 'J. C. K.' [Joseph Conrad* 25
*Korzeniowski], 'SAB' [Société Anonyme Belge] and 'GK' [Georges-
Antoine Klein], the SAB agent who died on the* Roi des Belges *and
a possible source for Kurtz in 'Heart of Darkness'. There are references
to three casks, 'cask 2' containing '150 p[ieces]' with 'poid [weight] –
lbs 364' [165.11 kg]. Calculations on page 46 consist primarily of* 30
counting in groups of five '╫╫'.]

UP-RIVER BOOK
1890

Up-river book.
Commenced –
3.Augst 1890–
S. S. "Roi des Belges"

[2]

On leaving – from A After passing the two islands steer for
clump – high tree. two isl[and] points – Sandy beach

[*Two combined sketches of a sandy beach area at Stanley Pool. Marked:
four islands indicated by rectangles with an area of stones marked by a
circular broken line. Words written: 'trees', 'sandy', 'point', 'To [two?]
isl[ands] bay', 'foul [?]', 'stones', 'A', 'A' and 'Nº 1'.*]

Nº II Steer for inside sandy point then keep out. (about East by
the sun – as you approach coast breaks out into islands – B steer
for Bend marked B. From position C. a further point visible. C –
Steer for sandbank II, behind hazy clumps of trees visible on a III

[3]

Nº III – IV. point of land. No islands visible. Left bank island
presents appearance of main land. Bank II covered at H[igh]
W[ater]
Come up right to the bank I. Pass near islet Y. Leave Bank II –
on port side – Steer for sandy patch on S[ou]th shore –
Position. D.
Point **a** looks low now.
S[ou]th side sandbank cov[ered] at H[igh] W[ater].
The opening narrows. Point a advancing. –
Position E.

138

Low land and outlying sandbanks a little to port. Steering for
a little square white patch. Stick on it – Pass close to the sands –
Cautiously!

[4]

N° V. (and also IV)   5
Position F. ENE – Patch about ESE – Pass along sand shore not
far from point △ Steering well in. Island X on the starboard side
and generally kept ahead. On the port side (left bank) extensive
and dangerous sand bank. 1 ¹/₂ foot (Capt Koch). As you proceed in point ⊙ seems closed in with Island X and apparently no   10
passage – further on it opens again. A small grassy patch marks
the end of point ⊙. High hills right ahead looming behind
island X
Come right up to the island then steer along shore with point
⊙ a little on the port bow as   15

[5]

Va. V and IV.
from position F.a. – Coming up to a white patch after opening a
small channel cutting X in two. A small island app[arent]^{ly} closes
the passage. When nearing the end of X must keep close and steer   20
into the bay 8 getting the clump of trees on the port side. Going
out the highest mountain will be right ahead –
Always keep the high mountain ahead crossing over to the left
bank. To port of highest mount a low black point. Opposite a long
island stretching across. The shore is wooded –   25
IV. V. Va

[6]

V. Va.
As you approach the shore the black point and the island close
in together – No danger – Steering close to the mainland between   30
the island and the grassy sandbank, towards the high mount[ain]^{s}.
Steering close to the left bank of the river all the time. Entered.

VI   On left bank wooded point
Right valley. – 1st Reach nearly North.
2^{d} Reach – about NNE.
Left bank. Wooded point.
5   3^{d} Reach the same and wooded point. –
4th Reach NbyE.
Point III. Stones off.
IV Before getting abreast there is a rocky shoal $\frac{1}{3}$ out

[7]

10   VI
2 hours after entering the river sighted "2 sago-trees point" not
at all remarkable – Low flat at the foot of the hills. –
The appearance of point VI is bushy – Rather low. Round shape
behind as per sketch.
15   Just before coming up to p[oin]^{t} VI got bottom at 6 feet
stones – Hauled out
Point VII called "Sandstone P[oin]t." with a small ledge of rock
outside of it
Before closing with it – cross over to the right bank
20   Moored to – grassy Beach backed by trees – 25 miles from the
entrance – 5^{h}30

[8]

4th Augst VII
This reach is about E
25   Shortly after leaving, point A opens out double in peculiar
shape.
Off point VIII long stone ridge.
Point A has a small sand-spit covered at full river. –
Right below the point there is a small sandbank along the
30   shore. – Wooding place – May get in between sandbank and the
shore
After passing A point in the middle of the river there is a rocky
ledge now above water – Covered at F[ull] W[ater].
River rather narrow – Steering well off the right bank
35   Snake tree point has a ledge of Rock lying well

[9]

off – To give a wide berth

Here begins a reach about NE – (by the sun). – On the left bank many palms visible –

After passing Sn[ake] Tree point on the left bank entrance to 5
Black River – A remark[ab]$^{\underline{le}}$ clump little further on

R[iver] bank – Point C.

Off point C – cross over – On the left bank on point XI one palm rather conspicuous when coming up. –

After turning point C. You open up a remarkable point running 10
from high mountains called point Licha

Wooding place. – (6h am) –

[10]

On the right bank past point C – Sandy beaches to be met often –
On left bank a little past XI point there is a market place. – Rocky 15
shoals near in shore. –

(from Licha point up. –

VIII

From Licha – crossing over to right bank where there is outcrop
of rock – Small sandy beach near. 20

		Left. 6.15	
Bearing –	Licha S 15° W	Time	
Point C –	S 25° W	6.35 –	
Point XII.	N 48° E –	6$^{h.}$ 35^m | 7.15	
Point D.	N 34° E –		25
Point F	N 36° E –		
Rate about 3$^1/_2$ miles per $^{\underline{h}}$			

[11]

VIII

After leaving Licha keep in the middle 30

B[earing].	T[ime].	
G. N33° E	9$^{\underline{h}}$20^m	bearing from p[oin]^t XII.
P[oin]t XIII	8.15	opposite XII rocky cliff with ledges extending

P[oin]t XIV from
P[oin]^t ⊗
By NEbyNE   After point XII Indented shore
with a low flat running at the foot
5   of the hills – After passing XIII
Rocky sweep – This reach is
NEbyN. – Steer by the left bank 2
low points
Point H   with many palms in the bight
10   at 10^{h}5^m an island in the middle of the
bight. – Before closing with G
point small S[and] B[ank] parallel

[12]

IX

15   to the shore – pass[age] inside (?)
P[oin]t XV bore   good wooding place. –
NEbyN$^1/_2$N   After passing 1st island open
from ⊗ p[oin]^t up a point and sight a long and a very small
island
20   P[oin]^t K bore   Island N° 2 long wooded – small
NNE from   islet N° 3 – This reach is NE
Is[lan]^d 3   by N nearly. –
Islet N° 3   Between Is[lan]^d N° 2 and N° 3 rocky
at 10^{h}50^m ledges and no passage. From abreast p[oin]^t
25   H it seems as if Is[land] 3 was abreast Point
XIV. The NW end of Is[lan]^d 2 has a palm
grove – The island lays NW – SE.
All along right shore small beaches – and
dead wood on most of them

30   [13]
IX
After passing point XIV a long stretch of low land on left bank
with islands (very small).
A remarkable clump of trees as per chart –

Island N° 4   and many palm trees on
at noon   the low shore
Island   This stretch of low land
N° 4   continues for a long time
   to   with many palms –   5
Point M   General appearance light green –
NEbyE   Long reach with a regular sweep on the
    left bank. From
$2^h 30^m$ p.m.   Island N° 4 $2\frac{1}{2}$ up.

[14]   10

X. This Reach is <u>NEbyN</u>.
Directly after passing P[oin]^t M – on the right shore rocky shoals
extending good way out
Afterwards same appearance
Hills to water's edge with small sandy beaches   15
Over p[oin]t XVI curious yellow path on a hill.
Steering a little over on the right bank side. On the other side
villages on slope of hill.
After point N another p[oin]^t forming a high plain. A little
further ridge of rocks.   20

At N   Before coming to high plain
$3^h 45^m$ P[oin]^t N° 2 there is a wooding place.

[15]

X
P[oin]^t P bore. NEbyN at $4^{\underline{h}}$ $25^{\underline{m}}$ from high plain p[oin]t$^{\prime\prime}$ N°   25
2 –
Abreast point XVII at $5^{\underline{h}}10^m$ – (length of reach $5\frac{1}{2}$ <u>m[iles]</u>
The new reach about NE$\frac{1}{2}$N –
Abreast point XVII a long parallel ridge of rocks well off the
shore –   30
Off Point P a long rocky ridge extending into the river
(from here in one day to Ki[n]chassa down stream. 12 hours
steaming).

All the time keeping over to the French shore.
Hills on left shore present a reddish appearance

[16]

X. All the right bank fringed with trees
5   At the small beach near Point P at 5^h50^m – moored. –
Wooding places – Villages on the opposite bank. –

Point P.6.^{h}o^m.
End of point –
10   Bankap bore
NEbyN from mid[d]^{le}
of the river. –
a little past
P[oin]^t P.
15   7^h45^m at point
XVIII

Left. Cross over from the beach
below the Point P.
Here commences a reach
about NE –
After rounding P[oin]^t P. There
is a wooding place. Narrow
beach.
From there steer a little
over where there is a small Island not
app[aren]^t. No passage – After that
keep nearly

[17]

20

25   XI.

from camp to
XVIII – 6 miles
$1\frac{h3}{4}$
30   P[oin]^t XVIII at 7^h45^m
times

from XVIII
Reach – NEbyN$^1/_2$N.

X in the middle. – All that shore is a
low flat fringed by trees backed by low
hills – Bordered by reefs – Steer in the
middle – till abreast p[oin]^t Q. Then
a little over to the right bank –
After p[oin]^t XVIII a[n] invisible
sandbank stretches along
the right shore. Keep off –
nearly in center –

Bankab – NEbyN
Point R from m[id]^{dle} NNE.
On p[oin]^t Bankab two
high trees – One broad
another less spreading

[18]

XI
to p[oin]t QR.
at 9^h am
from XVIII to
R. 1^{h}45^m at
say 6 miles –

NEbyN$^1/_2$N:

About 1 hour after passing
P[oin]t XVIII – passing the wooded
false points rocks extend out
into the river P[oin]t Q bearing   5
about Nth and Bankab
about NNE

On nearing p[oin]^t Bankab on French
shore to the Nth p[oin]^t Q small   10
island (N° 6) and long sandbank over
which from the middle of the river
you see Ganchu P[oin]^t bearing about
NbyE.

Bankab P[oin]^t
9^{h}15^m
Ganchu bore
N$^1/_2$W.

The islet N° 6 has a few   15
trees and a dead palm
on it. Opp[osi]te on same
shore in a Ravine small vill[ag]^e –
Round Bank[ab] in back curr[ent].

[19]   20

XI.

When rounding Bankab keep on
Right side and enter the current
sweeping out of the bight cautiously
and end on nearly –
(On coming down follow the current   25
round the bight.)
When about the middle of the open
stretch steer right across to clear
Ganchu's Point
Pass the point cautiously.   30
Stones – Then steer straight for
P[oin]t XIX. – Along the left shore
below that point stretches off a sand
bank

P[oin]t XIX at
10^{h}40^m
P[oin]^t S bore N.

ressembling [*sic*] a beach but   35
covered at F[ull] W[ater]. –

[20]

XI

From p[oin]^t XIX cross over a little af[te]^r a small beach on the opposite side by compass about NbyW$^1/_2$W –

5   This short Reach is about <u>NNE</u>.

Next short Reach is about NE by N$^1/_2$N.

Keeping a little over on the right shore. – On the left bank bushes grow-

10   ing down to the water. Right shore low, undulating. Wooded (coming down from S the False XIX point would be alone visible

P[oin]t. S. – <u>at Noon</u> 12^h.

15   P[oin]t XX bore N$^1/_2$E.

Entrance of Riv[er] Kassai. NEbyN.

Point on right bank. white patch bore N$^1/_2$W.

Next p[oin]t to S. N$^3/_4$W.

20   [21]

XII. Entrance to Kassai rather broad. On Sth side a bright beach with a spreading dead tree above it mark the mouth.

At the Cath[oli]^c mission moor along-side the head of the beach. –

25   From P[oin]t S' to Mission – NNE. 1$^{\underline{h}}$

Made fast at 1^h pm.

Pt XX. bore N 5° W

Left the mission at 2$^1/_2$ –

In the bight between the miss[ion]

30   and P[oin]^t XX rocky ledges – Of[f] p[oin]t XX a stony ridge partially cover[e]^d

from XX.   at high water –

P[oin]^t T   Off P[oin]t XX at 3^h 20$^{\underline{m}}$ making it

35   bore   about 2^h from the P[oin]^t S' –

NbyE$^1/_2$E
at 3^{h}20^m pm.

[22]

XII.   After passing P[oin]^t XX follow the
                             left shore at some distance to the   5
                             p[oin]t with the grassy slope about
                             NNE. From there cross over towards
                             point T. –
                             Sandbank always covered in the bight.
                             Current easier in the middle. –   10
                             Probably
off   there is a passage between
Point T   the sand and the left
at 5^{h}25^m bank.
Point XXI bore   This reach about N.   15
N¾ E.   (Stopped at 5^{h}45^m
                             Left stopping place at 7$^\underline{h}$ am.

[23]

XII On <u>Right bank</u>.
From stopping place sighted a dark green p[oin]t – a long spit   20
of sand cov[ere]^d at full water with high rocks also cov[ere]^d at
very full water. –
On <u>left shore</u> a sandb[an]k always covered extends 1/3^d into
the river.
Got soundings below the dark green P[oin]t. bearing   25
NbyW$^1/_2$W
P[oin]t XXI bore NEbyE – <u>3f[a]th[oms] and 4f[a]th[oms]</u>
Opening Lawson river with sandbank across the mouth and
rocks

[24]   30

XIII stretching off. – Further along cut beach. – P[oin]t XXI
gets indistinct on nearer approach – No danger on that side. – A
small rocky ledge on the point
Past Pt XXI – at –

This reach about N by E –
After passing P[oin]ᵗ XXI – R[i]g[h]t bank low scrubby and
trees – Sm[all] hills – To the left higher hills with bare tops and a
belt of forest half way up from the water's edge
5   At p[oin]t U – Wooding places

Caution   The landing must be approached cautiously on
              account of stones and snags
              Round P[oin]ᵗ U cautiously – When entering the
              reach

10   [25]

XIII keep rather on the outer edge of the current following the
right shore – Sandbank on left shore not visible –
From 3 fath[oms] position the P[oin]t XXII bears NEbyE The
middle of uncovered S[and] B[an]K bears about N$\frac{1}{2}$E.
15 A spit with 1$\frac{1}{2}$ f[a]th[oms] at less than $\frac{1}{2}$ full river extends
towards U high land
On rounding p[oin]t XXII give a wide berth. There is [*sic.*] 2
stony ledges – of which the outer one is cov[ere]ᵈ

                           [26]

20 XIII at full river. – This reach about NEbyN before passing Mission
P[oin]ᵗ. You open out False P[oin]ᵗ W which is not noticeable. Also
a point on the left shore.
Coast in perfect semicircle sand, swamp and trees – hills opened
out there. A few high thin trees dispersed in that stretch
25 As you near the end of the semicircle the M[issio]ⁿ marked
A in sketch disappears: from the same place Island N°7 – bore
N$\frac{3}{4}$E –
From point (Eng[lish] Mission) at Grenfell p[oin]t – at
4ʰ p. m.
30   When passing the dangerous sandbank called

                           [27]

XIII mission sands keep close in with M[issi]ᵒⁿ Point and have
the island either on port bow or starboard quarter till you clear
M[issi]ᵒⁿ Point.

[28]

*[Sketch of Mission Point with a dotted line suggesting a channel through
sand banks, snags and islands (including one designated as 'wooded';
others have 'clump B', 'palms' and 'bush') with instructions such as
'Island 11 Careful of snags opposite the dead tree'. At the top of the map* 5
*are 'NE. EbyN. NEbyE – NE – Square little beach ahead – Δ and bore
S[ou]th NNW Nth from S[and] B[ank]'. Fathoms are marked 1½ 1 1;
and sections of land are numbered 8 9 10.]*

[29]

Passage inside island 10 at full water 10
Passage inside small islet off 2 Palm P[oin]^t at full water when
<u>must keep</u> close inshore

	Keep close to island 12 – over a bank with 2
	fath[oms] –
Koch's passage	After passing Is[lan]^d 12 steer for bush on end 15
	of the long island.

From there for bush point on the m[ai]^n land follow cut bank
then cross over towards Low island –
Sandbank right across after approaching it steer along it toward
the trees on it and pass between 20

[30]

XIV it and the m[ai]^n land (when nearing 1 f[a]th[om] to 1½
f[a]th[oms]).
Steer in middle of passage and then for XXIV p[oin]^t following
the bight of the shore from p[oin]t XXIV steer between two small 25
islands keeping over to starboard
Soundings in 1, 1½, 1 fath[om] – variable
Bolobo village. Landing place

A few minutes after passing the mission keep out a little into 30
the river:
This reach from the mission is about NE –

Follow the right bank the courses being from NE to E till you
open the bend of low shore. Then P[oin]^t of

[31]

M[ai]^n Land bearing NEbyE and small island bearing EbyN$^{\underline{th}}$
5   Steer in the bend a little watching for edge of sandbank – Leave
the small island on St[arboar]^d side.
Sandbanks on both sides with spits across the course
After nearing island 12 another small island is seen to be left to
starb[oar]$^{\underline{d}}$
10   General direction of land from there is ENE –
After passing the island keep at mod[era]^{te} distances off
When app[roa]ch[in]$^{\underline{g}}$ long islands there is a bank with 1
f[a]th[om]

[32]

15   XV at $^1/_2$ full. Close in a little with the main[lan]^d –
After passing steep round bank steer in with the bend
When off the swamp spit all the islands on the southern bearing
seem one land
XVa Arrived at stopping place at 5^{h}30^m –
20   Village. –

Left stopping place at 6 am –
Steering for P[oin]t XXV keep in with the bend.
Remarkable. Islands. –

[33]

25   XVI
Island bearing NNE.
square clump. light green follow the island 15th shore all the
time – remarkable palm –
Second small island then steer for little grassy islet –
30   Soundings in 1$^1/_2$ and 1 f[a]th[om].
Course about ENE. –
Leave grassy islet on St[arboar]^d hand and steer in 1$^1/_2$ to 2
f[a]th[oms] for Island bearing ENE N$^{\underline{o}}$ 16

[34]

XVII

Follow the shore of island N$\underline{o}$ 16 on an NE$^1/_2$E course –
Mind the snags along Island N$\underline{o}$ 16.
Cross over well before getting to Roof P[oin]$\underline{t}$ 5
Cross to where higher trees begin
When nearing M[ai]^n Land P[oin]t – you will see the open
passage between Is[lan]$\underline{d}$ 17 and 18

[35]

XVIII –   10
The entrance to the Oubangi is barred on the up river side by
extensive sandbanks –
The opposite Congo shore forms a $^1/_2$ circle from the F[ren]$\underline{ch}$
mission to p[oin]t XXVI. –
When rounding P[oin]t XXVI the current is very strong. – Rocks   15
off the P[oin]t –
Sandbank stretching close from the N$\underline{th}$ towards it always covered
but impassable at any state of the river –
Inside the bight steer close in to guard against

[36]   20

XVIII
dangerous snags. –
Rounding the points pretty close you sight to port the commence-
ment of a long island called Flat Is[lan]$\underline{d}$
Proceeding on Past the village of Pressinbi then Irebu –   25
Sharp bend in the shore where the mouth of the R[iver
Oubangi] is. From elbow cross over to the flat island: avoiding
S[and]B[an]ks and snags – then where a few Palms form clump
cross over again and follow main shore
Rounding another point still follow main shore   30

[37]

at times only 2 to 1$^1/_2$ fath[oms] water – Otherwise passage not
intricate

Otherwise keep generally by the line indicated on the chart. –
After leaving Irebu there is no wooding place for some time.
XXIII XXIII.A.

[38]

5   XXIII. and A. Thursday. 14th Augst
Left stopping place at 6.10^m.
Pass outside the sm[all] islet in the first bend after leaving
The general direction since yesterday [not recorded]
Entering the next narrow reach keep on but at a little dist[an]^{ce}
10   from left shore – Snags –
This reach is safe across (Koch)
A succession of canal like bends – The shore covered with dense
forest right down to water's edge.
– The river opens suddenly disclosing more islands –

15   # [39]

XXIV
After rounding the last P[oin]t of the narrow part the channel lies
SE – Then ahead you have 3 islands looking at first like one – As
you near the point opposite them they open out. Off that point
20   sand-bank runs over to the islands – go over it XXV –
Then a wide bight of the main shore is entered – on the
P[or]t side many islands presenting varied aspects from different
places. –
The general direction is NE$\frac{1}{2}$N about

25   # [40]

XXV –
Keep pretty well on the main shore watching for snags all
along –
On the port side extensive sandbanks – partly visible but mostly
30   covered at $\frac{1}{2}$ F[ull] W[ater]. Both shores heavily timbered with
dense undergrowth –

After sighting a long island and following it for some time you enter a NbyE. reach: then you enter a narrow pass[a]^{ge} between two islands NEbyE.

At the end of short passage islands in sight again and the river broadens out – 5

[41]

XXVI

A broad stretch where the course is about NE$^1/_2$E. All islands seen from the broad passage are now shut together into one.

XXVI 10

Entering another broad expansion of the river follow cautiously the courses set on the chart XXVI

V[i]ll[a]ge of Ikongo – Bad –

X[X]VII

Rounding the next 2 points there is another broad stretch com- 15 paratively free of sandb[an]ks

Steer from p[oin]^t to p[oin]^t

[42]

XXVII

on the main shore having always the Islands on your P[or]t 20 hand. –

General direction about NE. –

Main shore less thickly overgrown now – Islands all heavily timbered

After passing Lower Mission Point a small bay with stones in it. 25 Beaches colored red.

After passing 2 more points you sight the Am[erican] Mission in the bottom of a small bight

Hardly vis[i]ble. A big dead tree marks it exactly

[43] 30

II. Part
in N[or]^{th} Lat[itu]^{de}
from Equator to Bangala –

[44]

Charts in N[or]th Lat[itu]^{de}
$\overline{\text{Saturday} - 16\text{th Aug}^{\text{th}}\,[\textit{sic}].\ 1890\ -}$
$7^{\text{h}}.30^{\text{m}}$

5   Left Equator – follow the bank. Short distance round the first
point pass State Station –
River narrowed by islands. App[arent]^{ly} no sandbanks.
After passing the 2^d point the next reach broadens out –
Courses – NNE – NE and ENE.
10 After passing a point with tall trees you open out a reach about
E
A low point of land without trees bearing east marks the
appr[oa]^{ch} of Berouki R[iver].
The other bank of the Berouki

[45]

15

I.N.
is covered with forest growth –
Two sm[all] islands mark the entrance of the south arm of the
delta –
20 Steering about NE close to two small islands to port of you you
app[roa]^{ch} the point of the second arm of the Berouki delta –
Steer close to it pass[a]^g[e] over 3 f[a]th[oms]: the next reach
being NbyW very nearly.
Soon another branch of the delta is passed. Very narrow.
25 The NbyW reach ends at a low point after pass[in]^g a sm[all]
clearing and a one limbed tree – Pass small river

II N.   The next reach opens on about the same width; two small
islands facing the bend. Direction Nth

[46]

30 II. N.
River perhaps a little wider in this reach – The same appearance
of the banks – Dense growth of bushes and not very tall trees of a
dark green tint. – On the port side S[and]–B[ank] visible before
reach. Point. After passing the point a straight reach due North –
35 not very long.

$\frac{2}{3}\underline{\text{ds}}$ up pass over the S[and]–B[ank] – Sound[in]^{gs} in 2.1. fath[oms] & 4 feet. Steer right in shore minding the snags – Snags to be looked out for all the way here.

Rounding the point by a fine large tree & then 2 palms enter a short reach N.b[y].E – 5

After a point another long reach N.b[y].E. Some small islands open out on the port side –

[47]

II N (A).

Long reach to a curved point. Great quantity of dangerous snags 10 along the starb[oar]$^{\underline{d}}$ shore – Follow the slight bend of the shore with caution –

The middle of the channel is a S[and]–B[ank] – always covered.

The more northerly of the 2 islands has its lower end bare of trees covered with grass a light green low bushes. Then a low flat 15 and the upper end is timbered with light trees of a darker green tint

A long sandbank unc[overe]$^{\underline{d}}$ at $^1/_2$ Full [Water] stretches in to the S[ou]th[war]$^{\underline{d}}$. No passage inside the islands –

After rounding the point 20

[48]

II N (A).

a broad reach opens out towards NNE.

On the port side some small islands. – Starboard shore makes a great sweep to the next point – 25

The middle of this expansion of the river is fouled by extensive sands always covered (Koch).

Follow the bend of the shore keeping pretty well in but not to brush the bank.

Both shores uniform dark green forest. When nearing the limit 30 point of the reach you will close with some sm[all] islands – Leave them to port. S[and] B[ank] between the islands and the point – Keeping to starboard you get

[49]

III. N.
over it in 2.1 fath[oms].
Broad bend follows.
5 The direction of the short reach being NNE –
In the bend itself extensive sandbank to be left to port side –
Patches on this bank uncovered at ¹/₂ F[ull] water. –
The channel is pretty wide; there is no necessity in shaving the
starboard bank to[o] close –
10 After this a straight long reach on N¹/₂E bearing
Keep nearly in the middle but more to starboard – St[arboar]$^{\underline{d}}$
side islands divided by very narrow channels on

[50]

III N
15 port app[a]r[en]^{tly} one island only –
Usual app[earan]$^{\underline{ce}}$ of dense vegetation dow[n] to water's edge.
Nth end sm[all] S[and] B[an]k 2 f[a]th[oms] at the Nth end sharp
bend and then broad sweep – NbyE to NEbyN and N. –
To starb[oar]$^{\underline{d}}$ wide branch dividing islands before mentionned
20 [sic] from m[ai]^{n} land.
IV N
Next reach NNE nearly – follow the starb[oar]$^{\underline{d}}$ side now M[ai]^{n}
L[an]$^{\underline{d}}$ river broad – same app[earan]$^{\underline{ce}}$ on Starb[oar]^{d} side past
a little narrow branch opening island again.
25 This reach ends like the last by a straight shore across its upper
end where there is a

[51]

IV N
[word missing] of triangular expansion.
30 Next reach nearly North –
– After passing the limit point reach nearly north. –
A small double island green on the Starb[oar]$^{\underline{d}}$ side.
After this first more islands open up with pretty broad channels
between, through which the back shore can be V.N. seen – River

very broad here. All the islands are laying on a line of bearing about NbyE from the last point. – Point ahead on a bearing $\frac{1}{2}$ a point more northerly

[52]

[Sketch of the river showing large and small islands with a line marking 5
the channel.]

[53]

V. N. –
Many large snags along the shores of the islands. –
Bush & trees to the water's edge –   10
After passing a narrow island take the channel where there is a small islet with a conspicuous tree in the middle of it
This channel is at first NE then gradually sweeps up to NbyE. and narrows greatly.
After coming out of it you enter a broad expanse with an islet   15
about East and two larger islands with passage between about NNE

[54]

[A sketch representing a reach of the river with the channel marked through several islands with the directions 'NE' and 'NNE' and the words 'big tree' written at the upper end of the sketch.]   20

[55]

V N.
This expanse is bounded to the Eastward by the M[ai][n] Land.
Heavy sandb[an]ks show between the further Northern and the upper eastern islands   25
The passage is narrow mostly NNE with a slight easterly bend on its upper end nearly NEbyN – : The main land is seen right across when coming out to the N[orthw]ard
Passage clear.

[56]

VI N.

M[ai]^n Land runs nearly N and S. Almost oppo[si]^{te} the Is[lan]$^{\underline{d}}$ Pass[a]$^{\underline{ge}}$ there is a wooding place.

5   Rounding the Nth point of the first straight stretch there is a L$^{\underline{d}}$ elbow and then again a straight Nth stretch.

To Port there is 3 islands on the bend and another long island further up with some more behind it.

On M[ai]^n Shore after passing a dead stem with a few palms
10   growing near it there is a point with a rocky ledge off it

[57]

VI N.

The northern expansion of this expansion is perceived with islets and islands. The course is between these and the M[ai]^n
15   L[an]$^{\underline{d}}$. – Off the m[ai]^n shore there are rocky ledges under water in several places.

Rocks when the little N[orth]$^{\underline{ern}}$ islet bears North going along the shore. Many villages on this shore

Leaving all the islands on the Portside cross the mouth of the
20   Loulanga R[iver] and steer along M[ai]n shore the reach lying about NbyW^1/$_2$W. –

It presents a narrow appearance.

[58]

[*The first of seven continuing sketches (others are at 61, 63–65, 67*
25   *and 69) of the Lulanga river passage. A sketch of a reach of the Congo*
with the directions 'N' and 'NNW'. The river channel is marked between
a 'shallow S[and] B[ank]' on the port side, sketches of islands and a
starboard shore marked 'grassy plain with large trees on the bank' (see
p. 187).]

30   ## [59]

Loulanga – R[iver] –
and French Factory –
Direction NE – first reach –

Entering, islet to port – Keep mod[era]^te dist[ance] from star[boar]^d shore

River turns northerly –

To starb[oar]^d Low circular island – passage round – In this back channel is the factory

Approaching landing mind the stones – High bank make fast to a tree there – small, bad land[in]^g place –

Arr[ived] at F[rench] F[actory] 8^h 15^m

[60]

VII N Left the F[rench] F[actory] 12^h45^m

(The back island passage through <u>Lulanga</u>).

Leaving the F[ren]^ch F[acto]^ry steer NNE when clear of round islet facing it and then NNW to enter the narrow channel between two wooded Is[lan]^ds. Lulanga left on the starb[oar]^d side. Extensive sandbanks to port of you. Pass over in 2 fath[oms] or perhaps 9 feet at ½ full water

– The first reach – narrow – about N.b[y].W.

Keep in the middle.

A short bend Nb[y]E.

[61]

↕ N^th VII. The back passage

[*The sketch of the Lulanga river passage continues with the boat's course designated by a broken line marked 'NNW', 'NWbyN' and 'N', with two soundings in fathoms of 2 and 2. The port side is marked 'S[and] B[ank]', 'grass bank', 'Bush' and 'trees'; the starboard bank is marked 'grassbank'.*]

[62]

VII

The next reach is about NWbyN –

A straight due North –

A long bend. Come over to P[or]t side – snags almost in the middle of passage. –

A reach due N^th.

Another stretch NbyE –
Pass channel, to starb[oar]^d leading to Baringu – sand beach
facing it stretch towards NbyW Water shallows to 9 & 7 feet

[63–65]

5   [*Three consecutive pages continue the sketch of the Lulanga river passage. The dotted line representing the route of the* Roi des Belges
*is marked 'N', 'N', 'Nb[y]E', 'Nb[y]W', 'NE', 'NNE', 'NE', 'NbyE'
and 'NNE'. The port side is marked 'grassb[an]k', 'Bush', 'Sm[all]
beach', 'Grass', 'grass'; the starboard side is marked 'Snags', 'To
10   Baringu', 'Grass', 'Swampy', 'Swamp grass' and 'Highbushed point'.
Time required to negotiate passage: '2^h 30^m'.*]

[66]

VI –
A Reach to NE follows. – grassy banks – off port bank sand
15   shallows –
After rounding that point channels branch off – follow the more
easterly small islet in it.
A long straight about NbyE^1/$_2$E
Passage broadens out with islands coming in sight

20   ## [67]

[*The penultimate sketch of the Lulanga passage, with a dotted line
indicating the channel around several islands drawn in mid-stream.
Time designated on the port side with arrows pointing to a small island
in the centre of the river indicate '3.^{h}30^m' to reach that point. A 'S[and]-
25   B[ank]' enters from the starboard side. Direction is 'N^1/$_2$E'; and river
depth is indicated by three soundings in fathoms – 2, 2 and 2.*]

[68]

Steering for a small island bearing Nth leave it on St[arboar]$^{\underline{d}}$
side –
30   Towards the upper end of it cross over to port avoiding snags
follow the Port shore. –

In the elbow must go close in to avoid extensive S[and]B[an]k
stretching right in from the island –
Before passing the two small islets get soundings in 2 fath[oms]
and less. – Keep well in shore. Mind the snags –
A Broad straight NbyE nearly   5

[69]

[*The final sketch of the Lulanga passage. The channel is marked 'NbyE*
to NNE'. On the port side is marked 'Snags'. Within the river banks
two small islands are sketched, and the words 'S[and] B[ank]' and
'S[and]-B[an]ks' are written, including the fathom markings 2, 2, 2, 10
1, 1, 2, 2, 2 and 2.]

[70]

VII
When following it must keep close over to port avoiding however
sunken trees –   15
Passing over tails of the great sandb[an]k with less than one
fath[om] up to 2 fath[oms] – soundings.
Arriving at the end of this straight cross over on a NE course
and enter the main route up the river
_____   20
End of Lulanga Pass[age]

[71]

Main River [*An elongated arrow points NNE.*]

[72]

VII N   25
Long NE$^{1}/_{2}$N reach; pretty straight – Island to port in a bend
of the shore – Off it 2 S[and]B[an]ks on opposite shore with 2
fath[oms] at $^{1}/_{2}$ full. Steering along the starb[oar]^{d} bank many
snags stranded well off the shore –
The point closing this reach on the Port Side has a high tree 30
on it

After passing this there is a broad straight channel at the end
of which a point is seen. –
The Broad channel

[73]

5   runs NbyW[ester]$^{\underline{ly}}$ –
Sandbanks. – Take the narrow channel
Directly inside, camp[in]^g place. Indifferent wood –
VIII. N.
A narrow reach about NEbyN –
10   Left camp at south end of it at 6^h a.m.
Curve to the NNE and a little broader reach.

[74]

VIII N
This reach expands in a NEbyE direction – to Port several islands
15   and a small islet bushy on one end, low on the other – follow the
M[ai]^n Land on the Starb[oar]$^{\underline{d}}$ side – Great many snags lining
the shore
On the Port side probably shallow water (K[och]).
At the end of this broad long stretch appear 2 islands –
20   The little islet to port has a long S[and]-B[an]k on its southern
end
The main shore runs

[75]

VIII N.
25   North-Easterly.
The next point to port after pass[in]^g the islet has an extensive
S[and]-B[ank] uncovered in places at $^1/_2$ F[ull water] stretching
away along shore to next sm[all] island – from here an island
appears in the middle of river beari[n]^g <u>NNE</u>.
30   Steering nearly for it after passing second islet to port the river
opens out to starboard into islands laying NE&SW nearly or little
more Easterly

[76]

VIII N –
Steer for the middle island about NbyE$\frac{1}{2}$E. Then into the broad
reach on its port side leaving it to starb[oar]$^{\underline{d}}$
Taking this route the M[ai]^n Land of the right bank is left and   5
course taken to Left or north bank.
(This is not the usual course not safe to follow at less than $\frac{1}{2}$
full water).

IX N.

– Keep a little nearer to the middle island than to the islands   10
on your Port side

[77]

IX N
Proceeding cautiously must feel your way in 12 to 8 feet water.
The shore on the port side is the north Bank of the river. –   15
Snags along but not much off. After passing two little islands
you sight a dead trunk of a tree and villages begin. – In many
places cut bank. – Excellent wooding places up to the point and
in the great bend – (10^{h}50)
Left 11.30   20
Rounding the 1st point after the dead tree you open the 2^d
point bearing a$^{\underline{b[ou]t}}$ NE where this reach ends – To starb[oar]$^{\underline{d}}$
seve-

[78]

IX N   25
ral islands of which two are prominent. – Land backing them in
a semicircle at a great distance – M[ain]^n Land on the Sth Bank
not visible. –
The river very broad here.
Follow close in the bend as there is a large sandbank between   30
the island and the main shore.
Nearing the P[oin]t sounding in 12 to 10 feet (at $\frac{1}{2}$ F[ull]
W[ater]).
Mind a very bad snag nearly off the point

After a bit of straight Shore and a small poin[t] ab[ou]^{t} ENE open out

[79]

X.N.

5 2 small islets come in sight. – Steer along the m[ai]^{n} shore. When pass[in]^{g} the islets much caution and good look out – Sandbanks.

10 [*A sketch of the river, showing two islands mid-stream with a 'S[and]B[ank]' extending from the northernmost, and the caption below the island 'Cov[ered]* $^{1}/_{2}$ *F[ull water] less 3 feet'. A 'NE' course is marked with soundings in feet: 10, 10, 10, 6, 6, 6, 6 and 6. 'Village' is recorded on the port side.*]

[80]

[*A sketch that has been erased and is indecipherable appears here.*]

[81]

15 X – N –

Following the bend – When approaching the P[or]^{t} SandB[an]k extends from islet to st[arboar]^{d}. A snag stranded on outer edge – Pass between the shore and the snag. Another [Sand]–B[an]k on the point and snags off it. Must steer very close 20 to the bank which is steep to –

River expands broadly here – The general direction of the main shore to the end of the expansion is ENE nearly. –

For some considerable distance the starb[oar]^{d} shore is low & grassy. After rounding the shutting in point leave the broad

[82]

25 XI N

reach and follow the main land by a narrower channel laying about NEbyN and turning towards the NE or more easterly still. Coming out of this channel again into the broad part a great number of 30 islands come in sight.

Steer carefully amongst sand bank watching for the edges –

– Cross over to the island and back to where 2^d village down is. At big clearing cross over again and enter another back passage – Sound[in]g^s in 10 to 6 feet. – Many snags

[83]

XII.   5
and some of them right in the fairway. –

Between a long low island and the main sandb[an]ks across with less than 6 feet water over them.

The passage rather intricate from islet N° 19. –

The North[er]^n end of that pass[a]^{ge} has a S[and]–B[an]k with   10
10–6 feet of water at $^1/_2$ F[ull] W[ater].

Coming out of it you follow a broad stretch on a NEbyE$^1/_2$E course (about) and then keep off the broad channel to the

[84]

XII N   15
NE between the M[ai]^n Land and an island –

Passage narrow – where it broadens 2 islets in the bend. One of them has a thin tall dead tree with one green branch on it. It looks like a flagstaff with a bough tied up to it at right angles

Steering in always keep closer to the main shore. – Good many   20
nasty snags all along

After passing the second of the 2 islets you may notice a third – Small – The main shore runs

[85]

XIIA. N.   25
NEbyE. on the Starb[oar]^d side many islands close together form an almost contin[u]ous shore. –

The channel is not deep from 10 to 6 feet of water some little distance up after passing the 2^d of two islets.

After that no soundings in 12 feet. –   30

Several small islets on the starb[oar]^d side –

On the islands on the starb[oar]^d side good many

[86]

[An indistinct sketch – two square figures presumably representing islands in an enclosed U-shaped image – perhaps images of the two islets referred to above.]

5

[87]

XIIA N.

dead palms

Further on a sandbank right across – 6 – 10 feet

At large clearing stopped. Firewood – snags –

10   XIII Left at 6^h 30^m

A straight reach NE^1/$_2$N.

When approaching the P[oin]t (to Port) ending the straight steer over to the other side to avoid sandbank

On starb[oar]^d side small islets in the bights of the shore which

15   is composed of long islands overlapping each

[88]

XIII N

other and appearing like one land when steaming up the river. –

20   Round in back again in 9 feet of water. –

Following the main shore care should be taken to avoid snags which are stranded right along it in great quantities.

2d reach before coming to end of it cross over to the island

20 – Right close in to the upp[e]^r end – in 9 to 5 feet –

25   Sandbank off the main shore –

[89]

XIII N

Pass close point on starb[oar]^d side and steer to leave next island on starb[oar]^d side nearly in midchannel. – Sandbank along the

30   M[ai]^n shore – Cross over to upper end of vill[a]^{ge} clearing. –

Follow the shore – Opposite sm[a]ll beach in isl[an]^d to star$^{b[oard]}$ sound[in]^{gs} 9 feet –

After passing this, steer off the M[ai]^n shore and steer across in 9 to 5 feet to leave the small islet to port. Keep nearly in the middle when entering the pass[a]$\underline{ge}$

Then steer rather over to starb[oar]^d shore (big island) Snags –

Coming out of the back channel you sight a very [word missing]

[90]

XIII N.

clearing bearing Nth. – Steer a little below it passing over 10 feet sound[in]^{gs} – When nearing the bank water deepens

Follow the cut bank pretty close – Safe. no snags there. –

Half round reach follows in a EbyN direction. Forest. Snags again. Keep a little off. – a very small creek hardly noticeable before coming to the closing P[oin]t on P[or]^t side sound[in]gs 10 feet.

Another bend where you keep nearly in the middle 10 feet s[oun]d[in]gs in one place –

This bend terminates in a NE direction.

There is now a double chan-

[91]

XIV

nel – one broad about EbyN another narrow nearly NE –

Leave the island to star$\underline{b}$[oard] and follow its inner shore to take the narrow p[assa]$\underline{ge}$ Sound[in]$\underline{gs}$ 9. to 5 feet

This passage is between the M[ai]^n Land on portside and 2 islands on starb[oar]$\underline{d}$ where the 1st Is[lan]$\underline{d}$ finishes there is a sandbank –

Steering close in to the islands in s[ou]nd[ing]s 10 to 5 feet – Then over to M[ai]^n shore and back again – All the way about 7 feet of water. Less in places

After leaving this narrow passage and rounding the point another similar

[92]

XIV

passage presents itself – Keep nearly in the middle where 7 to 9 feet water are obtained at $^1/_2$ F[ull] W[ater]. –

Another narrow passage presenting the same features only a little narrower – About 10 feet of water – Passage ends on an Eastern bearing. –

Coming out of this last the main stream is entered – River
5 broadens. This is the upper end

[93]

XV
of the northern bank passage

UNCOLLECTED ESSAYS

THE SILENCE OF THE SEA
1909

SOME FIVE YEARS AGO – time passes and the sea alone
remains unchanged – I had the pleasure of contributing to this
very page of *The Daily Mail* a paper on the theme of "overdue" and 5
"missing" ships – a record of feelings remembered in tranquillity,
very personal in tone, and illustrated by the instance of a certain
narrow escape of my own. It was but a subjective piece of writing,
a bit of prose, saved, if saved at all, by its sincerity. No great merit
that. No man who has lived for many years with and by the sea, 10
and even in certain measure *for* the sea, could be willfully false to
that character-moulding element and continue to live on in the
hope of saving his soul. Yet, true as it was, remorselessly true to the
writer's own sensations, the paper was not very instructive; and as
to "actuality," in the journalistic sense of that word, it had, I am 15
thankful to say, none at all at that particular time.

This is not to say that there has ever passed a year of this or any
other era in which some ships, big or little, have not been posted
as "overdue" – posted as "missing". So it was in the beginning,
and so it shall be as long as the science and craft of navigation 20
are not lost to the world – or out of the world. Those two leaden
words of doubt and resignation belong to the very realm of the
ocean, which, conquered as it may be to its innermost depths
and most secret recesses by the curiosity and hardihood of untold
generations, is not to be tamed altogether by the ingenuity of 25
inventive mankind.

Thus, as I have said before, there is no year in which ships are not
posted as "overdue" and given up as "missing". These words have
a perpetual sinister actuality. But it does not often happen that
an "overdue" ship looms large in the eyes of the anxious world, 30
a ghostly craft growing indistinct in the mist of an uncertain fate,
tragic with the freight of hopes and dread.

Many hearts in two hemispheres are straining with intolerable
anxiety for some sight of the steamship *Waratah.* Her looming
form grows more ghostly from hour to hour – though, of course, 35

"never say die". We on shore should whisper the precept to ourselves, since we may be certain that the responsible men on board
would be acting on it from the first moment of trouble to the very
last moment of existence. But the ship has been overdue now for,
5 roughly speaking, six weeks. And this is the sort of anxiety that
does not grow stale.

All the world is in possession of the only sea facts which are
certain: the ship left for a short coastwise run along the curve of
the southern seaboard of the African continent; she left her port
10 of call in threatening weather, which developed quickly into a very
heavy gale from the westward, and therefore generally adverse to
her on all the courses she had to steer while pursuing her way
parallel to the contour of the African shore.

And she has been six weeks overdue! The sea does not give up
15 all its secrets to the prying anxiety of men. The anguish of hearts
is nothing to it. It is not tamed enough to surrender what terrors
have been left to it by the progress of science and the records of
experience, by patient surveys and patent sounding machines, by
the alliance of iron and fire, by the accumulated knowledge of
20 a multitude of seamen, and by the perfect riveting of water-tight
bulkheads. No. Not tamed enough yet, not sufficiently stripped of
its robe of mystery. Within the rent and tattered folds of the sombre garment there may lurk yet the form of some inconceivable
disaster. But – never say die!

25 The first "missing" record in the history of the passenger service
was, I believe, the paddle steamship *President*, bound from England
to New York in the early 'forties. She was supposed to have run
full tilt against an iceberg. That is, very likely, the true explanation
of her disappearance. She must have gone down like a stone.

30 This is one of the dangers of the sea; yet within the recollection of my seagoing life the steamship *Arizona*, one of the ocean
greyhounds of the middle 'eighties, repeated the supposed performance of the *President*. There can be no doubt that she *did* run
against an iceberg, because she lived to tell the tale and exhibit
35 her wonderfully smashed bows. Verily the water-tight bulkhead
has robbed the ocean of some of its terrors. But, considered in
relation to the fate of the *Waratah*, this danger of the sea, peculiar
mainly to the North Atlantic and to the far southern water routes
of the globe, may be dismissed as inconceivable. It *is* inconceiv-
40 able that a treacherous floe should have come all the way from

the Polar ice-cap to fish for steamers on the African coast – and in
the dead of winter too!

Water-logged wrecks and uncharted rocks are among the dangers of the sea. But water-logged wrecks are only to be found in
the tracks of the timber trade, and are very rare now, because   5
the corpse of an iron ship, even if stuffed full of planks, generally
manages to sink out of the way of the living in a very short time.
As to rocks, the coast skirted by the *Waratah* is perfectly charted,
if very rocky in many places.

The fog is the most wicked accomplice of all the dangers of the   10
sea; but we know that there was no fog. There was a gale. What
a seaman would call very heavy weather. Against this were pitted
the seamanlike qualities of the men who manned her and the
seaworthiness of the ship – product of the science, the skill, the
honesty of other men whose hands drafted her lines, put together   15
the hull and engines, and launched her upon the sea.

In those matters the writer can depend upon the testimony
of his senses. One of the dangers of the ocean is the seas. I use
that word in the sense of waves, a term which does not come
glib to a seaman's tongue and refuses to slip easily under a pen   20
accustomed to record the memories of a time far removed from
the modes of thought and speech common to the shore. On the
edge of the Agulhas Bank the seas, driven by a westerly gale, are
terrible in their steepness. In sailor's phrase, they come at one
like a wall. In the month of August of the year 1884 the writer   25
was involved, on the very path which the *Waratah* should have
pursued, in a case which missed narrowly being the case of a
missing ship. The vessel on board of which he served went on
her beam ends and remained lying thus on her side for thirty
hours among these steep seas, whose menacing aspect and vicious   30
rush are not to be forgotten. It was a long-drawn experience, an
agonisingly prolonged opportunity to "never say die". I suppose
we never said it (from the habit and tradition of restraint in that
professional matter), though we certainly believed that the time
had come for us to do that thing which is never to be spoken of   35
as long as one's ship remains afloat.

Yet dangerous in character as the seas can grow when driven
by the headlong winds of that part of the world, it is not to be
suggested for a moment that they could by their sheer weight and
fury ever overwhelm a steamship like the *Waratah* handled by an   40

experienced seaman, not deeply loaded, of the size and build to
defy the worst the sea has been known to do. And should she by a
most improbable mischance have become disabled in her engine-
room at the height of the gale there are resources in seamanship
5 to meet such a grave eventuality.

But there is another steamer overdue in the same quarter
of the globe; and the mind of a seaman brooding over the fate of
ships and the dangers of the sea cannot overlook the possibility of
collision.

10 We have seen lately in the case of a big Atlantic liner that this,
the worst danger of the modern sea, is robbed of much of its
deadlines by the invention of water-tight bulkheads. Yet more than
once both colliding ships have been known to sink at one stroke.
And a collision in heavy weather, even if not immediately fatal to
15 either, is bound to put both ships in extreme jeopardy, for no ship
thus wounded, and with one or more of her compartments full of
water, can face with the buoyant courage of a good sea boat the
stress of the gale and the blows of the assaulting seas.

Reluctantly the possibility of this very thing having happened
20 must be faced – the combination of two dangers of the sea. But
he who remembers the tales passing from lips to lips in the world
of great waters, tales of ships lost and found again, all these tales
belonging to the tradition of the wonders of the sea, will never
say die. Never. At first in hope, afterwards perhaps because men's
25 grave silence is the only dignified answer upon the cruel mysteries
of the sea.

And, after all, ships have been lost not only for weeks on this
small and stormy world of ours, but for months – whole months
strung on end together to the number of three and more. One
30 remembers brave tales, wonderful instances too long to tell of
here; but whose moral is that we must never say die.

AUTHOR'S NOTE TO *YOUTH*
AND GASPAR RUIZ
1920

"YOUTH" was not my first contribution to "Maga." It was the
second. But that story marks the first appearance in the
world of the man Marlow, with whom my relations have grown
very intimate in the course of years. The origins of that gentleman
(nobody as far as I know had ever hinted that he was anything
but that) – his origins have been the subject of some literary
speculation of, I am glad to say, a friendly nature.
    One would think that I am the proper person to throw a light on
the matter; but in truth I find that it isn't so easy. It is pleasant to
remember that nobody had charged him with fraudulent purposes
or looked down on him as a charlatan; but apart from that he was
supposed to be all sorts of things: a clever screen, a mere device,
a "personator," a familiar spirit, a whispering "dæmon." I myself
have been suspected of a meditated plan for his capture.
    That is not so. I made no plans. The man Marlow and I came
together in the casual manner of those health-resort acquaintances which sometimes ripen into friendships. This one has
ripened. For all his assertiveness in matters of opinion he is not an
intrusive person. He haunts my hours of solitude, when, in silence,
we lay our heads together in great comfort and harmony; but as
we part at the end of a tale I am never sure that it may not be for
the last time. Yet I don't think that either of us would care much to
survive the other. In his case, at any rate, his occupation would be
gone and he would suffer from that extinction, because I suspect
him of some vanity. I don't mean vanity in the Solomonian sense.
Of all my people he's the one that has never been a vexation to
my spirit. A most discreet, understanding man . . . .
    Even before appearing in book form "Youth" was very well
received. It lies on me to confess at last, and this is as good a
place for it as another, that I have been all my life – all my two
lives – the spoiled adopted child of Great Britain and even of the
Empire; for it was Australia that gave me my first command. I

break out into this declaration not because of a lurking tendency to megalomania, but, on the contrary, as a man who has no very notable illusions about himself. I follow the instincts of vain-glory and humility natural to all mankind. For it can hardly be denied 5 that it is not their own deserts that men are most proud of, but rather of their prodigious luck, of their marvellous fortune: of that in their lives for which thanks and sacrifices must be offered on the altars of the inscrutable gods.

The story "Gaspar Ruiz" is not a piece of personal experience 10 like "Youth." It is truly fiction, by which I do not mean that it is merely invented but that it is truly imagined from hints of things that have really happened and of people that have really existed at that time, in that locality and under those special conditions of life. It can be easily understood that for that sort of work which is of 15 course of a creative (not reminiscent) nature, a certain knowledge of the epoch, the outcome of reading and mental assimilation, was necessary. I need not say that such knowledge as I had was used throughout with a scrupulous regard to the truth of it. No incident was introduced arbitrarily but only as a necessary touch 20 in the general picture. In this arrangement consists the art of story-telling as distinguished from the style. My suggestion for "Gaspar Ruiz" I found in an old book of travels published in 1830, both as to his personal appearance and as to certain facts and adventures of his life. The real name of the man was Benavides 25 and he was really for a time chief of a band of Partisans during the Independence War in South America, in the years 1822–24. He *did* change sides, his wife *was* betrayed to one of his enemies, as in the story, together with his little girl, and his character really *was* audacious, ruthless and enterprising. He was really visited by 30 the officers of a British man-of-war in reference to the release of some captured Englishmen. But all this information was contained perhaps in less than a full page of the book. I had to imagine the motives of actions, the various states of peoples' minds and the personal characters of all the persons involved in the tale. 35 Yet no incident or touch of character has been introduced for the sake of its mere sensational value, but only in order to give a true presentation of the feelings, perplexities and passions roused in human breasts by a sequence of certain events which, in the strictest truth, might have happened, and for the most part *did* 40 actually happen, at that time and place.

The episode of the gun fired from the man's back is a reminiscence of my boyhood's reading. Much later in life I heard of it again as an undoubted fact. I am assured that, supposing the gun an old brass four-pounder, considering the exceptional physique of Gaspar Ruiz and the use of such a comparatively mild explosive 5 as the gunpowder of that time, it is not impossible.

INTRODUCTORY NOTE TO
A HUGH WALPOLE ANTHOLOGY
1921

THIS IS NOT the place nor the occasion to enter into a pro-
5   founder appreciation of Mr Hugh Walpole's work. An anthology should speak for itself, and the anthology so intelligently compiled, within its limits, in this little book is bound to offer a sample
of literary shade for every reader's sympathy. Sophistication is the
only shade that does not exist in Mr Walpole's prose.
10   Of the general soundness of Mr Walpole's work I am perfectly
convinced. Let no modern and malicious mind take this declaration for a left-handed compliment. Mr Walpole's soundness is
not of conventions but of convictions; and even as to these let
no one suppose that Mr Walpole's convictions are old-fashioned.
15 He is distinctly a man of his time; and it is just because of that
modernity, informed by a sane judgment of urgent problems and
a wide and deep sympathy with all mankind, that we look forward
hopefully to the growth and increased importance of his work. In
his style, so level, so consistent, Mr Hugh Walpole does not seek
20 so much for novel as for individual expression; and this search,
this ambition so natural to an artist, is often rewarded by success.
Old and young interest him alike and he treats both with a sure
touch and in the kindest manner. I cannot here refer specifically
to passages contained in this excellent selection. In each of them
25 we see Mr Walpole grappling with the truth of things spiritual and
material with his characteristic earnestness, and in the whole of
them we can discern other characteristics of this acute and sympathetic explorer of human nature: his love of adventure and the
serious audacity he brings to the task of recording the changes
30 of human fate and the moments of human emotion, in the quiet
backwaters or in the tumultuous open streams of existence.

FOREWORD TO
LANDSCAPES OF CORSICA AND IRELAND BY A. S. KINKEAD
1921

IN THIS EXHIBITION of landscapes from two islands, of which one has a hold on the very heart of the artist and the other has appealed irresistibly to her artistic perceptions, will be found not alone complete fidelity to the natural features of the land but also the expression of the inner character of things which demands interpretation and is, so to speak, personal to the interpreter.

The first thing suggested by this collection is that Corsica is not a subject for every painter. After a short visit in the far-off days of boyhood, on revisiting it again this year that vague thought had become an absolute conviction.

No! Corsican landscape is not everybody's subject. It is dangerous by the apparent facility of its Alpine type which, like certain types of very fine faces, lends itself to commonplace, as if it were a mask rather than the envelope of the soul. Nothing could be made more banal by the exercise of mere skill or even by a vision not frankly and delicately personal than snow-crags, tormented rock-faces, fantastic pinnacles bordered by a blue sea. The truth of Corsican landscape is a matter of deeper vision; its features do not impose themselves by mere grandeur of desolation or exceptionality of form – things easy to capture on the canvas. Yet all those things are there! But in this series of pictures something more has been captured, something extremely subtle, composed of amenity and ruggedness which may be felt obscurely by any one but which this artist, so faithful in her technique has rendered with imaginative and touching insight. These pictures, so full of light and truth, contain all the wildness and all the transparent suavity, *suavità de aiere*, which give its unique charm to the Corsican landscape.

So much for Corsica. As to the other, her native island, there must be added to her individual and appreciative vision of beauty

179

as found in the world at large, the deeper sense of pathos born
of love, something on which the emotions of a non-native are not
perhaps capable of pronouncing a worthy appreciation. An artist
who had perceived the inner truth of a foreign landscape by the
5 power of imaginative sympathy could not fail to render still more
finely the spirit of her native land shining upon its outward face;
to respond more intimately still to the tie of old association, an
association going back into the soil, an association that, like all
manifestations of inherited personality, is really unanalysable in
10 its profounder appeal.

FOREWORD TO *BRITAIN'S LIFE-BOATS: THE STORY OF A CENTURY OF HEROIC SERVICE* BY A. J. DAWSON

1923

5

N O   V O L U N T A R Y   O R G A N I S A T I O N for a humane end has the reputation and the prestige of the Royal National Life-boat Institution, a clearer record of efficiency and, one may say, of brotherly devotion. But it is only those who have followed the 10 sea for their livelihood that know with what confidence the Life-boat Service is looked upon by those for whose benefit it has been founded by the generosity of people who live ashore. Myself a British seaman, with something like twenty years' service, I can testify to that feeling, and to the comfort the existence of Life- 15 boat Stations, with their ever ready crews, brings to the hearts of men on board ships of all nations approaching our shores in dangerous weather. I can bear witness to our unshakable belief in the Life-boat organisation and to our pride in the achievements of our fellow seamen, who, husbands and fathers, would go out 20 on a black night without hesitation to dispute our homeless fate with the angry seas. I remember well how affectionately we looked at those white and blue boats of characteristic shape into which (through a slot in the deck) we used to drop a little silver on paying-off days; feeling that we could do but little in that way, but 25 daring to hope that we, too, serving the overseas commerce of this generous country, were not upon the whole unworthy of the assistance given us for the preservation of the property under our care and for the saving of our obscure lives.

Tasman's journal (which ~~had been~~ *was* published not a very long time ago) gives us a ~~fine~~ idea *of their perplexing difficulties. The early navigators had* ~~had no means of~~ ~~ascertaining~~ their exact position on the globe. They could calculate their latitudes but ~~the~~ *the problem of* longitude was ~~always~~ a matter *which bewildered* ~~of~~ *minds and often falsified their judgment. It was a matter of guess work.* Tasman and his officers ~~when they met on board~~ the Heemskirk anchored in Murderer's Bay to consider their further course in the light of their instructions, did not ~~~~ know where *any* ~~~~ *of the problematic places named in their instructions were* ~~~~ neither did they ~~~~ *where they themselves* were. ~~~~ *Tasman might have* ~~~~ *in the end he decided to sail* sailed north or east, but ~~~~ between the two, and circling about ~~~~ returned to Batavia ~~~~ was ~~~~ received ~~~~ *told* ~~~~ by his employers the Governor General and the ~~~~ *Council in Batavia. Their final judgment was* ~~that Abel Tasman was a skilful navigator but that he had shown himself* "~~remiss~~" in his investigations and ~~~~ *that he left certain problems unsolved.* ~~~~ *We are told that Tasman did not expect this arm-chair criticism* ~~~~ *and indeed even it looks surprising to an unprejudiced mind. It was* *the voyage during which, amongst other things, he had discovered Tasmania* *the island by which his name lives on the charts, took first contact with* *N. Zealand (which was not seen again till 130 years afterward)* *sailed over many thousands of miles & uncharted seas bringing* *with him a journal which was of much value afterwards* *for his exploring successor. It may be he was*

[1] First typescript of 'Geography and Some Explorers', page 9

[2] Typescript of 'The *Torrens*: A Personal Tribute', page 3

Saturday 5th July. 94.
Left at 6.15. Morning cool, even
cold and very damp. Sky overcast.
by overcast. Gentle breeze from NE –
Road through a narrow plain –
up to R. Kwilu. Swift flowing
and deep 50yds wide – Passed in
canoe – After up and down very
steep hills intersected by deep
ravine – Main chain of heights
running mostly NW–SE or
N and at times. Stopped at
Manyamba – Camp place
bad – in a hollow – water very
indifferent. Tents set at 10¼
Section of to day's road
NNE ½ N dist 13 miles

To day's march –
direction NNE½N distce 13 miles

Saw another dead body lying
by the path in an attitude
of meditative repose. –
In the evening 3 women
of whom one albino passed
our camp – horrid chalky
white with pink blotches –
Red eyes. Red hair. features
very negroid and ugly –
Mosquitos. At night when
the moon rose heard shouts and
drumming in distant villages
Passed a bad night.

Monday. 28th

Left camp at 6.30 after
breakfasting with Mecha —
Road as first hilly. Steep
walking along the ridges of
hill chains with valleys on
both sides — The country more
open and there is much more
trees growing on large
clumps in the ravines. —
Passed Njungi and Camped
11ᵗʰ on the right bank of Ngoma
a rapid little river with
a rocky bed. Village on a
hill to the right. —

General direction 2.N.E.
Distance   14 miles
No sunshine. Gloomy cold day. Squall —

Tuesday – 29ᵗʰ

Off camp at 7ᵗʰ after a good night's
rest. Continuous ascent; rather easy
at first — Crossed worked ravines
& the river Lukanga by a — very
descent-bridge —
ahy. h Mas Mr.Gonetta. Ascending
a sick agent of the [Comp?] back
to Matadi — looking very well.
Had news from up the river — All
the steamers disabled. One
wrecked. — Country wooded —
At 10.30 Camped on Infwica —

General direction E.N.E
[Distance] 15 miles
Sun visible at 6.30. Very warm
day. —

[4] Entry for 'Monday. 28th', 'Tuesday – 29th', 'The Congo Diary', pages [24–5]

[5] 'XII Entrance to Kassai rather broad' and 'XII After passing Pt xx follow', 'Up-river Book', pages [21–2]

Dazed Scientific Investigator (who has been ordered horse exercise for his health). "WHERE AM I? WHAT'S HAPPENED? HAS SOME SILLY FOOL EXPLODED AN ATOM?"

[7] 'Dazed Scientific Investigator', *Punch, or The London Charivari*, 19 July 1922, page 67

THE TEXTS
AN ESSAY

A<small>FTER</small> C<small>ONRAD</small>'<small>S</small> <small>DEATH</small> on 3 August 1924, interest in publishing his uncollected work was expressed almost immediately. On 14 August, a representative of Chapman & Hall, a firm with no previous history of publishing the writer, sensed an opportunity, contacting J. B. Pinker & Sons, Conrad's literary agent, about publishing a volume of 'unfinished writings'.[1] The topic was discussed by Eric S. Pinker and Richard Curle, Conrad's de facto literary executor, certainly well before late August, when Curle mentioned he had 'copies of all the articles that will make up the Last Essays'.[2] For his part, Pinker, who was keenly aware of his late client's market value, wasted little time in beginning negotiations for this final collection of essays and reminiscences, and at the end of the month was already seeking permission from Thomas Beer to include Conrad's introduction to Beer's *Stephen Crane: A Study in American Letters* 'in a volume of Mr. Conrad's Essays which have not hitherto appeared in book form'.[3] Pinker had predicted publication of this volume for 1925,[4] but, to avoid glutting the market with posthumous work by Conrad, it was published in England in 1926, by J. M. Dent & Sons on 3 March and in America by Doubleday, Page & Company on 26 March.

Conrad's friend Richard Curle, who took on editing the collection, had in the interim seen various unpublished items into print, including *Suspense* (1925), left unfinished on Conrad's death.[5] At that time on the staff of the *Daily Mail*, he arranged for 'Legends' to appear in his newspaper on 15 August 1924, twelve days after the novelist's death, and a few days later negotiated with *The Times* to print 'The

---

[1] Chapman & Hall to Eric S. Pinker, 14 August 1924 (Berg).
[2] Richard Curle to Pinker, 29 August 1924 (Berg).
[3] Pinker's request is mentioned in a statement about rights to the essay; see Kellogg, Emery, Inness, Brown, & Cuthell to S. A. Everitt (Doubleday, Page & Company), 13 July 1926 (copy Yale-S).
[4] Pinker to J. M. Dent, 3 November 1924 (Berg).
[5] For the text of Conrad's will, see 'Conrad's Last Will and Testament', ed. Hans van Marle, *Documents*, pp. 245–51.

Unlighted Coast' for the first time. He continued to publish Conrad's literary remains even as he was gathering material for this volume: he placed 'A Glance at Two Books' in *T. P.'s & Cassell's Weekly* and the *Forum* (1925) and arranged for 'The Congo Diary' to appear in the *Blue Peter* (1925), the *Yale Review* (1926) and as a pamphlet (January 1926). These efforts not only kept Conrad's name before the public, but also fulfilled Curle's duties as executor in obtaining income for the writer's widow and sons, and ensured that copyright in unpublished items remained with the estate.[1]

Although not involved in the selection, revision or editing of this volume, Conrad had delegated authority to Curle years earlier to edit and market some of the essays brought together in it. The material ranges widely in subject matter and time, the earliest writing dating back to 1890, the last to 1924. It includes previously unpublished pieces (the second part of 'The Future of Constantinople' and the 'Memorandum') and a manuscript fragment found on Conrad's desk after his death ('Legends'). Curle's thematic arrangement possibly took its cue from *Notes on Life and Letters*, with its dual focus: *Last Essays* directs attention first to the sea – these writings comprising about half the book – then to literature (two essays on Stephen Crane and miscellaneous prefaces and reviews) and, lastly, to geopolitics, closing with 'The Congo Diary'. The present edition retains Curle's organization, but restores the complete record of Conrad's Congo experience, substituting for Curle's abridgement of 'The Congo Diary' the full text and adding 'Up-river Book'.

The history of *Last Essays* is distinct from the histories of its individual parts before Curle began to draw together the scattered pieces to make up a volume. (This textual situation thus closely resembles that of *Notes on Life and Letters* (1921), whose production Conrad himself oversaw during autumn 1920 and early 1921, and for which Curle helped to gather copy.) The discussion here is hence organized as follows: the history of the volume's publication in the first English and American editions and later printings is presented; editorial issues involving the volume as a whole are discussed, including general policies for the

---

[1] The concern about copyright is witnessed in the following: 'Can you tell me what has happened about the 2 unpublished articles, "The Unlighted Coast" & "Notes on Two Books"? I think the typescripts were both bought at the sale for U.S.A., & I am rather nervous lest the purchaser pirate them unless we are first in the field & obtain copyright' (Curle to Eric S. Pinker, 27 March 1925 (Berg)).

adoption of copy-texts and emendation; and, finally, each essay's composition and publication history is established and its textual situations
examined. The discussion of the individual essays follows the order of
the contents of the volume, not of writing and publication.

BOOK EDITIONS

CONRAD MENTIONED an eventual posthumous collection to his
literary agent as early as the spring of 1923,[1] but he made no real
plans for such a project, nor did he compose an 'Author's Note' in
anticipation of its eventual appearance. In the event, Curle wrote the
Introduction to *Last Essays*,[2] his title for this miscellaneous gathering,
during a voyage to New York in early October 1925, a trip undertaken
to discuss the book's publication with F. N. Doubleday, Conrad's American publisher, and to consult the manuscript of 'The Congo Diary' at
Harvard University.[3] Curle had long since made his selection of what
to include and had also decided upon the order of the volume's contents. He was apparently well advanced with (or had even finished)
providing Pinker with copy for the book, not a difficult task as he possessed a substantial collection of Conradiana. This may have occurred
on a piecemeal basis: for instance, he sent the introduction to Crane's
Red Badge of Courage in early December 1924, forwarded 'The Congo
Diary' in mid-February 1925 and posted a typescript of 'A Glance at
Two Books' in early March.[4] On the whole, his editing of the typescripts he had prepared was light, despite his stated policy as regards
punctuation when he read through G. Jean-Aubry's transcriptions for
his two-volume collection of Conrad's letters: 'These Letters, as in previous instances, have been very carefully punctuated by me. I hope all
my punctuation is having careful consideration, as very frequently it

---

[1] Conrad to Eric S. Pinker, 23 March 1923 (*Letters*, VIII, 59).
[2] More accurately, there are two versions of this text, Dent's and Doubleday's, the
Introduction being set, as variants establish, from different (now-lost) typescripts
and distinguished as well by house-styling. For a discussion, see the headnote to
Appendix A.
[3] He sailed on the *Mauretania* from Southampton on 3 October (Passenger Lists Leaving
UK, 1890–1960, BT27/1107/8, National Archives), arriving in New York on the 9th
(*New York Times*, 10 October 1925, p. 31). He returned to England on 3 November,
arriving in Southampton on the *Berengaria* from New York (Passenger Lists Leaving
UK, 1890–1960, BT26/806/40, National Archives). Curle mentions his consultation
of 'The Congo Diary' in his Introduction (see Appendix A).
[4] Curle to Eric S. Pinker, 4 December 1924; 15 February 1925; 5 March 1925 (Berg).

makes the meaning clear, and, in any case, it gives to the book, what
every book should have, – proper punctuation, which it has not got
at present.'[1] In the end, however, he was little moved to correct grammar or tidy idiom, but he was presumably responsible for altering the
subtitles of some of the essays, using the word 'preface' consistently
for prefatory statements that were variously titled.

   Pinker was not always comfortable with Curle's role, questioning
whether Conrad's executor might be holding things back. Curle
rejected Pinker's insinuation, insisting that he had been 'unusually
direct' in fulfilling his trust to the Conrad estate and family: 'how
much simpler it would have been for me, how much time and worry
I would have saved, perhaps, even money out of my own pocket, had
not I endeavoured to do what I could for the people entrusted to
my care'.[2] Six months later and in a more congenial mood, Curle
apologized for not keeping Pinker up to date about progress on the
volume, writing, when plans for publication were fairly far advanced:
'Very Sorry I forgot to answer your letter about the frontispiece to
"Last Essays."'[3] Pinker's enquiry may well have been pressing as he
was about to leave on a business trip to New York, during which plans
for the production of *Last Essays* were surely to be discussed.[4] No
documents survive, however, to establish what precise arrangements
were made or what percentages of the royalties the Conrad estate and
Curle, respectively, were to receive from sales.[5]

   The lack of documents relating to the history of the transmission
of the text to Dent and Doubleday, Conrad's long-term English and
American publishers, disallows certainty about the book's progress
through production. The textual evidence, however, provides some
clues as to what might have occurred. No typescripts sent to the publishers survive; this is unsurprising given that the general practice

---

[1] Curle to Pinker, 24 June 1926 (Berg).   [2] Curle to Pinker, 16 July 1925 (Berg).
[3] Curle to Pinker, 1 December 1925 (Berg). At issue is the facsimile reproducing the
   final words Conrad wrote, the last leaf of 'Legends'. See the frontispiece to the present
   volume, and, for further details, see the discussion of 'Legends' below.
[4] Pinker sailed to New York on the *Majestic*, departing from Southampton on 15
   December 1925 (Passenger Lists Leaving UK, 1890–1960, BT27/1109/5, National
   Archives).
[5] Arrangements for publication of the volume in the two markets varied. For instance,
   Doubleday, Page & Company requested Thomas Beer's permission to reprint Conrad's
   introduction to his biography of Stephen Crane in *Last Essays*, Knopf having informed
   the firm that Beer held American copyright in the piece (Doubleday, Page Editorial
   Department (signed Lillian M. Robins) to Thomas Beer, 5 November 1925 (Yale)).

in the trade was to discard setting-copy typescripts after use. Frustrat-
ingly, however, the extant correspondence between Curle and Pinker
yields no information about the state of the text the printers received,
when the publishers got copy and whether Curle passed proofs. Dent's
publication ledger, cited below, contains useful information about production, but not about the processes involved in the volume's being
readied for print; the Dent archives (University of North Carolina
at Chapel Hill) are silent about this, and enquiries to Doubleday's
archivists have uncovered no records of publication or correspondence relating to *Last Essays*. In any event, given that Curle returned
from America in early November, preparations were presumably ongoing from that month to some point in mid- or possibly late January
1926, with Dent taking delivery of its first copies in February.

As was usual, the two publishers pursued their plans and schedules
independently, and there appears to have been little attempt to coordinate publication in England and America,[1] other than its falling within
the same month. The fact that publication by Dent and by Doubleday
occurred within a few weeks, together with the general agreement
of the texts,[2] makes it unlikely, even impossible, that printer's copy
was a batch of disparate materials consisting of typescripts, serializations, pamphlets and typed transcriptions. Curle must have arranged
to have a typescript (or typescripts) made shortly after he returned
from America; thus the (now-lost) typescript(s) for the volume were
prepared sometime between early November 1925 and, at the latest,
January 1926. Thus, both publishers possessed typescripts of the volume, setting up their editions from them, or one publisher set up

---

[1] Doubleday cabled Pinker on 14 July 1926 (Berg) asking for the date of English
publication, for the firm's records as the cable is dated after publication. An unknown
hand wrote on the cable 'March 3rd', the English publication date.

[2] This conclusion is based upon the collations made for the present edition. Because
the posthumously published *Last Essays* was compiled and edited by Curle, multiple
collations using the Lindstrand Comparator and the Hinman Collator of multiple
exemplars of the first English and American editions – central to establishing critical
texts for the book versions – do not assist in establishing Conrad's intentions evolving
from multiple and various copy-texts. Given that type of E1 was distributed after
printing, multiple collations were unnecessary, as is true for serials, which were printed
only once. The book texts were electronically collated against other forms in the line
of transmission using the suite of programs called CASE (Computer Assisted Scholarly
Editing) or the JUXTA program developed by Applied Research in Paracriticism at
The University of Virginia. The transcriptions of the serial and pamphlet forms were
checked against originals or facsimile copies thereof over the quarter-century that the
editing of *Last Essays* was in process.

its text from typescript and forwarded a set of proofs to the other, a common enough practice.[1]

The survival in Doubleday's edition (A1) of British spellings (see below) indicates,[2] with certainty, that Doubleday used as their setting copy either a typescript prepared in England or a set of Dent proofs, it being impossible to entertain a scenario whereby Doubleday's editors or compositors installed British spellings into a text destined for the American market. Another advantage of Doubleday's use of Dent's proofs would have been that Curle would have needed to pass only a single set of proofs. Given his professionalism and the concern he showed elsewhere for his own work as well as that of his late friend, the assumption that he read Dent's proofs is a reasonable one. On the other hand, several casual errors survive in Dent's edition (E1), and Curle's proofreading, if undertaken, was imperfect.

The evidence gathered from collation trumps theoretical possibilities, however, and tends to suggest that the two publishers set up their texts independently from typescript, an original ribbon-copy and a duplicate probably being at issue.[3] E1's house-styling can, with some confidence, be identified,[4] and, had Doubleday used Dent's proofs, some of E1's styling would have been retained in Doubleday's edition (A1), whereas A1 is much less heavily house-styled. The typescript prepared for the volume on Curle's direction can occasionally be glimpsed through the common departures from his copy in E1 and A1, whether intentional, in the form of editing, or casual (errors or missed-out matter). Thus, for instance, both E1 and A1 share '*Marco Polo's* sails' (36.24), the wrongly italicized possessive marker being, probably, a typing error in the lost typescripts, although it is possible that compositors working independently made the same mistake.

---

[1] Curle's Introduction was obviously handled separately from the main text, as variants establish. See the headnote to Appendix A.

[2] The sigla used throughout this essay are fully explained in 'Emendation and Variation'. Standard abbreviations (MS for manuscript, for example) require no comment; otherwise, whether in book or serial form, A designates publication in America and E publication in England. The following sigla are also used: C = publication in a book not by Conrad; S = serialization. Lower-case letters are explained as follows: c = carbon copy; p = proofs; r = revised; t = as typed.

[3] That there would have been two typescripts made (at least a ribbon-copy and a carbon) is also probable, even if only out of caution against possible loss.

[4] For examples and a discussion of Dent's house-style, see, in particular, the essay on 'The Future of Constantinople' below.

Differences between the two editions fall into several categories. Some are obviously the result of transmissional error and house-styling, with, for example, E1 placing the titles of books and plays in italics and A1 placing such matter in double inverted commas. A likewise indifferent matter with respect to meaning is indentation and layout, and these differ significantly, particularly in the 'Memorandum' and 'The Congo Diary'. E1's text is more attractively set out in both cases, and its wider margins and more generous spacing in general account for its greater bulk – 272 pages as opposed to A1's 190, including blank pages and prelims.

Case and hyphenation also differ: E1 has 'exercise of his Art' (101.5)[1] and 'noble Red Man' (113.4) to A1's 'exercise of his art' and 'Noble Red Man'; and E1 has 'wool-clippers' (18.15), 'breakfast-bell' (26.5) and 'dug-out' (92.20), whereas these are unhyphenated in A1. Numerals are varyingly treated, A1 giving figures for E1's 'sixty', 'eighty' and 'five hundred', and styling differs as well, in, for example, E1's 'reluctance – hesitatingly – till' (40.36–37) and A1's 'reluctance, hesitatingly, till'.

Spellings differ with respect to terminal '-ise'/'-isation' and '-ize'/'-ization', the former as expected in E1, and there are other Americanizations in A1: 'halo round' (40.19) became 'halo around', and 'grey-yellowish' (125.6) became 'gray-yellowish'. More surprisingly, however, A1 not only allows terminal '-our' forms ('honourable', 'ill-humour') to stand,[2] but also retains typically British spellings such as 'towards' (throughout the volume), 'defence' and 'defenceless' (39.4, 118.12), 'traveller' and 'travelling' (e.g., 64.21, 65.11) and 'manœuvre' (63.18).[3] This may suggest that the book was hurriedly set and casually proofed, but there is also evidence to the contrary: an editorial hand was evidently at work in A1's text, with, for example, E1's

---

[1] Citations of the page and line numbers of this edition refer throughout to its critical texts and to the variants listed in the 'Apparatus'. Lower-case letters immediately following page–line numbers (e.g., 1.2a, 1.2b) distinguish entries that have readings in the same line.

[2] It might be noted in passing that British orthography during Conrad's career was apparently more fluid than is contemporary practice. For example, 'civilized' and 'civilization', now considered 'American', were standard in *The Times* of the period, whereas Dent (or Curle's typist) preferred 'civilised' (3.13). On the other hand, Dent allows 'judgment' (93.24), once widely used in Britain but now also generally considered an American spelling, rather than 'judgement'.

[3] Other examples include 'labour-saving' (53.4), 'splendour' (67.20) and 'behaviour' (85.9).

'the impression, and toil of the day' reading 'the impressions, and toil of his day' (3.16–17) and 'The worth of sentiment' reading 'The worth of a sentiment' (44.3). Moreover, A1 has the correct 'Africa' (12.24), 'Jugra River' (69.24), 'Hübner' (65.34), '*Comédie*' (80.8, 80.13), '*Mémoires*' (91.7) and 'San Stefano' (117.26) to E1's erroneous 'African', 'Juga River', 'Hubner', '*Comedie*', '*Memoires*' and 'San Stepano'. A1 also expands 'd. w. capacity' (54.16–17) to 'dead weight capacity' and declines to hyphenate 'imaginatively-written' (30.13), no doubt an E1 house-styling. In short, A1 often displays a scrupulous attention to detail, being at several points more 'correct' than E1; however, it also simultaneously exhibits a curiously mixed styling policy with most of the setting-copy's British spellings remaining unaltered.

PUBLICATION

DENT'S EDITION, printed at the Temple Press, Letchworth, Hertfordshire, was published on 3 March 1926, selling for 7s 6d. (The British Museum deposit copy is date-stamped '1 MAR 26', and the Bodleian Library registered its copy on 1 June.) The number of copies ordered – 7,200 – suggests confidence in sales. A volume of essays always sells less well than fiction even for a well-known and adroitly marketed author, and the print run is smaller than that Dent ordered for *Notes on Life and Letters*.[1] On 12 February 1926, the first 3,500 copies were received, the other 3,700 arriving four days later. Moulds were made and type distributed after the first printing. On 5 February, 3,000 copies were ordered bound; these were received during the week of the 18th–26th. Binding orders for 1,000 copies followed on 5 March (received by the 17th), and 350 additional copies were ordered bound on 6 June (received 15 September). Smaller orders for binding followed, such as the one for twenty bound copies on 28 February 1929. In addition, 750 copies were issued in colonial cloth. Of these, 500 were ordered on 5 February 1926 (received 1 March), and an additional 250 on 19 July (received by 27 September 1926).[2]

---

[1] In 1921, Dent printed 9,350 copies of *Notes on Life and Letters*; the smaller print run of *Last Essays* probably reflects a scaled-down sense of sales potential (see 'The Texts', *Notes on Life and Letters*, ed. J. H. Stape (2004), p. 221).
[2] Dent stock ledger (cited in *Bibliography*).

Doubleday, Page & Company published its edition, printed at its works, the Country Life Press at Garden City, New York, on 26 March 1926, at $2.00. The number of copies printed is unrecorded, but early sales proved disappointing. In late May, lawyers representing Doubleday in a dispute about publication rights to the essay 'Stephen Crane' reported that the book 'had not done nearly so well as expected, only some 2,300 copies having been sold at a net loss of several hundred dollars'.[1]

After the publication of the first editions, *Last Essays* was reprinted in various bindings and formats over the following few decades, the volume next appearing in Doubleday's 'Memorial' (1925),[2] 'Special', 'Deep Sea' and 'Malay' editions (so-called, as they are merely issues of A1) of 1928. In 1938, it was reprinted in Doran & Company's 'Collected' edition and published separately with *The Nature of a Crime* (along with, although not specified on the title-page, the plays *Laughing Anne* and *One Day More*). 'Dent's Uniform Edition' of 1928 and 'Dent's Collected Edition' of 1955, both descending from Doubleday's 1926 plates and hence issues of A1, placed it between the same covers as *Tales of Hearsay*, Conrad's posthumously published collection of short stories, as did the Penguin edition of 1944. None of these are new settings of text, aside from the Penguin edition, and thus there have been only three editions, the first English (E1) and first American (A1), both published in March 1926, and Penguin's. All subsequent printings, including those published by Dent, are issues of A1, with Dent, in fact, selling in England the Doubleday text rather than their own, type of which, as mentioned, was distributed after printing.

COPY-TEXTS

THE PRINCIPLE guiding the selection of copy-texts for this critical edition of *Last Essays* is that well established in modern textual practice:

---

[1] Wickes and Neilson (signed Nathan F. George) to Thomas Beer, 26 May 1926 (Yale-S). The issue of contested rights over the essay involved a claim by Beer that Doubleday had failed to consult him. Although the firm had, in fact, twice informed him of its intentions, in the end it paid out $500 in compensation; see Doubleday, Page Editorial Department (signed Lillian M. Robins) to Beer, 5 November 1925; Nathan F. George to Doubleday, Page & Company, 6 May 1926; Russell Doubleday to George, 11 May 1926; George to Doubleday, 17 May 1926; and Kellogg, Emery, Innis-Brown & Cutheil on behalf of Doubleday, Page & Company to George, 26 May 1926 (Yale-S).

[2] By mid-June 1926, Curle had given Doubleday permission to add *Last Essays* to the 'Memorial Edition' (Curle to Eric S. Pinker, 15 June 1926 (Berg)).

where appropriate, the copy-text chosen is the document closest to the hypothetical 'fair copy' that Conrad himself would have wished to have seen printed, had he been able to effect this choice. During his lifetime, his texts, despite his best and most conscientious efforts, often made their way into print in varyingly defective forms, and as regards fidelity and accuracy this is no less true of this posthumous volume, seen through printing by his friend and executor. The reprinting of the 1926 volume edited by Richard Curle, whether E1 or A1 cosmetically corrected, would offer the convenience of a unitary copy-text, but would ill serve the aim of presenting Conrad's work as he presumably would have wished it to appear, and is unhesitatingly rejected.

In addition to changes to Conrad's texts made by Curle, these editions incorporate the errors made by the typist (or typists) who prepared the setting-copy typescript(s) and hence perpetuate preferences with respect to punctuation, spelling and word-division that certainly did not originate with Conrad, nor have the possibility of his approval.[1] Moreover, Dent's and Doubleday's editors and compositors also intervened in these matters, either casually in terms of their own preferences as they worked to close deadlines, or systematically in a layer of house-styling, whether imposed by them or by copy-editors assigned to the volume. In short, the texts Curle saw into print are often, and perhaps normally, at several removes from Conrad's own work, and while it can often be a subtle matter, these interventions collectively impact upon and alter the rhythms and cadences of the prose of a writer renowned for his individual voice and for an elegant and self-aware prose style. The critical texts, then, attempt to reconstruct Conrad's evident intention – his cadences, achieved through his punctuation – by the choice of the earliest polished and developed document. (This is usually not a manuscript, these typically being rough drafts.) The selection of copy-texts on this basis guarantees the least intrusion by uninvited collaborators, however well-meaning and at times necessary their interventions.

The individual circumstances of composition, revision and printing of the pieces collected in *Last Essays* are highly varied and must be

---

[1] Much of Conrad's late work was dictated, and presumably choices as regards spelling and pointing were made by Miss Hallowes rather than by him in the course of dictation. None the less, his typist's choices were open to alteration as typescripts moved into print, and the situation is not identical to that in E1 or A1 texts, with changes imposed by Curle or his typist(s) or the books' compositors. On this subject, see also 'The Texts', *Suspense*, ed. Gene M. Moore (forthcoming 2011).

established and examined in order to arrive at copy-texts that best represent Conrad's work. Even then, an ideal text at times proves elusive. At points Conrad's handwriting remains open to varying interpretation, particularly with respect to capitals and in the placement of hyphens, which seem at times to be represented by two words continuously written and joined with a short line that may or may not indicate hyphenation. It is unsurprising that his typists and compositors variously interpreted these elements in documents in which his hand was at work.

The loss of critical documents is an even more serious impediment to the quest for an ideal text; in such cases, there is no way of knowing what the author himself would have preferred, and one must reluctantly make do simply with what happens to survive. Consequently, for instance, the copy-text for the essay section of the 'Future of Constantinople' and for 'The Silence of the Sea' ('Uncollected Essays') derive, respectively, from A1 and the *Daily Mail*. In the first case, of the two texts extant A1 is the least house-styled; in the second, the *Daily Mail* text is the only one surviving. These are printed here in an awareness that they almost certainly fail to present the author's work as he may have wished, the one text based on a now-lost typescript that provided setting copy for the book, the other on a newspaper printing, both certain to have undergone alteration by typists, editors and compositors.

Rationales for the selection of the copy-texts are presented in the individual textual essays below, which follow a discussion of the general principles of emendation employed throughout the present volume.

EMENDATION

THE MISCELLANEOUS TEXTS collected by Richard Curle after Conrad's death, like the posthumous volumes *Suspense* and *Tales of Hearsay* (both published in 1925), offer special editorial problems. Conrad had no opportunity to revise or correct the texts of these uncollected essays. On balance, it can be confidently assumed that he would have wished to do so. He polished the pieces brought together in *Notes on Life and Letters*, and although his overall revision eventually proved light, his interest in the volume was close and attentive, and he made many small and deft alterations. And throughout his career he attended to his prose with a concern that was professional and painstaking.

The original conditions under which the texts in *Last Essays* were created and printed were, as with *Notes on Life and Letters*, highly diverse, and emendation of the selected copy-texts, with respect to both accidentals and, occasionally, substantives, is necessary. With a few special exceptions discussed below, the copy-texts have been emended to eliminate outright errors, whether of inscription or transmission, and, where identifiable, to restore Conrad's punctuation when it was misunderstood or altered by his original typists or effaced by subsequent editorial intervention or house-styling.

The present edition departs from the practice of the historical editions of *Last Essays* in supplying beneath the title of each essay the year of first publication or, in the case of posthumously published work (for example, 'The Congo Diary', 'A Glance at Two Books' and 'Legends'), the year of writing. This is in accord with the practice of *Notes on Life and Letters*, a volume Conrad himself saw through printing and which *Last Essays* resembles in content. The addition of these dates is not reported in the 'Emendation and Variation' list.

Conrad's general practices are respected, although foreign words are placed in italics and spelled correctly. The general policy of the Cambridge Edition is to adhere to the conventions of the language in question as regards case and accents rather than to follow idiosyncrasies in a document that may represent an unpolished state of the work, subject – had the author been able to effect it – to later revision and correction that, for varied reasons, could not or did not occur. Whatever their styling in the copy-texts, titles of books, plays and newspapers and the names of ships appear in italics, and the titles of short stories and articles appear within inverted commas. (These editorial policies are not applied to Richard Curle's texts in Appendix A, which appear integrally as printed in E1.) Ampersands and abbreviations (including ''tho') are silently expanded; numerals are written out (thus, 'nineteenth' and 'ten' for '19th' and '10') when exact measurements are not at issue; and haplography and dittography are likewise not reported in the 'Emendation and Variation' list, these properly part of a diplomatic transcription of a document rather than an element of the text(s) contained in it.

Conrad's spelling was inconsistent throughout his career, and is particularly so in texts written, as were those collected in *Last Essays*, over several decades. Moreover, as mentioned, in dictated texts this element was often determined by his typist, Conrad's passive 'acceptance' of it being no guarantee of an actual preference. However that may be, spelling is retained here as in the selected copy-texts. Obvious spelling errors (including failures to provide an apostrophe with possessives) are silently corrected, and typing or compositorial errors or variant spellings that represent an editorial or compositorial imposition of a preference – as, for instance, the straightforward replacement of English spellings or usages in American editions (for example, 'towards' instead of 'toward' and 'amongst' instead of 'among') – are similarly unreported. Hyphenation proves equally problematic, subject to a typist's whims; when Conrad's own preference can be established, it is restored.

Misspelled proper names are adjusted, their correction being reported in the 'Emendation and Variation' list in the 'Apparatus': for example, 'H. R. Angel' (21.13, 21.27) replaces the erroneous 'H. R. Angell'. Hyphenation varies across the texts and can vary even in a single essay, with, for example, 'sea legend' and 'sea-legend' (36.11, 36.17) appearing on the same manuscript leaf. In an edition that seeks to eschew the standardization that was so often, and sometimes so deleteriously, applied to Conrad's writings, these inconsistencies, mainly without impact on meaning or rhythm, are allowed to stand. Necessarily, then, a volume based upon copy-texts at various states of polishing has a slightly rougher, and certainly a less consistent, texture in its accidentals than one based upon a unitary copy-text.

At times, in the flow of composition Conrad simply left certain elements for later settling, and he sometimes omitted a closing inverted comma or a full stop during rapid composition. While such matters can easily be identified and corrected, work never intended for print – the 'Memorandum', 'The Congo Diary' and 'Up-river Book' – offers unique challenges, as does 'Legends', an unrevised and unfinished draft cut short by Conrad's death. The errors and idiosyncrasies of these texts are, with some exceptions, preserved. In the case of the Congo notebooks, part of their interest lies precisely in their immediacy as records of private experience, and, thus, the nature of these documents determines that Conrad's incorrect spellings of certain words and of place-names (possibly only heard rather than seen in print) remain unaltered. Thus, too, missing or odd punctuation and the many superscripts with Conrad's inconsistent underlining have been left unemended in the Congo notebooks. Abbreviations, however, have, where required, been expanded in square brackets in an effort to make these texts accessible to the reader. The several casual misspellings in 'Legends' are a different matter. These have been corrected on the assumption that Conrad would obviously have done this himself or authorized an amanuensis to do so. No editor allowed them to stand, and to preserve them here would be fussily to enshrine, even to fetishize, the moment of writing and thus to present a diplomatic transcription at the expense of the protocols of the language. It seems more appropriate to follow through on probable (although, granted, unstated and occasionally elusive) authorial intentions.

This volume conforms to certain policies and conventions observed throughout the Cambridge Edition. Superior letters (for example, 'M^r') in the original documents have been lowered (that is, to 'Mr'), with the exception of the Congo notebooks, where Conrad's manuscript practices are preserved. The beginnings of paragraphs are represented by standard modern indentation regardless of the various conventions of the documents, and Conrad's combination of an en-rule and opening inverted commas ('–"') to introduce dialogue is reduced to simple inverted commas. Long dashes of variable lengths are printed as spaced one-en rules, and commas and full stops in quotations are consistently presented. Thus, whatever the varying practices of the copy-texts (with the exception of the Congo notebooks), the following rubrics apply: a comma precedes inverted commas (,"); when complete sentences are at issue, full stops appear inside the closing inverted commas (."); and when words or phrases are in question, the full stop is placed outside the inverted commas (".). Other typographical elements in the texts and titles of the original documents (for example, display capitals, chapter headings, running titles) have been standardized. Throughout the present volume decorative elements that have no effect on meaning and diverge from the highly varying practices of the individual copy-texts receive no report. Likewise, formal conventions of the documents, as such, are ignored (Conrad's signatures, serial by-lines, editorial headings, in-text divisions and instalment statements).

Reports of emendations, with the exceptions specified, appear in the 'Emendations of Accidentals' list in the 'Apparatus'.

THE ESSAYS

THE TEXTUAL HISTORIES that follow trace the evolution of the texts brought together in *Last Essays* from the earliest records in Conrad's letters and other correspondence, as well as evidence gathered from the study of both the preprint and published texts. Even though each textual history addresses the unique circumstances relating to an essay's origins, and is intended to stand by itself, the individual histories below follow a general pattern. The circumstances of writing and publication are presented, and the extant preprint documents and the development of the text then described, with the selected copy-text briefly identified. There follows, where appropriate, an analysis of typescripts revised in hands other than Conrad's, and, in a few instances, of galley-proofs, corrected galley-proofs and previously published texts. The rationale for the selection of copy-text and, where necessary, a discussion of its emendation concludes each history. The individual discussions, at some slight cost of repetition, are constructed so that they can be read independently, although not without reference to the history of the book editions.

The section on the 'Uncollected Essays' follows the same general pattern as regards the discussion of the history of composition and publication, the selection of copy-text and emendation. These histories are independent from the story of *Last Essays* because Richard Curle was unaware of these pieces or decided to omit them from his collection.

GEOGRAPHY AND SOME EXPLORERS

RICHARD CURLE ACTED as intermediary between Conrad and the editor and publisher, J(ohn) A(lexander) Hammerton, in negotiations for the writing of this essay as the introduction to *Countries of the World*, a photo-illustrated gazetteer of the world's countries and regions published in forty-two parts during 1924 and 1925 by the Amalgamated Press, a Harmsworth enterprise. Hammerton had invited Curle, an established travel writer, to write some of the articles he required, and Curle, in turn, recommended that Conrad be invited to write the series' general preface.

The following preprint documents are extant: (1) the 62-leaf manuscript (MS Yale), titled 'Geography', sold to the rare book and manuscript dealer Hodgson through Richard Curle, with the first typescript, for £155 in January 1924;[1] (2) a 23-page double-spaced ribbon-copy typescript (TS1 Yale), measuring $8\frac{1}{8}$ in. $\times$ $10\frac{1}{2}$ in. (20.5 cm $\times$ 36.5 cm), with an additional holograph leaf, signed and inscribed

---

[1] See Conrad to Messrs Hodgson & Co., 17 January 1924 (*Letters*, VIII, 276); Curle to Hodgson, 14 January 1924 (Bodleian).

'first copy from MS', sold with the manuscript; (3) a 24-page double-spaced ribbon-copy typescript (TS2 Berg), measuring 8 in. × 10¼ in. (20.5 cm × 26 cm), revised, corrected and initialled by Conrad; (4) a 24-page double-spaced carbon-copy typescript (TS2c Berg), measuring 7½ in. × 10¼ in. (19 cm × 25 cm), with the revisions made in TS2 imperfectly copied in, not by Conrad, with corrections also by the copyist and bearing printer's tracking marks and numbers related to the now-lost galleys; (5) a 23-page ribbon-copy typescript, measuring 7⅞ in. × 9¾ in. (20 cm × 24.75 cm), copy-edited and readied for press by the editors of *National Geographic Magazine* (TS4 NGS); and (6) pamphlet proofs (Pp Colgate), bearing corrections in the hand of Richard Curle and another individual. The revised text in TS1 (TS1r) serves as copy-text.

After Hammerton 'jumped at the idea' Curle had suggested,[1] Conrad decided to wait for 'a helpful hint' before proceeding (*Letters*, VIII, 207). By 31 October 1923, he consented to the commission (worth £200),[2] mooted the title 'Geography and Exploration' and had roughed out some ideas for development, rapidly writing 1,200 words of a proposed 4,000 by 2 November.[3] (In the end, the total reached 6,500 words.) At a time when he was stalled with his major project, the long-evolving *Suspense*, he wrote rapidly and fluently.[4] On the 20th, he forwarded a typescript to Hammerton, most likely TS2, regretting that it was not 'clean', but excusing its state on the grounds that retyping would cause delayed delivery and requesting to see proofs in order to compensate for a text hastily prepared to meet Hammerton's deadline.[5] That he did, in fact, pass such proofs seems unlikely: the pamphlet and the two serial texts are close, the variants probably entered into setting-copy typescripts. At the proof stage, Conrad did not, it seems, feel the need to return to a text he had so thoroughly revised.

He lost no time in posting a typescript to Pinker for serialization in America, which his agent duly forwarded to the New York office of the Amalgamated Press. Rights were bought by *National Geographic*

---

[1] *Conrad to a Friend: 150 Selected Letters from Joseph Conrad to Richard Curle* (1928), p. 213.
[2] Conrad to Eric S. Pinker, 26 November 1923 (*Letters*, VIII, 230).
[3] Conrad to J. A. Hammerton, 31 October 1923; to Curle, 2 November 1923 (*Letters*, VIII, 209, 210).
[4] For a history of the novel's evolution, see 'The Texts', *Suspense* (forthcoming 2011).
[5] Conrad to Hammerton, 20 November 1923 (*Letters*, VIII, 225).

Magazine for $500, and by 5 January the essay had been set up in galleys.[1] By this time, Curle had negotiated with the London printer and bookbinder Strangeways to publish the essay in pamphlet form prior to its serial appearance to boost value among collectors.[2] Thus the essay's first appearance was as a pamphlet in January 1924, in a printing limited to thirty copies. It was published on 12 February, under the title 'The Romance of Travel', in *Countries of the World* (SE), with sub-headings supplied by the Amalgamated Press,[3] and in March in *National Geographic Magazine* (SA), Americanized and supplied with sub-headings as well as sixteen full-page illustrations unrelated to it.[4] A brief extract appeared in the *Oakland Tribune* on 24 August (p. 64).

The manuscript shows the usual signs of hasty and fluid writing: letters were not always inked as the pen moved quickly over the page ('dreadfu', 'befor'); words were dropped out in the flow of rapid composition; spelling went awry ('theoritical', 'burried', 'distincly'); apostrophes were carelessly added to possessives; and occasionally an initial thought that had been replaced by a later one was allowed to stand.[5] Moreover, the handwriting offered such formidable challenges that the typist – presumably Miss Hallowes, who was familiar with Conrad's practices – did not always successfully surmount them. This is particularly true in the case of majuscules, which are frequently formed in a way that defies definitive resolution, and, to complicate matters, used inconsistently. (For instance, whereas MS reads 'the great superiority of the science of Geography over the science of Geometry', TS1t gives 'the great superiority of the science of geography over the science of geometry'.) As a result, some effects were smoothed out in the usual quest for consistency, while some of the manuscript's idiosyncrasies were carried over into the final printed text. As usual, too, the typist's

---

[1] The date appears on page 1 of TS4 as follows: 'Set in Galley | 1/5/24'; see also the Amalgamated Press (signed Joseph T. Gleason) to Frederick S. Bigelow, 11 January 1924 (Berg).

[2] Richard Curle to Messrs John Strangeways & Sons, 25 December 1923 (Berg).

[3] The serial publication date is from Curle to James Bain, 13 January 1924 (Berg). The sub-headings are of a typically journalistic kind: 'Through Error to Truth', 'Unveiling Africa's Mystery', 'In the Foot-Prints of Discovery'.

[4] *Countries of the World*, 1 (February 1924), xviii–xxviii; *National Geographic Magazine*, 45 (March 1924), 239–74.

[5] Examples of the latter include 'to take my scalp at the yearly test exams', where 'test' was obviously replaced by 'exams' but none the less not explicitly deleted. Likewise, for instance, in the phrase 'whose [existence] was doubted, was denied', the first inscription ('was doubted') was replaced by the second more emphatic verb (see Appendix E).

preferences were asserted, with, for example, 'upon' replacing 'on' (5.29, 6.21a).

That typescript proves, in turn, to add complexities: a hybrid document, it contains both a typed text, only shards of which survived the rewriting process, and what amounts to a new holograph text on top of much of the typewritten one (see Fig. 1). Conrad indulged in his usual small-scale verbal polishing, but also thoroughly recast and expanded ideas. Thus, while the manuscript is the undoubted lineal ancestor of the final printed text (see Fig. 8), a second creative phase supplanted it to such a great extent that it seems reasonable, even imperative, to consider 'Geography' (to use the manuscript title) as having been, in a sense, discarded, with TS1r the starting-point for 'Geography and Some Explorers'.[1]

As a result of Conrad's massive revision of TS1, the making of another typescript was necessary. But he was moved to make yet further revisions in TS2, but also in another way, now impossible to determine, whether by verbal directions to the typist or in notes for her consultation during TS1r's transcription. Constructing this scenario is necessary because obviously authorial changes appear, for the first time in extant documents, not in TS1r but in TS2 and TS2c. This, for instance, explains the replacement of TS1r's vague 'dreary thing' by the more vivid 'bloodless thing' (10.40) and the expansion of 'entry' to 'entry of Tanganyika' (12.34–35). Similarly, the equivalent of TS1r's 'What I got was French [sic] translation' appears in TS2c as 'My copy was probably in French' (10.14–15), phrasing restoring that present in the manuscript. However they were made, these revisions, which descend to all later texts, bear an authorial imprimatur: it is inconceivable that the typist could have been responsible for alterations of this kind.

As it turns out, the typing of TS2 proved less than letter-perfect. Inclined to anticipation generally, the typist also changed the text importantly in misreading 'worthy adventurers and devoted men'

---

[1] In the interests of clarity and accessibility and in order more faithfully to reflect the essay's evolution, the manuscript text is presented in its entirety in Appendix E. Its variants and those in TS1t are consequently not reported in the 'Emendation and Variation' list in the 'Apparatus'. If included, these variants would bulk so large as to discourage and even compromise an understanding of the textual history. A somewhat analogous situation, although handled differently, exists with respect to the variant openings and conclusions of 'A Smile of Fortune', for a discussion of which see 'The Texts', *Twixt Land and Sea: Tales*, ed. J. A. Berthoud, Laura L. Davis and S. W. Reid (2008), pp. 243–4, and Appendix F in that volume.

MS
|
TS1

C ⟶

TS2   TS2c

C ⟶

[*TS3*]   TS4

[*SEp*]   [*SAp*]   Pp

SE   SA   P

C ⟶ Conrad's revisions
Inferred lost documents (e.g., TS3)

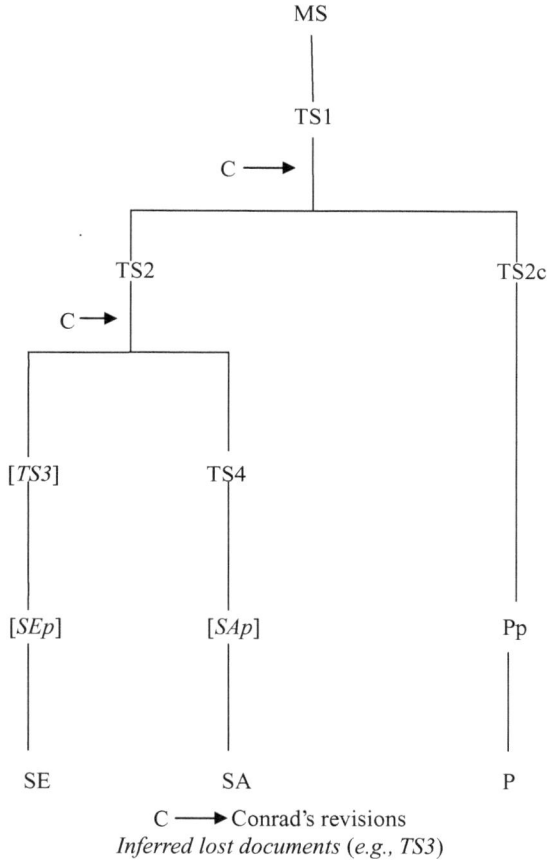

[8] Genealogy of 'Geography and Some Explorers'

(12.3) as 'worthy adventurous and devoted men', prompting Conrad in revision to add a comma after 'adventurous' and thus make a series; and she dropped the word 'blank' in 'blank spot' (14.8) in the most often quoted passage from this essay.

Conrad revised his text in TS2. At this stage, he rewrote sentences and made typical small verbal changes subtly altering his ideas: for example, 'difficulties' was revised to 'incertitudes' (7.14), 'guess-work' to 'pure guess work' (7.21) and 'much of an unscrupulous adventurer' to 'a taint of an unscrupulous adventurer' (8.11–12). He also repeatedly had to repair his text as the typist tended to miss out punctuation, and occasionally he had to supply words or phrases that the typist had dropped (5.34, 6.33, 9.34). On two occasions he was invited to fill in blanks where his handwriting had proved indecipherable to her (17.7, 17.27). As a result of all these changes, TS2c had to be retyped, these clean copies destined for the English and American serializations.

TS2c provided setting copy for the pamphlet, and was returned to Conrad after use. Lineation is identical with TS2, with, however, page 4 retyped. The first page bears the following indication in its upper right-hand corner: 'demy 8vo. | 21 wide | 37 deep | 40 pp.', and there are tracking marks throughout.[1] The revisions Conrad had made in TS2 were imperfectly copied into the carbon-copy typescript; some errors also occurred during this process, with, for example, the inadvertent alteration of 'pure cold water' (13.19) to 'cold pure water'. The handful of variants between this typescript and the pamphlet text represent compositorial correction or error. For instance, '130' was expanded on one occurrence (but not another) and a badly overwritten 'does' was misread as 'did'.

Conrad tinkered and made some minor revisions after completing his revisions in TS2, most likely in another typescript prepared by Miss Hallowes or in one prepared through Eric Pinker. Sorting out probable authorial alterations from those made by the typist is a somewhat vexed matter. For instance, while it seems certain that only Conrad could have been responsible for changing 'greatest drama' to 'darkest drama' (10.3) and 'imaginary' to 'mere imaginary' (10.27–28), the typist presumably altered the somewhat unconventional 'directive' (11.28) to 'directing' and normalized the characteristically Conradian 'had managed' (11.15) to 'managed'.

SE's setting-copy typescript does not survive. That used for setting the *National Geographic Magazine* text shows at least two hands at work in altering the text. Sub-headings were supplied; paragraph-breaks frequently inserted; spellings corrected and Americanized (for example, 'gray' for 'grey', 'draft' for 'draught', 'marvelous' for 'marvellous'); words were transposed; and case, punctuation and grammar altered.[2]

---

[1] The pamphlet, in fact, is comprised of forty pages. A proof title-page (two survive) bears the indication 'To be corrected' in Curle's hand, and corrections are in his and another individual's hand.

[2] Judged objectionable, the sentence fragment 'Too calm' (5.35) became 'It is too calm', and 'palpable' (5.1) was changed to 'palpably'.

Occasional adaptations were made with an eye to the magazine's audience: 'Great Lakes' (12.16) was expanded to the 'Great Lakes of Africa' (to avoid confusion with those in North America), and references to the missionary work of Protestant churches and to 'arm-chair geographers' (6.17, 6.18) were deleted. Conrad was rarely involved in seeing his work through serialization in America, and his passing of SA proofs or his approval of these changes can be discounted. In any case, the serial texts vary little, the differences, leaving aside the adaptations for the American market, amounting to some last-minute revisions in the typescript Conrad had to hand in England.[1]

As variants confirm, Curle used SE as copy for the *Last Essays* typescript. This is an expected choice: involved in securing Conrad's work for Hammerton's series, he was also keenly aware of the market value of pamphlets, especially ones signed by Conrad, and they played no role as copy.[2] He departed from the text to restore the title used for the pamphlet and SA, and, as a matter of course, deleted SE's subheadings.

Despite the layers of complexity, both textual and historical, the choice of copy-text among the surviving documents is straightforward. As has been argued, the manuscript is so heavily altered that it needs to be considered an independent text. TS2 inherits not only the work of the typist of the first typescript but also embodies the work of its own typist, and is not meticulous, particularly with respect to accidentals; TS2c contains most but not all of the revisions made in TS2, perpetuates its errors and was open to changes made on the initiative of the copyist; the *National Geographic* typescript (TS4) was independently altered, and its typewritten text (TS4t) is yet further distant from authority than that in TS2.[3] Thus, although TS1r in some ways evidences a work still in development, it is a preferable copy-text to any of the alternatives, and contains the heavily re-worked text, much of it holograph, from which all later texts descend. It is emended by reference to the manuscript, the spellings and styling of which were

---

[1] See, for example, 7.28, 9.7, 9.24.

[2] In this case, few pamphlets would have been available: of the thirty printed, twenty-five were purchased by an arrangement made prior to publication; see Curle to James Bain, 13 January 1924 (Berg).

[3] Given that the alterations in this document are the unauthorized work of in-house editors, they are not the subject of report in the 'Apparatus'. For a comprehensive discussion of this Americanized text, see Ray Stevens, 'Conrad, Gilbert Grosvenor, *The National Geographic Magazine*, and "Geography and Some Explorers"', *Conradiana*, 23 (1991), 197–202.

simply misunderstood or deliberately altered by an amanuensis in transcribing it, and to incorporate Conrad's revisions in TS2 and other authoritative states. Numerous subtle verbal effects and the author's spellings appear in print for the first time, and Conrad's rhythms, lost as the text was re-typed and as layers of formal punctuation and styling accumulated, have been restored in the critical text.

THE *TORRENS*
A PERSONAL TRIBUTE

CONRAD WROTE this essay at the request of F(rederick) A(rthur) Hook, founding editor of the *Blue Peter*, a popular and lavishly illustrated monthly magazine dealing with sea-travel that had begun publication in July 1921.[1] Richard Curle, who had contributed to the magazine, prompted Hook to approach Conrad.[2] The essay's publication came a month after the appearance in the September 1923 issue of a colour picture of the *Torrens* under sail.[3] Conrad, who later recalled the *Torrens* transaction as 'a pleasant affair altogether',[4] composed the essay rapidly in late August, deferring work on *Suspense*, then his major project. He reported to Curle, acting as go-between with F. A. Hook, that 'It took just three days from the first inception to the completing a copy fit for the printer' (*Letters*, VIII, 166). The essay's end is well documented: on 28 August, Conrad informed Curle that Hook needed the essay by mid-September, but that it would, in fact, be completed by the next day.[5] This date is confirmed by an inscription on the first leaf of the manuscript: 'finished | on the 29.8.23'.

The following preprint documents are extant: the manuscript, consisting of fourteen leaves (MS Yale), and an eight-page double-spaced carbon-copy typescript (TSc Boston). The typescript, typed in blue ink, bears the watermark 'CMK', featuring a ram's head;[6] the document

---

[1] A ship's flag featuring a blue background and a white square in the centre, a Blue Peter is flown to indicate readiness to sail immediately. For a detailed discussion of Conrad's relations with the magazine, see Robert Hampson, 'Conrad, Curle and *The Blue Peter*', *Modernist Writers and the Marketplace*, ed. Ian Willison, Warwick Gould and Warren Chernaik (1996), pp. 89–104.
[2] Conrad to Curle, 28 August 1923 (*Letters*, VIII, 163).
[3] On Spurling and his picture of the ship, see 'Explanatory Notes' (18.5–6*n*).
[4] Conrad to Curle, 5 November 1923 (*Letters*, VIII, 211).
[5] Conrad to Curle, 28 August 1923 (*Letters*, VIII, 162–3).
[6] This is a Chartham Mills watermark, but not of the usual kind, which bears the firm's name in full.

is revised throughout in black ink, a few typed words being deleted in blue pencil. Its first page bears the following authenticating note, initialled by Conrad, made for its sale: 'Note First and only copy | from the MS. with | my corrections. No other copy | corrected by me is in existence.' A single typescript page with holograph corrections, a prefatory note to the essay and not part of the main text, is preserved at Yale (see Appendix D). The revised text in the typescript (TScr) provides the copy-text for this edition.

Thomas J. Wise purchased both the manuscript and typescript from Conrad on 2 September for £35, being offered it during a visit to Oswalds.[1] When in town to see his agent on 3 September, Conrad himself delivered the clean-copy typescript destined for the printer's (now lost) to Curle at lunch on 3 September at the Royal Automobile Club.[2]

The essay appeared in the *Blue Peter* in October 1923 (SE),[3] accompanied by an autographed photo-portrait of the author and a facsimile of the first manuscript leaf. It was further illustrated by a photograph of the *Torrens* with a hole in her bow, taken after the ship collided with an iceberg in 1899. The essay was reprinted, with illustrations by John Richard Flanagan, on 27 October as 'A Clipper Ship I Knew' by *Collier's* (SA),[4] the American reprint magazine that had published Conrad's 'The Crime of Partition' in June 1919. During the same month the piece was issued as a privately printed limited-edition pamphlet (P) for Hook by Riddle, Smith & Duffus of Windsor House, London.[5] Described as 'Reprinted from "The Blue Peter," October, 1923', the

---

[1] Conrad to Curle, 28 August 1923, and to Thomas J. Wise, 4 September 1923 (*Letters*, VIII, 166, 169). Conrad received payment by cheque on 3 September, Wise taking the manuscript and corrected typescript with him upon leaving Oswalds. As a result of the speedy transaction, Hook had to go through Wise, by way of Curle, to publish the facsimile of the first leaf (*Documents*, p. 217).

[2] Conrad to Curle, 1 September 1923 (*Letters*, VIII, 167).

[3] *Blue Peter*, 3 (October 1923), 251–4.

[4] *Collier's*, 27 October 1923, p. 8. American negotiations were conducted through Brandt & Brandt, then acting in New York for J. B. Pinker & Sons. Other magazines being unable to take up the essay because of its prior publication in England, the offer from *Collier's* proved acceptable (telegram from Brandt & Brandt to Eric S. Pinker, 2 October 1923 (Berg)).

[5] In the printing of pamphlets, Conrad typically received a fee as well as reserving to himself a certain number of pamphlets, either for distribution to friends or for sale, not directly by himself but through an intermediary. Despite the fact that Hook appears as the issuer, the printing of the pamphlet, as extant correspondence establishes, was instigated by Conrad himself, with Curle assisting in the matter (see Conrad to Curle, 2 November 1923 (*Letters*, VIII, 211)).

pamphlet was limited to twenty copies. A note on a separate page bore
a handwritten numeral, testifying to its limited run, and each copy
was signed by Conrad, his only involvement in what he described as
a 'windfall' for which he had 'not done a stroke of work'.[1] As well as
proceeds from the pamphlet's sale, he received £50 from the *Blue Peter*
and $250 from *Collier's*.[2]

Conrad's description of the typescript as 'heavily corrected'[3] (meaning revised) is, in fact, only partly accurate: some pages of the original
typed text are almost wholly superseded by rewriting (see Fig. 2), and
the conclusion was altered and expanded. TScr is, in effect, a hybrid
text, both typed and holograph, the balance probably falling to the
latter. Variants between the MS and TSct texts reveal, moreover, a
complex process of writing, rewriting and revision that cannot now
be reconstructed much beyond guess-work. Revision apparently took
place in several stages: the deletions in the typescript in blue pencil
represent one,[4] the large-scale rewriting another.

Revision also occurred in documents that no longer survive. While
a poor typist could conceivably mangle MS's 'adaptability and just a
little imagination' as 'adaptability, justice and imagination', neither
anticipation nor eyeskip can account for complete sentences and
several variant wordings in TSct lacking a manuscript equivalent.[5]
For example, MS's 'composed almost without exception of willing
good seamen on whose smartness and efficiency one could depend'
has the TSct equivalent of 'composed of smart good seamen almost
without exception on whose good will and loyalty one could depend'.
The following sentences in TSct, obviously generated by Conrad, do
not appear in MS: 'To the captain's question the doctor answered
that of course he would not guarantee that the man would live as far
as Adelaide. He said that he would not guarantee any man's life for
twenty-four hours, even if he appeared as sound as this one, and he
too went.' Several other departures of this kind suggest that a now-lost
intermediate document must have been in play, perhaps a holograph
leaf (or two) containing alternative phrasings and rewritten passages,

---

[1] Ibid.   [2] *Documents*, p. 237.
[3] Conrad to Curle, 1 September 1923 (*Letters*, VIII, 166).
[4] Revision in this medium seems in a case or two to select between alternatives: for
example, in the sentence 'I myself launched myself on the seas waters of the Mediterranean', Conrad deleted the first 'myself' and 'seas'.
[5] This and other passages were revised so thoroughly as to disallow their being keyed
here to the critical text; see 'Emendation and Variation' list in the 'Apparatus'.

the typist being instructed to lay aside the manuscript and to work the inserted material into the typescript. Another alternative is that Conrad dictated material directly, working together with the typist as she struggled to make headway on transcribing the manuscript. However this may be, rewriting and revision were complex, thorough and painstaking, and verbal polishing and refining are responsible for textual cruxes in the extant carbon typescript.

Numerous variants between TScr and the serial texts establish that the essay underwent yet further revision in a document (or documents) no longer extant. Assuming that the clean-copy typescript was indeed 'clean' and that Conrad did not revise in it, this round of revision must have occurred in another typescript (now lost), or even two, the usual two typescripts of the final version being made, one for the *Blue Peter*, the other for circulation for sale in the American serial market.

In that market, the essay appeared in a shortened form. SA's editorial cuts fit the essay onto a single page, and the reference to 'a sea-travel magazine' was also deleted (18.6b). The serial texts otherwise differ slightly. Conrad's revisions in English serial proofs were rarely communicated to his American publishers, and, in a handful of instances, *Collier's* wordings are earlier forms.[1] This strengthens the case for the existence of two typescripts as well as revision in serial proofs. *Collier's* Americanized spelling and usage, changing, for instance, 'write to you' (22.20–21) to 'write you' and 'in the ship' to 'on the ship' (20.16b).[2] An editor also broke up lengthy paragraphs into smaller units. The *Last Essays* texts descend from the *Blue Peter*, either directly by way of a copy of the magazine or indirectly from a copy of the pamphlet. SE and P are textually identical, and either could have served as copy for Curle's typist.

Given the extent of revision in the typescript (and, possibly, in now-lost missing leaves), the manuscript is an even rougher draft than usual and must be rejected as copy-text. TScr, however, requires emendation to restore manuscript wordings mishandled by the typist as well as to incorporate Conrad's later revisions. In light of the text's complicated,

---

[1] E.g., 'good luck', 'absurd inconclusive', 'bursting' (shared with TScr), as opposed to SE's 'luck' (18.21c), 'inconclusive' (19.35) and 'burning' (20.15).

[2] This distinction has now largely disappeared in ordinary speech: in once-correct British usage, a seaman sailed 'in' a ship, whereas a passenger sailed 'on' one. (American usage seems never to have been firm about this, inclining generally even by Conrad's time to 'on'.)

even vexed, origins, however, emendation cannot be automatic and is of necessity both a delicate and perhaps, for the purist, a controversial matter: while some of the typist's interventions typically make sense of a hastily written draft, other variants originate with Conrad himself, effected either in a missing document or made verbally, as hypothesized above. For instance, MS's phrase 'some three months or so' rendered as 'three months' (20.29–30) in TSct is unlikely to have been altered by the typist on her own initiative: no obvious correction is called for, the alteration having been made on purely stylistic grounds.[1] The altered phrase has thus not been emended on the assumption that its revision was authorial, even though its first appearance is in TSct, and it would normally be rejected as a typist's intervention. On the other hand, the typist was, on balance, responsible for some small-scale changes: for instance, MS's 'at that epoch' (20.37) appears as 'of that epoch' in TSct, and the MS reading is restored. To adopt this policy of weighing the probable source of an alteration responds with nuance to the highly complicated textual situation witnessed in the surviving documents. A consistent, but chop-logic, policy whereby all readings first appearing in the TSct text would be rejected as originating with the typist would, whatever its theoretical purity, fail to respond to the actual circumstances. Textually the essay vies with 'Geography and Some Explorers' as the most complicated in this volume, and 'The *Torrens*: A Personal Tribute' is, like it, an eclectic text, composite in its origins and revised at several stages.

CHRISTMAS-DAY AT SEA

IN MID-1923, Conrad agreed to write the essay for publication in the popular women's magazine the *Delineator* (New York), to pay for gifts he bought for Florence and 'Patty' Doubleday, who, having accompanied him on his voyage home from New York, were then in England. He drafted and revised the essay between 14 June, the date he informed his agent that he was willing to undertake the commission, and 3 July, the date he posted it to him.[2] That Conrad wrote the essay in longhand, at a time when he was normally dictating to his secretary, suggests an even more precise date of composition. He

---

[1] Likewise, for example, the typist typed 'the passenger' as in MS and then interlinearly replaced 'the' with 'our poor' (22.4), a phrase not present in MS and obviously not introduced into the text by her; similarly, she replaced her originally typed 'knew' with 'had known', again interlinearly (21.27).

[2] Conrad to Eric S. Pinker, 14 June 1923 and [3 July 1923] (*Letters*, VIII, 113, 122).

complained of a 'painful wrist' on 14 June, the date he accepted the commission in a handwritten letter.[1] On the 21st, he noted Miss Hallowes's return to Oswalds, a return confirmed by the resumption of typed correspondence.[2] Despite lamentations on that date about his arm being 'still pretty bad' (*Letters*, VIII, 117), it seems that Conrad, although afflicted by the attack of gout, had managed to write the 1,500-word essay between 14 June and, at the latest, the 20th – that is, during his secretary's absence. Had she been available, he would presumably have dictated it to her.[3]

On 2 July, Conrad wrote to Eric Pinker that he would forward the essay to him the following day, adding that the manuscript would have 'to be put into shape and re-typed. It is about 800 words, but those people will be at liberty to cut it down to suit their space' (*Letters*, VIII, 121). The mention of possible cuts suggests that it had grown beyond its original word-limit, and Conrad's brief note accompanying the manuscript indicates that the essay had gone 'over 1000 w'.[4] On 5 July, Miss Hallowes wrote to Pinker to request that a duplicate copy be made for English use,[5] either emphasizing the suggestion Conrad had made when he had forwarded the manuscript to his agent or in response to an arrangement speedily contracted. Whatever the case, Pinker moved promptly on his client's request to secure English publication.[6] L(ewis) R(ose) Macleod, the *Daily Mail*'s literary editor, informed by Curle of the essay's availability for £60, made an offer on 10 July, and acknowledged receipt of this (now-lost) duplicate five days later.[7] Curle, on the paper's staff, had proved helpful, with Conrad thanking him in mid-July for the role he played in 'the successful negociation [*sic*]'.[8]

The manuscript, consisting of ten leaves, survives at the Harry Ransom Center, University of Texas at Austin (MS HRC). Titled 'Christmas-day at Sea' and identified as the 'First Draft', it is signed and dated '1st July. '23' on its last leaf. On 8 July 1923, Richard Curle

---

[1] Conrad to Pinker, 14 June 1923 (*Letters*, VIII, 113).
[2] Conrad to Pinker, 21 June 1923 (*Letters*, VIII, 117).
[3] Typed letters dated 21, 23, 25 and 27 June 1923 add weight to this scenario.
[4] Conrad to Eric S. Pinker, [3 July 1923] (*Letters*, VIII, 122).
[5] L. M. Hallowes to Pinker, 5 July 1923 (Berg).
[6] Pinker's efforts proved profitable for himself (his standard fee being 10 per cent) and for his client: the *Delineator* paid $500 for the essay, the *Daily Mail* £60 (*Documents*, p. 237). On payment from the *Delineator*, see also E. Kilday to Pinker, 17 August 1923 (Berg).
[7] L. R. Macleod to Eric S. Pinker, 10 July 1923 and 15 July 1923 (Berg).
[8] Conrad to Curle, 17 July 1923 (*Letters*, VIII, 134).

purchased this document for £25 along with the original six-page corrected and revised double-spaced ribbon-copy typescript (TS1 HRC)
made from it, bearing on its first page the authenticating note 'First
type. | J. Conrad'.[1] Two other corrected typescripts are also extant:
(1) a six-page doubled-spaced ribbon-copy typescript (TS2 HRC), formerly part of the Alfred A. Knopf Archive, initialled 'J. C.' at the bottom of the last page; and (2) a seven-page double-spaced carbon-copy
typescript corrected and revised by Conrad (TS3c TTU). Also surviving are two sets of corrected *Daily Mail* (SE) galley-proofs (SEp1 HRC
and SEp2 TTU). None of the extant typescripts served as setting-copy
for either the English or American serializations: Curle added TS1 to
his Conrad collection shortly after it was created, while the very survival of the other typescripts (such setting-copy typescripts normally
being discarded after use by the printers) and the lack of printers'
marks on them suggest that they were never in the printers' hands. At
least two other typescripts of the essay, then, must have once existed,
one for typesetting in England, the other used in America. For reasons
argued below, the revised text in TS1 (TS1r) provides the copy-text.

The essay appeared first in America in the *Delineator*'s December
1923 issue (SA1)[2] in a section titled 'I Remember a Christmas', which
also included recollections by the American writers Edith Wharton,
Booth Tarkington and the now-forgotten Ida M. Tarbell. This turns
out to be a truncated version, the second, third and final paragraphs
omitted, as were some sentences. It was subsequently published in full
in the *Daily Mail* (SE) on 24 December 1923, in two three-quarter-
length columns with a photograph of Conrad and his signature. (It
was reprinted in the December 1928 issue of *Country Life* (New York),
Doubleday's book text (A1) providing copy for that printing.)

The holograph text was drafted with what appears to be considerable ease.[3] TS1, on the other hand, is extensively revised. The typescript stage witnessed typical expansion (23.28a, 24.11), and characteristic small-scale polishing: for example, 'used to call them lunatic
asylums then' was revised to 'used to call them madhouses then in

---

[1] *Documents*, p. 217. Both MS and TS1 appeared in Curle's sale held at the American
    Art Association, New York, on 28 April 1927.
[2] *The Delineator* (December 1923), 10–11 (10).
[3] For a more detailed discussion of the context and textual history, see Ray Stevens and
    Robert W. Trogdon, '"Christmas Day at Sea": A Whaler, a Bundle of Papers, Two Boxes
    of Figs, Bibliographical Completeness, and Biographical and Textual Inaccuracies of
    Hemispheric Proportions', *Conradiana*, 33 (2001), 251–63.

our rude, cave-man way' (24.35–36). Despite offering no particular difficulties for the transcriber, MS's text came in for several kinds of misadventure: among other things, the typist failed to install a word chosen in final revision (23.5a); included deleted matter (see 'Textual Notes') and dropped out a phrase (23.6); and on occasion freely altered punctuation, replacing round brackets with commas, for instance, or an em-dash by a colon. Indeed, the typescript is so poorly typed that it is difficult to credit it as Miss Hallowes's work.

The typewritten text in the second typescript (TS2t) varies from TS1r only slightly: the typist twice altered punctuation, divided 'sometime' into 'some time' (24.38) and supplied an indefinite article (24.34). In TS2, Conrad made several revisions in wording and phrasing: for example, he changed 'It was' to 'We were' (23.26), 'there was no wind' to 'not a breath of wind anywhere' (23.28) and 'groping their way' to 'groping blindly' (23.30).

Two identical sets of unrevised galley-proofs were composed from the typescript that Miss Hallowes had requested Pinker's office to prepare. Conrad again revised in these, making several small but telling changes. Filed in the Macleod papers (TTU) with the second galley-proof, the carbon-copy typescript (TS3c) bears the note 'Return this proof to Mr MLeod'. The only corrections in that typescript are a half-dozen obvious typing errors.

The revised proofs illustrate that no matter how diligent an author may be, newspaper and serial editors get the last word – even if this proves to be erroneous. SE's text has two significant errors. An editor or compositor changed 'New Bedford' to 'New York' after Conrad had returned proofs to Macleod, perhaps thinking that English readers would not recognize the name of the once-famous American whaling port, or simply making an error of anticipation. The second change also skewed geography. When altering punctuation in both sets of proofs to emulate the signals coming from the *Alaska*, Conrad wrote: 'her name was: Alaska – two years out from New Bedford – last from Honolulu'. In heavy black ink on porous proof paper, he penned a lower case 'l' over the upper case 'L' of 'Last' in the unrevised proof because he had changed a full stop to a dash. The proof reveals that the top of the upper case 'L' protrudes enough through the black ink so that an editor or typesetter could misread the letter 'l' for a lower case 'e'. Thus, 'last' became 'east', and a suggestion of increased distance became the banal assertion that New York lies east of Honolulu.

A rough draft, MS is not the 'fair copy' traditionally adopted by editors as copy-text, with Conrad developing his work extensively in his first typescript and then tinkering with it further in TS2 and in serial proofs. Indeed, the essay, despite its brevity – or surely because of it – went through considerable revision from first impulse to final version. TS1r serves as the copy-text for the present edition, MS being overridden by Conrad's extensive rewriting and polishing in the 'draft' typescript. The adoption of that typescript, however, entails more emendation than usual in order to reinstate usages, styling and wordings mangled, misunderstood or simply changed by the typist. It is also emended to incorporate authorial revisions made in TS2 and in serial proofs. This text, whose evolution in several preprint documents was complex and at times even fraught, appears here in an authoritative form, with the interventions of its original typist finally expunged and the author's preferences restored. Dropped words and various subtle touches lost through slipshod typing – the appearance of 'fish' (that is, whales) in inverted commas, the placement of 'Season's Greetings' in upper case – appear in print for the first time.

OCEAN TRAVEL

CONRAD COMPLETED 'Ocean Travel' during his voyage to New York on the *Tuscania* between 21 April and 1 May 1923, a trip undertaken to promote sales of his books in America and to meet with his American publisher, F. N. Doubleday. He had planned to write while travelling, informing Eric S. Pinker on 9 April that he had an essay 'in my head which I may begin here [at Oswalds] and finish on board. Another one will suggest itself in due course, no doubt, and for all I expect to do, those 3 ought to be enough' (*Letters*, VIII, 74). The three essays, written in part to assist with travel expenses, were 'Ocean Travel', the preface to Thomas Beer's *Stephen Crane*, finished on 23 March, and perhaps 'Christmas-day at Sea', written not long after Conrad's return to England.

The date '29. Ap. 23', presumably that of completion, appears on the last leaf of MS (HRC), which consists of seven numbered leaves $8^1/_2$ in. × 13 in. ($21^1/_2$ cm × 33 cm). Likewise on this final leaf are initialled directions addressed to Richard Curle: '*Please correct, cut, arrange or alter as you think fit.*' In a letter on the leaf Conrad makes the comment: 'It's the best I can do. It is very poor, but I trust you will be able to make something of it. I can not look these pages over'

(*Letters*, VIII, 87). He added that, upon arriving in New York on the morning of 1 May, he would attempt to dispatch the piece by the noon mail-boat, and concluded that pain in his left wrist had impeded the text's expeditious completion.[1]

The essay appeared in the *Evening News* on 15 May 1923 (S), while Conrad was abroad.[2] It was spread across three half-columns and accompanied by two illustrations: one of two ships sailing beside one another, and a sketch of Conrad from a photograph by Charles Beresford. The *Evening News* paid £50 for publication.[3]

MS serves as copy-text. The holograph text is remarkably clear and the writing fluid, with only eleven lines deleted and then recast. It features, however, slips of the pen and casual misspellings, and some required punctuation is lacking. The document appeared in Curle's 1927 sale (item 7),[4] with the following catalogue description: 'It is perhaps unique among his later manuscripts in that no author's corrected typescript was ever made.' Since newspapers did not usually set copy from manuscripts and the holograph's preservation would have required special, even extraordinary, handling, a typescript was obviously made, possibly through Pinker. This would typically have been discarded after setting. Given Curle's close involvement in handling this piece, he probably passed proofs. Either Curle or an editor provided a paragraph-break not present in MS and the serial subtitle – Conrad's own title on the first leaf of MS is tentative: 'Ocean Travel (?)'.

Some of the alterations to accidentals made by Curle or the editor at the *Evening News* are necessary and would, no doubt, have been expected by Conrad, including the correction of misspellings and of a mere slip of the pen (29.2). Adoption of MS as copy-text ensures that Conrad's lighter pointing is restored, while S's sophistications, particularly its commas in compound sentences, are rejected, as are, likewise, the verbal tidyings effected by Curle or an in-house editor

---

[1] The journalist Christopher Morley reported that when Conrad arrived in New York, his left arm was bandaged (J. H. Stape, *The Several Lives of Joseph Conrad* (2007), p. 249).

[2] 'My Hotel in Mid-Atlantic. Modern Day Luxury – A Contrast with the Sailing-Ship Days', *Evening News*, 15 May 1923, p. 4.

[3] The amount of payment is extrapolated from Conrad's request to his agent to debit his account for a commission of £5; see Conrad to Eric S. Pinker, 2 July 1923 (*Letters*, VIII, 121).

[4] American Art Association, New York, 28 April 1927. The manuscript also appeared in the American Art Association sales catalogue of 1 June 1950 (*Register*, p. 45).

at the *Evening News*. The former interventions affect the rhythms of Conrad's prose, which are fluid and direct in MS; the latter make Conrad a more correct writer of English than he sometimes was. Ironically, however, a typist mis-read *suprême de volaille* (29.17) as *suprême au volaille*, calling into question Conrad's mastery of French. (In a revised phrase she also misread 'This' as 'It' (27.15) and seems simply to have dropped off the 's' in 'conditions' (27.19)).

Although Curle had the manuscript in his possession when he was gathering material for *Last Essays*, printer's copy for the book-text typescript was provided by a typescript made from S. As regards substantives, E1 and A1 differ from S in correcting agreement (28.2). E1 typically parts company with MS, S and A1 in its handling of compounds,[1] while the typist of the book typescript deleted hyphens in 'sea-travel' (27.21) and 'sea-voyage' (27.22), clearly present in MS and carried over into S. Adopting MS restores Conrad's own spelling ('can not' (29.32) as opposed to 'cannot') and, to the degree that it can be ascertained, his hyphenation.[2]

OUTSIDE LITERATURE

CONRAD WROTE 'Outside Literature' at the request of James Bone, the *Manchester Guardian*'s London editor, who wanted a contribution from him for the newspaper's 'Annual Literary Supplement' of 1922. On 11 November 1922, Conrad was at work on the essay,[3] on the very day the stage adaptation of *The Secret Agent* closed after a brief run at London's Ambassadors Theatre. The essay was finished, and two clean-copy typescripts made from the first draft typescript, by 14 November, the day on which Conrad forwarded a typescript to the *Manchester Guardian*, six days before the submission deadline (*Letters*, VII, 590). Conrad sent another typescript to Pinker on 16 November. Observing that he had retained American rights, he asked his agent

---

[1] S and A1 share MS's forms in the following instances: 'sea-life' (28.20), 'live stock' (28.31) and 'promenade decks' (29.10); E1 has no hyphen in the first instance and supplies one in the others.

[2] In some instances, the latter proves open to widely varying interpretation; for example, 'sea-life' (28.20) and 'four-footed' (28.32) may be seen differently by different readers, Conrad having run the words together with what can be interpreted as a short linking stroke.

[3] Conrad to Eric S. Pinker, 11 November 1922 (*Letters*, VII, 579–80).

to pursue placing the piece in that market 'if the thing itself seems to you worthwhile' (*Letters*, VII, 589). On 29 November, Thomas J. Wise received the extant first-draft typescript (TS Yale) 'in exchange for the MS of the Preface for R Curle's book' that he had been 'good enough to give' to Conrad (*Letters*, VII, 604).[1] The revised text (TSr) of that document serves as copy-text for the present edition.

'Outside Literature' first appeared, under the title 'Notices to Mariners', in the *Supplement to The Manchester Guardian* (SE1) on 4 December 1922; it was reprinted in the *Manchester Guardian Weekly* (SE2) on 8 December with the same title under the heading 'Gift-Books for Christmas'.[2] The latter printing features a photograph of the author by Alvin Langdon Coburn. The essay also appeared in the New York *Bookman* (SA) for February 1923 as 'Outside Literature',[3] the title at the top of the extant typescript.

Conrad complained to Pinker on 19 November that the *Guardian* had failed to acknowledge the essay's receipt and asked him to confirm this and to ascertain the publication date (*Letters*, VII, 590–91). His annoyance went unabated, the newspaper having failed to supply the requested information. On 14 December, Conrad complained once again that he had received neither copies of the article nor his fee (£10 10s 0d). Even though he had written the essay in his 'own time' (that is, his agent had not arranged the commission), he promised Pinker a guinea commission upon payment (*Letters*, VII, 618).[4] On 31 January 1923, Conrad acknowledged Pinker's communication that the essay had appeared in America (*Letters*, VIII, 15).

The typescript, typed in blue ink, is of bond paper bearing the water-mark 'ORIGINAL | CHARTHAM MILLS | KENT'.[5] The double-spaced pages, numbered 1–6 in type, were subsequently renumbered 1–8 by hand (not Conrad's) in order to accommodate a holograph

---

[1] *Documents*, p. 217. Curle subsequently acquired the draft typescript, George T. Keating buying it at the Curle sale of April 1927. Conrad's reference is to his Introduction to Curle's *Into the East*, originally consigned to Wise.

[2] *Supplement to the Manchester Guardian*, 4 December 1922, p. iii; *Manchester Guardian Weekly*, 8 December 1922, p. 453.

[3] *Bookman* (February 1923), 680–82. Copyright was applied for on 24 January 1923 (B571651), United States Copyright Office, *Catalog of Copyright Entries (Renewals), Part 1: January–June 1950*, p. 41. The publishers of the *Bookman*, George H. Doran Company, sent a cheque for $50; *The Bookman* (initialled 'R', perhaps S. M. Rinehart) to Eric S. Pinker, 26 January 1923 (Berg).

[4] A guinea (21s) would be Pinker's customary 10 per cent fee.

[5] For an illustration of this watermark, see *Register*, p. 91.

title-page made and signed by Conrad to authenticate the document: 'Outside Literature written for the Manchester Guardian (Literary Supplement for 1922)'. The second hand-numbered page consists of a typed and initialled note by Curle that provides information about the document's history and state: 'The typescript of this article . . . was dictated direct to his secretary by Joseph Conrad and then revised by him as shown. No holograph was ever made.' Written in Conrad's hand across the top of the first page of text is 'M[anchest]^{er} G[uar]^{dan} [*sic*]' and his signature.

Given the extensive revision in the extant typescript and the forwarding of typescripts to Pinker and to the *Manchester Guardian*, it is evident that a second typescript was prepared from TS in duplicate, these copies serving as printer's copy for the serials. Substantive alterations – as regards usage (31.24, 32.15, 32.23b) and additions or deletions (30.15, 30.33–34) – indicate common descent of the serials from that now-lost ancestor. SE2 was almost certainly set directly from SE1 (their texts are identical). Despite his frustrated letters to Pinker relating to the *Manchester Guardian*'s uncommunicativeness, Conrad probably saw SE proofs.

Curle's choice of SA as copy for *Last Essays* means that the hitherto received texts do not reflect Conrad's final revisions. In addition to Americanizing orthography ('toward' and 'civilization'), SA corrected an obvious error in agreement (30.29), allowed to stand in the SE texts. Curle's typist reversed the changes in spelling, but SA's editorial normalizations and errors of anticipation descended to the book texts. Thus, for instance, 'printing press', 'never learned' and 'question' were substituted for Conrad's own 'a printing press' (30.27), 'could never learn' (33.9) and 'doubt' (33.18), while the intensifier 'very' (33.6a) and 'as a remarkable play' (33.15) disappeared altogether, words having dropped out during setting or as the result of editorial intrusion. Selecting TSr as copy-text restores the author's own preferences and wordings, although the document's casual misspellings have, of course, been corrected.

LEGENDS

FOUND UNFINISHED on his desk when Conrad died on 3 August 1924, this essay was rushed into print in the *Daily Mail* (SE) by Curle, and appeared a few weeks later in the *New York Times Magazine* (SA), with extracts subsequently appearing in trade journals.[1] The holograph (MS Morgan) serves as copy-text. The heavily revised fragment is written on twelve leaves of cream wove, very faintly lined paper bearing the watermark 'Wm: N E W T O N B O N D '. All but the last leaf is numbered in Conrad's hand.[2] The final two paragraphs, totalling 139 words, are little more than notes that would have been expanded, perhaps by some 400 words, to reach the originally proposed total of 1,600. The typed transcriptions that Curle sent to the newspapers have not survived.

The essay had been the subject of discussion between Conrad and Curle by early July 1924, with plans to place it with the *Daily Mail*, Curle's employer: on the 8th, Conrad informed him that the article would deal with 'Sailors Saints University Dons etc.', apparently suggesting a tentative title, 'Subjects of Legend' (*Letters*, VIII, 400). On the same day, Conrad told his agent that he was calculating possible payments – '£80 for here and US and perhaps £20 for the MS' – suggesting that if in the end the *Daily Mail* declined the piece, *World's Work* might take it (*Letters*, VIII, 401–02). In late July, he told Pinker that he was awaiting Miss Hallowes's return from holidays to complete the essay as only she 'could make out that mess'. He also indicated that he would, in due course, forward two clean-copy typescripts, one for the *Daily Mail*, the other for the yet-to-be-determined American serial.[3]

Curle estimated that the essay was approximately three-quarters complete on Conrad's death, and acted to see it quickly printed and placed on the manuscript market. On 8 August, less than a week

---

[1] *Daily Mail*, 15 August 1924, p. 8; *New York Times Magazine Section*, 7 September 1924, pp. 1–2. A substantial extract from the *Daily Mail*, under the title 'Conrad's Great Tribute to Miss C. Fox-Smith', appeared in the fortnightly trade journal *The Publishers' Circular and Booksellers' Record*, 23 August 1924 (pp. 257, 259), and, to publicize *Last Essays*, Dent's house journal, *Bookmark*, printed extracts from this essay and 'John Galsworthy' in its spring 1926 issue (pp. 2–3, 3–4).

[2] Responding to a letter of condolence from J. E. Hodgson, Curle wrote on 7 August that he would 'probably wish to consult you about the sale of his last (uncompleted) MS' (*Portrait in Letters*, p. 248). Curle did offer it to Thomas J. Wise, who declined it on the grounds that it was 'incomplete' and would, no doubt, prove to be too expensive (Wise to Curle, 14 August 1924 (Indiana)). Offered for sale through J. A. Allen & Company of London in September 1924 for £250, the manuscript was acquired by A. S. W. Rosenbach of Philadelphia, and later sold to the American art and literary manuscripts collector Herschel V. Jones through whom it came to the Morgan (*Register*, p. 31).

[3] Conrad to Eric S. Pinker, 27 July 1924 (*Letters*, VIII, 409).

after that event, the American literary agent Carl Brandt of Brandt & Kirkpatrick, at the time the usual agent in New York for J. B. Pinker & Sons, sent a telegram to Eric Pinker proposing a payment of $2,000 to Conrad's executors for American rights should the essay run to 3,000 words, and insisting that publication in the *Daily Mail* bear a United States copyright notice.[1] On 12 August, Pinker notified Brandt that he was sending facsimiles of the manuscript and Conrad's signature to America, receiving an offer of $500 the next day, the amount reduced because the 1,250-word essay was shorter than originally assumed.[2] It was expected that syndication would bring a further $1,000.

'Joseph Conrad's Last Article' appeared on the *Daily Mail*'s page 8, accompanied by Curle's note, a reproduction of the manuscript's final leaf and facsimile of Conrad's signature, a photograph of the author and an editorial note, which stated that Conrad was writing 'within a couple of hours of being stricken by the illness which proved fatal' and that he told Curle the day before his death that he 'hoped from this one article . . . would spring a volume of intimate memories of the saliors [*sic*] he had met which would be a kind of pendent volume to "The Mirror of the Sea"'.

The *New York Times Magazine*, which published the fragment under the title 'Joseph Conrad's Last Writing | The Truth Which Rebukes the Legend of the Sailor's Life as It Does That of the Saint's', embellished the fragment in several ways. A facsimile of the last leaf appeared as a half-page illustration, framed by sea gods holding tridents in a storm-tossed ocean; the caption reads 'The Last Paragraph of the Last Unfinished Writing'. Also included were a photograph of Conrad on his arrival in New York in May 1923 and an essay of reminiscence mainly focussing on that visit. Inset at the bottom of the first page is a similar note, with two additional paragraphs commenting that on the day before his death Conrad had discussed 'Legends' with Curle, who had seen the last page of the essay just as 'the motor car was announced that was to take them for the drive during which Conrad was seized with his last illness'.

MS witnesses characteristic revision at the moment of inscription, with Conrad typically searching for stylistic effects and greater precision of expression: for example, he substituted his original 'done

---

[1] Carl Brandt to Pinker, 8 August 1924 (Berg). The following note appeared after the essay's close: 'Copyright 1924 United States of America. Reprinting in whole or part expressly forbidden.'

[2] Pinker to Brandt, 12 August 1924 (Berg).

with' by 'finished and done with' (34.5), and in 'notoriously uncritical' (34.21) dropped the adverb; he qualified 'decorative' with the phrase 'upon the whole' (34.8) and, altering tone, inserted 'I take it' (34.33). There are false starts as well as the usual elaborations. This draft has all the hallmarks of hasty writing, both in its various misspellings and in its missed-out words, to say nothing of the general roughness of the prose, particularly that of the last few paragraphs.

Responding to a text left unrevised by its author, Curle or an in-house editor, or possibly both, made it acceptable for print by correcting slips of the pen (35.27a) and spelling errors and by adding necessary articles and dropped words – 'when' (35.27b) and 'of' (35.20). In a few cases grammar was adjusted and wording tidied (35.35b).[1] Hyphenation and upper and lower case were typically tampered with. As to the former, however, 'Marco-Polo', a ship's name, was carried over by SE where it is placed neither in italics nor inverted commas, the hyphen a French styling for ship or street names, or a borrowing from a practice then somewhat dated in English (for example, Fleet-street). Curle, who corrected one factual error, changing 'Percy' to 'Basil' Lubbock (36.23), created another, mistakenly deleting the phrase 'Miss C. Fox-Smith's book' (36.25). In line with normal newspaper practice to avoid long uninterrupted swathes of text, a number of paragraph-breaks were inserted, particularly in SA.

SA and SE differ significantly, which suggests that the *New York Times* had access to the facsimile that Pinker had sent to Brandt or to a typescript made from MS, in addition to Curle's corrected typescript. SA varies from SE in a handful of instances affecting substantives, with SA dropping out words (35.37), misconstruing them (35.40) or declining to alter where SE does so.[2] On the whole, SA is not only more lightly edited, but it also more closely agrees with MS's text. For *Last Essays* Curle relied not on the manuscript text but on SE, in which he had possibly earlier had a hand. E1 typically departs from SE in placing 'Nature' in upper case (34.7), in hyphenating 'rudely-woven' (35.23) and in slightly heavier pointing. (In these instances, A1 has lower case and lacks hyphens.)

The text as Conrad left it requires, and indeed insists upon, several adjustments for print, the writer's death preventing not only its

---

[1] The grammatical changes at issue are as follows: 'had' was changed to 'have had' (34.14), 'it records' to 'they record' (36.8a) and 'its' to 'his' (36.28). Articles, some required and an aspect of English grammar characteristically problematic for Conrad, were added (e.g., 34.17, 35.22, 36.12).

[2] See, for example, 34.17, 36.8b, 36.19.

completion but also its revision and correction. Missing words and full stops are supplied, and, as throughout the present edition and the Cambridge Edition generally, impossible spellings (for instance, 'renounciation' and 'knowdge') are corrected silently. Either Curle or the serial editors supplied punctuation missed out in rapid writing, this adjustment necessary to prevent the reader from being distracted and in accord with the universal practices of the language. Again, the unfinished state of this text urges this as reasonable practice, the sort of minimal correction that Conrad would have expected from professional typists, editors and compositors. In these instances, then, the critical text likewise departs from the copy-text in order to avoid mere oddity.[1] A diplomatic transcription, whatever its interest to a specialist audience, would depart from, and even contravene, the spirit of the volume that Curle conceived and saw into print; moreover, had Conrad lived to finish this piece he would surely have effected the minimal adjustments made here.

THE UNLIGHTED COAST

THE ONLY ARTICLE of a proposed three to be written for the Admiralty as propaganda for the war-effort, 'The Unlighted Coast' was drafted during late December 1916 and early 1917 when Conrad was at work on an early version of *The Arrow of Gold*.[2] In the end, the Admiralty found it unsuitable for its purposes. J. B. Pinker apparently attempted to place the piece for serialization in early 1917, but his efforts, complicated by the fact that Conrad could not receive payment by terms of his arrangements with the Admiralty, failed.[3] The essay remained unpublished until after the writer's death, when Richard Curle, acting for the Conrad estate, arranged for its publication in *The Times*.[4]

---

[1] See the 'Emendations of Accidentals' list and 'Textual Notes'.
[2] See Conrad to J. B. Pinker, [2 January 1917] and [early January 1917] (*Letters*, VI, 4–5, 7–8).
[3] Conrad to J. B. Pinker, [23 January 1917] and [24 January 1917] (*Letters*, VI, 15–16).
[4] 'The Unlighted Coast. A Lost Article by Conrad', *The Times*, 18 August 1925, pp. 13–14. The copyright notice was exclusive, asserting rights in the United States and Canada. An attempt to place the essay in the United States through an American agent, however, proved unsuccessful: it was rejected by *Collier's*, the *Saturday Evening Post*, *Everybody's*, *Liberty*, the *Pictorial Review* and *McCall's* as well as by three firms with journals – Harper's, McClure's and Scribner's; see Nannie V. Joseph to J. B. Pinker & Sons, 17 December 1925 (Northwestern University).

Sold to John Quinn in early March 1920,[1] the manuscript, consisting of twenty-one leaves, was purchased for $1,750 at the 1923 Quinn sale by the American composer and book collector Jerome Kern, who issued the text as a privately printed limited-edition pamphlet for Christmas 1925. After the Brick Row Book Shop of New York acquired the manuscript in the Kern sale of January 1929,[2] it disappeared from sight until surfacing recently in a private collection. The typescript submitted to the Admiralty has eluded efforts to trace it,[3] and is apparently lost. The sole surviving exemplar of at least three typescripts is a sixteen-page double-spaced ribbon-copy typescript corrected and revised by Conrad (TS Colgate),[4] auctioned at the Hodgson sale and subsequently sold by Swift & Spencer of London in spring 1935 to Henry A. Colgate,[5] who donated it to Colgate University. The revised text in it serves as copy-text.

Conrad met with Captain Sir Douglas Brownrigg, Chief Censor, then recruiting prominent public figures to publicize the navy's role in the war, on 5 September 1916, and later visited naval bases in Scotland and the North to gather copy. Brownrigg hoped that the articles might be 'ready for issue early in November & during that month',[6] but Conrad made no progress on this project until late December,[7] and in the end wrote only one of the promised essays.

The manuscript (MS Private) is in black ink on twenty-one leaves of lined paper removed from a writing-tablet. Some verso leaves are inscribed, and the last four leaves are paginated A–D. The writing is characteristic throughout: there are the usual false starts, deletions,

---

[1] Conrad to John Quinn, 4 March 1920 (*Letters*, VII, 44).
[2] *The Library of Jerome Kern, New York City... To be Sold by His Order at Unreserved Public Sale* (Anderson Galleries, 1929).
[3] Enquiries have established that it is preserved neither in the National Archives nor at the Admiralty.
[4] TS bears the pencilled note '2 copies' in Conrad's hand, an indication that 'clean' copies were, as usual, to be made.
[5] *Register*, p. 85. (Location information has been corrected and updated in the online version of this resource, available on the Joseph Conrad Society (UK) website at www.josephconradsociety.org.) For the items in the sale, see *A Catalogue of Books, Manuscripts and Corrected Typescripts from the Library of the late Joseph Conrad* (1925). Jessie Conrad owned most of the items sold; however, the pamphlet proofs used by Conrad to pull together *Notes on Life and Letters* were Richard Curle's property.
[6] Captain Sir Douglas Brownrigg to Conrad, 13 October 1916, *Portrait in Letters*, p. 116.
[7] The first leaf of MS bears in Conrad's hand the description 'Written in pen and ink in Jany 1917', but the letter to J. B. Pinker of [2 January 1917], assuming dating is relatively secure, suggests that writing must have begun prior to the turn of the year.

interlinear additions and stylistic tinkering. Conrad revised extensively in the extant typescript and at this stage supplied a title.[1] In transcribing MS the typist altered spellings, dropped and misunderstood words and failed to provide emphases; thus, the text eventually printed not only perpetuated her errors but also at times represented her preferences. On a more positive note, her interventions involved supplying missing terminal punctuation. This revised typescript was transcribed to produce the now-lost clean-copy typescripts forwarded to the Admiralty and to J. B. Pinker.

The version of the essay in *The Times* (S), two and a half columns beginning on the leader page and continuing onto the next, is preceded by introductory remarks. In accordance with newspaper practice, the text is divided by an in-house editor's sub-headings, and *The Times*'s preferred '-ize'/'-ization' spelling is imposed on 'civilisation' and 'harmonising' (MS's and TS's spelling). Pointing is heavier than in the manuscript, and commas were provided in series to conform to the newspaper's house-style; an editor or compositor also adjusted the document for print, adding necessary (as well as conventional) punctuation left out during rapid inscription and not supplied in TS. Kern's pamphlet, a transcription of the manuscript by an unknown individual made for private distribution as a Christmas present, has no authority and lies outside the line of transmission. Its variants go unreported in the 'Apparatus'.

Curle used S as copy for the *Last Essays* typescripts, with the result that the received text, in addition to perpetuating the original typist's misprisions, also enshrines those of S's editor, including the division of one sentence into two, with the consequence that sense becomes muddled.[2] Conrad revised in typescript so extensively as to make MS only a rough draft, and TSr provides copy-text, repaired as required by reference to MS.

THE DOVER PATROL

ACCORDING TO Richard Curle, Conrad wrote this essay on the request of Lord Northcliffe, finishing it, as a note on the extant

---

[1] MS lacks a title, being designated, apparently, 'Paper for Admiralty', which was later revised to '1st and only Admiralty Paper'.

[2] A full stop wrongly follows 'task' (39.28) in S as well, of course, as in the book texts derived from it.

typescript indicates, on 23 July 1921.[1] Given the essay's length, drafting presumably began a few days before that date, for Conrad reported to his agent at around this time that he was 'working all the morning and gasping most of the afternoon'.[2] The essay, published in *The Times* under the title 'Heroes of the Straits | Dover Patrol Memorial. | Mr. Joseph Conrad's Tribute', appeared on the day of the unveiling of the monument to the Dover Patrol by the Prince of Wales (later Edward VIII).[3]

The following preprint documents survive: (1) a single holograph leaf (MS Yale) containing a draft of the essay's second paragraph and the first sentence of the third; (2) a single draft page, numbered 8 in type (TS1 Yale), containing a typewritten text followed by an addition in holograph;[4] (3) a ten-page complete typescript (TS2 BL Ashley 2942), corrected and extensively revised by Conrad, on white laid paper bearing the watermark 'CHARTHAM MILLS | KENT', accompanied by a signed, holograph title-page created for the document's sale to Thomas J. Wise. The revised text of the complete typescript (TS2r) serves as copy-text.

The MS leaf bears in its top left-hand corner a description in Miss Hallowes's hand as follows: 'The Dover Patrol. Page 1 | slight variation from text'. MS's text appears integrally in the typewritten text of the British Library typescript (TS2t); however, the third paragraph varies, and the procedures involved in the essay's production cannot be recovered. Conrad may have begun dictating the piece, with immediate revision of what had been done sparking off writing. In any event, the surviving leaf is almost certainly the only one written out by Conrad in longhand, the hypothesis that no complete manuscript ever existed being supported by the fact that Conrad's manuscripts were preciously preserved for sale to Wise, typescripts being sold for less. However that may be, the typescript's survival indicates that a clean-copy typescript was made from it and that (now-lost) document was sent to *The Times* to serve as printer's copy.

---

[1] See Appendix A. The essay's writing is undocumented in extant correspondence, although several letters of August and September 1921 concern payment for it (*Letters*, VII, 325–7, 329, 332, 333–4, 336, 337).

[2] Conrad to J. B. Pinker, [20 or 21 July 1921] (*Letters*, VII, 318).

[3] *The Times*, 27 July 1921, pp. 11–12.

[4] The MS leaf and composite page (typescript/holograph) appeared along with a copy of the pamphlet of the essay in Heffer's catalogue 289 (item 171) of 15 July 1927, priced at £21 (*Register*, p. 17).

The surviving documents suggest complex procedures involving several rounds of revision and typing. The single manuscript leaf and a half-typed and half-holograph page (TS1), both of which are drafts of material in the complete typescript, represent earlier stages in the text's development. The scant revisions on page 4 of TS2, compared with those throughout and the fact that page 3 only fills a quarter of the page and page 6 half of one, likewise hint at a separate drafting stage and the later incorporation of material into typescript. Conrad also revised heavily in the Wise typescript; he expanded and characteristically refined his phrasing. The typist's preferences and errors also became part of the historical text: she twice gave 'great war' upper-case initials, not following the manuscript, and, by forgetting to indent at the top of page 4, missed out a paragraph-break. (This is reinstated in the critical text at 45.20.)

The substantive variants between TS2r and S are authorial, but whether Conrad made a handful of further changes in the now-lost clean-copy typescript made from the Wise typescript or in serial proofs, or in both documents, is unclear. Even given the short lead-time between completion and publication, he would probably have been afforded an opportunity to see proofs: this piece was commissioned and his renown, as the sub-heading in S makes clear, was being used to celebrate the occasion.

The essay was published as a pamphlet (P) printed by H. J. Goulden, Ltd, of Canterbury in September or October 1922. Only a few textual variants separate it from S, some obviously compositor's errors. That it possibly derived from a carbon of the clean-copy typescript is suggested by its sharing with TSr the phrase 'embodied in', whereas only the word 'in' (47.3) appears in S. In any event, Conrad would typically have been little involved in its production, and its few departures from the Wise typescript and serial text, although part of the textual record, are irrelevant to the construction of a critical text.

For publication in *The Times*, an editor divided the piece with four sub-headings, altered paragraphing and upper and lower case and added punctuation, but was otherwise mainly content with minor tidying (the addition of hyphens in several compounds) and house-styling, which included the alteration of spelling – 'judgement' to 'judgment' (45.3) and 'jeopardising' to 'jeopardizing' (49.4). The editor likewise imposed consistency on TS2r's varying use of commas in series.

Adopting TS2r reinstates Conrad's loose, but effective, punctuation and his more fluid, even conversational, rhythms as well as his own capitalization practices. In a handful of instances, however, necessary commas missing in TS2r have been imported from S.

MEMORANDUM

CONRAD WROTE this memorandum at the invitation of Lawrence Durning Holt, junior partner in and managing director of Liverpool's Ocean Steam Ship Company, who, on 16 July 1920, asked for Conrad's observations on constructing a five-masted sailing ship that his company wished to build to train cadets for the Merchant Service.[1] On 20 July, Conrad agreed to write on this subject, and on 24 July promised to forward to Holt a discussion of about fourteen pages with a letter that would explain the concept of 'classical training' at sea.[2] Holt and his designer lunched at Oswalds on 3 August to discuss the project and to afford Holt the opportunity to examine the text, which Conrad promised to post in two days' time. Upon enquiring in August 1920 about possible publication of the memorandum in pamphlet form, Thomas J. Wise was told that Conrad had no plans to publish the document.[3] Its first appearance in print was in *Last Essays*.

Two ribbon-copy typescripts are extant: (1) the first draft (TS1 BL Ashley MS. 4788), dictated by Conrad to his secretary on 23 July, consisting of nineteen pages typed in blue ribbon on white wove paper with the watermark 'CHARTHAM MILLS | KENT';[4] and (2) the twelve-page clean-copy typescript (TS2 Private), sent to Holt on 25 July with a letter outlining Conrad's concept of classical sea training (*Letters*, VII, 149–50).[5] TS2 remained in the possession of Holt's heirs until it was sold in London in 1994 for £12,500, along with

[1] Lawrence Durning Holt to Conrad, 16 July 1920, *Portrait in Letters*, pp. 159–60.
[2] Conrad to Holt, 20 July 1920 and 24 July 1920 (*Letters*, VII, 144–5, 148–9).
[3] Hallowes to Wise, 23 August 1920 (BL Ashley 2953).
[4] TS1's pages are varyingly numbered at the top centre beginning on page 2 and running consecutively. Some numbers are typed, while others are (presumably) in Miss Hallowes's hand. Conrad himself numbered pages 2, 3 and 4. A holograph title-page added by Conrad bears the following title: 'Memorandum | on the Scheme for building | and equipping a Sailing Ship | for perfecting the training | of Merchant Service Officers'. When this was added, the pages were re-numbered 1–20 in the upper right-hand corner, in another hand. The first typed page bears the description 'July 1920. First Draft' in Conrad's hand in red crayon, and he signed the typescript at the top of page 1 and the bottom of page 20.
[5] Some of TS2's pages are double-spaced and some not: more than half are single-spaced and indented. The last page is signed.

correspondence related to it.[1] The revised text (TS1r) serves as the copy-text for the present edition.

As was typical of Conrad's working habits at this period, the typescript was – apart from its final paragraphs – dictated. Vestiges of dictation may be witnessed, for example, in TSt's spelling of 'combing' for 'coaming' (54.28) and 'tackel fawls' for 'tackle-falls' (58.18–19). The various media suggest that Conrad revised at several stages: most of the revisions are in black ink, but there are occasional insertions in grey pencil in the first few pages; alterations in blue pencil begin on page 5 and alterations in grey pencil occur on the last three pages. Wise purchased this typescript, which he rightly describes as 'heavily interlined and corrected in manuscript' (that is, by hand). Alterations are of various kinds, as Conrad tinkered with diction and vocabulary, refined his ideas and typically attempted greater precision, deleting as well as adding material. The title went through several changes.[2]

Set up as a working document for Conrad's meeting with Holt and his designer, TS2 is Conrad's corrected and revised version. He added roman numerals to mark transitions, and made deletions.[3] On the whole, the texts of TS1r and TS2 vary little, although in transcribing from TS1 the typist freely intervened with regard to punctuation.

The text published in *Last Essays* derives from TS2r. Jean Aubry,[4] engaged in collecting materials for *Joseph Conrad: Life & Letters* (1927), borrowed Holt's copy of the memorandum for three weeks, explaining that Curle wished to include the piece in *Last Essays*, for which material was then being assembled. Aubry acknowledged receipt of the typescript from Holt on 19 August 1925, and returned it, with a letter of thanks, on 8 September 1925.[5] During this period, Curle had a copy made (probably in duplicate) from it, which served as printer's copy for *Last Essays*. Differences between E1 and A1 are primarily presentational, but Curle also intervened in the text, correcting what

---

[1] R. A. Gekoski, Bookseller, *Catalogue 19* (1995), item 28.
[2] The typewritten title on page 1 is '*Memorandum*', with the following subtitle below it in Conrad's hand: 'Relating to a sailing-ship for perfecting the training of Merchant Service officers belonging to the Port of Liverpool'. The styling adopted in the present edition for the subtitle, however, is that of TS2, approved by him, with a hyphen in 'sailing-ship' but none in 'fitting out'.
[3] I.e., 55.27, 56.6, 56.16, 58.17b.
[4] Aubry used the pen-name 'G. Jean-Aubry'; here a distinction is made between the name under which he published and that he actually bore.
[5] Aubry to Lawrence Durning Holt, 19 August 1925 and 8 September 1925 (Private).

is, in fact, an error, altering TS2's 'for 3 years' for Conrad's service in the *Torrens* to 'for two years' (55.1–2); in doing so, he may have blurred an impression Conrad wished to create.[1]

Adopting TS1r as copy-text has the advantage of more reliably presenting Conrad's choices, although, given that this was a dictated text, this is a relative matter. In any event, the selection gives more focus to the interventions in TS2, which, in the case of necessary punctuation, can be weighed on individual merit. The selection of TS1r as copy-text allows the reader so interested to examine Conrad's subsequent changes by reference to the 'Apparatus'. Conrad's accidentals in TS1r are more consistent with his usual practices than are those in typescripts prepared by his typist, the single-spaced paragraphs of TS2 apart. It should be remembered, moreover, that TS2 was not prepared for publication but intended as a document for discussion with two seasoned ship-builders over luncheon at Conrad's home, and that its address was not to a general but to a private audience, the essay remaining unprinted until its appearance in *Last Essays*.

Two presentational matters require comment. The text of the present edition more closely resembles A1 in its traditional paragraphing and spacing for more than half the text of TS2t, which is indented and single-spaced, presumably on Conrad's direction, in order to set it off from double-spaced text. To represent single-spaced passages Dent's text reduced the font size but declined to adopt the five-space indentation of TS2t. Numbers have been allowed to stand as they are in the copy-text, with their styling for print by Curle's typist or the book editors rejected; again, the special status of this as a document for private circulation argues that its casual character be retained. The critical text does, however, adopt the roman numerals that Conrad added in TS2 to designate breaks. Published posthumously, the essay, like 'The Congo Diary' and 'Up-river Book', has circulated in print in forms not supervised by Conrad himself but by Richard Curle and the other agents who saw it into print.

THE LOSS OF THE *DALGONAR*

'THE LOSS OF THE *DALGONAR*', a letter to the editor of the *London Mercury*, was published in the journal's December 1921 issue

---

[1] For more on the decision to retain the original, see 'Textual Notes'.

(p. 187). Conrad was responding to a query by L. C. Gane in the October issue that questioned a detail in W. A. H. Mull's September article, 'A True Story. Log and Record of the Wreck of the Ship *Dalgonar* of Liverpool, bound from Callao to Taltal'. (See Appendix B for the full texts of Gane and Mull.) No preprint texts survive, and the letter as published in the *London Mercury* (S) serves as copy-text.

Two corrected typescripts found in Conrad's papers on his death and sold at the Hodgson sale to Spencer & Swift for £21 remain unlocated (Hodgson 181). The first was offered for sale again by the New York rare book dealer Edgar H. Wells, and a facsimile of its third and final page reproduced in the sales catalogue (item 79).[1] The facsimile consists of three lines of corrected typescript, which constitutes part of the letter's last sentence, beginning at 'put on the endurance'. A holograph addition at the bottom of the same page appears in the letter published in the *London Mercury* (62.31–63.4), and Conrad later added a sentence either in the typescript sent to the *Mercury* or in proofs (if such were sent to him) that appears in S: 'And *there* was the danger' (63.3–4).

E1's text differs from S and A1 in several ways: in presentation; in transposing, either inadvertently or as an editorial alteration, 'then was' to 'was then' (62.24); in placing 'Chief Officer' (63.25) in lower case; and in matters of house-style. The typist of Curle's setting-copy typescript dropped a word (63.14) in transcribing the serial, which was then omitted from both E1 and A1. The facsimile's styling, with its lighter – and authoritative – pointing, is imported into the critical text for the two sentences it contains, and Conrad's signature and farewell replace those given in the *London Mercury*.

TRAVEL
PREFACE TO RICHARD CURLE'S *INTO THE EAST*

THIS PREFACE was written at the request of Richard Curle, who first asked Conrad for an introduction to his travel book, *Into the East: Notes on Burma and Malaya*, in late 1921.[2] Conrad did not, however, settle to its writing until after he had completed *The Rover*. He began drafting the essay towards the end of July 1922, promising an end within the

---

[1] Edgar H. Wells & Co., Inc. *A Catalogue of books, including an important collection of original typescripts and books from the library of Joseph Conrad, with presentation copies from W. H. Hudson, Henry James and Arthur Symons* (1925), p. 14.
[2] Conrad to Curle, 12 November 1921 (*Letters*, VII, 369).

week;[1] the date on the draft typescript (TS1 Yale), 1 August, gives a completion date. The book apparently took some time to make its way through printing, as Curle had received his typescript back from his typist in early September.[2] The preface was not serialized,[3] but first issued in December by Curle, with Conrad's involvement, as a limited-edition pamphlet, printed by R. & R. Clark of Edinburgh.[4] Curle's *Into the East* (C) was published by Macmillan on 20 March 1923,[5] a limited large-paper issue of 125 copies having been released the week before.[6] (The British Museum deposit copy of the regular issue is date-stamped '6 APR 23'.) The revised text in the draft typescript (TS1r Yale) serves as copy-text.

Two typescripts are extant: (1) a dictated, heavily revised typescript (TS1 Yale), signed in full and dated '1st Augst 1922' on its last page, comprised of twelve double-spaced pages on cream wove paper bearing the watermark 'RYMANS HERTFORD BANK | LONDON'; and (2) a twelve-page double-spaced clean-copy typescript revised in Conrad's hand (TS2 Rosenbach) and signed by him but with the date as above typed in. Sold at the Curle sale of 1927, TS1 has been at Yale since 1982, part of the Arnold S. Askin Bequest. TS2, having been sold twice by Sotheby's (in 1928 and in 1930), was ultimately acquired by A. S. W. Rosenbach and is preserved in the Rosenbach Museum and Library, Philadelphia.[7]

Conrad's revisions in TS1 were thorough, particularly in the last few pages where the changes amount to rewriting. In making the 'clean copy', TS2's typist coped well but, in addition to adding some required punctuation, dropped the word 'mere' (66.24). She omitted hyphens in 'game-killing' (66.20) and 'good-will' (69.34), added a hyphen to 'travel book' and, in a few instances, substituted semi-colons for TS1's commas. Conrad tinkered with TS2's text: he altered wording in a handful of instances and made punctuation both more rhetorical and conventional.

[1] Conrad to Curle, 24 July 1922 (*Letters*, VII, 497).
[2] Curle to Eric S. Pinker, 6 September 1922 (Berg).
[3] The reported serialization of this preface in a double issue of *Blue Peter* of September–October 1922 in Theodore G. Ehrsam's *Bibliography of Joseph Conrad* (1969) is an error, the work in question being 'Joseph Conrad in the East' by Curle (pp. 184–8).
[4] See R. & R. Clark invoice to Curle (for £3 7s 6d) for twenty copies, 6 December 1922 and stamped 'Paid' 18 December 1922 (HRC). Conrad received £60 for fifteen copies; cheque drawn on Lloyds Bank Limited, dated 5 January 1923, endorsed by him, paid out 9 January 1923 (HRC).
[5] 'Next Week's Books', *The Times*, 9 March 1923, p. 8.
[6] The number of copies is stated in the edition.   [7] *Register*, p. 81.

He revised the essay yet again – 'I pulled together the phrasing here and [there]' – in a set of pamphlet proofs in late November.[1] These changes polish the prose: for example, he altered 'be' to the more vivid 'grow' (66.11), 'done so' to 'achieved it' (67.8–9) and 'simple' to 'cruel' (69.4), while correcting 'Sudan' to 'Nigeria' (68.4). He also called the reader's attention to Curle's three volumes of tales (70.17–18), the latter insertion being left up to Curle, who in the end agreed to make it. Punctuation underwent rigorous conventionalizing either by Curle or at the printer's. A few verbal changes are also suspect as to their derivation: for instance, 'that's' was changed to 'that is' (65.1), the characteristically Conradian (if unidiomatic) 'had written' was altered to 'has written' (65.9) and 'men that' to the grammatically correct 'men who' (66.40). While Conrad *may* have made these verbal changes, they are characteristic of the kind made by the agents who tidied his work for print, and have not been adopted in the critical text.

It seems probable that either a pamphlet or the proof in which Conrad had worked was provided to Macmillan as copy for their book, the text recently laboured over and supervised by Conrad. Although Curle had to hand the extant typescripts, the *Last Essays* text descends either from the pamphlet or the book text (C). The extremely close agreement of these texts disallows identifying which served as setting copy for the *Last Essays* typescript.

The selection of TS1r as copy-text ensures that Conrad's preferences as regards spelling, capitalization and styling are restored, although, inevitably in a dictated work, some of these decisions were the typist's. Emendation is required from TS2r to incorporate Conrad's alterations of wording and punctuation in that document, the latter relatively thoroughgoing, and also from the pamphlet in which, apart from the questionable instances mentioned above, the verbal variants can confidently be attributed to him.

STEPHEN CRANE
INTRODUCTION TO THOMAS BEER'S
STEPHEN CRANE

COMMISSIONED BY the American short-story writer and lawyer Thomas Beer to write an introduction to his biography *Stephen Crane:*

---

[1] Conrad to Curle, [21 November 1922] (*Letters*, VII, 597). Given that Curle's book did not appear until March, the proof in question at this juncture was almost certainly that for the pamphlet.

A Study in American Letters,[1] Conrad set to work on 12 or 13 March 1923, shortly after Beer, in the company of Alfred A. Knopf, called on him at Oswalds to discuss the project.[2] Although he was initially uncertain about being able to complete the essay in time for his agent to take with him on a business trip to New York,[3] progress on the 8,300- word piece was rapid. Conrad finished his task, more or less, on the 23rd, the date inscribed on the final leaf of the extant manuscript, and the same day that he reported to his agent that the introduction was 'ready'.[4] As planned, Pinker was thus able to deliver the essay in person,[5] and the book made its way through the press over the next few months. Conrad revised lightly in proofs. Although Conrad envisaged issuing a privately printed pamphlet of the introduction, this plan was strenuously opposed by Knopf, who asserted his firm's rights.[6] Its first appearance was thus in Beer's biography, published by Knopf in New York (CA) in a limited and a trade edition on 23 October 1923,[7] and by Heinemann (CE) on 28 August 1924.[8]

The following preprint documents are extant: (1) the 60-leaf holograph manuscript (MS Virginia), signed and dated 'Friday. 23 March.

[1] Published under the heading 'Introduction', in both England and America, the work was re-titled 'Preface' in Curle's edition of *Last Essays*. The original heading has been restored.
[2] On the visit, see Conrad to Edward Garnett, 10 March 1923 (*Letters*, VIII, 46). (Knopf's 1923 diary (HRC) does not cover this month.) Conrad gives both 12 and 13 March for the commencement of writing; see Conrad to Curle, 12 March 1923; to F. N. Doubleday, 13 March 1923 (*Letters*, VIII, 48, 49).
[3] Conrad to Eric S. Pinker, Wednesday [14 March 1923] (*Letters*, VIII, 51).
[4] Conrad to Pinker, 23 March 1923 (*Letters*, VIII, 56). A letter of the previous day also mentions that the 'Introduction' was 'finished'; however, the statement that corrections would be made on Saturday (the 24th) indicates that finishing touches were ongoing, possibly being made just before its posting to Pinker.
[5] Pinker and his wife left Southampton on the *Olympic* on 28 March, arriving in New York on 4 April (Passenger Lists Leaving UK, 1890–1960, BT27/1027/7, National Archives; 'List or Manifest of Alien Passengers for the United States', Ellis Island Archives). Shortly after arriving, he informed Beer that he had the Introduction for him, offered to meet for lunch and added that he would like to discuss inclusion of the essay in a future volume (Pinker to Thomas Beer, 6 April 1923 (Yale-S)).
[6] See Conrad to Pinker, 23 March 1923 (*Letters*, VIII, 57–9); Alfred A. Knopf to Pinker, 19 May 1923 (Berg); and Knopf to Thomas Beer, 11 June 1923 (Yale-S).
[7] The limited edition on Borzoi rag watermarked large paper was of 165 copies (150 for sale). The trade issue was 2,400 copies, with a second printing of 400 issued in February 1924; see Beer to Garnett, 4 March 1924 (HRC). The Garden City Publishing Company issued a reprint in its 'The Star' series in 1927.
[8] Publication dates from, respectively, the United States Copyright Office, *Catalog of Copyright Entries (Renewals), Part 2: July–December 1950*, and 'Next Week's Books', *The Times*, 22 August 1924, p. 15.

1923', sold to Thomas J. Wise for £110 on 29 March;[1] (2) a 24-page typescript marked by the printers (TSe Yale-S), date-stamped as received on '7/12/23';[2] and (3) pages 2–9 of the galley-proofs (CAp Yale-S), date-stamped 'July 13', and with the names of the compositors (Farley and Kennedy). The galley-proofs are corrected and revised by Conrad in black ink, with corrections and setting directions (in green ink) in another hand.[3] The 33-page ribbon-copy typescript revised by Conrad, and sold at the Hodgson sale, remains unlocated, and at this point in time can, with some confidence, be assumed lost. The copy-text for this edition is, of necessity, composite: TSe fills in for the missing first page (of nine) of the galley-proofs; for the remainder, the galleys provide the copy-text because of the extensive revisions of both wording and punctuation in them in Conrad's hand.

The manuscript is a typical rough draft, the text developed and worked up further in the missing typescript. Variants between the manuscript and extant setting-copy typescript indicate that revision was, as usual, thorough in the missing document, directed, characteristically, to small-scale stylistic polishing rather than the recasting of ideas or changes in direction. The fact that revision was under pressure of a tight deadline may have played a role in limiting revisions to what Conrad felt was strictly necessary.

The surviving typescript does not resemble others made for Conrad during this period, and may have been done rapidly through an agency, although its margins are extremely tight. In any event, the typing is mainly free from casual errors. The typist, however, added an extra space on a few occasions, possibly because of problems with the roller. These were interpreted as part-breaks, instated in the galleys by the words 'Blank lines' (not in Conrad's hand). These breaks descended to all printed texts; they are not retained here, lacking

---

[1] Conrad's page-count went off, with no leaves numbered 38 and 39; preserved with the manuscript is a holograph title-page made for Wise. On the sale to him, see Conrad to Wise, 26 and 29 March 1923 (*Letters*, VIII, 62–3); the cancelled cheque is also extant (Virginia).

[2] This date is given in American style. The typescript also bears indications for setting ('11 point Elzevir') and tracking marks.

[3] Conrad presented an extract of three double-spaced typed pages (TTU) to Edward Garnett, a supporter of Crane and actively interested in the preface's writing. Inscribed 'for E. Garnett' and headed 'extracts from the intro[ducti]on of Crane's biography (for E. G.)', the typescript's typing errors are corrected in Conrad's hand. For details, see Donald W. Rude, 'Recent Additions to the Texas Tech Conrad Collection', *Joseph Conrad Today*, 12 (1987), 318.

authority in the manuscript. Conrad himself corrected errors in the galley-proofs but revised little. Handled by two publishers, CA and CE vary in some trifling instances of styling and orthography. Curle presumably had the English edition of the Introduction transcribed for *Last Essays*, but the American and English texts are so close that this matter defies resolution.

Conrad's spellings and styling are reinstated by the choice of copy-text, and TS's preferred form 'Mr' (without the full stop) is imposed throughout, the galleys conforming to American usage ('Mr.') on this point. This statement suffices to signal the use of points; specific report of the other changes is made in the 'Emendations of Accidentals' list in the 'Apparatus'. On the whole, despite its length, the essay poses few textual problems and requires little emendation to restore Conrad's practices.

HIS WAR-BOOK
INTRODUCTION TO STEPHEN CRANE'S
THE RED BADGE OF COURAGE

CONRAD WROTE this introduction to Stephen Crane's *The Red Badge of Courage* in response to a request from the New York publisher Appleton & Company, in late September 1923.[1] By 9 October, he had finished the essay, written during a time when he was also preoccupied with getting together photographs for the frontispieces of Doubleday's 'Concord Edition'. Miss Hallowes forwarded a typescript to Eric Pinker on the 9th, accompanied by a letter reporting that in 'spare moments Mr Conrad has been doing this article on "The Red Badge of Courage" and he asks me to send it to you in order that you may have it at hand in the event of a satisfactory settlement with Appletons'.[2] She referred to Conrad's instructions in his letter to Pinker of the 26th, asking him to negotiate publication rights with a representative of the American firm, who would be in London within a week. The firm, however, declined. Perhaps the £50 fee was judged too high,[3] although it was in line with Conrad's standard rate at this

---

[1] Conrad to Eric S. Pinker, Wednesday [26 September 1923] (*Letters*, VIII, 183). The title varies: in MS and TS it is 'Introduction'; the original printing and Curle's version in *Last Essays* adopt 'Preface'. The title in the manuscript is restored here.

[2] Hallowes to Pinker, 9 October 1923 (Berg).

[3] Conrad to Pinker, Wednesday [26 September 1923] (*Letters*, VIII, 183).

time.[1] In any event, the matter languished until after his death, Pinker and Curle negotiating with Heinemann for the preface to appear in the firm's March 1925 reprinting of a novel it had first published in 1895. Curle sent a typescript, presumably to be used as Heinemann's printer's copy, to Pinker in early December 1924.[2]

Two preprint documents survive: (1) the fourteen-leaf holograph manuscript (BL Ashley MS. 4791), purchased by Thomas J. Wise for £15 on 12 October 1923;[3] and (2) a heavily corrected and revised seven-page ribbon-copy typescript (TS Dartmouth), apparently obtained from Wise by the American collector John A. Spoor and put up for auction in April 1939 after Spoor's death.[4] The manuscript is a rough draft superseded by revision at more than one stage, and the revised text of the typescript (TSr) serves as copy-text.

On 10⅝ in. × 8 in. (27cm × 20.5 cm) white paper, MS includes a holograph title-page made for Wise. The leaves were numbered twice: the first numbering (1–13) in Conrad's hand, the second, including the title-page in its count, typed in (2–14). At the top of the first leaf of text 'His War-book' replaces the word 'Introduction', which Conrad crossed out. MS is signed twice on its title-page and once again at the end; in addition, its second leaf has in the upper left-hand corner 'Red Badge of Courage | Stephen Crane'. Conrad's organization, argument and tone were set in this draft. There are typical additions, made at the time of initial inscription: for example, 'to whom the din and turmoil of the fray' became 'whose fiery spirit is soothed by the stress and clamour of the fray' (93.14–15).

The typescript, on Chartham Mills bond, is accompanied by an unnumbered holograph title-page and signed on both its first and last pages, Conrad's typical practice when authenticating a typescript for sale. At the top of page 1 is the note 'First draft | from MS | J. C.' and 'Int^{on} to S. Cranes "Red Badge of Courage"'. This separate title-page and the styling of the title in MS as 'His War-book' give authority for the altered title adopted in the present edition, so that the title now appears for the first time in print as the author wished it to. Further supporting evidence for Conrad's styling is offered by his insertion

---

[1] For a discussion of Conrad's fortunes in the literary marketplace during his later career, see 'Introduction', pp. xxxi–xxxvi.

[2] Curle to Pinker, 4 December 1924 (Berg).

[3] *Documents*, p. 217. (See also *Letters*, VIII, 197 n. 1, which wrongly cites this figure as £35.)

[4] *Register*, p. 26.

of 'war-book' during revision of the typescript (94.9), and 'war-book' also appears in MS (93.26), although the typist declined, or failed, to reproduce the hyphen.

Conrad's note on the state of the typescript proves accurate, and his thoroughgoing revision in this document likewise testifies to its status as a draft. The several substantive variants between MS and TSt are the consequence of typing so incompetent that, were Conrad's revisions not comprehensive in this document, one might on an initial examination conclude that an intermediate document might have once existed,[1] as witness the following examples: MS's 'strikingly genuine and as satisfying' appears as 'perfectly genuine, satisfying' (90.21–22) and 'sounds and sights' as 'confused movements and the sights' (91.22b).[2] However, the typist had a pronounced tendency to anticipation, and, moreover, intervened on several occasions, colourfully altering wordings. The former habit necessitated correction from the manuscript: for example, TSt has 'pages', 'Jean Marbot', 'wringing' and 'excitement', whereas MS and TSr share 'paper' (91.2), 'General Marbot' (91.7c), 'waving' (92.10.) and 'news' (92.12b). By mishandling a quotation from *The Red Badge of Courage*, the typist made Crane's words appear as Conrad's own (92.39). She also dropped words, both added and missed out punctuation, omitted two paragraph-breaks and substituted 'upon' for 'on' and 'on' for 'upon' (92.22b, 94.8a).

The generally poor typing has several consequences for the text, with Conrad responding to his typist's errors – not always, and perhaps only occasionally, with reference to his manuscript. For example, the typist's apparent misreading of a high dotted 'i' from a line below as a comma after 'interesting' (91.3) led Conrad to insert a comma to close a clause left half-punctuated, and the typist's omission of

---

[1] The handwriting in the holograph offers no special challenges, and the poor quality of the typing hints that it was probably not the work of Miss Hallowes, Conrad's usual typist. As the above discussion of composition indicates, she was at Oswalds during early October, dealing with the transmission of a clean-copy typescript to Eric Pinker. The fact that Conrad wrote this introduction out in longhand rather than dictating to her, as was his wont at this time, suggests that he possibly composed it whilst in London at the end of September (see *Letters*, VIII, 183–5), or that Miss Hallowes stayed in town longer than Conrad and his wife did.

[2] What at first sight might appear to be strong evidence for an intermediate document, proves otherwise on examination: TSt's phrase 'with his hands over his eyes' (92.20c) appears in MS although it was clearly deleted. Why the typist proceeded to type it is a mystery.

opening inverted commas led Conrad to position these differently from the way they appear in MS (92.25–26). In such instances, the manuscript preferences and choices have been restored. Despite TSt's manifold flaws, to adopt MS as copy-text on theoretical grounds would entail its being systematically over-ridden to accommodate thorough revision at the typescript stage with respect to both accidentals and wording. In this light, TSr's correction by reference to MS seems a more appropriate practical alternative than the massive emendation of the MS text.

Conrad's extensive revisions in the surviving typescript demonstrate a characteristic search for clarity that involved correcting his grammar, deleting superfluous words and occasionally changing wording. For example, 'something perfectly genuine' became 'a genuine revelation' (90.21–22). The first two paragraphs have changes typical of the whole: 'vivid' was revised to 'enduring' (90.6), 'of remarkable merit' to 'not devoid of merit' (90.10), 'be explosive' to 'give us shocks' (90.11), 'small bombardment' to 'small & lively bombardment' (90.13). Arguably the most significant change is the addition of the clause 'which was to give him his crumb of fame' (92.2). Whether Appleton & Co. returned the typescript after they rejected the essay is unknown. Similarly unknown is whether the typescript Curle sent to Pinker in December 1924 for Heinemann (C) was that document or a new typescript.

The variants in C establish that Conrad revised, as was his wont, in the (now-lost) clean-copy typescript or C proofs, or in both documents. C's text is heavily styled: an editor added more than twenty commas. Its new substantives cannot be straightforwardly adopted, both Conrad and an editor appearing to have been responsible for them, with those judged authorial imported into the critical text: 'lurks' was changed to 'lives' (91.11), a word Crane used in a paragraph later discussed by Conrad,[1] and 'that untried' was altered to 'his unblooded' (93.6–7), neither the kind of changes tidying editors normally make. On the other hand, there was a process of normalization and 'correction'; for example, 'unbelief' was altered to 'disbelief' (92.16).[2] The present edition accepts C's styling of a quotation of Heinemann's first edition

---

[1] 'He contemplated the lurking menaces of the future, and failed in an effort to see himself standing stoutly in the midst of them': *The Red Badge of Courage* (1896), pp. 11–12.

[2] For a discussion of this and other instances of rejected alterations, see 'Textual Notes'.

of *The Red Badge of Courage* (93.39–94.2), on the reasonable assumption that Conrad wished this quotation to be correctly transcribed (as it is in C). In MS, he had supplied only the page number, and had failed to check his typist's finished work against the original: not only did she give 'great death' in upper-case initials wrongly, but she also omitted three commas.

E1 and A1 derive from a typescript copy made from the book edition or from a copy of the typescript that Curle sent to Pinker. Apart from the different handling of titles in C and E1 (italics) and A1 (double inverted commas), the book texts vary in only three instances: E1 substitutes an exclamation point for a comma (93.1) and hyphenates 'dugout' (92.20), and A1 substitutes 'become' for 'became' (94.5). These editorial changes are rejected.

Despite its brevity, this essay has to date appeared in a defective, even corrupt, version: the textual problems, originating in the typescript, are further compounded by later non-authorial intervention. The various adjustments made to the copy-text now ensure that this introduction more closely approximates what Conrad would have liked to see into print. Despite his own involvement and best efforts, a compromised text has represented his work, and this piece serves as an object lesson about any theory advocating his 'passive' approval of the work of others.

JOHN GALSWORTHY
AN APPRECIATION

SEVERAL MONTHS BEFORE Conrad wrote this review of *The Man of Property* in Montpellier in early March 1906, the *Outlook*'s editor asked him to contribute opinions to the periodical 'upon the current questions of our time'.[1] Declining the invitation, Conrad kept open the possibility of future contributions, and consequently had a willing publisher for a review of his friend's book. Conrad laid aside work on other projects to compose it, informing his agent that he had been 'hindered' from sending additional leaves of 'Verloc' (later *The Secret Agent*) and the corrected proof of 'Gaspar Ruiz' by the need to write the review '*at once*',[2] a task, if his lament to Pinker of 28 March can be believed, that put him off his 'stride' for three days (*Letters*, III,

---

[1] Conrad to James L. Garvin, 11 January 1906 (*Letters*, III, 309).
[2] Conrad to J. B. Pinker, [mid-March? 1906] (*Letters*, III, 321).

323) and delayed his return to 'Verloc'. Conrad posted the essay to the weekly on 20 March 1906, informing Galsworthy on the 22nd that he had hinted it should appear about a fortnight after the novel's publication (*Letters*, III, 322), which occurred on 23 March.

The review, under the title 'A Middle Class Family', appeared in the 'Book of the Week' column on 31 March (pp. 449–50), and was issued as a privately printed limited-edition pamphlet in 1921. No preprint documents are extant, and the serial text (S) by default serves as copy-text for the present edition.

The history of the essay after its initial publication is confusing. Conrad's faulty memory led to its omission from *Notes on Life and Letters* (1921),[1] and, recognizing his oversight, he wrote to Galsworthy apologetically on 8 June 1921, expressing a hope that it could be included in the collected editions then being prepared by Doubleday and Heinemann. He reported that he had 'sent a typed copy to America and another to Hein[emann] with the intimation that it *must* go in' (*Letters*, VII, 299).[2] In the end, both publishers, understandably reluctant to alter the contents of a volume already in print, declined to include the essay in their editions of *Notes on Life and Letters*.

A galley-proof (Ep Indiana), consisting of two-and-a-half sheets in Heinemann's setting, is extant. The upper-right corner of this document's first page bears the date-stamp '16 JUN 1921' of 'MORRISON & GIBB LIMITED | EDINBURGH', the printers of Heinemann's collected edition of Conrad. A note on these proofs reads: 'Note to Printer: This essay on John Galsworthy is to be placed between the article on Anatole France (p 43) and Turgenev (p 61). Make the necessary alteration in the table of contents.' (The pagination refers to Dent's first edition.) The galley-proof contains nine pages of text, five of which are numbered (002, 004, 006, 008, 009); the pages are additionally numbered '61–69' by hand in order to ensure the essay's correct placement in the volume.

The two extant texts that Conrad is reputed to have seen in 1921 and 1922 were created from a now-lost typed copy of the 1906 *Outlook*

---

[1] On the omission of the review of Galsworthy from that volume, see *Notes on Life and Letters* (2004), p. xxxix.

[2] Galsworthy replied as follows on 12 June 1921: 'As to the article on the M of P. it was a very good article; but I quite understand its slipping your memory, nor in a way do I see why you should put it in, being on a particular book. It would never have occurred to me to expect it to be in': *'My Dear Friend': Further Letters to and about Joseph Conrad*, ed. Owen Knowles (2008), p. 114.

text, prepared through Pinker's office prior to 8 June 1921. The first is the 1921 galley-proof of the essay prepared by Heinemann for *Notes on Life and Letters*. The second is the 1922 corrected pamphlet proof (Ppr Colgate), set either from the typescript prepared through Pinker or the corrected galley-proof (Epe), which also derived from the Pinker typescript.

In the margin of page 8, Ep has a correction attributed, in an unknown hand, to Conrad – 'all sorts of respects' to 'every respect' (99.13); the alteration appears in no printed text.[1] An accompanying note identifies other changes to the galley-proof as made by Richard Curle. By a route difficult to reconstruct with certainty, the corrections to Ep identified as Curle's – five alterations of 'shall' to 'will', the change from 'this talent' to 'his genius' (98.37) and the correction of the obvious printer's error, 'poverty' to 'property' (98.25) – are incorporated into the pamphlet and *Last Essays* texts. Although Curle's alterations appear in the pamphlet, why the change in Epe attributed to Conrad was not adopted is unknown; perhaps it was simply overlooked, or Conrad preferred his original version.

Conrad's hand is clearly evident on the title-page of the corrected pamphlet proofs (Ppr) but nowhere else in the document. The pamphlet was issued twice, the issues textually identical but distinguished by binding and watermark. In his Introduction to *Last Essays*, Curle comments that Conrad corrected the 'oversight' of not including the essay in *Notes on Life and Letters* by 'privately printing a few copies' (Appendix A, p. 364). This figure is given somewhat more precision in A1, which specifies 'about fifty copies' (p. xii), but, in fact, the pamphlet's two printings totalled seventy-five copies.[2]

The choice of S as copy-text is axiomatic: all later printings evidence non-authorial intervention, and S is the extant document closest to the lost original. Intervention appears to have been relatively light, as several idiosyncratic turns of phrase that normally attracted the attention of tidying editors were permitted to stand. S's adoption as

---

[1] The *English Literature, First and Early Editions* catalogue (1931) offering the proofs describes them as follows: 'Galley-proofs of Conrad's review of "The Man of Property", with a few MS corrections of Richard Curle and one by Conrad . . . £2 12s 6d'. The proofs appeared in Heffer's catalogues in 1926 and 1927 (see *Register*, p. 28) but apparently went unsold until 1931, as indicated by a record of sale in a note accompanying the galley-proof: '2½ galleys no cover Harrard. Heffer. Cambridge, Eng. April 6, 1931. List £2 12s 6d'.

[2] George T. Keating, comp., *A Conrad Memorial Library: The Collection of George T. Keating* (1929), p. 391.

copy-text restores Conrad's own grammatical usages, in particular the emphatic 'shall' over the less insistent 'will'. Restored in the critical text is a brief paragraph about Irene Forsyte (97.9–13) that disappeared from the typescript made for Ep and the pamphlet, and absent not only from them but also – Curle having used the pamphlet as copy for the book – from the book texts of *Last Essays*. Also restored is a phrase cut from Ep (96.35–36), one stylistically clumsy but typically Conradian when writing and revision occurred under pressure; more importantly, it is essential to his sense, which is controverted by its omission.

The present edition unhesitatingly rejects Curle's editorial changes, as well as the single one attributed to Conrad, its source not being sufficiently attested. There is no evidence in Epe that Conrad revised in it, and the only intervention undoubtedly his in Ppr affects the title-page only. The typescript for the book text has an editorial change or typist's error, the phrase 'earthy foundations' replacing 'earthly foundation' (96.23).

The critical text does not retain the house-styling of 'Mr' followed by a full stop, Conrad's customary practice, as it is in the manuscript of 'His War-book', being 'Mʳ', a styling standardized in this edition to 'Mr' (see above). (This alteration is not reported in the 'Emendations to Accidentals' list.) Likewise, the present edition rejects the serial title and that in the Heinemann proofs and adopts that of the pamphlet, *John Galsworthy | An Appreciation*, a printing issued with author's imprimatur. This fuller title also accords with 'Henry James | An Appreciation' (1904) in *Notes on Life and Letters*, and is consistent with Conrad's description of the review in late March 1906 as 'an appreciation of that book' (*Letters*, III, 323). Lastly, it more accurately suggests the essay's contents, which focus not on Galsworthy himself but on his work. Curle apparently preferred the tidiness of a title parallel to 'Stephen Crane', an essay that, however, more narrowly focusses on biography.

A GLANCE AT TWO BOOKS

INTENDED FOR the *Pall Mall Gazette*, this review was dispatched to J. B. Pinker on 2 March 1904, Conrad having probably drafted it shortly beforehand by arrangement with the magazine.[1] It did not appear, however, and was first printed after Conrad's death. Richard Curle arranged for publication in *T. P.'s & Cassell's Weekly* (SE), where the piece was published under the title 'The Enterprise of Writing

---

[1] Conrad to J. B. Pinker, 2 March 1904 (*Letters*, III, 119).

a Book', and in *Forum* (New York), where, in the 'Opinions about Books' section, it appeared under the heading 'Joseph Conrad as Critic', prefaced by a note giving the title as 'A Glance at Two Books' (SA).[1] It was also picked up by the *Living Age* (Boston), a reprint magazine that had re-circulated several Conrad pieces.[2] The revised text in the extant typescript (TSr Colgate) provides the copy-text for this edition.

The surviving eight-page double-spaced ribbon-copy typescript (TS Colgate) is signed and dated '2d Mch 1904' on the last page. Given its preservation and the extent of revision in it, this copy was probably laid aside for safekeeping, a now-lost clean-copy being forwarded to Pinker. TS's first three pages are typed in black ribbon; purple ribbon begins on page 4 and continues thereafter. (The number of lines per page is also greater on the first few pages, which are less generously spaced than the later ones.) The paper, which lacks a watermark, appears to be uniform. Auctioned off at the Hodgson sale and acquired by Spencer & Swift of London, the typescript was subsequently purchased by Henry A. Colgate and is now preserved at Colgate University.

Curle had copies prepared from the surviving typescript found among Conrad's papers for the serial publications. Not well typed, the document's spellings, punctuation and erratic styling of titles (which appear both in italics and in inverted commas) required adjustment, Conrad having neglected to correct several oddities.[3] On the other hand, Curle or his typist also conventionalized the text. Characteristically loose and light in Conrad's manuscript drafts, punctuation was typically a matter left for settling after composition, as occurred in the case of this review where it is sometimes more rhetorical than rule-bound, calling forth different responses from different editors.[4]

---

[1] *T. P.'s & Cassell's Weekly*, 1 August 1925, pp. 474, 495; *Forum* (August 1925), 308–10.

[2] *Living Age*, 5 September 1925, pp. 514–17. The title on the magazine's cover is 'How to Write Novels', but the title of the essay is identical to that in *T. P.'s & Cassell's Weekly*, the publication footnoted as its source. A mere reprinting of SA, it goes unreported in the 'Apparatus'.

[3] For example, 'a thousands heads' (103.21) and 'shadows oft the forest leaves' (104.23–24) are uncorrected, and Conrad changed 'the *Island Pharisees*' to '*The Island Pharisees*' in one instance but allowed the small-case 't' and unitalicized and unsignalled title to stand only a few lines later. As well, the spellings 'Turgeniev' and 'Turgenieff' varyingly appear, and commas are inconsistently used in series.

[4] For example, in TS's phrase 'Mr Osborne the hard merchant, father of Captain Osborne, is more definite and flawless, than many of Thackeray's good characters' (101.32–34), SE's editor placed a comma after the first 'Osborne', while SA's editor did not, and the typist who prepared the serial typescripts removed the comma after 'flawless' so that it appears in no published text.

Not only Curle (presumably) but the serial editors also provided necessary punctuation.[1] Even perhaps more intrusive, at the stage of Curle's involvement, was the effacing of the essay's division into two parts (a division effected in TS by a roman 'I' and an arabic numeral '2').

SE provided sub-headings in the usual way of magazines and newspapers, and both American serials typically altered spellings for their market, with *Forum* adding, as well, commas in series (so-called 'Oxford' commas). Whatever TS's flaws, it provides a copy-text that more accurately reflects Conrad's preferences than do the published versions of the essay. Repaired as required by the protocols of the language and in order not to enshrine outright *currente calamo* and typing errors, the document's misspellings are silently corrected; necessary changes to its punctuation, in line with the general policy of this edition, are, however, duly reported in the 'Apparatus'. Given the somewhat unpolished and unsatisfactory state of TS, which, despite Conrad's revision, was corrected perfunctorily, the emendation of accidentals is more frequently required than is usual in a typescript that passed through the author's hands. In addition, the extract from Hudson's *Green Mansions* requires several adjustments, its mistranscription being the work either of the original typist or of Conrad himself. In the latter case, his copying of the passage was casual and inexact.

PREFACE TO *THE SHORTER TALES OF JOSEPH CONRAD*

NOT PUBLISHED by Doubleday, Page & Company until after the author's death and excluded from the English market, *The Shorter Tales of Joseph Conrad* appeared in New York on 30 October 1924,[2] its publication date a marketing decision that anticipated the Christmas trade. Written at the end of April and in early May 1924, the preface exists in five preprint states. The text in the second revised typescript (TS2r Dartmouth) serves as the copy-text for the present edition.

---

[1] The original typist, for instance, missed commas preceding 'perhaps' (102.2) and 'in fact' (102.11), leaving anomalous forms that prompted varied responses: in the first case, the comma disappeared; in the second, the initial comma was supplied.

[2] Publication date from United States Copyright Office, *Catalog of Copyright Entries (Renewals), Part 2: June–December 1951*, p. 638.

The following preprint documents are extant: (1) the 21-leaf holograph manuscript (MS Yale), on lined paper measuring 7⅞ in. × 10¼ in. (20 cm × 26 cm) featuring an indecipherable watermark, a gift from George T. Keating to Yale University in 1938 and bound with (2) a ten-page ribbon-copy first draft typescript (TS1 Yale) typed in blue ribbon on bond paper measuring 7⅞ in. × 10¼ in. (20 cm × 26 cm) and bearing the watermark 'CHARTHAM MILLS | KENT';[1] (3) a ten-page ribbon-copy bearing holograph revisions in Conrad's hand (TS2 Dartmouth);[2] (4) a ten-page carbon-copy typescript of TS2 (TS2c), purchased by the Yale Library Associates from Charles Retz;[3] (5) an eight-page printer's copy typescript (TS3 Berg), bearing the watermark 'HAMMERMILL BOND | MADE IN U.S.A.',[4] corrected in an unidentified hand, a gift to the Berg Collection from Doubleday & Company in April 1973.[5] In addition to these, distinct from the text's evolution and constituting part of the essay's pre-history, are two ribbon-copy typescripts (Yale), each consisting of two pages that contain alternative draft openings.[6]

Conrad worked with Doubleday's S. A. Everitt to select the narratives to be included in the volume. Everitt envisaged a book of approximately 500 pages amounting to 'upwards of 200,000 words' that, prefaced by Conrad's friend Muirhead Bone, would bring together all Conrad's short fiction of 20,000 words or less and include the 42,000-word 'Heart of Darkness'.[7] Objecting to Everitt's view of the collection, and by way of a 'counter-scheme', Conrad offered to write a preface of 'some five thousand words' for a volume of about 124,000 words (*Letters*, VIII, 309). Thematically focussed, the volume would

---

[1] TS1 features the typed abbreviation 'R. D.' [= Rough Draft] on each page.
[2] Page 1 is typed in blue ink; pages 2–10 are in purple ink. On page 1's verso is a transposed carbon impression of the page, the result of the carbon paper's having been improperly inserted into the typewriter.
[3] An employee at Scribner's, Retz later headed Parke-Bernet's Book Department; see David Anton Randall, *Dukedom Large Enough: Reminiscences of a Rare Book Dealer, 1929–1956* (1969), p. 13. The Yale Library Associates were established in the mid-1920s to procure rare books and manuscripts for the university.
[4] On the firm, see Michael J. Mcquillen and William P. Garvey, *'The Best Known Name in Paper': Hammerhill, A History of the Company* (1985).
[5] On this donation, see 'Doubleday Donates its Conrad File to NYPL', *Publisher's Weekly*, 9 April 1973, and *Staff News: The New York Public Library*, 62, no. 5 (1973), 79.
[6] Conrad presented these drafts to his friend Jean Aubry. They are published for the first time in Appendix C.
[7] Conrad to Eric S. Pinker, 12 February 1924 (*Letters*, VIII, 309). Two of the final eight choices, 'Typhoon' and 'Falk', are, in fact, novellas of more than 30,000 words.

bring together eight stories dealing 'with seamen in their various rela-
tions, professional and with people ashore'.[1] Everitt, who agreed to
Conrad's suggestions, requested that the preface arrive at the Country
Life Press, Doubleday's Garden City works, by mid-May.[2]

As this deadline loomed, Conrad reported to his agent on 1 May
that he was 'now working at the Preface for the vol. of Selected Tales'
(*Letters*, VIII, 350), having possibly begun it a day or two before.[3] He
finished the piece on the 5th, posting it the next day, 'in time to catch
the "Majestic"', scheduled to sail from Southampton for New York on
the 7th.[4] In reporting this to his American publisher, Conrad also
indicated that he had adopted Doubleday's suggestion not to identify
the volumes in which the tales had originally appeared.[5]

Conrad revised his preface at several stages. Most of his revisions
in MS were at the original draft stage: for example, he revised 'paper
ships' to 'paper-boats' (109.30) and 'sea' to 'ocean' (109.31). There
is a single correction in pencil: the insertion of the dropped word
'one' (108.10). The typewritten transcription (TS1t) closely follows
the text in the revised manuscript, although the typist adjusted lower
to upper case, altered pronouns and supplied a missing word. Conrad
thoroughly revised in black ink, and in three lines deleted phrases in
blue pencil.

Differences between the texts of TS1r and TS2 suggest that a
now-lost typescript intervened, incorporating corrections by the typist and a few small revisions by Conrad. Substantive revisions in TS2
in black ink show Conrad typically working for clarity of expression.
He altered verbs and verbal phrases, revising 'engaged in producing' to 'volunteering' (106.33), 'called strictly' to 'regarded as purely'
(111.13) and 'Each of them has' to 'In each there lurks' (111.36).
He divided a single sentence into two (111.14–17) and altered punctuation throughout. Written by him at the top of page 1 of TS2 is the

[1] For a detailed discussion of Conrad's role in the volume, see Donald W. Rude, 'Conrad
as Editor: The Preparation of *The Shorter Tales*', *Joseph Conrad: Theory and World Fiction*,
ed. Wolodymyr T. Zyla and Wendell M. Aycock (1974), pp. 189–96.
[2] S. A. Everitt to Eric S. Pinker, 29 February 1924 (Berg).
[3] A date for the beginning of writing prior to 27 April can be ruled out: the Conrads
spent 25–6 April in London, and immediately before that Miss Hallowes was absent
from Oswalds (*Letters*, VIII, 344).
[4] Conrad to Eric S. Pinker, Tuesday [6 May 1924]; to Doubleday, 8 May 1924 (*Letters*, VIII, 353, 355). The *Majestic*'s passenger list confirms her departure on 7 May
(Passenger Lists Leaving UK, 1890–1960, BT 27/1064, National Archives).
[5] Draft of cablegram from Conrad to F. N. Doubleday, 8 May 1924 (Yale).

following direction: 'Please let the proof-reader compare this T.S. with the proof, with special care as regards the final, red-ink corrections. J. C.' A second note confirms an agreement made with Everitt prior to the essay's writing not to delay publication by forwarding proofs to England: 'Attention to this request will save the delay and trouble of sending a proof to the author. J. C.'[1] Thus, TS2 was revised twice, the first revision in black ink, the second in red.

Conrad copied the corrections he had made in black ink into a carbon copy of TS2t (TS2cr) that was then sent to Doubleday. Three exceptions apart, TS2c is identical to TS2r, as revised in black ink: TS2c retains 'ever' (106.21), inserted in black ink and subsequently deleted in TS2, and has two additional commas after the words 'tales' and 'little' in the following phrases: 'successive sets of tales' and 'written of the sea very little' (107.8, 109.26). As he prepared final copy for the proofreader to compare with the proof, Conrad paid careful attention to punctuation, which had been characteristically light at the first draft stage. One instance of capitalization attracted particular attention, as it involves meaning: TS2t's 'eternal shadow' became 'eternal Shadow' in black ink and was further revised to 'Eternal Shadow' (110.2) in red ink. In revising, Conrad typically sought *le mot juste*: for example, he changed 'good fortune' to 'fortune' (106.12), 'revelatory' to 'sincere' (106.34) and 'abhor' to 'hate' (108.29). In the concluding paragraph, he added 'As I have said before in another preface' (111.33) and changed TS2t's 'each successive reader' to 'my readers' in black ink and to 'the readers' in red ink (111.40).

The existence of yet another typescript indicates that TS2c was retyped at Doubleday's office to serve as printer's copy. This double-spaced typed transcription was altered by an in-house editor at Doubleday's (TS3e) to incorporate Conrad's final revisions in red ink from TS2. An editor's note on the first page and references to galley-proofs on pages 4 and 6 – 'Gal. 2' and 'Gal. 3' – confirm that TS3e was used to set up type for galley-proofs. That Conrad's alterations in red ink to TS2r were incorporated into TS3 by hand indicates that TS2r arrived at Doubleday's Long Island works *after* TS3 had been typed. Doubleday's book text incorporates all of Conrad's changes, both those in black and those in red ink. Except for the title, 'Tales' being substituted for 'Stories', other changes are to accidentals. These changes, by an editor or compositor, impose standard American usage on the

---

[1] See Everitt to Eric S. Pinker, 29 February 1924 (Berg).

text, and these, as a matter of course, provide no emendations to the copy-text.

The typescript incorporating Conrad's revisions in an editor's hand (TS3e) was the source of the 'Preface' in Doubleday's *The Shorter Tales of Joseph Conrad* (C), the typesetting from which the *Last Essays* text descends. The latter also evidences intervention – whether a typist's, Curle's, a compositor's or, indeed, by more than one of these agents – particularly with respect to accidentals. Either in preparation of the book typescript or during setting, an entire sentence dropped out (110.5–6), and the phrase 'very force of things, to enter for a considerable part into the body of my work' (109.19–20) was mangled, becoming 'the very force of my work'.

Although the manuscript contains Conrad's styling, it is a typical rough draft superseded by several stages of revisions affecting both accidentals and substantives. Given Conrad's own characterization of TS1 as a rough draft and the further development of the text by him in TS2, the most suitable copy-text is TS2r. It requires only a few emendations to recover styling effaced by the typist. The present edition, as in similar instances, retains the book texts' title, by which this essay has been known since 1926.

COOKERY
PREFACE TO JESSIE CONRAD'S *A HANDBOOK OF COOKERY FOR A SMALL HOUSE*

CONRAD FIRST ANNOUNCED his intention to write a preface to a cookery book by his wife in early January 1907, when the book was to be published by Alston Rivers & Company.[1] Despite payment of a £25 advance to Jessie Conrad,[2] the firm let its option expire, and the preface and *Handbook* did not appear until fourteen years later. The preface first appeared in September 1921 as a pamphlet (P). Jessie Conrad's cookery book began a six-part run in August 1922, prefaced by Conrad's essay, in New York's *Delineator* (SA), a popular women's magazine,[3] and in mid-October, the *Woman's Pictorial Magazine* (SE) printed the essay to mark the beginning of a series of extracts from

---

[1] Conrad to Ernest Dawson, 3 January 1907 (*Letters*, III, 399).   [2] Ibid.
[3] A1's copyright notice acknowledges the Butterick Publishing Company, the firm that established the *Delineator* in 1873 (originally simply to market Butterick's sewing patterns but then quickly expanding into a general-interest magazine for women).

the cookery book.[1] The book form of Conrad's preface appeared in February 1923, published by Heinemann (a firm then largely owned by F. N. Doubleday), and in March by Doubleday, Page & Company.[2] The final version of this essay varies little from that which Conrad described to Ford Madox Ford (then Hueffer) in late January 1907 as 'a mock serious thing into which I dragged Red Indians and other incongruities' (*Letters*, III, 410). No preprint documents of the preface survive, and the copy-text for the present edition is the first edition text published by Doubleday (CA). That brought out by Heinemann descends from Doubleday's plates and is thus an issue of the American edition (CAa).

On 25 January 1907, Conrad informed Ford, then serving as intermediary with the publisher (Ford's own), that the preface and 130 of the book's recipes were ready for final typing and suggested the title 'Cooking Precepts for a Little House – or something of that kind' (*Letters*, III, 410). Given the brevity of the preface, writing possibly occurred during the first few weeks of January, as the Conrads were settling in in Montpellier, although it could have been written during the latter part of 1906 just before their departure for France.

In March 1921, Samuel A. Everitt of Doubleday's enquired of Conrad's literary agent if it were true, 'as the literary notes are now pointing out', that Mrs Conrad had written a cookery book, and he expressed an interest in publishing it.[3] Negotiations got underway and, in early May, Jessie Conrad promised Pinker the 'Cookery Book', now enlarged to 191 entries, by the month's close.[4] The 'literary notes' Everitt mentions were perhaps inspired by Marie M. Meloney, editor of the *Delineator*, who visited the Conrads in June 1920; her introductory note to the book's first instalment describes after-dinner coffee at Oswalds as follows: 'when a maid entered and asked if the wife of Doctor___ could copy the recipe for Yorkshire pudding. A cabinet was unlocked and the cook-book... brought forth.' Meloney mentioned that the recipes were kept in 'a big, leather-bound ledger'.[5] Interest in publishing the cookery book was not limited to Meloney. On 21 September 1921, Mary Austin, an American journalist and feminist

---

[1] 'Preface—by Joseph Conrad', *Woman's Pictorial Magazine*, 14 October 1922, p. 14.
[2] The preface was reprinted in Jessie Conrad's book *Home Cookery* (pp. v–viii), published by Jerrolds (London) in January 1936.
[3] Samuel A. Everitt to J. B. Pinker, 4 March 1921 (Berg).
[4] Jessie Conrad to J. B. Pinker, 10 May 1921 (Berg).
[5] *Delineator* (August 1922), 11.

who had met the Conrads in England, also learned of Mrs Conrad's project, and asked Conrad whether or not his wife would 'like to sell some of that to a Magazine, or to the women's news service . . . we'd like to have some of it'.[1]

Everitt's letter rekindled interest in publishing the cookery book, and Pinker began successful negotiations with the *Delineator*, Heinemann and Doubleday. When and under what conditions Conrad arranged for the pamphlet's publication is uncertain. Since Pinker was involved in its distribution, he was presumably involved in arranging for publication, with London the probable place of printing.[2] The printer remains unidentified, however, no records having been located. One hundred copies were printed, an extraordinarily high number, given that the Conrad pamphlets issued by C. K. Shorter and Thomas J. Wise were limited to runs of twenty-five copies. The pamphlet was being distributed by late September 1921, Jessie Conrad then writing to Pinker of her pleasure 'about the preface' and informing him that money from its sale was arriving.[3]

In mid-November, Conrad, who himself became involved in the volume's presentation (even to the point of fussiness), forwarded to his agent 'the completed, corrected and arranged text of the famous Cookery Book', save for its prelims and preface, the latter 'quite correct'.[4] He also suggested that only one copy be made through Pinker's office for forwarding to Doubleday, who, he assumed, would 'set up and send galley slips' to England, 'from which after correction Heinemann will be able to set up on this side'. Pinker followed these wishes, with Conrad returning the typescript to his agent on 21 November 1921, including 'all the pre[li]ms, Contents and Preface, OK for the printers', and requesting that Doubleday be asked to send proofs in galley form 'in case of small alterations' (*Letters*, VII, 378).

Everitt acknowledged receipt of the preface and cookery book in mid-December, and agreed to attempt to carry out Conrad's quite explicit suggestions about the volume's production.[5] These, sent to

---

[1] *Portrait in Letters*, p. 185.
[2] Conrad to J. B. Pinker, 4 October 1921 (*Letters*, VII, 347). A clover-leaf design appears on the title-page, but whether this is a house logo or merely a decorative element is unknown. Ehrsam's *Bibliography of Joseph Conrad* gives London as place of publication (p. 331), but records no publisher.
[3] Jessie Conrad to J. B. Pinker, 27 September 1921 (Berg).
[4] Conrad to J. B. Pinker, 14 November 1921 (*Letters*, VII, 370).
[5] Everitt to J. B. Pinker, 16 December 1921 (Berg).

Pinker (*Letters*, VII, 370), were followed to the letter, down to the provision of red and blue ribbon-markers, the one exception being the altered layout of the title. Conrad returned corrected galley-proofs to Doubleday's secretary, Lillian M. Robins, on 22 February 1922, explaining that he and Miss Hallowes, in the ten days that they worked on them, had responded to the editor's queries about usage specific to the English kitchen and requesting that the editor 'cast his eye over the slips before they go back to the printers' (*Letters*, VII, 423).

The pamphlet's appearance caused concern about American serialization. While Conrad was working with the typescript and galley-proofs for Doubleday, Meloney, who had arranged to have the cookery book published in the *Delineator*, was apparently confused about the publication, believing it to be a book: on 8 December 1921, she had been notified that 100 copies of the '"Preface to Mrs Conrad's Cook Book", which is being published by Heinemann or Dent', had appeared in America, and stated that 'Doubleday Page . . . will hold up publication' until the editors of the *Delineator* had decided about serial rights.[1] Meloney questioned Pinker about the appearance of the 'Conrad book', wondering whether more than a few copies had been sent to the United States. If so, Meloney continued, the *Delineator* might have to reconsider serialization.[2]

The contretemps over American serialization continued, with Doubleday's secretary writing to Pinker in late December that plans to publish on 12 May 1922 might have to be deferred because of the *Delineator*'s serialization of the book.[3] That, however, did not prevent Everitt from forwarding the Conrads a contract on 11 January 1922,[4] and Robins later confirmed a tentative publication date of 12 May.[5] On a business trip to America in April, S. S. Pawling, long involved in Conrad's work for the firm and at that time dealing with Heinemann's collected edition of the author, called on Everitt on Conrad's behalf to help allay any lingering confusion.[6] Pawling suggested that Jessie Conrad write a 'personal request to consent to the publication

[1] Memorandum from Miss Burke to Meloney, 8 December 1921 (Berg).
[2] Meloney to J. B. Pinker, 9 December 1921 (Berg).
[3] Lillian M. Robins to J. B. Pinker, 22 December 1921 (Berg).
[4] Its terms were that the Conrads' royalties would be 10 per cent on 5,000 copies, 12.5 per cent on the next 5,000 and 15 per cent thereafter; see Everitt to J. B. Pinker, 16 December 1921 (Berg).
[5] Everitt to J. B. Pinker, 11 January 1922; Robins to J. B. Pinker, 19 January 1922 (Berg).
[6] Pawling arrived in New York on 13 April 1921 (Ellis Island Passenger Records).

of the Cookery Book'.[1] The book's six-issue run began in the *Delineator* (SA) in August 1922. As foreseen, serial publication did result in the postponement of Heinemann's book until February 1923; Doubleday's application for American copyright was made on 9 March (A705031).[2]

SA was set either from the pamphlet or a typescript derived from it: in twelve instances both SA and P feature commas to be found in no other text, and both place 'noble red man' in lower case, in contrast to the upper-case initials of CA and SE. SA imposes American spellings ('somber', 'skillful', 'neighbors').

Conrad's preface appeared in the *Woman's Pictorial Magazine* (SE), accompanied by a photograph of him, as part of a two-page spread opening the first series of extracts from his wife's book ('The Conrad Way with Apples', 'Out-of-the-Ordinary Breakfast Dishes' and 'Pastry for Meat Pies and Puddings') in a popular magazine that printed light fiction and mingled society and royal news with practical tips for the middle-class homemaker.[3] The printer's copy for this was identical in wording with the (now-lost) typescript sent to Doubleday to set up its edition. The texts of SE and CA are clearly later, more revised versions of the preface: for example, Conrad himself obviously revised the pamphlet's and serial's 'benevolent', 'painstaking' and 'exactitude' to 'affectionate' (112.13), 'clear and concise' (113.40–114.1) and 'soundness' (114.4), and altered 'suffered cruelly' to 'suffered' (113.3). The pamphlet and American serial texts also evidence formal, more rhetorical punctuation systems, uncharacteristic of Conrad generally. For example, 'discussed and even mistrusted' (112.9), 'modestly but gratefully' (112.18) and 'irritability which follows' (113.10) appear, respectively, as 'discussed, and even mistrusted', 'modestly, but gratefully' and 'irritability, which follows'.

SE would at first sight, given its publication in England, appear to represent a more authoritative text, but its slightly heavy punctuation suggests an editorial hand. For instance, of the five additional commas, the first appears after 'industry' (112.7) in the opening sentence, while the phrase 'by rendering easy the processes of digestion' (112.30) is set off. These have rhetorical impact, and CA, on balance, closer to

---

[1] Conrad to Eric S. Pinker, 16 May 1922 (*Letters*, VII, 469).
[2] United States Copyright Office, *Catalog of Copyright Entries (Renewals), Part 1: January–June 1950*, p. 22.
[3] Extracts from Jessie Conrad's cookery book ran weekly (on Wednesdays) until 10 February 1923.

Conrad's characteristic pointing, has been chosen as copy-text. Apart, however, from the silent alteration of an Americanized spelling ('skillful' to 'skilful') and the title, the copy-text calls for no emendation. Curle necessarily altered the title for *Last Essays*, this being merely 'Preface' in SE and CA. The present edition accepts his title and subtitle, the essay having been referred to as 'Cookery' since 1926.

THE FUTURE OF CONSTANTINOPLE

CONRAD'S LETTER to *The Times* on the progress of the First Balkan War was the only private comment in the newspaper's 'Imperial and Foreign Intelligence' section (p. 5) of 7 November 1912 (S). The second part of this essay, which takes up his ideas further, was printed in *Last Essays* for the first time.

No preprint documents survive. Curle identified his source for the second part as an unpublished typescript (now lost) discovered among Conrad's papers (see Appendix A). The text of the letter to *The Times* provides the copy-text for the first part; the copy-text of the second part is, for reasons given below, the text as published in A1.

A typescript of the letter that appeared in *The Times* arrived at Pinker's office on 6 November, accompanied by a letter in which Conrad questioned the propriety of its publication, a somewhat odd reluctance given that he had commented some months earlier on the *Titanic* affair both in essays and in letters to the daily press. Whatever his reservations, he none the less directed Pinker to telephone *The Times* to ask if 'they would print a letter from Conrad on the fate of Constantinople'. Should its editors decline, he speculated that 'some other paper perhaps would' be interested (*Letters*, v, 129). He also informed his agent that he was sending a copy to Paris to his French translator, H.-D. Davray, to be submitted to *Débats* or *Le Temps* or *Le Figaro*. Pinker acted quickly, as did *The Times*, which rushed the letter into print the day after Pinker's office received it.[1] If, indeed, Davray translated and circulated the letter, French newspapers declined to print it.

Conrad's letter in *The Times* prompted an editor at the *Daily News and Leader* to wire a request for an 'expanded article (1000 w)' on the letter to *The Times* (*Letters*, v, 132). Conrad responded rapidly by

---

[1] See also *The Times* form acknowledging receipt and indicating intention to publish, 6 November 1912 (Berg).

writing an article on 7 November and forwarding a typescript to Pinker the next day, along with the suggestion that his agent decide whether to send it on to the *Daily News*. In the end, the article did not make its way into print, but no evidence establishes why.[1] Pinker perhaps took Conrad at his word and decided to kill it, but, given Conrad's hostility towards the newspaper that had asked for it – 'I don't like the D. News & Leader and would much prefer some other paper' (*Letters*, v, 132) – he may have hawked it about unsuccessfully. Equally possible is that an editor at the *Daily News* decided that public interest had peaked or that the article simply did not suit the paper.

Unaware of the history of the piece, Curle concluded, in the first instance, that it was a letter (despite the lack of greeting, farewell and signature), and, in the second, that it was written 'evidently a few days later to an untraceable correspondent'.[2] (Why he failed to preserve the document that turned up – presumably a carbon copy, the original having been sent to Pinker – is unknown.)

Adopting S as copy-text for the letter to *The Times* allows the reinstatement of the word 'and' in the phrase 'the old and obscure colony' (115.14) and 'a' in 'a neutralized Bosporus' (116.8), missing from both E1 and A1, and hence dropped out during preparation of the setting-copy typescript. An evident trace of the text's styling by Curle (or his typist) is the placement of the phrase 'to a certain extent' (118.39) within commas, shared by E1 and A1 but not present in S, and the treatment of the farewell and signature. Of greater importance is the unimpeachable evidence of E1's heavy house-styling as witnessed by the lower-case initials of 'Imperial' (115.19), 'Senate' (115.25), 'Burgomaster' (115.26), 'Patrician' (115.27), 'Courts' (116.2), 'State' (116.6) and even 'Sir' (116.9), all in upper case in S and A1. Also typically house-styled in E1 was S's 'civilization', 'organization' and 'neutralized' to '-isation'/'-ised' forms. In addition, E1's editors removed commas in one series and left them in another. Their inclusion was house-style in *The Times*, and A1 likewise preferred commas in series. (Conrad's own practice varied.)

Given E1's intrusive styling of the first part of the essay, A1's orthography and styling in the pendent piece are, on balance, almost certainly closer to the now-lost setting-copy typescript. (As witness, for

---

[1] A search by Laurence Davies of *The Times, Daily Chronicle, Daily Express, Daily Mail, Daily Telegraph, Morning Post, Pall Mall Gazette, Standard* and *Westminster Gazette* discovered no evidence of publication (*Letters*, v, 132 n. 4).

[2] See Appendix A, p. 365.

instance, its 'Imperial City' (117.19) compared to E1's mistakenly imposed lower-case form.)[1] Contrary, then, to what might perhaps be expected – that an English edition of a Conrad text be chosen by default – A1 serves as copy-text for the second part of this essay. It has required emendation only with respect to the spelling of 'Bosporus', used in *The Times* for the first part of this essay but in the *Last Essays* typescript or proofs appearing as 'Bosphorus'.

THE CONGO NOTEBOOKS

THE RECORD of Conrad's experience in the Congo Free State in 1890 is contained in two notebooks. 'The Congo Diary', the title that Richard Curle gave to the first, relates Conrad's overland expedition from Matadi to Nselemba, near Stanley Pool, covering the period 13 June to 1 August. The 'Up-river Book' (the author's own title) records Conrad's observations during the first half of his up-river voyage on the Congo in August–September as a supernumerary aboard, and briefly captain of, the *Roi des Belges* (see 138.6n.) on the return to Kinshasa. The notebooks are preserved at Harvard University's Houghton Library. The texts contained in them serve as the copy-texts for the present edition.

As Jessie Conrad recorded, the holograph texts of both 'The Congo Diary' and 'Up-river Book' are 'written in pencil in two little sixpenny notebooks with shiny black covers' that, she observed, 'must have been in some queer places'.[2] Curle stated that the two notebooks, bound in black leather, 'were originally given to me by Mrs. Conrad, after Conrad's death; but, as was only proper, I had them sold for the benefit of the estate'.[3] The notebooks measure $6\frac{1}{4}$ in. × 4 in. (15.7 cm × 10 cm). Stamped on the last page of the first is 'Waterlow & Sons | Limited | Manufacturing | Export Stationery | [. . .] | London'.

THE CONGO DIARY

MOST OF THE FIRST PAGE of this notebook, presumably the original holograph title-page, has been torn out, with perhaps a quarter remaining attached. Discernible is 'N° 1' followed by what looks to

---

[1] On this name, see 119.8n.
[2] Jessie Conrad, *Joseph Conrad as I Knew Him* (1926), p. 153.
[3] Note inscribed in *Joseph Conrad's Diary of his Journey up the Valley of the Congo in 1890* (Keating Collection, Yale).

be an upper case 'J'. Above that is written 'Jo' followed by the portion of a letter, probably 'u'; presumably, this originally read 'N° 1
Jou[rnal]' – or 'Jou[rney]', followed by other words designating the
contents, comparable to the second notebook's title-page (see below).
The damaged page is followed by thirty-three lined pages recording
the progress of the overland trek from Matadi to Nselemba, and the
diary is followed by twelve pages of miscellaneous notes. The primary
record of the diary is Conrad's overland experience from his arrival
on 13 June 1890 at Matadi, about 90 miles (144 km) inland from
the mouth of the Congo and the farthest inland point reachable by
ocean-going vessels, until he reached Nselemba, near Stanley Pool and
Kinshasa, some 230 miles (368 km) upstream, on 1 August. The trek,
rather than a journey by river, was made necessary by the same reason
the railway line was being constructed in 1890 when Conrad arrived:
the Congo's thirty-two cataracts constitute the impassable Livingstone
Falls in the Crystal Mountains.

After Conrad's death, Curle wasted little time seeing into print a
heavily edited and abridged version of 'The Congo Diary', with negotiations underway by mid-March 1925.[1] This text appeared in print
three times prior to its publication in *Last Essays*; it was published
in serials in England and the United States and issued as a privately
printed limited-edition pamphlet.[2] By 15 February 1925, Curle had
a typed version of both the text – 'a very curious document' that 'I
think, would be easy to sell' – and his notes, and promised Eric Pinker
a map of Conrad's overland trek.[3] On 3 March, Curle forwarded the
abridged text of 'The Congo Diary' and map to Pinker, suggesting
that he offer the diary to *National Geographic Magazine*, and remind-
ing him that the magazine had offered Conrad $750 for an article to
follow 'Geography and Some Explorers'.[4] Curle soon wrote to Pinker
again, requesting two copies of his edited text for circulating to English
and American literary agents.[5] In mid-April, F. A. Hook, publisher of

---

[1] Curle to Eric S. Pinker, 18 March 1925 (Berg).
[2] 'Joseph Conrad's Diary (hitherto unpublished) of his Journey up the Valley of the
    Congo in 1890', *Blue Peter*, 5, no. 43 (October 1925), 319–25; 'Conrad's Diary', *Yale
    Review*, n.s. 15 (January 1926), 254–66; and *Joseph Conrad's Diary of His Journey Up the
    Valley of the Congo in 1890* (January 1926).
[3] Curle to Pinker, 15 February 1925 (Berg). An updated and emended version of
    Curle's map is included in the present edition (see Map 1).
[4] Curle to Pinker, 3 March 1925 (Berg).
[5] Curle to Pinker, 6 March 1925 (Berg).

the *Blue Peter*, asked when the text would be available, as he hoped to publish a British version simultaneously with the American serial text.[1] Curle had also been in contact with the editor of the *Empire Review*, Commander Oliver Locker-Lampson, but in the end accepted an offer from the *Blue Peter* for £40.[2] Not until late November, however, were arrangements finally confirmed, with Pinker being informed that the *Yale Review*, not *National Geographic*, would publish the diary in America, and that the magazine's editors would coordinate publication with Doubleday, Page & Company, then already making plans to release *Last Essays*.[3]

An integral part of the diary are twelve detailed sketches of the terrain Conrad traversed as he followed the overland trail that parallels the Congo river. These sketches were not published by Curle in his 1925–6 texts. Photographic reproductions of four of these sketches are included in the present edition (Figs. 3–6), and descriptions of all of them appear within square brackets in the critical text.

Curle's version of the diary, abridged and heavily edited for reasons he explained in his Introduction to 'The Congo Diary' (see Appendix A, pp. 366–68), is rejected out of hand as a possible copy-text. The present edition unhesitatingly retains his title, however, because the document has been known by it since its initial publication. The editorial policies in preparing the transcription are identical to those used in presenting 'Up-river Book' and are discussed below.

UP-RIVER BOOK

THE TEXT in this notebook was first published in Poland in 1972 by Józef Miłobędski, who provided a Polish translation in columns parallel to the original.[4] Although it was omitted by Curle from *Last Essays*, 'Up-river Book' appears in the present edition because it forms an integral part of the documentary record of the writer's experience in the Congo and is an essential supplement to 'The Congo Diary',

---

[1] Hook to Pinker, 14 April 1925 (Berg).
[2] Curle to Pinker, 5 March 1925; 18 March 1925; 17 May 1925 (Berg).
[3] *Yale Review* (signed NVJ) to Pinker, 27 November 1925 (Berg).
[4] 'Joseph Conrad's Congo Diary', *Nautologia* (Gydinia), 7, no. 1 (1972), 7–53. The notebook has also been published in *CDP* (pp. 1–38) and in a *face-en-face* English and Italian version in *Heart of Darkness – Congo Diary* (1994), originally edited by Ugo Mursia, with revisions and notes by Mario Curreli.

which Curle added to the Conrad canon. The holograph (MS Harvard) serves as copy-text.

The notebook containing this document is identical in size to that in which 'The Congo Diary' appears. The writing covers ninety-three pages, with an additional twenty-five pages left blank, possibly to allow for the addition of further material.[1] Conrad follows the same pattern of recording observations as he does in 'The Congo Diary'.

Given that his role as supernumerary involved studying the Congo river and learning the essentials for navigating it, it seems probable that his initial plan was to chart the Congo from Kinshasa at Stanley Pool to Kisangani at Stanley Falls, 985 miles (1,576 km) upstream. He fell short of that goal, however, only recording notes as far as Bangala, about half-way up the river.[2] His observations include geographical features, navigational hazards and details of human activity (factories, plantations, missions, governmental outposts and stations of the Société Anonyme Belge pour le Commerce du Haut-Congo). Charts and sketches provide information in visual form, with line-drawings depicting river channels, bends, bights, bores, islands and sandbanks. As Conrad steamed up the Congo, his handwriting occasionally exhibited less control than when he began the diary at Matadi, as can be observed by contrasting the handwriting in the last illustrated page of 'Up-river Book' with the tighter, more controlled script in 'The Congo Diary' and with an earlier page of 'Up-river Book' (see Figs. 3–6).

'Up-river Book' is divided into two parts and various sections. The first part is not explicitly identified as such, the title-page serving to indicate the notebook's subject. The second part is labelled 'II. Part | in Nth Lat^{de} | from Equator to Bangala'. Each part, divided into sections

---

[1] Several blank pages testify to a narrative gap, and there is a break in the serial enumeration of the various sections. Given the record of Conrad's several bouts with illness whilst in the Congo, it is possible that the gap results from an inability to continue taking notes.

[2] Why Conrad stopped taking notes near Bangala is unknown. Suggestions vary: his experience of three attacks of a tropical fever by the time he arrived at Stanley Falls (*CDP*, p. 5); his decision to leave the Congo after his voyage in the *Roi des Belges* was completed; knowledge that he would never be appointed to a command by Camille Delcommune, the deputy director of the station at Kinshasa, despite promises that Conrad believed were made by Albert Thys, the company's deputy director in Brussels, who had hired him; and his disgust not only with the exploitation he had witnessed but also with most of the Europeans he had met. Another possibility, first mooted by Curle (see Appendix A, p. 366), is that Conrad wrote additional notes that have not survived. Miłobędski agrees with this view, believing that Conrad continued to record observations as far as Stanley Falls in another notebook, now lost.

designated by roman numerals, was probably linked to a chart or map to which Conrad had access.[1] The numbers of the first part run consecutively from I to XVIII, followed by a hiatus; they begin again with XXIIIA and conclude with XXVII; the second part runs consecutively from I.N through XV.

The critical texts of 'The Congo Diary' and 'Up-river Book' in the present edition follow Conrad's own practices but make some necessary concessions for the reader. Dashes of varying lengths are standardized to unspaced en-rules, but the texts follow the practices of the documents in using both full stops and dashes to conclude sentences or larger narrative sections. This idiosyncrasy is preserved especially because of the lack of traditional paragraph-breaks, the texts relying instead upon inconsistent end-line punctuation or an occasional space resembling a skipped line to separate sections. The original's pages are unnumbered; page numbers are supplied here in square brackets in order to compensate for the absence of paragraph-breaks.

Marginalia appear with the main narrative separated from it either by brackets extending as much as three lines or by a line or several lines drawn vertically. This is necessary to distinguish otherwise marginal glosses from the main text. In such cases marginalia are separated from the main narrative by several spaces in order to indicate the distinct separation Conrad intended. An illustration (Fig. 5) demonstrates his usual practice. The infrequent indentation of several lines of text is also preserved. Finally, brief descriptions of the sketches of the Congo river are recorded within square brackets at appropriate places. (See Fig. 6 for a record of the vagaries of the Lulanga river passage south of Bangala.)

---

[1] Archival searches and enquiries to many scholars have failed to locate or identify the document(s) in the possession of the ship's captain, a Dane, Ludvig Rasmus Koch, to which Conrad keyed his narrative, the series of roman numerals referring to an itinerary prepared for captains of the Société Anonyme Belge pour le Commerce du Haut-Congo and perhaps for other company officials travelling on the Congo. (Archives contacted in the search for these missing charts include, among others, the Baptist Missionary Society Archives, Oxford; the Central African Museum, Tervuren; the Geographical Society, London; and the Library of Congress and the National Geographic Society Archives, Washington, DC.) Conrad did have access to maps of the river, especially that recently completed (1884–9) by the Baptist missionary George Grenfell (148.28n.), who worked closely with the company. This detailed ten-panel map, with Grenfell's notes, was published as 'The Upper Congo as a Waterway' in the *Geographical Journal* of November 1902. It is the main document used here to identify locations recorded cryptically in the text.

The critical text follows Conrad's orthography, making minimal adjustments. Thus superscripts are preserved in contracted words, and letters missing from words are supplied in square brackets. Conrad's inconsistent use of the underline in superscripted letters of abbreviated words is preserved. Occasional misspellings are silently corrected. Certain place-names mentioned lacked a standard orthography, being variously spelled in the literature and on maps, and thus Conrad's usages, even if idiosyncratic, are followed, with any exceptions noted. Spelling (for example, 'Kinshasa' and 'Kinchassa') and capitalization vary.

UNCOLLECTED ESSAYS

RICHARD CURLE'S Introduction to *Last Essays* explains that he decided not to include in the collection 'a few short prefaces and some interesting letters to newspapers' by Conrad on the grounds that they were 'of no particular importance' (362). With the exception of the addition of 'Up-river Book' to the main text (as discussed above), the present edition maintains the integrity of Curle's volume as published, but it also reprints five occasional pieces that Curle either did not know of or rejected.[1] The 'interesting' letters he mentions have found their rightful place in *The Collected Letters of Joseph Conrad* and are not reprinted in this volume. Likewise excluded are the rough drafts of Conrad's speeches made in April and May 1923, respectively, to the Life-Boat Institution in London and to F. N. Doubleday's employees in Garden City, New York,[2] work generically different from that collected in *Last Essays*.

For these five pieces, preprint documents survive only for the 'Foreword to *Landscapes of Corsica and Ireland*' and for the section that deals with 'Gaspar Ruiz' in the 'Author's Note' to *Youth and Gaspar Ruiz*. The texts of the extant revised typescripts serve as copy-texts in the present edition, and variants are recorded in the 'Emendation and Variation' list. In the other cases, with the exception of the section on 'Youth', the copy-text adopted is the original publication, details of which are provided in the discussions below. Chronological order

---

[1] In addition to their original publication, the items have appeared in *CDP*.

[2] These texts are available in *CDP*, pp. 110–11, and in Donald W. Rude, 'Joseph Conrad's Speeches in America: His Texts Recovered', *L'Époque Conradienne*, 13 (May 1987), 21–32.

of appearance is followed in the organization of the items themselves and in presenting them here. The editing of these pieces follows the principles laid out in the section on emendation above, with by-lines and signatures omitted. Dates of publication are supplied under the titles.

THE SILENCE OF THE SEA

CONRAD SUMMARIZED the writing of this essay as follows: 'The history of my composition to the Daily Mail is this: Reply prepaid wire asking me if I would write 1200 wds on Waratah case. My reply yes twelve guineas. A wire accepting terms. I wrote the column that night.'[1] The night in question was almost certainly close to the essay's mid-September 1909 publication in the *Daily Mail*,[2] but no details are known. At the time, Conrad was struggling to make headway with 'Razumov' (later *Under Western Eyes*), but his activities during this month are otherwise poorly documented.

Given his need to justify the essay's writing to his agent, who apparently thought it a diversion from work on the novel then in hand, a typescript could not have been made through Pinker. Unless he forwarded his manuscript to the newspaper, a somewhat unlikely procedure, Conrad must have arranged for typing elsewhere, perhaps relying upon his wife. (His correspondence of the period is handwritten, and he was at that point writing out 'Razumov', not dictating it to a secretary.) Whether he was afforded an opportunity to see proofs is an open question, but given that the essay was commissioned, its placement prominent – it appeared on the same page as the leader of the day on the government's just-delivered budget – and the fee generous (a guinea per 100 words), it made its way into print with due care. No preprint documents exist, and the history of the essay's writing and production cannot be further established.[3]

Curle may well have been unaware of this piece when he was compiling materials for inclusion in *Last Essays*. Its interest is arguably greater than some items he included in the collection: the essay touches on

[1] Conrad to J. B. Pinker, 11 October 1909 (*Letters*, IV, 277).
[2] *Daily Mail*, 18 September 1909, p. 4.
[3] The essay was reprinted in the *Baltimore Sun*, 3 October 1909, p. 14, *The Star* (Christchurch), 22 November 1909, p. 2, and, save for its opening sentence, the essay's sixth paragraph was printed in the *Evening Post* (Wellington, New Zealand) in its column 'Ships and the Sea', 13 November 1909, p. 12.

Conrad's life at sea, a topic of interest to his readers, and the dramatically charged event it describes may still have had resonance in popular memory.

The copy-text of the present edition is the text as published in the *Daily Mail* (S). Four sub-headings dividing the essay were doubtless the work of an in-house editor and are not retained. In accordance with usual newspaper practice, the name *Watarah* did not appear in italics or in inverted commas; the usual italics are supplied here, an alteration not recorded in the 'Emendations of Accidentals' list.

AUTHOR'S NOTE TO *YOUTH AND GASPAR RUIZ*

THIS VOLUME of two stories was specifically designed for use in schools. Hugh R. Dent first mooted its production during a visit to Oswalds on 27 January 1920 (*Letters*, VII, 18–19), but only on 12 May did Conrad sign a contract for British and colonial rights, its terms providing for payment of £150 on publication and a royalty of 1 $^1/_2$d. per copy.[1] The note on *Youth* was with Dent's compositors by the end of April, and the firm was then promising to send proofs to Conrad 'in the course of a week or two'.[2] *Youth and Gaspar Ruiz* was published by J. M. Dent & Sons of London (C2) in late July or early August 1920[3] as Volume 8 in the King's Treasuries of Literature series under the general editorship of Professor Sir A. T. Quiller-Couch.[4] The prefatory note (pp. 165–8) is placed after the texts of the stories and prior to a 'Conrad Catechism', a series of questions directed to students. The book was reprinted several times over the next few decades,[5] and, like

---

[1] *Documents*, p. 216. The terms were on 25,000 copies; see Hugh R. Dent to Eric S. Pinker, 9 April 1920 (Berg).

[2] Dent to Pinker, 28 April 1920 (Berg).

[3] Conrad received an advance copy from Dent's on 13 July 1920 (*Letters*, VII, 136). The British Museum deposit copy is date-stamped '5 AUG 20'. *The English Catalogue of Books* gives a publication date of December 1920 but, if not a transcription error, this must refer to a second printing.

[4] The series, which by 1928 comprised 160 volumes, had a character similar to Dent's Everyman Edition but also included literature for younger readers such as, for example, *Theras: The Story of an Athenian Boy* by Caroline Dale Snedeker and *Heroes of Fiction* by Mary Somerville. In December 1926, a compilation of Conrad stories titled *Four Stories*, edited by S. F. Moscrop, was also published in it.

[5] Copies noted include reprints dated as follows: 1922, 1926, 1931, 1939, 1943, 1945, 1949 and 1951.

other volumes in the King's Treasuries of Literature series, was also brought out by E. P. Dutton of New York. In 1920, (C2a), an American issue of Dent's edition, appeared.

The copy-text for the present edition is, of necessity, hybrid. No preprint documents survive for the section on the writing of 'Youth', and thus, among the historical texts, the text in *Youth and Gaspar Ruiz* (C2) has for this section been selected as copy-text. This text, save for an unhyphenated form, is identical with C1. The section of the 'Author's Note' dealing with 'Gaspar Ruiz' has as copy-text the revised text (TSr) in the surviving typescript.

A corrected and revised two-page ribbon-copy typescript, in black ink, of the section dealing with 'Gaspar Ruiz' survives (TS NYU). Signed on its first page, the typescript bears the following note in Conrad's hand: 'This was an introduction written for the School book consisting of *Youth* and *G. R.*'

The discussion that follows takes up the section on 'Youth' first. Conrad's note on the second page authenticating the typescript for sale is confirmed by a comparison of the texts: 'The part of the introduction relating to *Youth* has been taken from Dent's 5/– reprint of the *Youth volume* (1916 [*sic*])'. The introduction referred to was first published in Dent's September 1917 edition of *Youth, A Narrative, and Two Other Stories* (C1), the second English edition of the *Youth* volume.[1] As Conrad stated, the 1917 and 1920 texts are identical, separated only by a single instance of styling: C1 fussily has 'book-form' (175.31), whereas C2's version is unhyphenated. These texts are likewise identical to that published in *Notes on My Books*, a compilation of Conrad's prefaces first typeset during the autumn of 1920 and, after laborious effort – it was entirely re-set to accommodate Conrad's preferences – brought out by Doubleday (C3) and by Heinemann (C3a) in the spring of 1921.[2]

No evidence survives about the precise date of writing the 'Gaspar' section, but the note appears in a list of works sold to Thomas J. Wise on 20 May 1920, and dictation to Miss Hallowes not too long prior

---

[1] For the composition and publication history of the 'Author's Note' to the 1917 edition of *Youth, A Narrative, and Two Other Stories*, see 'The Texts', *Youth, Heart of Darkness, The End of the Tether*, ed. Owen Knowles (2010), pp. 320–22.

[2] On the production of this volume, see 'The Texts', *The Secret Agent*, ed. Bruce Harkness and S. W. Reid (1990), pp. 317–19.

to this date is probable.[1] During April and May Conrad was in what might be characterized as an enforced reminiscent vein, composing for his collected edition the prefaces to *A Set of Six*, *Under Western Eyes*, *Chance*, *Victory*, *Within the Tides* and *The Shadow-Line*. This introduction, if shorter, is similar in tone.

Conrad's revisions in the extant typescript mainly represent stylistic polishing, including the addition of emphases to several verbs – '*did* change', '*was* betrayed', '*was* audacious' (176.27a, 176.27b, 176.29) – and the addition of both necessary and rhetorical punctuation left out during dictation. At this stage he also added the final paragraph.

The copy-text for the 'Youth' section has been emended as follows: a footnote identifying 'Maga' as *Blackwood's Magazine* has been deleted, on the grounds that this was unlikely to have been supplied by Conrad; moreover, its information is relevant only in the original publishing context. Story titles in the 'Gaspar Ruiz' section have been placed within inverted commas rather than italicized as in the copy-text.

INTRODUCTORY NOTE TO
A HUGH WALPOLE ANTHOLOGY

CONRAD'S PREFACE to the Hugh Walpole anthology in the King's Treasuries of Literature series, yet another spin-off from his successful connection with J. M. Dent & Sons, was published in May 1921 (C).[2] E. P. Dutton of New York brought out an American issue of the English edition (CA). Conrad's extant correspondence makes no mention of the writing of this note, but Hugh Walpole is on record as having requested him to write the preface on 8 January 1921 during a visit to Oswalds.[3] Although preoccupied with plans for his departure for Corsica, Conrad may have managed to compose it hastily just before leaving at month's end, or, assuming he did not write it whilst abroad, wrote or dictated it shortly after his return to England in early April. No preprint document is known (none is recorded in sales or auction catalogues), and the copy-text for the present edition is that of the note's first publication. Full stops have been removed from 'Mr.', this

---

[1] *Documents*, p. 219; *Letters*, VII, 98–9. Wise apparently paid £5 for the note, the total coming to £50 for four prefaces (sold at £10 each) with a draft of a cablegram and the note on 'Gaspar Ruiz' making up the batch.
[2] Month of publication from *The English Catalogue of Books*.
[3] Walpole diary entry, 8 January 1921, in J. H. Stape, 'Sketches from the Life: The Conrads in the Diaries of Hugh Walpole', *The Conradian*, 34, no. 1 (2009), 176.

being an obvious house-styling; Conrad's own practice is invariably a superscript 'r', without terminal punctuation.

FOREWORD TO *LANDSCAPES OF CORSICA AND IRELAND* BY A. S. KINKEAD

CONRAD WROTE this foreword at the request of the Irish artist Alice Kinkead, who, in early October 1921, asked him to provide a prefatory note for an exhibition catalogue of her pictures at London's United Arts Gallery. Kinkead's request was made on the basis of an acquaintanceship struck up in Corsica, where she was on a painting trip, sometime during February to March whilst Conrad was there on a working-holiday. Diffident about his fitness for the task – 'I don't know how the thing looks or ought to look; and my fundamental ignorance of the art of painting frightens me more than I can say' – Conrad none the less agreed on 10 October 'to send...something' (*Letters*, VII, 351). He drafted the note, revising it at least twice during the course of the next week, and sent it to Kinkead on 17 October.[1] As payment he stipulated six 'free copies' of the catalogue, apparently to be sold to a dealer. (They eventually appeared in the Hodgson sale.)

The following revised and corrected documents survive: (1) a manuscript leaf of only two sentences (MS Yale), sold at the Hodgson sale (item 185) along with (2) a two-page double-spaced ribbon-copy typescript draft in black ink (TS1 Yale), inscribed on its first page 'For Kinkie';[2] (3) an incomplete double-spaced ribbon-copy typescript consisting of one page in blue ink, numbered page 2 (TS2 Bryn Mawr), sold with Conrad's letter to Kinkead of 10 October 1921;[3] and (4) a two-page double-spaced ribbon-copy typescript in blue ink (TS3 HRC), sold by Heffer's of Cambridge in 1927. The revised text in the last-mentioned document (TS3r), the author's most developed version, provides the copy-text for the present edition.

If it is not a trying out of phrasing before dictation, the MS fragment contains what may be the essay's initial opening. A major theme is announced – 'Corsican landscape is not everybodys [*sic*] subject'; the

---

[1] Conrad to J. B. Pinker, [17 October 1921] (*Letters*, VII, 354).
[2] The inscription does not mean that Kinkead owned the typescript; its appearance at the Hodgson sale means that it was among Conrad's papers on his death.
[3] The upper left-hand corner of the page bears the following inscription in blue pencil (neither in Conrad's hand nor in that of Miss Hallowes): 'Kinneard [*sic*] | Landscapes | Corsica', possibly related to its sale or merely identifying it (as it is a fragment).

essential word 'landscape' is an insertion, indicating a mind one step ahead of the hand. The revision of a phrase interrupted in mid-flow, 'the soul that dwells in' to 'the soul', similarly displays the writer in his workshop. This fragment suggests that Conrad possibly intended to draft the short piece in longhand but then decided to resort to dictation. (That his correspondence for October is both holograph and typewritten establishes that Miss Hallowes must have been present at Oswalds on and off throughout the month.) Another possibility is that these sentences, absent from TS1, may be related to later revisions.

The typescripts' survival and the fact that none of them is 'clean copy' suggest that the typescript that Conrad sent to Alice Kinkead provided printer's copy for the catalogue. It was either discarded after setting or returned to Kinkead and subsequently lost. The catalogue, printed between mid-October and the exhibition's November opening, does not identify the printer, almost certainly one based in London.

Considering that this was unpaid writing for a friend, the essay underwent a surprising amount of revision, with the almost obsessive search for the *mot juste* and the right rhythm necessitating several re-typings. Conrad's pains over his prose are evident in several recastings of phrasing.

FOREWORD TO *BRITAIN'S LIFE-BOATS: THE STORY OF A CENTURY OF HEROIC SERVICE* BY A. J. DAWSON

CONRAD'S PREFATORY NOTE to Alec Dawson's official history of, and centenary tribute to, the Royal National Life-boat Institution appeared during the first week of November 1923, published by Hodder and Stoughton (p. v) in a trade edition priced at 7s 6d as well as in an *edition de luxe* limited to 1,000 copies. The latter was released in December.[1] Conrad reported to his friend G. F. W. ('Fountaine') Hope that he had been requested to compose the preface by the Institution, a letter no doubt coming from its secretary.[2] No further details of the essay's writing are known, nor is there any record of preprint

---

[1] The date for the trade issue is from an advertisement in *The Times* of 26 October 1923 (p. 7). The date for the *edition de luxe* is from *The English Catalogue of Books*.
[2] Conrad to Fountaine Hope, 6 December 1923 (*Letters*, VIII, 243).

documents having been put up for sale or auction. By default the copy-text is that of the first printing.

THE CAMBRIDGE TEXTS

THE CAMBRIDGE EDITION presents to the modern reader deliberately eclectic texts of the various pieces collected in *Last Essays* based on the original documents or, where these are no longer extant, on the forms closest to the lost originals.

The copy-texts for the essays are variously 'fair copy' manuscripts, revised typescripts or, where such documents no longer exist, the printed texts closest to the lost originals. Conrad's revisions, made at several stages as a manuscript or dictated typescript moved into print, supply emendations to the copy-texts. The Cambridge Edition texts also incorporate both editorial corrections and readings found in other documents when analysis of the history of composition, transmission, revision and publication indicate that these would more faithfully represent Conrad's work.

This new Cambridge text of *Last Essays* removes from the received texts successive layers of non-authorial intervention affecting wording and 'accidentals' (punctuation, spelling and word-division). Such alterations, both inadvertent and intentional, by the typists, compositors and publishers who first saw Conrad's texts into print and by later copy-editors and compositors who 'corrected', 'improved' and house-styled his writings when his essays were gathered together for publication as a collection, have been removed to the extent that the surviving documents and historical evidence allow. To the degree that is has been possible, then, Conrad's own words, pointing, emphases and orthography have been restored to the occasional writings that he himself first saw into print in journals and newspapers and as introductions and forewords to books.

The same policies have been adapted, as appropriate, to deal with works that were published for the first time after his death. Those texts were similarly subjected to a regularizing impulse as Richard Curle, an experienced journalist, conscientiously and professionally prepared them for print; at times, however, he and his typist(s) substituted their preferences and those prevalent during the period for Conrad's own, which could occasionally be idiosyncratic. Dent intrusively house-styled the typescript it received as setting-copy for the volume, with the result that the Doubleday text (later circulated in England by

Dent) proves superior to it. However that may be, neither book can be considered authoritative, and the individually selected copy-texts are the only reliable means of identifying the author's own preferences.

The Cambridge Edition publishes Conrad's 'The Congo Diary' unabridged and unemended, and includes 'Up-river Book' as an integral part of this collection. Other writings, not known to or rejected by Curle when preparing his volume, find their proper place alongside Conrad's other excursions into occasional prose. 'Legends' and 'The Unlighted Coast' appear here for the first time with the author's paragraph-breaks; words that fell out during preparation of the book typescript are restored to 'Legends', and a sentence never understood by the agents who saw into print Conrad's last written words finally appears as it should. Wording that dropped out during preparation of the book text typescript is restored to several essays – the letter in 'The Future of Constantinople', particularly – and an entire paragraph is reinstated in 'John Galsworthy: An Appreciation'. In the present edition that essay is also at long last given its correct title, as are 'His War-book' (a piece that, because of inadequate typing, has previously appeared in a corrupt version) and 'Christmas-day at Sea'. The 'Memorandum' is here styled as it appears in Conrad's first revised typescript. 'A Glance at Two Books' for the first time features its part divisions, as Conrad wished, and the author's rhythms, effaced by an over-zealous editor, are restored. Numerous subtle touches can, at last, be appreciated in this diverse collection of reminiscences, occasional essays and letters to the press. The individual pieces in *Last Essays* are published here in forms that are more authoritative than those in which they have hitherto appeared in print.

APPARATUS

EMENDATION AND VARIATION

This list records the present edition's emendations of substantive readings together with the variants in substantive readings amongst the texts collated. A separate list records emendations of accidentals.

Each note provides the full history of the readings in the collated texts. The reading of the Cambridge Edition text appears immediately after the page–line citation. It is followed by a square bracket, then by a siglum (or sigla) identifying the text(s) in which it occurs, and then by the variant reading(s) of the remaining texts and their sigla. A substantive variant shared by the copy-text and other text(s) appears here in the form (the 'accidentals') it takes in the copy-text or, otherwise, in the earliest recorded one. (As a consequence, a report may not always reflect the accidental form of the copy-text; e.g., 11.7b, 16.37). Where an editorial alteration of punctuation, spelling, word-division or capitalization has the effect of a substantive change, it is reported below (e.g., 4.13).

Formal conventions and appurtenances in the documents – Conrad's signatures, serial bylines, editorial headings and instalment statements – are ignored unless they bear upon variants otherwise being reported, as are differences in typography and styling (see p. 202). Excluded in the same way, and with the same proviso, are impossible word forms created by mere typographical errors, including dittography, as well as those containing unreadable or uncertain characters (usually an original typewritten text that has been thoroughly blotted out during revision). Not reported as such are legitimate variant word forms (e.g., 'towards'/'toward', 'among'/'amongst'), including abbreviations. Likewise not reported, unless meaning is potentially at issue, are instances of misspelling (unless of proper names), haplography or casual inscription errors, as, for example, when Conrad omitted to add an apostrophe in a possessive. A question mark in round brackets in reports of a variant title is Conrad's, indicating that a title in the state reported was tentative. A question mark in square brackets indicates a conjectural reading.

The following conventions are used in the reports below:

(a) Emendations to the copy-texts are recorded in entries headed by page–line citations in bold-face (e.g., **3.8a**).

(b) Lower-case letters immediately follow page–line citations when lemmas occur in the same line (e.g., 3.23a, 3.23b).

(c) The en-rule appears between sigla when three or more texts in sequence agree in a given reading; when all subsequent texts agree, no siglum follows the en-rule (e.g., **TSr–**).

(d) Cross-references to entries in the 'Textual Notes' that discuss an instance of variation appear in italics within square brackets (i.e., *n.*), as do editorial statements.

The following symbols are used in the reports below:

¶	a new paragraph begins
...	a report omits one or more words in a series
. . .	an omission occurs in the text itself
***	an unreadable character appears in an early text
[*]	characters, words or phrases missing through manuscript or typescript damage
|	a break occurs between lines
||	a typed interlinear insertion occurs
ED	a reading is adopted for the first time in this edition; that is, it is not present in the texts collated.

Reports on major variation, usually in the preprint or serial texts, employ two special symbols:

(1) OM (omitted) appears when one text or more lacks the entire passage in which occur those words that are the subject of the note, and
(2) VAR (variant) when such a passage is present in a text, but in a version different from that in the other texts reported (owing, for instance, to general revision or recasting).

Listed in sequence below their headings are the sigla used for *Last Essays* and the uncollected essays as well as the collated texts they represent. Those for the following are not repeated, because they are uniform throughout:

E1	first English edition (Dent, 1926)
A1	first American edition (Doubleday, 1926)

LAST ESSAYS

GEOGRAPHY AND SOME EXPLORERS

MS	holograph manuscript (Yale) [*See Appendix E*]
TS1	typescript (Yale)
TS1r	revised text of **TS1** (incorporating Conrad's alterations): copy-text
TS2	ribbon-copy typescript (Berg)
TS2t	typewritten (unrevised) text of **TS2** superseded by revision
TS2r	revised text of **TS2** (incorporating Conrad's alterations)
TS2c	carbon-copy typescript (Berg) [*page 4 ribbon-copy:* 4.37–5.22: 'certainly royal' *to* 'nations is']
TS2ct	typewritten (unrevised) text of **TS2c**
TS2ce	altered text of **TS2c** with Conrad's alterations in **TS2r** copied in by another hand
P	*Geography and Some Explorers* (John Strangeways & Sons, January 1924)
SE	*Countries of the World*, 1 (February 1924), xviii–xxviii
SA	*National Geographic Magazine*, 45 (March 1924), 239–74

3.1–2 Geography and Some Explorers] **TS1r–P SA–** The Romance of Travel **SE**

3.8a a figure] **TS2r SE–** any figure **TS1r TS2t TS2c P**

3.8b sections] **TS1r–SE E1–** section **SA**

3.9 are] **TS2r SA** are all **TS1r TS2t TS2c–SE E1–**

3.16a impressions] **TS1r–SA A1** impression **E1**

3.16b his] **TS1r–SA A1** the **E1**

3.21 is always] **TS1r–P SA** is **SE E1–**

3.23a outward] **TS2r SE–** the outward **TS1r TS2t TS2c P**

3.23b perhaps] **SE–** so often **TS1r TS2t TS2c P** so perhaps **TS2r**

3.24 undistinguishable] **TS1r–TS2c SE–** indistinguishable **P**

3.28–29 their bars] **TS1r–P SA** bars **SE E1–**

3.33a experiments] **TS2r SE–** the experiments **TS1r TS2t TS2c P**

3.33b that] **TS2r SE–** the **TS1r TS2c P** th [*sic*] **TS2t**

4.3 from the play] **TS2r SE–** the play **TS1r TS2t TS2c P**

4.9 as some] **TS1r–E1** as are some **A1**

4.10 pictures] **TS2r TS2ce–** the pictures **TS1r TS2t TS2ct**

4.13 lions,] **ED** lions **TS1r–**

4.14 haunted] **TS1r** or haunted **TS2–**

4.21 men's] **TS2r TS2ce–** a [*sic*] any man's **TS1r** any man's **TS2t TS2ct**

4.22 for solemn fooling] **ED** solemn fooling for solemn fooling **TS1r–**

4.26 never aimed] **TS2r TS2ce–** did never aim **TS1r TS2t TS2ct**

4.28 may be] **TS1r–SE E1–** maybe **SA**

4.31a modern geography] **TS2r TS2ce–** geography **TS1r TS2t TS2ct**

4.31b to] **TS2r TS2ce–** to go to **TS1r TS2t TS2ct**

4.31c was at one] **TS2–** one **TS1r**

4.32 remains] **TS1r TS2r TS2ce–** is **TS2t TS2ct**

4.37 discovery] **TS1r TS2r–** discoverer **TS2t**

4.38 was the occasion of] **TS2–** did call out **TS1r**

4.39a cruelty and greed] **TS2–** cruelty, greed **TS1r**

4.39b say this] **TS2r SE–** say **TS1r TS2t TS2ce P** say that **TS2ct**

5.2 lure] **TS2r SE–** lured **TS1r TS2t TS2c P**

5.4 than that] **TS1r TS2c–** than **TS2**

5.5 Conquistadors] **TS1r TS2r** Conquistadores **TS2c–** conquistadors **TS2t**

5.9 floundered] **TS1r TS2r–** floundering **TS2t**

5.14–15 which ... geography.] **TS1r TS2r–** that one is sorry it ever happened. I console myself however with the reflection that **TS2t**

5.14 to do] **TS1r TS2c–** to **TS2r** v a r **TS2t**

5.16 beyond] **TS1r TS2r–** beyond even **TS2t**

5.17 Cortez] **TS1r–P SA** Cortés **SE A1** Cortes **E1**

5.18a Conquerors] **TS2r–** conqueror **TS1r TS2t**

5.18b de Vaca] **TS1r TS2r–** di Vaca **TS2t**

5.19 humanely] TS1r P–
humanly TS2 TS2c

5.26a that the history of] TS2–
that TS1r

5.26b the Conquest] TS1r TS2r
TS2ce– its conquest TS2t
TS2ct

5.27 geographical] TS1r
geographically TS2–

5.28 Vasco Núñez] A1 Vasco
Nuñez TS1r P–E1 Fernan
Nunez TS2t TS2ct Vasco
Nunez TS2r TS2ce

5.29 on] TS1r upon TS2–

5.30 which] TS2– which
portion of the TS1r

5.34–35 is one ... globe] TS1r
TS2r TS2ce– OM TS2t
TS2ct

5.34 one of the] TS1r TS2ce–
one TS2r OM TS2t
TS2ct

6.2 the fiercest tempest]
TS1r TS2r TS2ce– them
TS2t TS2ct

6.5 its serene] TS1r TS2r
TS2ce– the serene TS2t
TS2ct

6.6 the Indies] TS1r TS2r
TS2ce– India TS2t TS2ct

6.8 what] TS2– was TS1r

6.10 sown] TS1r TS2r– sewn
TS2t

6.11 groups of] TS1r TS2r
TS2ce– groups and TS2t
TS2ct

6.14 thousands of] TS2r SE–
some thousands of TS1r
TS2ce P some ten
thousand TS2t TS2ct

6.16a adventure and] TS1r
TS2r TS2ce– adventurous
TS2t TS2ct

6.16b the missionary] TS1r
TS2r TS2ce–SE E1– the
mission TS2t TS2ct
missionary SA

6.17 of, mainly, Protestant
churches] TS1r–SE E1–
OM SA

6.18 arm chair] TS1r–SE E1–
some SA

6.21a on] TS1r upon TS2–

6.21b inventions] TS1r TS2r
TS2ce– invention TS2t
TS2ct

6.22a oneself] TS1r TS2r
SE–E1 yourself TS2t
TS2ct one's self TS2ce
P A1

6.22b geography] TS1r TS2r
SE– the geography TS2t
TS2c P

6.24a was] TS1r TS2r TS2ce– is
TS2t TS2ct

6.24b land on] TS2– land of
TS1r

6.25a would] TS1r TS2r could TS2–

6.25b the fitness] TS2– fitness
TS1r

6.27 a matter] TS2– matter
TS1r

6.28 will be free] TS2r TS2ce
– will be able TS1r are
free TS2t TS2ct

6.30 so far] SE E1– as far
TS1r–P SA

6.33 What is] TS2r TS2ce–
What is really TS1r is
really TS2t TS2ct

6.37–38 arm chair people]
TS1r–SE E1– people
SA

7.1 Australis Incognita] TS2r
TS2ce– Australis TS1r
TS2t TS2ct

7.3 seventeenth century
explorers] ED explorers
TS1r TS2t TS2ct 17th
century explorers TS2r
TS2ce–

7.4 that went forth] TS2r
TS2ce– came out TS1r
TS2t TS2ct

7.6 enough there] TS2r
TS2ce– enough TS1r
TS2t TS2ct

7.6–7 bit ... line] TS1r a line
TS2t TS2ct bit of the
coast TS2r TS2ce–

7.13 of unknown seas] TS2–
or of unknown a sea TS1r

7.14a incertitudes] TS2r
TS2ce– difficulties TS1r
TS2t TS2ct

7.14b the first explorers in]
TS2r SE– the explorers of
TS1r TS2t TS2ct
explorers in TS2ce P

7.16a was] TS1r TS2ce–SE E1–
has been TS2 TS2ct SA

7.16b a very long time] MS a
very long TS1r so very
long TS2–

7.17 some] TS2– a some TS1r

7.19 latitudes] TS1r latitude
TS2–

7.21a had to be] TS2r TS2ce–
was TS1r TS2t TS2ct

7.21b pure guess-work] TS2r
SE– guess work TS1r
TS2t TS2c P

7.22a they met] TS2r TS2ce–
they me [sic] TS1r sat
down TS2t TS2ct

7.22b Heemskerck] ED
Heemskirk TS1r–

7.23 Murderers' Bay] TS2–
Murderer's Bay TS1r

7.26 they know] TS2– they
TS1r

7.28 where he was] TS2ce–SE
E1– was TS1r–TS2ct SA

7.29a employers] TS1r TS2r
TS2ce– employers, by
TS2t TS2ct

7.29b Honorable Governor
General] TS2r SE–
Governor General TS1r
Governor-General TS2t
TS2c P

7.31–32 had ... leaving] TS2r
TS2ce– left TS1r TS2t
TS2ct

7.34 arm-chair criticism]
TS1r–SE E1– criticism SA

7.35a even now,] TS2– even
TS1r

7.35b seems] TS2r TS2ce–
looks TS1r TS2t TS2ct

7.37 Tasman discovered the
island] TS2r TS2ce– he
had discover [discover =
discovered TS2t TS2ct]
Tasmania the island TS1r
TS2t TS2ct

7.38 New Zealand] TS2– N.
Zealand TS1r

7.39 130] TS1r–TS2c SE SA
A1 a hundred and thirty
P one hundred and thirty
E1

7.40 bringing] TS1r bringing
back TS2–

8.1 successors] TS2–
successor TS1r

8.2a of ... Council] TS2r
TS2ce– OM TS1r TS2t
TS2ct

8.2b does] TS1r TS2ce did
TS2 TS2ct P–

8.4 asked] TS1r TS2r TS2ce–
asked the Council TS2t
TS2ct

8.8 achievement] TS2r SE–
achievements TS1r TS2t
TS2c P

8.10 medalist [sic] ... Society]
TS2r TS2ce– OM TS1r
TS2t TS2ct

8.11–12 But ... an] TS2ce SE–
There was much of an
TS1r TS2t TS2ct But
there was a taint TS2r But
there was a taint of P

8.12 certain that] TS2– certain
TS1r

8.13 his patron] TS1r TS2r–
the his patron TS2t

8.15 transactions] TS1r
transactions of their own
TS2–

8.18 business negotiation]
TS2r TS2ce– business (or
other) negotiation TS1r
business or other
negotiation or other TS2t
TS2ct

8.19 Acheen] TS1r Achin
TS2–

8.23	he] **TS1r–SE E1**– Tasman **SA**	9.8b	problem] **TS1r TS2r TS2ce**– problems **TS2t TS2ct**
8.26a	The action] **ED** The decision **TS1r** This decision **TS2t TS2ct** This action **TS2r TS2ce**–	9.9	ship of] **TS1r** ship which carried him on **TS2**–
		9.11–12	on his second expedition] **TS1r TS2r TS2ce**– **OM TS2t TS2ct**
8.26b	the character] **TS1r TS2r TS2ce**– that character **TS2t TS2ct**	9.13	say that it was] **TS2r TS2ce**– say **TS1r TS2t TS2ct**
8.27a	any scandalous story] **TS2r TS2ce**– anything else **TS1r TS2t TS2ct**	9.14	man.] **TS2r TS2ce**– man. A new spirit entered the Pacific in his train. **TS1r TS2t TS2ct**
8.27b	He was valuable] **TS2r TS2ce**– Valuable **TS1r TS2t TS2ct**	9.15	idea] **TS2r TS2ce**– desire **TS1r TS2t TS2ct**
8.28	these] **TS1r P A1** those **TS2 TS2c SE–E1**	9.16–17	in more ... fine] **TS2r SE**– in fine **TS1r TS2t TS2ct** more or less in fine **TS2ce P**
8.34	now] **TS2ce P** which now **TS1r** which is now **TS2 TS2ct SE**–		
8.35	Commonwealth] **TS2r TS2ce**– nation **TS1r TS2t TS2ct**	9.17	were] **TS1r** are **TS2**–
		9.19a	His deeds] **TS2r TS2ce**– and his deeds **TS1r TS2t TS2ct**
8.37a	that in that] **TS1r SE**– that that **TS2 TS2ct** that in the **TS2ce P**	9.19b	speak] **TS2r TS2ce**– spoke **TS1r TS2t TS2ct**
8.37b	the Elysian] **TS2**– Elysian **TS1r**	9.20–21	single-minded explorers] **TS2r TS2ce**– explorers **TS1r TS2t TS2ct**
9.1	130] **TS1r TS2 SE A1** a hundred and thirty **TS2c P SA** one hundred and thirty **E1**	9.21	nineteenth] **P**– XIX **TS1r** 19th **TS2 TS2c**
		9.24	main] **SE E1**– great **TS1r–P SA**
9.3–4	the geography ... day] **TS2r TS2ce**– geography for all time **TS1r TS2t TS2ct**	9.26	a century] **TS1r** the century **TS2**–
		9.32	the nineteenth] **P**– VAR **TS1** 19th **TS2 TS2c**
9.5a	shadow] **TS1r** shade **TS2**–	9.34a	but on] **TS1r TS2r TS2ce**– but by **TS2t TS2ct**
9.5b	or] **TS1r TS2c P E1** nor **TS2 SE SA A1**		
9.6	achievement] **TS1r** achievements **TS2**–	9.34b	professional] **TS2 TS2ct SE**– the professional **TS1r** his professional **TS2ce P**
9.7	the masters] **TS2ce–SE E1**– the great masters **TS1r** great masters **TS2 TS2ct SA**	9.34c	high personal] **TS1r TS2r TS2ce**– personal **TS2t TS2ct**
9.8a	worked at] **TS1r TS2r TS2ce**– settled **TS2t TS2ct**	9.34d	character] **TS2r TS2ce**– character distinguished man **TS1r** character of

	that distinguished man TS2t TS2ct
9.35	returned home] TS1r TS2r TS2ce– returned TS2t TS2ct
9.37	his fate] TS1r this fate TS2–
9.40	the first two] TS2r TS2ce SE– two TS1r TS2t TS2ct P
10.2	the time the] TS1r TS2r TS2ce– the TS2t TS2ct
10.3	darkest] SE E1– greatest TS1r–P SA
10.6	Leopold M'Clintock] TS2 TS2ct SA L. M'Clintock TS1r Leopold McClintock TS2ce–SE E1–
10.7	little] TS2r TS2ce– great TS1r TS2t TS2ct
10.7–8	it ... tale] TS2r TS2ce– has great record worthy in its manly simplicity of a its [a its = its TS2t TS2ct] poignant subject TS1r TS2t TS2ct
10.9a	I ... publication] TS2r TS2ce– year [year = the year TS2t TS2ct] of its publication was the first year of my life TS1r TS2t TS2ct
10.9b	Therefore,] TS2r TS2ce– So TS1r TS2t TS2ct
10.11a	only] TS2r TS2ce– not even TS1r TS2t TS2ct
10.11b	it falling] TS2r TS2ce– the way it fell TS1r TS2t TS2ct
10.11c	by] TS2r– unless by TS1r TS2t
10.12	John] TS2– J. TS1r
10.13a	that] TS2– the TS1r
10.13b	Leopold M'Clintock's] TS2 TS2ct SA L M'Clintock's TS1r Leopold McClintock's TS2ce–SE E1–
10.14–15	My ... French. But] TS2– What I got was French [sic] translation but TS1r
10.16	popular edition] TS2– popular TS1r
10.17	It contains] TS2r TS2ce– containing TS1r TS2t TS2ct
10.18	two ships] ED ships' TS1r ship's work TS2t TS2ct two ship's work TS2r TS2ce–
10.21	M'Clintock] TS2 TS2ct SA MClintock TS1r McClintock TS2ce P SE E1–
10.21–22	under ... just] TS2r TS2ce– its date was TS1r TS2t TS2ct
10.23	their deadly] TS2r TS2ce– their TS1r the TS2t TS2ct
10.24a	began.] TS2r TS2ce– began. I remember the profound impression I received of the dramatic quality in the life of men. TS1r TS2t TS2ct
10.24b	have been imagined] TS2ce– have been TS1r TS2t TS2ct have imagined TS2r
10.25a	to let] TS1r for letting TS2–
10.25b	the breath ... romance] TS2r TS2ce– a the [sic] breath TS1r the breath TS2t TS2ct
10.26a	existence] TS2r TS2ce– life TS1r TS2t TS2ct
10.26b	knowledge of] TS2r TS2ce– knowledge with TS1r relations with TS2t TS2ct
10.27	an abstract] TS2ce– merely of shadowy TS1r a shadowy TS2t TS2ct a [sic] abstract TS2r
10.27–28	mere imaginary] TS2ce–SE E1– the

	imaginary **TS1r TS2 TS2ct SA**	11.5–6	And ... myself] **TS2r TS2ce–** and the
10.28	ends] **TS1r TS2r TS2ce–** end **TS2t TS2ct**		geography to which I was devoted **TS1r TS2t TS2ct**
10.29a	great ... realities] **TS2r TS2ce–** noble realism **TS1r TS2t TS2ct**	11.6–7	built up on] **TS1r–SA A1** built upon **E1**
10.29b	romantic] **TS1r–P** the romantic **SE–**	11.7a	devoted ... air,] **TS2r TS2ce–** devotion i [*sic*] **TS1r** devotion, work **TS2t**
10.30a	explorations ... self;] **TS2r TS2ce–** exploration of my own **TS1r TS2t TS2ct**		**TS2ct**
10.30b	taste for] **TS1r–E1** taste of **A1**	11.7b	old geography] **TS1r TS2t TS2ct** geography **TS2r TS2ce–**
10.31a	maps] **SE E1–** land and sea maps **TS1r–P SA**	11.8	already ... approaching] **TS2r TS2ce–** fated to come to an **TS1r TS2t**
10.31b	revealed] **TS1r–TS2ct SA** and revealed **TS2ce–SE E1–**		**TS2ct**
10.31c	existence of] **TS2r–** existence **TS1r TS2t**	11.8–9	with the death of] **TS2r TS2ce–** with **TS1r TS2t TS2ct**
10.31d	a latent] **TS1r TS2r TS2ce–** latent **TS2t TS2ct**	11.13a	certainly] **TS2r TS2ce–** really **TS1r TS2t TS2ct**
10.35–36	of no ... possibilities] **TS2r TS2ce–** with no a [*sic*] romantic sense of the great realities **TS1r** who had n [*sic*] without romantic sense **TS2t TS2ct**	11.13b	of] **TS2r TS2ce–** about **TS1r TS2t TS2ct**
		11.15a	knowledge] **TS2r TS2ce–** knowledge of it **TS1r TS2t TS2ct**
		11.15b	had managed] **TS1r** managed **TS2–**
10.36	with no] **TS2r TS2ce–** no **TS1r TS2t TS2ct**	11.16	my enthusiasm] **TS1r TS2r TS2ce–** in enthusiasm **TS2t TS2ct**
10.37	wide ... world] **TS2r TS2ce–** world **TS1r TS2t TS2ct**	11.19a	have been] **TS2r TS2ce–** be **TS1r TS2t TS2ct**
10.39	And their] **TS1r TS2r TS2ce–** and whose conception of **TS2t TS2ct**	11.19b	on reading] **TS1r** in reading **TS2–**
10.40	bloodless] **TS2–** dreary **TS1r**	11.28a	directive] **TS1r–TS2ct SA** directing **TS2ce–SE E1–**
11.1	uninteresting] **TS2–** statistical **TS1r**	11.28b	sane] **TS1r–TS2ct SE–** a sane **TS2ce P**
11.1–2	ashamed of] **TS2–** ashamed **TS1r**	11.29	precision to one's] **TS2r TS2ce–** direction to **TS1r TS2t TS2ct**
11.2	has been] **TS1r–TS2c SE–** had been **P**	11.30	nineteenth] **P– XIX TS1r** 19th **TS2 TS2c**
11.3	now for nearly] **TS2–** nearly **TS1r**	11.32	was extended later to] **TS2r TS2ce–** extended to **TS1r** extended too to **TS2t TS2ct**
11.4	exams] **ED** test exams **TS1r** examinations **TS2–**		

11.35 eighteenth] **P–** 18 **TS1r**
18th **TS2 TS2c**
11.36 had been] **TS2r TS2ce–**
was **TS1r TS2t TS2ct**
11.39 out of] **SE–** of **TS1r–P**
11.40–12.1 wonders ... ages] **TS2r**
TS2ce– the wonders **TS1r**
wonders **TS2t TS2ct**
12.1–2 spaces ... unknown!] **TS2r**
TS2ce– blank spaces over
with **TS1r** blank spaces
over which **TS2t TS2ct**
12.2–3 itself there] **TS2r TS2ce–**
itself **TS1r TS2t TS2ct**
12.3 adventurers] **TS1r**
adventurous **TS2–**
12.4 attacking] **TS2r TS2ce–**
attacking it **TS1r TS2t**
TS2ct
12.6a up by] **TS2r TS2ce–** up
victims of **TS1r TS2t**
TS2ct
12.6b their hearts were] **TS2–**
their were **TS1r**
12.10 The fame ... had] **TS2r**
TS2ce– Their fame was
had **TS1r** Their fame had
TS2t TS2ct
12.12a their story] **TS2–** their
TS1r
12.12b novel] **TS2–** noble **TS1r**
12.12–13 me, for the] **TS2r TS2ce–**
me. The **TS1r TS2t TS2ct**
12.13 been whispered] **TS2–**
whispered **TS1r**
12.16 Great Lakes] **TS1r–SE**
E1– Great Lakes of Africa
SA
12.19a done my] **TS1r TS2r**
TS2ce– my **TS2t TS2ct**
12.19b paid] **TS2r TS2ce–** pay
TS1r TS2t TS2ct
12.20 their first] **TS2r TS2ce–**
the **TS1r TS2t TS2ct**
12.22 in about] **TS1r** about
TS2–
12.23 Great Lakes] **TS2–** Great
TS1r
12.24 Africa] **TS1r–SA A1**
African **E1**

12.25 prompted] **TS2r TS2ce–**
could have prompted
TS1r TS2t TS2ct
12.26 accuracy of] **TS1r TS2r**
TS2ce– accuracy with
TS2t TS2ct
12.27 very] **TS2r TS2ce–** very
first **TS1r TS2t TS2ct**
12.30a second] **TS1r–TS2ct SE–**
a second **TS2ce P**
12.30b has been] **TS1r–TS2ct SA**
was **TS2ce–SE E1–**
12.31 charts] **TS1r** the charts
TS2–
12.32a Admiralty] **TS1r** the
Admiralty **TS2–**
12.32b conscientiously] **SE E1–**
conscientiously of course
TS1r–P SA
12.33 sense of responsibility;]
TS2r TS2ce– certain
interest **TS1r TS2t TS2ct**
12.34–35 entry of Tanganyika]
TS2– entry **TS1r**
12.38 problems] **TS1r**
problems of each **TS2–**
13.6 best ... lives] **TS2r SE–**
greatest effort and all
their lives **TS1r** greatest
effort of their life **TS2t**
TS2ct greatest effort of
their lives **TS2ce P**
13.9 some] **TS2r TS2ce–** each
TS1r TS2t TS2ct
13.9–10 soon formed] **TS2r**
TS2ce– formed **TS1r**
TS2t TS2ct
13.10 an image] **TS2r TS2ce–** a
cherished image **TS1r**
TS2t TS2ct
13.14 of a young] **TS2–** young
TS1r
13.15 gasping] **TS2r TS2ce–**
lying very ill and gasping
TS1r TS2t TS2ct
13.15–16 and lying on] **TS2r P–** on
TS1r TS2t TS2ct and
while lying on **TS2ce**
13.17 while from] **TS2–** while
TS1r

13.18–19	full of pure cold] TS2r SE– of pure cold TS1r full of cold TS2t TS2ct full of cold pure TS2ce P		me the image of TS1r evoke for the the [*sic*] image TS2t TS2ct
13.19–20	of which, according to	13.35	a rugged] TS2– rugged
	himself,] P E1 A1 which		TS1r
	TS1r which according to	13.36	at ... black] TS2r TS2ce–
	himself TS2 TS2c SE SA		with only a few TS1r TS2t
13.20a	seems] SE– seemed		TS2ct
	TS1r–P	13.37–38	native ... clinging in]
13.20b	effected] TS2– affected		TS2r TS2ce– hut where
	TS1r		he died while clinging to
13.23a	wearing a turban] TS2r		TS1r TS2t TS2ct
	TS2ce– a turban TS1r	13.38	hour] TS2r TS2ce–
	TS2t TS2ct		moment TS1r TS2t
13.23b	his head] TS1r TS2r		TS2ct
	TS2ce– its head TS2t	13.39a	his] TS1r TS2r TS2ce–
	TS2ct		the his TS2t TS2ct
13.23c	towards a gate in] TS2r	13.39b	unappeased desire] TS2r
	TS2ce– towards TS1r		TS2ce– desire TS1r TS2t
	TS2t TS2ct		TS2ct
13.24	from which] TS2r TS2ce–	13.39–40	That passion had] TS2r
	while TS1r TS2t TS2ct		TS2ce– That is what TS1r
13.26a	subsidised by] TS2r		TS2t TS2ct
	TS2ce– traveling [*sic*] at	13.40a	in ... from] TS2r TS2ce–
	the expense of TS1r TS2t		from TS1r TS2t TS2ct
	TS2ct	13.40b	explorer] TS2– explorers
13.26b	the British] SE– the TS1r		TS1r
	TS2t TS2c P our TS2r	14.1	home any more] TS2r
13.27a	Kano] TS1r TS2r TS2c–		TS2ce– home TS1r TS2t
	Karno TS2t		TS2ct
13.27b	has seen] TS1r had seen	14.2a	exalted] TS2r TS2ce–
	TS2–		honoured TS1r TS2t
13.27–28	forty years later] SE– only		TS2ct
	last year TS1r–P	14.2b	militant geography] TS2r
13.29a	had travelled] TS2r		TS2ce– geography TS1r
	TS2ce P had visited TS1r		TS2t TS2ct
	TS2t TS2ct travelled SE–	14.2–4	and ... afford to] TS2r
13.29b	in order to] TS2r		TS2ce– he can TS1r TS2t
	TS2ce–SE E1– to TS1r		TS2ct
	TS2t TS2ct in a day to SA	14.2–3	with his memory]
13.30	many pictures] TS2r		TS2ce–SE E1– V A R TS1r
	TS2ce– pictures TS1r		TS2t TS2ct his memory
	figures pictures TS2t		TS2r SA
	TS2ct	14.4	fatal delusion] TS2r
13.33	by all sorts of] TS2r		TS2ce– only failure TS1r
	TS2ce– by TS1r TS2t		TS2t TS2ct
	TS2ct	14.6	objects] TS1r–P SA the
13.34–35	bring before my eyes]		objects SE E1–
	TS2r TS2ce– evoke for	14.7	Only once] TS1r Once
			only TS2–

14.8   blank spot] **TS1r** spot
             TS2–
14.9   very ... white] **TS2r SE–**
             very **TS1r** very then **TS2t**
             TS2c P
14.10a   that some day] **TS2r**
             TS2ce– that **TS1r TS2t**
             TS2ct
14.10b   go] **TS1r TS2r TS2ce–**
             get **TS2t TS2ct**
14.12   mere vapouring] **TS2r**
             TS2ce– that vapouring
             statement **TS1r TS2t**
             TS2ct
14.13   afterwards] **TS1r TS2r**
             TS2ce– afterwards while
             TS2t TS2ct
14.15a   Everything was] **TS2r**
             TS2ce– floating all **TS1r**
             TS2t TS2ct
14.15b   Every other] **TS2ce–**
             Every **TS1r–TS2t**
14.16   I ... alone] **TS2r TS2ce–**
             while I remained **TS1r**
             TS2t TS2ct
14.18a   mutter] **TS2r TS2ce–**
             noise **TS1r TS2t TS2ct**
14.18b   Stanley Falls] **TS1r** the
             Stanley Falls **TS2–**
14.20   in ... above] **TS2r TS2ce–**
             just beyond **TS1r TS2t**
             TS2ct
14.20–21 yet unbroken] **TS2–**
             unbroken **TS1r**
14.21–22 Their ... over. Away] **TS2r**
             TS2ce– in Reshid's camp.
             On a dark island, away
             TS1r in Reshid's camp on
             a dark island away **TS2t**
             TS2ct
14.22–23 on ... black] **TS2r TS2ce–**
             almost **TS1r TS2t TS2ct**
14.23a   black] **TS2ce–SE E1–**
             VAR TS1r TS2t TS2ct
             dark **TS2r SA**
14.23b   foam] **TS2r SE–** very
             foam **TS1r TS2t TS2c P**
14.23c   solitary] **TS2r TS2ce–**
             dim solitary **TS1r TS2t**
             TS2ct

14.24–25 I said ... boast.] **TS2r**
              TS2ce– I tasted the
              first melancholy moment
              of my life. The
              unexpected fulfillment of
              a boyish boast. Yes, this
              was the very spot. **TS1r** I
              tasted the first melancholt
              [*sic*] moment of my life.
              Yes, this was the very spot.
              The unexpected
              fulfilment [*sic*] of a
              boyish boast. **TS2t**
              TS2ct
14.26–27 shadowy ... in] **TS2r**
              TS2ce– great figure for
              me there to haunt **TS1r**
              TS2t TS2ct
14.27   the enormous] **TS1r–SA**
              A1 enormous **E1**
14.28   haunting memory] **TS2r**
              TS2ce– memory **TS1r**
              TS2t TS2ct
14.29a   prosaic] **TS2r TS2ce–**
              successful **TS1r TS2t**
              TS2ct
14.29b   distasteful] **TS2–**
              distressful **TS1r**
14.30a   vilest] **TS2r TS2ce–**
              basest **TS1r** base **TS2t**
              TS2ct
14.30b   history] **TS1r TS2r**
              TS2ce– countenance
              TS2t TS2ct
14.32   idealised] **TS1r TS2r**
              TS2ce– idolised **TS2t**
              TS2ct
14.33–34   hard ... now, in] **TS2r**
              TS2ce– quite extraneous
              to **TS1r TS2t TS2ct**
14.34   Still] **TS2r TS2ce–** But
              TS1r TS2t TS2ct
14.35a   the pipe] **TS1r** a pipe
              TS2–
14.35b   at midnight in] **TS2r**
              TS2ce– in **TS1r** in the
              very cen [*sic*] at **TS2t**
              TS2ct
14.36a   the African] **TS2–** African
              TS1r

14.36b   and] **TS2r TS2ce–** and
found it dark **TS1r TS2t
TS2ct**

14.37a   There I] **TS2r TS2ce–** I
TS1r TS2t TS2ct

14.37b   because] **TS2ce P** there.
TS1r TS2t TS2ct because
there **TS2r SE–**

14.38   lacked company] **TS2r
TS2ce–** lacked company
there **TS1r TS2t
TS2ct**

14.38–39 grown up friends] **TS2r
TS2ce–** friends **TS1r TS2t
TS2ct**

15.2a   things that commanded]
TS2r TS2ce– that had
TS1r TS2t TS2ct

15.2b   profound] **TS1r**
profoundest **TS2–**

15.2c   loyalty] **TS2r TS2ce–**
sympathies **TS1r TS2t
TS2ct**

15.2d   perhaps it is] **TS2–**
perhaps **TS1r**

15.4–5   scientific ... sail] **TS2r
TS2ce–** navigators
[navigators = navigator
TS2 TS2ct] it has been
given to me to pass **TS1r
TS2t TS2ct**

15.5   old Pacific] **TS2r SE–**
Pacific **TS1r TS2t
TS2c P**

15.6a   a region which] **TS2r SE–**
which **TS1r TS2t TS2c P**

15.6b   imperfectly] **TS1r** very
imperfectly **TS2–**

15.10   deep lying] **TS2r TS2ce–**
profound **TS1r TS2t
TS2ct**

15.14a   way of] **TS2–** way **TS1r**

15.14b   Torres Straits] **TS1r–P**
Torres Strait **SE–**

15.16a   unheard of] **TS2–**
unheard **TS1r**

15.16b   I must ... awaited] **TS2r
TS2ce–** and I must I await
TS1r and I must say I
awaited **TS2t TS2ct**

15.16c   the reply] **TS2r TS2ce
SE–** their reply **TS1r TS2t
TS2ct P**

15.18a   chiding] **TS1r** the
chiding **TS2–**

15.18b   simply called] **TS2–**
called **TS1r**

15.20–21 and so on] **TS1r** and so
on and so on **TS2–**

15.21   however we] **TS2–** we
TS1r

15.22   Torres Straits] **TS1r–P**
Torres Strait **SE–**

15.26   not been] **TS2–** no [sic]
been **TS1r**

15.27   was because] **TS2–** was
TS1r

15.28–29 my responsibility] **TS2r
TS2ce–** me **TS1r TS2t
TS2ct**

15.30   Sons'] **TS2r P–** Sons **TS1r
TS2t TS2c**

15.30–31 that I regret] **TS2–** I
regretted **TS1r**

15.33a   Torres Straits] **TS1r–P**
Torres Strait **SE–**

15.33b   their] **TS1r–P** its **SE–**

15.34   on along] **TS1r TS2r
TS2ce–** on on **TS2t TS2ct**

15.35–36 I ... gale] **TS2r TS2ce–** I
left Sydney in a **TS1r** on a
day when a heavy gale of
wind from the south-east
TS2t TS2ct

15.35   was insistent] **ED VAR
TS1r TS2t TS2ct** insistent
TS2r insisted **TS2ce–**

15.37   they hastened to leave]
TS2– left **TS1r**

15.38   while still inside] **TS2r
TS2ce–** inside **TS1r TS2t
TS2ct**

15.40   Torres Straits] **TS1r–P**
Torres Strait **SE–**

16.4   of the solid] **TS1r** solid
TS2–

16.5   Straits] **TS1r–P** Strait **SE–**

16.6–7a   doubted ... over] **TS2r
TS2ce–** discussed **TS1r
TS2t TS2ct**

16.6	about] **TS2r TS2ce–SE E1–** VAR **TS1r TS2t TS2ct** OM **SA**
16.6–7b	squabbled over] **TS2ce–SE E1–** VAR **TS1r TS2t TS2ct** squabbled **TS2r** squabbled about **SA**
16.7	even denied by] **TS2r TS2ce–** absolutely denied by the man who knew most about them **TS1r TS2t TS2ct**
16.7–8	and skilful] **TS1r** but skilful **TS2–**
16.9a	true] **TS2r TS2ce–** first **TS1r TS2t TS2ct**
16.9b	first laid] **TS2r TS2ce–** laid **TS1r TS2t TS2ct**
16.11	later seamen-fathers] ED seamen-fathers **TS1r TS2t TS2ct** later sea-men fathers **TS2r SE–** later seaman fathers **TS2ce P**
16.13	benevolently by] **TS2r TS2ce–** by **TS1r TS2t TS2ct**
16.14	spirit] **TS1r SE E1–** animus **TS2 TS2c P SA**
16.16	pig-headed] **TS2r TS2ce–** obstinate **TS1r TS2t TS2ct**
16.18	only fifty] **TS2r SE–** fifty **TS1r TS2t TS2c P**
16.20a	question] **TS2–** problem **TS1r**
16.20b	and left] **TS2–** a left **TS1r**
16.21	of the Pacific behind] **TS2r TS2ce–** after **TS1r TS2t TS2ct**
16.23	a certain emotion] **TS2–** emotion **TS1r**
16.25	her head at daybreak] **TS2r TS2ce–** at the first break of day her head **TS1r TS2t TS2ct**
16.26	Bligh's Entrance] **TS1r–SE E1–** Bligh Entrance **SA**
16.27	Windswept,] **TS2ce–** A wind-swept **TS1r–TS2ct**
16.30	looked like] **TS2r TS2ce–** was **TS1r TS2t TS2ct**
16.32	in the] **TS1r** with the **TS2–**
16.33	They] **TS2–** There **TS1r**
16.35a	known by now] **TS2–** known **TS1r**
16.35b	winds] **TS2–** wind **TS1r**
16.36a	round] **TS1r** around **TS2–**
16.36b	remains] **TS1r TS2r TS2ce–** manes **TS2t TS2ct**
16.36c	the very sand] **TS2r TS2ce–** sand **TS1r** the sand **TS2t TS2ct**
16.37	36] **TS1r TS2r TS2ce–** Thirty two **TS2t TS2ct**
16.37–38	of ... approaching] **TS2r TS2ce–** I sighted at **TS1r TS2t TS2ct**
16.38	Straits] **TS1r–P** Strait **SE–**
16.39	I sighted a gaunt] **TS2ce–** a gaunt **TS1r–TS2ct**
16.40	southernmost] **TS1r TS2r TS2ce–** southern coast **TS2t TS2ct**
16.40–17.1	I ... years.] **TS1r** She had been there for years. I had heard of her. **TS2–**
17.2a	sinister, an enormous] ED sinister, all enormous **TS1r** a sinister and enormous **TS2–**
17.2b	refraction] **TS1r** the refraction **TS2–**
17.2c	on] ED of **TS1r–**
17.3a	serene] **TS2r TS2ce–** calm **TS1r TS2t TS2ct**
17.3b	far away] **TS2r TS2ce–** serene **TS1r TS2t TS2ct**
17.3–4	horizon ... sun] **TS2r TS2ce–** horizon **TS1r TS2t TS2ct**
17.5a	Torres Straits] **TS1r–P** Torres Strait **SE–**

17.5b	dusk] **TS1r** the dusk **TS2–**	17.22b	laced coat] **TS2r TS2ce–** coat **TS1r TS2t TS2ct**
17.6a	Just] **TS2r TS2ce–** and just **TS1r TS2t TS2ct**	17.23	the rocky] **TS2–** ston [*sic*] rocky **TS1r**
17.6b	a clear sun] **TS1r TS2r SE–** the sun a clear sun **TS2t TS2ct** the clear sun **TS2ce P**	17.23–24	ship's boat] **SE–** boat **TS1r TS2t TS2ct P** ships-boat **TS2r** ships' boat **TS2ce**
17.7	a little island] **TS1r TS2r TS2ce–** the ___ **TS2t TS2ct**	17.24	her oars] **TS1r TS2r TS2ce–** the oars **TS2t TS2ct**
17.8	advanced sentinel] **TS2–** sentinel **TS1r**	17.24–25	kept ... hand] **TS2r TS2ce–** watches for a sign of the captain's hand **TS1r** sits watchful for a sign of the keeps his eyes on him watching for a sign **TS2t TS2ct**
17.9	to watch the approaches] **TS2r TS2ce–** watching the approach **TS1r TS2t TS2ct**	
17.10	a hallowed] **TS2–** hallowed **TS1r**	
17.11a	that] **TS1r TS2r TS2ce–** that Captain Cook had landed on it **TS2t TS2ct**	17.27	have peopled it] **SE E1–** had peopled [peopled = ___ **TS2t TS2ct**] it for me **TS1r–SA**
17.11b	in the year 1762] **TS2r TS2ce–** OM **TS1r TS2t TS2ct**	17.28a	unforgettable] **TS1r TS2r TS2ce–** un- [*sic*] **TS2t TS2ct**
17.13	do] **TS2r SE–** do there **TS1r TS2t TS2c P**	17.28b	shades of the masters] **TS1r TS2r TS2ce–** shadows of men, great **TS2t TS2ct**
17.14a	alone] **TS2r TS2ce–** alone there **TS1r TS2t TS2ct**	17.28–29	in ... too] **TS2r TS2ce–** was [was = was which **TS2t TS2ct**] to be mine too in a humble sense **TS1r TS2t TS2ct**
17.14b	his thoughts] **TS2–** thoughts **TS1r**	
17.15	triumphs] **TS1r** the triumph **TS2t TS2c P** the triumphs **TS2r SE–**	17.29	their endeavour] **TS2–** endeavour **TS1r**
17.17	tempered] **TS1r TS2r TS2ce–** steeled tempered **TS2t TS2ct**	17.30a	successes] **TS1r TS2r TS2ce–** success **TS2t TS2ct**
17.19a	task] **TS2r–** strenuous task **TS1r** great task **TS2t**	17.30b	men who] **TS2r SE–** who **TS1r TS2t TS2c P**
17.19b	It may ... this] **TS2r TS2ce–** Perhaps on that **TS1r TS2t TS2ct**	17.31	lights and] **TS2r SE–** character **TS1r** character and **TS2t TS2ct** light and **TS2ce P**
17.21	famous] **SE E1–** great **TS1r–P SA**	17.32a	a spark] **TS1r TS2r TS2ce–** the spark **TS2t TS2ct**
17.22a	three cornered] **TS2r TS2ce–** tricornered **TS1r TS2t TS2ct**	17.32b	the sacred] **TS2r TS2ce–** a sacred **TS1r TS2t TS2ct**

THE *TORRENS*
A PERSONAL TRIBUTE

MS   holograph manuscript (Yale)
TSc   carbon-copy typescript (Boston)
  TSct   typewritten (unrevised) text of **TSc** superseded by revision
  TScr   revised text of **TSc** (incorporating Conrad's alterations): copy-text
SE   *Blue Peter*, 3 (October 1923), 251–4
SA   *Collier's*, 27 October 1923, p. 8
P   *The Torrens: A Personal Tribute* (F. A. Hook, 1923)

18.1–2   The ... Tribute] **MS TScr**
            SE P– The Torrens | A
            Personal Note **TSct** A
            Clipper Ship I Knew **SA**
18.6a   evoked] **TScr–** called out
            MS pulled out **TSct**
18.6b   by a sea-travel magazine]
            MS–SE P– o m **SA**
18.6c   before] **TScr–** to pass
            before **MS TSct**
18.8a   Personally ... them] **TScr–**
            Not **MS TSct**
18.8b   Personally I] **SE– v a r**
            MS TSct I personally **TScr**
18.9a   needlessly sophisticated]
            TScr– curiously
            sophisticated as it seems
            to me **MS TSct**
18.9b   However] **TScr–** But **MS**
            TSct
18.9c   opinion] **TScr–**
            impression **MS TSct**
18.10a   wildly wrong.] **TScr–**
            wrong. I have travelled by
            sea very little and I even
            have seen very few people
            doing that thing. **MS TSct**
18.10–12   I am ... few.] **TScr–** o m
            MS TSct
18.10b the demands of] **SE– o m**
            MS TSc
18.12a few] **SE– o m MS TSct** a
            few **TScr**
18.12b   My two ... in the] **TScr–**
            The **MS TSct**
18.13   only professional] **TScr–**
            only **MS TSct**
18.14–18   though ... fortunate]
            TScr– there can be [can

            be = is **TSct**] no doubt
            that it was extremely
            lucky **MS TSct**
18.14   we – officers] **SE– v a r**
            MS TSct we **TScr**
18.14–15   strenuous Indiamen and
            famous] **SE P– v a r MS**
            TSct iron **TScr** smart
            Indiamen and famous **SA**
18.16   with] **SE– v a r MS TSct**
            with luck from every
            point of view the end of
            my sea life with **TScr**
18.19   marking] **TScr–**
            enriching **MS TSct**
18.19–20   new impressions, pleasant
            memories] **MS** pleasant
            memories, new
            impressions **TSc–**
18.20   precious] **TScr–** enduring
            MS TSct
18.21a   include] **TScr–** extend to
            MS TSct
18.21b   companies] **TScr–**
            company **MS TSct**
18.21c it was my luck] **SE P–** it
            was my good luck **MS SA**
            we had || it was my good
            luck || **TSc**
18.21–22   to work with on] **SE P–** to
            have to work with on **MS**
            on **TSc SA**
18.22a   voyages.] **TScr–** voyages.
            They were composed
            almost without exception
            of willing good seamen
            on whose smartness and
            efficiency one could
            depend absolutely. **MS**

Both were composed of smart good seamen almost without exception on whose goodwill and loyalty one could depend absolutely. **TSct**

18.22b But the] **MS–SE P–** The **SA**

18.22c fame] **TScr–** name **MS TSct**

18.23–26 and when ... again] **MS–SE P–** OM **SA**

18.24a her chief officer had] **TScr SE P–** there was **MS TSct** OM **SA**

18.24b large and promising crowd] **TScr SE P–** promising crowd for the chief officer **MS TSct** OM **SA**

18.25 was in it] **TScr SE P–** was **MS TSct** OM **SA**

18.26 and were ... again] **TScr SE P–** OM **MS TSct SA**

18.27a apart] **MS** for apart **TSc–**

18.27b qualities, such as] **TScr–** qualities **MS TSct**

18.27–28 her celebrated] **TScr–** sheer **MS TSct**

18.29 regarded] **TScr–** looked upon **MS TSct**

18.31–19.1 I cannot ... sailing] **MS–SE P–** OM **SA**

18.31 cannot] **SE P–** can't **MS TSc** OM **SA**

18.32 experienced] **SE P–** had any **MS TSc** OM **SA**

18.33–34 "very ... style)] **TScr SE P–** the "strong gales" **MS TSct** OM **SA**

18.34 that] **TScr–** that the way she had **MS TSct** OM **SA**

19.1a the way ... letting] **TScr–** to let **MS TSct**

19.1b big] **SE–** the big **MS TSc**

19.2 one's] **TSc–** ones **MS**

19.3 an ... skill] **TScr–** a display of grace and unerring intelligence **MS TSct**

19.3–4 could fascinate] **TScr–** fascinated **MS TSct**

19.6 any] **MS TSct SE–** an **TScr**

19.6–7 whose ... shore] **TScr–** possessed of an ordinary share of adaptability and just a little imagination **MS** possessed of an ordinary share of adaptability, justice and imagination **TSct**

19.8 There are of course] **TScr–** Of course there were **MS** There were **TSct**

19.8–9 even to the incurable] **TScr–** OM **MS TSct**

19.9–10 A gentleman ... however,] **SE–** and [and = and it **TSct**] a gentleman whom we had on board on my first voyage presented an extreme case of it by offering the captain progressive amounts up to £300 to be put ashore on the first convenient land, which in this case could be only Madeira. But that was a morbid display. **MS TSct** A [*sic*] extreme instance which certainly **TScr**

19.10–12 trenched ... moments] **TScr–** OM **MS TSct**

19.11 excessive] **SE–** OM **MS TSct** display of **TScr**

19.12a more than ten] **TScr–** 10 **MS TSct**

19.12b out from] **TScr–** out of **MS TSct**

19.13–14 took ... voyage] **TScr–** came to the conclusion that he could not survive the passage **MS TSct**

19.14–15 Note ... that] **TScr–** OM **MS TSct**

19.16 at sea] **TScr–** of it, he declared (he had not had

an hour of sea-sickness)
MS TSct

19.16–20.23 him.] **TScr–** him. The sea
would do it. There were
pathetic moments in this
comedy of sea inspired
fright. He used to
produce his bank
pass-book to almost
anybody to prove his
means. What was money
as against a chance of life.
I was called into counsel
into the captains [*sic*]
room one day and having
not much say was quite
impressed by our
passenger's self
controlled pleading
earnestness, the captains
[*sic*] perplexity and the
doctor's rather grim
attitude. Having
examined the man and
testified that there was
nothing wrong
organically he stood by in
non committal silence
except for a word thrown
in at times in a curt
positive tone. And so the
inconclusive conference
went on. He would not
take no for an answer and
the thing threatened to
become interminable and
the situation became
absurd with a tinge of
cruelty in it. So I struck in
a pause simply asking the
captain to let me know in
time next to-day so that I
could get the anchors
ready at leisure. Upon I
withdrew perfectly certain
that the anchors would
not be used but the effect
I expect was produce.
The mere sound of the
word anchors quietened

the man. He consented to
leave the question open
for another 24 hours and
went out of the cabin.
Next day we passed
Teneriffe at 30 miles off
with light winds. Our man
put in one more plea and
then watched the island
steadily till it faded in the
dusk without addressing a
word to anybody that day.
He must have had a dose
to stoicism in his
character. For the rest of
the passage nor ghost of
allusion or a word of
complaint escaped his
lips. He kept himself
apart yet not surlily. His
manners were very good.
But hated us all. He went
ashore in Adelaide
without shaking hands
with anybody – except
myself. Hadn't I
mentionned [*sic*] anchors
on that occasion of his
last appeal for life. I
suppose anchor was the
most humane word I
could have used in his
hearing without
committing myself. But
the idea of having been
refused one chance of life
must have been pretty
hard to bear for eighty
days or so. **MS** The sea
would do it. There were
pathetic moments in his
persistent and hopeless
negotiations with what
must have appeared to
him absolutely heartless
monster. He produced
this bold possibility to
almost anybody to prove
his means. What was
money against life? I was

called in to council into
the captain's room one
day and it was very
impressive and having
not much to say was quite
impressed by our
passenger's
self-controlled
earnestness. The captain's
perplexity and the
doctor's grim attitude.
Having examined the
man and testified that
there was nothing wrong
organically he stood by in
non-committal silence
except for a word thrown
in at times in a curt but
positive tone, and so the
inconclusive conference
went on. He would not
take no for an answer and
the thing threatened to
become interminable and
the situation became
absurd, with a tinge of
cruelty to it, so I struck in
in a pause simply asking
the captain to let me
know in time next day so
that I could get the
anchors ready at leisure.
Upon that I withdrew
perfectly certain that the
anchor would not be used
but the effect expected
was produced. The mere
sound of the word
anchors quietened the
man and he consented to
leave the question open
for another twenty-four
hours and went out of the
cabin. ¶ To the captain's
question the doctor
answered that of course
he would not guarantee
that the man would live as
far as Adelaide. He said
that he would not

guarantee any man's life
for twenty-four hours,
even if he appeared as
sound as this one, and he
too went Next day we
passed Teneriffe at thirty
miles off with light winds.
Our man put in one more
plea and then watched
the island steadily till it
faded in the dusk without
addressing a word to
anybody that day. He
must have had a dose of
stoicism in his character.
For the rest of the passage
not a ghost of allusion or
a word of complaint
escaped his lips. He kept
himself apart, but not
surlily. His manners were
very good, but he hated
us all. He went ashore in
Adelaide without shaking
hands with anybody
except myself. Had I not
mentioned anchors on
that occasion of his last
appeal for life. ¶ I
suppose anchor was the
most humane word I
could have used without
committing myself. But
the loss of having been
refused one's chance of
life must have been
pretty hard to bear for
eighty days or so.

TSct

19.17	persistent] **SE– OM MS TSct** sort of **TScr**
19.19a	Teneriffe] **TScr SA E1–** OM **MS TSct** Tenerife **SE P**
19.19b	is not] **SE–** not **MS TSc**
19.19–29	But ... more.] **TScr SE P–** VAR **MS TSct** OM **SA**
19.23	especially as] **SE P–** VAR **MS TSct** since **TScr** OM **SA**

19.25	organic] SE P– VAR MS TSct any organic TScr OM SA
19.26	the man] SE P– VAR MS TSct him TScr OM SA
19.28	£300] SE P– VAR MS TSct 300 pounds TScr OM SA
19.29	those] TScr SE P– VAR MS TSct these SA
19.30	argument] SE– VAR MS TSct pleading TScr
19.31–33	He ... silence.] TScr SE P– VAR MS TSct OM SA
19.35	inconclusive] SE P– VAR MS TSct absurd inconclusive TScr SA
19.37	remarked] SE– VAR MS TSct said TScr
20.1	instantaneous] SE– VAR MS TSct extraordinary TScr
20.2	was at last] SE P– VAR MS TSct apparently was TScr at last was SA
20.5	Teneriffe] TScr SA E1– VAR MS TSct Tenerife SE P
20.8a	was the] SE– VAR MS TSct was like a TScr
20.8b	death-sentence] SE– VAR MS TSct sentence of death TScr
20.12	civil] SE– VAR MS TSct polite TScr
20.14a	expended] SE– VAR MS TSct expended in vain TScr
20.14b	in vain] SE– VAR MS TSct OM TScr
20.15	burning] SE P– VAR MS TSct bursting TScr SA
20.16a	notice] SE– VAR MS TSct leave TScr
20.16b	in] TScr SE P– VAR MS TSct on SA
20.18	at least] SE– VAR MS TSct least TScr
20.18–22	If I ... last.] TScr SE P– VAR MS TSct OM SA

20.20	abhorred] SE P– VAR MS TSct hated TScr OM SA
20.20–21	have been exposed] SE P– VAR MS TSct have TScr OM SA
20.21	was] SE P– VAR MS TSct is TScr OM SA
20.23	our] SE– VAR MS TSct the both lots of our passengers TScr
20.25a	removed ... of] MS TSct SE– re- [sic] TScr [n.]
20.25b	Ritz hotels] MS the Ritz Hotel TSct SE– VAR TScr
20.26a	the sea] SE– life at sea MS TSct sea TScr
20.26b	than ... shore] TScr– OM MS TSct
20.27a	visible remedy] TScr– remedy MS TSct
20.27b	no] TScr– there no [sic] MS there are no TSct
20.28–29	contains ... some] SE– is full or was full then of MS TSc
20.29–30	three months] TSc– some three months or so MS
20.30–37	The ... crowded.] MS–SE P– OM SA
20.30a	The feeling] SE P– The sense MS TSct As to the sense TScr OM SA
20.30b	close confinement] TScr SE P– confinement MS TSct OM SA
20.30c	in a sailing ship] SE P– in a ship MS TSct that in a ship TScr OM SA
20.30–31	with ... air] SE P– whose rigging leads the eye aloft MS TSct of which the propelling power leads the eye aloft TScr OM SA
20.31–33	with ... oppressive] SE P– whose life goes on before your eyes with an interest much [much = much more TSct] human than mechanical, is much less pronounced MS TSct a

	daily life going on in one's sight presenting a more human than mechanical interest – is less pronounced **TScr** OM **SA**		21.2c	some of our] **TScr**– one or two of our [our = the **TSct**] **MS TSct**
			21.3–4	who ... hornpipe] **TScr**– could take lessons in hornpipe dancing **MS TSct**
20.34	even many] **SE P**– many **MS TSct** even of many **TScr** OM **SA**		21.3	seized] **SE**– VAR **MS TSct** took **TScr**
20.34–35	Besides ... neither] **SE P**– and there is no **MS TScr** and there is never | no **TSct** OM **SA**		21.4	professor] **TScr**– expert **MS TSct**
			21.4–5	could pursue their studies] **TScr**– OM **MS TSct**
20.35	nor] **SE P**– or **MS TSc** OM **SA**		21.5a	studies] **SE**– OM **MS TSct** study **TScr**
20.35–36	actively wearisome] **SE P**– wearisome **MS TSc** OM **SA**		21.5b	in] **TScr**– in the privacy of **MS TSct**
20.36	Another advantage was that] **TScr SE P**– And of course **MS TSct** OM **SA**		21.5–6	for its practice] **TScr**– OM **MS TSct**
20.37a	at that] **MS** of that **TSc SE P**– OM **SA**		21.6–7	I can assure you] **SE**– OM **MS TSc**
20.37b	cabins of the Torrens] **TScr**– cabin's **MS** cabins **TSct**		21.7	Much more.] **TScr**– OM **MS TSct**
			21.8a	The] **SE**– I see [see = have just learned **TScr**] from a book of reference that the **MS TSc**
20.38a	each] **MS TScr**– in each **TSct**			
20.38b	they were] **TScr**– were **MS TSct**		21.8b	only a] **TScr**– a **MS TSct**
20.38c	overfurnished with] **SE**– overfurnished **MS TSct** over furnished by **TScr**		21.9a	had managed] **TScr**– managed **MS** OM **TSct**
			21.9b	after ... launch] **TScr**– after much tribulation to launch **MS** I launched **TSct**
20.39	all ... called] **TScr**– OM **MS TSct**			
20.40–21.1	three ... them] ED three berths in them **MS** three berths **TSct** three or four berths **TScr**–		21.9c	waters] **MS TScr**– seas waters **TSct**
			21.10a	began our careers about] **MS SE**– began our sea life together **TSct** did begin our careers about **TScr**
21.1a	their ... numbered] **TScr**– the very couch having a berth number [berth number = number **TSct**] **MS TSct**			
			21.10b	the same] **MS TScr**– same **TSct**
			21.11	was by far] **TScr**– was **MS TSct**
21.1b	very couches] **TScr SE P**– VAR **MS TSct** couches **SA**		21.12a	It] **MS TSct SE**– which **TScr**
21.2a	big as ours] **TScr**– big **MS TSct**		21.12b	went on growing] **TScr**– lasted **MS TSct**
21.2b	Not half as big] **SE**– Not half **MS TSc**		21.13a	Captain] **TSc**– Capt. **MS**

21.13b Angel] **MS** Angell **TSc–**
21.13c whose] **MS TScr–** He left
        her whose **TSct**
21.13–14 own long] **TScr–** long **MS**
        TSct
21.14 the greatest ... three] **SE–**
        also a great success **MS**
        TSct perhaps the great
        success of the three **TScr**
21.15–18 and ... responsible]
        MS–SE P– O M **SA**
21.15 his ship's] **SE P–** her **MS**
        TSct his ships **TScr** O M
        SA
21.16 The Torrens certainly]
        TScr SE P– She **MS TSct**
        O M **SA**
21.17 sudden accidents] **TScr**
        SE P– accidents **MS TSct**
        O M **SA**
21.18a be made] **TSc SE P–** be
        MS O M **SA**
21.18b afterwards] **TScr–** after
        MS after a year after in
        TSct
21.19a 2nd of November] **SE P–**
        2^{d}of Nov. **MS** the end of
        October **TSct** 2nd Nov
        TScr 2d of November **SA**
21.19b London,] **TScr–** London,
        sailing from Plymouth
        where we used to call for
        the bulk of our
        passengers on the 25 of
        the month **MS** London,
        sailing from Plymouth
        where we used to call for
        the bulk of our
        passengers on the 25th of
        November, **TSct**
21.20 15th] **TSc–** 15 **MS**
21.20–21 October, 1893] **TSc–** Oct
        1893 **MS**
21.21a in London Dock I] **SE–** I
        MS TSct I in the Lond:
        dock **TScr**
21.21b look from the quay]
        TScr– farewell look **MS**
        last look and a last
        farewell **TSct**

21.22a at ... care] **TScr** at that
        last of my sea-homes from
        the quay **MS** and at last of
        my sea-homes from the
        quay **TSct** that last of
        ships I ever had under
        my care **SE–**
21.22b stepping] **TScr–** turning
        MS TSct
21.23–24 a tall ... time] **TScr–** the
        warehouse **MS TSct**
21.24 stepped] **TScr–** stepped
        out **MS TSct**
21.25a owed] **TScr–** owe **MS**
        TSct
21.25b my close] **SE–** this **MS**
        TSct close **TScr**
21.26a my acquaintance with]
        SE– the kindness of **MS**
        TSc
21.26b Captain] **TSc–** Capt **MS**
21.27a Captain H. R. Angel] **E D**
        Capt. R. H. Angel **MS**
        Capt. H. R. Angell **TSc**
        Captain H. R. Angell **SE–**
21.27–32 I had ... particularly]
        MS–SE P– O M **SA**
21.27b had known] **TScr SE P–**
        knew **MS** knew || had
        known || **TSct** O M **SA**
21.27–28 some ... slightly] **TScr SE**
        P– slightly some years
        before **MS TSct** O M **SA**
21.28 I knew ... been] **SE P–**
        Capt Cope was **MS TSct** I
        knew that he was **TScr**
        O M **SA**
21.29–31 that ... way] **TScr SE P–**
        serving afterwards in mail
        boats of great Liverpool
        steamship line **MS** sailing
        afterwards in the
        mailboats of a great ***
        steamship line **TSct** O M
        SA
21.29 he had had] **SE–** V A R **MS**
        TSct had **TScr** O M **SA**
21.30 steamer service] **E D V A R**
        MS TSct service **TScr**
        steamer **SE P–** O M **SA**

21.31–32	But ... particularly.] TScr– OM MS TSct SA	22.5a	lasted out] ED lasted for MS TSct lasted out for TScr–
21.31	believe that] SE– OM MS TSct SA believe TScr	22.5b	voyages,] MS TScr– voyages, I could not have bee [sic] TSct
21.32	However on hearing] TScr SE P– Hearing MS TSct SA	22.5c	discharges] MS TScr– two discharges TSct
21.33a	sent] TSc– send MS	22.6	Lubbock ... Clippers,] SE–
21.33b	the Torrens] TScr– he MS TSct		Lubbock's book MS TSct Lubbock in his history of
21.34	as ... me] TScr– OM MS TSct	22.8a	Colonial Clippers TScr stay] MS–SE P– to stay
21.35a	recovering slowly] TScr– recovering MS TSct	22.8b	SA Thus my] TScr– My MS
21.35b	a most] SE– one the [sic] most MS one of the most TSc	22.9	TSct by many years] TScr– OM MS TSct
21.36a	tropical disease] SE– of tropical diseases MS TSc	22.10a	life ... than I] TScr– life MS TSct
21.36b	which I had caught] TScr– which I caught MS caught TSct	22.10b	it was at least] TScr– it was MS and it was TSct
21.37	river Congo] TScr– Congo MS TSct	22.11a	unavailing regrets] TScr– regrets MS regret TSct
21.37–38	Yet ... doubts of] TScr– I hesitated about MS TSct	22.11b	escaped] TScr– was spared MS TSct
21.39–40	he ... and] TScr– the temptation was great and he MS TSct	22.11c	fate] TScr– end MS TSct
		22.13a	put so much] MS TScr– write with such put so
21.40–22.1	It was clear that] SE– I suppose my looks MS TSct I suppose too, that TScr	22.13b	much TSct interesting knowledge] TScr– knowledge MS TSct
22.1a	goes] TScr– is MS TSct	22.14a	right feeling] TScr– feeling MS TSct
22.1b	my looks did] TScr– did MS TSct	22.14b	studies of] SE– writings about MS TSc
22.1c	argued] TScr– assured me MS TSct	22.14c	calls] MS TScr– called TSct
22.2a	so far] SE P– as far MS TSc SA	22.15	Her fascinations] TScr– And her fascination MS
22.2b	seem to be] TSc– seem MS		and her fascinations TSct
22.3a	me] TSc– [t]hose MS	22.15–16	have ... men] TScr– live still in some memories
22.3b	could ... half] SE– could not have been anything MS TScr was not half TSct	22.16a	MS TSct marks] SE P– VAR MS TSct mark TScr SA
22.4	our poor] TScr– the MS the || our poor TSct	22.16b	received] TScr– had MS TSct

22.17   remembered having] SE–
         had MS TSct remember
         having TScr
22.18   invoking confidently]
         TScr– invoking MS TSct
22.19   Mr] TSc– the Mr MS
22.20   when ... 1891] TScr in
         1892 MS in 1891 TSct
22.20–21 write to] MS–SE P– write
         SA
22.21   friendly, quiet] MS TScr–
         friendly TSct
22.21   seaman's letter] TScr
         letter MS TSct
22.22   I know of] TScr– there is
         in Massachusetts MS TSct
22.23   in Massachusetts] TScr–
         OM MS TSct
22.23–25 a model ... service] TScr–
         her model from memory
         MS her model from || in
         || memory TSct
22.25a   had no] SE P– could find
         no MS had not TSc SA
22.25b   go and] MS TSc SA go to
         SE P–
22.25–26a to gaze ... hands] TScr–
         the pious work of his
         hands in memory of her
         who was so worthy of
         men's loyal service MS
         the pious work of his
         hands TSct

22.25–26b at the] SE– VAR MS TSct
         on the TScr
22.28–29 Genoa ... broken up]
         TSc– Genova after a
         stranding MS
22.30a   the perfections ... build]
         TScr– construction MS
         TSct
22.30b   perfections] TScr SE P–
         VAR MS TSct perfection
         SA
22.31   went to work instead]
         TScr– went to work MS
         repaired her went to work
         TSct
22.32a   few more years] SE– little
         while longer MS TSc
22.32b   was] TScr– had been MS
         TSct
22.33–34 in ... up] TScr– she was
         broken up in the end MS
         TSct
22.34   reverence] TScr–
         reverence, and her spirit
         has entered now upon its
         eternal rest MS TSct
22.34–40 And ... while.] TScr– OM
         MS TSct
22.35   last] SE– OM MS TSct
         first TScr
22.37   sunlit sea] SE– OM MS
         TSct sea TScr
22.39   renowned,] SE– OM MS
         TSct fearless sunlit TScr

CHRISTMAS-DAY AT SEA

MS   holograph manuscript (HRC)
TS1   typescript (HRC)
TS1t   typewritten (unrevised) text of TS1 superseded by revision
TS1r   revised text of TS1 (incorporating Conrad's alterations): copy-text
TS2   typescript (HRC)
TS2t   typewritten (unrevised) text of TS2 superseded by revision
TS2r   revised text of TS2 (incorporating Conrad's alterations)
TS3c   carbon-copy typescript (TTU)
TS3ct   typewritten (unrevised) text of TS3c superseded by revision
TS3cr   revised text of TS3c (incorporating Conrad's alterations)
SA   *Delineator*, December 1923, p. 10
SEp1   *Daily Mail* galley-proofs (HRC)

SEp1u   unrevised text of **SEp1**
SEp1r   revised text of **SEp1** (incorporating Conrad's alterations)
SEp2   *Daily Mail* galley-proofs (TTU)
SEp2u   unrevised text of **SEp2**
SEp2r   revised text of **SEp2** (incorporating Conrad's alterations)
SE   *Daily Mail*, 24 December 1923, p. 4

23.3	Christmas Day] **TS1**– it **MS**		**TS2t SA**– ship's company **TS3c SEp1u**
23.4a	sinful] **TS1r**– redeemed **MS TS1t**	23.14a	got] **TS1r**– do get **MS TS1t**
23.4b	but this] **TS1r**– This is an **MS TS1t**	23.14b	of some sort] **TS1r**– OM **MS TS1t**
23.4c	is so] **TS1r**– so **MS TS1t**	**23.14c**	appears] **MS TS1t TS2r**–
23.5a	the human] **MS TS1r** **TS2t SA E1**– the young **TS1t** human **TS2r TS3c SEp1**–SE	23.15a	appeared **TS1r TS2t** for the first time] **TS1r**– OM **MS TS1t**
23.5b	fails] **MS** refuses **TS1**–	23.15b	the officer] **TS1**– to officer [*sic*] **MS**
23.6	Perhaps ... face it] **MS** perhaps **TS1r**– OM **TS1t**	**23.15c**	greets] **TS2r**– meets **MS TS1t** greeted **TS1r** **TS2t**
23.7	for ... blame] **TS1r**– which of course is not its fault **MS TS1t**	23.16	Christmas] **TS1**– Xmas **MS**
23.8a	It prefers to concentrate] **TS1r**– and thus concentrates **MS** a **TS1t**	23.17a	Anything] **TS1r**– for anything **MS TS1t**
23.8b	ceremonial] **MS TS2r**– the ceremonial **TS1 TS2t**	23.17b	would] **MS–SEp1u** would be **SEp1r**–
23.9	such] **MS TS1r**– such as **TS1t**	**23.17c**	of] **MS** in **TS1**–
23.10	as giving] **MS TS1r**– giving **TS1t**	23.17–18	not have been] **TS1r** **TS2t** not be considered **MS TS1t** be not
23.11a	conventional point] **TS1r**– point **MS TS1t**	23.18–19	**TS2r–SEp1u** not **SEp1r**– Normally ... shape of] **TS1r**– And the usual
23.11b	view] **MS TS1r**– view and the **TS1t**		answer to this would be **MS** And the measured
23.12a	weak distinctly weak] **MS** distinctly weak **TS1**–		answer to this would be **TS1t**
23.12b	distinctly weak] **TS1r**– distinctly weak, in its conventional manifestations **MS TS1t**	**23.18**	may] **SEp1r**– VAR **MS TS1t** could **TS1r TS2t** can **TS2r–SEp1u**
23.12–13	The opportunities ... lacking.] **TS1r**– OM **MS TS1t**	23.20a	He ... it] **TS1r**– Not **MS TS1t**
23.13	a ship's company] **TS2r** the men **MS TS1t** the ship's company **TS1r**	**23.20b**	does] **TS2r**– VAR **MS TS1t** did **TS1r TS2t**
		23.21–24.15	One ... other.] **MS–TS3c SEp1**– OM **SA**
		23.21	Christmas] **TS1–TS3c SEp1**– Xmas **MS** OM **SA**

23.22	correct] TS1r–TS3c SEp1– right MS TS1t OM SA	23.29	as motionless] TS2r TS3c SEp1– motionless MS–TS2t OM SA
23.23	doesn't] TS1r–TS3c SEp1– don't MS TS1t OM SA	23.30a	the wretched steamboats] TS2r TS3c SEp1– any wretched steamboat MS wretched steamboat TS1t wretched steamboats TS1r TS2t OM SA
23.24a	Nothing] TS1r–TS3c SEp1– and nothing MS TS1t OM SA		
23.24–25	three ... dense forg [sic]] TS1r–TS3c SEp– fog had come on MS TS1t OM SA	23.30b	groping blindly] TS2r TS3c SEp1– groping its way MS wrapping its way TS1t groping their way TS1r TS2t OM SA
23.24b	less] TS2 TS3c SEp1– OM MS SA less come TS1	23.31a	felt] TS1r–TS3c SEp1– never felt MS TS1t OM SA
23.25	up] TS2r out on deck MS out TS1 TS2t OM TS3c–	23.31b	I had behaved tactlessly] TS1r–TS3c SEp1– so tactless in my life, and MS so tactless and TS1t OM SA
23.26a	orders] MS TS1r–TS3c SEp1– order TS1t OM SA		
23.26b	We were] TS2r TS3c SEp1– It was MS–TS2t OM SA	23.33	difficult] TS2r TS3c SEp1– difficult ever MS–TS2t OM SA
23.26c	chops of] MS TS1r–TS3c SEp1– chops in TS1t OM SA	23.33–34	when one is] TS1r–TS3c SEp1– especially for the MS TS1t OM SA
23.26–27	with the] TS2r TS3c SEp1– the MS–TS2t OM SA	23.34	from my gaucherie] TS1r–TS3c SEp1– OM MS TS1t SA
23.27a	Scilly islands] TS1r–TS3c SEp1– Scillies MS TS1t OM SA	23.35a	when in] TS1–TS3c SEp1– when MS OM SA
23.27b	on a vague bearing] TS1r–TS3c SEp1– were somewhere MS were TS1t OM SA	23.35b	hour] TS1t SEp1r– hour afterwards MS TS1r–TS3c SEp1u OM SA
23.27c	thirty miles of us] TS1r–TS3c SEp1– thirty miles MS thirteen miles TS1t OM SA	24.2a	warning sound] TS2r TS3c SEp1– sound MS TS1 TS2t OM SA
23.28a	not ... anywhere] TS2r TS3c SEp1– there was no wind MS TS1 TS2t OM SA	24.2b	like a] TS2r TS3c SEp1– in the guise of MS TS1 TS2t OM SA
23.28b	There the ship remained] TS2r TS3c SEp1– And there we were MS TS1t There the ship stood TS1r TS2t OM SA	24.2c	blot] TS2r TS3c SEp1– blob MS TS1 TS2t OM SA
		24.3a	bow. She] SEp1r– bow, and MS–TS3c SEp1u OM SA
23.28c	wrapped] MS wrapped up TS1–TS3c SEp1– OM SA	24.3b	took on] MS TS2r TS3c SEp1– took TS1 TS2t OM SA

24.3c	the shape ... ship] **TS2r** **TS3c SEp1–** ships [*sic*] shape **MS–TS2t** O M **SA**	24.13b	straining] **TS2r TS3c SEp1u–** strained **MS–TS2t** O M **SA**
24.5–6	into nothing] **TS1r–TS3c SEp1–** away **MS TS1t** O M **SA**	24.14	impending marine] **TS1r–TS3c SEp1–** marine **MS TS1t** O M **SA**
24.6a	long before] **TS1–TS3c SEp1–** long **MS** O M **SA**	24.16a	of course] **MS–TS3c SEp1–** O M **SA**
24.6b	beastly noise] **TS1r–TS3c SEp1–** uproar **MS TS1t** O M **SA**	24.16b	Christmas] **TS1–** Xmas **MS**
24.7	her people] **TS2r TS3c SEp1–** the people on board **MS TS1t** people on board of her **TS1r TS2t** O M **SA**	24.16–17	would hardly take] **TS1r–** is not likely to come in **MS** which casts a shadow is not likely to come in **TS1t**
24.8a	them] **MS** her **TS1–TS3c SEp1–** O M **SA**	24.17	than] **MS TS1t TS3cr SEp1–** but **TS1r–TS3ct SA**
24.8b	by way of] **TS1r–TS3c SEp1–** for **MS TS1t** O M **SA**	24.19a	which] **TS1r–** that **MS TS1t**
24.8c	Christmas] **TS1–TS3c SEp1–** Xmas **MS** O M **SA**	24.19b	Christmas] **TS1r–** a Ch'as day **MS** Christmas day **TS1t**
24.9	more] **MS TS1r–TS3c SEp1–** more un-Christian could be imagine [*sic*] **TS1t** O M **SA** [*n.*]	24.19	upon] **MS** on **TS1–**
		24.20	consists] **TS1–** consist **MS**
24.10	and I ... that] **TS2r TS3c SEp1–** O M **MS–TS2t** S A	24.20–21	worry ... sea] **ED** giving of presents at sea **MS** giving of presents **TS1t** worry about presents **TS1r–**
24.10–11	whole ship's company get] **TS1r–TS3c SEp1–** ship's company **MS TS1t** O M **SA**	24.21a	Presents] **TS1r–** A present **MS TS1t**
24.11	one ... calls"] **TS2r TS3c SEp1–** a mere chance **MS TS1t** a mere close call **TS1r TS2t** O M **SA**	24.21b	unexpected things] **TS1r–** an unexpected thing **MS TS1t**
		24.22	seems ... hypocritical] **TS1r–** is a strangely savourless **MS TS1t**
24.12a	We remained] **TS1r–TS3c SEp1–** They **MS** They remained **TS1t** O M **SA**	24.23a	like] **TS1r–** It is like **MS TS1t**
24.12b	the morning] **TS1r–TS3c SEp1** day **MS TS1t** O M **SA**	24.23b	gifts of] **TS1r–** O M **MS TS1t**
24.12c	consumed] **TS1r–TS3c SEp1–** we ate **MS** we eat **TS1t** O M **SA**	24.23c	proof] **TS1r–** a season **MS TS1t**
		24.24–25	the fruits] **TS1r–** The gifts **MS** And the gifts **TS1t**
24.13a	Christmas] **TS1–TS3c SEp1–** Xmas **MS** O M **SA**	24.25a	chances to gather] **TS2r–** may find **MS TS1t** may gather **TS1r TS2t**
		24.25b	on] **MS–TS3c SEp1r–** of **SEp1u**

24.25c as salt as tears] **MS** of sawdust **TS1t** salt as tears **TS1r–**

24.25d as bitter] **MS–SEp1u** bitter **SEp1r–**

24.27a all my] **TS1r–** my **MS TS1t**

24.27b over] **MS TS1r–** about | over **TS1t**

24.28a Christmas] **TS1–** Xmas **MS**

24.28b celebrated] **TS1r–** marked **MS TS1t**

24.29 proper] **TS2r–** OM **MS–TS2t**

24.30 no] **TS1r–** and no **MS TS1t**

24.30–31 and ... recording.] **TS1r–** but that opinion depends upon the view one takes of the value of a bundle of old newspapers. That's how it happened. **MS TS1t**

24.31 Let] **TS1r–** But let **MS TS1t**

24.32–33 wireless telegraphy] **MS** wireless **TS1t** wireless messages **TS1r–**

24.33–34 prophesy broadcasting] **TS1r–** prophecy its coming **MS TS1t**

24.34a regarded] **TS1r–** looked upon **MS TS1t**

24.34b a particularly] **TS1t TS2–** particularly **MS TS1r**

24.34c offensive nuisance] **TS1r–** objectionable lunatic **MS TS1t**

24.35a probably sent] **TS1r–** sent off **MS TS1t**

24.35b We] **TS1r–** we **MS** – as we **TS1t**

24.36 madhouses ... way] **TS1r–** lunatic asylums then **MS TS1t**

24.37a The daybreak of] **TS1r–** The day break of the **MS** Christmas Day of the year

1879 | The daybreak of the **TS1t**

24.37b Christmas] **TS1–** Chris^as **MS**

24.37c '79] **MS** 1879 **TS1–**

24.38 sometime] **TS1r–** somewhere **MS TS1t**

24.38–39 sombre expanse] **TS1r–** solitary wastes **MS** solitary waters **TS1t**

24.39 Lat.] **MS** latitude **TS1–**

25.1a sighted] **MS TS1r–** reported | sighted **TS1t**

25.1b swell] **TS1r–** sea **MS TS1t**

25.2 "Merry Christmas"] ED Merry Xmas **MS** a happy Christmas **TS1 TS2t** a "Merry Christmas" **TS2r–**

25.3a still sleepy] **TS1r–** sleepy **MS TS1t**

25.3b reported] **TS1r–** pointed in the direction of **MS TS1t**

25.3c to him] **TS1r–** OM **MS TS1t**

25.5 her] **MS TS1r–** them **TS1t**

25.5–8 I ... theory.] **MS–TS3c SEp1–** OM **SA**

25.6a she had all her] **TS1r–TS3c SEp1–** her **MS TS1t** OM **SA**

25.6b furled] **TS1r–TS3c SEp1–** were furled **MS TS1t** OM **SA**

25.6c brought to] **SEp1r–** by **MS–TS2t** brought by **TS2r TS3c** brought up by **SEp1u** OM **SA**

25.8 glasses] **MS TS1r–** glass **TS1t**

25.9a stripped] **TS2r–** OM **MS–TS2t**

25.9b resembling three Swedish safety] **TS1r–** the size of three **MS TS1t**

25.10 ridiculously] **TS1r–** OM **MS TS1t**

25.11	heaving ... countless] TS1r– austere solitude of moving MS TS1t	25.24a	companion stairs] TS2r– companion MS–TS2t
25.12	yawned] TS1r– yawned callously MS TS1t	25.24b	Have you any] MS TS1r– Any TS1t
25.12–13	This ... shock] TS1r– It was a shock to me MS TS1t	25.24c	newspapers] TS2r– papers MS–TS2t
25.14	comparative stranger] TS1r– novice MS TS1t	25.26	We ... before.] MS–TS3c SEp1– O M SA
25.14–15	in ... waters] TS1r– in those regions of the water-world MS TS1t	25.27a	several old] TS1r– lots of MS TS1t
25.16a	a captain's] TS1r– the captain's MS TS1t	25.27b	Telegraphs,] MS–SE A1 Telegraphs, and E1
25.16b	disappeared] TS1r– had disappeared MS TS1t	25.28	a few] TS1r– some MS TS1t
25.17a	and] MS TS1t TS2r– but TS1r TS2t	25.29–32	The ... eccentricities.] TS1r– O M MS TS1t
25.17b	our] TS2r– the MS–TS2t	25.32	at them] TS1r– O M MS TS1t
25.17c	the poop ladder] TS1r– on the poop MS TS1t	25.33	with] TS1r– in on MS TS1t
25.18a	an empty, small] TS2r– a MS an empty TS1t a small TS1r TS2t	25.34a	and ... particular] TS1r– O M MS TS1t
25.18b	the sort in which] TS1r– the sort MS which TS1t	25.34b	be loafing] TS1r– loaf MS TS1t
25.19a	packed.] TS2r– packed in. But it was empty. He said: Here it is [Here it is = "Here's this, TS1t] sir." MS TS1t packed, but it was empty TS1r TS2t	25.35a	on the ... storms] TS1r– over those stormy regions of the globe MS TS1t
		25.35b	very] TS2r– V A R MS TS1t O M TS1r TS2t
25.19–20	What ... Chips?] TS1r–TS3c SEp1– I don't want it here. MS TS1t	25.35c	the gloomy] TS2r– V A R MS TS1t that gloomy TS1r TS2t
25.19b	mean by] TS2r– V A R MS TS1t mean TS1r TS2t	25.36a	hour] TS1r– O M MS TS1t
25.20	sir] TS1r– O M MS TS1t	25.36b	learned] TS1r– discovered MS TS1t
25.21	explained shortly] TS1r– explained MS TS1t	25.37	this nonchalant ship] TS1r– she MS TS1t
25.22a	Christmas] TS1– Xmas MS	25.37–38	She was the] TS1r– The MS This was the TS1t
25.22b	and he went away] TS1r– O M MS TS1t	25.38	had hoisted] TS1r– flew MS TS1t
25.23a	to speak] TS1r– that spoke MS TS1t	25.39	at her peak] TS1r– O M MS TS1t
25.23b	up] MS TS2r– to TS1 TS2t	26.1a	her name was: Alaska] SEp1r– she was the "Alaska" MS–SEp1u
		26.1b	out from] TS2r– from MS–TS2t

26.1–2 New ... Honolulu]
TS1r–SEp2 and had been
away MS TS1t New York –
east from Honolulu
SE–

26.2a days] TS1r– days from
Honolulu MS TS1t

26.2b the] TS2r– her MS–TS2t

26.5a our] TS1r– the MS TS1t

26.5b captain] TS1– Cap¹ MS

26.6a held up aloft] MS–TS2
held aloof TS3ct held
aloft TS3cr–

26.6b three] MS O M TS1–

26.9a day] TS1r– day, I suppose
MS TS1t

26.9b flung ... rail] TS1r– cast it
overboard and MS TS1t

26.9c flung it] TS2– V A R MS
TS1t flung TS1r

26.9d far] TS1r TS2 SA V A R
MS TS1t far out TS3c
SEp1–

26.10a sliding] TS1r– slid away
from it MS TS1t

26.10b a high] TS1– high MS

26.10–11 swell ... wake] TS1r– swell
MS swell *** TS1t

26.11a flourished] TS1r– raised
MS TS1t

26.11b an] TS2r– his MS–TS2t

26.12a a much bewhiskered
person] TS1r– much
bewhiskered MS TS1t

26.12b forward] MS TS2–
forwards TS1

26.13 ready and smart] TS1r–
smart and sure MS
TS1t

26.14a desperately] TS1r–
heavily MS TS1t

26.14b one of her boats] TS1r– a
boat MS TS1t

26.15a southern ocean] MS
TS1r– eternal hills
Southern ocean TS1t

26.15b went on tossing] TS1r–
tossed MS TS1t

26.15c ships] TS1r– ships up and
down MS TS1t

26.17 instantly ... catapult]
TS2r– instantly MS TS1

26.18 lost not] TS1r– did not
lose MS TS1t

26.19a her Christmas] TS1r– the
Xmas MS that Christmas
TS1t

26.19b the] TS2r– an MS–TS2t

26.20 had increased] TS1r–
increased MS TS1t

26.21 thanks and] TS1r– thanks
MS TS1t

26.22 paid them] TS1r– paid
MS TS1t

26.23 days] MS days of risk and
toil spent TS1t days of
risk and toil TS1r–

26.23–24 the sounds ... world]
TS1r– all sound and sight
of mankind MS TS1t

26.24 beyond ... life] TS1r– on
the outermost edge
[outermost edge = edge
TS1t] of the world MS
TS1t

26.25a lonely] MS and lonely
TS1–

26.25b penance] TS1r– toil MS
TS1t

26.26–31 Christmas ... ticket.]
MS–TS3c SEp1– O M SA

26.26–27 at sea ... atrocious] TS1r–
are various MS are very
various TS1t O M SA

26.27 In ... include] TS1r–
There are for instance
MS TS1t O M SA

26.28a Christmas] TS1– Xmas
MS O M SA

26.28b the passenger] MS
passenger TS1– O M SA

26.29a sister] TS1r– a sister MS
TS1t O M SA

26.29b and ... way] TS1r– O M
MS TS1t SA

26.30a days] MS Christmas Days
TS1– O M SA

26.30b what I suppose] MS I
suppose what TS1–TS3
SE1p–SE O M SA

26.30c   conventional] **TS2r**–   26.31   included ... ticket]
          commonplace   **TS1–TS3 SE1p–SE** O M
          conventional **MS–TS2t**   **MS TS1t SA**

OCEAN TRAVEL

MS   holograph manuscript, final text (HRC): copy-text
S   *Evening News*, 15 May 1923, p. 4

27.1   Ocean Travel] **E1**– Ocean   **28.26**   indubitably] **S**–
           Travel (?) **MS** My Hotel in   undubitably **MS**
           Mid-Atlantic. Modern   28.27   which] **MS** that **S**–
           Ocean Luxury – A   28.28   used] **MS** had **S**–
           Contrast With the   28.35   boxed up] **MS** boxed and
           Sailing-Ship Days. **S**   **S**–
27.3   be safely] **MS** safely be **S**– **29.2**   than] **S**– that **MS**
27.15   This] **MS** It **S**–   **29.11**   to walk] **S**– walk **MS**
27.19   conditions] **MS** condition   29.13   that] **MS** this **S**–
           S–   29.14   frequent] **MS** regular **S**–
27.23   applies] **MS** applied **S**– 29.17   de] **MS** *au* **S**–
27.27   a hotel] **MS** hotel **S**–   29.19   a nice] **MS** nice **S**–
28.2   ferry] **MS S** ferries **E1**– 29.26   lay] **MS** lie **S**–
28.4   as much] **MS** much **S**–   29.32   they] **MS** that they **S**–

OUTSIDE LITERATURE

TS   typescript (Yale)
  TSr revised text of **TS**: copy-text
SE1   *Supplement to the Manchester Guardian*, 4 December 1922, p. iii
SE2   *Manchester Guardian Weekly*, 8 December 1922, p. 453
SA   *Bookman* (New York), 56 (February 1923), 680–82

30.15   appreciated] **SE1**–   **31.4**   Notices] **SE1**– a Notice
              properly appreciated   **TSr**
              TSr   31.6   of] **SE1**– in **TSr**
30.16   their style] **SE1**– the style 31.9   a quiet] **SE1**– quiet **TSr**
              of Notices to Mariners   31.14   civilisation] **TSr** a
              TSr   civilisation **SE1**–
30.23   it doesn't] **SE1**– they 31.24   subjects] **SE1**– matters
              don't **TSr**   **TSr**
30.27   a printing-press] **TSr–SE2** 31.27   have tried] **SE1**– like **TSr**
              printing press **SA**–   31.31   acquiring] **SE1**– forming
30.29   is] **SA**– are **TSr–SE2**   **TSr**
30.31   ideal] **TSr** an ideal **SE1**– 32.3a has happened] **TSr**
30.33–34 smile ... it] **SE1**– smile   happened **SE1**–
              TSr   32.3b   course] **SE1**– march **TSr**
30.34–35 expounding the] **SE1 SE2** 32.15   detected] **SE1**– read on
              expressing the **TSr** of **SA**–   my face **TSr**

32.19–20	in ... hand] **SE1**– sheepishly **TSr**		**33.6b**	I lost] **SE1**– lost **TSr**
32.21–22	had been] **SE1**– was **TSr**		**33.6c**	trusted] **SE1**– trustworthy **TSr**
32.23a	tried] **SE1 SA**– wanted **TSr** tired **SE2**		33.9	could never learn] **TSr–SE2** never learned **SA**–
32.23b	give me a hint] **SE1**– put me on the track **TSr**		**33.12**	us at] **SE1**– over **TSr**
32.28–29	my captain one morning] **TSr** one morning my captain **SE1**–		**33.14**	Wasn't it] **SE1**– Was it not **TSr**
32.30	that] **TSr**– the **SE1 SE2**		33.15	Hamlet ... play] **TSr**– *Hamlet* **SA**–
32.31	their] **SE1**– her **TSr**		33.18	doubt] **TSr**– question **SA**–
32.35–36	of beckoning] **SE1**– with him **TSr**		**33.19–20**	Mariners ... literature,] **SE1**– Mariners **TSr**
32.36	say of it] **SE1**– say **TSr**		**33.20**	fidelity] **SE1**– successful fidelity **TSr**
33.6a	very last] **TSr–SE2** last **SA**–			

LEGENDS

MS manuscript (Morgan): copy-text
SE *Daily Mail*, 15 August 1924, p. 8
SA *New York Times Magazine*, 7 September 1924, pp. 1–2

34.14	had] **MS SA** have had **SE E1**–		**35.35a**	speaks] **E D** He speaks **MS**–
34.17	gentle] **MS SA** the gentle **SE E1**–		35.35b	inner] **MS** much **SE**–
34.22	be not] **MS SE E1**– not be **SA**		35.37	collective soul] **MS SE E1**– soul **SA**
35.3	would] **MS SA** could **SE E1**–		35.40	foot] **MS SE E1**– fact **SA**
35.11	vocational] **SE**– was vocational **MS** [*n.*]		36.8a	it records] **MS SA** they record **SE E1**–
35.14	men] **MS** man **SE**–		36.8b	its] **MS SA** their **SE E1**–
35.20	of manhood] **SE**– manhood **MS**		**36.9–10**	the celebration] **SE E1**– celebration **MS SA**
35.22	countless] **MS SA** the countless **SE E1**–		**36.12**	an era] **SE**– era **MS**
35.23	rushes] **SE**– rushed **MS**		**36.18**	sign of adversity] **E D** of adversity **MS SA** adversity **SE E1**
35.27a	lies in] **SE**– lies is **MS**		36.19	the details] **MS SE E1**– details **SA**
35.27b	when the] **SE**– the **MS**		**36.23**	Basil] **SE E1**– Percy **MS SA**
35.31a	had] **SE**– has **MS**		36.25	one ... book] **MS** one reviewer **SE E1**– and reviewers of the book **SA**
35.31b	Mr Basil] **MS SE E1**– Basil **SA**			
35.34	if not] **MS SA** is now **SE E1**–		36.28	his] **SE**– its **MS**

THE UNLIGHTED COAST

MS	holograph manuscript, final text (Private collection)
TS	typescript (Colgate)
TSt	typewritten (unrevised) text of **TS** superseded by revision
TSr	revised text of **TSt** (incorporating Conrad's alterations): copy-text
S	*The Times*, 18 August 1925, pp. 13–14

37.1 The Unlighted Coast] TSr– OM **MS TSt**

37.3a came] **TSr–** have come **MS TSt**

37.3b the most] **MS TS** most **S–**

37.5 darkness in] **MS TSr–** a darkness in **TSt**

37.6 the contact] **MS TS** contact **S–**

37.9a water] **TSr–** the water **MS TSt**

37.9b mariners'] **MS TSr–** mariner's **TSt**

37.10 exploration.] **TSr–** exploration. ¶ I knew from my own small experience that often on the wildest coasts [coasts = night **TSt**] a light of some sort – if only a chance bushfire on a hillside meets a mariner's eye. But here there was nothing; neither the complex brilliant display of a system of lighthouses nor the halo-like loom of conglomerated human habitations, nor [nor = not a **TSt**] spark, gleam or glow. Nothing. **MS TSt**

37.11 To] **TSr–** And to **MS TSt**

37.11–12 behold ... sea-passages] **TSr–** behold **MS TSt**

37.12 the English coast] **TSr–** that coast after long sea-passages **MS TSt**

37.13 sleepless] **MS** a sleepless **TSt–**

37.13–14 for sleepless toil] **TSr–** sleepless toil **MS TSt**

37.14 like] **TSr–** something like **MS TSt**

37.15a truth.] **TSr–** truth. It was as if pestilence had smitten that land destroying the faithful keepers of the lights, the feasters, the toilers and the towns of the coast sleeping under their diffused ruddy glow on which stood out here and there the black shoulder of a cliff or a dark fragment from the contour of a point of land. **MS TSt**

37.15b Fires in the night] **TSr–** At night it is fires that **MS TSt**

37.16a There were] **TSr–** And there was **MS TSt**

37.16b signs] **S–** sign **MS TS**

37.18a unlighted] **TSr–** lightless **MS TSt**

37.18b known] **TSr–** had known **MS TSt**

37.19a departed from] **MS** departed **TSt–**

37.19b only its] **TSr–** the **MS TSt**

37.20 no longer there.] **TSr–** gone – which had turned that land the home of seamen unfailingly bestarred with the guiding [guiding = guarding **TSt**] lights for ships into that long featureless shadow. I don't recognise it. Even my imagination fails to give it shape and yet eight

	and thirty years ago when the young eyes the eager mind took impressions quickly I used to know by heart almost every curve and point of that coast, placid in the sunshine stern under the clouds and never so lightless so lifeless as this in its secure slumbers **MS TSt**
37.21	The ... shadow.] **TSr–** O M **MS TSt**
37.22a	Of] **TSr–** Yet of **MS TSt**
37.22b	scourges] **TSr–** the scourges **MS TSt**
37.26a	Breathing] **TSr–** And breathing **MS TSt**
37.26b	air of the night] **TSr–** air **MS TSt**
37.29a	obscured] **TSr–** unsubstiantial [*sic*] **MS TSt**
37.29b	That] **TSr–** a **MS TSt**
37.32	appearances.] **TSr** appearances. That air of death-like slumber, this, this [this, this = this **TSt**] aspect of unhabited [unhabited = uninhabited **TSt**] shore, the surface peace of the sea, mere appearances, mere [mere = were **TSt**] disguises of the great merciless reality commanding the hearts and the thoughts of men. **MS TSt** appearance. S–
38.3	this] **TSr–** this (and when it was comparatively an uninhabited waste) and that it was left for us now when it was teeming with millions to behold this perfection **MS TSt**
38.4–5	was heard] **TSr–** said **MS TSt**
38.6	messages] **TSr–** messages which **MS TSt**
38.7	was] **TSr–** was yet **MS TSt**
38.17	messages] **TSr–** messages and **MS TSt**
38.19	overlighted.] **TSr–** overlighted. One could not get rid at first of the absurd notion that it must be visible afar a blazing beacon for hostile eyes in the neutral night which like all the other neutrals would find it difficult to hold an even balance and from the nature of things is bound to be more favourable to attack than to defence [defence = defend **TSt**]. **MS TSt**
38.21	phrases; but] **TSr–** expression. **MS TSt**
38.22–23	an enemy] **MS** a hostile **TS–**
38.24	addressed ... at sea] **TSr–** O M **MS TSt**
38.28a	unmoral] **MS TSr–** immoral **TSt**
38.28b	that] **MS TSr–** than **TSt**
38.31	flows on unheard] **TSr–** unheard flows on **MS TSt**
38.32	clouds.] **TSr–** clouds. There was a feeling of profound and amused satisfaction in turning the arbitrary groups of letters into understandable short phrases and the whole sample of war-talk stand forth in its concise clearness. **MS TSt**
38.34a	around] **MS** round **TS–**
38.34b	war] **TSr–** war. For its philosophy, its rhetoric and even its eloquence suggests a welter [welter = matter **TSt**] of personal emotions, of diverse faiths, doubts convictions the existence of individual scruples and even purposes **MS TSt**

38.36	The other] **TSr–** But **MS TSt**	39.33c	From] **TSr–** It is from **MS TSt**
38.37	almost] **TSr–** which is almost **MS TSt**	39.34	it must be] **TSr–** a **MS TSt**
38.38	purpose] **TSr–** directness **MS TSt**	39.36	some of] **TSr–** o m **MS TSt**
39.1a	all] **TSr–** o m **MS TSt**	40.1	the tale] **TSr–** of it **MS TSt**
39.1b	the correct] **TSr–** correct **MS TSt**	40.4	clean] **MS TSr–** clear **TSt**
39.4a	all] **TSr–** o m **MS TSt**	40.5	effectually as] **TSr–** if **MS TSt**
39.4b	the true] **MS TS** a true **S–**	40.14a	But the] **TSr–** The **MS TSt**
39.5	too in] **TSr–** its own purely **MS TSt**	40.14b	in his direction] **TSr–** his way **MS TSt**
39.6	had] **TSr–** has **MS TSt**	40.22	that life] **MS–S A1** life **E1**
39.8	half] **TSr–** a half **MS TSt**	40.24a	crowded upon me] **TSr–** were very present in my mind **MS** o m **TSt**
39.10	sense] **TSr–** appreciation **MS TSt**		
39.12	from] **TSr–** in **MS TSt**	40.24b	memories] **TSr–** very characterised memories **MS TSt**
39.13	that] **TSr–** the **MS TSt**		
39.14	the force,] **TSr–** o m **MS TSt**	40.24c	temperaments] **TSr–** aspects **MS TSt**
39.15	the sun] **TSr–** heaven **MS TSt**	40.25	And looking at him] **TSr–** and **MS TSt**
39.17	RNR] **MS TS** the R. N. R. **S–**	40.26a	down] **TSr–** o m **MS TSt**
39.19	to it] **TSr–** all **MS TSt**	40.26b	He] **TSr–** and he **MS TSt**
39.25	points] **TS–** point **MS**	40.26–27	no haste] **TSr–** haste **MS TSt**
39.27	activities] **TSr–** work **MS TSt**	40.28	"descriptive"] **TSr–** that descriptive **MS TSt**
39.28a	the circumstances] **TSr–** its circumstances **MS TSt**		
39.28b	the conditions] **TSr–** of its conditions **MS TSt**	40.32	untrue] **TSr–** wrong **MS TSt**
39.28c	the incidents ... task] **TSr–** its incidents – and of the feelings **MS TSt**	40.33	we parted and] **TSr–** o m **MS TSt**
		40.33–34	him ... as] **TSr–** he was **MS TSt**
39.29	too, more] **TSr–** o m **MS TSt**	40.36	with ... reluctance] **TSr–** about the peculiarities of sea-fogs **MS TSt**
39.30	than of detailed description] **TSr–** of the men and of the work **MS TSt**		
		40.37	mentioned to] **TSr–** assured **MS TSt**
39.30–31	the work itself] **TSr–** that last **MS TSt**	40.38–39	He ... mine] **TSr–** and that there was nothing in the behaviour of sea-fogs that could either surprise or shock me. After that **MS TSt**
39.31	now] **TSr–** here **MS TSt**		
39.33a	proportion] **TSr–** great proportion **MS TSt**		
39.33b	truth] **TSr–** truth though not the whole truth **MS TSt**	40.40a	became] **TSr–** got **MS TSt**

40.40b   Not much tho'] **TSr**– but not much **MS TSt**

41.1a   again] **TSr**– then **MS TSt**

41.1b   spoke] **TSr**– talked **MS TSt**

41.2   a low tone] **TSr**– low tones **MS** w low [*sic*] tones **TSt**

41.3   delivered] **TSr**– gave **MS TSt**

41.4   a man] **TS**– man **MS**

41.7   outside] **TSr**– outside, steering some course between north and west **MS TSt**

41.8a   unnecessary description] **TSr**– description **MS TSt**

41.8b   best give] **TSr**– give **MS TSt**

41.8–9   the size ... command] **TSr**– her size **MS TSt**

41.10a   breech] **S A1** breach **MS TS E1**

41.10b   gun] **TSr**– gun, also in repose **MS TSt**

41.12   that] **TSr**– which **MS TSt**

41.12–13   move then] **TSr**– move **MS TSt**

41.13   than] **TS**– that **MS**

41.14   thick weather] **TSr**– a fog **MS TSt**

41.16   and thickening] **TSr**– thickening **MS TSt**

41.17–18   wink sometimes] **TSr**– shutter **MS TSt**

41.19   walking up and down] **TSr**– walking **MS TSt**

41.21   layer of fog] **TSr**– layer **MS TSt**

41.21–22   for succeeding minutes] **TSr** o m **MS TSt**

41.22   ship's] **TS**– ships **MS**

41.24–25   the Zeppelin] **TSr**– her **MS TSt**

41.25   the engines] **TSr**– her engines **MS TSt**

41.26a   soon as] **TS**– soon **MS**

41.26b   regained ... words] **TSr**– could speak he commanded **MS TSt**

41.28   that at] **TSr**– at **MS TSt**

41.29a   In fact it] **TSr**– But the Zeppelin **MS TSt**

41.29b   not anything] **TSr**– not **MS TSt**

41.30a   coming up astern] **TSr**– astern **MS TSt**

41.30b   a little ... side] **TSr**– not exactly so **MS TSt**

41.32   very close indeed] **TSr**– indeed very close **MS TSt**

41.35a   need] **TSr**– want **MS TSt**

41.35b   watch] **TSr**– follow **MS TSt**

41.40   fire] **TSr**– on him **MS TSt**

42.7   for ... own] **TSr**– o m **MS TSt**

42.8   and discomposed him] **TSr**– him cruelly **MS TSt**

42.8–9   insistent whispering] **TSr**– whispering **MS TSt**

42.9   crept up] **MS** crept **TS**–

42.10a   waste] **TSr**– loose [*sic*] **MS TSt**

42.10b   moment] **MS S**– coment [*sic*] **TS**

42.10c   the beggar] **TSr**– him **MS TSt**

42.11   Ordering] **TSr**– and ordering **MS TSt**

42.12   skipper] **TSr**– man **MS TSt**

42.14   and ... side] **TSr**– o m **MS TSt**

42.20–21   The ... boundless.] **TSr**– o m **MS TSt**

42.22a   very much] **MS** very **TS**–

42.22b   became] **TSr**– was **MS TSt**

42.22–23   eyes below] **TSr**– naked eye **MS TSt**

42.25   I saw ... plainly.] **TSr**– o m **MS TSt**

42.26   single one] **TSr**– one **MS TSt**

42.29a   without more ado] **TSr**– o m **MS TSt**

42.29b   own speed] **TSr**– own **MS TSt**

42.30   fog blowing over] **TSr**– fog **MS TSt**

42.31	faintest] **TSr**– merest **MS TSt**	43.23b	anybody] **TSr**– any one **MS TSt**
42.37	fog] **TSr**– air **MS TSt**	43.24	anxious searchers] **TSr**–
42.38a	nearer than before] **TSr**– о м **MS TSt**		searchers **MS TSt**
42.38b	downwards] **TSr**– down **MS TSt**	43.27	a desert] **TSr**– the desert **MS TSt**
42.39	angle.] **TSr**– angle. And even nearer than before. **MS TSt**	43.28	for ... shore] **TSr**– о м **MS TSt**
		43.28–29	to this one] **TSr**– with him **MS TSt**
43.5	of them] **TSr**– together **MS TSt**	43.30a	had merely] **TSr**– merely had **MS TSt**
43.6	He] **TSr**– It **MS TSt**	43.30b	unskilled in speech] **TSr**–
43.8	awful] **MS** the awful **TS**–		sparing of words **MS TSt**
43.10a	You] **TSr**– He **MS TSt**	43.31–32	for ... impression] **TSr**–
43.10b	made him] **TSr**– been very **MS TSt**		but [but = and **TSt**] somehow I fancied **MS TSt**
43.14	Damaged] **TSr**– of a damaged **MS TSt**	43.33	official report] **TSr**– report **MS TSt**
43.17	his protecting work] **TSr**– work **MS TSt**	43.33–34	remained ... choice] **TSr**– been **MS TSt**
43.18–19	strained, hopeful vigilance] **TSr**– vigilance **MS TSt**	43.34–35	I ... than] **TSr**– He would not have liked to **MS TSt**
43.20	as our coasters say] **TSr**– о м **MS TSt**	43.35	immense] **TSr**– great **MS TSt**
43.22	will come] **TSr**– come **MS TSt**	43.36a	in the world] **TSr**– о м **MS TS**
43.23a	having seen no one] **TSr**– о м **MS TSt**	43.36b	he] **TSr**– but **MS TSt**

THE DOVER PATROL

MS	holograph leaf, final text (Yale): 44.11–17 ['The story' *to* 'war too.']
TS1	draft typescript with holograph addition, 1 page (Yale)
TS1t	typewritten text of **TS1**: 47.31–36 ['mostly fisher' *to* 'in them.']
TS1r	revised text of **TS1** (incorporating Conrad's alterations)
TS1h	holograph addition to **TS1**: 47.37–48.6 ['They were' *to* 'country']
TS2	typescript (BL)
TS2r	revised text of **TS2** (incorporating Conrad's alterations): copy-text
S	*The Times*, 27 July 1921, pp. 11–12
P	*The Dover Patrol* (H. J. Goulden, 1922)

44.3	of a] **S P A1** of **TS2r E1**	44.12b	protective] **TS2r**– great, vital **MS**
44.4	ideals are] **S**– idealism is **TS2r**	44.13	simplicity] **TS2r**– nobility **MS**
44.12a	greater proud record] **TS2r**– national pride in and consciousness **MS**	44.14–15	yet ... importance] **TS2r**– о м **MS**

44.16a opening ... nineteenth] **TS2r**– 19 **MS**

44.16b their] **TS2r**– its **MS**

44.17 too] **TS2r**– too, its great effort, and its dominant figure **MS**

44.22a people] **S**– population **TS2r**

44.22b gave up] **S**– gave **TS2r**

44.28 of Europe] **S**– the Europe **TS2r**

44.29 new force] **S**– force **TS2r**

44.30 if] **S**– but **TS2r**

44.33 its thoughts and emotions] **S**– mind and conscience **TS2r**

44.34 Men's] **S**– Mens **TS2r**

45.2 cruel negations] **S**– negations **TS2r**

45.3 men's] **S**– man's **TS2r**

45.7 and patrolling] **TS2r** patrolling **S**–

45.18 and] **S**– but **TS2r**

45.19 its] **S**– its own **TS2r**

45.26a exaltation] **S**– force **TS2r**

45.26b which] **TS2r S E1**– with **P**

45.27 his] **S**– its **TS2r**

45.36 very] **S**– a very **TS2r**

45.39 appreciated] **S**– guaged [*sic*] **TS2r**

46.3 a superior] **TS2r S E1**– the **P**

46.6 just for] **TS2r** for just **S**–

46.7 small] **S**– small a **TS2r**

46.8 men ... command] **S**– men **TS2r**

46.11 hard skilled] **TS2r** skilled hard **S**–

46.14 millions] **TS2r P**– million **S**

46.19 a hundred] **S**– hundred **TS2r**

46.25 can] **S**– could **TS2r**

46.26 since no one could] **S**– for who would **TS2r**

46.29a hand] **S**– hands **TS2r**

46.29b the dreadful] **S**– this dreadful **TS2r**

46.34 were to be] **S**– were **TS2r**

46.37 the desperate] **S E1**– a desperate **TS2r P**

46.38 and day] **S**– or day **TS2r**

47.3 in] **S E1**– embodied in **TS2r P**

47.11 The work] **S**– All this **TS2r**

47.13 drifters] **S**– drifters, and all this **TS2r**

47.15 an attack] **S**– any operation **TS2r**

47.17 The routine ... Patrol] **S**– Those tasks **TS2r**

47.24 a national] **TS2r–E1** national **A1**

47.25 was bound to be] **S**– was **TS2r**

47.32 addition of] **TS2r**– addition of a large proportion of **TS1t TS1r**

47.33 of R.N.R. ... ratings] **TS2r**– R.N.R. officers **TS1t TS1r**

47.33–34 Though properly speaking] **TS2r**– Though **TS1t TS1r**

47.34 the fighting] **TS2r**– a fighting **TS1t TS1r**

47.35 own] **TS1t TS1r** old **TS2r**–

47.37a sufficient.] **TS2r**– sufficient. [sufficient. = sufficient for the trust reposed in them. **TS1r**] ¶ Apart from the naval problems with its purely seamans work the Patrol acted also in cooperation with the land army on its left wing, render an assistance fully acknowledged by the shore command in October and November 1914 and later by the systemmatic [systemmatic = systematic **TS1r**] bombardments of the Flanders shore [shore = short later **TS1r**] in the

	years 1916 and 1917 **TS1t TS1r**	48.6	country] **TS2r–** country all went through **TS1h**
47.37b	No] **TS2r–** No greater **TS1h**	48.10	of which ... consequences] **TS2r S** the fatal consequences of which **P–**
47.39	imposed upon] **TS2r–** demanded from **TS1h**		
47.40	Originating in the] **TS2r–** Starting as a **TS1h**	48.13	planning and execution] **S–** elaboration and carrying out **TS2r**
48.1–2	under ... at] **TS2r–** depending on **TS1h**	48.16	compel the admiration] **S–** warm the heart **TS2r**
48.2	developed an] **TS2r–** came into **TS1h**	48.21	These men] **S–** They **TS2r**
48.3a	by] **TS1h–S E1 A1** through **P**	48.26	they] **S–** these men **TS2r**
48.3b	of fortified] **TS2r–** fortified **TS1h**	48.28	exploding] **TS2r** the exploding **S–**
48.5a	defence] **TS2r–** warfare **TS1h**	49.2	which] **S–** what **TS2r**
48.5b	well be] **TS2r–** be very well **TS1h**	49.3–4	disastrously ... night] **S–** on any night disastrously **TS2r**
		49.5	were] **TS2r–P** was **E1 A1**

MEMORANDUM

TS1	typescript (BL)
TS1t	typewritten (unrevised) text of **TS1** superseded by revision
TS1r	revised text of **TS1** (incorporating Conrad's alterations): copy-text
TS2	typescript (Private collection)
TS2t	revised text of **TS2** superseded by revision
TS2r	revised text of **TS2t** (incorporating Conrad's alterations)

50.2a	on the scheme for] **TS2–** OM **TS1t** Relating to **TS1r**	50.16	such a] **TS1r–** that **TS1t**
50.2b	fitting out] **TS2–** OM **TS1t** building and equipping **TS1r**	50.17	the healthy] **TS1r–** healthy **TS1t**
50.2–3	the purpose of *perfecting*] **TS2r–** OM **TS1t** perfecting **TS1r** the purpose of perfecting **TS2t**	50.19–20	facility of the voyage] **TS1r–** facility **TS1t**
		50.20–21	general experience] **TS1r–** experience **TS1t**
		50.21	offer] **TS1r–** give **TS1t**
		50.26	his] **TS1r–** the **TS1t**
50.3–4	belonging ... Liverpool] **TS2–** OM **TS1**	50.28	I] **TS1r–** OM **TS1t**
50.8	equipping of] **ED** equipping **TS1–**	50.29–30	be self-supporting] **TS1r–** earn her expenses **TS1t**
50.12	will] **TS1r–** may **TS1t**	50.31	size] **TS1r–** tonnage **TS1t**
50.15	(including New Zealand)] **TS1r–** OM **TS1t**	51.1a	pay her expenses] **TS1r–** answer that requirement **TS1t**
		51.1b	venture] **TS1r–** make bold then **TS1t**

51.2	who] **TS1r**– accustomed to **TS1t**	51.27	great] **TS1r**– more **TS1t**
51.3a	manage] **TS1r**– administer **TS1t**	51.28a	three] **TS1r**– between two or three **TS1t**
51.3b	steamships)] **TS1r**– steamships for the training ship size **TS1t**	51.28b	and over makes] **TS1r**– or more made **TS1t**
		51.29	anything but quick] **TS1r**– certainly not smart **TS1t**
51.3c	14 to 1500] **TS1r TS2** 14 to 1400 **TS1t** 1400–1500 **E1** fourteen to fifteen hundred **A1**		
		51.29–30	and renders them] **TS1r**– and **TS1t**
51.4	earning of] **TS1r** perfectly sound proposition that the ship should pay **TS1t**	51.30	from] **TS1r**– by **TS1t**
		51.31	serious damage] **TS1r**– accidental disablement **TS1t**
51.4–5	expenses ... ship] **TS1r**– expenses **TS1t**	51.32	that] **TS1r**– that quickness in **TS1t**
51.6	is] **TS1r**– may be **TS1t**	51.32–33	develops a corresponding] **TS1r**– somehow instinctively develops the **TS1t**
51.9	all what] **TS1r** all that **TS1t TS2**–		
51.14	qualities] **TS1r**– qualities, actual speed **TS1t**	51.33	in] **TS1r**– of **TS1t**
		51.35	person] **TS1r**– man **TS1t**
51.15	quickness] **TS1r**– smartness **TS1t**	51.36	merchant] **TS1 TS2** Merchant Service **E1**–
51.16	position] **TS1r**– position, by unexpected change of the weather or other circumstances than cannot be always guarded against **TS1t**	51.38a	think about] **TS1r**– think it over **TS1t**
		51.38b	meditate over] **TS1r**– meditate **TS1t**
		52.1	question of the ship's] **TS1r**– mere beauty of **TS1t**
51.17	have] **TS1r**– carry as near as possible in **TS1t**		
51.17–18	a dead ... about] **TS1r**– weight **TS1t**	52.2	adding] **TS2**– and adding **TS1**
51.18	half] **TS1r**– half of **TS1t**	52.4a	arouses one's admiration] **TS1r**– is very attractive **TS1t**
51.19	comfort in] **TS1r**– fort in a sea *ay **TS1t**		
51.20a	remembered] **TS1r**– remembered that **TS1t**	52.4b	vessel] **TS1r**– ship **TS1t**
		52.5–6	giving an impression] **TS1r**– the suggestion of giving that sort of suggestion **TS1t**
51.20b	propelling] **TS1r**– actual **TS1t**		
51.21	remain ... sheltered] **TS1r**– perforce be on deck and not **TS1t**	52.6	defined] **TS1r**– expressed **TS1t**
51.22	latest big] **TS1r**– ultra modern **TS1t**	52.7	but] **TS1r**– b [*sic*] to whom **TS1t**
51.23	is generally] **TS1r**– was **TS1t**	52.8a	sailor's] **E1** sailor **TS1** sailors' **TS2 A1**
51.25	heavy sea] **TS1r**– gale **TS1t**	52.8b	graphic] **TS1r**– expressive **TS1t**

52.8c	in justice] **TS1r**– very well **TS1**t
52.10a	a sailing ... is] **TS1r**– such a ship **TS1**t
52.10b	to *perfect*] **TS1r**– the perfect **TS1**t
52.11a	officers] **TS1r**– the officers **TS1**t
52.11b	certain ideal elements] **TS1r**– considerations of moral influence **TS1**t
52.11–12	taken into consideration] **TS1r**– given due weight **TS1**t
52.13a	grow attached] **TS1r**– be proud **TS1**t
52.13b	to their] **TS2**– of their **TS1**
52.13–14	do) be proud] **TS1r**– be **TS1**t
52.14–15	of their ... her] **TS1r**– O M **TS1**t
52.17–18	great ... experience] **TS1r**– good and useful time which **TS1**t
52.18	seamen] **TS1r**– the seamen **TS1**t
52.19	a time to] **TS1r**– and which can **TS1**t
52.20	somewhat as an old] **TS1r**– with something of the same sentiment which the **TS1**t
52.21a	at] **TS1 TS2 A1** to **E1**
52.21b	old buildings] **TS1r**– building **TS1**t
52.22	achievements] **TS1r**– feats **TS1**t
52.23	seamen] **TS1r**– teamship inits [*sic*] more recent history **TS1**t
52.24a	to] **TS1 TS2 A1** and **E1**
52.24b	record] **TS1r**– quick **TS1**t
52.26	in of] **TS1r**– in **TS1**t
52.27a	seamanship] **TS1r**– means **TS1**t
52.27b	determination ... assistance] **TS1r**– ingenuity in their use **TS1**t

52.28	is made that] **TS1r**– that **TS1**t
52.28–29	advocating things hopelessly] **TS1r**– advocating **TS1**t
52.29a	date] **TS1r**– date things is made **TS1**t
52.29b	scheme] **TS1r**– matter **TS1**t
52.30a	associated] **TS1r**– involving associated **TS1**t
52.30b	closely] **TS1r**– close **TS1**t
52.30c	men's *morale*] **TS1r**– moral **TS1**t
52.30d	and with] **TS1r**– and **TS1**t
52.31	apply] **TS1r**– exist **TS1**t
52.32	On the practical side] **TS1r**– Practically **TS1**t
52.34	future officers] **TS1r**– officers **TS1**t
52.34–35	the finest modern] **TS1r**– modern **TS1**t
52.35	give them] **TS1r**– select **TS1**t
52.36a	most] **TS1r**– absolutely **TS1**t
52.36b	sailing] **TS1r**– the sailing**TS1**t
52.38–39	and service] **TS1r**– O M **TS1**t
53.3	tendency] **TS1r**– propensity **TS1**t
53.3–4	(on ... effectively)] **TS1r**– from the mere expense of sufficient manning **TS1**t
53.5a	This] **TS1r**– And this **TS1**t
53.5b	postulate which] **TS1r**– postulate **TS1**t
53.6	I am most anxious] **TS1r**– which I wish **TS1**t
53.6–7	it is this:] **TS1r**– O M **TS1**t
53.8	11] **TS2r A1** 2. **E1** O M **TS1 TS2**t
53.13	vertical] **TS1r**– donkey **TS1**t
53.14a	heaving up] **TS1r**– raising **TS1**t
53.14b	may] **TS1r**– should **TS1**t

53.15	should ... which] TS1r– ought to be one that TS1t
53.17	this insistence ... use of] TS1r– the above suggestions *** the TS1t
53.20	on that point] TS1r– of that TS1t
53.21	of an] TS1r– and of a certain TS1t
53.22	with] TS1r– with the, say, TS1t
53.23a	and some other] TS1r– of the usual TS1t
53.23b	the officers] TS1r– they TS1t
53.25	laid down] E1– laid TS1 TS2
53.28–29	wishing to fit himself] TS1r– wishing TS1t
53.29	good officer] TS1r– sailor TS1t
53.30	into] TS1r– to TS1t
53.30–31	all ... others] TS1r– heart in associations TS1t
53.32	it ... youths] TS1r– the boys will be brought TS1t
53.35	that] TS1r– the TS1t
53.35–36	was ... mere] TS1r– has been in the nature of a TS1t
53.36	branches of labour] TS1r– mechanical occupations TS1t
54.1	life at sea] TS1r– it TS1t
54.2a	healthy] TS1r– helpful TS1t
54.2b	owing] TS1r– owing also TS1t
54.2c	very] TS1r– OM TS1t
54.3a	exertions] TS1r– exertion TS1t
54.3b	affirm] TS1r– say TS1t
54.4	sailing ... excellent] TS1r– it is a very good TS1t
54.5	a delicate youngster] TS1r– very delicate specimens TS1t
54.6	change] TS1r– develop TS1t
54.7	during] TS1r– in TS1t
54.8	break down] TS1r– go under TS1t
54.9	any] TS1r– this TS1t
54.10	a special] TS1r– in *** TS1t
54.10–11	it ... sailor-mentality] TS1r– the sea mentality TS1t
54.11	a valuable] TS1r– the most valuable TS1t
54.13	III.] TS2r A1 OM TS1 TS2t 3. E1
54.14	sailing ship] TS1r– ship TS1t
54.16a	14–15 ... reg.] TS1r 14–15 hundred tons TS1t 14–1500 tons reg. TS2 1400–1500 tons register E1 1400 and 1500 tons register A1
54.16b	d.w.] TS1r TS2 E1 small dw TS1t dead weight A1
54.19	2000 tons reg.] TS1r TS2 200 tons register TS1t 2000 tons register E1–
54.22	if ... three-masted] TS1r– in a three, [sic] masted vessel TS1t
54.24	This] TS1r– which TS1t
54.28a	on ... deck-house] TS1r– to bear a house TS1t
54.28b	coaming] TS1r– combing TS1t
54.29–30	across at each end] TS1r– between these and the ends TS1t
54.30a	having] TS1r– leaving TS1t
54.30b	The house] TS1r– It TS1t accomodation [sic]]
54.32	TS1r– space TS1t
54.34a	at the sides] TS2r– for TS1t on the sides TS1r TS2t
54.34b	various] TS1r– the various TS1t
54.34c	or] TS1r– and TS1t
54.36	All that however] TS1r– but all that TS1t

55.1–2	(for 3 years)] **TS2r** OM **TS1 TS2t** (for two years) **E1–**
55.2	a chief] **TS1** chief **TS2–**
55.3	its] **TS1 TS2** her **E1–**
55.7	reg.] **TS1–E1** register **A1**
55.18	The] **TS1r–** This apart from the **TS1t**
55.19a	consisted] **TS1r–** which consisted **TS1t**
55.19b	stern] **TS1r–** spare **TS1t**
55.23a	under] **TS1r–** on **TS1t**
55.23b	poop] **TS1r–** upper **TS1t**
55.25	in] **TS1r–** on **TS1t**
55.27a	assuming] **TS2–** assuming that **TS1**
55.27b	being berthed] **TS1 TS2** are berthed **E1** berthed **A1**
55.37	at sea too] **TS1r–** himself, when at sea **TS1t**
55.38–39	position of commanding] **TS1r–** command of **TS1t**
55.40	as is] **TS1t TS2r** as **TS1r TS2t E1–**
56.5	42] **TS1 TS2** forty-four **E1–**
56.6	and be made] **TS1t TS2r–** accessible to **TS1r TS2t**
56.7	may be] **TS1r–** would be there **TS1t**
56.8	daylight down there] **TS1r–** daylight **TS1t**
56.12	time or other] **TS1r–** time **TS1t**
56.13	This] **TS1r–** which **TS1t**
56.15a	cared for] **TS1r–** studied **TS1t**
56.15b	within] **TS1r–** between **TS1t**
56.16	health] **TS1r–** health and **TS1t**
56.19	I believe that] **TS1r–** OM **TS1t**
56.20	will] **TS1r–** would **TS1t**
56.25	all of them] **TS1r–** all **TS1t**
56.26	apprenticeship] **TS1r–** training **TS1t**
56.27	officer] **TS1 TS2t E1–** office **TS2r**
56.28	whether] **TS1r–** whether it will be **TS1t**
56.32	the three] **TS2t–** three **TS1**
56.33	shifts] **TS2r–** shifting **TS1 TS2t**
56.34	the boys] **TS1r–** them **TS1t**
56.35	habit] **TS1r–** mere habit **TS1t**
56.36	should] **TS1 TS2** would **E1–**
56.37	suggest that] **TS1r–** suggest **TS1t**
56.38	had obtained] **TS1r–** had **TS1t**
57.1	be] **TS1r–** should be **TS1t**
57.4	main through] **TS1r** to main through **TS1t** through main and **TS2–**
57.5	be selected from] **TS1r–** fall to **TS1t**
57.6	the training] **TS1r–** their training **TS1t**
57.7	some luck in her] **TS1r–** any luck as to **TS1t**
57.8	at] **TS1r–** on **TS1t**
57.11	on the] **TS1r–** in **TS1t**
57.14a	stream] **TS1r–** streams **TS1t**
57.14b	this] **TS1r–** that **TS1t**
57.17	hove up] **TS1r–** raised **TS1t**
57.18–19	under ... help] **TS1r–** by the means **TS1t**
57.21–22	four or three] **TS2r–** three **TS1 TS2t**
57.22	I suggest] **TS1r–** OM **TS1t**
57.23a	The] **TS1r–** I suggest that the **TS1t**
57.23b	may] **TS1r–** should **TS1t**
57.27	fair weather] **TS1r–** OM **TS1t**
57.28	at] **TS1r–** with all winds at **TS1t**
57.29	abaft] **TS1r–** above **TS1t**

57.32	traditional practice] TS1r– practise TS1t
57.34	led] TS1r– laid TS1t
57.35	furling] TS1r– folding TS1t
57.36	is] TS1 TS2 was E1–
57.39	was likely ... itself] TS1r– would free itself in the wind TS1t
57.40	from] TS1r– in TS1t
58.2	with ... sail] TS1r– OM TS1t
58.4	is] TS1 TS2 were E1–
58.11a	fell in] TS1r– consented TS1t
58.11b	with] TS1r– to TS1t
58.12	back to] TS1r– to TS1t
58.13	properly.] TS1r– properly. ¶ That this is the practice which has been abandoned almost completely in the last ten years is no argument for the ship is not meant to train modern sailing ship men but to perfect the training of officers destined for modern steamships. TS1t
58.14	boats ... refer] TS1r– the boats referring TS1t
58.16	carried in her, aft,] TS1r– carried TS1t
58.17a	They] TS1r– which TS1t
58.17b	water] TS1t TS2r E1– water there TS1r TS2t
58.18	a lanyard] TS1r– the lanyard TS1t
58.18–19	tackle falls] TS1r– tackle fawls TS1t
58.19	coiled clear on deck] TS1r– called clear TS1t
58.20	were ready] TS1r– ready TS1t
58.22	get] TS1r– go TS1t
58.24a	falls] TS1r– fawls TS1t
58.24b	test of quickness] TS1r– test TS1t
58.25	happened] TS1r– was TS1t
58.26	luffed ... quarter-boats] TS1r– brought to and the boat TS1t
58.27	had flown] TS1r– flew TS1t
58.28a	having been] TS1r– being TS1t
58.28b	at the time] TS1r– OM TS1t
58.28c	all this] TS1r– it TS1t
58.32	abaft] TS1r– above TS1t
58.33	But the] TS1r– The other two and TS1t
58.34	very roomy] TS1r– enormous TS1t
58.35a	abaft] TS1r– above TS1t
58.35b	fore] TS1r– aft TS1t
58.35c	chocks and] TS1r– chocks TS1t
58.36	fore-and-afted] TS1r– fore and aft TS1t
58.37a	falls] TS1r– fawls TS1t
58.37b	tubs] TS1r– boxes on hoo[ks] TS1t
58.38	deck-house] TS1r– forward house on deck TS1t
58.38–39	life-boats] TS1r– boats TS1t
58.39	fitted] TS1r– lifted TS1t
58.40a	oil-bags, oars] TS1r– oars TS1t
58.40b	breakers] TS1–E1 beakers A1
59.3–4	davits and bolts] TS1r– bolts TS1t
59.5	out those life-|boats] TS1r– life-|boats out TS1t
59.5–6	Now and again] TS1r– From time to time TS1t
59.7a	I managed] TS1r– managed TS1t
59.7b	things] TS1r– it TS1t
59.9	of the order] TS1r– I said TS1t
59.10	swung ... chocks] TS1r– returned landed in the chock TS1t
59.11	starboard] TS1r– port TS1t

59.12a   third] **TS1r**– third mate
          TS1t

59.12b   port side] **TS1r**–
          starboard **TS1t**

59.16–17 homeward ... of] **TS1r**–
          going or returning, in
          TS1t

59.17   it ... that] **TS1r**– directly
          the fog horn came into
          use **TS1t**

59.18–19 immediately ... these]
          TS1r– without [delay?]
          swung those **TS1t**

59.19   that] **TS1r**– which **TS1t**

59.20a   weather permitting]
          TS1r– if possible **TS1t**

59.20b   fog] **TS1r**– weather **TS1t**

59.20c   cleared.] **TS1r**– cleared.
          The davits were slightly in
          the way of the fore braces
          especially in the case of
          tacking ship but we
          remedied that by tricing
          them up in a large
          wooden hoop attached by
          a long lanyard to one of
          the back stays. **TS1t**

59.22a   very few] **TS1 TS2 A1** few
          E1

59.22b   sailing ship] **TS1r**– O M
          TS1t

59.23a   have] **TS1r**– have ever
          TS1t

59.23b   the care of] **TS1r**– O M
          TS1t

59.24   ship.] **TS1r**– ship. I may
          also mention as a trait of
          old times that when
          tacking ship with the
          watch in day time the
          stewards were called out
          and manned the after
          braces. They also went
          aloft in the day time to
          help to furl the mainsail
          and in their short black
          jackets were very
          noticeable on the yards
          amongst the seamen.
          When all hands were on

deck those men of course
were never called away
from their proper duties,
nor yet in very bad
weather for which they
were not equipped. In
case however of a sudden
emergency and of any
definite order for boat
stations those men came
automatically under the
order of the chief
officers, and it was
surprising to see how
some of them who came
in straight from steamers
got into the habits of
sailing ship life. **TS1t**

59.25   be given] **TS1r**– get **TS1t**

59.26–27 proper stowage] **TS1r**–
          stowage **TS1t**

59.28   sailing powers] **TS1r** the
          length of the passage
          TS1t her sailing powers
          TS2–

59.31–32 It is ... order] **TS1r**– and
          also different in its
          nature. The order **TS1t**

59.32   is a] **TS1r**– being of
          TS1t

59.33a   disposition] **TS1r**–
          arrangement **TS1t**

59.33b   a steamship's cargo]
          TS1r– the loading **TS1t**

59.34–35 found useful on occasion]
          TS1r– even useful **TS1t**

59.37   propulsion] **TS1r**–
          mechanical power for
          propulsion **TS1t**

59.38a this may] **TS2**– it will
          TS1t it this **TS1r**

59.38b   rate] **TS1r**– question
          TS1t

60.1   thought] **TS1r**– thought
          himself in greater danger
          because the ship was **TS1t**

60.1–2   less ... steamship] **TS1r**–
          O M **TS1t**

60.2a A ship's] **TS2t**– Her **TS1t**
          A ships [*sic*] **TS1r**

60.2b	rests] **TS1r**– is **TS1t**
60.3	are aboard] **ED** man **TS1t**
	aboard **TS1r** are aboard
	of **TS2**–
60.5a	a ship ... would] **TS1r**–
	her more secure and the
	space could **TS1t**
60.5b	useful for] **TS1r**– more
	useful for many **TS1t**
60.7a	The ship] **TS1r**– She
	TS1t
60.7b	make use of] **TS1r**– take
	TS1t
60.8a	her] **TS1r**– each of her
	TS1t
60.8–9	This ... get] **TS1r**– and
	this will be practice for
	the cadets, give the cadets
	TS1t
60.8b	afford to] **TS1r TS2** VAR
	TS1t afford **E1**–
60.8c	the opportunity] **TS1r**
	VAR **TS1t** an opportunity
	TS2–
60.9–10	various ... operations]
	TS1r– operations, and
	manoevres **TS1t**
60.10–11	steel ... them] **TS1r**– the
	tow rope would be in
	itself **TS1t**
60.13a	Lawrence] **ED** Laurence
	TS1–
60.13b	speaks of] **TS1r**– suggests
	TS1t
60.13c	60–80] **TS1r**– 65 **TS1t**
60.14	suggest] **TS1r**– suggest if
	possible **TS1t**
60.15	my mind] **TS1r**– mind
	TS1t
60.16a	some accident] **TS1r**–
	accidents **TS1t**
60.16b	best] **TS1r**– best found
	and best officered
	TS1t
60.17	and its] **TS1r**– its **TS1t**
60.17–18	Regard ... facility of]
	TS1r– and the actual
	facility in **TS1t**
60.18a	a lesser] **TS1r**– the lesser
	TS1t

60.18b	out of] **TS1r**– away from
	TS1t
60.19a	them all] **TS1r**– them
	TS1t
60.19b	a shipwreck] **TS1r**–
	shipwreck **TS1t**
60.21	his apprenticeship]
	TS2r– to make up his
	passing time **TS1t**
	apprenticeship **TS1r**
	TS2t
60.22	sea service allowed for]
	TS1r– for **TS1t**
60.23a	last] **TS1r**– rest of the
	time, a **TS1t**
60.23b	as] **TS1r**– being served as
	TS1t
60.24	a steamship] **TS1r**– steam
	TS1t
60.27a	finish] **TS1r**– then
	finishing **TS1t**
60.27b	steam.] **TS1r**– steam. ¶ In
	conclusion I beg to thank
	the originators of the
	scheme for giving me the
	opportunity to make
	these remarks and to
	ascribe their length and
	perhaps superabundant
	detail not to vain garrulity
	but to whole-hearted
	interest in their project
	combined with the
	greatest sympathy with
	their guiding idea of
	perfecting the training of
	the officers destined to
	serve them afloat with
	that same fidelity and
	devotion which has been
	displayed by their
	forefathers. **TS1t**
60.28–61.8	I don't ... ranks.] **TS1r**–
	OM **TS1t**
60.35	aloft that] **TS2**– OM **TS1t**
	aloft **TS1r**
61.3	a cricket] **TS2**– OM **TS1t**
	cricket **TS1r**
61.7	ship's] **TS2**– OM **TS1t**
	ships **TS1r**

THE LOSS OF THE *DALGONAR*

TS   partial facsimile: Edgar H. Wells Catalogue (1925), item 79, p. 3 only: 62.31–63.4 ['I can not' *to* 'event!'] and 63.32–37 ['put on' *to* 'Conrad.']

TS1t   typescript text (facsimile) of **TS1** superseded by revision

TS1r   revised text with holograph insertion (facsimile) of **TS1** (incorporating Conrad's alterations)

S   *London Mercury*, 5 (December 1921), 187: copy-text

62.24	then was] **S A1** was then **E1**	63.33a	in] **TSr–** and in **TSt**
		63.33b	vigilance and plucky]
	[*TS holograph insertion begins here.*]		**TSr–** [***] vigilance and **TSt**
63.1	too] **S–** a little too **TS**	63.34	to remain by and] **S–** OM
63.3–4	And ... danger.] **S–** OM **TS**		**TSt** to stand by and **TSr**
	[*TS fragment ends*]	63.34–35	take off] **TSr–** save **TSt**
63.14	etc., etc.] **S** etc. **E1–**	63.36	I am etc etc] **TSr** OM **TSt**
	[*TS fragment resumes here.*]		Yours, etc., **S–**
63.32	put ... of the] **TSr–** [***] **TSt**	63.37	J. Conrad] **TSr** OM **TSt**
			JOSEPH CONRAD **S–**

TRAVEL
PREFACE TO RICHARD CURLE'S *INTO THE EAST*

TS1   typescript (Yale)

TS1r   revised text of **TS1** (incorporating Conrad's alterations): copy-text

TS2   typescript (Rosenbach)

TS2t   typewritten text (unrevised) of **TS2** superseded by revision

TS2r   revised text of **TS2** (incorporating Conrad's alterations)

P   *Travel. A Preface to 'Into the East: Notes on Burma and Malaya'* (R. & R. Clark, December 1922)

C   Richard Curle, *Into the East: Notes on Burma and Malaya* (Macmillan, 1923)

64.1–3	Travel ... *East*] **E1–** OM **TS1t** Preface **TS1r TS2** C	**65.24**	mass] **TS2r–** multitude **TS1 TS2t**
	Travel │ A Preface to *Into the East: Notes on Burma and Malaya* **P**	**66.11**	grow] **P–** be **TS1 TS2**
		66.24	mere sport] **TS1** sport **TS2–**
64.34	the capacity] **TS1r TS2** capacity **P–**	66.30	manly] **TS1–C A1** mainly **E1**
65.1	that's] **TS1 TS2** that is **P–**	**66.34**	– those] **TS2r C–** The **TS1 TS2t** – these **P**
65.9	had written] **TS1 TS2** has written **P–**	66.40	that] **TS1 TS2** who **P–**
65.12	the One] **P–** one **TS1 TS2**	**67.8–9**	achieved it] **P–** done so **TS1 TS2**
65.14	they visited] **P–** OM **TS1 TS2**	**67.15**	globe] **TS2r–** world **TS1 TS2t**

67.20	historian's] TS2r– historian TS1 TS2t		68.38	these] TS1 E1 those TS2–C A1
67.35	interview] P– OM TS1 TS2		69.3 69.4	Asiatic] P– OM TS1 TS2 cruel] P– simple TS1 TS2
67.38	marvel at a] P– even some TS1 TS2		69.15	to think that] P– OM TS1 TS2
67.39	some old-time] P– some TS1 TS2t an old-time TS2r		69.18 69.22–23	having listened] P– after listening TS1 TS2 ought to have been] P–
67.40	Relation] TS1–C A1 Relations E1			properly speaking, should be TS1 TS2
68.4	Nigeria] P– Sudan TS1 TS2		69.24 70.2	Jugra] TS1–C A1 Juga E1 fact] TS1 TS2 E1 facts P
68.10	were] TS2r are TS1 P– OM TS2t		70.7	C A1 This] TS1 TS2r– Thus
68.19	or] TS1 TS2 and P–			TS2t
68.23a	laid aside] P– closed TS1 TS2		70.8 70.10	on] TS1 of TS2t– few] TS2r– twenty-four
68.23b	MS.] P– book TS1 TS2			TS1 TS2t
68.23c	publishing] P– writing TS1 TS2		70.17–18	of whose ... tales] P– OM TS1 TS2
68.28	longer] TS1 P– more TS2		70.21	alive to] P– recognising
68.37a	presented to] P– for TS1 TS2		70.22	TS1 TS2 and while pursuing] P–
68.37b	to their] TS1 P– for their TS2			pursues TS1 TS2t and pursuing TS2r
			70.23	he] TS2r– and TS1 TS2t

STEPHEN CRANE
INTRODUCTION TO THOMAS BEER'S
STEPHEN CRANE

MS	holograph manuscript, final text (Virginia)
TS	typescript (Yale-S)
TSt	typewritten uncorrected text of TS (printer's copy) superseded by revision
TSe	altered text of TS (incorporating Conrad's alterations in unidentified hand): copy-text pp. 1–3 ['Introduction' *to* 'far only']: 71.2–73.11
CAp	galley-proofs, partial (pp. 2–9) ['about myself' *to* 'Joseph.'''] 73.11–89.30: Thomas Beer, *Stephen Crane: A Study in American Letters* (Knopf, 1923) (Yale-S)
CApu	unrevised galley-proofs
CApr	revised galley-proofs (incorporating Conrad's alterations): copy-text 73.11–89.30
CA	Thomas Beer, *Stephen Crane: A Study in American Letters* (Knopf, 1923), pp. 1–33
CE	Thomas Beer, *Stephen Crane: A Study in American Letters* (Heinemann, 1924), pp. 1–35

71.1–3	Stephen ... *Crane*] ED	72.32	my] **TS**– its **MS**
	Personal Recollections of	72.35	hard put] **TS**– put hard
	My Friendship with		**MS**
	Stephen Crane **MS**	72.36	my complex intentions]
	Introduction **TS–CE**		**TS**– it **MS**
	Stephen Crane	A	72.37	which] **TS**– that **MS**
	Preface to Thomas Beer's	72.39	world] **TS**– larger world
	"Stephen Crane" **E1**–		of men **MS**
71.22	our] **E1**– their **MS–CE**	**73.1**	"The Red Badge"] **CA**–
71.32–72.7	¶ I was ... writing.] **TS**–		his Badge of Courage **MS**
	OM **MS**		the "The Red Badge" **TS**
71.32	asked] **CA**– OM **MS**	**73.7**	intimate friends] **CA**–
	Crane was asked **TS**		intimates **MS TS**
71.33	Crane] **CA**– OM **MS** he	73.8a	W. E. Henley's] **E1**– W. H.
	TS		Henley **MS** W. H.
72.8a	say that] **TS**– that **MS**		Henley's **TS–CE**
72.8b	precious friendship] **TS**–	73.8b	acceptance of my tale]
	friendship **MS**		**TS**– acceptance **MS**
72.14a	the author] **TS**– author		[*TSe ceases to be copy-text;*
	MS		*CAp reported from here:*]
72.14b	my] **TS**– that **MS**	73.11	talking so far only] **TS**–
72.17	conditions] **CA**–		writing too much **MS**
	demands **MS TS**	73.12	that] **TSe**– this **MS TSt**
72.19a	temperament tried by]	73.13	trace what] **TS**– try to
	TS– nature brought to		record the trace that **MS**
	MS	73.15	record] **TS**– statement
72.19b	emotions] **TS**– test **MS**		**MS**
72.19c	a battlefield] **TS**– the	73.16	And out] **TS**– But **MS**
	battlefield **MS**	73.18	visit] **TS**– later visit **MS**
72.20	his] **TS**– that **MS**	73.19	Even] **TS**– And even **MS**
72.21a	I – in mine – had] **TS**–	73.23	made it] **TS**– made **MS**
	had **MS**	73.24	own visions] **TS**– social
72.21b	same subject] **TS**– subject		engagements **MS**
	MS	73.25	he had more] **TS**– more
72.22	and] **TS**– but **MS**		**MS**
72.23	of a] **TS**– of **MS**	73.26	time] **TS**– spare time **MS**
72.25a	connection] **TS**–	73.27	that as] **TS**– as **MS**
	similitude **MS**	73.28a	my] **TS**– me **MS**
72.25b	two works] **TS**– works **MS**	73.28b	and] **TS**– an **MS**
72.26a	too] **CA**– very **MS** to [*sic*]	73.29	affected humility] **TS**–
	TS		humility **MS**
72.26b	here] **TS**– at this distance	73.30	you] **TS**– one **MS**
	of time **MS**	73.31	revelatory] **TS**–
72.27	at the time. It] **TS**– then		indefinable **MS**
	and it **MS**	73.33a	quality] **TS**– thing **MS**
72.28	virtue] **TS**– the virtue **MS**	73.33b	care-free] **TS**– careless
72.28–29	his ... as] **TS**– gifts		**MS**
	disclosed in that work **MS**	73.34a	have had my answer] **TS**–
72.31	sincerity] **TS**– seriousness		can see through that
	of intention **MS**		unconscious enigma **MS**

73.34b have had] **CApr**– V A R
MS have **TS CApu**

73.34–35 his ... earth] **TS**– he will
soon die **MS**

73.37 memories] **TS**– memory
MS

73.38 his] **TS**– that **MS**

74.1 friends. It was] **CA**–
friends, and **MS** friends
TS CApu

74.1–2 under the] **TS**– under **MS**

74.2 Sydney] **MS CE**– Sidney
TS–CA

74.3a voice] **TS**– chest voice **MS**

74.3b looked] **TS**– did look **MS**

74.5 the] **TS**– the result of the
MS

74.10a a meal] **TS**– meal **MS**

74.10b Crane] **TS**– Pawling sat at
ease, Crane **MS**

74.11a deliberate] **TS**– quiet **MS**

74.11b Greece, at war] **TS**–
Greece I believe **MS**

74.12a sensed] **TS**– become
aware of **MS**

74.12b his] **CApr**– that **MS–CApu**

74.13 for his] **TS**– his **MS**

74.14 was careless] **TS**–
sounded careless **MS**

74.17 in the deep] **MS** the deep
TS–

74.21 life] **TS**– short life **MS**

74.23 heritage, not] **TS**–
heritage and not **MS**

74.29 temper] **CApr**– fine stuff
MS stuff **TS–CApu**

74.31 fitting occasions] **TS**–
occasions **MS**

74.34 affectation] **CApr**–
meanness **MS–CApu**

74.36 its relief] **TS**– an issue **MS**

74.37 ¶ Many] **CApr**– I believe
many **TS–CApu**

74.37 imagined] **MS TS CApr**–
imagine **CApu**

75.2a pause] **TS**– pose **MS**

75.2b he not] **TS**– not **MS**

75.3 did flag] **CApr**– flickered
MS–CApu

75.8 cast] **TS**– character **MS**

75.12 its charm] **TS**– the
interest **MS**

75.13a acute] **TS**– attractive **MS**

75.13b view] **TS**– expression **MS**

75.14 expressed ...
deliberation] **TS**– as a
rule in a very few words
MS

75.15 whom he] **MS–E1** he **A1**

75.16 felt he] **TS**– he **MS**

75.19a idiots] **TS**– and familiar
idiots **MS**

75.19b brood] **TS**– brooded **MS**

75.21a from] **TS**– from that
cloud **MS**

75.21b had sent out] **TS**– would
come **MS**

75.21c a few] **TS**– rare **MS**

75.22 heavy] **TS**– few heavy **MS**

75.23 if] **CApr**– though
MS–CApu

75.24–25 have been] **MS CApr**– be
TS CApu

75.27 with an effect as] **TS**– like
the effect **MS**

75.31 life] **TS**– private history
MS

75.33 from] **TS**– through all
MS

75.34 first. Our affection] **TS**–
course of our friendship
which **MS**

75.34–35 "everlasting" ... it] **TS**–
durable **MS**

75.35 the jealous death] **TS**–
death **MS**

75.36 man.] **TS**– man. I never
asked him about his past.
MS

75.39 early days] **TS**– days **MS**

75.40 men kindly] **TSe**– even
were merely **MS** were
kind or **TSt**

76.1a he used ... lovingly] **TS**–
O M **MS**

76.1b used to utter] **CApr**– O M
MS uttered **TS CApu**

76.3a ¶ It] **TS**– But it **MS**

76.3b heard] **CApr**– have heard
MS–CApu

76.3–4   trials, privations] **TS–**
         trials **MS**
76.4   I ... many.] **TS–** O M **MS**
76.6   I could ... would] **TS–**
         would **MS**
76.7   shaken] **TS–** affected **MS**
76.8   is] **TS–** may be **MS**
76.9a   may sound] **TS–** sound
         MS
76.9b   will] **TS–** must **MS**
76.10   Crane] **TS–** Crane's
         nature **MS**
76.10–11 trust with one's life] **TS–**
         deal with **MS**
76.13   an] **TS–** a **MS**
76.14a   too may] **TS–** may **MS**
76.14b   Some men] **TS–** Some
         MS
76.15   the office they hold] **TS–**
         office **MS**
76.19a   because] **TS–** only
         because **MS**
76.19b   great] **MS–CE A1** greater
         E1
76.23   everything] **CAp–**
         anything **MS TS**
76.26a   I think] **TS** for I think
         MS
76.26b   I have] **TS–** have **MS**
76.28a   confident he will receive]
         TS– assured of **MS**
76.28b   humane and] **TS–**
         humanely **MS**
76.29   discovered ... was] **TS–**
         sure of however, is **MS**
76.32 S. S. Pawling] **TS CApu**
         CE– SS Pawling **MS** M. S.
         Pawling **CApr CA**
76.33   friendly] **TS–** pleased,
         friendly **MS**
76.34   big, prosperous] **TS–**
         prosperous **MS**
76.36a   was] **TS–** looked **MS**
76.36b   in the tales too] **TS–** too
         MS
76.37   of it is] **TS–** that he was
         really is in the fact **MS**
77.1   consideration ... duty]
         TS– considerations **MS**

77.1–2   and myself] **TS–** or myself
         MS
77.3   may] **TS–** might **MS**
77.4   was the] **TS–** was a **MS**
77.5a   last century] **TS–** century
         MS
77.5b   of] **MS TS CApr–** about
         CApu
77.6a   missish] **TS–** missyish
         MS
77.6b   but even] **CApr–** but
         MS–CApu
77.6–7   entering formally into a]
         TS– any **MS**
77.7   to remain together] **TS–**
         not to part **MS**
77.9a   occupation, or] **TS–** or
         occupation or even
         MS
77.9b   care] **CApr–** even care
         MS–CApu
77.9c   next night's] **TS–** night's
         MS
77.12   made answer] **TS–**
         answered **MS**
77.13 had never] **MS** never had
         TS–
77.14a   since the] **TS–** the **MS**
77.14b   had] **TS–** having **MS**
77.15   feeling] **MS TSe–** feeling
         that **TSt**
77.15–16 said shyly] **TS–** said **MS**
77.17   more] **TS–** more
         professionally **MS**
77.18   till] **CApr–** till long
         MS–CApu
77.19   with his] **TS–** with **MS**
77.20   can just] **CAp–** just can
         MS TS
77.21a   characteristic] **TS–**
         significant **MS**
77.21b   depth of] **TS–** depth
         reached by **MS**
77.22   should] **TS–** would **MS**
77.23   praise] **TS–** evidence of
         insight into the other's
         art **MS**
77.24   made that afternoon]
         TS– made **MS**

77.25 Indeed] **TS**– on that afternoon. And indeed **MS**

77.26 time, and then] **CApr**– time **MS–CApu**

77.29 would have expected more] **TS**– might have misunderstood **MS**

77.30a Crane and I had] **TS**– we were **MS**

77.30b never been] **TS**– never **MS**

77.30–31 other's work] **TS**– other **MS**

77.33 mutual recognition] **TS**– the remarks **MS**

77.33–34 It consisted] **CApr** consisted **MS**–

77.34 sometimes of the mention] **TS**– the mention **MS**

77.35 or of] **TS**– or **MS**

77.36a caught] **TS**– struck **MS**

77.36b applied] **TS**– fitted **MS**

77.37 turns] **TS**– needs **MS**

77.39a They] **TS**– which **MS**

77.39b that] **TS**– his **MS**

77.40 by him to] **TS**– to **MS**

78.1 as seen by] **TS**– from the point of view of **MS**

78.3 these words] **TS**– they **MS**

78.4 at] **TS**– at the first page of **MS**

78.5 has remained an object] **TS**– was always a great favorite **MS**

78.5–6 my confirmed admiration] **TS**– mine **MS**

78.9 As] **CApr**– and as **MS–CApu**

78.12a possible] **TS**– possibly **MS**

78.12b my] **TS**– that **MS**

78.13 invariably] **TS**– invariable **MS**

78.14 after all] **TS**– after **MS**

78.16 of presentation] **TS**– on presentation **MS**

78.18 phrase] **TS**– statement **MS**

78.19a what is to follow] **TS**– the extremity of these castaways **MS**

78.19b acquires] **MS TS CApr**– acquired **CApu**

78.19–20 the poignancy ... universal] **TS**– an almost universal poignancy of meaning **MS**

78.22 living then] **TS**– living **MS**

78.23 for the moment as] **TS**– as **MS**

78.24a the couch] **TS**– a couch **MS**

78.24b opposite. After] **CApr**– and after **MS** opposite and after **TS CApu**

78.25a which] **TS**– which no doubt **MS**

78.25b could have felt] **TS**– felt **MS**

78.26a a deadly] **TS**– deadly **MS**

78.26b adventure] **TS**– sort of adventure **MS**

78.30 had struck him] **TS**– striking him at once **MS**

78.31–32 Don't ... quotation?] **TS**– It's a quotation **MS**

78.32a asked] **TS**– said **MS**

78.32b These words form] **TS**– That was in fact **MS**

78.34 quietly] **TS**– quickly **MS**

78.35 leisure] **TS**– much leisure **MS**

78.37 say that] **TS**– say **MS**

78.39 is] **TS**– was **MS**

79.2 character of] **TS**– character **MS**

79.6 overspreading] **CApr**– spreading over **MS–CApu**

79.8 grimy brick houses] **TS**– houses **MS**

79.9a things] **TS**– thing **MS**

79.9b were] **TS**– was **MS**

79.9c impressions] **CApr**– impression **MS–CApu**

79.10	New Mexico] **MS** Mexico **TS**–	80.5b	he knew] **TS**– O M **MS**
79.12	whether] **TS**– why **MS**	80.6–7	now suddenly] **TS**– now **MS**
79.13	indoors ... country] **TS**– indoors **MS**	80.7	ten] **CApr**– 9 **MS** nine **TS** **CApu**
79.14a	any people] **TS**– anybody **MS**	80.9	plan,] **TS**– plan, its details **MS**
79.14b	except for] **TS**– except **MS**	80.10	critical description] **TS**– cursory view at least **MS**
79.15	then, unreal] **TS**– then **MS**	**80.12**	Monico's] **E1**– Monico **MS–CE**
79.16	was stopped ... seems] **TS**– seemed stopped, but **MS**	80.15	rush of hundreds] **TS**– rush **MS**
79.19	had] **TS**– had perhaps **MS**	80.15–16	tons of crockery] **TS**– crockery **MS**
79.20	London's] **TS**– the London's **MS**	80.16	could] **TS**– did **MS**
79.21	know] **TS**– am certain of **MS**	80.16–17	with Balzac)] **TS**– to know of Balzac?) **MS**
79.22	but our] **TS**– Our intense **MS**	80.18	led] **MS** **CAp**– lead **TS**
79.23–24	and gave ... stoicism] **TS**– O M **MS**	80.19a	not know] **TS**– not **MS**
79.25a	let] **TS**– allowed **MS**	80.19b	to understand] **TS**– understand **MS**
79.25b	sit] **TS**– to sit **MS**	80.20	it all] **TS**– it **MS**
79.25–26	To be left alone] **CApr**– This **MS** It **TS** **CApu**	80.24	again,] **TS**– again, without even exchanging addresses **MS**
79.26	had then] **TS**– then had **MS**	80.25a	childhood] **TS**– our earliest days **MS**
79.30	and weary, yet] **TS**– and **MS**	80.25b	each other] **TS**– each **MS**
79.31	ever, and] **TS**– ever yet, **MS**	80.30a	might] **TS**– could **MS**
79.34	by] **TS**– with **MS**	80.30b	was received as] **TS**– already almost **MS**
79.37a	then was, I believe] **TSe**– was then **MS** was, I believe **TSt**	80.31	day] **TS**– day he **MS**
		80.32	and sincere as] **TS**– as **MS**
79.37b	London] **TS**– London, I believe **MS**	80.33a	friendship] **TS**– affection **MS**
79.40	streets, forgetting] **ED** regions as it were, disdaining **MS** mazes the streets, forgetting **TS**–	80.33b	was] **TS**– was a durable sentiment **MS**
		80.34	child, a boy] **TS**– boy **MS**
		80.35–36	was that] **TS**– that **MS**
80.1	standing] **TS**– having accomplished a circle **MS**	80.36a	Stephen Crane] **TS**– Stephen **MS**
80.2	blinking at] **CApr**– dazed with **MS–CApu**	80.36b	in] **TS**– was in **MS**
		80.38a	invited to come] **TS**– invited **MS**
80.5a	curiosities] **TS**– conversation **MS**	80.38b	visit to] **TS**– stay in **MS**
		81.4	it is ... awful] **TS**– it a very [*sic*] **MS**
		81.5	best yet] **TS**– best **MS**

81.8 and yet] **TS**– in their movements, but **MS**
81.11 a dog] **TS**– one or more **MS**
81.16a ¶ A scratching] **TS**– There **MS**
81.16b heard] **TS**– a scratch **MS**
81.17 throw it open] **TS**– go and open it **MS**
81.19 for a while with] **TS**– with **MS**
81.20a by] **TS**– by sometimes even **MS**
81.20b perhaps as] **TS**– as **MS**
81.21 the dogs] **TS**– they **MS**
81.22 direct their foot-steps] **TS**– proceed **MS**
81.22–23 an impressive and] **TS**– an **MS**
81.24–25a before ... panel] **TS**– and then the senior dog I suppose gave the signal **MS**
81.24–25b scratching on] **CApr**– **VAR MS** scratching **TS CApu**
81.25 never] **TS**– but never **MS**
81.26 go meekly] **TS**– go **MS**
81.31 I] **TS**– And I too **MS**
81.32 on ... repetition] **TS**– OM **MS**
81.33a loud interminable] **TS**– bitter **MS**
81.33b and] **TS**– on the fifth or sixth repetition. And **MS**
81.36a learned] **TS**– knew **MS**
81.36b secret] **TS**– truth **MS**
81.39 indeed] **TS–CE A1** Indeed **MS** OM **E1**
81.40 which] **TS–CE A1** which indeed **E1**
82.1 might] **TS**– may **MS**
82.2 our child] **CApr**– that child **MS–CApu**
82.4 The two] **TS**– It **MS**
82.10a "The Red Badge"] **TS**– the Red Badge of Courage **MS**
82.10b in all] **TS**– in **MS**

82.12 yet] **TS**– but **MS**
82.13 would be silence] **TS**– silence **MS**
82.16 beyond] **TS**– a matter beyond **MS**
82.17 ground] **TS**– grounds **MS**
82.19 taking] **TS**– to taking **MS**
82.20a part] **TS**– part against me **MS**
82.20b the baby] **TS**– that baby **MS**
82.22a seemed always] **TS**– always seemed **MS**
82.22b nurse] **TS**– have **MS**
82.24 a dog ... boy?] **TS**– him a dog **MS**
82.25a made] **MS E1**– made me **TS–CE**
82.25b imply] **MS TSe**– imply that **TSt**
82.26 to go and] **MS** and go and **TS** and go **CAp**–
82.28 It was ... answer] **TS**– OM **MS**
82.29 said] **TS**– only said **MS**
82.34 on which] **TS**– when **MS**
82.35a He dropped] **TS**– Dropping **MS**
82.35b theme] **TS**– theme he left me **MS**
82.36 boy ... work] **TS**– boy **MS**
82.38 Joseph,] **TS**– OM **MS**
83.1 The happiest] **TS**– He was a very fine horseman. The happiest **MS**
83.3 looked at] **TS**– looked **MS**
83.4a must have] **TS**– must **MS**
83.4b As usual] **TS**– and usually **MS**
83.5 went on] **TS**– was **MS**
83.6 your] **TS**– that **MS**
83.9 green slopes] **TS**– slopes **MS**
83.10–11 the confident] **TS**– an assured **MS**
83.11 very sure] **TS**– sure **MS**
83.12a and of] **TS**– and **MS**
83.12b All because] **TS**– And perhaps **MS**

83.14	give a man] **TS**– a give [*sic*] a man such **MS**
83.15	believe] **TS**– believe that **MS**
83.15–16	it had really] **TS**– really it had **MS**
83.16	given] **TS**– given to **MS**
83.17a	of hours ... it] **TS**– or hours It **MS**
83.17b	this spell] **TS**– that spell I believe **MS**
83.18	when at] **CApr**– at **MS–CApu**
83.19	After] **CApr**– When **MS–CApu**
83.20a	no] **MS TSe**– not **TSt**
83.20b	it would be] **TS**– he meant **MS**
83.21	slim] **TS**– slender **MS**
83.21–22	to ... head] **TS**– very shyly **MS**
83.22–23	to me of ... verse] **TS**– spoken of it to **MS**
83.22	It] **TS**– I **MS**
83.23	the book] **TS**– it **MS**
83.24a	they] **TS**– those verses **MS**
83.24b	years before in] **TS**– in **MS**
83.26a	or] **TS**– or a **MS**
83.26b	which we] **TS**– we **MS**
83.28	the words ... many] **TS**– there were more words **MS**
83.29	time.] **TS**– time, I cannot help thinking, for **MS**
83.30a	was even] **TS**– even **MS**
83.30b	of a critic than] **TS**– than **MS**
83.31	very] **TS**– sometimes so **MS**
83.33a	could convey] **TS**– conveyed **MS**
83.33b	between us] **TS**– as it were **MS**
83.34	literary conscience] **TS**– conscience **MS**
83.36	art] **TS**– style and genius **MS**

83.36–37	London Academy] **TS**– Academy **MS**
83.38–39	Alfred A. Knopf. 1922. New York.] **TS**– O M **MS**
84.1	Edward's almost uncanny] **TS**– characteristic **MS**
84.1	well balanced] **TS–CA** a helpful **MS** a well-balanced **CE**–
84.2	the blind, pathetic] **TS**– a more or less unconscious **MS**
84.4a	Crane's] **TS**– that **MS**
84.4b	recorded in] **TS**– evidenced by **MS**
84.4c	conclusions] **TS**– conclusion **MS**
84.6	such] **TS**– such deliberately **MS**
84.7	as:] **TS**– as "Mr Crane's talent is unique", ... **MS**
84.7–8	age ... unique"] **TS**– age," **MS**
84.9	very ... confidently] **TS**– last lines contain the pronouncement **MS**
84.10	it ... who] **TS**– of Am: writers Mr Crane **MS**
84.12a	not] **TS**– mainly **MS**
84.12b	critic] **TS**– no critic **MS**
84.12c	of private] **TS**– a private **MS**
84.14	might] **TS**– may **MS**
84.15a	will] **TS**– it will **MS**
84.15b	to be based on] **TS**– a display of **MS**
84.17a	cause of letters,] **TS**– letters **MS**
84.17b	always summon for] **TS**– apply to **MS**
84.19	re-read it] **TS**– it **MS**
84.20	of great] **TS**– a great **MS**
84.21	record] **TS**– records **MS**
84.25	faculties] **TS**– gift **MS**
84.26	On] **MS–E1** Of **A1**
84.27a	look] **CApr**– look close **MS–CApu**
84.27b	Crane's] **TS**– his **MS**

84.28	closing] **CApr**– bringing **MS–CApu**	85.22	base humanity] **TS**– humanity offspring of ignorance **MS**
84.29	my friend] **CApr**– our friendship to a close **MS–CApu**	85.23a	would often] **TS**– was prone to **MS**
84.30a	do not] **TS**– don't **MS**	85.23b	any exceptional] **TS**– a **MS**
84.30b	ever] **TS**– being **MS**		
84.30c	had] **TS**– thus forced **MS**	85.23c	man] **TS**– man of peculiar talents **MS**
84.31	work ... proceedings] **TS**– overexert himself **MS**	85.24–25	just ... kind] **TS**– the usual contemptible talk of some
84.32	ever "dunned"] **TS**– "dunned" **MS**		periodical outburst of unholy festivities in town – of course of the vaguest
84.33	spendthrift] **TS**– man **MS**		
84.34	the prices] **TS**– the **MS**		**MS**
84.35–36	and I will not] **TS**– but I won't **MS**	85.25	in its] **TSe**– V A R **MS** its **TSt**
84.37	Brede Place] **TS**– Brede **MS**	85.25–26	I have heard one] **TS**– One **MS**
84.40	least] **TS**– rooms. [*sic*] which even then looked **MS**	85.26	"friends" ... Philistines] **TS**– friends I heard myself hinting **MS**
84.40–85.1	rooms ... bare] **TS**– O M **MS**	85.27a	write] **TS**– compose **MS**
85.2	but that] **TS**– But this **MS**	85.27b	without getting drunk!] **TS**– unless stimulated by liquor. **MS**
85.7	company] **TS**– company of **MS**		
85.8	chose] **TS**– choose **MS**	85.28	gross palpable] **TS**– obvious **MS**
85.9	Having ... decency] **TS**– Indeed having a certain sense of shades **MS**	85.29a	gave out as an] **TS**– thought another **MS**
85.10	the Cranes'] **TSe**– his **MS** the Crane's **TSt**	85.29b	the artistic] **TS**– artistic **MS**
85.14	silence] **TS**– a silence **MS**	85.31a	foundation of] **MS TSe** **CApr**– foundation to **TSt** **CApu**
85.15	secretly envious] **TS**– secretly **MS**		
85.17	with] **TS**– to **MS**	85.31b	piece of gossip] **TS**– romantic detail **MS**
85.18	may be] **CApr**– are **MS–CApu**	85.32	the] **TS**– his **MS**
85.19a	yet. They] **CApr**– yet – were ever hardly anything else – and would **MS** still. They **TS CApu**	85.33	at about] **MS TSe**– about **TSt**
		85.34	the long] **TS**– a long **MS**
		85.36	with] **TS**– but with **MS**
		85.37a	sound] **TS**– word **MS**
85.19b	one] **TS**– and one **MS**	85.37b	heard] **TS**– spoken **MS**
85.20	the legend] **CApr**– that legend **MS–CApu**	85.38a	Crane] **TS**– I **MS**
		85.38b	say suddenly] **TS**– hear him say **MS**
85.21a	and contemptible gossip] **TS**– gossip **MS**	85.38c	won't] **MS TS CApr**– don't **CApu**
85.21b	in order to] **TS**– to **MS**		

85.38d	now] **MS TSe**– no **TSt**	86.27	MS] **CApu**– original MS
85.39	his regular] **TS**– his **MS**		**MS TS**
85.40	half a] **MS TSe**– a half	86.30	Stokes' invitation to
	TSt		come] **TS**– Stokes
86.1	seemed] **TS**– always		invitation **MS**
	seemed **MS**	86.31	remembrances] **TSe**–
86.2	to ... miracle] **TS**–		remembrance **MS TSt**
	perfectly miraculous **MS**	86.34	Stephen] **TS**– (signed)
86.3a	Most] **TS**– And most **MS**		Stephen **MS**
86.3b	the ale] **TS**– that ale **MS**	86.35	P.S.] **TS**– o m **MS**
86.5–6	drain ... drop of] **TS**–	86.37	We] **TS**– and we **MS**
	always finish **MS**	87.2	we went and] **TS**– we **MS**
86.8	gleeful] **TS**– amiable **MS**	87.3	existed then] **TS**– then
86.8–12	making up ... suggestive.]		existed **MS**
	TS– of which I had a hint	87.4a	have] **TS**– keep **MS**
	or two. The authority of	87.4b	this awful debauch] **TS**–
	the rest of the legend that		these awful debaucheries
	used to be mouthed		**MS**
	confidentially with a sort	87.10	he said] **TS**– o m **MS**
	of glee and hypocritical	87.10–11	an unrestrainedly] **TS**– a
	assumption of regret has		**MS**
	about the same value.	87.11a	temperament.] **TS**–
	MS		temperament. There also
86.12	on] **TS**– of **MS**		temperaments that are let
86.14	to spend] **TS**– spend **MS**		us say perfidious. **MS**
86.15a	his supposed] **TS**– those	87.11b	pass] **TS**– be **MS**
	unholy **MS**	87.12	because] **TS**– for **MS**
86.15b	yet have] **TS**– yet had **MS**	87.14	how it was] **TS**– why **MS**
86.17	own to] **TS**– own **MS**	87.15	had suddenly grown] **TS**–
86.19a	have been] **TS**– have		was simply **MS**
	MS	87.16	on this] **TS**– this **MS**
86.19b	I daresay] **TS**– But I dare	87.17	then ... break for] **TS**–
	say that **MS**		that practically was **MS**
86.20a	in which] **TS**– with which	87.17–18	last train. Afterwards we]
	MS		**TS**– end of it. We **MS**
86.20b	asked me] **TS**– asks **MS**	87.18	our] **TS**– the **MS**
86.21	join him] **TS**– associate	87.22a	experience] **TS**–
	myself **MS**		inexperience **MS**
86.21–22	kept from] **TS**– preserved	87.22b	subject] **TS**– theme **MS**
	of **MS**	87.28	boundless] **TS**– wide **MS**
86.22	very few] **TS**– few **MS**	87.29	objections] **TS**–
86.23	possessions.] **TS**–		difficulties **MS**
	possessions. | Letter |	87.30	a sunset] **TS**– the sunset
	Copy of Stephen Crane's		**MS**
	letter when sending me	87.32	horses] **TS**– horses
	the ms of "The Five White		(however small) **MS**
	Mice". **MS**	87.35	penetrated] **TS**– moved
86.26	17 March.] **TS**– March 17		**MS**
	MS	87.36a	and of] **TS**– and **MS**

87.36b	spirit of] **MS TSe–** spirit of the **TSt**
87.38a	prophetic sense] **TS–** sense **MS**
87.38b	have been] **TS–** have **MS**
87.40	writings] **TS–** work **MS**
88.1	come] **MS–CE** have come **E1–**
88.9	which could create] **TS–** which **MS**
88.10a	that fascinating] **TS–** created the **MS**
88.10b	is] **TS–** was **MS**
88.13	could not be] **CAp–** could be not **MS TS**
88.15	alas it stood] **TS–** it was **MS**
88.16	would fail to make] **TS–** was fated to fail in making **MS**
88.17	remember, a brotherly] **TS–** remember like a **MS**
88.25	succeeded] **TS–** succeed **MS**
88.26	away] **CApr–** away from one **MS TSe CApu** away from on **TSt**
88.28a	¶ The cloudy] **TS–** That **MS**
88.28b	two ... over] **TS–** rushed about **MS**
88.30a	£60] **CApr–** sixty pounds that day **MS** 60 at once **TSt** £60 at once **TSe CApu**
88.30b	the sun set] **TS–** sunset **MS**
88.33	£60] **TSe–** sixty pounds **MS** 60 **TSt**
88.34	various offices] **TS–** one or two places **MS**
88.34–35	we had] **TS–** had **MS**
88.35	money hunting] **TS–** such **MS**
88.36a	would take] **CApr–** took **MS–CApu**
88.36b	interest] **TS–** stock **MS**
88.37	the Spanish-American] **TS–** Spanish-American **MS**
88.38–39	have liked ... over] **TS–** like to think about it till tomorrow **MS**
88.39	downstairs] **TS–** down the stairs **MS**
88.40	it occurred to me] **TS–** I had the idea **MS**
89.1	William] **TS–** Wm. **MS**
89.2a	received ... Presently] **TS–** listened to and **MS**
89.2b	Presently] **TSe–** VAR **MS** Presumably **TSt**
89.3	home] **MS TSe–** him **TSt CApu**
89.4a	"for the war"] **TS–** OM **MS**
89.4b	next day] **TS–** next morning **MS**
89.5	the reason] **TS–** why **MS**
89.6–7	has done ... pay] **TS–** paid **MS**
89.8a	though that afternoon] **TS–** though **MS**
89.8b	by the hand] **TS–** OM **MS**
89.9	But] **TS–** though **MS**
89.14	was] **MS** were **TS–**
89.15	not a] **TS–** not the **MS**
89.15–16	but merely] **TS–** but **MS**
89.18a	a bird-haunted reef] **TS–** the bird haunted reefs **MS**
89.18b	the mere] **TS–** a mere **MS**
89.19	but] **TS–** yet **MS**
89.21a	come] **TS–** come in **MS**
89.21b	came.] **TS–** came and **MS**
89.21–22	I received ... words] **MS TSe–** came **TSt**
89.21c	received] **TSe–** had **MS** VAR **TSt**
89.22a	suggestions] **TSe–** suggestion **MS** VAR **TSt**
89.22b	words] **TSe–** mortal words **MS** VAR **TSt**
89.24a	alive] **TS–** alive today **MS**
89.24b	be] **TS–** have been **MS**
89.27	a line] **TS–** line **MS**

89.27–28	then looking] **TS–** looking **MS**	89.29a	say] **TS–** say very deliberately **MS**
89.28	into my eyes] **TS–** at me **MS**	89.29b	the] **TS–** that **MS**

HIS WAR-BOOK
INTRODUCTION TO STEPHEN CRANE'S
THE RED BADGE OF COURAGE

MS   holograph manuscript, final text (BL)
TS   typescript (Dartmouth)
   TSt   typewritten (unrevised) text of **TS** superseded by revision
   TSr   revised text of **TSt** (incorporating Conrad's alterations): copy-text
C   Stephen Crane, *The Red Badge of Courage* (Heinemann, 1925), pp. 5–12

90.6	enduring] **TSr–** vivid early **MS** vivid **TSt**	90.27	with an] **TSr–** an **MS** only an **TSt**
90.7a	is] **MS TSr–** was **TSt**	90.28a	in order] **TSr–** O M **MS** **TSt**
90.7b	in] **TS–** in England in **MS**		
90.7c	1895] **C–** 1898 **MS TS**	90.28b	give us] **TS–** give **MS**
90.8a	Crane's] **C–** the **MS** Cranes **TS**	**90.29**	him] **MS C–** it **TS**
		91.2	paper] **MS TSr–** pages **TSt**
90.8b	volume] **TS–** vol: **MS**		
90.8c	Mr] **TS–** Mr. W **MS**	91.3	One of the] **TSr–** The most interesting if not the **MS** The **TSt**
90.10a	at] **MS** of **TS–**		
90.10b	not devoid of] **TSr–** of remarkable **MS TSt**	91.4	criticisms] **TSr–** criticism **MS TSt**
90.11a	the series] **TSr–** that it **MS TSt**	91.5	letters] **TS–** letters too **MS**
90.11b	give us shocks] **TSr–** be explosive **MS TSt**	91.7a	with] **TSr–** with Zola in *La Debacle* and Tolstoi in *War and Peace* as works of art [art = art, and **TSt**] **MS TSt**
90.11c	far as] **C–** far **MS TS**		
90.12	all] **TSr–** us **MS TSt**		
90.13	& lively] **TSr–** O M **MS TSt**		
90.14	Crane's] **TS–** Cranes **MS**	91.7b	*Memoires*] **TS–** Memoirs **MS**
90.15	impact and force] **TSr–** force **MS TSt**	91.7c	General] **TSr–** Gen. **MS** Jean **TSt**
90.21	it was] **MS TSr–** was **TSt**	91.8a	famous *Diary*] **TSr–** diary **MS TSt**
90.21–22	a genuine revelation] **TSr–** something strikingly genuine and as **MS** something perfectly genuine **TSt**	**91.8b**	personal] **MS** a personal **TS–**
		91.9	rendered] **TSr–** renders **MS TSt**
90.22	war and love] **TSr–** love and war **MS TSt**	91.9–10	what ... confessed] **TSr–** these but concludes **MS TSt**
90.23	the subjects] **MS TS** subjects **C–**		
90.25	we had] **TSr–** was **MS TSt**	**91.11a**	lurks] **C–** lives **MS TS**
90.26	on] **TSr–** in **MS TSt**	91.11b	men] **TS–** even **MS**

91.12a	aspects] **TSr**– O M **MS TSt**
91.12b	reactions] **TSr**– aspect **MS** aspects **TSt**
91.12c	a] **TSr**– any given **MS TSt**
91.13	with his] **TSr**– with the **MS TSt**
91.14a	what] **MS TSt** C– the what **TSr**
91.14b	the truth ... is] **TSr**– things are **MS TSt**
91.14–15	He ... that] **TSr**– And he concludes [concludes = concluded **TSt**] **MS TSt**
91.17a	Contrived] **TSr**– Contrives **MS TSt**
91.17b	that ... last word] **MS TSr**– is not exactly the word which **TSt**
91.18	any piece of work] **TSr**– anything done **MS TSt**
91.22a	accord of] **TSr**– adjustment in **MS TSt**
91.22b	impressionistic ... on] **TSr**– tonality of narrative depiction of the sounds and sights of **MS** tonality of narrative depicting the confused movements and the sights of **TSt**
91.23	the imaged style of] **TSr** C A1 O M **MS TSt** the imagined style of **E1**
91.23–24	the emotions] **TSr**– emotions the record **MS** emotion, the minute record **TSt**
91.24a	in the inward moral] **TSr**– of inward **MS TSt**
91.24b	struggle going on] **TSr**– struggle [struggle = struggles **TSt**] with the greatest doubt of all **MS TSt**
91.25	Young Soldier] **TSr**– "young soldier" *par excellence* **MS TSt**
91.26	of the monodrama] **TSr**– monodrama **MS** of that monodrama **TSt**
91.26–27	presented ... phrases] **TSr**– embodied in a most picturesquely worded narrative **MS TSt**
91.28a	Stephen] **TS**– Steph: **MS**
91.28b	his Young Soldier] **TSr**– him **MS TSt**
91.28c	an] **TSr**– a young and **MS TSt**
91.29	this] **TSr**– that **MS TSt**
91.29–30	a spontaneous] **TSr**– an [an = a **TSt**] imaginative **MS TSt**
91.31a	writer's] **TS**– writers **MS**
91.31b	In order that] **TSr**– That **MS TSt**
91.32	has] **TSr**– had **MS TSt**
91.33	which he would have] **TSr**– to be **MS TSt**
91.34	matured ... of] **TSr**– conscious of its achievemt [*sic*] and **MS TSt**
91.35	His] **C**– That **MS TS**
91.37	as merely] **TSr**– but **MS TSt**
91.38	had] **TSr**– has **MS TSt**
91.39a	idle and fretting] **TSr**– waiting, waiting **MS TSt**
91.39b	moment] **TSr**– morning **MS TSt**
91.40	at ... simplicity] **TSr**– with the words **MS** with the opening words of his book **TSt**
92.1a	These] **TSr**– – which **MS TSt**
92.1b	first] **TSr**– opening **MS TSt**
92.1–2	war-book ... fame.] **TSr**– book. **MS** book. And that opening paragraph is wonderful in its homely dignity of statement description at the break of the day before the battle. **TSt**
92.3	of that opening paragraph] **TSr**– opening par: of the R. B. of C **MS**

	opening paragraph of the	**92.22b**	on] **MS** upon **TS–**
	Red B. of C. **TSt**	92.22c	historical] **TS–** a
92.4	dignity of] **MS TSt C–**		historical **MS**
	dignity in **TSr**	**92.23**	had never believed] **C–**
92.4–5	the indicated … army]		can not believe **MS** does
	TSr– mainly		not believe	can not
	topographical description		believe **TSt**
	MS TSt	**92.24**	had been a] **C–** was some
92.5a	shivering] **C–** VAR **MS**		sort of **MS TS**
	TSt shuddering **TSr**	92.25	has despaired] **TSr–**
92.5b	at the break] **TS–** at		despaired **MS TSt**
	break **MS** in the light at	92.29a	this touch] **TSr–** this **MS**
	daybreak **TSt**		**TSt**
92.6–7	with … narrative] **TSr–**	92.29b	We can remember] **MS**
	OM **MS TSt**		**TSr–** If he had these	We
92.8a	forming] **TSr–** which **MS**		can remember **TSt**
	TSt	92.31	and … ignorance] **TSr**
92.8b	the subject] **C–** is the		OM **MS TSt**
	subject **MS TS**	92.32a	His] **TS–** He and his **MS**
92.8c	subject] **MS–C A1**	92.32b	had listened to] **TSr–** had
	subjects **E1**		heard **MS TSt**
92.9	going] **MS TSr–** who had	92.32c	the tales of] **TSr–** tales
	gone	going **TSt**		from various **MS TSt**
92.10	waving] **MS TSr–**	92.34a	he can] **TSr–** they could
	wringing **TSt**		**MS TSt**
92.11	from somebody that]	92.34b	his faith] **TSr–** whole **MS**
	TSr– that **MS TSt**		all faith **TSt**
92.12a	only immediate] **TSr–**	**92.36**	lies.] **C–** lies. They had
	first **MS *** TSt**		shouted "Fresh fish after
92.12b	piece of news] **TSr–** news		the [the = his **TSr**]
	MS excitement **TSt**		regiment so often that
92.13	a wooden] **TS–** wooden		**MS TS**
	MS	92.37	And the] **TSr–** The **MS**
92.14	deserted] **TSr–** alone **MS**		**TSt**
	TSt	92.38a	whether] **MS TSr–** is
92.15	excitement … by] **TSr–**		whether **TSt**
	excitement [excitement	92.38b	will or will not] **TSr–** will
	= news **TSt**] meets with		or will **MS** would	will or
	MS TSt		will not **TSt**
92.16	unbelief] **MS TS** disbelief	**92.39a**	He can] **C–** And he can
	C–		**MS TS**
92.18	noticed] **TS–** noted **MS**	**92.39b**	panic-fear] **MS** panic fear
92.20a	a rather] **MS TSr–** the		**TS–**
	rather **TSt**	**92.39c**	enters] **C–** grew in **MS**
92.20b	dugout] **TS–** OM **MS**		**TS**
92.20c	down] **MS** down with his	93.1a	jumps] **TS–** jump **MS**
	hands over his eyes **TS–**	93.1b	Lord] **TS–** God **MS**
92.21	Thus the] **C–** The **MS TS**	93.3a	his very words] **MS TSr**
92.22a	suddenly that] **C–** that		he was heard to speak **TSt**
	MS TS		his words **C–**

93.3b this] **TSr**– the **MS TSt**

93.4–5 He stands before] **TSr**– the fear of **MS TSt**

93.6–7 his unblooded] **C**– that untried **MS TS**

93.8a In] **TSr**– And in **MS TSt**

93.8b stands] **TS**– stand **MS**

93.8c the symbol] **TSr**– a symbol **MS TSt**

93.8–9 untried men] **TS** the Untried **MS**

93.10a estimated] **C**– pronounced **MS TS**

93.10b a morbid case] **MS TSr**– morbid **TSt**

93.11a The abnormal] **MS TSr**– Morbid | The abnormal **TSt**

93.11b at the] **MS** of **TSt** of the **TSr**–

93.11c of those] **C**– those **MS TS**

93.12a at ... sight of] **TSr**– before the **MS TSt**

93.12b of those] **TSr**– those **MS TSt**

93.13 Neither will I] **TSr**– And I don't [don't = do not **TSt**] **MS TSt**

93.14 only soothed] **TSr**– soothed **MS TSt**

93.15a fury] **TSr**– stress **MS TSt**

93.15b a battle] **C**– the fray **MS TS**

93.15–16 Of ... fame.] **TSr**– O M **MS TS**

93.16 lot of] **TS**– lot **MS**

93.17 fear of] **MS TSr**– fear if **TSt**

93.18a *Red Badge of Courage*] **C**– R B of Courage **MS** Red B. of C. **TS**

93.18b He ... because] **TSr**– but **MS TSt**

93.19a Stephen Crane's imagination] **MS C**– the imagination of Stephen Crane **TSt** the Stephen

Crane's imagination **TSr**

93.19b is] **TS**– he is **MS**

93.20a the insight] **MS TSr**– an artist's insight **TSt**

93.20b the power ... artist] **TSr**– the animating force of an artist **MS** power of expression. And thus he appears unique **TSt**

93.21 chief] E D foremost | chief **MS** foremost **TS**–

93.22 greatest] **TS**– great **MS**

93.24a fundamental] E D general **MS TSt** generalised fundamental **TSr**–

93.24b superficially] **TSr**– particularly **MS** particularly Crane's war book **TSt**

93.25a Tolstoy's] **MS** Tolstoi's **TS**–

93.25b were mentioned by critics] **TSr**– have been mentionned [*sic*] **MS TSt**

93.26–27 But ... with] **TSr**– was mainly concerned with depicting **MS** Zola was mainly concerned with the rendering of a depicting [*sic*] **TSt**

93.27a the Imperial regime] **TSr**– a regime **MS** a regime he hated. He **TSt**

93.27b he fancied] **MS C**– fancied **TS**

93.28 Tolstoy's book] E D Tolstoy **MS** Tolstoi **TSt** Tolstoi's book **TSr**–

93.29a first time] **TS**– first **MS**

93.29b a mere episode] **C**– merely episodic **MS TS**

93.30 in a mass of] **MS TSr**– O M **TSt**

93.32 elemental] **TSr**– the **MS TSt**

93.33 what is] **TSr**– the **MS TSt**

93.35a That is why] **TSr**– And **MS TSt**
93.35b Not ... pages.] **TSr**– OM **MS TSt**
93.36a a happy] **TSr** by a happy **MS TSt** happy **C**–
93.36b inspiration] **MS TSr**– instinct | inspiration **TSt**
93.37a had ... in] **TSr**– he had put in **MS** he has put into **TSt**
93.37b had] **TSr** VAR **MS TSt** has **C**–
93.38 words] **TS**– words on page one **MS**
93.39a a] **TSr**– the **MS TSt**
93.39b phrase] **MS TSr**– phrase in one of **TSt**
93.39c p. 194 of] ED p. 194 **MS** page 104 **TSt** page 194 of **TSr**–
93.39d edition which runs] **TSr**– edition. . . " quote (p 194) . . . **MS** editions on page on **TSt**
93.39–94.2 "He ... man."] **TS**– OM **MS**
94.3–4 We ... army] **TSr**– and the army is seen for the last time **MS TSt**
94.4–7 a "procession . . . sky. . . "] **TS**– quote (p 194) **MS**
94.5 became] **A1** OM **MS** become **TS–E1**

94.8a upon] **MS** on **TS**–
94.8b through a break in] **TSr**– through **MS TSt**
94.9a war-book] **TSr**– book **MS TSt**
94.9b so virile ... full] **TSr**– OM **MS TSt**
94.9c of gentle sympathy] **C**– OM **MS TSt** gentle sympathy **TSr**
94.9d which] **TSr**– which there is **MS TSt**
94.10–11 sentiment ... felicity] **TSr**– phrase to break the sustained verbal inspiration **MS TSt**
94.12a had] **C**– has **MS TS**
94.12b the herald] **TSr**– a herald **MS TSt**
94.13–14 and ... was] **TSr**– as if **MS TSt**
94.15 mortally wounded] **TSr**– OM **MS TSt**
94.15–16 snatching at the air] **TSr**– OM **MS TSt**
94.16 a] **TSr**– the middle of a [a = the **TSt**] **MS TSt**
94.16–17 meet ... terrified] **TSr**– die while the **MS TSt**
94.17 kind] **TSr**– OM **MS TSt**
94.18a stand by, silent] **TSr**– stand **MS TSt**
94.18b those] **MS TS** these **C**–
94.19 too] **TSr**– OM **MS TSt**

JOHN GALSWORTHY
AN APPRECIATION

S *Outlook*, 17 (31 March 1906), 449–50: copy-text
Ep Heinemann galley-proofs (Indiana)
Epu uncorrected Heinemann galley-proofs
Epe corrected Heinemann galley-proofs (corrections in another hand)
Pp pamphlet page-proofs (Colgate)
Ppu unrevised pamphlet page-proofs
Ppr revised pamphlet page-proofs (title-page only revised by Conrad)
P1 *John Galsworthy* (H. J. Goulden, 1922), 1st printing
P2 *John Galsworthy* (H. J. Goulden, 1922), 2nd printing

95.1–2	John Galsworthy | An Appreciation] **Ppr** A Middle-class Family. **S** John Galsworthy **Ep Ppu P1–**	97.21	a concrete] **S Epu Pp–** one concrete **Epe**
		97.30	right] **S–P2 A1** rights **E1**
		98.25	property] **S Epe–** poverty **Epu**
96.5	want] **S** wants **Ep–**	98.34	forms] **S Ep** form **Pp–**
96.15	shall] **S Epu** will **Epe–**	98.37	this talent] **S Epu Pp–** his genius **Epe**
96.23a	earthly] **S–P2** earthy **E1–**		
96.23b	foundation] **S–P2** foundations **E1–**	99.13	all sorts of respects] **S Epu Pp–** every respect **Epe**
96.35–36	and ... middle-class family] **S** O M **Ep–**	99.32	they shall] **S Epu P1 P2** that will **Epe** they will **Pp**
97.4	shall] **S Epu** will **Epe–**		**E–**
97.9–13	¶ Irene ... whatever.] **S** O M **Ep–**	99.33	shall] **S Epu** will **Epe–**
		99.39	shall] **S Epu** will **Epe–**

A GLANCE AT TWO BOOKS

TS	typescript (Colgate)
TSt	typewritten (unrevised) text of **TS** superseded by revision
TSr	revised text of **TS** (incorporating Conrad's alterations): copy-text
SE	*T. P.'s & Cassell's Weekly*, 1 August 1925, pp. 475, 494
SA	*Forum*, 74 (August 1925), 308–10

101.1	A ... Books] **E1–** O M **TSt** A Glance at Two Books (?) **TSr** The Enterprise of Writing a Book **SE** Joseph Conrad as Critic **SA**	103.5	delicacy] **TS** the delicacy **SE–**
		103.13	does uphold] **TS SA** upholds **SE E1–**
		103.21	thousand] **SE–** thousands **TS**
101.3	I] **TSr** O M **TSt SE–**		
101.28	own vision] **TS SA** vision **SE E1–**	103.21–22	a thousand] **TS SA E1–** thousand **SE**
101.31	altruistic] **E D** altruist **TS–**	**104.24**	of] **SE–** oft **TS**
102.22	II] **ED** 2 **TS** O M **SE–**	**104.29**	leaf] **E D** small leaf **TS–**
102.34	answer] **TS SE E1–** answers **SA**		

PREFACE TO *THE SHORTER TALES OF JOSEPH CONRAD*

MS	holograph manuscript, final text (Yale)
TS1	typescript (Yale)
TS1t	typewritten (unrevised) text of **TS1** superseded by revision
TS1r	revised text of **TS1** (incorporating Conrad's alterations)
TS2	typescript (Dartmouth)
TS2t	typewritten (unrevised) text of **TS2** superseded by revision
TS2r	revised text of **TS2** (incorporating Conrad's alterations): copy-text
TS2c	carbon-copy typescript (Yale) of **TS2**

TS2ct	typewritten (unrevised) carbon-copy text of **TS2**	
TS2cr	revised text of **TS2** (incorporating Conrad's alterations)	
TS3	typescript (Berg)	
TS3t	typewritten (unrevised) transcription of **TS3** superseded by alteration	
TS3e	revised text of **TS3** (incorporating Conrad's alterations to **TS2r** in an unidentified hand)	
C	Preface to *The Shorter Tales of Joseph Conrad* (Doubleday, 1924), pp. v–xii	

106.1–3   Preface ... *Conrad*] **E1**–
Preface to the Vol of
Selected Stories **MS**
Preface. To Volume of
Selected Stories. **TS1t** *The
Shorter Stories of Joseph
Conrad* | Preface
TS1r–TS3t C Preface
TS3e

106.5   selected] **TS1r**– coll^ed **MS**
collected **TS1t**

106.6   received] **TS1r**–
approached **MS TS1t**

106.7–8   So ... disclose] **TS1r**– It is
not the object of this
preface to expose **MS**
TS1t

106.8   the feelings] **TS1r**– my
feelings **MS TS1t**

106.8–9   with ... Preface] **TS1r**– at
the time **MS TS1t**

106.10a   the sense] **TS1r**– a sense
MS TS1t

106.10b   of being] **TS2r**– that it
was **MS–TS2t**

106.11   not] **MS TS1t TS2r**– is
TS1r TS2t

106.12a   fortune] **TS2r TS3e**–
work's good **MS TS1t**
good **TS1r TS2t TS2c**
TS3t

106.12b   The] **TS1r**– Those **MS**
These **TS1t**

106.15a   enough] **TS1r**– things
enough **MS TS1t**

106.15b   yet they] **TS1r**– yet **MS**
TS1t

106.15c   shapes] **TS1r**– a shape
MS TS1t

106.18   to only] **TS1r**– to **MS** only
to **TS1t**

106.20a   That consideration]
TS1r– These [These =
Those **TS1t**]
considerations **MS TS1t**

106.20b   seem to me] **TS2r TS3e**–
have been **MS TS1r TS2t**
have been be **TS1t** have
been, for me, **TS2c**
TS3t

106.20c   anyone] **TS2r**– о м **MS**–
TS2t

106.21a   writing any] **TS2r TS3e**–
the writing of this **MS**
TS1t writing of any **TS1r**
TS2t TS2ct ever writing
any **TS2cr TS3t**

106.21b   whatever] **TS1r**– о м **MS**
TS1t

106.21c   were not] **TS2r TS3e**–
had not been **MS–TS2t**
TS2c TS3t

106.21–22   for my ineradicable
suspicion] **TS1r TS2r**
TS3e– the thought **MS**
TS1t my ineradicable
suspicion **TS2t TS2c TS3t**

106.23a   merely as] **TS1r**– as **MS**
TS1t

106.23b   series] **TS2r**– scene
MS–TS2t

106.23c   our very] **TS1r**– even **MS**
TS1t

106.23–24   must ... meaning] **TS1r**–
have their reality **MS TS1t**

106.24   Are they not as] **TS1r**–
They are a characteristic
part **MS TS1t**

106.24–25 an individual ... opinions]
TS1r– a man – as much
MS TS1t

106.25 or ... face] TS1r– as the
shape of his cranium or
any trick of his manner
MS TS1t

106.26 being ... be] TS1r– they
MS they are **TS1t**

106.26–27 dangerously revelatory]
TS1r– revelatory **MS TS1t**

106.27 This is an] TS1r– An **MS
TS1t**

106.28a acquired callousness]
TS1r– callousness **MS
TS1t**

106.28b inborn] TS1r– simple **MS
TS1t**

106.29a has] TS1r– had **MS TS1t**

106.29b not] **MS TS1t TS2r**
TS3e– never **TS1r TS2t
TS2c TS3t**

106.30 from] **MS TS1r**– of **TS1t**

106.30–31 revelatory prefaces]
TS1r– prefaces **MS TS1t**

106.31 for ... account] TS1r–
The only quality that can
not be refused to them is
shortness **MS TS1t**

106.32a incensed man] TS1r–
man **MS TS1t**

106.32b with a shot-gun] TS1r–
O M **MS TS1t**

106.32–33 here ... desist] TS1r– on
me with a shot-gun to
destroy me as a public
nuisance **MS TS1t**

106.33 again volunteering]
TS2r– engaged [engaged
= again engaged **TS1r
TS2t**] in producing
MS–TS2t

106.34a more of these] TS1r–
more **MS TS1t**

106.34b sincere confessions] **TS2r
TS3e**– O M **MS TS1t**
voluntary confessions
TS1r TS2t revelatory
confessions **TS2c TS3t**

107.1a To begin with] TS1r– I
think **MS TS1t**

107.1b venture to affirm] **TS1r**–
safely say **MS TS1t**

107.2–3 from which those
included] **TS1r**–
included **MS TS1t**

107.3 have been selected was]
TS2r– has been **MS TS1t**
are [are = was **TS2t**]
selected has been **TS1r
TS2t**

107.4 problems] **TS1r**–
problem **MS TS1t**

107.5a their style] **TS1r**–
execution **MS TS1t**

107.5b upon] TS1r– on **MS** opon
[*sic*] **TS1t**

107.5c I have] TS1r– I had **MS** a
had **TS1t**

107.5–6 and on the nature] **TS2r
TS3e**– upon the sincerity
MS TS1t and on the
sincerity **TS1r TS2t TS2c
TS3t**

107.6 reactions] TS1r– reaction
MS TS1t

107.6–7 particular ... general]
TS2r– general **MS TS1t**
particular instances and
to the general **TS1r
TS2t**

107.7–10 This ... so.] TS1r– And
thus they got written,
generally in batches, at
various times, in various
moods, in different
mental conditions. This
gave them a sort of unity
from the first. **MS
TS1t**

107.7–8 each of the] **TS2**– V A R
MS TS1t the **TS1r**

107.8a sets of tales] **TS2r–C** V A R
MS TS1t sets **TS1r TS2t**
tales **E1**–

107.8b composed] **TS2r**– V A R
MS TS1t written **TS1r
TS2t**

107.8c   times] **TS2r**– VAR **MS**
           TS1t times of my writing
           life **TS1r TS2t**

107.8d   and in] **TS2**– VAR **MS**
           TS1t in **TS1r**

107.10   I had] **MS TS1r**– gentle
           *e**i* my first collected
           edition had **TS1t**

107.11   the Author's Notes]
           TS1r– prefaces **MS**
           TS1t

107.12   impression] **TS1r**– view
           MS TS1t

107.12–13 my short-story volumes]
           TS1r– the vols from
           which a selection has
           been [has been = was
           TS1t] made for this book
           MS TS1t

107.13–14 consistent ... wilderness]
           TS1r– distinct character
           of its own, whether the
           stories contained in it
           were **MS TS1t**

107.13   outlook] **TS2r**– VAR **MS**
           TS1t purpose **TS1r TS2t**

107.14   and life] **TS2r**– or of life
           MS or life **TS1 TS2t**

107.16a   It ... much] **TS1r**– I [I =
           Thus I **TS1t**] may venture
           MS TS1t

107.16b   not be] **TS2t**– VAR **MS**
           TS1t be not **TS1r**

107.16c   too] **TS2t**– VAR **MS TS1t**
           to [*sic*] **TS1r**

107.16d   this trait] **TS1r**– this **MS**
           TS1t

107.17   "Tales of Unrest"] **TS1r**–
           vol^me of *Tales of Unrest*,
           the very first of of [of of
           = collection of **TS1t**]
           short stories I ever
           published, where the
           localities range from the
           Malay Archipelago
           through Brittany and
           Central Africa to an
           upper middle-class house
           in a residential street of
           London **MS TS1t**

107.20–23 It ... London.] **TS1r**– OM
           MS TS1t

107.23   also seems to me] **TS2r**
           TS3e– is **MS–TS2t** seems
           to me **TS2c TS3t**

107.24   volume called] **TS2r**– vol.
           of **MS** volume of **TS1**
           TS2t

107.25   one story has] **TS1r**– the
           story The Brute **MS** this
           story "The Brute" **TS1t**

107.26–27 of ... presentation] **TS1r**–
           and in the artistic quality
           of its expression **MS**
           TS1t

107.28a   Yet, in] **TS1r**– In **MS TS1t**

107.28b   almost the whole] **TS2**–
           the whole **MS TS1t** the
           almost whole **TS1r**

107.30a   to end in] **TS1r**– into the
           sunshine of **MS TS1t**

107.30b   the South of Italy] **TS1r**–
           South Italy **MS TS1t**

107.31   was] **TS2r**– is **MS–TS2t**

107.32   and from my] **TS1r TS2r**–
           This, from a certain **MS**
           TS1t and from that **TS2t**

107.32–33 I accepted ... as a] **TS1r**–
           is a sort of **MS TS1t**

107.33a   this] **TS2r**– VAR **MS TS1t**
           it **TS1r TS2t**

107.33b   inner consistency] **TS1r**–
           unity **MS TS1t**

107.33–34 would claim] **TS1r**– claim
           MS TS1t

107.34a   set] **TS2r**– volume
           MS–TS2t

107.34b   shorter tales] **TS1r**– short
           stories, and I welcomed
           [welcomed = welcome
           TS1t] it on that ground
           MS TS1t

107.35a   volume] **TS1**– vol. of
           short stories published in
           MS

107.35b   I take] **TS1r**– OM **MS**
           TS1t

107.36–37 of the book ... being]
           TS1r– book was **MS** of it
           was **TS1t**

107.36	seemed to produce] TS2r– VAR MS TS1t produces TS1r TS2t	108.8a	sources profounder] TS2r TS3e– causes more profound MS TS1t causes
107.37	component parts] TS2r– parts MS–TS2t		profounder TS1r TS2t TS2c TS3t
107.37–38	as a confirmation] TS2r– seems to confirm MS TS1t It confirms TS1r TS2t	108.8b	a deliberate] TS1r TS2r– any preconceived MS TS1t a deliberated TS2t
107.38a	my] MS TS1r– the TS1t	108.9a	acquired learning]
107.38b	having welded the diversities] TS1r– artistic unity welding the diversity MS TS1t		TS1r–C some acquired learning MS TS1t acquiring learning E1–
107.39–40	consistency ... nature] TS1r– whole, characteristic MS TS1t	108.9b	let us say] TS1r– OM MS TS1t
108.1	The ... how] TS1r– It will be, then, understood by any friendly reader that MS TS1t	108.9c	lessons drawn from] TS2r TS3e– the lessons of an [an = a TS1t] MS TS1t the lessons drawn from TS1r TS2t TS2c TS3t
108.2a	productions] TS1r– productions [productions = production TS1t] in their original grouping MS TS1t	108.10a	practice] MS TS1r– experience TS1t
		108.10b	for ... with] TS1r– with me for this view in MS TS1t
108.2b	recoil at first] TS1r– feel an aversion MS TS1t	108.12	only] MS TS1r– only one TS1t
108.3	out of] TS1t– out MS	108.13	take for] TS1r– make MS take TS1t
108.4	belonged] MS TS1r– belong TS1t	108.15	individuality] TS1r– ultimate sum MS TS1t
108.5	because ... result] TS1r– do [do = so TS1t] that the effect produced was not outcome [outcome = the outcome TS1t] MS TS1t	108.16	suspect] MS TS1r– suspect that TS1t
		108.17a	I mean] TS1r– yes MS TS1t
		108.17b	precisely] TS1t– just precisely MS
108.6	happened] TS1r– happened so MS TS1t	108.17–18	the part the general] TS1r– that part which the general [the general = general** of TS1t] MS TS1t
108.6–7	in one's work seem] TS1r– are MS TS1t		
108.7a	impressive] TS1r– more impressive MS TS1t	108.18a	plays] MS TS1r– play TS1t
108.7b	valuable because] TS2r TS3e– more valuable since MS even more valuable since TS1t valuable since TS1r TS2t TS2c TS3t	108.18b	shaping] TS1r– general aspect MS TS1t
		108.19a	those] TS1– these MS
		108.19b	have "just happened"] TS1– "just happen" MS
		108.20a	or] TS1r– and even MS TS1t

108.20b   are] MS TS1r–C is TS1t
           E1–
108.21a   moments too] TS1r–
           moments MS TS1t
108.21b   when one's] TS2r– when
           his MS TS1t TS2t his
           TS1r
108.22–23 (for ... mysteries)] TS1r–
           OM MS TS1t
108.22   practical] TS2t– OM MS
           TS1t the practical
           TS1r
108.23   one] TS2r TS3e– him
           MS–TS2t TS2c TS3t
108.23–24 take up] TS1r– take a MS
           TS1t
108.24a   different] TS2– OM MS
           TS1t differing TS1r
108.24b   one's] TS2r TS3e– his
           MS–TS2t TS2c TS3t
108.26   that] TS1r– when MS
           TS1t
108.27a   came] TS2r TS3e– has
           been put MS–TS2t TS2c
           TS3t
108.27b   from] TS2r TS3e– by
           MS–TS2t TS2c TS3t
108.28a   friend and publisher]
           TS2– friends and
           publishers MS TS1
108.28b   Mr F. N.] TS2– Messers:
           MS Messrs. TS1
108.28c   is an idealist] TS2– are
           idealists MS TS1
108.29a   and who] TS2r– and
           MS–TS2t
108.29b   simply hate to] TS2r
           TS3e– on no account MS
           TS1t simply abhor to
           TS1r TS2t TS2c TS3t
108.29c   his] TS2– their MS TS1
108.30a   business. His ... mind]
           TS2r– business which MS
           TS1 TS2t
108.30b   consists, mainly,] TS1r–
           consists MS TS1t
108.30–31 the intermediary] TS2–
           intermediaries MS TS1
108.32   brain] TS2r TS3e– minds
           MS–TS2t TS2c TS3t

108.33   his ... on] TS2r TS3e–
           their conclusion
           [conclusion =
           conclusions TS1t] MS
           TS1t their way [their way
           = his ways TS1r] of
           carrying it out TS1r TS2t
           TS2c TS3t
108.34   his conclusions] TS2–
           their conclusions MS TS1
108.36   his words] TS2– their
           words MS TS1
108.37a   my own idealism] TS1r–
           me MS TS1t
108.37b   notion] TS1r– idea MS
           TS1t
108.39   native] TS1r– original MS
           TS1t
109.2a   has] TS1– it has MS
109.2b   advantage] TS2r– quality
           MS–TS2t
109.3   immune ... infection of]
           TS1r– least accessible to
           MS at least inaccessible to
           TS1t
109.4   I soon found that] TS1r–
           OM MS TS1t
109.4–5   simple ... sincere] TS1r–
           purpose was the simple
           MS TS1t
109.5–9   deeper ... End] TS1r–
           impressions and not the
           advancement
           [advancement =
           advocacy TS1t] of ideas
           or the description of any
           social phase, the
           application MS TS1t
109.5–6   more sympathetic] TS2r–
           VAR MS TS1t
           sympathetic TS1r TS2t
109.7   yet have] TS2r TS3e–
           VAR MS TS1t have TS1r
           TS2t TS2c TS3t
109.9–10   of the World ... all] TS2r
           TS3e– OM MS TS1t of
           the World, which when it
           comes will be only the
           vanishing of all vanities,
           the vainest thing of

all,**TS1r TS2c TS3t** of the
World, which when it
comes will be only
vanishing of all vanities,
the vainest think [*sic*] of
all, **TS2t**

109.10a not] **TS1r–** found not **MS**
TS1t

109.10b its application] **TS1r–**
practice **MS TS1t**

109.11 seemed to be] **TS1r–**
seemed **MS TS1t**

109.11–12 classed as] **TS1r–** called
MS TS1t

109.12 have always] **TS1r–** always
MS TS1t

109.13–14 a full text of] **TS2r TS3e–**
my **MS TS1t** the text of
TS1r TS2t TS2ct a text of
TS2cr TS3t

109.17 self-satisfying possession]
TS1r– self-satisfying
experience **MS** possession
self-satisfying experience
TS1t

109.18 Calderon] **TS1r–** was it
not Calderon who **MS**
TS1t

109.19 my past] **TS1r–** La vita
[*sic*] es sueño?) that
experience **MS TS1t**

109.19–20 things ... body of] **MS–C**
OM E1–

109.20 of what] **MS TS1r–** for
what **TS1t**

109.21 of the inner] **TS1r–** the
inner **MS** the native inner
TS1t

109.22a set] **MS–TS2** sets **TS2c–**

109.22b add here] **TS1r–** say **MS**
TS1t

109.23a those words] **TS1r–** that
phrase **MS TS1t**

109.23b after so] **TS1r–** in the
face of **MS TS1t**

109.24 for] **TS2r TS3e–** to
MS–TS2t TS2c TS3t

109.25 destined] **TS2r–** directed
MS–TS2t

109.27 has] **TS2–** had **MS TS1**

109.28a aim] **TS1r–** object **MS**
TS1t

109.28b It ... years] **TS1r–** After all
those years it is too late
MS TS1t

109.29 confess here] **TS1r–**
disclose **MS** confess
TS1t

109.30 first paper boats] **TS1r–**
paper-boats **MS TS1t**

109.32a unappeasable] **MS TS2–**
unappeased **TS1**

109.32b human] **TS1r–** mens **MS**
men's **TS1t**

109.33 trust] **TS1r–** hope **MS**
TS1t

109.35a Much time] **TS1r–** Time
MS TS1t

109.35b passed since] **TS1r–**
passed **MS TS1t**

109.36a my readers] **TS1r–** you
MS TS1t

109.36b than I do] **TS1r–** than **MS**
TS1t

109.37a these] **MS TS1t TS2–**
those **TS1r**

109.37b see now] **TS1r–** see **MS**
TS1t

109.38 were but] **TS1r–** were **MS**
very **TS1t**

109.39a a grown-up] **TS1–**
grown-up **MS**

109.39b dreams] **MS TS1r–** dream
TS1t

109.39c launched innocently]
TS1r– launched **MS TS1t**

109.40a that terrible] **TS1r–** a **MS**
TS1t

109.40b honest] **TS1r–** good **MS**
TS1t

109.40–
110.2 life ... Shadow] **TS1r–** life,
has [life, has = days life
has **TS1t**] no other limits
than a shadowy horizon
MS TS1t

110.3a Approaching] **TS1–** On
approaching **MS**

110.3b book] **TS1r–** volume **MS**
TS1t

110.3c the full] **TS1–** full **MS**

110.5   its own] **TS2**– a certain **MS TS1t** his own **TS1r**

110.5–6   Character ... patches.] **MS–C** OM **E1**–

110.6   Looking over the] **TS1r**– Reviewing thus [thus = the **TS1t**] certain **MS TS1t**

110.7a   discovered] **TS1r**– selected for **MS TS1t**

110.7b   guide in] **TS1r**– guide **MS TS1t**

110.8   me so often] **TS2**– me **MS TS1t** so often **TS1r**

110.8–9   cast early] **TS1r**– cast **MS TS1t**

110.9a   waters] **TS1r**– water **MS TS1t**

110.9b   Thus] **TS1r**– OM **MS TS1t**

110.9c   trait of the] **TS1r**– tone of these **MS** then **TS1t**

110.10a   consists] **TS1**– consist **MS**

110.10b   central ... being] **TS2r**– fact that in each of them **MS TS1t** central figure in each of them being **TS1r** central figure of them being **TS2t**

110.11a   presented either in the] **TS1r**– is a central figure in its **MS TS1t**

110.11b   relations] **TS1r**– various relations **MS TS1t**

110.11c   of his] **TS2r**– in its **MS–TS2t**

110.12a   his own kind] **TS2r TS2cr TS3**– others of its own kind **MS–TS2t TS2ct**

110.12–13   or ... that] **TS1r**– and also with the people and affairs ashore – that is with the **MS TS1t**

110.12b   lands men] **TS2r TS2cr TS3**– VAR **MS TS1t** men **TS1r TS2t TS2ct**

110.13   embroiled in the] **TS2r TS2cr TS3**– VAR **MS TS1t** the shore **TS1r TS2t TS2ct**

110.15   label] **TS1r**– characterise **MS TS1t**

110.16a   They] **TS1r**– for the [the = they **TS1t**] **MS TS1t**

110.16b   feelings] **TS1r**– the problems and feelings **MS** the problems **TS1t**

110.17–18   support given by a] **TS1r**– OM **MS TS1t**

110.18   which confronts] **TS1r**– with [with = which **TS1t**] regards **MS TS1t**

110.18–19   an elemental] **TS1**– elemental **MS**

110.19a   fury] **TS1r**– manifestation **MS TS1t**

110.19b   be met and] **TS2**– be **MS TS1t** met and **TS1r**

110.21   mere ideas] **TS2r**– an idea **MS TS1t** mere idea **TS1r** a mere idea **TS2t**

110.22a   and also] **TS2r TS3e**– and **MS–TS2t TS2c TS3t**

110.22b   articulate appeal] **TS1r**– appeal **MS TS1t**

110.24a   weakness] **TS2r**– weaknessess [*sic*] **MS** weaknesses **TS1 TS2t**

110.24b   many other] **TS1r**– other **MS TS1t**

110.25a   affect] **TS2r**– not only affect **MS–TS2t**

110.25b   and] **TS2r**– but **MS–TS2t**

110.26a   are meant to give] **TS2r**– even give **MS TS1t** give **TS1r TS2t**

110.26b   a colouring] **TS1**– the colouring **MS**

110.27a   even to] **TS1r**– even **MS TS1t**

110.27b   which is expected] **TS2**– expected **MS TS1t** which expected **TS1r**

110.27c   To] **TS1r**– But to **MS TS1t**

110.28   would have] **TS1r**– had **MS TS1t**

110.29   view of] **TS2**– regard to **MS TS1t** a view to **TS1r**

110.29–30 the private] **TS2r TS3e–**
everyday **MS** the everyday
TS1 TS2t TS2ct the
personal **TS2cr**
TS3t

110.30 incidents] **TS1r–** events
MS TS1t

110.30–31 title ... of] **TS1r–** title **MS**
TS1t

110.31 It ... by] **TS1r–** owing to
MS TS1t

110.32a will] **TS2r–** can **MS–TS2t**

110.32b nor] **TS1r–** or **MS TS1t**

110.33 blind antagonisms]
TS1r– antagonisms **MS**
antagonism **TS1t**

110.35 parts ... desire] **TS1r–**
sections arise [arise =
arises **TS1t**] partly from
the fact that I wanted **MS**
TS1t

110.37a autobiography] **TS1r–**
biography **MS TS1t**

110.37b emotions remembered]
TS2– remembered **MS**
TS1

110.38a which defined] **TS1r–**
which **MS TS1t**

110.38b a purely] **MS TS1t TS2–**
purely **TS1r**

110.38c descriptive] **TS1r–**
literary **MS TS1t**

110.39 the two] **TS1r–** my two
MS TS1t

110.39–40 which ... times] **TS1r–** OM
MS TS1t

111.3 part deals] **TS1r–** sec[on]
deal **MS** section deals
TS1t

111.4 parts there] **TS1r–** sec[ons]
MS sections **TS1t**

111.5 no ... order] **TS2–**
attempted **MS TS1t** no
attem [*sic*] chronological
order **TS1r**

111.6a neither] **TS1r–** no **MS**
TS1t

111.6b nor] **TS1r–** or **MS TS1t**

111.7 writer's] **TS1–** writers
MS

111.8a the book] **TS2r–** it **MS**
TS1t the volume **TS1r** the
TS2t

111.8b lies] **TS2r–** is **MS–TS2t**

111.9a Part First] **TS1r–** the first
section **MS TS1t**

111.9b speaks] **TS2r–** will speak
MS–TS2t

111.10a regrets] **MS TS1r–** regret
TS1t

111.10b second story] **TS1r–**
second **MS TS1t**

111.11a the "*esprit*] **TS2r–** esprit
MS–TS2t

111.11b deep fellowship] **TS1r–**
comradeship **MS TS1t**

111.12a seamen ... time] **TS1r–**
men [men = sea-men
TS1t] following the sea
MS TS1t

111.12b Those] **TS1r–** and those
MS TS1t

111.13 regarded as purely]
TS2r– called strictly
MS–TS2t

111.13–14 in Part First] **TS1r–** OM
MS TS1t

111.15 The last] **TS1r–** and the
other **MS TS1t**

111.15–16 effect ... fascination of]
TS1r– appeal **MS TS1t**

111.16a has ... lot of] **TS2r TS3e–**
has **MS–TS2t TS2c**
TS3t

111.16b for its] **TS2r TS3e–** the
MS for a **TS1t** for the
TS1r TS2t TS2c TS3t

111.17 interest] **TS2r TS3e–**
figure **MS–TS2t TS2c**
TS3t

111.18 Part] **TS1r–** Section **MS**
TS1t

111.19a which is being] **TS2r**
TS3e– being **MS–TS2t**
TS2c TS3t

111.19b Captain] **TS1–** Capt **MS**

111.20a it is] **TS1r–** OM **MS TS1t**

111.20b that ... symbolic] **TS1r–** is
felt to be the principal
MS TS1t

111.22a   to ... him] **TS1r**– wrecks
his life **MS** holds wrecks
his life **TS1t**

111.22b   spoils] **TS2**– V A R **MS**
TS1t a spoils **TS1r**

111.24   right] **MS TS1r**– right.
And in **** *Falk* **TS1t**

111.26   suggest ... of] **TS2r**–
render there is existence
MS render there is the
existence of **TS1 TS2t**

111.29a   pitilessly] **TS1r**–
mercilessly **MS TS1t**

111.29b   the crucial] **TS1r**– a
crucial **MS TS1t**

111.29–30   bizarre love-story] **TS1r**–
emotional life **MS TS1t**

111.32a   these] **MS TS2**– those
TS1

111.32b   are records] **MS–C** is a
record **E1**–

111.33–34   As ... they] **TS2r TS3e**–
They **MS TS1t** They are
all authentic because they
TS1r TS2t TS2c because
they **TS3t**

111.33   said before] **TS2r TS3e**–
V A R **MS TS1** O M
TS2tTS2c TS3t

111.35   had] **MS TS1t TS2r**
TS3e– has **TS1r TS2t**
TS2c TS3t

111.35–36   their ... exist] **TS1r**– them
MS TS1t

111.35   their] **TS1r TS2r**– V A R
MS TS1t that **TS2t**

111.36   In each there lurks]
TS2r– Each of them has
its **MS–TS2t**

111.37a   from] **TS1r**– by **MS TS1t**
111.37b   various] **MS** the various
TS1–

111.39   matter for a verdict]
TS2r– quite another
matter **MS TS1t** a matter
of judgment **TS1r TS2t**

111.40a   consciences] **TS2r**–
conscience **MS–TS2t**

111.40b   the readers] **TS2r TS3e**–
each successive reader
MS–TS2t my readers
TS2c TS3t

COOKERY

PREFACE TO JESSIE CONRAD'S *A HANDBOOK OF
COOKERY FOR A SMALL HOUSE*

P   *Simple Cooking Precepts for a Little House* (Publisher unknown, 1921)

SA   *Delineator* (New York), August 1922, 11

SE   *Woman's Pictorial Magazine* (London), 14 October 1922, p. 14

CA   Jessie Conrad, *A Handbook of Cookery for a Small House* (Doubleday, 1923): copy-text

CAa   Jessie Conrad, *A Handbook of Cookery for a Small House* (Heinemann, 1923): British issue of CA

112.7   that] **P SE**– which **SA**

112.10   one and unmistakable] **P**
SE– unmistakable **SA**

112.11   object] **P–CAa A1** objects
E1

112.13   affectionate] **SE**–
benevolent **P SA**

112.19   most successful] **SE**–
impeccable **P SA**

112.20   many priceless] **SE**– more
than fifteen **P SA**

112.25   cooking] **P–CAa** cookery
E1–

112.28   of the] **SE**– the **P SA**

113.3a   suffered] **SE**– suffered
cruelly **P SA**

113.3b   perpetual indigestion]
SE– indigestion **P SA**

113.20	apparently] **P–CAa** O M **E1–**	113.40– 114.1	clear and concise] **SE–** painstaking **P SA**
113.28	the honesty] **SE–** honesty **P SA**	114.4	soundness] **SE–** exactitude **P SA**
113.36	intention] **P SE–** intentions **SA**		

THE FUTURE OF CONSTANTINOPLE

S *The Times*, 7 November 1912, p. 5: copy-text for letter
A1 *Last Essays* (Doubleday, 1926), pp. 149–54: copy-text for essay

| 115.14 | old and] **S** old **E1–** | 116.8 | a neutralized] **S** neutralised **E1–** |

UNCOLLECTED ESSAYS

AUTHOR'S NOTE TO *YOUTH AND GASPAR RUIZ*

'GASPAR RUIZ'

TS typescript (NYU)
   TSt typewritten text (unrevised) of **TS** superseded by revision
   TSr revised text of **TS** (incorporating Conrad's alterations): copy-text (176.9–177.6)
C1 'Author's Note', *Youth, A Narrative, and Two Other Stories* (Dent, 1917), pp. vii–ix
C2 'Author's Note', *Youth and Gaspar Ruiz* (Dent, 1920), pp. 165–8: copy text (175.4–176.8)
   C2a 'Author's Note', *Youth and Gaspar Ruiz* (Dutton, 1920), pp. 165–8
C3 'Author's Note', *Notes on My Books* (Doubleday, 1921), pp. 33–8
   C3a 'Author's Note', *Notes on My Books* (Heinemann, 1921), pp. 33–8

175.1-2	Author's ... Ruiz] **ED** O M **TSt** Introductory Note for Gaspar Ruiz. **TSr** Author's Note **C1–**	176.15b 176.16	a certain] **TSr–** an [?] **TSt** the outcome] **TSr–** an outcome **TSt**
176.10	mean that] **TSr–** mean **TSt**	176.17 176.18	was] **TSr–** is **TSt** a scrupulous] **TSr–** complete **TSt**
176.11a	merely invented] **TSr–** invented **TSt**	176.19 176.20a	was] **TSr–** is **TSt** In this arrangement]
176.11b	truly imagined] **TSr–** imagined **TSt**	176.20b	**TSr–** And in that **TSt** consists] **TSr–** consist **TSt**
176.14	sort of work] **TSr–** work **TSt**	176.21	distinguished] **TSr–** apart **TSt**
176.15a	(not reminiscent) nature] **TSr–** nature (not reminiscent) **TSt**	176.22 176.23 176.24a	an old] **TSr–** a **TSt** and as to] **TSr–** and **TSt** of the man] **TSr–** O M **TSt**

176.24b	Benavides] **TSr**– Benavidas **TSt**	176.34	the personal ... all] **TSr**– his personal character. And so for the rest of **TSt**
176.25a	for a time] **TSr**– OM **TSt**		
176.25b	chief] **TSr**– a chief **TSt**	176.35	Yet] **TSr**– But **TSt**
176.25c	during] **TSr**– in **TSt**	176.36	but only] **TSr**– but **TSt**
176.26	in the] **TSr**– about the **TSt**	176.38a	human breasts] **TSr**– a human breast **TSt**
176.33a	actions] **TSr**– his actions **TSt**	176.38b	sequence] **TSr**– certain sequence **TSt**
176.33b	the various] **TSr**– his various **TSt**	176.38c	certain events] **TSr**– events **TSt**
176.33c	peoples' minds] **TSr**– mind **TSt**	177.1–6	The episode ... impossible.] **TSr**– OM **TSt**

FOREWORD TO *LANDSCAPES OF CORSICA AND IRELAND* BY A. S. KINKEAD

MS	holograph manuscript, one-leaf fragment (Yale): 179.16–19 ['Corsican landscape' *to* 'soul.']
TS1	typescript (Yale)
TS1t	typewritten (unrevised) text of **TS1** superseded by revision
TS1r	revised text of **TS1** (incorporating Conrad's alterations)
TS2	typescript, partial (Bryn Mawr): 179.30–180.10 [*from* 'rendered' *to the end*]
TS2t	typescript (unrevised) text of **TS2** superseded by revision
TS2r	revised text of **TS2** (incorporating Conrad's alterations)
TS3	typescript (HRC)
TS3t	typewritten (unrevised) text of **TS3** superseded by revision
TS3r	revised text of **TS3** (incorporating Conrad's alterations): copy-text
C	*Landscapes of Corsica and Ireland* (The United Arts Gallery, 1921), pp. [i–ii]

179.1–3	Foreword ... *Ireland*] **ED** OM **TS1 TS3t** Foreword to Catalogue of Corsican & Irish Landscapes. **TS3r** Foreword **C**	179.8c	the natural] **TS3**– OM **TS1t** natural **TS1r**
		179.8–9	features of the land] **TS1r**– OM **TS1t**
179.5	landscapes from] **TS1r TS3**– the scenery of **TS1t**	179.12	suggested by this collection] **TS1r**– that may be said **TS1t**
179.6	has a hold on] **TS1r**– is in **TS1t**	179.13a	a subject ... painter] **TS1r**– every painter's subject **TS1t**
179.7	perceptions] **TS1r**– emotions **TS1t**	179.13b	short visit] **TS3r**– first short glimpse of it **TS1** first short visit **TS3t**
179.8a	found not alone] **TS3**– found **TS1**		
179.8b	complete fidelity to] **TS1r**– truth to nature no doubt **TS1t**	179.14–15	had become] **TS3r**– becomes **TS1 TS3t**
		179.16a	No!] **TS3**– OM **MS TS1**

[*MS is extant for only
179.16–19*]

179.16b Corsican ... subject.] **MS
TS3**– For after all what is
it? [it? = Corsican
landscape **TS1r**] **TS1t
TS1r**

179.17–19 dangerous ... soul] **MS
TS3**– but Alpine scenery,
with **TS1t** in the main
Alpine scenery, with **TS1r**

179.17a Alpine type which] **TS3r**–
type which is the Alpine
type **MS** V A R **TS1** type,
which is the Alpine **TS3t**

179.17b like] **TS3r**– and like **MS
TS3t** V A R **TS1**

179.18 very fine] **MS TS3r**– V A R
TS1 fine **TS3t**

179.18–19 as if it were] **TS3r**– being
more like **MS TS3t** V A R
TS1

179.19 rather than] **TS3r**– than
MS TS3t V A R **TS1**

179.19–21 Nothing ... than] **TS3**–
O M **TS1**

179.21 snow-crags] **TS3r**– crag
and snow **TS1t** snow
plates **TS1r** its snow-crags
TS3t

179.22a tormented] **TS1 TS3r**– its
tormented **TS3t**

179.22b rock-faces] **TS3**– rock
face **TS1**

179.22c fantastic] **TS1 TS3r**– its
fantastic **TS3t**

179.22d a blue] **TS3r**– the blue
TS1 TS3t

179.22e sea.] **TS3**– sea. And
nothing could be made
more commonplace by
the exercise of the mere
skill or even by a vision
not frankly and delicately
personal. **TS1**

179.23a truth] **TS3**– truth and the
charm **TS1**

179.23b deeper vision; its] **TS3r**–
right response for the

179.24 **TS1** right response, its
TS3t

179.24 mere grandeur] **TS3r**–
imposing proportion, the
grandeur **TS1** grandeur
TS3t

179.25 or exceptionality] **TS3**–
of exceptionality **TS1**

179.26a this series] **TS3**– the
series **TS1**

179.26b pictures] **TS3**– the
pictures exhibited here
TS1

179.27 something more ...
captured] **TS3r**– there is
something more **TS1**
TS3t

179.28 ruggedness] **TS3r**–
charm **TS1 TS3t**

179.28–29 may ... any one] **TS3r**–
everybody can feel **TS1**
TS3t

179.29 so ... technique] **TS3r**–
more than any other **TS1**
TS3t

[*TS2 is extant from
'rendered' (179.30)*]

179.29–30 has rendered] **TS3**– had
seen and rendered
suggested **TS1** seen and
rendered **TS2t** rendered
TS2r

179.30a imaginative] **TS2**– an
imaginative **TS1**

179.30b insight] **TS1r**– precision
TS1t

179.30–33 These ... landscape.]
TS2r– And there is
nothing more faithful to
visual impressions can be
imagined than those little
landscapes full of light
and vigour. We see in
them the sincerity of the
artist reaching the soul
that is in things. **TS1**
Nothing more faithful to
visual impressions could
be created than these

little landscapes full of
light and vigour. **TS2t**

179.30c   These] **TS3**– VAR **TS1**
TS2t Those little **TS2r**

179.34   Corsica] **TS2**– Corsica
which may be considered
here as the opportunity
for an artist to express his
very subtle and most
sympathetic
understanding **TS1**

180.1   the deeper] **TS2r**– a
deeper **TS1 TS2t**

180.1–2   sense ... love] **TS2r**– sense
TS1 sense and pathos
TS2t

180.2   emotions] **TS2**– mere
emotions **TS1**
[*TS1 concludes with*
'worthy appreciation'
(180.3)]

180.4   had perceived] **TS2r**– can
so catch **TS2t**

180.5   render] **TS2r**– catch **TS2t**

180.7   to respond ... to] **TS2r**–
Looking at these pictures
one feels **TS2t**

180.9–10   unanalysable ... appeal.]
TS2r– unanalysable. In
the Corsican pictures it is
possible to see the efforts
of her creative gift, but in
the Irish pictures there is
no effort. They are a
spontaneous production
and, like the song of a
bird, have a natural
fidelity that no
self-conscious striving
could catch. **TS2t**

EMENDATIONS OF ACCIDENTALS

This list records the present edition's emendations of the accidentals of the copy-texts. A separate list records emendations of substantives.

The purpose of this list is not to provide a history of some particular readings in the texts collated, but to report the alterations made by the present editors to the punctuation and word forms of each copy-text and to record the earliest source for the emendation, whether one of the collated texts or the editors of the Cambridge Edition text.

Earlier texts may be assumed to agree, for present purposes, with the copy-text's reading in the absence of a statement to the contrary; if such a text offers a viable alternative to the adopted form, its rejected reading is reported in a separate line together with identifying siglum. Thus the list ordinarily does not record the typewriting errors found in copy-texts and rejected by Conrad while 'correcting' their texts. It should likewise be noted that cases can arise where the pick-up word in the copy-text is not shared by the historical source; for instance, in the following report, 'morning;] **MS**~∧' (24.12), the swung dash stands for a substantive and allows reference to the copy-text, whereas MS, in fact, reads 'day;', the semi-colon being restored to the critical text, but the wording superseded by authorial revision.

As stated in the headnote to the list recording emendations and variation in substantives, formal conventions of the documents are, as such, ignored (Conrad's signatures, serial bylines, editorial headings, in-text divisions and instalment statements), and ignored as well are changes in features of typography and styling, although such elements may occasionally appear in entries noting other alterations.

Likewise not reported here are corrections of impossible word forms and other obvious errors in the preprint texts, as when, for example, Conrad wrote 'renounciation' or 'irrevererent', or when a typist produced 'emake' or 'perople'. Unambiguous typographical errors (e.g., 'waher' for 'water') in the copy-text go unreported, and also not reported are certain categories of emendation discussed in 'The Texts: An Essay'.

Reports on manuscripts are based on their final readings, as are those on typescripts for which no earlier texts survive. Reports on all typescript texts ignore both part-words generated by false starts at the ends of lines (when they do not involve whole words or possible affixes) and characters x-ed out by the typist.

In each entry below, the reading of the Cambridge Edition text appears immediately after the page–line citation. It is followed by a square bracket, then by a siglum identifying the text in which the emendation first occurs, and then by the rejected reading of the copy-text, which concludes the main statement. When appropriate, reports on alternative readings in intermediate texts follow in the next line.

The following symbols are used in the reports below:

E D   a reading is adopted for the first time in this edition; that is, it is not present in the texts collated

~   the swung dash represents the same word as appears before the bracket; it occurs in records of variants in punctuation or other accidentals associated with that word, when the word itself is not the variant being noted

∧   the inferior caret signals the absence of punctuation.

The en-rule and other conventions of notation conform to those followed in the 'Emendation and Variation' list and explained in its headnote.

Listed in sequence below the headings for *Last Essays* and the uncollected essays are the collated texts relevant to the emendations adopted as well as the sigla used to represent them; those for the following are not repeated because they are uniform throughout:

E1 first English edition (Dent, 1926)
A1 first American edition (Doubleday, 1926)

LAST ESSAYS

GEOGRAPHY AND SOME EXPLORERS

MS	holograph manuscript (Yale)
TS1	typescript (Yale)
TS1r	revised text of **TS1** (incorporating Conrad's alterations): copy-text
TS2	ribbon-copy typescript (Berg)
TS2t	typewritten (unrevised) text of **TS2** superseded by revision
TS2r	revised text of **TS2** (incorporating Conrad's alterations)
TS2c	carbon-copy typescript (Berg) [*page 4 ribbon-copy*: 4.37–5.22: 'certainly royal' *to* 'nations is']
TS2ct	typewritten (unrevised) text of **TS2c**
TS2ce	altered text of **TS2c** with Conrad's alterations in **TS2r** copied in by another hand
P	*Geography and Some Explorers* (John Strangeways & Sons, January 1924)
SE	*Countries of the World*, 1 (February 1924), xviii–xxviii
SA	*National Geographic Magazine*, 45 (March 1924), 239–74

3.5	Geography] **MS** geography	4.23	order,] **TS2r** ~∧
3.5	Geometry] **MS** geometry	4.25	Geography] **MS** geography
3.13	man;] **TS2r** ~,	4.29	contumely,] **TS2r** ~.
3.16	campfire] **MS** camp fire	4.31	upon,] **TS2r** ~∧
		4.39	at least,] **TS2r** ~ ~∧
3.19	interesting,] **TS2r** ~∧	5.1	yet, as ever,] **TS2r** ~∧ ~ ~∧
3.20	advantage,] **TS2r** ~∧		
3.21	play,] **TS2r** ~∧	5.4	round,] **TS2r** ~∧
3.25	Geography] **MS** geography	5.18	Conquerors] **TS2r** conqueror [*sic*]
3.31	Geography] **MS** geography	5.22	territories,] **TS2t** ~∧
		5.28	Balboa,] **TS2t** ~∧
3.35	knowledge.] **TS2t** ~,	5.34	glance∧] **TS2r** glance,
4.12	Kingdoms] **MS** kingdoms	6.2–3	gulf∧pacific∧] **MS** ~, ~,
		6.17	churches,] **TS2r** churchs∧ [*sic*]
4.22	Yet,] **TS2r** ~∧		

THE *TORRENS*
A PERSONAL TRIBUTE

MS	holograph manuscript (Yale)
TSc	carbon-copy typescript (Boston)
TSct	typewritten (unrevised) text of **TSc** superseded by revision
TScr	revised text of **TSc** (incorporating Conrad's alterations): copy-text
SE	*Blue Peter*, 3 (October 1923), 251–4
SA	*Collier's*, 27 October 1923, p. 8
P	*The Torrens: A Personal Tribute* (F. A. Hook, 1923)

18.15	wool-clippers –] **SE** wool-clippers_∧	21.24	stepped,] **ED** ~_∧
		22.1	me_∧] **MS** ~,
19.6	sea-sense] **MS** sea sense	22.5	prove_∧] **MS** ~,
19.27	yet! . . .] **SE** ~!..	22.8	¶ But] **MS** But
20.12	himself. Though] **SE** ~ though	22.13	¶ Mr] **MS** Mr
20.26	bear_∧] **MS** ~,	22.15	Wonderful] **MS** wonderful
20.38	overfurnished] **MS** over furnished	22.19	Conrad_∧] **MS** ~,
21.2	Not half_∧] **SE** ~ ~.	22.19	chief officer] **MS** Chief Officer
21.2	– in] **SE** _∧In	22.34	reverence.] **ED** ~;
21.12	success.] **MS** ~,	22.38	winds,] **SE** ~_∧
21.20	is_∧] **MS** ~,	22.39	swift,] **SE** ~_∧
21.21	1893, when] **SE** ~. When		

CHRISTMAS-DAY AT SEA

MS	holograph manuscript (HRC)
TS1	typescript (HRC)
TS1t	typewritten (unrevised) text of **TS1** superseded by revision
TS1r	revised text of **TS1** (incorporating Conrad's alterations): copy-text
TS2	typescript (HRC)
TS2t	typewritten (unrevised) text of **TS2** superseded by revision
TS2r	revised text of **TS2** (incorporating Conrad's alterations)
TS3c	carbon-copy typescript (TTU)
TS3ct	typewritten (unrevised) text of **TS3c** superseded by revision
TS3cr	revised text of **TS3c** (incorporating Conrad's alterations)
SA	*Delineator*, December 1923, p. 10
SEp1	*Daily Mail* galley-proofs (HRC)
SEp1u	unrevised text of **SEp1**
SEp1r	revised text of **SEp1** (incorporating Conrad's alterations)
SEp2	*Daily Mail* galley-proofs (TTU)
SEp2u	unrevised text of **SEp2**
SEp2r	revised text of **SEp2** (incorporating Conrad's alterations)
SE	*Daily Mail*, 24 December 1923, p. 4

23.1	Christmas-day] **MS**	25.10	fro∧] **MS** ~,
	Christmas Day	25.11	water-hills∧] **MS**
23.3	Christmas-day] **MS**		water-hills,
	Christmas Day	25.16	captain∧] **MS** ~,
23.6	steadily. Perhaps] **MS** ~,	25.16	way∧] **MS** ~,
	perhaps	25.17	poop-ladder] **TS2r** poop
23.7	littleness (for] **MS** ~, ~		ladder
23.7	blame)] **MS** ~∧	25.19	surprised,] **TS2t** ~∧
23.10	plum puddings] **MS**	25.20	sir,] **TS2t** ~∧
	plum- | puddings	25.24	stairs.] **MS** ~∧
23.12	weak, distinctly] **ED** ~∧~	25.27	*Bulletins*∧] **MS** ~,
23.21	¶ One] **TS2r** One	26.1	was:] **SE1pr** ~∧
23.32	Season's Greetings] **MS**	26.1	"Alaska" –] **SE1pr** "~"∧
	season's greetings	26.1	New Bedford –] **SE1pr** ~
23.33	¶ It] **MS** It		~;
24.5	whistle. Her] **MS** ~, ~	26.2	Honolulu –] **SE1pr** ~∧
24.6	noise.] **ED** ~,	26.4	¶ We] **SE1pr** We
24.6	But] **MS** but	26.4	passed,] **TS2r** ~∧
24.10	imagined;] **TS2r** ~.	26.4	slowly,] **TS2r** ~∧
24.12	morning;] **MS** ~∧	26.6	aloft,] **TS2r** ~∧
24.23	Dead-Sea] **MS** Dead Sea	26.7	stern,] **MS** ~∧
24.30	Dead-Sea] **MS** Dead Sea	26.9	day. We] **TS2t** ~∧we
24.32	1879∧] **MS** ~,	26.15	southern] **MS** Southern
24.37	day break] **MS** daybreak	26.21	reported∧] **MS** ~,
24.39	Ocean] **SEp1** ocean	26.22	"fish"] **MS** ∧~∧
25.10	matches∧] **MS** ~,	26.30	be –] **MS** ~:
25.10	down∧] **MS** ~,	26.31	hotel∧] **TS2r** ~,

OCEAN TRAVEL

MS	holograph manuscript, final text (HRC): copy-text
S	*Evening News*, 15 May 1923, p. 4

27.25	man∧] **S** ~,	29.6	them.] **S** ~∧
28.2	Atlantic] **S** atlantic	29.20	steering.] **S** ~∧
29.1	mornings∧ (and] **S** ~, (~	29.22	seaman's] **S** seamans

LEGENDS

MS	manuscript (Morgan): copy-text
SE	*Daily Mail*, 15 August 1924, p. 8
SA	*New York Times Magazine*, 7 September 1924, pp. 1–2

34.11	decorative).] **SE** ~∧.	34.18	if∧] **SE** ~,
34.17	train,] **E1** ~∧	34.24	story.] **SE** ~∧

34.26	miracles,] **SA** ~∧	35.31	Lubbock] **SE** Lubock
35.9	it,] **SE** ~∧	35.36	C.] **SE** ~∧
35.14	sea-gods,] **SE** sea-gods∧	36.24	Marco-Polo's] **SE**
35.30	decadence.] **SE** ~∧		Marco-Polos

THE UNLIGHTED COAST

MS   holograph manuscript, final text (Private collection)
TS   typescript (Colgate)
  TSt   typewritten (unrevised) text of **TS** superseded by revision
  TSr   revised text of **TSt** (incorporating Conrad's alterations): copy-text
S   *The Times*, 18 August 1925, pp. 13–14

37.23	heaven] **MS** Heaven	40.15	Zeppelin-strafer.] **S**
37.26	calm air∧] **S**~ ~,		Zeppelin-strafer∧
37.26	night,] **S**~∧	40.16	*that*] **MS** that
38.1	For,] **MS** ~∧	40.24	temperaments,] **S**~∧
38.6	messages∧] **S**~,	40.29	friend,] **MS**~∧
38.7	wireless] **MS** Wireless	40.40	tho'.] **S** ~∧
38.12	said:] **S**~.	41.10	gun∧] **S** ~,
38.20	decode] **MS** de-code	41.38	judgment] **MS** judgement
39.11	judgment] **MS** judgement	42.10	now,] **S** ~∧
39.14	force,] **S**~∧	42.12	fortitude∧] **MS**~,
39.17	RNR] **MS** R. N. R [*sic*]	42.15	then,] **S**~∧
39.17	naval officers] **MS** Naval	42.15	said,] **S**~∧
	Officers	42.18	know,] **S**~∧
39.22	capacity,] **MS** ~∧	43.1	instantly,] **S**~∧
40.2	shedlike] **MS** shed-like	43.10	sick,] **S**~∧
40.8	watch,] **S** ~∧	43.11	*looked*] **MS** looked
40.9	figure,] **S** ~∧	43.11	indeed,] **S**~∧
40.10	R. N. R.] **S** ~. ~. ~∧	43.20	place,] **S**~∧
		43.34	choice,] **S**~∧

THE DOVER PATROL

MS   holograph leaf, final text (Yale): 44.11–17 ('The story' *to* 'war too.')
TS1   draft typescript with holograph addition, 1 page (Yale)
  TS1t   typewritten text of **TS1**: 47.31–36 ('mostly fisher' *to* 'in them.')
  TS1r   revised text of **TS1** (incorporating Conrad's alterations)
  TS1h   holograph addition to **TS1**: 47.37–48.6 ('They were' *to* 'country')
TS2   typescript (BL)
  TS2r   revised text of **TS2** (incorporating Conrad's alterations): copy-text
S   *The Times*, 27 July 1921, pp. 11–12
P   *The Dover Patrol* (H. J. Goulden, 1922)

44.13	great war] **MS** Great War	46.27	were inadequate,] **E D** ~
44.16–17	great war] **MS** Great War		~_∧
45.20	¶ Amongst] **S** Amongst	47.16	work,] **S** ~_∧
45.33	end,] **S**~_∧	48.6	country,] **S**~_∧
46.18	globe,] **S**~_∧	48.38	front,] **S**~_∧
46.25	blamed,] **S** ~ –		

MEMORANDUM

TS1	typescript (BL)
TS1t	typewritten (unrevised) text of **TS1** superseded by revision
TS1r	revised text of **TS1** (incorporating Conrad's alterations): copy-text
TS2	typescript (Private collection)
TS2t	revised text of **TS2** superseded by revision
TS2r	revised text of **TS2t** (incorporating Conrad's alterations)

50.3	*perfecting*] **TS2r** perfecting	55.10	live-stock] **E D** live | stock
		55.15	cargo,] **TS2t** ~_∧
50.8	*perfect*] **TS2r** perfect	55.16	all;] **TS2r** ~,
50.16	Horn,] **E D** ~_∧	55.26	*Torrens,*] **TS2r** ~_∧
51.3	tons,] **TS2r** ~_∧	55.26	candles,] **TS2r** ~_∧
52.10	"*perfect*] **TS2r** _∧~	55.28	above,] **TS2r** ~_∧
52.11	fleets,"] **TS2r** ~,_∧	55.29	them,] **TS2r** ~_∧
52.13	ship_∧] **E1** ~,	56.16	health,] **TS2r** ~_∧
52.13	do),] **TS2t** ~)_∧	57.3	be, I imagine,] **TS2t** ~_∧~ ~_∧
52.20	pride,] **TS2t** ~_∧		
52.24	passages_∧] **E1** ~,	57.21	*three*] **TS2r** three
52.36	ship_∧] **TS2t** ~,	58.16	her,] **TS2t** ~_∧
53.14	anchors,] **E1** ~_∧	58.18–19	tackle-falls] **TS2r** tackle falls
53.17	man-power] **E1** man power	58.24	had,] **TS2r** ~_∧
53.22	of,] **TS2t** ~_∧	59.2	way,] **TS2r** ~_∧
53.29	Thirdly,] **TS2t** ~_∧	59.3	Davits] **E1** davits
54.7	twelve-months'] **TS2t** twelve-month's	59.15	Islands_∧] **E1** ~,
		59.16	bound),] **E1** ~)_∧
55.4	*Macquarie*] **E D** Macquarrie		

THE LOSS OF THE *DALGONAR*

TS	partial facsimile: Edgar H. Wells Catalogue (1925), item 79, p. 3 only: 62.31–63.4 ('I can not' *to* 'event!') and 63.32–37 ('put on' *to* 'Conrad.')
TS1t	typescript text (facsimile) of **TS1** superseded by revision
TS1r	revised text with holograph insertion (facsimile) of **TS1** (incorporating Conrad's alterations)
S	*London Mercury*, 5 (December 1921), 187: copy-text

| 62.32 | not∧ however∧] **TS** ~, ~, | 63.2 | 1 ¹/₂] **TS** one and a half |
| 62.33 | afterwards∧] **TS** ~, | 63.3 | 2] **TS** two |

TRAVEL
PREFACE TO RICHARD CURLE'S
INTO THE EAST

TS1	typescript (Yale)
TS1r	revised text of **TS1** (incorporating Conrad's alterations): copy-text
TS2	typescript (Rosenbach)
TS2t	typewritten text (unrevised) of **TS2** superseded by revision
TS2r	revised text of **TS2** (incorporating Conrad's alterations)
P	*Travel. A Preface to 'Into the East: Notes on Burma and Malaya'* (R. & R. Clark, December 1922)
C	Richard Curle, *Into the East: Notes on Burma and Malaya* (Macmillan, 1923)

64.20	...!] **P** ..!	67.34	of, say,] **TS2r** ~∧ ~∧
65.25	for∧] **TS2r** ~,	67.34	miles,] **TS2r** ~∧
65.28	*cabinets de lecture*] **TS2r** cabinets de lecture	67.39	simply-worded,] **TS2r** simply worded∧
65.32	Women,] **TS2r** ~∧	68.10	cannibal-tribes] **TS2r** cannibal tribes
65.35	*World,*] **TS2r** ~∧		
65.37	remarks,] **TS2t** ~∧	68.13	chatter,] **TS2r** ~∧
65.39	seriousness,] **TS2r** ~∧	68.15	that,] **TS2r** ~∧
66.5	rest,] **TS2r** ~∧	68.16	mystery,] **TS2r** ~∧
66.10	sportsmen,] **TS2r** ~∧	68.16	substitute,] **TS2r** ~∧
66.15	half-apologetic] **P** half apologetic	68.27	importance,] **TS2r** ~∧
		69.3	gods,] **TS2t** ~∧
66.20	regulations;] **TS2r** ~∧	69.21	subjects,] **TS2r** ~∧
66.23	primitive∧] **TS2r** ~,	70.7	him,] **TS2r** ~∧
66.25	antelope∧] **TS2r** ~,	70.8	steamer,] **TS2r** ~∧
66.28	travel,] **TS2r** ~∧	70.18	tales; a] **P** ~. A
66.32	behind,] **TS2r** ~∧	70.19	day,] **TS2r** ~∧
66.37	jaunty;] **TS2r** ~,	70.19	tracks,] **TS2r** ~∧
66.38	tears;] **TS2r** ~,	70.20	on,] **TS2r** ~∧
67.6	stare,] **TS2r** ~∧	70.20	sensitive,] **TS2t** ~∧
67.30	had),] **TS2t** ~)∧	70.23	transition,] **TS2t** ~∧

STEPHEN CRANE
INTRODUCTION TO THOMAS BEER'S
STEPHEN CRANE

MS	holograph manuscript, final text (Virginia)
TS	typescript (Yale-S)
TSt	typewritten uncorrected text of **TS** (printer's copy) superseded by revision

TSe	altered text of **TS** (incorporating Conrad's alterations in unidentified hand): copy-text pp. 1–3 ['Introduction' *to* 'far only']: 71.2–73.11
CAp	galley-proofs, partial (pp. 2–9) ['about myself' *to* 'Joseph.'"] 73.11–89.30: Thomas Beer, *Stephen Crane: A Study in American Letters* (Knopf, 1923) (Yale-S)
CApu	unrevised galley-proofs
CApr	revised galley-proofs (incorporating Conrad's alterations): copy-text: 73.11–89.30
CA	Thomas Beer, *Stephen Crane: A Study in American Letters* (Knopf, 1923), pp. 1–33
CE	Thomas Beer, *Stephen Crane: A Study in American Letters* (Heinemann, 1924), pp. 1–35

73.9	the] **MS** *The*	81.31	gravity$_\wedge$] **MS** ~,
73.15	dates:] **MS** ~,	82.4	Arctic] **MS** arctic
75.9	"unique] **MS** $_\wedge$~	82.31	eye$_\wedge$] **MS** ~,
75.9	faculty"] **MS** ~$_\wedge$ [*n.*]	83.3	park] **MS** Park
75.9	Garnett] **MS** Garnet	83.37	December] **MS** Dec.,
76.11	recognisably] **MS** recognizably	84.32	"dunned"] **MS** $_\wedge$~$_\wedge$
76.38	now." It] **ED** ~," it	85.12	smiles$_\wedge$] **MS** ~,
77.12	*The*] **MS** the	85.20	legend$_\wedge$] **MS** ~,
77.16	general] **MS** General	86.26	March$_\wedge$] **MS** ~.
77.21–22	three-hour-old] **E1** three-hour old	86.35	*must*] **MS** must
78.10	contradistinction] **MS** contra-distinction	87.3	neighbourhood] **MS** neighborhood
78.28	mantlepiece [*sic*]] **MS** mantel-piece	87.29	ride. (A] **MS** ~, (~
		87.29	touch.)] **ED** ~).
79.12	Street] **MS** street	88.31	6.40] **MS** "six forty"
79.32	gods] **MS** Gods	89.13	"The Predecessor"$_\wedge$] **MS** ~,
80.29	post-card] **MS** postcard	89.15	predecessor] **MS** Predecessor

HIS WAR-BOOK
INTRODUCTION TO STEPHEN CRANE'S
THE RED BADGE OF COURAGE

MS	holograph manuscript, final text (BL)
TS	typescript (Dartmouth)
TSt	typewritten (unrevised) text of **TS** superseded by revision
TSr	revised text of **TSt** (incorporating Conrad's alterations): copy-text
C	Stephen Crane, *The Red Badge of Courage* (Heinemann, 1925), pp. 5–12

90.1	War-book] **MS** War Book	90.34	criticism$_\wedge$] **MS** ~,
90.17	us –] **MS** ~;	91.3	interesting$_\wedge$] **MS** ~,
90.18	consternation$_\wedge$] **MS** ~,	91.4	Wyndham –] **MS** ~,
90.19	one$_\wedge$] **C** ~,	91.7	*Mémoires*] **A1** *Memoires*
90.33	words$_\wedge$ and] **MS** ~, ~	91.7	Marbot$_\wedge$] **MS** ~,

91.12	battle,] MS ~∧	92.39	"A] ED ∧~
91.13	heaven given] MS	92.39	mind."] MS ~.∧
	heaven-given	93.1	Lord!] C ~,
91.17	sound,] ED ~∧	93.3	¶ This] MS This
91.19	Crane∧] MS ~,	93.4	itself.] C ~ –
91.21	that∧] MS ~,	93.6	battle, and] MS ~. And
91.23	battlefield∧] MS ~,	93.8	∧In] ED ¶ In
91.36	it,] ED ~∧	93.12	danger∧] MS ~,
91.37	"vast] MS ∧~	93.14	gods] MS Gods
91.38	demonstration."] MS ~.∧	93.20	artist,] MS ~∧
92.12	¶ The] MS The	93.22	impressionist∧] MS ~,
92.15	Tall Soldier's] C tall	93.23	way∧] MS ~,
	soldier's	93.26	war-book] MS war book
92.17	it∧] MS ~,	93.30	matter –] MS~,
92.18	is. Neither] MS ~, neither	94.1	great death,] C Great
92.19	Young Soldier] C young		Death∧
	soldier	94.1	that, after all,] C ~∧ ~ ~∧
92.25	months∧] MS ~,	94.2	great death] C Great
92.25	∧of] MS "~		Death
92.25	"a] MS ∧~	94.15	book –] MS ~∧
92.36	death∧] MS ~,	94.17	battle∧] ED ~ –
92.39	know:] MS ~.		

JOHN GALSWORTHY
AN APPRECIATION

S	*Outlook*, 17 (31 March 1906), 449–50: copy-text
Ep	Heinemann galley-proofs (Indiana)
Epu	uncorrected Heinemann galley-proofs
Epe	corrected Heinemann galley-proofs (corrections in another hand)
Pp	pamphlet page-proofs (Colgate)
Ppu	unrevised pamphlet page-proofs
Ppr	revised pamphlet page-proofs (title-page only revised by Conrad)
P1	*John Galsworthy* (H. J. Goulden, 1922), 1st printing
P2	*John Galsworthy* (H. J. Goulden, 1922), 2nd printing

95.6	Aunt] Epu aunt

A GLANCE AT TWO BOOKS

TS	typescript (Colgate)
TSt	typewritten (unrevised) text of TS superseded by revision
TSr	revised text of TS (incorporating Conrad's alterations): copy-text
SE	*T. P.'s & Cassell's Weekly*, 1 August 1925, pp. 475, 494
SA	*Forum*, 74 (August 1925), 308–10

101.10	deed,] **SE** ~∧	103.20	faithful,] **SE** ~∧
101.15	exclaim:] **SE** ~;	103.26	whisper,] **E D** ~∧
101.18	lyrically∧] **SE** ~;	103.34	delivered,] **SE** ~∧
101.19	moods:∧] **SE** ~: –	103.34	foot,] **SE** ~∧
101.29	B.] **SE** ~∧	104.14	phrasing,] **SE** ~∧
102.2	not,] **E D** ~∧	104.17	tender, is tranquil,] **SE**
102.9	Thackeray, we imagine,]		~∧ ~ ~∧
	SE ~∧ ~ ~∧	104.27	Now,] **E D** ~∧
102.11	was,] **SE** ~∧	104.28	spider,] **E D** ~∧
102.22	II∧] **E D** 2.	104.29	legs,] **E D** ~∧
102.26	one,] **SE** ~∧	104.29	on to] **SE** onto
102.26	*Pharisees*,] **SE** ~∧	104.30	colour∧] **E D** ~,
102.27	novel;] **E D** ~:	104.30	black∧] **E D** ~,
102.31	*The*] **SA** the	104.30	it,] **E D** ~;
102.32–33	Why is] **SE** why ~	104.39	It] **SE** it
103.6	Shelton –] **E D** ~,	105.4	men∧] **E D** ~,
103.20	errant,] **SE** ~∧		

PREFACE TO *THE SHORTER TALES OF JOSEPH CONRAD*

MS   holograph manuscript, final text (Yale)
TS1   typescript (Yale)
   TS1t   typewritten (unrevised) text of **TS1** superseded by revision
   TS1r   revised text of **TS1** (incorporating Conrad's alterations)
TS2   typescript (Dartmouth)
   TS2t   typewritten (unrevised) text of **TS2** superseded by revision
   TS2r   revised text of **TS2** (incorporating Conrad's alterations): copy-text
TS2c   carbon-copy typescript (Yale) of **TS2**
   TS2ct   typewritten (unrevised) carbon-copy text of **TS2**
   TS2cr   revised text of **TS2** (incorporating Conrad's alterations)
TS3   typescript (Berg)
   TS3t   typewritten (unrevised) transcription of **TS3** superseded by alteration
   TS3e   revised text of **TS3** (incorporating Conrad's alterations in **TS2r** in an unidentified hand)
C   Preface to *The Shorter Tales of Joseph Conrad* (Doubleday, 1924), pp. v–xii

109.30	paper-boats] **MS** paper boats	111.1	view∧ (that] **TS3e** ~, (~
		111.19	typhoon] **TS2t** Typhoon
109.32	vast:–] **E D** ~;–	111.20	MacWhirr] **E D** McWhirr
109.38	paper-boats] **MS** paper boats		

THE FUTURE OF CONSTANTINOPLE

S   *The Times*, 7 November 1912, p. 5: copy-text for letter
A1   *Last Essays* (Doubleday, 1926), pp. 149–54: copy-text for essay

116.8	Bosporus] **ED** Bosphorus	118.21	Bosporus] **ED** Bosphorus
116.31	Bosporus] **ED** Bosphorus	118.27	Bosporus] **ED** Bosphorus
117.3	peninsula] **ED** Peninsula		

APPENDICES

APPENDIX A

RICHARD CURLE'S INTRODUCTIONS TO
LAST ESSAYS AND 'THE CONGO DIARY'

INTRODUCTION TO *LAST ESSAYS*

Richard Curle's Introduction to the English and American first editions of *Last Essays* is reprinted below. The first English edition text serves as copy-text. A signed note by Curle in George T. Keating's copy of the volume (Yale) explains the circumstances of writing: 'I wrote this introduction on board the S/S *Mauretania* on my way to New York in October, 1925. Most of these garnered essays were, if I remember rightly, printed from copies in my own collection; at least a number were. Richard Curle, July 1928'. The Introduction, which serves mainly to indicate the place and date of the original publication of Conrad's essays, was composed between the SS *Mauretania*'s departure from Southampton on 3 October 1925 and her arrival in New York on the 9th.[1] Nothing is known of arrangements for its typing and printing, but Curle, a man of long experience in publishing, is sure to have carefully supervised production.

The version in A1 is styled for its American audience: on two occasions *The Times* was altered to 'the London *Times*' and *The Daily Mail* to 'the London *Daily Mail*'. Dates adopt American styling (for example, 'November 2, 1891' for E1's '2 November, 1891' and 'October, 1925' for 'October 1925'), and 'Laurence' was even changed to 'Lawrence'. On balance, A1 has the correct phrase 'saw the light', the definite article being dropped out during E1's setting (or missing in the setting-copy typescript).

More significantly, a handful of verbal variants suggest that the two publishers received slightly different versions of the piece, or that Curle took the opportunity to make some last-minute changes in E1 proofs, these not being communicated to Doubleday. The changes are not the kind made by an editor, and represent verbal tinkering and polishing.[2]

---

[1] List of Passengers Leaving the United Kingdom, 1890–1960, BT27/1107/8, National Archives; arrival in 'Shipping and Mails', *New York Times*, 10 October 1925, p. 31.

[2] Listed here are some of the most interesting differences, the reading found in E1 appearing before the bracket and that in A1 after it: warm regard] warm affection; written in 1904. Composed] done in 1904. Written; at the wish] at the instigation; Some years before he died] A few years before he died; a few copies] about fifty copies; keen historical imagination] impressive historical sense; towards the end of this book] at the end of this book.

The text is that as originally printed in E1 save that decorative capitals are treated as they are throughout the present edition (see 'The Texts', p. 202), and the full stop after the closing signature is omitted. Two further cosmetic alterations, indifferent matters of house-style, raise lower to upper case in the initial word of the subtitles 'A Personal Tribute' and 'A Study in American Letters'.

INTRODUCTION

Most of the contents of this volume were written subsequent to the publication of *Notes on Life and Letters* in 1921, and these two books together may be said to contain practically all Conrad's miscellaneous writings. There are, it is true, a few short prefaces and some interesting letters to newspapers which might have been included here, but they are of no particular importance, and the twenty separate pieces gathered between these covers are indeed the last essays of Joseph Conrad. But there remains a chance that some of his early essays and reviews may still rest undiscovered in the files of old newspapers and weeklies. Conrad had a very uncertain memory for his own work, and I recall that when the material for *Notes on Life and Letters* was being collected, he was frequently quite vague as to what he had written and where it had appeared. In proof of this, it may be mentioned that the essay entitled "John Galsworthy" in this volume was only omitted from the previous one through Conrad's forgetfulness of its existence. Therefore, as I say, discoveries may yet be made.

In the latter years of his life Conrad occasionally found relief from the toil and exhaustion of more creative work in the writing of reminiscent essays, and some of these rank, decidedly, among his finest efforts in this direction. *Last Essays* is just as remarkable a book as *Notes on Life and Letters*; it contains passages of extraordinary charm, serenity and eloquence. And particular care has been taken to avoid any aspect of absolute completeness, as though a dead author's desk had been ransacked for every fragment. All the articles included in this volume have been included for very definite reasons. Nothing has been printed merely for the purpose of adding to the bulk.

For some time Conrad had had the idea of writing a pendent volume to *The Mirror of the Sea*, and the unfinished article, "Legends," on which he was at work the day before he died, was, he told me, to have formed part of such a book. And I suspect that "The *Torrens*," "Christmas Day at Sea," "Ocean Travel," "Outside Literature," and part, at least, of "Geography and Some Explorers," would also have been incorporated into this book, and therefore I have placed them all together at the beginning of the volume. They form, as it were, the shadowy nucleus of a projected work.

"Geography and Some Explorers," the second longest essay in this collection, was written as a general introduction to a serial publication called *Countries of the World*. It appeared as "The Romance of Travel" in the first number, February 1924, and was reprinted under its proper title in *The National Geographic Magazine*, March 1924. In this fascinating essay Conrad, after discussing the feats of some of the early navigators and explorers, gives a memorable account of a passage he made in 1888 (when in command of the *Otago*) through the Torres Straits on a voyage from Sydney to Mauritius.

"The *Torrens*: A Personal Tribute," was published in *The Blue Peter* in October 1923. In the early 'nineties Conrad had been chief officer of this ship – he joined her on 2 November, 1891, and left her on 15 October, 1893 – and he made two journeys from England to Australia and back in that capacity. For her he always retained a warm regard, and when, in the September *Blue Peter* of 1923, there was issued a coloured illustration of the *Torrens*, he willingly consented to give a personal remembrance of her in the next number. The last words, in which he describes her end upon the shores of the Mediterranean, possess a rare and pensive beauty, which I recover in this following paragraph:

But in the end her body of iron and wood, so fair to look upon, had to be broken up – I hope with fitting reverence; and as I sit here, thirty years almost to a day since I last set eyes on her, I love to think that her perfect form found a merciful end on the shores of the sunlit sea of my boyhood's dreams, and that her fine spirit has returned to dwell in the regions of the great winds, the inspirers and the companions of her swift, renowned, sea-tossed life, which I, too, have been permitted to share for a little while.

"Christmas Day at Sea" was published in *The Daily Mail* on 24 December, 1923. It is concerned largely with an episode on one Christmas Day during Conrad's first voyage to Australia in the *Duke of Sutherland* in 1879, where he served as an A. B.

"Ocean Travel" made its first appearance in the London *Evening News* of 15 May, 1923, where it was named "My Hotel in Mid-Atlantic." It was written during Conrad's voyage to America in the *Tuscania* in the spring of that year, and was posted to me the moment he arrived in New York. It compares the old and the new life at sea, and, needless to say, the vote of affection is given for the old.

"Outside Literature," a short essay dealing with the subject of notices to mariners, appeared under the title "Notices to Mariners" in *The Manchester Guardian* of 4 December, 1922, and under its proper title in the American *Bookman* of February 1923.

"Legends," as I have mentioned, was the last article Conrad ever wrote; it was left unfinished upon his desk. It tells, with a strain of melancholy, of the breed of seamen who have disappeared with the disappearance of sailing ships and was printed, less than a fortnight after Conrad's death, in *The Daily Mail* of 15 August, 1924.

Next follow two essays which have the war at sea as background. "The Unlighted Coast" recalls Conrad's experiences in the North Sea during his ten days' cruise in the *Ready* in 1917 – a full account of this cruise is to be found in Captain Sutherland's *At Sea with Joseph Conrad* – and was written for the Admiralty. For some reason or other they never used it, and it first saw light in *The Times* of 18 August, 1925.

"The Dover Patrol," written at the request of the late Lord Northcliffe, was published in *The Times* of 27 July, 1921, the day on which the Prince of Wales unveiled the Dover Patrol Memorial. It is a glowing tribute to "the physical endurance, the inborn seamanship, the matter-of-fact, industrious, indefatigable enthusiasm" of the men who guarded unsleepingly and at extreme hazard the entrance to the Channel.

The "Memorandum on the Scheme for fitting-out a Sailing Ship" is here first printed. Written in 1919 for the Holt Steamship Company, who had proposed to fit out a sailing ship for the training of boys destined for the Mercantile Marine, it is an example of Conrad's intense and practical interest in such subjects. It is exactly what it purports to be – a memorandum, precise, technical, full of his accumulated experience and long-pondered ideas. Nothing came of the scheme:

as Mr. Laurence Holt wrote to me, it was "abandoned owing to the depression of trade which set in soon after my conversation with Mr. Conrad." The document from then to now has been in Mr. Holt's possession and cordial thanks are due to him for his permission to use it here.

"The Loss of the *Dalgonar*" is a further example of Conrad's interest in questions of seamanship. Indeed, I print it solely for that reason, because in itself it but refers to the contents of an article from another pen. It appeared as a letter to the editor in *The London Mercury* of December 1921, and was called forth by a paper in the September number entitled "A True Story: Log and Record of the Wreck of the Ship *Dalgonar* of Liverpool, bound from Callao to Taltal." This paper described the wreck of the barque *Loire*, which happened in October 1913, and Conrad's letter, while correcting some obvious mistakes in the narrative as printed, is a testimony to the gallantry and efficiency of the officers and crew.

The essay called "Travel" was written, I am proud to think, out of friendship for myself, and formed the preface to a book by me, *Into the East: Notes on Burma and, Malaya*, 1923. The effort to finish *The Rover* held up the writing of this preface for about a year, but it seems to me that in its evocation of the great travellers of old and of times that have gone for ever, it reaches the highest beauty and distinction. Let me quote one paragraph:

And these things, which stand as if imperishable in the pages of old books of travel, are all blown away, have vanished as utterly as the smoke of the travellers' camp fires in the icy night air of the Gobi Desert, as the smell of incense burned in the temples of strange gods, as the voices of Asiatic statesmen speculating with the cruel wisdom of past ages on matters of peace and war.

"Stephen Crane," the longest and most elaborate essay in the book, was written as an introduction to Mr. Thomas Beer's *Stephen Crane, A Study in American Letters*, 1923. Conrad, as is generally known, was a close friend of Crane during the last years of that meteoric life, when Crane was frequently a neighbour of his in southern England. In all, Conrad wrote three essays on Crane and his work. One appeared in *Notes on Life and Letters*, two are printed in this volume, and all breathe a spirit of affectionate admiration. This essay is a study in biographical side-lights and is undoubtedly the most personal and the most delightful of all reminiscences of Crane.

The short essay, "His War Book," which follows, was composed specifically as a preface to a new edition of Crane's best-known work, *The Red Badge of Courage* – the new edition came out at last in 1925 – and it gives clear indication of Conrad's feeling for the artist who could observe so truly and create with such economy.

"John Galsworthy," as I have said, was only accidentally omitted from the previous volume of Conrad's essays. It was composed as a review of *A Man of Property*, contained in a wider study of the author, and was published in *The Outlook* of 31 March, 1906, under the title of "A Middle Class Family." Some years before he died Conrad rectified, as far as he could, his oversight by privately printing a few copies of this essay, and he would certainly have included it in any future volume of essays.

The next piece, "A Glance at Two Books," dealing with Galsworthy's *The Island Pharisees* and Hudson's *Green Mansions*, dates from even earlier and was written in 1904. Composed obviously in answer to an editorial request, it was, for reasons unknown, never used, and the typescript, being found among Conrad's papers, was first printed in *T. P.'s and Cassell's Weekly* of 1 August, 1925.

A "Preface to his Shorter Tales" was written at the wish of his American publishers to introduce *The Shorter Tales of Joseph Conrad*, and the essay, like the selection, has never appeared in England. It was one of his last completed pieces – the volume was issued after his death in 1924 – and it throws a reminiscent glance upon the ideas that animated his work and upon his writing life.

The little note, "Cookery," charming in its playful fancy, was written as a send-off to his wife's book, *A Handbook of Cookery for a Small House*, 1922. I include it here for the sake of its association and for the unique quality of its tone.

The next two pieces, both of them letters, give glimpses of Conrad's abiding interest in international questions and the affairs of Europe. He was always a student of foreign politics, a student fortified by a keen historical imagination and by a great knowledge of Continental problems throughout the centuries, and these two letters, with their combined eloquence and hold on reality, throw light upon an aspect of Conrad's mind of which few people are aware.

The first letter, an appeal for a free Constantinople under the protection of the Powers, was published in *The Times* of 7 November, 1912, when the Balkan States were at war with Turkey and their armies already within striking distance of the capital.

The second letter, written evidently a few days later to an untraceable correspondent – a typescript only was found – who had criticised his printed observations, is an amplification of the previous one.

Finally comes "The Congo Diary," a reprint of the diary kept by Conrad in the Congo in 1890, which was first published in *The Blue Peter*, October 1925, and then in *The Yale Review*, January 1926. This diary calls for its own introduction and a series of explanatory notes, and these will be found with it towards the end of this book.

Here, then, are the twenty pieces which form this volume of *Last Essays*. They show as clearly as did the contents of *Notes on Life and Letters* the rich diversity of Conrad's mind, his powers of cogent argument, of fond memory, and of noble expression. His mastery over his chosen material never flagged, and these essays are a last witness to his consummate gifts.

RICHARD CURLE

INTRODUCTION TO *THE CONGO DIARY*

Richard Curle's Introduction to 'The Congo Diary' is reprinted below, the first English edition of *Last Essays* serving as copy-text. The map referred to in it faced the first page of Curle's Introduction in E1 and bore the following caption: 'Rough map of the route followed by Joseph Conrad on his overland journey in the Belgian Congo, from Matadi to Nselemba, in 1890'. In A1, the map bore no caption and was interleaved in the Introduction. A1 Americanized date forms and some spellings (for example, 'southeast', 'footnotes' and 'tantalizing' for E1's 'south-east', 'footnotes' and 'tantalising', but the British form 'sceptical' stands). For 'The pages of Messrs Dent's ordinary edition of *Youth*' it substitutes 'The pages of The Concord Edition of "Youth"' and likewise altered is 'only four, 75–78' to 'only three, 70–72'.

In the present edition, a modern and redrawn version of the Congo map replaces Curle's (see Map 1).

The text printed below is that originally printed in E1 save that decorative capitals are treated as they are throughout the present edition, and the full stop after the closing signature is omitted.

INTRODUCTION

The diary kept by Joseph Conrad in the Congo in 1890, or such of it as has survived (for there is no saying whether there was more or not), is contained in two small black penny notebooks, and is written in pencil. One carries his initials, J. C. K. – Joseph Conrad Korzeniowski. The first entry is dated 13 June, 1890, but in the second notebook dates are practically discarded, and it is impossible to say when the last entry was made. And names of places, also, are practically discarded in the second notebook, while abounding in the first, so that, though we can see that the diary was begun at Matadi, we cannot discover where it was ended. The last place mentioned is Lulanga, far up the great sweep of the Congo River to the north of the Equator, but there remain some twenty-four pages of the diary beyond that entry in which no name whatsoever appears. It must, indeed, have been continued into the very heart of that immense darkness where the crisis of his story, *Heart of Darkness*, is unfolded. We know from *A Personal Record* that he reached ultimately somewhere to the neighbourhood of Stanley Falls; and Stanley Falls are farther from Lulanga than Lulanga is from Stanley Pool.

And it is in this same book that we can read how the Polish boy, when nine years of age, looking upon a map of Africa, had put his finger upon its unexplored centre, and had said to himself, "When I grow up I shall go *there*." Go there he did, and these notebooks are the first expression of his fulfilled resolve.

The map will enable the reader to plot out, with reasonable accuracy, the exact route followed by Conrad on his overland journey, from Matadi, which is about one hundred miles above the mouth of the Congo, to Nselemba, on or near the south-east corner of Stanley Pool – a distance of probably more than two hundred and fifty miles from Matadi – where it was that he joined the *Roi des Belges*, as second in command, for the up-river voyage. The places and streams alluded to on this overland journey have been given on the map in Conrad's own spelling, even where their names have been altered (unless beyond recognition, which may have happened in certain instances) in existing atlases, many of which have been examined, or can be only placed approximately, owing to their not being mentioned at all. The mapping of the Congo is not in a very advanced state, and, what with the paucity of the entries and the contradictory nature of the information, precise accuracy is not attainable. All the same, it is easy enough to trace the general line of his march, which lay much nearer the banks of the Congo than lies the railway which now runs between Matadi and Kinshasa on Stanley Pool.

The following is a reproduction of the first notebook alone – not, however, of the list of names, persons, books, stores, and the calculations that fill the last pages – consisting of thirty-two manuscript pages, not all of which are full, and twelve of which are further curtailed by Conrad's sectional drawings of the day's march. The given spelling and abbreviations have been adhered to throughout – they help to heighten its true flavour – but the paragraphing and the punctuation have been freely altered.

I may mention that these two notebooks are now preserved in the library of Harvard University, and that when I was in America in 1925 I saw them again in their new and permanent home and checked the text once more.

As to the appended foot-notes, their chief purpose has been to show how closely some of the earlier pages of *Heart of Darkness* are a recollection of Conrad's own Congo journey. This story was serialised in *Blackwood's Magazine* between February and April 1899, and I remember Conrad telling me that its 40,000 words occupied only about a month in writing.

When we consider the painful, slow labour with which he usually composed, we can perceive how intensely vivid his memories of this experience must have been, and, to judge from the parallel passages, how intensely actual. But then the notebook only goes to prove the almost self-evident contention that much of Conrad's work is founded upon autobiographical remembrance. Conrad himself wrote of this story in his Author's Note to the new edition of the *Youth* volume in which it appeared: "*Heart of Darkness* is quite as authentic in fundamentals as *Youth*... it is experience pushed a little (and only a little) beyond the actual facts of the case." If only he had kept a diary of his meeting and association with Kurtz!

The pages of Messrs. Dent's ordinary edition of *Youth* – the edition always referred to in the notes – which bear direct reference to the first volume of the diary, are only four, 75–78, but in these few pages there are an astonishing number of touches strongly reminiscent of the diary. One would argue, indeed, that he must have consulted the diary when writing the story, but Mrs. Conrad assures me that it was not so. Twice had she saved it from the waste-paper basket, and probably by the time *Heart of Darkness* came to be written, Conrad had forgotten all about it, or did not dream that it had survived. He never spoke to me of it, and I never heard of its existence until after his death.

The second notebook, which is an entirely technical account of Congo navigation, written, no doubt, in relation to the then river charts, is not printed here, simply because it has no personal or literary interest. It is much longer than the first notebook, and is contained on seventy-nine pages, apart from several pages of rough outline maps. I reproduce a portion of one page, in order to show a sample:

11. N. (A) Long reach to a curved point. Great quantity of dangerous snags along the star^d shore. Follow the slight bend of the shore with caution. The Middle of the Channel is a S – B – [sand-bank] always covered. The more northerly of the two islands has its lower end bare of trees covered with grass and light green low bushes, then a low flat, and the upper end is timbered with light trees of a darker green tint.

It will be seen from this passage, which, though typical, is less technical than most, that the second notebook is not really, like the first, so much in the nature of a diary as of a specific aid to navigation. But those who recall the river journey in *Heart of Darkness*, with its dangers and its difficulties, will perceive how this notebook, too, has played its special and impersonal part in the construction of that story.

The title-page of the first notebook is almost all torn out, but the title-page of the second reads, "Up-river Book, commenced 3 August, 1890, S. S. *Roi des Belges*." Long ago, when I was making, from Conrad's dictation, a list of the ships he had sailed in, he wrote opposite *Roi des Belges* – "*Heart of Darkness, Outpost*." And, in truth, hints for *Heart of Darkness*, reminders of *Heart of Darkness*, lie thick upon the pages of the first notebook, though *An Outpost of Progress* – "the lightest part of the loot I carried off from Central Africa," to quote his Author's Note to *Tales of Unrest*, in which it was published – is only visible in the diary by the implication of the tropical African atmosphere.

No other diary of Conrad's is extant, and I am very sceptical as to whether he ever kept another. He was not at all that type of man, and his piercing memory for essentials was quite sufficient for him to re-create powerfully vanished scenes and figures for the purposes of his work. In 1890, of course, he had published nothing, and though we know that the unfinished MS. (seven chapters) of *Almayer's Folly* accompanied him on his Congo journey – *A Personal Record* describes how it was nearly lost on the river – yet it is doubtful whether he seriously envisaged its appearance in print at a future date. It was largely the breakdown of Conrad's health, due to this very trip, that caused him finally to abandon the sea, and if he had not abandoned the sea, how could he have become a novelist in the accepted sense? Unless we assume that genius must always find means of full expression – a big assumption and quite beyond proof – we owe it really to an accident that Conrad adopted writing as a career. Without this journey, and, therefore, without this diary, where would have been the great Conrad novels?

Thirty-four years to a day from beginning the second notebook, Conrad died – 3 August, 1924. Reading it again, I find, as I am continually finding, how many things there are which I would have liked to ask him and never did ask him, and how much I want to know which I never now can know. Well, that is always what happens when our friends depart. This diary is only a strange, tantalising fragment and must eternally remain so. Yet it has a value of its own, both real and romantic, and I am glad to be able to give it to the world.

RICHARD CURLE

APPENDIX B

THE *DALGONAR* INCIDENT: THE *LONDON MERCURY* TEXTS

Reprinted here from the *London Mercury* are documents providing the context for 'The Loss of the *Dalgonar*'. The story to which Conrad's letter to the editor responds appeared in the journal's September 1921 issue (pp. 482–8), prefaced by a brief editorial note. The reprinting below reproduces the article as it appeared, with, of course, altered lineation. Noted in square brackets is the correction of the nonsensical 'nil' and 'web', which, as Conrad points out in his letter, should read 'rail' and 'we', respectively. Other errors, involving technical matters and noted in his letter, are not, however, signalled.

A TRUE STORY

Log and Record of the Wreck of the Ship *Dalgonar* of Liverpool, bound from Callao to Taltal. By Mr. W. A. H. MULL, barque *Loire*. October 14th, 1913.

[*This record was written eight years ago. It carries its own description: we feel that any comment we could make on it would be otiose. But we cannot help expressing the opinion that there is no story in Hakluyt finer or more simple and powerfully told; and we make no excuses for publishing it, although its author was a stranger to conscious art and had no thought of a general audience.*—EDITOR.]

WE left Callao Dock September 20th at about 1 p.m. – ship's draft of water, 12 feet 2 inches aft and 11 feet 7 inches forward; main draft, 12 feet 2 inches – and anchored in the Bay.

Crew down in the hold levelling down the ballast in both hatches, shifting board all up and well lashed, having also diamond-shaped shifting bins in the square of each hatch, all well lashed, and the ballast covered fore and aft, and shored down between deck beams. We had also bulkheads at the end of each lot of ballast, 660 English tons in hatch No. 2, and 340 tons in hatch No. 3, and the ship was fumigated fore and aft and in the hold.

September 23rd, at 4 p.m., we left Callao, thirty hands on board all told, for Taltal; light S. E. wind and fine weather; set all sail. We found the vessel very stiff, steering by the wind on the port tack, heading S. W. by W. Moderate and fine weather continued until we reached the latitude 26 S. and longitude 84 W.

October 4th. — As well as can be remembered the wind gradually increased and we reduced sail accordingly.

October 8th, a.m. — We experienced east winds and squally weather; we were under topsails and foresails. I had a look down below and all was well. At noon all hands wore ship and put the vessel on the starboard tack, heading N. E. and N. N. E.; at 7 p.m. wind and sea were increasing, and we took in the mizzen fore upper topsail; at 11 p.m. wind and sea were still increasing: took in the mizzen and main upper topsails.

October 9th, a.m. — Hard gale and high increasing sea and very showery. The vessel was labouring and straining heavily. At 6 a.m. the second officer, Mr. Oxnord, went down the hold to see the ballast all right, and he reported everything was

well down there, 8 a.m. the wind moderated a little, but a terrific high sea from
the S. E.; ship's head N. E. and N. N. E. At 8.30 a.m. Captain Isbester[1] told me to
go down with the carpenter and see the ballast was all right. We found everything
well when we came down; but while we were standing looking at the ballast a squall
struck the vessel, and, the fore lower topsail carried away, the watch went up aloft
to pick up the remains; at the same time the vessel made an extra heavy roll and
the ballast shifted a little on the lee side. We called all hands on deck and down
below and trimmed the ballast back again and covered it well and shored it down
well, and at 11.30 a.m. Captain Isbester ordered the watch to go and get their
dinner. At noon the starboard watch came down the hold and relieved the port
watch, putting up extra shores, and the port watch went below: latitude at noon
31.45 S.; longitude 85.27 W. It was blowing a very hard gale, with a terrific high
sea and heavy rain squalls every half hour. At 2.30 p.m. a terrific squall struck the
vessel and at the same time a fearful high sea struck her on the starboard beam,
and heavy sprays flying over the vessel like steam, and threw the ship nearly on her
beam ends, and carrying away all the shores and throwing the ballast clean over
into the port wing. Some of the men in the starboard watch got their legs buried
in the ballast and had great difficulty in clearing themselves. They all scrambled
up on deck, some of them almost naked. The captain ordered the carpenter to
batten down the hatches. He then gave orders to put the ship on the port tack;
the helm was put hard over and web [= we] squared in the main and crossjack
yards and shivered the sails. Ship's head was N. E. when we put the helm up, and
she paid off to N. N. E., but would not go any further. The captain ordered me
to hoist up the inner and outer jibs to help pay her off, and, when doing this,
the foresheet, which was brand new, only recently made, carried away, and, with a
terrific lurch, the vessel was thrown on her beam ends, with the main and mizzen
topsail yard-arms in the water.

Captain Isbester and the carpenter rushed into the cabin and the captain told
the carpenter to get the axes out of the storeroom and stand by. The captain went
into his room for something, and they both came out on the main deck. The
carpenter asked Captain Isbester to come up on the poop, but he refused to come;
he ordered the port lifeboat to be cut away, which was done and got into the water
all right. Six or seven hands jumped into her, but she was immediately crushed by
the davits, and the men managed to scramble back on board again. The captain
then gave orders for the starboard lifeboat to be cut away, which was immediately
done, and Mr. May (third officer), the cook, sailmaker, R. Jones[2] (cabin boy),
A. Confrere, A. B., and two or three more men jumped into her, got her into the
water all right, but, try as they would, they could not get her away clear of the ship
on account of the backwash and the rolling of the vessel: the forward davit head
came down on the cook, who was in the bow of the boat, and crushed him and the
bow of the boat also. The remaining part of the boat turned over twice, throwing
all the men into the sea. They all managed to get back on board again, with the
exception of the cook, who was crushed, the sailmaker, who was drowned; and

---

[1] John Isbester (b. 1852), a native of the Shetlands, a resident of Whiteness, was married
in 1884, and father of three sons and a daughter. Owned by Gracie, Beasley & Coma-
pany of Liverpool, the *Dalgonar* had been under his command for about fourteen
years when she foundered, and was well known in Australian waters.

[2] Richard Leonard Jones, a Londoner (perhaps born in Kingston in 1895), was on his
first voyage.

A. Confrere, A. B., managed to get on board again, but got entangled in the braces and hung there under the main rail for two days after: we could not get anywhere near him, and he was washed away piece by piece. When our poor captain saw the starboard lifeboat being crushed he evidently must have lost his senses, for he lost his hold and went with his head up against the after-davit, which must have fractured his head: he never spoke or moved again, and the backwash took him away and we saw him no more. I was scrambling along the outside of the ship with the men I had with me to set the jibs when I saw the poor captain go over the side.

I immediately ordered the masts to be cut away, and the carpenter and Mr. Oxnord (second officer) and one man cut away the mizzen rigging; and I sent three or four men forward to try and get axes out of the carpenter's shop, and they managed to get them by the aid of ropes, and started to cut away the fore backstays and lower rigging. The mizzenmast went first; it broke about ten feet above the deck, and broke again just outside the rail. I cheered our gallant officers and men up all I could to give them courage at their work, and in about forty minutes the three masts were over the side.

The mainmast was the next cut away by Mr. Oxnord, the carpenter, and some of the men; it also broke about eight or ten feet above the deck, and again outside the rail, then the foremast the same way; but with the rolling of the ship the head of the foremast lifted up about ten feet and came down with a terrific force on the keelson: if it had missed once it would have certainly gone through the ship's bottom. Every time it came down it shook the ship terribly, and we did not expect to see many hours more; but, anyway, after the masts were cut away it made her lee rail visible once more. We could not get at the lee rigging to cut away, as the sea was washing half way up to the hatches, and all the rooms in the cabins on the lee side were full of water, and broke up everything that was in them. Every moment we were expecting the spars to poke a hole in her side or else turn over altogether. I cheered everybody up and told them to trust in God and He would help us all.

It was now about 8 p.m. and the gale still continued with violent rain squalls and a fearful high sea. We all mustered on the outside of the nil [= rail] on the half round. Mr. Oxnord and Mr. May, with some of the men, went down into the saloon by the aid of ropes through the skylight and down through the charthouse, and they secured a chair in the saloon and lowered me down out of the weather. We were all wringing wet and cold, but we managed to get some dry clothes from the slop-chest and some biscuits. After this we resigned ourselves to God Almighty, as we did not expect to see another day dawn on us; we were too far south and not far enough west for any homeward-bounders to fall across us: but, anyway, I set one officer and two men on watch, as there is nothing impossible for God, and the rest took shelter in the charthouse and in the saloon by my side, but everyone of us had a lifeline round us to enable us to get on deck again. I sat all night in my chair praying to God with all my heart and soul, and I have no doubt that they were all doing the same. At midnight the gale was raging heavily, with a very high sea and heavy rain squalls, the ship rolling heavily, sometimes the decks being perpendicular, and we were expecting her to turn over at any moment.

October 10*th.* — Mr. May and his two men on watch saw a green light on the port bow. We quickly got some rockets and blue light out of the charthouse, and we fired rocket after rocket and blue light after blue light, but we had not fired more than two or three when the ship answered with a blue light. Oh, how we all cheered and thanked God, no tongue can tell; the Lord had heard our prayer and sent this ship to our rescue, and at daybreak we saw her coming down on us with square yards on our starboard quarter: she came close round our stern and under our lee, and everybody that was capable joined in with three cheers.

The vessel's name was *Loire* of Dunkirk, and she flew the French ensign, with the signal, "Do you wish to abandon," which we answered in the affirmative. She sailed round us four times this day, but could not render assistance owing to the fearful gale and high sea that was raging; at the same time several of the men that could swim wanted to jump overboard when the vessel was close to us, but I advised them not to try it, as I felt sure they could never reach the ship, and they took my advice. At daylight we found that all three masts had gone and broken off just outside of the rail and taken with them the jibboom: it had broken off just outside of the inner jib stay-band and the screws had carried away just below the boxes. This made our hearts feel a little lighter when we saw this.

There is one thing I wish to say about my good officers and men. I am very proud to say that Mr. Oxnord, second officer, and Mr. May, third officer, have done their duty like true British seamen, and carried out my orders to the letter and at all times cool and collected, and great praise is due to them. Our carpenter, Mr. Dunker, behaved like a hero, very cool and collected, and stuck to his great work like a man, cheering up the men that were working with him in cutting away the masts, and I must say he is worthy of great praise; great praise is also due to all the men. They all kept very cool and collected and carried out my orders like noble British seamen: may God bless them and protect them.

At 3 p.m., when we found it impossible to be rescued this day, we tried to get some biscuits and water and put on dry clothes, and we were successful in getting it by the aid of ropes. We found the freshwater pump working all right, and we were very glad of that, as we were getting very thirsty now. At 4 p.m. our companion, the four-masted barque *Loire*, sailed round us the fourth and last time this day and went close under our stern. The captain waved his hand and begged us to be cool and patient, and he hoisted the signal that he would stand by us, and we joined in with three cheers again, which he retaliated, and lightened our hearts considerably: we then prepared for the night as before, having flare-up lights for stand-by in case of emergency, and then resigned ourselves to God to protect us against the perils of the deep.

October 11*th.* — At daylight we were a little disheartened at not seeing the French vessel. Our hero carpenter and three or four of the men volunteered to go forward and cut away the port anchor, which was lashed on the forecastle head, and they were successful in doing so, which lightened the vessel a little; then they volunteered to be lowered down the hold from the fore-hatch to ascertain if anything could be done with the ballast, but when down there they found all the ballast over on the port side and up under the tweendeck beams and utterly impossible to do anything to such a ballast as we had; it was rolling about like marbles with the rolling of the vessel. They also found water fore and aft in the tweendecks, but they kept that quiet from all the men, as it might have caused a panic. At 10 a.m. the French barque hove in sight again on our starboard quarter, and in a few minutes we could see her bearing down on us with square yards. No one but those who have experienced such a terrible situation can understand how the sight of her lightened our hearts, and we once more knew that our prayers had been heard by our Great Creator. The gale was still blowing with great force and high sea; we had our lifebelts on and prepared for the worst. Our merciful friend sailed round us twice this day, and the second time he hoisted a signal, "Wait until the weather moderates." Oh, how we cheered and thanked him. We now felt sure that he would not leave us, but see the last of us or save us. Then we resigned ourselves to God for another night and kept a keen watch. At midnight it was still blowing very hard and a mountain of sea; no boat could live in it, and every now and then we could hear something giving away down below; it would go off like a gun, and the vessel was shaking and trembling terribly.

October 13*th*, a.m. — The gale still continued with a high sea, and, as near as I could judge, the vessel was drifting in the N. N. W. direction, at about two and a half miles an hour, which proved pretty correct when we were safe on board our good ship *Loire*. At daylight our good ship was not in sight, but we could not see very far, as it was very squally, with heavy showers of rain.

At about 9 a.m. we got a Bible and prayer-book which one of the men had in his pocket, and we held a funeral service for our poor Captain Isbester and H. Unger, cook and steward, H. J. Cousin, A. B., who had lost their lives. The service was conducted by Mr. A. L. May, third officer, he being a clergyman's son and the most suitable for the occasion, singing hymns and thanking God for His most wonderful mercy in sending this ship to our rescue: we had not seen a single ship since we left Callao. After the service was over our friend hove in sight again and came close round our stern and under our lee, but still impossible to put out a lifeboat: the gale was still raging with violent rain squalls.

We were all shaking like leaves and getting wet all the time with the sprays and rain.

This day our friend kept within our sight all the time, and when night came on we kept a flare-up light going at intervals, which she answered. At midnight the gale abated a little and the sea went down considerably.

October 14*th*. — At daylight the wind started to freshen again, but the sea had gone down a good deal.

Our friend the four-mast barque was hove to on our weather beam; under the topsail and foresail she had two flag signals flying, saying, "I am coming to your assistance," and in a few minutes we saw them launching the lifeboat and coming to our weather quarter. The chief officer, M. Yves Cadic, was in charge at the risk of their lives, for the wind was rapidly increasing with a very high sea. We had a two-inch rope bent to a lifebuoy, and floated it to them, as they could not come any nearer than sixty fathoms on account of the high sea. They picked this up, and we bent a three and a half rope to it, and they hauled it in and made it fast in the stern of the boat. They also had a sea-anchor out with fifteen fathoms of line forward to prevent the boat from being thrown end over end to the sea; then we took our new deep-sea line which we had on the poop and bent it to another buoy and floated it to them; then we made a bowline in the middle of the lead-line. The carpenter took a turn with the lead-line round the rail, and one A. B. went in the bowline: the carpenter then lowered away into the water, and the chief officer and his boatswain sat in the stern of the boat and hauled away and got the man safe in the lifeboat.

I was in the lifeboat and had with me the ship's papers, but my logbook is lost. I tried to get it out of my room after our first night's outing on the half round, but my room was full of water and everything broken and mixed up.

They then made the lifebuoys fast to the lines again and let them go and rowed away for the ship. Mr. Oxnord hoisted up on a little pole the letter R, according to our captain friend's instructions to his officer, to let him know that the boat was coming back again. We got alongside safe and stood by to jump when the boat was level with the ship's rail and her crew were ready to catch us: thirteen of us got all safe on board, and the chief officer, M. Cadic, did not wait one moment with his gallant crew, but gallantly pulled back again at the risk of their lives to save the rest of our shipmates, and they were successful in doing so. The carpenter was the last man to leave the wreck; the letter R was flying, and he lowered himself down, and when in the sea he let go the line, and they hauled him safe into the lifeboat, and she got safe alongside and all on board in the same manner as before; they then hooked on the lifeboat, and we all helped to run her up quick in order to prevent her from getting smashed up, and landed her on deck.

We all went on the quarter-deck and thanked God, the captain, officers and his crew, and gave them all three hearty cheers for saving our lives at the risk of their own. They had the second lifeboat ready in tackles to put out in case anything happened to us in the first: they had also very large bags full of oil hanging over the bow and stern which prevented the heavy rollers from breaking and swamping the boat. When the first boatload were safe on deck I saw the captain standing on the bridge and crying like a child, and I rushed up to him and thanked him. He then told me that he would never have left us if he had had to stand by us for thirty days: he would see the last of us or save us.

We were all safe on board at noon in latitude 28.58 S. and longitude 87.4 W., the wind south and rapidly increasing again to a strong gale. They trimmed the yards and steered by the wind on the port tack, and the captain, officers, and crew gave us dry clothes and something to drink; they treated us with the utmost kindness. The men all got a bunk each down in the forepeak, and the carpenter and some men were making shavings to serve as beds, and the captain sacrificed two good sails, cut them up and made blankets for them all: it was very nice and warm down in the fore peak, and the men were all very comfortable. The captain and myself attended to all those that got hurt, and gave them quarters. R. Jones was the first attended to; his arm was swollen to a terrible size from the shoulder to the finger-ends, but the bone was not fractured. The captain bandaged him up and gave him a room in the quarter-deckhouse. Our carpenter got badly bruised about the hip and knee and also his foot got hurt and cut. The captain bandaged him up and also gave him quarters with the ship's carpenter.

E. Maganske, Charles Ellison, James Kavanagh, Mitchell Singer, and B. Mullvaney all got more or less bruised about the arms and legs, but the captain attended to them regularly every day. Myself and Mr. Oxnord got a room in the saloon, and Mr. May got quarters with the third officer of the *Loire*, so that everybody was made very comfortable. There are twenty-six of us saved and the ship's crew all told is thirty-three – total, fifty-nine lives on board, which made it absolutely necessary to put all hands on half rations. The ship's crew were willing to do so for our sakes, and I hope they will all be highly rewarded on our arrival home, and may God bless and protect our rescuers wherever they go.

Great praise is due to Captain Michel Jaffré, master of the good ship *Loire*, for his heroic action in standing by us for four days, working his vessel all the time. He never had his foot off the deck from the time he saw our rockets until we were saved, and also to the chief officer, M. Yves Cadic, who was in charge of the boat, and his crew for the seamanlike manner he handled the lifeboat at the risk of their lives to save ours, and also to the second officer, M. Paul Boulet, and crew for their smartness in handling their vessel in order to save our lives. I hope that God our heavenly Father will bless and protect them all and highly reward them all for their heroic action.

November 11 *th.* — The third day after we were saved my head swelled up terribly, and I was very ill for a week, and the chief officer, M. Cadic, was also laid up through the exposure in the lifeboat with a very heavy cold, and was off duty for one week, but he is not well yet, and has been under the captain's care all the time. The rest of us are all well at present, thank God.

LETTER BY L. C. GANE TO THE *LONDON MERCURY*

Conrad refers to the following letter, which appeared in the October 1921 issue of the *London Mercury* (p. 642):

SIR,– In "A True Story," published in your September issue, I notice what appears to be a contradiction in terms. The writer states that in reducing sail they took in the "mizzen fore upper topsail." The words "mizzen" and "fore" seem to me irreconcilable. The vessel is specifically stated to be a "ship." A full-rigged ship has three masts – fore, main, and mizzen. Four-masted square-rigged ships are invariably barques, the two after-masts being termed mizzen and jigger masts, so in any case "mizzen fore" does not seem sense.

I am not a sailor, and should be very pleased to be corrected if I am wrong. I write because I think that the value and interest of a record such as this depend on its absolute technical accuracy. – Yours, etc.,

L. C. GANE.
97 North Gate, Regent's Park, N. W., September 9th.

APPENDIX C

PREFACE TO *THE SHORTER TALES OF JOSEPH CONRAD*: TWO REJECTED DRAFTS

Published here for the first time are two rejected drafts of the opening of the preface to Conrad's selection of short stories brought out posthumously by Doubleday, Page & Company on 30 October 1924. Housed in the Beinecke Rare Book and Manuscript Library, Yale University, the ribbon-copy typescripts (in blue ink) are comprised of two pages each. According to the Beinecke's catalogue, the typescripts were gifts from Conrad to his friend Jean Aubry, from whom the library acquired a significant collection of Conradiana. The history of the essay's writing is detailed in 'The Texts'.

The drafts are undated, and there is no indication to suggest the sequence of their writing. On balance, however, that printed first below seems more likely to represent initial thoughts. In the transcriptions, paragraph openings of first paragraphs are adjusted flush left (standard throughout the Cambridge Edition), and lineation is continuous. A missing word is supplied in square brackets.

Draft 1 features a comma added by hand, probably by Conrad, after the phrase 'will be found'. He filled in a blank left in the typewritten text, where presumably the typist was unable to read his handwriting, with the word 'modes'. Conrad's hand is undoubtedly present in Draft 2: he added the title 'Preface.' and substituted the phrase 'The publication of this vol: of coll^d stories when once decided upon' for 'The idea of this selection is not apparent on the surface, but'.

The typescripts do not appear to have been dictated, as the typing is fluid and exact, with no corrections required. Conrad may have begun writing this preface by hand, then had the first opening typed, but rejected it and began again. The adjustments to the second draft show that he probably intended to recast his material directly in the typescript, but upon deciding to take another tack altogether, he likewise laid it aside. Circumstances then changed, with his secretary being absent, and he drafted the whole in manuscript.

[DRAFT 1]

This is a selection of my stories – not haphazard – not meant to show a particular mood of the writer, or a particular locality, or even a certain type of story.

In a selection out of all one's shorter work one would have expected that the earliest of them would naturally find place. Here this is not the case, for the idea of this selection is not to show development of the author's gift, or even feelings in the face of certain facts and situations. Thus "The Lagoon" which is the first story I ever wrote will not be found;[1] but the latest will be found, mainly for the reason

---

[1] In the 'Author's Note' to *Tales of Unrest* (1919), another retrospective statement, Conrad also makes the claim that 'The Lagoon' was the first story he ever wrote. This not only discounts 'The Black Mate' (whose origins lie as far back as 1884) but also contradicts evidence in extant correspondence from his time in Brittany indicating

that the privileged person in it is a seaman and this selection has been made in reference very much to the people that appear in it rather than the surroundings in which the events take place. The milieu then is of no importance in the general view of these tales, and though many of them take place at sea they can not be called sea stories in any sense. In fact they are mixed, and one of them even passes on land altogether. No ship plays a part in it. Yet those that reach this story in the following pages will see at once why it has been included in the collection, the idea of which is a study of seamen, portraits in action of men who had much or little to do with the sea, not only in professional relation in the elements, though that is the [case] in Typhoon, but in the general scheme of life and problems of humanity to which they belong.

I do not want to lay myself open to be classified. That was always my great fear, my great dislike, because the only classification to which I stuck was modes of life, of which I had personal knowledge, or which I had made my own by personal meditation.

[DRAFT 2]

The idea of this selection is not apparent on the surface, but has been the subject, however, of a good deal of thought leading to some sort of examination of the writer's own impulses and more obscure feelings.

Primarily a story-teller, that is a man applying his creative instinct to a definite episode in the private history of an individual, he has been obscurely conscious – yet certainly conscious – of those general principles which apply to humanity as a whole and place the episode in relation to the rest, as it were, with the whole sum of existence.

In a writer who is primarily not a writer of short stories in the sense which is generally given to them by the general consent of literary critics and editors of magazines, once the idea of such a volume has occurred the necessity of a principle of selection is presented at once. At the end of more than a quarter of a century of literary life the first principle which offers itself to the mind would be naturally a series illustrative of the author's development by a careful arrangement of the order in which they would be printed. For reasons however into which it is difficult to enter upon in this preface that principle has never been contemplated. Readers of the pages that follow will not find in them the very first short tale of this author, which of course would be the proper starting point of an illustrative series; though they will, as a matter of fact, find in them the very last short production he has written up to date, though it would not be the last in the order of contents.

that he wrote 'The Idiots' and 'An Outpost of Progress' before 'The Lagoon'. For a discussion, see 'The Texts', *Tales of Unrest*, ed. Allan H. Simmons and J. H. Stape (forthcoming).

APPENDIX D

NOTE ON THE *TORRENS* AND
NOTES FOR 'TRAVEL'

NOTE ON THE *TORRENS*

A prefatory statement by Conrad to his essay on the *Torrens*, summarizing historical information from Basil Lubbock's *The Colonial Clipper Ships* (1921), accompanied the essay in *Collier's Weekly*. It may have been composed upon the magazine's request. The note was printed in italics, which are not reproduced here.

The Torrens composite ship, built in 1875 by James Laing, is authoritatively stated by Mr. Basil Lubbock in his monograph on Australian clippers as one of the most successful ships ever launched. Captain R. H Angell [*sic*] sailed her with the greatest success between London and Adelaide for fifteen years, making some wonderfully quick passages, which are the more remarkable because, out of regard for the comfort of her passengers, the Torrens was never hard driven.

Her length was just over 230 feet over all, of which the poop took up 80 feet. Her accommodation was mainly for the first-class, but there was a limited accommodation for a few second class passengers. Altogether fifty-two very roomy berths. She was the last sailing passenger ship out of London. Her last voyage under the British flag ended in 1906.

J. C.

A draft of this prefatory note is extant and is printed below for the first time. The one-page typescript text, revised in Conrad's hand, is preserved in the Beinecke Rare Book and Manuscript Library, Yale University. A list of superseded readings follows the revised text.

The TORRENS composite ship, built in 1875 by James Laing is authoritatively stated by Mr Basil Lubbock in his monograph on Australian Clippers as one of the most successful ships ever launched. She was managed by Messrs Elder & Co, London & Adelaide, and mainly owned by Capt. R. H Angell [*sic*], who had previously commanded the ships "Glenosmond" [*sic*] and "Collingrove" notable in their day. He supervised the building of the Torrens and sailed her with the greatest success between London and Adelaide for 15 years, making some wonderfully quick passages which are the more remarkable because out of regard for the comfort of her passengers the TORRENS was never hard-driven. Her length was just over 230 feet over all, of which the poop took up 80. Her accom[m]odation was mainly for the first class, but there was a limited accom[m]odation for a few second class passengers. Altogether 52 very roomy berths. She was the last sailing passenger ship out of London. Her last voyage under the British flag ended in 1906.

The original wordings over-ridden by revision appear following the square bracket:

composite ship] ship
monograph on] monograph of
launched] built

previously commanded] commanded
Collingrove] Coningrove
He supervised the building] Before he took command
and sailed] sailing
wonderfully] wonderful
Her accommodation was mainly for the] Her passengers were mostly
passengers. Altogether 52 very roomy berths.] passengers too.

NOTES FOR 'TRAVEL'

These notes, published here for the first time, if not precisely a draft, are vestiges
of Conrad's preliminary thoughts to be worked up for the preface that Richard
Curle requested him to write to his travel book *Into the East* (1923). The matter in inverted commas is a quotation from Curle's book: 'an exquisite feeling
of well-being, harmonious as first love or as music heard in dreams, fills and
overpowers me with a Dionysian joy' (p. 110), as is the sentence about the 'whisper of innumerable hills' (p. 111), the latter quoted in the final version of the
essay.

The line-by-line transcription is of two holograph leaves written in ink, undated
and unsigned, held at the Beinecke Rare Book and Manuscript Library, Yale
University. The transcription does not report deletions but is of the final text.
No history of sale is known, and the leaves presumably once belonged to
Conrad's friend Jean Aubry, from whom the library acquired a significant col-
lection of Conradiana. The history of the writing of this preface is detailed in 'The
Texts'.

[*leaf 1*]

The traveller at moments tasting the flavour of expecta
tion "harmonious as first
love – as the music of dreams".
So that in travel one can
yet find those moments
when it is good to be
alone.
    It was in the frontier town of Bhamo where
they live on rumours that he
heard the whisper of
the innumerable hills
passing to one another the
restless murmurs of men's
hearts.
    Whether vanity consist in revolt
against facts but in the final acceptance of life or in
in conformity with
all its forms and a hidden rejected
of life is also one of the questions
that suggest themselves as he
goes voyaging to this traveller

so susceptible to inner
promptings so responsive
to visual impressions.

[*leaf*] 2

He who travels to-day beholds
a world in transition.
    How diff[eren]ᵗ M. Polo
who seemed to progress
amongst immutable things – a
continuity of the unchanging
of the splendid and the
bizarre – an everlasting
shape of wonder.
    The observation that Bur-
mah is antipathetic to
Indian ideals puts a
special character on the
descriptive characterization
in which this traveller abounds.
    Man rebels in his heart agains[t]
the wilderness which he may
love —— Travel brings the
sense of the intolerable and interesting contradictions of our inner
life. That is because the
traveller is the only true spectator who knows that he can
not go home to sleep at the end
of the day.

APPENDIX E

'GEOGRAPHY': UR-VERSION OF 'GEOGRAPHY AND SOME EXPLORERS'

Conrad never expected to see this draft version of his essay printed, and its rough-ness, an essential part of its texture, is largely retained in the transcription below. Abbreviations have not been expanded, nor have erratic capitals been regular-ized or altered. On the other hand, some accommodation for the reader seems reasonable, and this is neither a diplomatic nor a line-by-line transcription of the extant manuscript, preserved in the Beinecke Rare Book and Manuscript Library, Yale University.[1] Where a dropped-out word might cause particular awkwardness in reading, one has been suggested in square brackets, but textual cruxes have oth-erwise been allowed to stand as likewise have half-thoughts and instances where revision was imperfect or alternatives unresolved (for example, 'was doubted, was denied', 'in my me', 'test exams'). Conrad's majuscules and minuscules offer chal-lenges, and other readers might resolve these in ways different from those below.

Certain conventions governing the texts published in the Cambridge Edition generally are applied: misspellings (for example, 'dimmension', 'Mauritious') are silently corrected; haplography is not reported; and missing apostrophes and full stops have been supplied. Contrary to the general practice, however, where no styling appears, ship's names have been placed within inverted commas, the pro-tocol (where there is one) of the manuscript.

GEOGRAPHY

It seems to me that for most of mankind the great superiority of the science of Geography over the science of Geometry lies in the appeal of the figures, the graphic representations appertaining to those. It may be an incorrigible frivolity inherent in human nature but there can be no doubt that a map is [a]   5
much more fascinating thing than any figure in a treatise on conic sections –
at any rate for the simple minds which are the inheritance of the great majority
of the dwellers on this earth.

No doubt a trigonometrical survey may be a romantic undertaking striding
over deserts and leaping over the valleys never before seen by the eye of   10
civilised man but its accurate operations can never have the charm of the
fascination of the first hazardous footsteps of a venturesome, sometimes lonely
explorer recording by his campfire the events and the toil of his day. For a
long time yet a few suggestive words grappling with things seen will have
the advantage over a long array of precise, no doubt interesting and even   15
profitable figures. The earth is a stage and though it may be an advantage,
even to right comprehension of the play to know its exact dimension it is
always the drama that will [be] the thing with its inner passions expressed

---

[1] For a discussion of the manuscript and the reasons for its presentation in full
here, see 'The Texts', pp. 205–06.

by its outward action marching so often blindly to success or failure which themselves are often undistinguishable from each other at first.

Of all the sciences Geography finds its origin in action, and what is more in adventurous action of the kind that appeals to sedentary people who like
5   to dream of arduous adventure like prisoners safe behind their bars dream of all the risks and hazards of liberty dear to the heart of man.

Descriptive Geography like any kind of science rested on the experience of certain Phenomena and on the experiment prompted by the unappeasable curiosity of men which their intelligence has elevated into a quite respectable
10 passion for acquiring knowledge, and like other sciences it has fought its way to truth through the errors of a love for the marvellous, of credulity, of rash and unwarrantable assumptions, the play of unbridled fancy. Its cartography [is] a graphic record of phantastic theories produced in the 12th century a chart in which our first parents in the company of the serpent are represented
15 realistically at the very top of the circle, (where the north pole should have been) the rest of its contents whether representing land and water being strangely rectilinear and incomprehensible that I must believe that its meaning can not be geographical but of a symbolic representation now of a view impenetrable to our matured minds. Later the making of maps seemed to
20 be an exercise of unbridled fancy. Geography had its period of extravagance which is not to be regretted for if it did not represent the shape of continents it gives us an idea of the mediæval states of mind in the face of the problems relating to the knowledge of the earth its products and its inhabitants. Its cartography was pictorial placing illustrations of strange pageants, strange
25 trees, strange beasts in the midst of purely theoretical continents. It had its Kingdoms of Monomotapa and of Prester John, its regions inhabited by lions and others by men with reversed feet or eyes in the middle of their breasts most convincingly labelled on charts apparently meant for the use of serious travellers – makers of geography. But what of that! Has not chemistry passed
30 through its phase [of] alchemy and our knowledge of the serene stars been arrived through the cruel deceptions of astrology? Solemn fooling for solemn fooling of the scientific order I prefer yet the kind that does not exploit the fears and the cupidities of men. From that point of view Geography is the most guileless of sciences. Its marvellous side did not lend itself to cheating
35 simple mortals (who are a multitude) out of their peace of mind or their money. At most it lead[s] some of them to leave their homes, to obscure death may be, now and then to a little disputed glory never to a high fortune, not seldom to contumely. The most distinguished of workers for the advance of geography was at one time loaded with chains and thrown into prison.
40 That was not the fault of the science [of] Geography however. The guilt must be looked for in the imperfections of [the] human heart which must be accepted with resignation. And if the discovery of America did call out the greatest outburst of reckless greed in history we may say at least that the gold of Mexico and Peru unlike the gold of alchemists was really there. But the
45 conquest of the New World tho' it helped the advance of our knowledge of our globe belongs properly speaking not to the development of the guileless science of the geographer but to the art [of] the historian who works indoors and puts what complexion he likes on the acts of rapine, policy, devotion, chicane, heroism that go to make up the tale of the fatality which drives races
50 and generation[s] to struggle amongst themselves for the possession of the

Earth which for so long they had peopled with monstrous beings and stored
with untold wealth, but of whose very size and shape they had no definite idea
for ages. I suppose it not very charitable on my part but I must say that even
at this day I think with malicious pleasure of the many disappointments of
those heroic searchers for Eldorado who cared not for mountains and rivers   5
except as obstacles to their personal desires and ambitions. Not for them the
serene joys of research – Geographical research – but many broken heads and
precious little gold to share (however few they were) in then [*sic*] end. And
serve them right too, though I will not put on the appearance of a virtue I do
not possess, for who knows, if my life had been cast in those times when the   10
beginning of modern Geography took place, I too might have joined them.
I suspect a certain proportion of my contemporaries would have joined too.
Well, we have missed that chance to which perhaps we would not have been
equal, for that deplorable business was by no means child's play. We may console ourselves however by the reflexion that our geographical knowledge [is]   15
of the kind that [lay] beyond even the conception of the hardy followers of
Cortez and Pizarro and of the estimable gentleman called Cabeza de Vaca who
was famous for his gentle dealing with the heathen nations whose territories
he traversed in search of some Eldorado. They are described as appreciating
him greatly – and they assisted him on his way. Thus he traversed their ter-   20
ritories and now the very name of these nations is lost while their territories
are being traversed many times in every twenty-four hours by the trains of the
Southern Pacific R. R.

I must however own that the Conquest which really, both in its aims and
the interrelations of individuals is a rather squalid romance, contains one   25
great moment – I mean a geographical great moment, when the leader of
[the] party crossing the Isthmus of Panama set his eyes for the first time upon
the tranquil portion of the great ocean, which in his haste he misnamed the
pacific.

That privileged individual surrendered to his first impression but he can   30
hardly be blamed, for that portion of the waters of the globe called the G. of
Panama is a calm and serene spot. Too calm. So that the navigators considered
[it] a dangerous region where one might have been caught and lie becalmed
for weeks with a crew slowly dying of thirst under a cloudless sky. A dreadful
fate in its quietness which gave you time to feel yourself die in a long agony.   35
How much preferable a region of storms where man and ship can at least
put up a fight and keep-up the illusion almost to the last. I will not say that
tempest[s] at sea are a delightful experience; but a desperate fight is better
than a fate of helpless torture, and a fight with a storm gives you, at least, a
chance off victorious – and a[n] illusion of greatness even in defeat. Balboa   40
was deceived. What he saw was only a gulf pacific even to deadliness, a prison-
house for uncautious caravels and a place of torture for their crews. But Balboa
knew nothing of that. Or dead [= did] he perhaps have the intuition that he
was looking at a mass of waters comparable in extent to the view of a firmament
and sown all over with groups of islands resembling the constellations of   45
the sky.

The tale goes that in the first transports of his enthusiasm he waded knee-
deep into the water naked sword in hand to take possession of his discovery
in the name of the King of Spain. But whatever his feelings he could not
possibly know that this first glance of his added, as it were, 10000 miles to   50

the circumference of the globe and opened an immense field for adventurers
and for the missionaries of the XIX century – and an enormous canvas where
study-Geographers for a couple of centuries employed their exuberant fancies
in inventing various southern continents.

5   I will not quarrel with th[e] old cartographers for their wild and
monotonous inventions. The geographers of those days did not seem able
to reconcile themselves to the idea that there is much more water than land
on this globe. Nothing would satisfy them but enormous and fanciful southern continents in that great region of the south where as a matter of fact the

10   great seas of the stormy latitudes can chase each other all round the globe. I
suppose, being landsmen they could not somehow accept the indication that
our world as far [as the] apportioning of space goes seems to have been created mostly for the fishes. What is really surprising to me is that the seamen of
the time should have believed that these study-made theories ought to be true

15   and that there must be a great austral continent which it was their business to
track out and describe. At bottom it was a desire for symmetry which seems
natural to the human mind. The large spaces of land to the North of the
Equator demanded as a matter of good art or sound science to be balanced
by corresponding continental structures in the southern hemisphere. And

20   the seamen of the 16th and 17th centuries seemed also to become fascinated
by a such reasonable assumption. Every bit of coast line discovered, every
island glimpsed in the distance had to be dragged into the scheme as a head-
land or outlying archipelago that [was] irrepressible. Even Tasman the best
seaman of them all before James Cook that most accomplished of explorers

25   and navigators to whom it was given by the virtue of genius and character to
settle the geography of the Pacific – even Tasman after hanging about the
north island of New Zealand long enough to trace roughly a bit of the coast
and lose a boat's crew in a sudden affray with the Maoris seemed to take it for
granted that what he had discov[er]ed was but the Western end of an enor-

30   mous continent extending clear away the to the continent of Sth America.
Mighty is the power of a theory especially if based on such a common sense
notion as the balance of continents.

It is difficult now to realize the frightful difficulties of the early explorers of
these Pacific wastes which are now so well known in their innermost recesses,

35   contain a great if young commonwealths [sic] have been the scene of momentous events in the history of civilised mankind no more than 250 years after
Tasman's important voyage.

His journal (which has been published not a very long time ago) gives us
a good idea. The early navigators had no means of ascertaining their exact

40   position on the globe. They could calculate their Lat$^{\underline{de}}$ but the Long^{de} was
always a matter of wild guesswork. Tasman and his officers sitting down in
the cabin of the Heemskirk anchored in Murderer's Bay to consider their
further course in the light of their instructions did not, to speak plainly, know
where they were, neither did they know where various places named in their

45   instructions were. No small handicap you will admit. He could have sailed
north or east but as a matter of fact he sailed more or less between the two,
and circling about he returned to Batavia where he was not received as well
as he might have expected, by his employers the Gov: Gen: and the council,
who declared him somewhat "remiss" in his investigations. In my youth, when

50   reading voyages of discovery I used to take it for granted that except from one

bourne the traveller does always return. Now after having had half a lifetime at sea the matter for astonishment is that any of them did ever return. It is for this rather than for their discoveries that I give the early navigators my profound professional respect. For those were the professional achievements about which the[re] could be no doubt, whereas discoveries belong to science and are achievements of the kind about which people sitting in comfort by their firesides could wrangle endlessly, extol and depreciate according to their whims, jealousies and preconceived notions.

Thus they judged Abel Tasman remiss – a poor reward to come back to. The truth is, I am sorry to say, that Tasman's character, other than professional, was not of the kind to cause governors and councils to treat him with particular consideration. Except in professional competency and [a] certain audacity in handling his ships on unknown coasts and amongst unknown dangers he is not comparable for a moment to Capt Cook, another humble son of the soil – a man of great and sober genius, associate of the most learned in the land and honoured by his Sovereign and a Captain in [the] Royal Navy. In Tasman was a mere adventurer; and it is certain that the Hon Council gave him employment on some rather dubious business of their own, connected with the Japan trade. There's no doubt also that once he kidnapped a Chinaman, who probably was a worthless person, but even that can not make the transaction honourable. In his old age he got into some disreputable scrape and received a dismissa[l] from employment though not actually from the Service of the States General. Those and many other scandalous tales I have only learned recently tho' I admit that my early admiration for Tasman as a man of Geographical research is not affected very much by it. Hadn't he mapped 8000 miles of an island which almost deserving the name of a continent – a very old continent which will be presently the home of a young nation, with all the possibilities of material and intellectual splendours hidden in its future. I like to think that in that portion of the Elysian Fields set apart for great navigators James Cook would not refuse to acknowledge the civilities of Abel Tasman, the man who sighted New Zealand first in the perplexed bewildered way of those times, 130 years before Capt Cook on that voyage which laid for good and all the ghost of the great southern continent, saw and added N. Zealand to the scientific domain of geography – also for all time.

No shadow of remissness or doubtful motive rests upon the achievement of Capt Cook who came out of a labourer's cottage to take his place at the head of the great masters of maritime exploration, who settled the great geographical problem of the Pacific. "Endeavour" was the name of the ship of his first voyage and it was the watchword of his professional life. "Resolution" was the name of the ship he commanded himself on his second expedition, and it was the determining quality of his soul. I won't say the greatest, for he had all the other manly qualities of a great man. A new spirit entered the Pacific in his train. The voyages of the early explorers were prompted by an acquisit[iv]e spirit, the desire of lucre in some form, the desire of trade, or the desire of loot disguised in fine words. But Cook's three voyages were free from any taint of that sort. His aims needed no disguise. They were scientific – and the deeds spoke for themselves with the masterly simplicity of a hard-won success.

In that respect he seems to belong to the explorers of the XIXth century, the late Fathers of Militant Geography whose only object was the search for truth. Geography is a science of facts and they devoted themselves to the discovery of facts in the configuration and feature[s] of the great continents.

It was a century of landsmen investigators. In saying this I do not forget the Polar Explorers whose aims were certainly as pure as the air of those high
5   latitudes where not a few of them laid down their live[s] for the advancement of Geography.

Seamen, men of science, it is difficult to speak of them without admirative emotion and the dominating figure of the first half of the 19 cent seamen explorers was of course that of Sir John Franklin not only by the extent of his
10 discoveries by the personal character of that distinguished man, who is one of those navigators that never returned and by the persistent efforts extending over ten years to ascertain his fate.

When fully revealed to the world it appeared the more tragic as all through two years the way of that expedition seems to be the leading to a desired
15 and important success while in fact it was all the time the way to a life and death struggle in which every man had to go down knowing in his heart how hopeless from the first must be the issue of the drama played behind the curtain of arctic mystery.

The corner of it concealing the tragic last days of "Erebus" and "Terror"
20 was lifted when I was about a year old by Sir L. M'Clintock when in the "Fox," the last ship that went out in search of Sir J: Fr. "The Voyage of the 'Fox' in the Arctic Seas" is a great little book. Tho' I was not living in the way of such literature it fell into my hands when I was about eleven years old. I can only account for it by the interest all Europe took in the mystery of Sir John's
25 fate. The "Voy[ge] of the 'Fox'" – a little yacht of 170 tons – was translated I believe into every language of the white races and my copy was probably in French. But I have glanced through it many times since. I got a popular copy not [a] long time ago, got [up] exactly as I remember my first one with the touching facsimile of a printed report form to put under a cairn giving a
30 summary record of the ships' work with "Sir John Frank. commanding the Exp[e]dition" and its underlined confident "*All well*" less than a year before the ships were abandoned and the crews long and vain struggle against cold and starvation began. There could [not] have been a better book to let in a breath of polar atmosphere into a life whose relations with the poles of
35 the earth had been merely a formal, official kind as the imaginary ends of the imaginary axis upon which the earth turns. It sent me into a realistic-romantic exploration of my own – developed an inborn taste probably for poring over the maps (which interfered with my school-work) and roused a[n] ardent devotion to geography which on examination I tried to make my
40 great stand-by. Unfortunately the marks awarded for that subject were as few almost as the hours apportioned to it in the school curriculum by people who had no poetry, no imagination no desire for roaming the world mere bored professors who were not only middle aged but looked to me as though they had never been young. And their geography was very much like themselves a
45 dreary thing with a dry skin covering a repulsive armature of statistical bones. I would be ashamed of digging up a hatchet which has been buried nearly fifty years ago, if those fellows had not tried so often to take my scalp at the yearly test exams. There are things that [one] does not forget and the geography to which I was devoted was the Geography of open spaces and wide horizons
50 built up on men's devoted work, the old Geography, still militant but fated

to come to an end with the last great explorer. Thus it happened that I got
no marks at all for my paper on arctic geography which I wrote at [the] age
of thirteen. It was for my tender year[s] an erudite performance. I really did
know something about geography, but what I [was] after really I suppose was
the history of arctic exploration. My knowledge of it had considerable gaps   5
but I had managed to compress my enthusiasm into just two pages which in
itself was a sort of merit. Yet I got no marks. For one thing it was not a "set
subject." I believe the only comment made about it to my private tutor was
that I seemed to be wasting my time on reading books of travel instead of
attending to my studies. I tell you these fellows were always trying to take my   10
scalp. On another occasion I just saved in by proficiency in map-drawing. It
must have been good I suppose but all I know about it is that it was done in a
loving spirit. Star-gazing is a fine occupation if it leads you unto the borders
of the unattainable but map-gazing to which I became addicted early runs
it close in bringing great spaces into stimulating contact with the faculty of   15
directed imagination. A change had come upon the spirit of map-making.
A generation had come which possessed of the true figure of the continents
had given up the practice of filling them with of [sic] imaginary detail born
from all fables and legends and old reveries that were both extravagant and
wearisome. They were honestly replaced by great blanks [sic] places, places of   20
mystery, much more stimulating than the precise if mendacious statements
about regions inhabited by lions or by men with dog's heads (mere baboons
I imagine) or imaginary kingdoms appearing full of towns with phantastic
names and watered by wriggly non existent rivers taking their source perhaps
in some strange rectilinear range of mountains which aroused one's profound   25
scepticism.

Yes, all through the 18th century the business of map-making was growing
into an honest occupation, registering the hard-won knowledge but also, in
a scientific spirit recording the geographical ignorance of its time. And it
was Africa, the continent of which the Romans said "some new thing was   30
always coming" that got cleared and swept out first and the wonders of it were
replaced by a blank mystery with adventurers and enduring men nibbling at
its edge, attacking it from North and South and East and West, conquering a
bit here and a bit there, sometimes swallowed up themselves by the mystery
they were so persistently attacking.   35

Mungo Park of Western Sudan and Bruce of Abyssinia were I believe the
first two names I heard when I began to take notice – I mean geographical
notice – of the world into which I was born. Their fame was European and
already historical by then. But the geographical news that could have been
whispered to me in my cradle as the very latest was the discovery of Tanganyika   40
by Burton and the first glimpse of Victoria Nyanza obtained by Speke in their
joint expedition into Eastern Africa. It didn't occur to anybody to take that
trouble and it was only in the later sixties that I did my first bit of map-drawing.
It consisted in entering in pencil the outline of Tanganyika on my old atlas
which having [been] published in about '52 did of course contain none of the   45
great lakes, a prophetic bit of voluntary work, since later as second officer of
various ships I [= it] has been my lot to correct the ship's charts according to
the Admiralty notices, but I did it I must own without the slightest excitement.
But my first contact with the region of great Lakes on the fringe of the last
large blank space on the Map of Africa furnished a lot of excitement to my   50

boyish days. However I did not give up the polar regions completely on that
account. My interest swung between the frigid and torrid zone, fascinated by
the mystery no doubt but more yet by the men who like Great Masters of an
art worked each in his own way to complete the picture of the earth. Almost
5 each day of my school-boy life had its hour spent in their company. It was a
very good company of which no two individuals were alike, and of each of
whom I had formed for myself an image cherished in boyish mind.

    Not the least interesting part in the study of geographical discovery is the
insight it gives one into the characters of that special kind of men who gave
10 all their efforts and all their life to geographical exploration. In the world of
mentality and imagination it is they and not characters of fiction who were
my first friends. Of each of them I had formed for myself a cherished image
indissolubly connected with their achievement. For instance tho' I could
even now sketch in from memory the western bulge of the African coast, and
15 could place pretty correctly the course of principal rivers and other features of
Western Sudan, my intimate impression of that part of Africa is represented by
a fair-haired (I don't know I assume M Park to have had fair hair) young man,
clad simply in tattered shirt and damaged breeches, very ill and fevered, lying
down in the shade of an enormous tree (species unknown) gasping painfully
20 for breath, with a black-skinned woman (she must have been a Mandingo)
bringing him a calabash full of pure cold water, which seems to have effected
a miraculous cure. The representative of Central Sudan in the court of my
memory is a very different person, the self-confident and keen-eyed (he noted
and figured the forms of every cooking pot used by the various tribes) Dr Barth
25 on horseback, in a long cloak and a sort [of] turban on his head, approaching
the mud-walls of Kano thronged by an excited population that Kano which no
white man's eye had seen till then, but when only last year my friend Sir Hugh
Clifford had opened a college with much ceremony. I have no doubt that
abode of learning will be furnished with an electric-light plant. Its windows
30 will blaze on the African night and dispel in time every other kind of darkness
no doubt. A great thing, this torch of education, that has been set burning on
the other side of [the] Sahara. But to me it will be like a torch burning on the
grave of the Old Geography, so dear to some little boys of the years 1865–75,
but which has completed its work and has passed away now leaving behind
35 the memory of a few great figures, such for instance as David Livingstone,
the Conqueror for Science of so much of Africa, and captured by its dark
spell, wandering amongst the reed-fringed lakes of the Congo head-waters
and clinging in his last hour to his heart's desire of discovering the sources
of the Nile. A notable figure with a world wide name, a rugged kind face and
40 a thick clipped grey moustache, a great explorer turned in his last days in a
restless wanderer, on[e] of those that can not go home. The greatest object
perhaps of my early geographical enthusiasms.

    But my enthusiasm was always reasonable, it was also discreet. Once only I
exposed myself to the derision of a couple of my school boy chums by putting
45 my finger on a blank spot in the centre, almost, of Africa and declaring that
I would get there. It was perfectly justifiable. I myself was almost ashamed of
having been betrayed into that sort of vapouring. Yet no more than 18 years
afterwards while a wretched little stern wheel steamboat lay moored to the
bank all dark under the stars, I lingered late on deck smoking the pipe of
50 peace after an anxious day. The faint thundering noise of the Stanley Falls

hung in the heavy night air of the Upper Congo. And on the other side of the rapids the unbroken power of the Congo Arabs lay slumbering before the last effort to keep its hold on the immense forests to the eastward. On a dark island lying in the middle of the stream almost in the very foam of the rapids, a dim little light glimmered – and I said to myself: "Yes. This is the very spot," 5 without elation but with considerable surprise. I may well have wondered at what I was doing there, for it was merely an extraneous episode not justifiable on any reasonable ground in the life of a seaman. And truth to say for me no great figure haunted that spot, so unknown to the civilised world, but the unholy memory of a newspaper stunt, and a most unseemly scramble for loot 10 that ever disfigured the history of geographical exploration. But I won't dig up that old hatchet now. The fact remains that I have smoked the pipe of peace in the very center [sic] of what used to be [a] mysterious continent – and that I felt very lonely there. But not so at sea. I never felt lonely there. Perhaps it was because I had a vocation. But mainly I believe because its unchangeable salt 15 waters bring home to you better the sense of the past, the memory of things accomplished which have always temperamentally appealed to my profound sympathies. And I have been lucky, because neither explorer or navigator, it has been given to me also to pass through a central place in the history of sea exploration which has been for long a place of mystery to the civilised world, 20 and even in my time was very imperfectly charted and very lonely.

It was in 1888 while in command of a ship loading in Sydney for Mauritius that all of a sudden all the romantic sense of the past that was in my me [sic] surged up to the surface one day and urged me to write a letter to my owners suggesting that instead [of] the usual Southern route I should take the ship 25 to Mauritius through Torres Straits. I ought to have received a severe rap on knuckles for it for the arguments I advanced in my letter were distinctly thin. The answer came after some little delay and by that time I was sorry I had written. But instead of the opening sentence "You must be crazy" it began by calling my attention that "there would be an additional insurance to pay" and 30 then going on "on the whole however we have no objection to your taking the ship through Torres St^{ts} if you are certain that the season is not too far advanced to endanger the success [of] your passage through the calms that might prevail in the Arafura Sea" and in my heart I felt compunctious, for indeed the season was advanced and my argumentation beside being thin 35 had not been exactly honest. But I must have struck a lucky day in Messrs H. Simpson & Sons' offices, a romantic day. And I don't regret my villainy – for what my sea life would have been for me if it had not included a passage through Torres Straits in its fullest length from the mouth of the Great Fly River to Thursday island. 40

I left Sydney in a gale of wind, in such heavy weather that both the pilot and the tug left me to my own devices inside Sydney Heads, and that in the first twenty minutes after we got outside most of the crockery in the ship got smashed. We were short of cups and plates all that passage, but what was the deprivation in comparison with the hardship of the early navigators. Nine 45 days afterwards I was outside the Bligh entrance in the last ship perhaps that went with a cargo from Sydney to Mauritius through Torres Straits, named first after the determined and reticent Spaniard who first went through them in the 17th century without knowing where he was, without suspicion he had solid New Guinea on one side of him and the whole solid Australian continent 50

on the other (he was passing through an Archipelago) the straits whose [existence] was doubted, was denied by that good navigator and disreputable person Abel Tasman (who thought it was a large bay) who certainly was a little "remiss" in not pushing his investigations further – and whose first contours
5   were laid down on the map by James Cook, the navigator without fear and without reproach, the explorer's infinite pains audacious and persevering and so generally estimable as to be invested with a romantic halo by the very perfection of his virtues.

     If the dead haunt the scene of their earthly exploits then I went by well
10   attended by those shades, the determined Spaniard, so disdainful that in his report he does not condescend to say a single word about the appalling difficulties and dangers of his passage; the mule-headed Hollander who made up his mind that there was no passage there, but a great navigator all the same; and the Englishman, a son of the soil but with the soul of a great navigator in
15   him, a great professional seaman who solved that question like some others leaving no doubtful spot after him. All friends of my youth!

     That morning after entering into the strait a black speck caught my attention, and it was the half-buried old remnant of a little schooner. She marked conveniently the end of a long sandbank which I passed close in order to
20   make out the faded letters on her stern. Her name was: "Honolulu." The port I could not read. Her story by now is known to God alone, and the winds were drifting around what remained of her form a quiet grave of sand. Thirty hours afterwards of which about ten were spent at anchor under Saddle Island, I was at the other end of the Strait whose end was marked to me by the gaunt
25   grey wreck of a big American ship lying high and dry on the Warrior Reef. I had heard of her. She had been there for years and loomed up sinister and enormous raised by refraction of this calm evening above of the far horizon. And thus at dusk I passed out of Torres Straits, I hardly hoped noticed by the three Great Shades. The last sailing vessel perhaps that has passed that way
30   on her purely commercial errand. I do not know if it is to their favour and especially that of Abel Tasman who was the man of his time who knew the most of the Arafura Sea that just escaping the season of calms in that lonely region I made a good passage to my destination.

     What is certain is that while making that passage my mind was haunted
35   by the prestige of my achievement. Thus the sea for me has never been a lonely waste. The company of my boyhood attended the grown man and I shall never regret wasting my time in reading books of travel and exploration by sea and land, for which those professor[s] were always trying to take my scalp (but I have forgiven them) considering it a reprehensible waste of time,
40   those books that told me of great endeavour and hard-won successes, and of the men great in their calling of varied characters and going with varied motives, laudable or sinful but each nursing in his breast a spark of the sacred fire.

TEXTUAL NOTES

The notes below justify or gloss decisions related to emendations to the copy-texts, or otherwise comment upon textual issues at a level of detail inappropriate to 'The Texts: An Essay', which lays out the editorial policy of the Cambridge Edition and of this critical edition of *Last Essays*.

In notes dealing with alternative readings – whether in the early texts or proposed as emendations (adopted here or not) – a bracket follows the reading drawn from the text (the lemma) and a statement of variation precedes the commentary. Conventions of notation conform to those followed in the 'Emendation and Variation' list and explained in its headnote on pp. 273–4. The policies governing reports are also laid out there. The sigla for the texts and explanations for the abbreviations used are to be found in the same headnote and in the headnotes for the individual essays.

LAST ESSAYS

GEOGRAPHY AND SOME EXPLORERS

4.22   **for solemn fooling**] ED solemn fooling for solemn fooling TS1r– Conrad appears to have merely rewritten his phrase on a new line to include 'for', but then forgot to delete his initial inscription. This is a characteristic fault in revision in manuscripts and typescripts, and, as occurs here, vestiges of original formulations not explicitly deleted remain in a final text sometimes to awkward effect.

5.11   **infinite toil**] TS1r TS2t TS2ct infinite toil, TS2r TS2ce– Punctuation added by Conrad in hasty or careless revision so vigorously disrupts sense that returning to the original is imperative.

7.6–7   **bit of the coast line**] TS1r a line TS2t TS2ct bit of the coast TS2r TS2ce– The original formulation, effaced by a typing error, is preferred to a revision made on the typist's terms.

7.22   *Heemskerck*] ED Heemskirk TS1r– Conrad's error may derive from his previous misspelling of the name of his character Heemskirk in 'Freya of the Seven Isles'. (Abel Tasman's ship was named after the town in the Netherlands.)

8.15   **transactions**] TS1r transactions of their own TS2– The typist mistakenly carried over the phrase 'of their own' from TS1t. It is clearly deleted but occurs at a point where Conrad's heavy holograph revisions meet up with the typewritten text. His failure to delete the phrase in TS2t does not warrant its retention; as in other instances of this kind, this would be to adopt phrasing whose authority lies with the typist.

8.34   now] **TS2ce P** which now **TS1r** which is now **TS2 TS2ct SE–** Conrad's muddled draft required repair. TS2's typist addressed this issue by adding a verb, whereas the individual responsible for copying revisions into TS2c either followed verbal directions given by Conrad or intervened by cutting 'which is'. The latter is the more satisfactory solution since the phrasing is tangled up with the earlier 'which ... now' in this sentence.

9.34   **professional]** **TS2 TS2ct SE–** the professional **TS1r** his professional **TS2ce P** Although the typist made an error in dropping the definite article, Conrad's thorough revision of his phrasing serendipitously requires its omission.

10.22   **two ships]** ED ships' **TS1r** ship's work **TS2t TS2ct** two ship's work **TS2r TS2ce–** The anomalous possessive in **TS1r** apparently urged on the typist of TS2 to supply a noun, not required if the faulty possessive is corrected.

11.7   **old Geography]** **TS1r TS2t TS2ct** geography **TS2r TS2ce–** Conrad's deletion of 'old' so obviously works against the sense of his passage, otherwise dominated by rewriting and recasting, that, on balance, it must have been inadvertent.

14.37   **because]** **TS2ce P** there. **TS1r TS2t** because there **TS2r SE–** Conrad added 'There' at the opening of his sentence, but his replacement of his original terminal phrase (with its new sentence) 'there. I never' with 'because I never' was imperfect: he deleted the full stop, but then failed to delete 'there'. The alteration made in TS2c is a reasonable clarification.

15.6   **imperfectly]** **TS1r** very imperfectly **TS2–** Rather than representing revision in a now-lost document, the first appearance of 'very' here is suspect; in TS2 the word occurs on the line above ('very heart') in the same sentence. On balance, this represents either eyeskip or anticipation.

15.35   **was insistent]** ED VAR **TS1r TS2t TS2ct** insistent **TS2r** insisted **TS2ce–** Conrad's flawed revision in TS2 presumably inspired radical tidying by his typist; his intention, however, seems clear, and the emendation follows it through.

16.37–38   **of ... approaching]** **TS2r TS2ce–** I sighted at **TS1r TS2t TS2ct** In revising TS2, Conrad replaced 'I sighted at' with 'approaching', then failed to supply a verb to his revised sentence. The historical texts opt to restore the phrase he explicitly deleted, whereas the meaning and rhythm of the sentence are better served by following through on what appears to have been his initial intention and placing the verb where it would logically occur.

17.2   **on]** ED of **TS1r–** Rather than asserting that an image of the wrecked ship had been raised by 'refraction' *of* the afternoon, Conrad, by way of contrast, is recalling the incongruity of sighting a reminder of death *on* a 'serene afternoon'.

THE *TORRENS*
A PERSONAL TRIBUTE

18.27   **apart]** **MS** for apart **TSc–** In a making a revision at the bottom of the first page, Conrad carried over the typist's phrasing from the top of the next, preserving a word she had introduced and thus, without reference to his original, altering his work on her terms. MS's phrasing, more grammatical, is unhesitatingly restored.

19.10   **an extreme instance of it**] SE– and a **MS** and an extreme case of it **TSct** A [*sic*] extreme instance which certainly **TScr** This is a case among several in this typescript where the typist recuperated a deletion in MS. TSct's version is, in fact, Conrad's original inscription, which he then altered, first, in revising the typescript and, later, for the serial. For a detailed discussion of the typist's transcription of deletions in the manuscript, see 'The Texts', pp. 212–14.

20.25   **removed ... ideals of**] **MS TSct SE**– re- **TScr** Conrad deleted matter during revision, perhaps intending to replace it, but in the end failed to do so. Restoration of MS's text occurs as a matter of course to avoid a lacuna.

20.40–21.1   **three or four berths in them**] ED three berths in them **MS** three berths **TSct** three or four berths **TScr**– On balance, the typist was responsible for dropping 'in them', and thus inspired Conrad to revise on her terms.

21.22   **at ... care**] **TScr** at that last of my sea-homes from the quay **MS** and at last of my sea-homes from the quay **TSct** that last of ships I ever had under my care **SE**– Conrad's handwriting in the typescript is so difficult to decipher and the revision so hard to follow that SE's somewhat awkward phrasing is, probably, a typist's reconstruction from the material rather than a case of authorial revision in a later typescript.

21.30   **steamer service**] ED VAR **MS TSct SA** service **TScr** steamer **SE** P– The addition of 'steamer' and the dropping of the word 'service' in SE led to an error that made the name of a river appear to be that of a ship: E1 reads '*Hoogh1y* pilot-steamer'. TScr provides the grounds for emendation: at issue is a regular service supplied by a company, not a single vessel.

22.5   **lasted out**] ED lasted for **MS TSct** lasted out for **TScr**– While at times faulty, idiomatic control here is so radically and atypically askew as to make ineffective revision probable. In revising, Conrad seems inadvertently to have forgotten to delete 'for' while he replaced it with 'out'. Similar slips occur several times across his texts.

22.19   **Mr Conrad**] TSc– the Mr Conrad **MS** Failure to adjust MS's awkward syntax during revision seems more likely responsible for phrasing than does a poor sense of idiom, the impression of the latter compounded by the addition of a comma in TSct after 'Conrad'. Phrasing apparently altered in mid-flow, and the typist's intervention seems an acceptable solution to the problem generated by a half-completed revision.

22.25   **go and**] **MS TSc SA** go to **SE** P– Although Conrad revised SE proofs, this change towards 'correct' usage is sufficiently suspicious to be rejected as an editorial sophistication.

CHRISTMAS-DAY AT SEA

23.1   **Christmas-day**] **MS** Christmas Day **TS1**– Conrad's usage, more common in the early and mid nineteenth century, presumably fell before the typist's conventionalizing instinct. Conrad uses this form only in the title and first paragraph, later resorting, in the haste of writing, to various abbreviations ('Xmas', 'Ch'[as], 'Chris[as]') before the word 'day'. Although he obviously expected these to be expanded by his typist, here she rejected a clearly expressed preference.

23.5 **fails**] **MS** refuses **TS1**– Conrad first wrote 'is unable', revising that to 'refuses', and then finally hit upon 'fails', writing that word in the margin of the next line and crossing out 'refuses'. The typist, oddly, typed the initial crossed-out inscription and then replaced that by 'refuses' (easily legible); in the end, however, she missed Conrad's final revision.

23.6 **Perhaps ... face it**] **MS** OM **TS1t** perhaps **TS1r**– The typist skipped a line, and Conrad revised in TS1 without reference to his original, with the typist's error altering his drift.

23.12 **weak, distinctly weak**] **MS** distinctly weak **TS1**– The typist either missed out the first word or considered the phrasing redundant; in any case, Conrad's wording and colloquial tone disappear. In the critical text, a comma is added after the first 'weak'.

23.13 **a ship's company**] **TS2r** the men **MS TS1t** the ship's company **TS1r TS2t SEp1r**– ship's company **TS3 SEp1u** The dropping out of the indefinite article during the typing of TS3 caused Conrad to correct in SEp1 on the basis of an error. His revision in TS2 takes precedence over a revision spawned by his typist's mistake.

24.9 **more**] **MS TS1r–TS3 SEp1**– more un-Christian could be imagine [*sic*] **TS1t** OM **SA** This is not a fit of creative writing by the typist: what she transcribed is Conrad's original inscription that he deleted in the manuscript. See 23.5*n.* and 26.23*n.*, which describe similar situations where matter clearly deleted in the manuscript none the less found its way into the typescript.

24.25 **as bitter**] **MS–TS3 SEp1u SA** bitter **SEP1r**– Conrad's revision in SE proofs, made to effect balance, was inspired by a typing error, his phrase 'as salt as tears' (MS) being mangled by the typist. Restoration of the original formulation is axiomatic.

24.32–33 **wireless telegraphy**] **MS** wireless **TS1t** wireless messages **TS1r**– The typist's omission of the word 'telegraphy' necessitated an adjustment during revision. On balance, Conrad's initial wording seems preferable to a correction made when his hand was forced.

24.34 **a particularly**] **TS1t TS3**– particularly **MS TS1r** The initial inscription reveals a characteristic problem with articles. In TS1, however, Conrad's first impulse towards revision was the phrase 'regarded as particularly offensive' and he thus crossed out the indefinite article supplied by his typist. In further revision he added 'nuisance', failing, however, to reinstate the now necessary article.

25.2 **"Merry Christmas"**] ED Merry Xmas **MS** a happy Christmas **TS1 TS2t** a "Merry Christmas" **TS2r**– The typescript in which Conrad revised inherited the indefinite article supplied by the typist of TS1; it is expunged here.

26.23 **days**] **MS** days of risk and toil spent **TS1t** days of risk and toil **TS1r**– In MS, Conrad revised his initial phrase 'days spent in risk and toil' to 'days', but the typist reinstated the deleted material (as she did in several other instances) and also misplaced the word 'spent'.

OUTSIDE LITERATURE

30.29   **is**] SA E1 A1 are TS SE1 SE2 The alteration by SA's editor, also made by Curle (or his typist), seems a reasonable correction of a flagrant and highly disruptive error in agreement in a dictated text produced under pressure and rapidly revised.

30.31   **ideal**] TS an ideal SE1– On balance, the reading in the printed texts represents normalization by the typist.

31.14   **civilisation,**] TS a civilisation SE1– See the preceding note, with normalization again suspected here. The deletion of TS's comma necessitates adding the indefinite article and alters not only the balance of the sentence but also the meaning of the assertion.

32.3   **has happened**] TS happened SE1– The unidiomatic verb form is so characteristically Conradian that tidying at the second typescript stage on the part of the typist seems a greater likelihood than authorial revision. As in similar instances discussed here, retaining the reading in the copy-text is more compelling.

32.28–29   **my captain one morning**] TS one morning my captain SE1– The case for revision seems weaker than that to be made for mechanical error or eyeskip. The re-casting in the printed texts renders the sentence less typically Conradian in rhythm.

LEGENDS

34.25   **itself, the**] MS itself. The SE– Conrad's revisions to his original inscription were misunderstood in such a way as to create two sentences – one an awkward fragment – where, in fact, only a single sentence is at issue. Conrad first wrote 'The Golden Legend suffers of it'. He then added 'itself' after 'Legend', and deleted 'it' and 'suffers of' and, finally, dashed a badly formed comma into the margin. The comma was apparently read as a mere stray mark, and the absence of punctuation after 'miracles' further confused the issue, so that the editor missed the point that an explanatory clause was intended.

35.11   **vocational**] SE– was vocational MS The elimination of a redundant 'was' is necessary, although that after 'believe' could just as easily be selected for deletion. The solution offered by the historical texts is, however, reasonable and allowed to stand. Conrad tends to repeat verbs after long parenthetical phrases, but the repetition here is not only clumsy but also disruptive.

35.35   **speaks**] ED He speaks MS– The copy-text is so obviously defective as to require repair. The historic texts do so by muddling sense, claiming for Basil Lubbock, apparently on no evidentiary basis, a trip round Cape Horn. Conrad's prior conditional 'if', retained only by SA, moves in an altogether different direction: it suggests that, although not having faced the perils of Cape Horn, Lubbock none the less possessed the intimate knowledge of a seaman who had experienced them.

36.9–10   **the celebration**] SE E1– celebration MS SA As a native speaker of Polish, Conrad typically had problems with articles in English, but in this case, the omission of the definite article was due to a slip of the pen as he revised. He originally wrote 'the illustration of Holiness', and on substituting this phrase deleted 'the' inadvertently.

36.18　**sign of adversity**] ED of adversity **MS SA** adversity **SE E1–** SE's solution to a textual crux is insensitive to Conrad's meaning: the word clearly intended here simply failed to make its way onto the page.

36.23　**Basil**] **SE E1–** Percy **MS SA** In preparing this essay for publication, Richard Curle corrected this casual error to avoid confusing the reader, and, presumably, on the assumption that, had Conrad been able to revise his essay, he would have corrected his mistake. Percy Lubbock (1879–1965), Basil Lubbock's first cousin, was a Cambridge literary critic, essayist and biographer, his best-known work being *The Craft of Fiction* (1921).

36.24–25　**sails, one**] ED one (sails **MS** sails – one **SE–** Conrad's writing in a paragraph with several problems is so tangled and Curle's response sufficiently arbitrary to make comment advisable. Conrad seemingly first placed the phrase 'one reviewer ... mean' within en-rules. (The first en-rule is uncertain as the writing is unclear.) He then placed a round bracket before 'one reviewer' and deleted the closing en-rule so as to form a full stop but failed to supply a closing round bracket. The emendation offers a less dramatic handling of this crux than that of the historical texts. Curle's or the serial editor's en-rule, overly forceful, also reverts to a form Conrad rejected.

36.30　**to tell**] **SE–** it tell **MS** Curle's is a logical solution to impossible wording in a phrase Conrad tinkered with, having initially written 'I wonder who first sent it about?', then replacing that with 'I wonder who was the man who invented it?' Stylistically flat, the final version is also garbled.

THE UNLIGHTED COAST

37.13　**sleepless feast**] **MS** a sleepless feast **TS–** The typist's normalization or error of anticipation effaces a balanced stylistic effect: the absence of the indefinite article, if somewhat unusual, is not grammatically wrong.

37.16　**signs**] **S–** sign **MS TS** In revising the typescript, Conrad changed 'And there was' to 'There were' but failed to follow through with the required change in number.

38.22–23　**an enemy**] **MS** a hostile **TS–** Conrad's initial inscription, which he replaced during revision of the manuscript, made its way into the typescript, the typist overlooking the clearly made change, and Conrad not referring back to his original during revision.

42.22　**very much**] **MS** very **TS–** The typist missed out 'much', with the result that Conrad, when expanding this section by the addition of two short sentences, and after initially crossing out the phrase, recopied what had been typed, unknowingly altering his work on the typist's terms.

43.8　**awful**] **MS** the awful **TS–** The typist was moved to normalize, or this is a case of anticipation. The definite article, not grammatically necessary, slows the pace.

THE DOVER PATROL

47.35 own] **TS1** old TSr– The distinction between professional mariners, whether naval or belonging to the Merchant Service, and fisher-folk involved in the war effort is more effectively maintained by TS1's wording, which the typist normalized or mistyped in copying this draft page.

MEMORANDUM

50.8 **equipping of**] **ED** equipping **TS1**– The ungrammatical phrase most likely results from a typist's error, the required preposition having dropped out during dictation. Although prone to problems in the correct use of articles, Conrad is unlikely to have had problems here with the use of 'of'.

51.9 **what**] **TS1r** that **TS1t TS2** TS2's typist normalized, rejecting what appeared to be an odd formulation for the more expected and idiomatic 'that'. The phrasing, however, is distinctly Conradian: 'All what I have said is true ... ': *Almayer's Folly* (1990), p. 41.21.

51.18 **once and a half**] **TS1**– Emendation suggests itself if 'once' is viewed as a typing error for 'one'. Although qualifying it as 'rare', the *OED* notes this sense: 'Denoting numerical proportion; multiplied by one'.

52.8 **sailor's**] **E1** sailor **TS1** sailors' **TS2 A1** 'Sailor phrase' is acceptable usage. Cf. '"if you once give a dog a bad name" – as the sailor-phrase is': Richard Henry Dana, Jr, *Two Years before the Mast* (1840), or '"Laying off and on" – a sailor phrase sufficiently well understood by landsmen': *Daily Union*, 22 May 1866 in *Mark Twain's Letters from Hawaii*, ed. A. Grove Day (1975), p. 83. TS2's typist, however, rightly saw the awkwardness of the formulation 'sailor expressive phrase' (revised to 'sailor graphic phrase'). Her possessive plural, however, is less compelling than the singular possessive, in line with TS1 and also favoured by E1's compositor.

52.13 **attached to**] **TS2**– attached of **TS1** The typist reasonably responded to Conrad's failure to carry through a revision: having changed 'be proud of' to 'grow attached', he failed to alter the preposition.

53.25 **laid down**] **E1**– laid **TS1 TS2** The addition by Curle or his typist sensibly repairs a flaw in the typescripts, the word perhaps having been missed out during dictation.

55.1–2 **(for 3 years)**] **TS2r** OM **TS1 TS2t** (for two years) **E1**– Aware that Conrad had spent 1891–3 in the *Torrens*, the ship alluded to, Curle assumed that this was a slip and adjusted the period to two years. It is quite possible that, in adding this detail in revising TS2, Conrad simply misremembered the length of his service. His general tendency to exaggerate the time he spent at sea suggests that this should remain unemended, even if at odds with fact.

60.3 **are aboard**] **ED** man **TS1t** aboard **TS1r** are aboard of **TS2**– The historical texts perpetuate a typist's awkward addition made in transcribing TS1r and not caught by Conrad in his revision of TS2. On the other hand, her decision to supply an obviously missing verb in this phrase is a reasonable, and indeed necessary, way of coping with one missed out during dictation.

TRAVEL
PREFACE TO RICHARD CURLE'S *INTO THE EAST*

68.10　**were**] **TS2r** are **TS1** P– OM **TS2t** Conrad's revision, probably made without reference to TS1, is a response to a dropped word. The required verb reflects genuine second thought rather than his revising on the typist's terms. The syntax of this sentence remains awkward, but it seems preferable to take TS2r's clear authority rather than to rely upon the uncertain source for a return to the present tense in P.

70.8　**on**] **TS1** of **TS2**– The typist normalized Conrad's nautically inflected and acceptable phrase that positions the deck 'on' the steamer.

STEPHEN CRANE
INTRODUCTION TO THOMAS BEER'S
STEPHEN CRANE

74.17　**in the deep**] **MS** the deep **TS**– That 'in' dropped out during typing trumps the possibility of revision: the rhythm of the phrase demands the repeated preposition.

75.9　**faculty"**] **MS** The restoration of the inverted commas to this phrase is the only matter at issue here. MS lacks the comma that appears after 'faculty' in the critical text, and thus this report does not include it.

77.13　**had never**] **MS** never had **TS**– On balance, it seems plausible that the manuscript's thoroughly idiomatic phrasing was transposed by the typist.

79.40　**streets**] **ED VAR MS** mazes the streets **TS**– This redundancy in the typescript is a typical example of an inscription not deleted on second thought and managing to survive through revision and imperfect proofreading. The definite article also suggests the possibility of another idea not followed through.

HIS WAR-BOOK
INTRODUCTION TO STEPHEN CRANE'S
THE RED BADGE OF COURAGE

92.16　**unbelief**] **MS TS** disbelief **C**– Although not impossible here, revision seems less probable than editorial intervention, with authorial wording falling to an editor's 'correcting' impulse, 'unbelief' being, properly, a rejection of belief rather than incredulity or scepticism. The rejected 'disbelief' is, moreover, redundant since 'incredulity' is already specifically mentioned.

92.20　**down**] **MS** down with his hands over his eyes **TS**– Although Conrad's deletion of the phrase in MS is unambiguous, it made its way into the typescript, which is otherwise the work of a poor typist whose interventions compromise this text at several points.

93.1 **Lord!**] **E1** God! **MS** Lord, **TS C–** The punctuation in the manuscript gives authority for adopting E1's reading, the formulation in the lost clean-copy typescript being presumably a typist's error.

93.3 **very words**] **MS TS** words **C–** Emendation is again declined on another occasion where the standardizing energies of the American editor seem more probable than authorial revision.

93.4 **itself.**] **C–** itself – the **MS** itself– He **TS** The editorial adjustment of punctuation is justified, the typist having mistakenly carried over the en-rule belonging to a superseded formulation.

93.8 **In**] **ED** And in **MS** ¶ In **TS–** The typist installed a paragraph-break not present in MS. Whatever Conrad's revised wording, MS authorizes the elimination of this break.

93.11 **at the**] **MS** of **TSt** of the **TSr–** The typist's dropping out of 'the' puts into question her transcription of 'of' as well, and, on balance, the manuscript's phrasing, also more logical, has stronger claims. Conrad revised on terms he was unaware of and probably made no reference to his original.

93.21 **chief**] **ED** foremost | chief **MS** foremost **TS–** Conrad first wrote 'foremost' and on beginning a new leaf inscribed the word 'chief' without, however, deleting 'foremost' on the previous page. The typist presumably viewed 'chief' as redundant.

93.24 **fundamental**] **ED** general **MS TSt** generalised fundamental **TSr–** Conrad altered his original wording and when, in further revision, he rejected 'generalised' for 'fundamental', failed to delete his first revision. As a result, awkward and even redundant phrasing descended to the historical texts.

A GLANCE AT TWO BOOKS

101.31 **altruistic**] **ED** altruist **TS–** The *OED* gives no warrant for the adjectival use of this word, and Conrad employs the correct adjectival form in the manuscripts of 'Heart of Darkness' (*Youth* (2010), p. 95.38) and *The Secret Agent* (p. 14.2). Rather than a nonce usage, this is apparently a slip (possibly influenced by the French adjective *altruiste*), uncaught in the revision of a rather poorly produced typescript in which Conrad also failed to correct several even more obvious errors. A case could be made that this is an error for 'altruists', but that seems less plausible.

104.29 **leaf**] **ED** small leaf **TS–** It is a toss-up whether Conrad or his typist was responsible for the defective mistranscription of W. H. Hudson's text in this and several other instances (see 'Emendations of Accidentals'). In TS, the occurrence of the word 'small' four times in relatively close proximity allows for eyeskip during the typing of the (lost) manuscript, a possibility supported by the fact that this typist was not careful in her work here generally. Conrad himself may, of course, have mistranscribed the passage and failed to check it. Assuming, however, that he intended to copy these sentences correctly and to have his typist copy his work aright, it is preferable to revert to Hudson's original.

EXPLANATORY NOTES

Topics sufficiently explained in a standard desk dictionary receive no notice. Place-names and other topographical matters identified by the maps at the end of this volume are also disregarded except when contextual or historical information might be useful. Where place-names have changed since Conrad's time, the present-day name is given only on its first occurrence, an exception being made for 'The Congo Diary' and 'Up-river Book', documents probably to be read for reference, independently from the other essays here. Vocabulary related to shipping and maritime matters is listed and briefly explained in the 'Glossary of Nautical Terms'. Wherever possible, the sources cited here are those that Conrad and his first readers could have known: thus, late nineteenth-century and early twentieth-century documents are preferred to later, retrospective studies.

LAST ESSAYS

GEOGRAPHY AND SOME EXPLORERS

3.8 **conic sections** In mathematics, a conic section is a curve formed by the intersection of a plane and a cone. It is either a circle, ellipse, parabola or hyperbola.

3.19 **earth is a stage** 'All the world's a stage, / And all the men and women merely players': Shakespeare, *As You Like It*, II.vii.139–40.

3.21–22 **the play ... the thing** A possible echo of 'The play's the thing / Wherein I'll catch the conscience of the king': Shakespeare, *Hamlet*, II.ii.641–2.

4.9 **pictorial ... modern newspapers** Early newspapers rarely featured illustrations. The weekly *Illustrated London News* (founded 1842) both created and responded to a market need, and, as technology developed, pictorial elements became increasingly prominent in the daily press, particularly in the popular mass-circulation newspapers established during the late-Victorian boom in journalism.

4.13 **Monomotapa ... Prester John** 'Monomotapa' was an early sixteenth-century Portuguese adaptation of *Mwene Mutapa* ('Ravager of the Lands'), the name given to a paramount chief of a group living between the Zambezi and Limpopo rivers in south-eastern Africa. The name eventually appeared on maps as the Kingdom of Mutapa. Prester John (also Presbyter John) was a legendary Christian ruler-priest, about whom legends flourished from the mid twelfth to the seventeenth centuries. He was first believed to have ruled over a utopian kingdom in Asia, but later legends shifted the scene of his activities to Africa and, by the fourteenth century, specifically to Abyssinia (present-day Ethiopia).

4.14–15   **eyes ... breasts** The source for this myth is in Herodotus: 'Here are also the Cynocephali, as well as the Acephali, who, if the Libyans may be credited, have eyes in the breasts': *The Histories*, IV.111 (trans. Revd William Beloe, 1840). Mention is made of these creatures throughout the centuries. See, for example, the comment of the French essayist Michel de Montaigne: 'there are countries, where men are born without heads, having their mouth and eyes in their breast': *The Essays of Michel de Montaigne*, trans. Charles Cotton (1908), p. 223; and Sir Thomas Browne: 'we relinquish as fabulous what is delivered of *sternophthalmi*, or men with eyes in their breast': *Pseudodoxia Epidemica* (1646), Bk III, ch. 19 in *The Works of Sir Thomas Browne*, ed. Simon Wilkins (1852), I, 316–17.
   An early nineteenth-century article on 'Superstition' attacks the assertion that such men existed – 'It is false and irrational to say that there ever lived on earth a race of men who walked on one leg, and had their eyes in their breast': *The London Encyclopædia, or Universal Dictionary*, ed. Thomas Curtis (1829), XXII, 418. A mid-nineteenth-century travel book commenting on the Africa constructed by Pliny and Herodotus observes: 'The men with dogs' heads [the Cynocephali], of whom Herodotus speaks, are the barking baboons which I saw in the Senegal; the men with their heads under their shoulders, their eyes in their breast, are the ill-formed negroes, whose shoulders are shrugged up, and whose heads drop on their breasts': W. Winwood Reade, *Savage Africa: being The Narrative of a Tour in Equatorial, Southwestern, and Northwestern Africa* (1864), p. 369.

4.24   **fears ... cupidities of men** Commonplace in religious and philosophical discourse, the phrase is possibly derived from 'All sins in men are caused by two things, fear and cupidity': St Augustine's Commentary on Psalm 79.

4.32   **chains ... Columbus** After 'discovering' the Americas in 1492 and returning to Spain, the Italian explorer Christopher Columbus (Cristoforo Colombo or Cristoval Colón, 1451–1506) was initially honoured, but his fortunes soon waned. In 1500, he was transported from Hispaniola back to Spain in chains, and on a subsequent expedition marooned on Jamaica.

5.1–2   **Fata Morgana** A mirage, specifically attributed to Morgan le Fay of Arthurian legend: looking at the Strait of Messina, between Calabria and Sicily, a spectator on the shore sees images of men, houses, ships and so forth, sometimes in the water, sometimes in the air, with the images observed often seeming to have two identical images, one inverted.

5.4–5   **the Conquistadors** The Spanish conquerors of Peru and Mexico during the sixteenth century.

5.8   **Eldorado** 'The Golden City' (Spanish). A legendary city of gold (also spelled 'El Dorado') was believed to be located on the Amazon river, although others placed it on the Orinoco. The latter location particularly interested English adventurers such as Sir Walter Raleigh (1552–1618).

5.17–18   **Cortez ... Pizarro ... Cabeza de Vaca** The most notable Spanish explorers of the Americas: Hernán Cortés or Cortez (1485–1547), known primarily for the conquest of Mexico, arrived at Tenochtitlán (present-day Mexico City) and subjugated the Aztec ruler Montezuma in 1519. He later sent expeditions into northern Central America. On returning to Spain in 1540, he fell out of favour and was neglected by the Court. The greed and ambition of the conqueror of Peru, Francisco Pizarro (*c.* 1476–1541), alienated his followers, and he was assassinated.

Álvar Núñez Cabeza de Vaca (*c.* 1490 – *c.* 1557) explored the south-west of what is now the United States after an unsuccessful time as treasurer of an expedition to Florida in 1528. He escaped to an island off present-day Texas, where he was enslaved by Indians. Escaping again, he travelled west to what is now Texas, New Mexico and Arizona, and perhaps as far as California, gaining respect as a healer, because many cures were considered the result of his prayers.

5.24 **Southern Pacific Railroad** The pre-eminent railway of the south-western United States (founded in 1865), eventually growing to include more than 13,000 miles (20,800 km) of track.

5.28 **Balboa** The Spaniard Vasco Núñez de Balboa (*c.* 1475–1519), who 'discovered' the Pacific Ocean in 1513, claimed it and all the territories surrounding it for Spain.

5.31 **named the Pacific** In fact, the Portuguese explorer Ferdinand Magellan (*c.* 1480–1521), not Balboa, named the Pacific Ocean.

6.19 **theory ... southern continent** From at least the time of first-century Greek astronomer and geographer Ptolemy, the theory existed that a great continent in the southern oceans would one day be discovered. An early report, Cornelius Wytfliet's *Descriptionis Ptolemaicæ Augmentum* (1598), commented that *Australis Terra* is 'separated from New Guinea by a narrow strait. Its shores are hitherto but little known ... [It] begins at one or two degrees from the equator, and is ascertained by some to be of so great an extent, that if it were thoroughly explored it would be regarded as a fifth part of the world': *Encyclopædia Britannica*, 9th edn (1890), III, 103.

7.2 **Tasman ... Cook** Abel Janszoon Tasman (*c.* 1603–59), a Dutch navigator for the Dutch East India Company during 1632–53, was a trader and explorer in the Pacific and Indian Oceans who reached the Philippines, Taiwan and Japan. In 1642, he discovered Van Diemen's Land (present-day Tasmania, Australia) and New Zealand and sailed by the Tonga Islands. He returned to Batavia (7.28*n.*) the next year having circumnavigated Australia, proving that its land mass was unattached to Antarctica. The English explorer and navigator James Cook (1728–79) joined the Royal Navy and later explored and surveyed parts of eastern and western Canada, New Zealand and Australia, in the process circumnavigating the globe. He disproved the existence of *Terra Australis Incognita*.

7.16 **Tasman's journal** The complete journal of Tasman's first voyage survives only in two abridged versions or extracts, neither confirmed as being in his hand. The translation referred to, by J. De Hoop Scheffer and C. Stoffel, appears in *Abel Janszoon Tasman's Journal of his Discovery of Van Diemen's Land and New Zealand in 1642 with Documents relating to his Exploration of Australia in 1644*, edited by J(an) E(rnst) Heeres and published by Frederick Muller of Amsterdam in 1898. In addition to learned commentary in Dutch and English and facsimiles of the surviving document, it also included a life of Tasman by Heeres.

7.22–23 *Heemskerck* ... **Murderers' Bay** Tasman's flagship, the *Heemskerck*, accommodated a crew of about sixty. Tasman bestowed the name Murderers' (Mordenaars) Bay (present-day Golden Bay) on a bay near Nelson, New Zealand, in memory of a Maori attack on 19 December 1642 on the *Zeehaen*, the *Heemskerck*'s companion-ship. Three sailors were bludgeoned to death and a fourth mortally wounded.

7.28   **Batavia** Founded by the Dutch (*c.* 1619), the city (present-day Jakarta, Indonesia) on the Java Sea became the headquarters of the Dutch East India Company and the de facto administrative centre of the colonial government, becoming in time Java's most important city.

7.37   **name lives** Tasmania, the large island located about 150 miles (240 km) south-east of the Australian continent, was renamed in 1855 to honour its discoverer. From 1642 to 1855, it had been called Van Diemen's Land (see 8.13*n.*).

7.39   **130 years** The rounding off is doubtless for rhetorical effect: Captain Cook arrived 127 years later, in October 1769.

8.10–11   **medallist of the Royal Society** Founded in 1660 and incorporated in 1662 as the Royal Society of London for Improving Natural Knowledge, the Society commissioned Cook's Pacific voyages from 1768 to 1771 and from 1772 to 1775. On Cook's return from his second voyage, he was elected to a Fellowship for his work in cartography, navigation and astronomy, and in 1776 received the Society's oldest award, the Copley Medal, given annually for outstanding research in any branch of science. The medal, awarded in the physical or biological sciences in alternate years, honours in Cook's case the measures he had taken to preserve the health of his crew.

8.13   **van Diemen** Dutch statesman, general manager of the Dutch East India Company and Governor of the Dutch East Indies, Anton van Diemen (1593–1645) sent Tasman on the exploratory expedition during which he discovered Tasmania.

8.19   **Acheen** The sultanate, also Achin or Atjeh (present-day Aceh), of northern Sumatra in the Dutch East Indies. Strategically located on the Strait of Malacca, Aceh during the early seventeenth century was much contested for by the Dutch, Danish, English, Portuguese and Chinese, all of whom attempted to gain trading supremacy over the area.

8.29   **amusing and interesting book** See 7.16*n.*

8.33–34   **common consent ... continent** That is, Australia. The designation 'continent' has diverse meanings: the Americas, for example, being considered by some, and particularly by the Hispanic world, as a single continent and Antarctica dismissed, making a total of five rather than, as in the English-speaking world, seven continents.

8.35   **young Commonwealth** An allusion to the official name, the Commonwealth of Australia, formed in 1901 on the federation of six colonies (the states of the new nation).

8.37   **the Elysian Fields** In Greek mythology, the blissful place reserved in the after-life for heroes and the virtuous favoured by the gods. Its pleasures are variously presented by the writers of Antiquity; in Virgil, it was a place enjoying eternal springtime and featuring shady groves.

9.33   **Franklin** After serving in the Royal Navy and seeing action in the Battle of Trafalgar, John Franklin (1786–1847; knighted 1829) began his explorations in northern Canada and the Arctic in 1819. His expeditions are recorded in *Narrative of a Journey to the Shores of the Polar Sea* (1823) and *Narrative of a Second Expedition to the Shores of the Polar Sea* (1828). After an interlude as Governor of Van Diemen's

Land (1836–43), he set out to search for the Northwest Passage. His ships became ice-bound, and he and his crew perished. The opening of 'Heart of Darkness' recalls him and his ships.

10.6   **M'Clintock** (Francis) Leopold McClintock (1819–1907; knighted 1860) began his search for Franklin on the expedition of Sir James Clark Ross in 1848, and led one of more than forty expeditions to search for Franklin when Lady Franklin gave him command of the *Fox* in 1857. He explored Prince Wales and King William Islands, discovering evidence that Franklin and his men had left the *Erebus* and *Terror* alive and had proceeded on foot to Hudson Bay. McClintock, who argued that Franklin had discovered the Northwest Passage, recorded his search in *The Voyage of the 'Fox' in Arctic Seas: A Narrative of the Discovery of the Fate of Sir John Franklin and his Companions* (1859).

10.9   **born ... publication** A slip: Conrad was born in December 1857.

10.14–15   **copy ... in French** Presumably, either the full translation by V(ictor)-A(dolphe) Malte-Brun under the name Francis-Léopold Mac-Clintock: *La Destinée de Sir John Franklin dévoilée. Rapport du capitaine Mac-Clintock ... suivi d'un résumé analytique de l'expédition des navires 'Erebus' et 'Terror' et accompagné d'une carte des découvertes arctiques* (Paris, 1860); or Ferdinand de Lanoye's retelling for the adolescent market: *La Mer polaire: Voyage de l'Erebe et de la Terreur et Expéditions à la recherche de Franklin* (Paris, 1865), also with charts and maps.

11.18   **my private tutor** Adam Marek Pulman (1846–91), who studied medicine at the Jagiellonian University from 1868 to 1875. Conrad's schooling was somewhat erratic and irregular because of his ill-health. He had previously been tutored by his father and had perhaps received some formal lessons during his period in Cracow. Conrad describes holidays spent with Pulman and their relationship in *A Personal Record*.

11.39   **Romans ... new thing** 'Ex Africa semper aliquid novi' ('Out of Africa something new is always coming') is the phrase of the Roman scholar and natural historian Pliny the Elder (AD 23–79). The idea, however, has been traced back to Greece of the fourth century BC; see Harvey M. Feinberg and Joseph B. Solodow, 'Out of Africa', *Journal of African History*, 43 (2002), 255–61.

12.2   **Regions unknown** An echo of the Latin phrase *terra incognita*. The phrase still appeared on maps published in Conrad's boyhood.

12.7   **Park ... Bruce** Employed by the African Association to explore the Niger river, the Scottish explorer Mungo Park (1771–1806) travelled about 300 miles (482 km) northward from Segu to Bamako, and recorded his findings in *Travels in the Interior Districts of Africa* (1799). Attempting to trace the Niger to its mouth, he was drowned near Bussa when natives attacked his canoes. Park's fellow Scot, explorer James Bruce (1730–94), known as 'the Abyssinian', travelled extensively in Abyssinia, visiting the capital Gondar, exploring the Blue Nile and travelling to its confluence with the White Nile. His excursions are recorded in *Travels to Discover the Source of the Nile, 1768–73* (1790).

12.14   **Burton and Speke** Captain Richard Francis Burton (1821–90; knighted 1886) travelled with fellow English explorer Captain John Hanning Speke (1827–64) to central Africa to discover the source of the Nile, where he found Lake Tanganyika in 1858. Speke then travelled alone to discover Victoria Nyanza or N'yanza (Lake Victoria), which he believed to be the source of the Nile. In 1862, he discovered that the Victoria Nile flows from the north end of Victoria Nyanza over Ripon Falls. Conrad possibly knew his *Journal of the Discovery of the Source of the Nile* (1863), also available in French translation as *Les Sources du Nil* (1864).

12.23 **Great Lakes** Part of the Congo river system in east central Africa, Lake Tanganyika is the world's longest freshwater lake, Victoria Nyanza being its second largest. Other major lakes in the area are Lakes Albert, Edward, Nyasa and Mweru.

12.24 **heart ... white and big** Areas of Africa unexplored by Westerners were often indicated on maps by blank or white areas, colonized areas being coloured according to a scheme of national colours. Marlow describes this colour-coded mapping system in 'Heart of Darkness'.

12.30 **second officer** Conrad passed his second-mate's examination on 28 May 1880. The second mate is often the ship's navigator. On Admiralty notices, formally Notices to Mariners, see 30.4*n*.

13.13 **episode ... Park's life** Conrad's description of this, based on a memory of childhood reading, apparently conflates and embroiders two experiences in ch. 15 of Park's *Travels*, which has as one of its sub-headings 'Compassionate Treatment of a Negro Woman'. Refused hospitality by the Dooty of Doolinkeaboo, other than a restorative drink of water, he later, whilst continuing his journey, finds himself shunned by the local community but is treated with kindness by a woman:

I was regarded with astonishment and fear, and was obliged to sit all day without victuals in the shade of a tree; and the night threatened to be very uncomfortable ... About sunset, however ... a woman returning from the labours of the field and perceiving that I was weary and dejected, inquired into my situation ... Having conducted me into her hut, she lighted up a lamp, spread a mat on the floor, and told me I might remain there for the night. Finding that I was very hungry she said she would procure me something to eat ... I was oppressed by such unexpected kindness, and sleep fled from my eyes. (*Travels in the Interior Districts of Africa*, 1878 edn, pp. 181–2)

In the early and mid nineteenth century, the episode circulated in anthologies intended for children, including *Introduction to the English Reader* by Lindley Murray (31st printing, 1836) where it appears under the title 'The Hospitable Negro Woman', and Bk IV of *Laurie's Graduated Series of Reading Lesson Books* (1866) by James Stuart Laurie, where it is given the title 'Mungo Park and the Negro Woman'.

13.25–26 **Dr Barth ... Lord Palmerston** Heinrich Barth (1821–65), a German explorer who, on the Prussian ambassador's recommendation, worked with the British government, joining an expedition to the Western Sudan in 1849. He explored Chad before travelling to Kano and Sokoto in northern Nigeria. His account was published as *Travels and Discoveries in North and Central Africa, being a Journal of an Expedition undertaken under the Auspices of H. B. M.'s Government in the Years 1849–1855* (5 vols., 1857–8). When he sponsored Barth, Henry John Temple, Viscount Palmerston (1784–1865), was serving, for the fourth time in his long political career, as Foreign Secretary. In 1855, after a brief spell as Home Secretary, he became Prime Minister, and twice held that office.

13.28–29 **Clifford ... College** A colonial administrator and writer of various studies of and stories about the Malay Peninsula where he spent his early career, Hugh Charles Clifford (1866–1941; knighted 1909) was colonial secretary at Trinidad and Ceylon (present-day Sri Lanka) and later appointed Governor of the Gold

Coast (present-day Ghana), Nigeria, Ceylon and the Straits Settlements, respectively. He served as Governor General of Nigeria from 1919 to 1925. The specific reference is to his opening on 5 March 1922 of Katsina College (present-day Barewa College), in a remote and difficult-to-reach area of northern Nigeria. The college was founded for the teacher-training of Muslims. For further details, see James P. Hubbard, *Education under Colonial Rule: A History of Katsina College, 1921–1942* (2000).

13.30–31   **many pictures ... illustrated papers** Conrad's reference remains elusive: no such pictures appeared from March to August in the *Graphic*, the *Graphic* (weekly), *Sphere*, *Westminster Gazette*, *Sketch*, *Illustrated Sunday Herald* or *Lloyds Illustrated*, and neither the *Scotsman* nor *The Times* report on the event.

13.34   **Livingstone** The Scottish explorer and missionary, David Livingstone (1813–73) wanted to introduce Christianity into Africa in part to combat the slave trade. His many expeditions led to significant geographic discoveries, such as Lake Ngami, the Zambezi river, Victoria Falls and Lakes Mweru and Bangwuela. Becoming ill, he convalesced at Ujiji on Lake Tanganyika, where Henry M. Stanley famously 'found' him in 1871. Stanley and Livingstone explored the Lake Tanganyika area jointly during 1871–2.

14.3   **memory enshrined** Livingstone died in Africa on 1 May 1873. His remains were returned to England for burial in Westminster Abbey, where the interment ceremony was held on 18 April 1874. His tombstone in the Abbey describes him as 'Missionary, Traveller, Philanthropist'.

14.9–10   **declared ... would go there** Marlow in 'Heart of Darkness' records a similar experience: 'there were many blank spaces on the earth and when I saw one that looked particularly inviting on a map ... I would put my finger on it and say: When I grow up I will go there': *Youth, Heart of Darkness, End of the Tether*, ed. Owen Knowles (2010), p. 48.16–19. Conrad recounts this in similar terms, as follows:

It was in 1868, when nine years old or thereabouts, that while looking at a map of Africa of the time and putting my finger on the blank space then representing the unsolved mystery of that continent, I said to myself with absolute assurance and an amazing audacity which are no longer in my character now: "When I grow up I will go *there*." (*A Personal Record*, ed. Zdzisław Najder and J. H. Stape (2008), p. 26.29–35)

Boyhood fascination with the map of Africa is a common motif in travellers' accounts of the period. Of these, the closest to Conrad's version is perhaps this by the English explorer E(dward) J(ames) Glave (1862–95):

But I remember that, even at school, Africa had a peculiar fascination for me. A great map of the 'Dark Continent' hung on the walls of my class-room; the tentative way in which the geographers of that day had marked down localities in almost unknown equatorial regions seemed to me delightful and mysterious. There were rivers with great estuaries ... and territories of whose extent and characteristics, ignorance was openly confessed by vast unnamed blank spaces. (*In Savage Africa, or Six Years of Adventure in Congo-Land* (1892), p. 16)

For a detailed discussion of Conrad's interest in maps, see Robert Hampson, '"A Passion for Maps": Conrad, Africa, Australia, and South-East Asia', *The Conradian*, 28, no. 1 (2003), 34–56.

14.14 **stern wheel steamboat** The *Roi des Belges* ('King of the Belgians' – that is, Leopold II) of which Conrad took temporary command in the Congo during August–September 1890. See 'Up-river Book'.

14.18 **Stanley Falls** On the Upper Congo river basin between Kisangani and Ubundu, Stanley Falls 'consists of seven distinct cataracts extended along a curving stretch of fifty-six statute miles': Henry M. Stanley, *The Congo* (1885), II, 155.

14.20 **Reshid's camp** The nephew of Tippu Tibb (or Hamid Ibn Muhammad, 1837?–1905), Reshid bin Mohammed (1855?–?), like his uncle and many other Arabs in the Congo, was involved in the ivory and slave trades. The Arabs' seat of power was the Stanley Falls area, and Tippu Tibb, a notorious Zanzibari ivory trader and slaver, was the uncrowned king of the Arabs of the region and characterized as 'the Bismarck of Central Africa'. (Modern historians tend to spell his name Tib or Tip; this, in any case, was a nickname, allegedly inspired by the sound of his guns. His actual name is a chain of Arab patronymics a line or so long, his father a Muscat Arab and his mother African.) In 1887, recognizing the importance of Tibb to the success of their plans, Stanley expediently persuaded Leopold II of Belgium to appoint Tippu Tibb Governor of the Falls. Tibb played a central role in the Emin Pasha Relief Expedition, on which see Iain R. Smith, *The Emin Pasha Relief Expedition, 1886–1890* (1972).

14.29–30 **newspaper stunt ... scramble** References to Stanley's 'discovery' of Livingstone (13.34*n*.) in 1871, while employed as special correspondent by the *New York Herald*, and to exploitation of the Congo Free State and surrounding territories by colonial powers, especially Leopold II.

15.8 **ship loading in Sydney** The mixed cargo of the 367-tonne barque *Otago* consisted of fertilizer, soap and tallow. Conrad was master of her, his only command (January 1888 – March 1889), apart from a brief time as temporary captain of the *Roi des Belges* (14.14*n*.).

15.14 **Torres Straits** Discovered in 1606 by the Spanish explorer Luis Vaez de Torres (*c.* 1565–1613?), the passage between New Guinea and the Cape York Peninsula of Australia connects the Coral and Arafura Seas, the latter separating New Guinea and Australia. Passage for ships is perilous because of its many reefs, shallow waters and islands, some of which are coral. (The *OED* notes that the word when used as a proper geographical name is usually plural but has a singular sense, and that, in a few particular cases, including Torres Strait(s), usage is divided.)

15.16 **the reply** Conrad preserved three letters from the *Otago*'s owners (see *Portrait in Letters*, pp. 3–5), but that cited here – if, in fact, not simply reconstituted from memory – is not known to survive.

15.25 **Arafura Sea** See 15.14*n*.

15.30 **Simpson & Sons' offices** That is, Henry Simpson & Sons of Adelaide, a large firm established and owned by Captain Henry Simpson (1815–84), who had arrived in South Australia in 1836. For a history of the firm, see R. H. Parsons, *The Black Diamond Line of Colliers (Henry Simpson & Sons, Port Adelaide)* (1972).

15.34   **Great Fly River** New Guinea's largest river, the Fly runs approximately 650 miles (965 km) from the Victor Emmanuel Range to the Gulf of Papua.

15.36   **south-east gale** Conrad left Sydney for Mauritius in the mid-July to September monsoon season, which possibly accounts for the heavy south-east gale.

15.38   **Sydney Heads** North Head and South Head are promontories stretching out into the sea, guarding the entrance to Sydney (Port Jackson) Harbour.

16.10   **without fear and without reproach** The proverbial description of Pierre du Terrail, Seigneur de Bayard (*c.* 1475–1524), as 'le chevalier sans peur et sans reproche' ('the knight without fear and above reproach'). Conrad uses the phrase in 'Books' (1905), *Notes on Life and Letters*, ed. J. H. Stape (2004), p. 10.5–6, and it appears in a letter to R. B. Cunninghame Graham, 16 February 1905 (*Letters*, III, 217).

16.14–18   **Spaniard ... Hollander ... Englishman**   Respectively,   de   Torres (15.14*n.*), and Tasman and Cook (7.2*n*).

16.26   **Bligh's Entrance** On the south coast of Papua New Guinea, an area (present-day Bligh Boat Entrance) notable for swift tides that rise and fall almost three fathoms. It is named after Captain William Bligh (1754–1817) who, mainly recalled for the mutiny on the *Bounty* in 1789, enjoyed a long career: as sailing master of Captain Cook's final voyage (1776–9) and as a commander in the wars with France. He was also Governor of New South Wales from 1805 to 1808, when he was sent home and imprisoned for two years. In 1811, Bligh was promoted to rear admiral, rising three years later to a vice admiralship.

16.33   *Honolulu* This is probably the brig wrecked in Torres Straits in September 1870.

16.35   **known ... to God alone** A description on a tombstone for a deceased person whose identity is unknown, the phrase was given currency during the Great War. Although not specifically used, it is alluded to in the quotations 'The Lord knoweth them that are his' and 'Unknown and yet well known, dying and behold we live' on the tomb of the Unknown Warrior in Westminster Abbey (dedicated 11 November 1921).

16.39–40   **wreck ... Warrior Reefs** Perhaps the 1,725-tonne *John de Costa*, wrecked in July 1885, and perhaps legendary because there was no loss of human life although she lost most of her cargo of horses. For details, see [Harold Ray Stevens], 'A *Memento Mori*, Conrad, and the Torres Strait', *Joseph Conrad Today*, 29, no. 1 (2004), 4–5. The Warrior Reefs are rocky, coral reefs – extensions of the Great Barrier Reef off the Australian coast – that impede the exit from Torres Strait.

17.2   *memento mori* 'Reminder of death' (Latin).

17.6   **a clear sun** Although the use of 'clear' to denote 'brightness' or 'luminousness' is not without historical precedent in English (see the *OED*'s 'Expressing the vividness or intensity of light: brightly shining, bright, brilliant'), Conrad's usage may be influenced by the Polish *jasne* or French *clair*, both of which translate into English as 'clear' but connote 'brightly shining'. Conrad uses 'clear' in this way throughout his career, perhaps the examples most relevant to the usage here being the following from *Lord Jim*: 'clear stars' (p. 128), 'clear sunshine' (p. 157) and 'clear yellow glow' (p. 322).

17.11 **in the year 1762** An error: the *Endeavour* was only commissioned in 1768, sailing under Cook from Plymouth in August. Conrad possibly misremembered Cook's landing at Possession Island, one of the Strait's more than 275 islands, where, on 23 August 1770, Cook claimed New South Wales for England, after charting the east coast of what was later to become Australia, from Point Hicks to Possession Island.

17.32 **sacred fire** Sacred fires occur in several cultural contexts, including that tended by the Vestal Virgins in ancient Rome. The phrase seems to be one of Conrad's favourites. Cf. 'bearers of a spark from the sacred fire': 'Heart of Darkness', *Youth* (2010), p. 45.5–6; 'The root of the matter – which is expression – is there, and the sacred fire, too': Conrad to Arnold Bennett, 10 March 1902 (*Letters*, II, 389); 'Their own masters had not handed the sacred fire into the keeping of their cold and skilful hands', *The Mirror of the Sea*, p. 33; 'his instinct acted as though he were the last of mankind nursing that law like the only spark of a sacred fire', 'Falk', *Typhoon and Other Stories*, p. 198.

THE *TORRENS*
A PERSONAL TRIBUTE

18.1 *Torrens* Built in 1875 by James Laing of Sunderland and launched in October that year, the ship was owned by A. L. Elder & Company of London. The passenger clipper of 1,334 gross tonnage was engaged on the Plymouth–Adelaide run. By the time Conrad joined her, she had gained considerable fame for speed, having made the run under Captain H. R. Angel (21.13*n.*) in sixty-four days in 1880, a record never beaten. In over fifteen voyages to Adelaide, the *Torrens* averaged seventy-four days at sea.

18.5–6 **beautiful ship ... evoked** The reference is to the oil-on-canvas picture of the *Torrens* under full sail by Jack Spurling (1870–1933), reproduced on the cover of the September 1923 issue of the *Blue Peter* (18.6–8*n.*). The picture was later collected, with a commentary by Basil Lubbock, in *Sail*, ed. F. A. Hook (3 vols., 1927–36), a series that also reprints this essay (II, 87–90).

18.6–8 **sea-travel magazine ... different conditions** The attractively illustrated *Blue Peter*, founded and edited by F(rederick) A(rthur) Hook (1864–1935), a Fellow of the Royal Geographic Society who had earlier worked for the P. & O. shipping line, was first published in July 1921. It was addressed to those with a keen interest in maritime traditions and to sea-travellers, then making their passages in large, comfortable, steam-powered ocean liners holding upwards of 1,000 passengers, and different in all respects from the more intimate, small-scale conditions in sailing ships such as the *Torrens*.

18.11 **know ... nothing of sea-travel** To cite only Conrad's travels as a passenger on long-distance ships: he sailed on the *Nürnberg* from Adelaide to Southampton (1889), on the *Ville de Maceio* from Bordeaux to Léopoldville (now Kinshasa, Congo) and from Léopoldville to Europe (1890). He, of course, made several trips to and from the Continent from the 1890s onwards. At the time of writing, he had recently made voyages on the *Tuscania* from Glasgow to New York and on the *Majestic* from New York to Southampton.

18.12   **My two years** Conrad signed on on 19 November 1891, and signed off after his second voyage on 27 July 1893. For details about his service in the ship, see Jerry Allen, *The Sea Years of Joseph Conrad* (1965), pp. 324–5; J. H. Stape and Hans van Marle, '"Pleasant Memories" and "Precious Friendships": Conrad's *Torrens* Connection and Unpublished Letters from the 1890s', *Conradiana*, 27 (1995), 39 n. 1; and Knowles and Stape.

18.15   **wool-clippers** The wool-clippers Conrad saw service in were the *Duke of Sutherland* and *Loch Etive* (see 'Chronology').

18.17   **till all was blue** That is, sailing the ship so hard that the air was blue with curses. The *OED* cites 'to make the air blue' with curses from J. S. Farmer and W. E. Henley's *Slang and its Analogues* (1890). The expression is still in use in the United Kingdom. The *OED* also yields an alternative possibility: '*Till all's Blue*: carried to the utmost – a phrase borrowed from the idea of a vessel making out of port, and getting into blue water': Admiral W. H. Smyth, *The Sailor's Word-Book* (1867).

18.19   **end of my sea-life** After leaving the *Torrens*, Conrad, in fact, served in the *Adowa*, leaving London on 26 November 1893 for Rouen to pick up emigrants from France and then to proceed to Québec and Montréal. The Franco-Canadian Transport Company, which had chartered the *Adowa*, soon failed as the result of a lack of interest in its trade, and Conrad spent much of his time in port maintaining the ship and writing *Almayer's Folly*. He signed off in London on 17 January 1894. He recalls his experience in *A Personal Record* (ch. 1).

18.20   **friendships** Most notably with John Galsworthy (1867–1933), then a recently graduated barrister, and E(dward) L(ancelot) ('Ted') Sanderson (1867–1939), a Cambridge man, who had read Classics and in time followed his father's footsteps into school-mastering. Conrad met them on the return voyage to England from Adelaide in March 1893. Both encouraged Conrad's writing-career and became close and life-long friends. Galsworthy, who came from a well-to-do family and helped his friend financially, became a popular novelist and dramatist and was awarded the Nobel Prize for literature in 1932.

Conrad remained in friendly contact with other passengers for varying periods after his service in the ship, among them Walter Banks, a civil engineer; Caroline A. Madden, a nurse who assisted Mrs Conrad while the latter was recuperating from medical problems in 1904; and E. B. Redmayne, to whom Conrad sent a presentation copy of *Almayer's Folly*, and Nita B. Wall, his daughter, whose 'skilful touch made even the voice of the old Torrens' piano a delight to my ears' (*Letters*, IX, 16). On the topic of Conrad's *Torrens* friendships, see Martin Ray, 'Conrad and "Civilized Women": Miss Madden, Passenger on the *Torrens*', *The Conradian*, 33, no. 1 (2008), 158–61; and Knowles and Stape.

19.9   **my first voyage** The ship departed Gravesend on 21 November 1891 for Plymouth, with an arrival in Adelaide on 28 February 1892, and a return to London Dock on 2 September. For a detailed log of the voyage, see Knowles and Stape.

19.10   **trenched upon** The *OED* describes this sense of the phrase ('to border closely upon; to verge upon; to approach towards' as 'in vaguer use') with its last reference dating to 1876.

19.12–13   **out from Plymouth** After leaving the Port of London, ships usually loaded passengers and provisions at Plymouth in Devon, allowing passengers to avoid much of the English Channel passage and shortening the number of days at sea. On Conrad's first voyage in the *Torrens*, she arrived in Plymouth on 24 November 1891, departing the next day.

19.19   **Teneriffe** The largest of the Canary Islands (now usually spelled Tenerife, as in Spanish), and the last feasible stop off the coast of Africa before many days on the open ocean.

19.22   **invalidated the ship's insurance** Conrad was aware of the hazards of the Australia run and of the specifics of insurance, a topic he refers to in 'Geography and Some Explorers'. Almost 10 per cent of the more than 8,000 recorded shipwrecks occurred on this run (*Encyclopædia of Australian Shipwrecks* (2006)).

19.24   **the doctor** His identity is problematic: although T(homas) Archibald Dukes (b. 1866 – after 1931), a Londoner, recently licensed (1890), signed on for his first sea service on 21 November 1891 at Gravesend, the Agreement and Account of Crew (National Archives), which lacks his signature, indicates that he 'did not appear'. A student at Epsom Downs Royal Benevolent College and a graduate of London University, Dukes, later long in practice in Croydon and its district medical officer, occasionally wrote on medical issues. His 'recollections' of Conrad in the *Torrens* were published in the *Spectator* in 1928 (rpt 'Memories of Joseph Conrad', *Joseph Conrad: Interviews and Recollections*, ed. Martin Ray (1990), pp. 59–60).

19.25   **my captain** See 21.13 n.

19.36   **neurasthenic myself** After his experience in the Congo, Conrad returned to London in January 1891 in ill-health, passing some months in extreme physical and nervous disorder. He spent March and part of April in the German Hospital, Dalston, and in May left for a hydrotherapy cure in Switzerland, returning to England in mid-June. On Conrad's illnesses and treatments, see Martin Bock, *Joseph Conrad and Psychological Medicine* (2002).

20.5–6   **towering and majestic shadow** The island could be seen from a great distance because of the loftiness of its principal mountain, El Teide, a volcano 12,198 ft (3,718 m) high.

20.13   **few words to give** If not quite a Gallicism, at least influenced by French, more idiomatic English being 'few words to say to anybody'. *Donner* ('to give') is normally linked with *parole* ('word') in French.

20.18–19   **an Irishman's privilege** A phrase of widely divergent meanings, here seemingly meaning plain-speaking. The phrase generally means the right to answer a question by posing one, as, for example, 'Now as he has asked the question how this can be, I avail myself of an Irishman's privilege, and reply to that question by asking another': Revd John Cumming and Daniel French, *The Hammersmith Protestant Discussion* (1852), p. 120. (Other uses suggest a phrase of some versatility; cf. 'members [of the House of Commons] enjoyed for an hour or two the Englishman's full privilege – which in this case was the Irishman's privilege also – of a good grumble': *The Times*, 6 June 1884, p. 9; 'I will avail myself of an Irishman's privilege ... of adding a postscript to his letter as long as the letter itself': *Complete Works of Rev. Thomas Smyth, D. D.* (1908), IV, 885.) Conrad, however, apparently intends 'Irish bull', that is, an incongruous statement somewhat along the lines of an oxymoron. The expression, very common in the nineteenth century, featured in countless *Punch* cartoons; it derives from 'bullish' as in having a pair of horns. 'Irish bulls' were often taken by outsiders as picturesquely silly and illogical, whereas insiders saw them as jokes, comic exaggerations, ingenious paradoxes or rhetorical delights.

20.24   **homely** In British parlance, comfortable, domestic and agreeable (in contradistinction to American usage, in which the word denotes the unattractive or dowdy).

20.25   **ideals of Ritz hotels** The chain of luxury hotels – Paris (1898), London (1906) and New York (1907) – was established by the Swiss businessman César Ritz (1850–1918). Patronized by the wealthy and fashionable, they quickly became a by-word for luxury and elegance.

20.40   **modern passenger steamship** Either the *Tuscania* on which Conrad sailed to America in late April 1923 or the *Majestic* on which he returned in early June 1923. Built for the Anchor Line by Fairfield Shipbuilding of Glasgow, the *Tuscania*, launched in 1921, had a gross tonnage of 16,991, and was much smaller than the *Majestic*, which, at more than 56,000 gross tonnage, was then the largest passenger ship in service. Built by Blohm & Voss of Hamburg for the Hamburg-Amerika Line in 1914 and launched as the *Bismarck*, she was purchased and re-named by the White Star Line in 1922 for its transatlantic service.

21.8–9   **1875 ... trouble ... launch myself** The *Torrens* was launched in October 1875. The 'trouble' possibly refers to French shipping regulations, which dogged Conrad's career in France, but may also be read as an allusion to his family's staunch opposition to his pursuit of a career at sea. Conrad's own launching at sea was his joining the *Mont-Blanc* at Marseilles, aged seventeen, on 8 December 1874, officially a passenger, making a voyage to the French Antilles, although he in effect served as part of the ship's crew. His second voyage (June–December 1875) was as a ship's boy, and was thus officially his first berth.

21.11–12   **the greater success** Conrad's career at sea was coloured by the decline of sail as steam came to the fore and opportunities for employment contracted. He encountered difficulties in finding berths at the level of his qualifications and, by force of circumstances, was more often than not under-employed and underpaid.

21.13   **H. R. Angel** H(enry) R(obert) Angel (1829–1921) was one of the owners of the *Torrens*, which was built to his specifications. He served as her captain from her launch in 1875 until his retirement in 1890. He had previously worked for A. L. Elder & Company of London, engaged in the passenger and cargo trade between Britain and South Australia. In retirement, he lived in South Devon. For a history of the *Torrens* under his command, see Basil Lubbock, *The Colonial Clippers* (1921), pp. 159–61, and E. C. Bowden-Smith, *Land Ho!* (1931).

21.16   **lost ... masts** Caught in a sudden squall on 30 November 1890, the *Torrens* lost her foremast at the deck, everything above the cap of the main lower mast, her mizzen topgallant and almost all the yards on her mizzenmast. Towing into Pernambuco for repairs took eight days and cost the owners £2,000, with new spars costing a further £700.

21.18–21   **joined her ... 1893** Conrad's dates are incorrect: see 18.12 *n*.

21.24   **stepped ... sea life** Possibly an omission of fact for artistic effect: after Conrad left the *Torrens* he served as second mate in the *Adowa* (18.19 *n*.) for almost two months.

21.26 **W. H. Cope** W(alter) H(enry) Cope (1849–1918) served as the *Torrens*'s master from 1890 to 1895, making six return voyages from London to Adelaide. On leaving her, he was for a time in the employ of the North of Scotland, Orkney & Shetland Steam Navigation Company, as a skipper and nautical advisor. In retirement, he and his wife lived in Herne Bay, Kent.

21.29 **Conway boy** That is, a student in or a man graduated from the HMS School Ship *Conway*, a training-ship for merchant seamen moored in the Mersey river near Liverpool. Between 1859 and 1941, three successive vessels were moored there under the name. Naval cadets served a year in her, followed by three at sea. (The Conway naval school closed in 1974.) Conrad refers to the training-ship by name in 'Youth' and 'The Secret Sharer', and alludes to her in *Lord Jim* (ch. 1).

21.30 **Hooghly pilot steamer service** The Hooghly river in the Indian state of West Bengal is a part of the Ganges river complex, giving access to Calcutta (present-day Kolkata) from the Bay of Bengal. The pilot-steamers of the Hooghly Pilot Service guided ocean liners through channels featuring numerous shoals and shifting quicksand that were constantly being dredged to keep sea lanes open. A contemporary account suggests the high prestige involved in such a command:

Under the East India Company's rule the pilot service could not be entered at all without great influence; but once entered, the pilot had a position from which only misconduct could remove him, receiving excellent pay while on duty and a substantial pension at the right time. Men of education too they often were, and are, sometimes speaking several languages, and always men of character. ... His rule was law. His dignity beyond mortal reach. (James Routledge, 'Indian Notes. III. Commerce and Manufactures', *Macmillan's Magazine* (May 1875), 457–8)

21.35–36 **break-down ... tropical disease** Conrad apparently contracted malaria whilst working in the Congo, and suffered from depression on his return to Europe, going into hospital in the spring of 1891 and then taking a hydropathic cure in Switzerland.

21.37 **steamer on the river Congo** On Conrad's stint as temporary captain of the SS *Roi des Belges* and his experience in Africa generally, see 'The Congo Diary' and 'Up-river Book' in the present volume.

22.6 **Lubbock ... *The Colonial Clippers*** Basil Lubbock (1876–1944), who came from a family of bankers, scientists and politicians, was educated at Eton. He participated in the Klondike Gold Rush, fought in the Boer and First World Wars and had shipped before the mast. Conrad received his copy of *The Colonial Clippers* (1921) as a gift from Sydney Cockerell in early 1922 (*Letters*, VII, 438).

22.14–15 **studies ... "The Wonderful *Torrens*"** In addition to *The Colonial Clippers*, Lubbock's several anecdotal histories of ships and shipping include *The China Clippers* (1914), *The Log of the 'Cutty Sark'* (1924) and *The Opium Clippers* (1933). Conrad cites Lubbock's heading for his discussion of the ship in *The Colonial Clippers* (p. 157).

22.17 **a letter ... seaman** Harald Leofurn Clarke (1874–1942), who served as an indentured apprentice (not as an able seaman) on Conrad's first voyage in the *Torrens*, wrote to Conrad on 11 November 1922. (The date of this letter is given in G. Jean-Aubry, ed., *Joseph Conrad: Life & Letters* (1928), II, 359); the letter itself is not extant.) Conrad replied on 2 January 1923, stating that he had 'the best recollection of the ship's company' and thanking him for being remembered by 'an old shipmate' (*Letters*, VIII, 4). Clarke earned a master's certificate, and was later Harbour Master at Suva in Fiji.

22.25   **no time … see him** An allusion to Conrad's then-recent visit to America, made on the invitation of his publisher, F. N. Doubleday (108.28*n*.). Mainly in New York City and on Long Island, Conrad also spent some days in Connecticut and Massachusetts, including a visit to Boston, in May 1923.

22.27–30   **to read … build** Cf. the following:

With the change of ownership as with the change of skippers, evil luck again struck the celebrated old ship, for the Italians soon after ran her ashore and after getting her off again sent her to Genoa to be broken up. But when the Genoese shipbreakers saw the beauty of her model and construction, they went to the expense of repairing her, only again to bump her on the rocks. (Lubbock, *The Colonial Clippers*, p. 162)

22.28–29   **transfer … broken up** Unable to compete with steamers for cargo, the ship was sold to Italians in 1903 for £1,500, and broken up in 1910.

CHRISTMAS-DAY AT SEA

23.21–24   **young then … my captain** Given the geographical information provided and Conrad's whereabouts in Decembers when he was at sea, the incident appears to be a mixture of near-fact, outright invention and faulty recollection. The time-frame points to his service in the steamer *Europa*, which passed through Dover on 14 December 1879 on her way to the Mediterranean via Penzance. However, she was unlikely to have been still in or near the Channel on Christmas Day, and had a crew of twenty-one (not thirty-six: see 24.7–8*n*.). The ship's captain was Alexander Munro.

23.26–27   **chops of the Channel … Scilly islands** Respectively, the area where tides meet to cause an irregular sea, or where a channel meets the sea, from, 'chops' meaning 'mouth' or 'entrance'. The 'chops' here refer to the entrance to the English Channel from the Atlantic, between the Scilly Isles and Ushant (Oeussant) Isle, and an archipelago of about 150 small islands and rocky islets, about 30 miles (48 km) south-west of Land's End in Cornwall, an area noted for shipwrecks. The largest of the five inhabited and often fog-enshrouded isles is St Mary's, about 1,500 acres (607 ha).

23.28–29   **wrapped … blanket** That is, covered over by a heavy fog.

24.7–8   **thirty-six throats** The complement of officers and men aboard the sailing ship in question; neither the *Europa* nor any other ship Conrad recalls in this essay had such a large company.

24.23–26   **Dead-Sea fruit … ashes** A legendary fruit (also known as apples of Sodom) particularly attractive to the eye but dissolving into smoke and ashes when held; thus, an outwardly desirable object that turns out, in fact, to be worthless. The actual species of yellow fruit on which the legendary one is based is full of small black grains that have a bitter taste. The phrase, now obsolete, has a long history. The Victorian novelist Mary Elizabeth Braddon published a novel titled

Dead-Sea Fruit (1868); cf. also 'Like to the apples on the Dead Sea shore / All ashes to the taste': Lord Byron, *Childe Harold's Pilgrimage* (1812–18), III.34; and

> Greedily they pluck'd
> The fruitage, fair to sight, like that which grew
> Near that bituminous lake where Sodom flamed;
> This more delusive, not the touch, but taste
> Deceived: they fondly thinking to allay
> Their appetite with gust, instead of fruit
> Chew'd bitter ashes ...
> (John Milton, *Paradise Lost* (1667), Bk x, 560–65)

24.27 **twenty years** Conrad's career at sea began in 1874 in Marseilles, and he left the *Adowa* in January 1894. He spent about a decade actually at sea, the rest of the time passed on shore, either loading ships or seeking employment.

24.32 **the year 1879** Conrad, who misremembered the year, conflates several experiences: he was outbound for Australia in the *Duke of Sutherland* on Christmas Day in 1878, having passed the Cape of Good Hope on Christmas Eve rather than having left Sydney 'eighteen days before' (25.26). On Christmas Day 1879, he was on a voyage to the Mediterranean in the *Europa*, and on the same date in 1880, the *Loch Etive* was docked in Sydney. For details of Conrad's service in the *Duke*, see Allan H. Simmons, 'Conrad and the *Duke of Sutherland*', *The Conradian*, 35, no. 1 (2010), 101–25.

24.32–34 **wireless telegraphy ... broadcasting** The Italian inventor Guglielmo Marconi (1834–1937) established Marconi's Wireless Telegraph Company in London after patenting his wireless telegraphy (radio telegraphy) system in 1896, building upon the theoretical work of the British scientist James Clerk Maxwell in the 1860s and the more practical applications of the German and Russian physicists Heinrich Hertz in the 1880s and Aleksandr Popov in the 1890s. In 1913, the American engineer Edwin H(oward) Armstrong patented a circuit for the regenerating radio receiver that made long-range radio reception practicable.

24.39 **Southern Ocean** Known also as the Great Southern Ocean, the Antarctic Ocean and the South Polar Ocean, this body of water includes the southernmost parts of the Indian, Atlantic and Pacific Oceans as they extend into Antarctic regions.

25.5–8 **pointed out ... theory** Although positioned to take advantage of the powerful westerlies for which the Roaring Forties and Furious Fifties are notorious, most of her sails were furled.

25.9–10 **Swedish safety matches** In common use at the time, the matches, patented in the mid-1840s by the Swedish chemist Gustaf Erik Pasch (1788–1862) but only becoming commercially viable a decade later, replaced those containing poisonous white phosphorus; they evoke the crow's-nest atop the mainmast, visible when the sails are furled.

25.20 **Chips** The traditional nickname (from wooden shavings or 'chips') for a ship's carpenter.

25.27 ***Heralds, Telegraphs, Bulletins*** The *Sydney Morning Herald* (founded 1831) and *Daily Telegraph* (founded 1879) were then dailies (the *Herald* having begun life as a weekly newspaper). The weekly *Bulletin* (published 1880–2008) emphasized political and business commentary and featured some literary content.

25.35   home of storms Given that the ship is many thousands of miles east of the Cape of Good Hope, also known as the 'Cape of Storms', and seemingly headed nowhere in particular, this is perhaps a reference to myth: the palace of Æolus, god of the winds, was the home of storms.

26.1   *Alaska* ... New Bedford Conrad may have seen the *Alaska* sailing in the Southern Ocean in January 1881, when she was then off New Zealand. She departed New Bedford, in south-eastern Massachusetts, for the South Pacific under Captain Charles W. Fisher on 14 September 1880, returning home in November 1884. (Her log-book is held at the New Bedford Whaling Museum.) New Bedford, which lies south of Boston, was the world capital of the whaling industry prior to the American Civil War, and remained a busy whaling port until the industry's decline towards the close of the nineteenth century. The town remained active in the trade until 1927 when its last whaling ship went out.

OCEAN TRAVEL

27.4–5   different now elementally An allusion to the four elements of Greek cosmology (earth, air, fire and water), providing a contrast between the methods of travel by steam (fire) and by sail (air).

27.10   travelling multitudes For example, the Cunard Line's *Tuscania*, aboard which Conrad wrote this essay on his way to New York City, could accommodate more than 2,000 passengers.

27.27   sort of a hotel Conrad likewise decries the provision of shipboard luxuries – a factor of modern travel that, in his view, necessitated overly large ships – in his essays on the *Titanic*: see 'Some Reflexions on the Loss of the *Titanic*' and 'Certain Aspects of the Admirable Inquiry into the Loss of the *Titanic*' (1912), *Notes on Life and Letters* (2004), pp. 167–78, 179–93.

28.2   territorial names Among the day's more famous Cunard ocean liners were, for example, the *Tuscania* (named after Tuscany), the *Lusitania* (named after ancient Portugal), the *Aquitania* (named after the old French territory of Aquitaine) and the *Mauretania* (named after a Roman province in North Africa).

28.14   Ritz hotel See 20.25*n*.

28.22   a sailing passenger ship The *Torrens*, in which Conrad was first mate. See 'The *Torrens*: A Personal Tribute' and 'Chronology'.

28.22–23   port of London In general, the port extends from the City of London down the Thames to the sea, but a more specific historic designation has been the 14 miles (22 km) of river-front constituting Greenwich, Lewisham, Southwark, Newham and the Tower Hamlets. By 1886 the docks extended 26 miles (42 km) downstream to Tilbury.

28.24–25   about sixty This figure refers only to the maximum number of passengers and does not include the crew. In Conrad's own experience, there could be considerably fewer passengers: on his second homeward return from Adelaide in

October 1892, for example, there were twenty first-class and five saloon passengers. (For the *Torrens* passenger lists at the time of Conrad's service, see Knowles and Stape.)

28.30 **Plymouth** See 19.12–13 *n*.

29.2 **dreamt of ... philosophy** Cf. 'There are more things in heaven and earth, Horatio, / Than are dreamt of in your philosophy': Shakespeare, *Hamlet*, I.v.166–7.

29.16–17 **bread ... suprême de volaille** An allusion to the Torah's 'Man doth not live by bread only' (Deuteronomy viii.3), also quoted by Christ in his temptation by Satan as 'Man shall not live by bread alone': Luke iv.4 and Matthew iv.4. The dish referred to consists of poultry, invariably a chicken breast and sometimes the wing, poached and served in *sauce suprême* (chicken stock, cream and egg yolks).

OUTSIDE LITERATURE

30.4 **Notices to Mariners** Technically and formally, information sent out to ships at sea by the Admiralty or other maritime authorities.

30.18 **Maxims of La Rochefoucauld** *Réflexions ou sentences et maximes morales* (1685) by François, duc de La Rochefoucauld (1613–80), a collection of some 600 pithy aphorisms, is known for the polished brilliance and wit of its dissection of the foibles of human character and conduct.

31.1 **Mr Punch** *Punch, or the London Charivari*, the English weekly comic journal of wit, humour and satire in poetry and prose first appeared in July 1841, and soon became an institution (ceased publication 2002). The magazine was named at an early meeting at which it was decided it should be 'like a good Punch mixture – nothing without Lemon' (a punning reference to Mark Lemon, its first editor).

31.3–4 **lately ... explosive atom** A reference to a cartoon that appeared on 19 July 1922, p. 67 (see Fig. 7). Atomic explosions were the subject of scientific discussion and speculation at the time. For example, when Ernest Rutherford received the Nobel Prize for Chemistry in December 1908, his lecture referred to the expulsion of alpha-particles from radioactive elements as the consequence of 'an intense atomic explosion'. Invoking Rutherford's work with Frederick Soddy on radioactivity, H. G. Wells imagines the dangers of nuclear weaponry in his novel *The World Set Free* (1914).

31.9–10 **angel ... poor Jack** Cf. 'They say there's a sweet little cherub sits up aloft, / To keep watch for the life of poor Jack!': 'Poor Jack' (*c.* 1788), a song by the British actor, dramatist and song writer Charles Dibdin (1745–1814).

31.26 **mortal envelope** A figure of speech derived from *enveloppe mortel* (French), that is, the body as the receptacle of the soul. Cf. 'the mortal envelope of Mr Verloc had not hastened unduly along the streets': *The Secret Agent* (1990), p. 33.35–36.

31.28–29 **vanities of the world ... Trappists** A Roman Catholic (Cistercian) order founded in the twelfth century, the Trappists were re-dedicated from the seventeenth century onwards to the ideal of discipline, including perpetual prayer, self-abnegation, continual reminders of the brevity of life and seclusion from worldly affairs.

31.30   *memento mori ... nothing else* See 17.2*n*. There may be here an allusion to the then-widespread misconception that Trappists, by the rules of their order, slept in their coffins.

32.4–8   **W ... E ... azimuth paper** Azimuth, from Arabic *sumat* ('way' or 'direction'), is a navigational term used to indicate the bearing of a celestial body relative to a specific observation point, usually on the earth's surface. The 'W' and 'E' refer to positions on the 'azimuth angle', the compass bearing relative to the true geographic North. The fact that angles are measured in degrees, *minutes* and seconds presumably accounts for Conrad's feeling that he had been given 'a hint'.

32.5–6   **an examination** The Board of Trade examination for advancement to first mate, among whose duties is keeping the ship's log, which includes recording Notices to Mariners. Conrad's memory is selective: he failed on his first attempt on 17 November 1884 but was successful on 3 December 1884. He deals at length with his professional examinations (omitting mention of his failures) in *A Personal Record*.

32.26–27   **bound to Calcutta** Conrad signed on as second mate of the *Tilkhurst* on 24 April 1885, four months after his first mate's examination, for a voyage to Calcutta, departing London on 27 April and arriving on 19 November, to remain in port until 12 January 1886, when she set out on her homeward voyage.

32.28   **my captain** E(dwin) J(ohn) Blake (1838–86), of Plymouth. Conrad recalls him as 'short, stout, dignified, perhaps a little pompous, he was a man of singularly well-informed mind, the least sailor-like in aspect, but certainly one of the best seamen whom it has been my good luck to serve under': *The Mirror of the Sea*, p. 9.

32.31–32   **truck to keelson** See 'Glossary of Nautical Terms'. Literally, the length of the mainmast, from top to bottom.

32.39   **proper Admiralty sheet** That is, the official ship's record.

33.12   **Angel watches** See 31.9–10*n*.

33.14–15   **papa Augier ... *Hamlet*** (Guillaume-Victor) Émile Augier (1820–89) was a prolific French dramatist prominent for verse drama (*La Ciguë*), comedies about middle-class life (*Un Homme de Bien*) and plays with a highly moral character (*Gabrielle*). He was also a librettist, most notably of the opera *Sapho* (1851), set to music by Charles Gounod. Conrad recalls (and reframes) an anecdote about Augier's visit on 17 December 1885 to Jules Claretie, director of the Comédie française, who had long wished to mount a production of Shakespeare's best-known play, with Augier arguing for the mounting of one of his own dramas.

33.16–17   **"*Vous ... vous?*"** 'Call that a play, do you?' (French)

LEGENDS

34.6   **bones ... seen myself** Possibly a recollection of Conrad's experience in Africa in 1890, partly fictionalized in 'Heart of Darkness', in which Marlow comes upon his predecessor Fresleven's remains; cf. 'the grass growing through his ribs was tall enough to hide his bones': *Youth* (2010), p. 50.4–5.

34.25 *The Golden Legend* Compiled in Latin by the Italian archbishop Jacobus de Voragine or Varagine (1230–92), *Aurea Legenda* (*c.* 1275) was the most popular and most printed religious folk book of the Middle Ages. It recounts miraculous events and miracles performed by the saints. Brought out in English translation by William Caxton in 1483 as *The Golden Legend, or Lives of the Saints*, in Conrad's day it circulated in seven volumes in Dent's Temple Classics series (1900).

35.18 *La mort sans phrases* Literally, 'death without phrases' (or 'death without fine words', that is, 'Death – with no need for discussion'). The contemptuous phrase is varyingly attributed to the Abbé de Sièyes and to Danton on voting for the execution of Louis XVI. Conrad alludes to it in 'Amy Foster', *Typhoon and Other Stories*, and in a letter to Henry Arthur Jones of 7 November 1922 (*Letters*, VII, 571). The subject here is death in the silence of the sea.

35.25 **winking of an eye** Perhaps a variation on the commoner 'twinkling of an eye' derived from 'We shall all be changed, in a moment, in the twinkling of an eye': 1 Corinthians xv.51–2. The passage forms part of the 'Order for the Burial of the Dead', *Book of Common Prayer* (1623), which Conrad knew from burials at sea. The phrase also occurs in 'Youth' and *Lord Jim*.

35.31 **Basil Lubbock** See 22.6*n*.

35.35 **ceremonies ... Cape Horn passage** Taking its cue from traditional shipboard initiation rites and festivities on crossing the Equator, the reference is to travel round the southernmost point of South America through the Strait of Magellan, which separates the Tierra del Fuego archipelago from mainland South America. Travel there is especially harrowing, given the strong currents, ferocious winds and high waves, the occasional 'Cape Horn snorters' (particularly hazardous squalls) and icebergs that sometimes drift from Antarctica.

35.36 **C. Fox-Smith** The tales and poems about the sea and seamen of C(ecily) Fox-Smith (1882–1954) appeared regularly in the *London Mercury* and *Punch*, her work being collected in such volumes as *Sea Songs and Ballads, 1917–1922* and *Sailor Town Days* (both 1923). Among her books about ships are the *Return of the Cutty Sark* and *A Book of Famous Ships* (both 1924).

36.15–19 *Marco-Polo ... Forbes ... short career* Launched at Saint John, New Brunswick, in 1851, the *Marco Polo* was known as the 'fastest ship involved in the Australia passenger trade'. Her Scottish captain, James Nicol ('Bully') Forbes (1821–74), set the record for a return voyage from London to Melbourne in 1852 in less than six months, and is supposed to have done improbable things to set records for sailing. An epidemic of measles among the children aboard caused some fifty deaths during the voyage. Forbes commanded the ship only during 1852–3. For details on him and the ship, see Lubbock's *The Colonial Clippers*, pp. 26–40.

36.26 **timid ... crew** Cf. 'It was on this voyage, also, that he was said to have kept his crew in order at the point of the revolver, and adopted the methods of the American clipper captains, padlocking his sheets and halyards as a precaution against interference on the part of the more timid members of the ship's company': Fox-Smith, *A Book of Famous Ships*, p. 24.

36.32–33 **tell it ... Horse-Marines** An allusion to the once commonplace idiom 'Go tell it to the Marines', a phrase used to express a complete lack of credibility in something just said, from the sailor's contempt for the marine's ignorance of seamanship. According to *Brewer's Dictionary of Phrase and Fable*, its origins lie in the diarist Samuel Pepys's mention of flying fish to Charles II, when re-telling stories gathered from the navy. The courtiers were sceptical, but an officer of the Maritime Regiment of Foot said that he too had seen such fish. The King, accepting this evidence, said, 'From the very nature of their calling no class of our subjects can have so wide a knowledge of seas and lands as the officers and men of Our Loyal Maritime Regiment. Henceforward ere ever we cast doubts upon a tale that lacks likelihood we will first "Tell it to the Marines".'

Both the Royal Marines and the United States Marine Corps occasionally deployed mounted squadrons on inland expeditions: the British, for example, on Java during the Napoleonic Wars (1811), and the Americans in North Africa during the Barbary Wars (1805) and in China during the Boxer Rising (1900). Across the English-speaking world, however, the horse marines were widely assumed to be a comic fiction, the subject of drama, songs and jokes. A song popular in Conrad's day was 'I'm Captain Jinks of the Horse Marines' (1868) by William Horace Lingard. Clyde Fitch's *Captain Jinks of the Horse Marines* (1901), an American comedy that enjoyed a long London run, adapted Lingard's song. Rudyard Kipling's story 'The Horse Marines' appeared in *A Diversity of Creatures* (1917).

THE UNLIGHTED COAST

37.3   **I came ashore** On 16 November 1916, Conrad disembarked at Bridlington, Yorkshire, after a ten-day voyage in the armed brigantine HMS *Ready*, a Q-ship (a merchant vessel armed with concealed guns to lure and destroy German submarines). He had joined her after participating in several other war-related activities with the naval services to gather material for articles for the Admiralty. Under the command of Captain J. G. Sutherland, the *Ready*, renamed *Freya* in Conrad's honour, was disguised as a Norwegian timber-freighter. She had a civilian crew of seven and a naval crew of forty. According to Conrad, she was a '110 ton (Special Services) fitting out in October 1916 | Name painted on the Stern: FREYA–BERGEN': notes inserted in the copy of Jerome Kern's pamphlet *Admiralty Paper* owned by George T. Keating; see *A Conrad Memorial Library: The Collection of George T. Keating* (1929), plate opposite p. 390.

37.4–6   **great darkness … watchers** Along the English coast no lights were visible at night because of the need to keep the enemy unaware of the presence of towns or military activities. Observers participated in coastal defences along the North Sea during the First World War, whether on shore or in Q-ships or other Royal Navy and Merchant Service vessels.

37.11–12   **long sea-passages** Conrad's service at sea involved passages by sail to the Far East and Australia, these typically taking several months each way, and involving periods with little contact with or sight of land.

37.22–24   **prays … pestilence … war** A recollection of the Litany of the Saints of the Roman Catholic Church, an antiphonal prayer involving various intercessions. In that alluded to, the officiating priest intones 'A peste, fame, et bello' ('From pestilence, famine and war'), with the congregation responding 'Libera nos, Domine' ('Deliver us, O Lord'). Cf. 'They have removed war from the list of heaven-sent visitations that could only be prayed against; they have erased its name from the supplication against the wrath of war, pestilence and famine as it is in the litanies of the Roman church': 'Autocracy and War' (1905), *Notes on Life and Letters* (2004), p. 89.14–17. Conrad also vaguely alludes to this phrase in the following: 'who feared emotion, enthusiasm, or failure more than fire, war, or mortal disease': 'The Return', *Tales of Unrest*, p. 120.

37.24–25   **dreaded company ... under the water** German aircraft, here Zeppelins (40.15*n*.), surface naval vessels, including destroyers and submarines.

38.2   **Cæsar's galleys ... Danish rovers** Gaius Julius Cæsar led Roman expeditions to the island of Britain in 55 and 54 BC. A more thoroughgoing invasion began in AD 43 on the orders of Tiberius Claudius Cæsar. Vikings from Denmark started to raid the coasts of Britain, Ireland and the Isle of Man in the late eighth century. During the ninth, they arrived in much larger numbers and began to settle, taking Dublin during the 830s, York in 866 and Nottingham in 867.

38.35–36   **To be ... arms** Cf. 'To be or not to be ... / Whether 'tis nobler in the mind to suffer / ... Or to take arms against a sea of troubles, / And by opposing end them': Shakespeare, *Hamlet*, III.i.56–60.

38.37   **sound and ... fury** Cf. 'Life's but a walking shadow ... / ... it is a tale / Told by an idiot, full of sound and fury, / Signifying nothing': Shakespeare, *Macbeth*, v.v.24–8.

39.1–2   **the correct foresight** German militarism and Anglo-German competition at sea had been a constant feature of international politics during the years immediately preceding the outbreak of war in August 1914. While many considered actual hostilities unthinkable, the British government in August 1913 had entered into a pact with France and Russia to act in concert in the event of conflict with Germany, and during the Agadir crisis between France and Germany (June–December 1911) had actively made preparations for war.

39.4–5   **true defence ... sword ... shield** Conrad invokes a standard principle of swordplay with respect to the shield, as advocated in such authorities as Giacomo di Grassi in his *Ragioni di adoprar sicuramente l'arme* (1570), George Silver in *Paradoxes of Defence* (1599) and Sir William Hope in *The Complete Fencing Master* (1692). The role of the war-time Q-ships was primarily defensive.

39.8–9   **half a life-time** Poetic licence rather than strict fact is at issue here: Conrad, who had turned fifty-nine on 3 December 1916 (shortly after the events described), could tally up a sea-career of twenty years, ten of those spent in port.

39.15   **under the sun** Conrad replaced his original phrase 'under heaven' with a more usual and commonplace phrase, possibly biblical in origin; see, for example, Ecclesiastes ii where several changes are rung on it.

39.17   **RNR** See 47.33*n*.

39.26   **uttermost ... Empire** An allusion to the contributions to the Allies' war-effort, in both manpower and moral support, from Australia and New Zealand, South Africa, Canada and Newfoundland.

40.15   **Zeppelin** A cigar-shaped dirigible named after its German inventor, Ferdinand, Count von Zeppelin (1838–1917). Originally in commercial use, during the war these non-rigid airships came to be relied upon extensively by the German forces for scouting and as bombers. A renaissance occurred in their commercial use during the 1920s and 1930s, when they provided a luxury service to a well-to-do clientele, but they had disappeared from the scene by 1940.

40.21   **since my time** Conrad's last service was in the *Adowa*, sailing only from London to Rouen and back, towards the close of 1893 and beginning of 1894.

41.7   **craft mounted one gun** According to Conrad's notes at Yale (see 37.3 *n.*), the *Ready* actually had 'two 18 hdw. 14. Pounders amidships / two 12 hdw. 14 pounders aft / Masked by screens simulating deck-load of pit-props'.

42.11–12   **Ordering the skipper away** A Merchant Service man, the skipper is, of course, the captain of his diminutive ship, but the gunner, an officer in the Royal Naval Reserve, is in terms of authority his superior.

42.20   **Fritz** A German combatant, or, more generally, the German forces (slang).

43.18   **fair or foul ... seeing** Perhaps an echo of 'So foul and fair a day I have not seen': Shakespeare, *Macbeth*, I.iii.38.

43.29   **Fortune ... fickle ... outrageous** Cf. 'Whether 'tis nobler in the mind to suffer / The slings and arrows of outrageous fortune': Shakespeare, *Hamlet*, III.i.57–8. The personification of luck and fate, the goddess Fortuna figured prominently in Roman mythology, and, without husband, children or lovers, was often represented as either veiled or blind. She was also sometimes called *Fortuna brevis* ('fickle fortune').

THE DOVER PATROL

44.1   **The Dover Patrol** Beginning in July 1914, even before the formal declaration of war, twelve Tribal class destroyers joined outdated destroyers already in Dover Harbour to make active the defence of the entrance to the North Sea. Eventually the Dover Patrol included armed yachts and motor-launches, minesweepers, air-craft and submarines to escort ships, lay and destroy mines in the sea lanes, build barrage nets, attack German installations along the Belgian coast, sink U-boats and, in general, protect the English Channel.

44.16–17   **nineteenth century ... great war** The wars waged from 1803 to 1815 by Napoleon (44.26 *n.*) intimately involved England, which, hostile to Napoleon, faced invasion by France and built up defences along her southern coast. The Napoleonic conflict singularly animated Conrad's imagination, members of his family having served in the Grande Armée (see *A Personal Record*), and at the time of writing he was at work on *Suspense* (1925), set against the backdrop of Napoleon's impending flight from Elba. *The Rover* (1923) is set during the French Revolution and the early years of the Napoleonic period, and the Napoleonic Wars provide the settings of 'The Duel' (1907) and 'Prince Roman' (1911).

44.17   **its duration** Conrad is likely to have thought in terms of a 'long' nineteenth century, and the fear of a French invasion (germane to this essay's context) went back to the early days of hostilities between France and England following the French Revolution. The Battle of the Nile (1798) was, for instance, a direct consequence of Napoleon's Egyptian expedition. The Napoleonic conflict thus spanned well over a decade as opposed to the First World War's four years (August 1914 to November 1918).

44.19 less intensely national While involving the nation's sentiments, the Napoleonic threat was felt more vividly in the south, particularly along the coast, whereas in the First World War troops were mustered from throughout the United Kingdom, and the war effort and hostilities touched every aspect of national life and affected daily routines.

44.26 great and dominant figure That is, Napoleon Bonaparte (1769–1821), Emperor of the French. For Conrad's mainly hostile attitude to him, see 'Autocracy and War' (1905), *Notes on Life and Letters*.

45.3–4 resentful character ... embittered A possible allusion to the animosity provoked by the Treaty of Versailles (1919), the instrument concluding the war, whereby the victorious Allies (not united in their vision of terms) imposed upon a defeated Germany a peace that included major territorial concessions, the payment of reparations, the reduction of her armed forces and the admission of full responsibility for beginning the war. Not represented at the Paris Peace Conference, Germany signed the treaty under protest, and the United States failed to ratify it. There was widespread dissatisfaction and anger in Germany over its terms, not least among ex-servicemen. In the United Kingdom, meanwhile, those who had served in the war often found it difficult to obtain jobs, medical care for bodily and psychic wounds, equitable pension rights and decent housing. Their resentment was considerable, as was their reluctance to sanction further wars. A number of veterans' organizations campaigned outspokenly on their behalf, joining together in 1921 to form the British Legion. Conrad's son, Borys, was among the many who continued to feel the war's effects.

45.6 hour of peace ... 1815 Napoleon's definitive defeat in the Battle of Waterloo came on 18 June 1815.

45.7 the Downs The anchorage off the east coast of Kent, lying inside the Goodwin Sands and between North and South Foreland.

45.10 never ... again Just as the First World War had come to be known as 'the war to end all wars', as early as 1914, Conrad's one-time friend H. G. Wells published a short book titled *The War That Will End War*.

45.12 occupation ... gone Cf. 'Farewell! Othello's occupation's gone!': Shakespeare, *Othello*, III.iii.357.

45.21 unveiling of the memorial Conrad's essay was published on 27 July 1921 to mark the unveiling of the Dover Patrol Memorial at Leathercote Point, on the east side of St Margaret's Bay, by the Prince of Wales (later Edward VIII; later Duke of Windsor). The 84-foot (25.6-metre) obelisk of Norwegian granite, situated on the highest peak of the cliffs of Dover and erected by public subscription, had been completed on 20 June 1921. The memorial commemorates the men of the British Merchant Service, the Royal Navy, the Royal Naval Reserves, the Royal Navy Volunteers Reserves and the 'fisher folk' who sacrificed their lives to keep the southern exit of the North Sea free from German U-boats, other vessels of war and mines that preyed upon troop transports and merchant ships.

45.27   **the Admiral** Two admirals commanded the Dover Patrol: Admiral Sir Reginald Hugh Spencer Bacon (1863–1947; knighted, 1916) until 31 December 1917, and thereafter Vice-Admiral Sir Roger John Brownlow Keyes (1872–1945; knighted 1918; 1st Baron Keyes of Zeebrugge and Dover, 1943).

45.28   **small drifter's crew** During the war the Royal Navy used such craft to patrol the coasts and carry supplies. (For 'drifters', see 'Glossary of Nautical Terms'.)

45.37   **the Grand Fleet** The name given on two occasions in Britain's naval history to the principal fleet gathered to prosecute the war: first, during the two wars against France, the Revolutionary (1793–1801) and Napoleonic (1803–15); and second, during 1914–18. During the First World War, the British Grand Fleet was comprised of thirty-five to forty battleships and battle-cruisers, and smaller ships such as destroyers and submarines. These forces contrasted with the less grand Tribal class destroyers and auxiliary craft constituting the Dover Patrol. The Grand Fleet's primary duties were to blockade the German coast, control entry into British coastal waters from the north and engage the enemy.

46.4–5   **established ... line** The reference is to the long-range artillery batteries along the Belgian coast, on the right flank of the German line of battle as conceived by Generals Alfred von Schlieffen (1833–1913) and Helmuth von Moltke (1848–1916).

47.12   **torpedo destroyers** Torpedo-boats were developed by most navies during the decade 1880–90 to take advantage of the Whitehead torpedo, then emerging as a significant naval weapon. The first torpedo-boat was HMS *Lightning*, launched in 1876. However, the threat of these boats in the hands of foreign navies spurred the Admiralty to try to discover the antidote and experiments led to the launching, in 1893, of HMS *Havelock* and HMS *Hornet*, two torpedo-boat destroyers.

47.13–14   **enemy of superior force** The Central Powers – Germany and Austria-Hungary – were, within a year after the declaration of war in August 1914, joined by the Ottoman Empire and Bulgaria. They were aligned against the Allied Powers, or the Triple Entente, consisting initially of the United Kingdom, France and Russia.

47.33   **R.N.R. and R.N.V.R.** Respectively, the Royal Naval Reserve and the Royal Naval Volunteer Reserve. The former, established in 1859, recruited merchant seamen and fishermen; the latter, established in 1903, recruited seasoned amateur sailors.

48.1   **Downs Boarding Flotilla** The men of this service, whose vessels consisted primarily of Tribal class destroyers and auxiliary patrol vessels, controlled access to the English Channel, their duties including patrolling the seas and examining ships' cargoes.

48.2   **Harwich** On the estuary of the Stour and Orwell rivers in Essex, the town is a major port and was long engaged in ship-building. During the war, it was a major naval command post and base for submarines.

48.19   **barrage nets** Barriers set to prevent enemy ships from travelling through the Straits of Dover. The barrage also included mines to curtail German incursions into coastal waters.

48.40–49.1   **system ... firing** Shore-installed artillery designed to strafe ships in the North Sea.

MEMORANDUM

50.6–7   **public spirit ... shipowners** The proposal by the Ocean Steam Ship Company of Liverpool to found and support a training-ship offering a complete education in sailing occasioned this piece. By the 1920s, conditions at sea in the new machine age were such that most young seamen had little experience under sail; in the event, however, plans for this training-ship fell through.

50.8   **southern-going** That is, in service from the United Kingdom to ports in South Africa, Australia and New Zealand.

50.15–16   **the Cape ... the Horn** Respectively, the Cape of Good Hope, at Africa's southern tip, and Cape Horn and the Tierra del Fuego archipelago at the southern tip of South America. Thus, the voyage proposed is one around the world.

51.3   **14 to 1500 tons** By way of comparison, the *Riversdale* was 1,490 gross tonnage, the *Narcissus* 1,336 and the *Tilkhurst* 1,570 (see 'Chronology').

51.7   **committee** The committee set up by Lawrence Durning Holt (53.19*n.*) of the Ocean Steam Ship Company to evaluate plans for establishing a cadet training-ship.

51.10   **my own experience** Conrad's career at sea began in December 1874, first as a passenger and later as apprentice in the *Mont-Blanc*, out of Marseilles to the French Antilles, but his time in the British Merchant Service amounted to sixteen years, beginning in 1878 as an unofficial apprentice in the *Mavis*, and continuing, with some hiatuses, until he signed off the *Adowa* in January 1894.

51.11   **trained ... British flag** Conrad had no formal training such as that provided by training-ships. He did undergo tutoring for his examinations, attending the courses offered at the London Sailors' Home, but his training was mainly of the hands-on kind, gained through practical experience, as he worked his way up through the ranks.

51.13   **in sail and steam** Conrad's experience at sea was mainly in sail during a time when steam, which was faster and allowed ships of larger cargo or passenger capacity, began to replace sail. The steamships in which he served include the *Mavis, Europa, Vidar, Roi des Belges* and the *Adowa* (see 'Chronology').

53.19   **Mr Holt** Lawrence Durning Holt (1882–1961) of the Ocean Steam Ship Company of Liverpool, who commissioned this memorandum. He was then a junior partner in the family firm, Alfred Holt & Company, in which he served from 1908 to 1953. City councillor from 1913 to 1932, he was also Lord Mayor of Liverpool in 1929–30. His interest in proper sea-training proved enduring, and in 1941 he co-founded the Outward Bound Sea School.

54.15   **the Liverpool *Sierras* ... '90** The Sierra Line was operated by Thompson, Anderson & Company of Liverpool under the name Sierra Shipping Company. Its fourteen ships, which carried cargo, all had names beginning with the word Sierra (for example, *Sierra Nevada, Sierra Blanca, Sierra Morena*). The company was in business during the 1870s, with Conrad emphasizing his own encounters with its ships on the high seas between England and Australia or in port. He may also have heard of the dramatic loss of the *Sierra Nevada* in 1900. The company ceased operations in 1913. For details, see Basil Lubbock, *Last of the Windjammers* (1929), Vol. 1.

55.1–2 **for 3 years** Conrad, in fact, served as first mate in the *Torrens* for two outward and two homeward voyages to Adelaide during 1891–3; for details, see 'The *Torrens*: A Personal Tribute'. On Curle's adjustment of this to 'two years', see 'Textual Notes'.

55.4 *Macquarie* Built in 1875 by R. & H. Green of the Blackwall Line for their run to Australia, the three-masted ship was originally named the *Melbourne*. When she was sold to Devitt & Moore in 1888, her destination port was altered from Melbourne to Sydney and her name was changed to *Macquarie*. (The name, familiar in Australia, crops up in the names of landforms, districts and streets named in honour of Lachlan Macquarie (1762–1824), the influential Governor of New South Wales.) One of that company's best-known vessels, she mainly carried passengers on her outward run; her second- and third-class cabins were dismantled to accommodate a cargo of wool on her homeward one. From 1897 to 1904 she was, as Conrad notes, a cadet training-ship in New Zealand waters. She was then sold to a Norwegian and renamed the *Fortuna*. In 1909, she became a coal hulk in Sydney Harbour, and in 1949 was converted to a coal-carrying barge. She was broken up in Sydney in 1953.

58.2 **less men** This grammatical slip probably betrays contamination from Polish or French (or both), neither of which distinguishes between countable and uncountable nouns as does English with the use of 'fewer' and 'less' and 'many' and 'much' (see also 69.10n.).

58.10 **Capt. Cope** See 21.26n.

58.11 **Conway boy** See 21.29n.

59.15 **chops of the Channel** See 23.26–27n.

59.15 **Western Islands** Here, specifically, the Azores; in Scotland, the Hebrides.

59.17 **thick weather** A usage rare in general parlance but current in maritime discourse, and usually connoting foggy, hazy or misty conditions. The *OED*'s first citation is to 1745. Cf. also 'a thick rain squall passed over the two boats': 'Youth', *Youth* (2010), p. 35.4.

THE LOSS OF THE *DALGONAR*

62.1 *Dalgonar* A three-masted, square-rigged steel ship of 2,665 gross tonnage, the *Dalgonar* was launched at Southampton in 1892. For a detailed description of the shipwreck, see Appendix B. *The Times* reported her loss on 6 December 1913 (p. 22). The *New York Times* reported on 11 December 1913 (p. 1) a sighting of the derelict and dismasted *Dalgonar* by a Captain Noricet of the French barque *Marie*. Noricet, who observed her on 28 October about 1,200 miles (1,920 km) west of the coast of Chile, recorded that she was 'lying almost on her beam ends' and appeared 'to have been caught in a hurricane which shifted her ballast'. He also reported that 'two of her small boats were gone, but the others still swung from the davits'.

62.6 **"True Story"** The *London Mercury* published the article (in fact, titled 'A True Story'), in its September issue (pp. 482–8). The complete text is reprinted in Appendix B.

62.11 **Mr L. C. Gane** See his letter in Appendix B. Presumably L(aurence) C(harles) Gane (1898–1984), long a London resident whose later life was spent in Cambridge. He served as a Lieutenant in the Royal Field Artillery in 1917, and was an agent dealing in the sale of wood. A voyage to Japan in August 1919 may have inspired his interest in nautical matters.

63.22–23 **crew of the *Dalgonar*** Of the ship's complement of thirty men, twenty-six were saved. A number of the crew had signed on at Callao, and the crew comprised, in addition to British nationals, a large number of Swedes. The heroic carpenter mentioned in the *London Mercury* article was one Hermann Dunker from Bremen.

63.25 **Mr Mull** For his account, see Appendix B.

63.26 **the *Loire*** A French four-masted steel barque of 3,094 gross tonnage launched in December 1896.

TRAVEL
PREFACE TO RICHARD CURLE'S *INTO THE EAST*

64.3 ***Into the East*** The full title of the book by Richard Curle (69.9–10*n*.), published in a trade edition on 20 March 1923 by Macmillan and the week previously in a special large-paper format limited to 125 copies, is *Into the East: Notes on Burma and Malaya*. The book brings together writing that had previously appeared in *The Times*, the *English Review*, the *Rangoon Times* and the *Blue Peter*.

64.5 **the fate of books** An allusion to 'Pro captu lectoris habent sua fata libelli' ('The reader's fancy makes the fate of books'), *De Syllabis*, l. 1286, by the Latin poet Terentianus Maurus (*fl.* 200). Cf. 'It has been said a long time ago that books have their fate': 'Books', *Notes on Life and Letters* (2004), p. 10.15.

64.18 **valley of tears** A reference to the universal lament of earthly life and its sorrows. The phrase goes back at least to Psalm xxiii.4: 'Yea though I walk through the valley of the shadow of death'. An early version of its counterpart, 'vale of tears', is found in the Roman Catholic hymn and prayer 'Salve, Regina': 'To thee do we send up our sighs, mourning and weeping in this vale of tears.'

65.2 **lovers of wonders** Possibly an allusion to the *Thousand and One Nights*, a book Conrad alludes to in 'Autocracy and War' (*Notes on Life and Letters*).

65.3 **"travelling is victory,"** Cited in *An Outcast of the Islands* (ch. 5), this phrase serves as Curle's epigraph, with Conrad's novel its probable source. Conrad's own source is Captain Sir Richard Burton's *Personal Narrative of a Pilgrimage to Al-Madinah and Meccah* (1855):

The conversation was the usual Oriental thing. It is, for instance, understood that you have seen strange things in strange lands.
   "Voyaging – is – victory," quotes the Mirza; the quotation is a hackneyed one, but it steps forth majestic as to pause and emphasis. (I, 87)

Man's heart bounds in his breast at the thought of measuring his puny force with Nature's might, and of emerging triumphant from trial. This explains the Arab's proverb, "Voyaging is victory." (I, 149)

Conrad also used the phrase in a letter, writing to R. B. Cunninghame Graham on Graham's return to England from North Africa – 'We shout cries of welcome. Travel[l]ing is victory': 9 November 1898 (*Letters*, II, 116).

65.8–9 **Arab traveller ... book** Probably Ibn Battutah or Battuta (1304–69?, Abu 'abd Allah Muhammad Ibn 'abd Allah Al-lawati At-Tanji Ibn Battutah), who began travelling in 1325, and continued for almost thirty years, primarily in the Islamic world, from North Africa to the Middle East, including the Hajj, and reaching Persia (present-day Iran), India, Ceylon, Malaya and China as well as Andalusia and western Africa. He dictated the record of his travels, translated as *Rihlah: My Travels*, to a scribe. See *Voyages d'Ibn Battutah, accompagné d'une traduction*, ed. C. Defremery and B. R. Sanguinetti (1853–8).

65.11 **travelling sword in hand** A complex reference, referring both to the tradition of forcible conversion, practised during the early Islamist period over swathes of the Middle East and elsewhere, and to Ottoman incursions into Europe during the preceding centuries.

65.14–15 **spiritual character ... shades of Vallombrosa** A multi-layered allusion. The Romantic poet William Wordsworth used the following lines from Milton's *Paradise Lost* (1.302–04) as the epigraph to section XVIII of his poem *Memorials of a Tour in Italy* (1837) titled 'At Vallombrosa': 'Thick as autumnal leaves that strow the brooks / In Vallombrosa where Etrurian shades / high overarched embower'. Wordsworth's poem itself transposed the shades as follows: 'Vallombrosa! Of thee I first heard in the page / Of that holiest of Bards ... / And, now, ye Miltonian shades! under you / I repose.' Milton's lines occur in a section of his epic poem in which Satan surveys his fellow fallen angels lying thick as leaves and in which he also recalls his own meeting with Galileo; Wordsworth responds both to the natural landscape and to his encounter with Milton's art. The fame of Milton's lines is attested to as follows: 'I found myself on the shadowy hills of Vallombrosa. Its very name, which Milton has made familiar to English ears, has a poetic and romantic attraction; and whenever it is pronounced, there rises in the memory his famous simile': W. W. Story, *Vallombrosa* (1881), p. 1.

Literally 'shady valley' (*Valle Ombrosa*), the village and vale of this name are about 18.5 miles (30 km) south-east of Florence at an altitude of 4,000 ft (1,219 m) in the Apennine forests. The climate made the locale a popular summer resort throughout the late-Victorian period (see 'Vallombrosa', *The Times*, 24 September 1875, p. 4). The phrase 'spiritual character' alludes to its Benedictine abbey, founded in 1038.

65.16–17 **successors ... pounds per head** A reference to travel agents, the great pioneer being Thomas Cook, in the early mid-Victorian period. On Conrad and modern travel and tourism, see Stephen Donovan, *Joseph Conrad and Popular Culture* (2005). The phenomenon of modern tourism is satirized in *Lord Jim* (ch. 7).

65.21 **Isthmus of Suez** The Suez Canal, built 1859–69, carved through the narrow neck of land connecting Asia and Africa, provided easier access to the Far East, avoiding the longer voyage round the tip of Africa. The Canal was prominent in geopolitical manœuvrings throughout Conrad's lifetime.

65.28 ***cabinets de lecture*** 'Circulating libraries' (French), that is, lending libraries hiring out books on a per-book basis and usually requiring an annual subscription.

65.34–35 **Hübner's *Voyage* ... World** *Promenade autour de monde* (1871) by the Austrian diplomat Joseph Alexander, Baron de Hübner (né Hafenbredl, 1811–92), was translated into English as *A Ramble Round the World 1871* (1874) in two volumes by Lady Herbert. Hübner's travels, detailed in almost 1,000 pages, including engravings, took him from Ireland to New York, and across North America to Japan and China. This popular work was in a sixth Paris edition by 1881. A later book of travel was his *À travers l'Empire Britannique* ['Through the British Empire'], *1883–84* (1886).

66.27 **heroes of my boyhood** These are discussed in 'Geography and Some Explorers'.

67.13–14 **protagonists ... Hannon** Conrad mistakenly uses the word 'protagonists' for 'precursors'. A Carthaginian navigator of *c.* 500 BC, Hannon founded towns on the coast of what is today Morocco and perhaps explored the African coast as far as present-day Sierra Leone.

67.16 *Periplus* Hannon's record of his voyage, *Periplus*, probably written in Punic, was originally deposited in a temple at Carthage. It survives only in Greek translation, and was translated into English in 1797. A more modern version is *The Periplus of Hanno; A Voyage of Discovery Down the West African Coast, by a Carthaginian Admiral of the Fifth Century, B.C., with Explanatory Passages Quoted from Numerous Authors*, trans. Wilfred H. Schoff (Philadelphia, 1912).

67.18–19 **Marco Polo** A Venetian traveller to the East, Marco Polo (1254? – *c.* 1324) became a favourite of Kublai Khan, for whom he conducted business of trade and state. Returning to Venice, he became a prisoner of war (1296) while fighting the Genoans, and he dictated an account of his travels, *Il Milione* (in English *The Books of Ser Marco Polo* or *The Travels of Marco Polo*), whilst in prison. Recent scholarship has cast doubts on his claims to have reached China.

67.25–26 **sun ... nothing new** A statement of conventional wisdom, an early example of which is 'There is nothing new under the sun': Ecclesiastes i.9.

67.32 **our daily bread** A favourite Conrad commonplace from 'The Lord's Prayer' – 'Give us this day our daily bread': Matthew vi.11.

68.4–5 **Barth ... Denham ... Clapperton ... Park** On Barth, see 13.25–26*n.* Dixon Denham (1786–1828) joined Hugh Clapperton (1788–1827) to explore western Africa, crossing the Sahara Desert and discovering Lake Chad in 1823, and dying of a fever in Sierra Leone five weeks after he was appointed governor in 1828. Clapperton explored Lake Chad with Denham and later tried to find the source of the Niger river, but died near Sokoto before he reached his goal. His servant, R. L. Lander, returned to England with Clapperton's records, published in 1829 as *Journal of a Second Expedition into the Interior of Africa*. On Mungo Park, see 12.7*n.*

69.2 **Gobi Desert** In East Asia, mostly in what is now the Mongolian People's Republic and the Inner Mongolian Autonomous Region of China, one of the world's largest deserts.

69.5–6 **Khan of Tartary's court** Jenghiz or Genghis Khan (1167?–1227) and his sons and grandsons ruled variously in Tartary (or Tatary) which, during the Middle Ages, included the central belt of Central Asia and Eastern Europe from the Sea of Japan to the Dnieper river. The Tartars (Tatars) of Russia are primarily remnants of the thirteenth-century Mongolian invasion, which pushed the Mongols and some Turkish populations of the Ural-Altaic region westwards.

69.7–9   **Kuala Kangsar ... Sultan of Perak ... K.C.M.G. ... Governor** Kuala Kangsar is the royal capital of the state of Perak in what was at the time of writing the Federated Malay States (part of present-day Malaysia). The Sultan was the hereditary and titular ruler, under a British advisor, the Sultan at issue being Alang Iskandar (1881–1938; r. 1918–38). The abbreviated decoration ('K.C.M.G.') is that of Knight Commander of the Order of St Michael and St George. Laurence Nunns Guillemard (1862–1951) was Governor of the Straits Settlements from 1919 to 1927. Curle records the ceremony he witnessed in the following terms: 'We had come to Kuala Kangsar to see the Sultan of Perak invested in his home with the K.C.M.G. by the High Commissioner, Sir Laurence Guillemard, Governor of the Straits Settlements. The function went off with perfect good breeding': *Into the East*, p. 210.

69.9   **Straits Settlements** The name of the British colonies in South-East Asia, comprising the territories of Penang, the Dindings, Singapore and Malacca, under unified administration as of 1826. In 1867, the Straits Settlements became a unitary British colony (dissolved 1946).

69.9–10   **This modern traveller** Born in Melrose, Scotland, Richard Henry Parnell Curle (1883–1968) established himself as a journalist and short-story writer in London after leaving Wellington College in 1901. From 1905, he worked in publishing, and was introduced to Conrad through Edward Garnett's Mont Blanc Restaurant circle. He wrote the first critical study of Conrad (1914). His other travel writings include *Caravansary and Conversation* (1937). Acting as one of Conrad's executors, he edited *Suspense, Last Essays* and a volume of Conrad's letters to himself. His *The Last Twelve Years of Joseph Conrad* (1928) provides an intimate portrait.

69.10   **less words** This ungrammatical phrase is probably contaminated by Polish usage (*mniej słów*); cf. also 'much more trees' influenced by *wiele wiecej drzew* in 'The Congo Diary' (130.28 *n.*).

69.18   **Selangor** A state in north-eastern Malaya (present-day Malaysia) on the Strait of Malacca (69.26 *n.*).

69.19–22   **Admiral ... "Hear ... game."** Conrad also draws on this incident, found in his wide reading on South-East Asia, in *Lord Jim*: 'When Jim had done there was a great stillness. Nobody seemed to breathe even; no one made a sound till the old Rajah sighed faintly, and looking up, with a toss of his head, said quickly, "You hear, my people! No more of these little games"' (ch. 25). The original reads as follows:

Our Admiral had an interview with the Sultan, who was surrounded by his chiefs and people, and in as much state as he was capable of showing. The Admiral, in referring to the barbarity of the Jugra piracy, advised and urged upon the Sultan [of Selangor] to caution his people against being guilty of such acts in future, pointing out how it was impossible that they could be left unpunished ...

The Sultan listened very attentively, and then turning quickly round to his people, he exclaimed: *Dungar lah, jangan kitah main main lagi!*— 'Hear now, my people! Don't let us have any more of this little game!' (Major Fred. McNair, *Perak and the Malays: Sārong and Krīs* (1878), p. 289)

Quashing pirate activities is a theme of writings about Sir James Brooke, the first Rajah of Sarawak, and forms the background for the Patusan section of *Lord Jim*, with Jim (in the event, temporarily) bringing the rule of law to a region where piracy and brazen theft were endemic.

69.24–25   **Jugra river ... era of security** A tidal creek in Selangor State, the Jugra joins the Langat river. Conrad's allusion is to the Jugra Piracy, discussed at length by McNair (see note above), whose account he knew. The incident involved the pirating of a Malay trading vessel and the killing of all but one of its crew members at the mouth of the Jugra in November 1873. British authorities reacted strongly to the affair, and set up a Commission to deal with it; the Sultan of Selangor, who initially characterized it as 'boys' play', in due course proved cooperative. The perpetrators were caught and executed, and the authority of the Sultan's viceroy greatly strengthened as the result of this turn of events. For more detail, see Sir Frank Swettenham, *British Malaya: An Account of the Origin and Progress of British Influence* (1907), p. 183.

69.26   **Straits of Malacca** The 500-mile (800-km) wide Strait of Malacca between the island of Sumatra and the Malay Peninsula, linking the Indian Ocean to the South China Sea, is one of the region's busiest and most important waterways.

69.35   **(as he himself observes)** Cf. the following from *Into the East*:

It is vain to speculate on the future of countries, but we all do it. Malaya is a small place and her great wealth has been acquired in a few years. But now, indeed, the hour of misfortune has struck, and with distress comes muttering. The capital that poured in from Europe, expanding like yeast upon these golden shores, is melting from week to week. But man overcomes his troubles because man must live, and Malaya, with her fertile soil, will never sink into a mere echo of past prosperity. (pp. 212–13)

70.8   **Irrawaddy flotilla steamer** Curle records, 'No, you can't escape your companions on an Irrawaddy Steamer': *Into the East*, p. 107. The Irrawaddy river is Burma's major waterway, flowing 1,000 miles (1,600 km) through the centre of the country and through Rangoon, its capital. The river valley is home to the country's primary cultural, business and political activity. Founded in 1865, the Irrawaddy Flotilla Company ran services on the main river, its delta and such tributaries as the Chindwin, carrying passengers and freight, including large quantities of rice and teak logs. The crews were chiefly Bengalis and the officers Scots. The vessels were built on the Clyde and reassembled in Burma. In his poem 'The Road to Mandalay' (1892), Rudyard Kipling evokes the clunking of their paddle wheels. At the height of its operations, in the 1920s, the company owned 600 vessels and carried 9 million passengers a year, justifying its claim to be 'the greatest river fleet on earth'.

70.10   **Bhamo** A small city on the Irrawaddy in Kachin State, Burma, the nearest port to the border with China. At the time Curle visited, its population was 9,000. Situated on the caravan route from Burma to India, Bhamo was important for the transportation of jade.

70.10–14   **frontier ... innumerable hills** The context of Curle's passage is the comment of a resident of Bhamo who had confessed to Curle 'On the frontier [of

China] ... we live on rumours', with Curle's response recorded as follows – 'I looked sharply at him, sitting there beside me in calm security, and suddenly I seemed to hear around me the whisper of innumerable hills': *Into the East*, p. 111.

70.18   **three volumes** An allusion to Curle's collections of short fiction: *Shadows out of the Crowd* (1912), *Life is a Dream* (1914) and *The Echo of Voices* (1917).

STEPHEN CRANE
INTRODUCTION TO THOMAS BEER'S
STEPHEN CRANE

71.5–6   **rainy day ... author** On 8 March 1923, Iowa-born Thomas Beer (1889–1940), a lawyer by profession, called on Conrad at his home, Oswalds, near Canterbury (*Letters*, VIII, 46) in the company of his publisher Alfred A. Knopf. Beer's *Stephen Crane: A Study in American Letters*, published by Knopf on 23 October 1923, was the first biography of the American novelist, short-story writer and war correspondent (1871–1900). Beer also wrote a biography of the American politician Mark Hanna (1929) and studied American manners in *The Mauve Decade: Life at the End of the Nineteenth Century* (1933). His biography of Crane has been discredited for fabricating evidence, particularly letters; see Stanley Wertheim and Paul Sorrentino, 'Thomas Beer: The Clay Feet of Stephen Crane Biography', *American Literary Realism*, 22, no. 3 (1990), 2–16.

71.10–11   **appear in my lifetime** Conrad describes Crane's fall into oblivion after his death as follows: 'Mere literary excellence won't save a man's memory. In fifty year's time some curious literary critic (of the professional scribbler kind) will perhaps rediscover him as a curiosity and write a short paper in order to earn five guineas. Sad but true': to Peter F. Somerville, 1915 (?) (*Letters*, V, 546).

71.20   **initial date ... friendship** If Edward Garnett's dating of a letter to him from Conrad is correct (*Letters*, I, 396 n. 1), Crane and Conrad met on 15 October 1897. *The Nigger of the 'Narcissus'* was then appearing serially in the *New Review*. For Conrad's account of his meeting and subsequent friendship with Crane, see also 'Stephen Crane: A Note without Dates', *Notes on Life and Letters* (2004), pp. 43–5. For a discussion of the relationship between the two writers, see Elsa Nettels, 'Conrad and Stephen Crane', *Conradiana*, 10 (1978), 267–83.

71.20–21   **life is but a dream** A commonplace, with several possible derivations, including, for instance, 'We are such stuff / As dreams are made on': Shakespeare, *The Tempest*, IV.i.156–8. It figures as the title of the drama *La vida es sueño* by the Spanish Golden Age dramatist Pedro Calderón de la Barca (1600–81), from which Conrad uses a quotation as the epigraph to *An Outcast of the Islands*. The play, set in an imaginary Poland, has long been popular among literary Poles, and Conrad may also have encountered it in his reading of Arthur Schopenhauer's *The World as Will and Representation* (1819). The popular nursery rhyme and song 'Row, row, row your boat' with its final line 'Life is but a dream' may also be at issue. (The well-known musical setting dates to 1881.)

71.21–22   **never kept a diary** Conrad forgets his 'Congo Diary' and 'Up-river Book'.

71.23   **another friend** Jessie Conrad (see 112.14–15*n*.).

71.27 **our Essex home** The Conrads moved to a semi-detached villa in Victoria Road, Stanford-le-Hope, Essex, in September 1896, and then to Ivy Walls, an Elizabethan farmhouse on the town's outskirts, in March 1897, remaining in Essex until March 1898.

71.29 **short paper** 'Stephen Crane: A Note without Dates' published in the *London Mercury*'s inaugural issue of December 1919 (pp. 192–3), and later collected in *Notes on Life and Letters*.

71.30–31 **Pawling ... firm of Mr Heinemann** S(ydney) S(outhgate) Pawling (1862–1923), partner in the publishing firm of William Heinemann, had met Conrad in 1896 at the urging of Edward Garnett, and was instrumental in advancing the writer's early career. Heinemann published *The Nigger of the 'Narcissus'* in December 1897, after it had appeared serially in the *New Review*, a journal published by the firm. Established in 1890, Heinemann built up an impressive list that included, among others, the rising writers Rudyard Kipling, Robert Louis Stevenson and H. G. Wells.

71.34 **notable journalist** The American novelist and journalist Harold Frederic (1856–98), then London correspondent for the *New York Times*, best remembered for his novel *The Damnation of Theron Ware* (1896).

72.4 *Red Badge of Courage* See 90.7 *n*.

73.8–9 **W. E. Henley's ... New Review** W(illiam) E(rnest) Henley (1849–1903) was a poet, critic and dramatist, and Robert Louis Stevenson's sometime collaborator. He edited the *New Review* from June 1889 until its demise in December 1897 (in which issue the final instalment of *The Nigger of the 'Narcissus'* appeared). Crane's sole contribution to the magazine, the story 'One Dash – Horses', appeared in February 1896.

73.17 **absence ... Spanish-American war** Crane left England in April 1898 to cover the war for Joseph Pulitzer's *New York World*, in time also writing for William Randolph Hearst's *New York Journal*. His experience involved six weeks on small boats, and visits to Havana and Guantánamo. He returned to England in January 1899. For a detailed discussion of his war journalism, see Michael Robertson, *Stephen Crane, Journalism, and the Making of Modern American Literature* (1997).

The Spanish-American War lasted from the retroactive declaration of war by the United States on 21 April 1898 until the surrender of the Spanish Army in Cuba on 17 July. It began as the result of Spanish repression of Cuba's fight for independence, the sinking of the US battleship *Maine* in Havana harbour, sensationalistic and exaggerated reporting by the press and war fever in the United States. Conrad took Spain's side in the conflict.

73.18–19 **visit ... last illness** Crane returned to England via New York in poor health on 11 January 1899 and continued to decline throughout the winter and spring. He died of tuberculosis on 5 June 1900 at a health spa in the Black Forest in Badenweiler, Germany, aged twenty-eight.

73.22 **different counties** Crane lived in Surrey at Ravensbrook Villa, Oxted, and later in Sussex at Brede Place, a fourteenth-century manor house (84.37 *n*.). The Conrads were then living in Kent on the outskirts of the village of Postling at Pent Farm (78.21 *n*.).

73.27–28   **as an author … senior** Crane's first novel, *Maggie, A Girl of the Streets*, appeared in 1893; Conrad's first novel, *Almayer's Folly*, in 1895.

74.2   **much bigger man** Pawling, who had a considerable reputation as a cricketer, was well over 6 ft (1.8 m) tall. For a photograph of him, see *Letters*, IX.

74.11   **Greece, at war** The Greco-Turkish War of 1897 was one of many conflicts related to the Ottoman Empire's gradual withdrawal from Europe. Crane had been a foreign correspondent in Greece during April–May 1896. For Conrad's views of the Eastern Question, see 'The Future of Constantinople'.

74.22   **stroll … rose-garden** Among other things, Crane left college after two years; lived a bohemian life in New York City (the basis for his novel *Maggie, A Girl of the Streets*); gained a reputation for profligate living, possibly involving drug addiction; survived shipwreck; covered two wars, contracting malaria to complicate his tuberculosis; and lived an unconventional life with Cora Howarth (80.36*n.*).

75.9–11   **Edward Garnett … simile** Cf. 'And he does it all straight from the surface; a few oaths, a genius for slang; an exquisite and unique faculty of exposing an individual scene by an odd simile': 'Mr. Stephen Crane: An Appreciation', *Academy*, 17 December 1898, p. 484. A publisher's reader for T. Fisher Unwin, Conrad's first publisher, and later for Heinemann and Duckworth, Edward William Garnett (1868–1937), who hailed from a bookish family, became a behind-the-scenes force in the rise of literary Modernism. He wrote plays and essays himself and mentored Conrad during his early career. Conrad wrote an introduction to his book on Turgenev (1917), and the friendship lasted until the writer's death.

75.28   *memento mori* See 17.2 *n.*

75.40–76.1   **Garland … Howells** American writers: the regional novelist Hamlin Garland (1860–1940) was an early champion and friend of Crane, and the editor, critic and realist William Dean Howells (1837–1920) mentored several young writers, including Crane. For a discussion of Garland's friendship with Crane and Conrad, see Owen Knowles and J. H. Stape, 'Conrad and Hamlin Garland: A Correspondence Recovered', *The Conradian*, 31, no. 2 (2006), 62–78.

76.14–16   **"honourable" by courtesy … popular assembly** The courtesy title (that is, one without legal status) 'the Honourable' (abbreviated 'Hon.') is given to the children of viscounts and barons. Privy Counsellors, most of them senior judges or government ministers, are styled 'the Right Honourable' ('Rt Hon.'). By strictly enforced convention, members of the House of Commons do not use each other's names in the chamber, referring instead to 'the honourable member' or, if belonging to the same party, 'my honourable friend'.

77.11   **Green Park railings** The tall, wrought-iron fences along the northern boundary of the 53-acre (21-ha) park, which is situated between Hyde and St James's Parks not far from Buckingham Palace, were moved to Devonshire House, on the north side of Piccadilly, in 1898, the year after Conrad and Crane met, and subsequently returned to their original location on the south side in 1921.

77.16   **your general** A minor character in *The Red Badge of Courage*, the general is knowledgeable and in command when he enters the battlefield: 'The general reined strongly at his charger's opened and foamy mouth and guided it with dexterous horsemanship past the man.' See especially ch. 18.

77.18–19 **Hyde Park Corner** Hyde Park Corner is at the south-east end of Hyde Park, at the junction of Knightsbridge, Piccadilly and Grosvenor Place. The 360-acre (146-ha) Hyde Park is adjacent to Kensington Gardens. Conrad and Crane's walk took them through a particularly fashionable part of London known for its shops, tea-rooms and restaurants.

77.20 **your young man** Young Charley of *The Nigger of the 'Narcissus'* – who is described thus: 'Young Charley was lean and long-necked. The ridge of his backbone made a chain of small hills under the old shirt. His face of a street-boy ... hung low over his bony knees' (p. 7) – is last seen on shore as his mother 'slobbered over him': '"Leggo of me," said Charley ... he gave me a humorous smile and a glance, ironic, courageous, and profound, that seemed to put all my knowledge of life to shame' (pp. 170–71).

77.39–40 **"barbarously abrupt" ... "The Open Boat"** Cf. 'These waves were most wrongfully and barbarously abrupt and tall, and each froth-top was a problem in small boat navigation.' Crane's short story 'The Open Boat', first published in *Scribner's Magazine* in June 1897, is based on a shipwreck Crane survived. It was collected in *The Open Boat and Other Stories*, published by Heinemann in April 1898.

78.21 **Pent Farm** The Conrads' home in the village of Postling, Kent, near Hythe, from October 1898 to September 1907. Perhaps named from an Old Kentish dialect word meaning 'incline', or 'sloping land', possibly derived from the French *pente* ('a slope or declivity'), the house is mentioned in a document related to land title dating to 1787. Set in rolling countryside and farmland, it lacks distant views.

78.33 **his tale** Crane's 'The Open Boat'.

79.4 **Kensington Gardens** Adjoining Hyde Park, Kensington Gardens, one of central London's five large parks, is comprised of 275 acres (111 ha) including Kensington Palace.

79.11–12 **the Painted Desert ... Oxford Street** Stretching from the north-eastern bank of the Little Colorado river in what is now northern Arizona southward about 220 miles (320 km) from the Grand Canyon, the desert includes the Petrified Forest. The colours described result from eroding layers of red and yellow sediment and bentonite clay. Oxford Street, a long thoroughfare in central London, is renowned for its shops.

79.21 **A.B.C. shop** A tea-room of the Aerated Bread Company (commonly abbreviated as 'A.B.C.'). Established as a bakery in 1862, the company opened the first of its self-service tea-rooms in 1865, and by 1923 had 150 branch bakeries and 250 tea-rooms throughout London.

79.26 **a club** At the time of writing, Conrad belonged to both the Royal Automobile Club, a favoured London haunt during his later years, and the prestigious Athenæum, to which he had been elected in 1918.

79.29–30 **world ... old and weary** A possible echo of 'How weary, stale, flat, and unprofitable / Seem to me all the uses of this world!': Shakespeare, *Hamlet*, I.ii.133–5.

80.1–2 **Piccadilly Circus ... night-birds** The centre of London's West End theatre district, with access to entertainment establishments, shopping and government offices. The principal thoroughfares converging there are Piccadilly, Shaftesbury

Avenue and Regent Street. During the late-Victorian era, the area had a reputation for loucheness and was a known haunt of prostitutes.

80.3–8   **Balzac ... Comédie Humaine** A series of short stories and novels written from about 1830 by the French novelist Honoré de Balzac (1799–1850), *La Comédie humaine* depicts contemporary French society of all classes and professions in precise detail, and has a searingly critical and unsentimental attitude towards the bases of human society and affection. On Conrad's interest in Balzac, see J. H. Stape, '"One could learn something from Balzac": Conrad and Balzac', *Conrad: Intertexts and Appropriations: Essays in Memory of Yves Hervouet*, ed. Gene M. Moore, Owen Knowles and J. H. Stape (1997), pp. 103–18.

80.12   **Monico's** A huge café-restaurant, Café Monico at 15 Tichborne Street, was founded in 1876 by Giacomo Monico, who left Gatti's (87.2n.) in 1872. In operation as an independent concern until the 1950s, it was then taken over by the Forte group. Expansion in 1888 gave it frontage on the east side of Piccadilly Circus.

80.22   **monumentally heavy ... Pavilion** The London Pavilion Theatre, from 1861 a variety theatre, had been rebuilt in 1885 after extensive renovations related to the construction of Shaftesbury Avenue. A lavish theatre for musical revues and popular entertainments, it features an elaborate and highly decorated stone façade with false columns.

80.34   **our first child** (Alfred) Borys (Leo) Conrad (d. 1978) was born at Stanford-le-Hope on 15 January 1898. The Conrads' second child, John Alexander, was born in 1906.

80.36   **his wife** Cora Ethel Eaton Howarth (1865–1910; alias Cora Taylor; alias Cora Stewart; later Mrs Hammond P. McNeil). The term 'wife' was a courtesy, as she and Crane were not legally married, H. G. Wells having presided over a makeshift ceremony. Crane met her in late 1896 or early 1897 when she was running a brothel; their union led to rumours that Crane was, among other things, a Satanist and drug addict, slander partly responsible for his move abroad. One of the earliest women war correspondents, she reported on the Greco-Turkish War for the New York press. After Crane's death, she remained in England until 1901, when she moved to Jacksonville, Florida, where she managed a high-class brothel and, in 1905, married unhappily.

80.40   **young aunt** Alice Dora ('Dolly') George (1884–1949; later Mrs John Harald Hawar; later Mrs George Harold Moor), the second youngest of Jessie Conrad's four sisters. Conrad helped pay for her education at the Bernardine Convent, Slough. She married a South African and later immigrated to his country. On her, see Keith Carabine and J. H. Stape, 'Family Letters: Conrad to a Sister-in-Law and Jessie Conrad on Conrad's Death', *The Conradian*, 30, no. 1 (2005), 127–31, and J. H. Stape and Keith Carabine, 'Further Light on Conrad's Sister-in-Law Dolly Moor', *The Conradian*, 31, no. 1 (2006), 128–9.

81.38   **man ... laughing animal** A commonplace dating to Antiquity, and variously treated; see, for example, ''Twas said of old, deny it who can, / The only laughing animal is man': William Whitehead, *On Ridicule* (1743); and 'Man is called a Laughing Animal: but do not the apes also laugh, or attempt to do it; and is the manliest man the greatest and oftenest laugher': Thomas Carlyle, *Sartor Resartus* (1833–4), Bk I, ch. 5. Conrad read Carlyle carefully, and 'Youth' specifically mentions *Sartor Resartus*.

82.9   **see more war** Borys Conrad was commissioned as a second-lieutenant in the Army Service Corps in September 1915. He was gassed and shell-shocked in France in late 1918, and was hospitalized for neurasthenia in early 1919.

82.29   **"Behold the boy"** Possibly an attempt at grim humour, recalling Pontius Pilate's famous phrase 'Ecce homo' ('Behold the man'), pronounced on presenting the scourged Christ to the hostile mob.

82.35   **the dog theme** Later, Crane gave Borys a spaniel, named 'Escamillo' after the toreador of Georges Bizet's *Carmen* (Conrad's favourite opera).

83.22   *The Black Riders* Crane's *The Black Riders and Other Lines* was published in Boston in mid-1895.

84.20   **collection of literary essays** In addition to that on Crane, *Friday Nights: Literary Criticisms and Appreciations* (1922) brought together essays on Conrad, D. H. Lawrence, W. H. Hudson, Robert Frost and other writers.

84.37   **Brede Place** The Cranes leased this picturesque but dilapidated sandstone manor house from Moreton Frewen (1853–1924), politician, author and erstwhile rancher. During the tenancy (1899–1900) their guests included Conrad, Ford Hueffer, Edward Garnett, H. G. Wells and Henry James. The Cranes' virtually baronial hospitality helped to make up for the dampness of the rooms, the dimness of the lighting, the absence of plumbing and the attentions of the resident ghost, Sir Goddard Oxenbridge. What remains of the house – largely destroyed by fire in 1979 – stands on an isolated site in the Brede Valley of Sussex, about 5.5 miles (9 km) west of Rye.

85.14   **those Indians** A reference to persons possessed of uncouth manners. Conrad himself often jokingly recalled America's native peoples when speaking of Americans generally, talking of taking scalps and the like.

85.18   *Pulvis et umbra sunt* 'They are but dust and shadow' (Latin). The usual quotation is 'Pulvis et umbra sumus' ('We are but dust and shadow'): Horace, *Carmina*, IV.vii.16.

85.32   **still smaller ale** Ale at its most innocuous: the expression survives in 'small beer' as applied to something trivial.

86.30   **Stokes' invitation** Crane's New York publisher Frederick A(bbott) Stokes (1857–1939) founded his firm in 1881 and was its president from 1890. Conrad had already refused this invitation (*Letters*, II, 45–6), but, on being further pressed, accepted it.

86.30–37   **the Savage ... Savages** Celebrating literature and the arts, particularly the theatre, the Savage Club was in Conrad's time housed in Adelphi Terrace near The Strand. (It has moved several times since, and is at present in the National Liberal Club in Whitehall Place.) Nowadays the all-male club refers to itself as 'one of the leading Bohemian Gentlemen's Clubs' of London, although ladies are invited to some dinners. Members refer to each other as 'Savages' or 'Brother Savages'.

87.2–3   **Gatti's ... Bodega** Established in a modest way in the 1860s by the Paris-born Agostino Gatti (1841–97) and Giacomo Monico, the eventual Gatti's Restaurant and Café at 430 Strand and Adelaide Street was by the late 1890s a famed gathering-place for bohemians, particularly on Sunday evenings. (On the Gatti family and their business dealings, see *DNB*.) A London chain of Spanish bars cum wineshops was named 'Bodega' (Spanish for 'wine shop'); that near Gatti's would have been the Covent Garden branch, the Bodega Bar in Bedford Street. It was favoured by a theatrical clientele.

87.20–21   *Lord Jim ... Blackwood* Conrad began the novel as a short story probably in May 1898, but was pressed by the need to complete 'The Rescuer' (later *The Rescue*) and then took up 'Heart of Darkness' and collaborated with Ford Madox Hueffer (later Ford) on *The Inheritors*. When he returned to the story, it rapidly grew into a full-length novel. *Lord Jim* was published in *Blackwood's Edinburgh Magazine* in thirteen monthly instalments (October 1899 – November 1900), and appeared in book form on 9 October 1900.

88.15   **stood already written** A probable allusion to a commonplace in Islamic culture, derived from the Koran, that an individual's destiny is written upon his forehead; cf. '"Every man carries his destiny on his forehead", say the Mohammedans': John Hutton Balfour Browne, *The Medical Jurisprudence of Insanity* (1875), p. 103. The idea is also found in Hindu beliefs about *karma*. Cf. 'As if the initial word of each our destiny were not graven in imperishable characters upon the face of a rock': *Lord Jim*, p. 186.

88.30   **that day ... sun set** The war's anticipated brevity accounted in part for Crane's wish to reach Cuba quickly.

88.35   **money hunting enterprises** Conrad's account of the day in London leaves out some significant facts. Crane was trying to obtain an advance rather than a loan, and thus the 'various offices' were those of publishers. When Conrad decided not to collaborate on the play, Crane rethought the subject as a novel to be written by himself alone and showed the publishers a 'prospectus' summarizing the plot. Towards the end of a long day, Crane and Conrad reached the office of the newspaper publisher C(yril) Arthur Pearson (1866–1921), where Crane's synopsis was refused yet again. In despair, Crane gave it to George Brown Burgin (1856–1944), a prolific novelist and Pearson's literary advisor, telling Burgin he could have the plot for his own use. Burgin kept the synopsis and published it in *More Memoirs and Some Travels* (1922), pp. 170–72, along with the story of its origin. There are two divergences from the play as described by Conrad: the partner does not try to impersonate the dead rancher, and the horses do not die. Perhaps Crane changed the story in response to Conrad's ridicule, or perhaps Conrad tinkered with the details so as to make a better anecdote.

88.36   **see about a dog** A once common euphemism for responding to the call of nature.

89.1   **Blackwood & Sons' London office** The firm (established 1817) was then located in the capital at 37 Paternoster Row, the centre of British publishing in the period; its main offices, however, were at 45 George Street, Edinburgh. The firm published Conrad's work from 1897 to 1902. For details of his dealings with it, see *Joseph Conrad: Letters to William Blackwood and David S. Meldrum*, ed. William Blackburn (1958), and Ivo Vidan, 'Conrad in his *Blackwood's* Context: An Essay in

Applied Reception Theory', *The Ugo Mursia Memorial Lectures*, ed. Mario Curreli (1988), pp. 399–422. Since Crane had already left the 'prospectus' with Burgin, the money from Blackwood's was not an advance on 'The Predecessor' but perhaps offered in the expectation of stories about the impending war.

89.3   **Charing Cross** One of the metropolis's main railway stations, with services to Surrey, Sussex and Kent and, at the time of writing, with boat-trains for Channel services.

89.5–6   **"The Price of the Harness"** The short story, published in the December 1898 issue of *Blackwood's Edinburgh Magazine*, Crane's sole contribution to the magazine, is one of a series of his sketches, essays and fictions about the Spanish-American War.

89.8   **led ... to his doom** Crane's health, already fragile, was further undermined by the vicissitudes to which he was exposed during his experience as a war correspondent, and by the time he returned to England in January 1899 he was seriously ill.

89.13–14   **short tales ...** *Metropolitan Magazine* The story alluded to is 'The Planter of Malata', which appeared in the June and July 1914 issues of New York's *Metropolitan Magazine*. Other Conrad works published in the *Metropolitan* were 'Laughing Anne' ('Because of the Dollars'), 'Freya of the Seven Isles' and 'The Inn of the Two Witches'. For a full discussion of Conrad's fortunes in the American serial market, see S. W. Reid, 'American Markets, Serials, and Conrad's Career', *The Conradian*, 28, no. 1 (2003), 57–99.

HIS WAR-BOOK
INTRODUCTION TO STEPHEN CRANE'S
THE RED BADGE OF COURAGE

90.7   **appearance in 1895** Serialized in 1894 and published in book form in America in September 1895, *The Red Badge of Courage: An Episode of the American Civil War* by Stephen Crane (1871–1900), was brought out in England by Heinemann on 27 November 1895. The 'Popular edition' (3s 6d), for which Conrad wrote this preface, appeared in March 1925.

90.9   **Heinemann's Pioneer Series** On Heinemann's, see 71.30–31*n*. The firm's Pioneer Series, distinguished by what *The Times* called 'ultra-Japanese designs' on its paper covers and intentionally limited to works of 'convenient length', included such works as the anonymously authored *The Green Carnation* (1894), *The Wings of Icarus* (1894) by Lawrence Alma-Tadema and *A Street in Suburbia* (1895) by Edwin W. Pugh.

90.12   **a term made familiar** Even before the First World War, 'dud' could mean something counterfeit or useless, as in 'a "dud" car' (*Westminster Gazette*, 1908). During the war, the word was applied to shells that had not exploded; the earliest examples cited in the *OED* date to 1915.

90.17   **great outcry** Despite some reservations – *The Times*, for instance, found the 'inflated' style 'monotonously irritating' (28 February 1896, p. 13) – the novel had a much greater critical success on its appearance in England than it had had in the United States, where, however, it found popular appeal, going through several printings in its first two years.

91.4–5   Wyndham ... man of letters The specific reference is to Wyndham's 'A Remarkable Book' published in the *New Review* in January 1896 (pp. 30–40) and reprinted as 'An Appreciation', the preface to Stephen Crane's *Pictures of War* (1898), a collection containing *The Red Badge of Courage* and six other stories.

A man of wide interests and experience, George Wyndham (1863–1913), a veteran of the Coldstream Guards, had fought in the Sudan, served as Chief Secretary to the Lord Lieutenant of Ireland and in the War Office, and was a Conservative Member of Parliament. Well versed in French literature (he produced an anthology of Ronsard and La Pléiade), he wrote on many topics for the *New Review* and *National Observer* and moved in literary circles as a good friend of his cousin, the poet Wilfrid Scawen Blunt.

91.7–8   comparisons ... *Mémoires ... Cavalry Officer* Cf. the following quotation:

Marbot's *Memoirs* and, in a lesser degree, Tomkinson's *Diary of a Cavalry Officer*, are both admirable as personal accounts of the Peninsular Campaign, but the warfare they describe is almost as obsolete as that of the Roses, and, even if it were not so, they scarcely attempt the recreation of intense moments by the revelation of their imprint on the minds that endured them. And, on the score of art and of reticence, one is glad that they do not. Their authors were gallant soldiers waging war in fact, and not artists reproducing it in fiction. They satisfy the special curiosity of men interested in strategy and tactics, not the universal curiosity of Man the potential Combatant. He is fascinated by the picturesque and emotional aspects of battle, and the experts tell him little of either. To gratify that curiosity you must turn from the Soldier to the Artist, who is trained both to see and tell, or inspired, even without seeing, to divine what things have been and must be. ('An Appreciation', *Pictures of War* (1898) by Stephen Crane, p. xi)

The diaries and memoirs of Jean-Baptiste-Antoine-Marcelin, baron de Marbot (1782–1854), chronicle the fortunes of Napoleon's Grande Armée. *The Diary of a Cavalry Officer in the Peninsular War and the Waterloo Campaign, 1809–1815* by Lt-Col. William Tomkinson (1790–1872), edited by his son James Tomkinson, was published in 1895.

91.16   "Mr Crane ... masterpiece." Cf. ' ... old themes re-handled anew in the light of novel experience, are the stuff out of which masterpieces are made, and in *The Red Badge of Courage* Mr. Crane has surely contrived a masterpiece'.

91.25   Young Soldier Conrad thought – a once common critical error – that the main figure was 'nameless' (see 'Stephen Crane: A Note without Dates', *Notes on Life and Letters* (2004), p. 43.13), whereas his name is Henry Fleming.

91.37–38   blue demonstration Cf. 'He had grown to regard himself merely as a part of a vast blue demonstration': Heinemann edition, pp. 9–10. The uniforms of the Union side in the American Civil War (1861–5) were blue.

92.25–26   Greek-like struggle Cf. 'From his home his youthful eyes had looked upon the war in his own country with distrust. It must be some sort of a play affair. He had long despaired of witnessing a Greek-like struggle. Such would be no more, he had said. Men were better, or more timid. Secular and religious education had effaced the throat-grappling instinct, or else firm finance held in check the passions': Heinemann edition, p. 5.

92.32–33   **grey bewhiskered hordes** Cf. 'Various veterans had told him tales. Some talked of grey, bewhiskered hordes who were advancing with relentless curses, and chewing tobacco with unspeakable valour – tremendous bodies of fierce soldiery who were sweeping along like the Huns': Heinemann edition, p. 10. ('Grey' functions ambiguously here, referring both to experienced and aged enemy soldiers and to the colour symbolic of the Confederacy, as blue was of the Union.)

92.39   **little panic-fear** Cf. 'A little panic-fear grew in his mind... He contemplated the lurking menaces of the future, and failed in an effort to see himself standing stoutly in the midst of them... He sprang from the bunk and began to pace nervously to and fro. "Good Lord, what's th' matter with me?" he said aloud': Heinemann edition, pp. 11–12.

93.15–16   **Picton of Peninsular fame** Lt-General Sir Thomas Picton (1758–1815) fought with distinction under Wellington in the Peninsular War (1808–14), being knighted and promoted to lieutenant-general in 1813. Parliament commended Picton seven times for his valorous exploits. Wounded at the Battle of Quatre-Bras on 16 June 1815, he was killed two days later at Waterloo.

93.21–23   **severe critic ... chief impressionist ... age** Cf. 'He is the chief impressionist of this age, as Sterne was the great impressionist, in a different manner, of his age': Edward Garnett, 'Mr. Stephen Crane: An Appreciation', *Academy*, 17 December 1898, pp. 483–4, a review of *The Open Boat* (see 77.39n.). When the subject of a biography of Crane was under discussion, Garnett wrote to Conrad as follows – 'I have tried to rub into those blasted Americans that Crane was a master': Garnett to Conrad, 19 March 1923 (*Portrait in Letters*, p. 207).

93.22   **Sterne** An eccentric Anglican clergyman, Laurence Sterne (1713–68) is best known for his association-of-ideas novels *The Life and Opinions of Tristram Shandy, Gentleman* (1759–67) and *A Sentimental Journey* (1768), the latter possibly influential on the structure and method of Conrad's *A Personal Record* (see 'Introduction', *A Personal Record* (2008), pp. xxxvi–xxxviii).

93.25   **La Débâcle ... War and Peace** *La Débâcle* (1892), by the French Naturalist Émile Zola (1840–1902), focusses on the Franco-Prussian War and is noted for its use of detail, unity of purpose and depiction of the horrors of war. Its central section spans the French defeat at Sedan, which ended the reign of Emperor Napoleon III. An epic novel about Napoleon's 1812 invasion of Russia and depicting individual men as pawns in the relentless movements of history, *War and Peace*, by Leo Tolstoy (1828–1910), was first serialized in 1865–9, and published in book form in 1869.

93.25   **mentioned by critics** Conrad has George Wyndham specifically in mind again:

Mr. Crane has composed his palette with these colours, and has painted a picture that challenges comparison with the most vivid scenes of Tolstoï's *La Guerre et la Paix* or of Zola's *La Débâcle*. This is unstinted praise, but I feel bound to give it after reading the book twice and comparing it with Zola's Sédan and Tolstoï's account of Rostow's squadron for the first time under fire. Indeed, I think that Mr. Crane's picture of war is more complete than Tolstoï's, more true than Zola's. (Crane, 'An Appreciation', pp. xiii–xiv)

94.18–19   **"those ceremonies … meeting"** Cf. 'The youth had watched, spell-bound, this ceremony at the place of meeting': *The Red Badge of Courage*, ch. 9.

JOHN GALSWORTHY
AN APPRECIATION

95.4–8   **When … book** Cf. the following from *The Man of Property* (1906):

Some of the Forsytes – Aunt Hester, for instance, who had always been musical – could not help regretting that Francie's music was not "classical"; the same with her poems. But then, as Aunt Hester said, they didn't see any poetry nowadays, all the poems were "little light things." There was nobody who could write a poem like "Paradise Lost," or "Childe Harold"; either of which made you feel that you really had read something ('Afternoon at Timothy's', Part II, ch. 7)

95.9   **Galsworthy's latest volume** *The Man of Property*, published in March 1906 by Heinemann, was the sixth volume of fiction by John Galsworthy (1867–1933) and the first volume of what would evolve into *The Forsyte Saga*. Galsworthy met Conrad on the *Torrens* on returning from Australia in 1893, and the two became life-long friends. In addition to novels and short stories, Galsworthy wrote volumes of critical essays and more than twenty dramas. A humanitarian of international stature, he won the Nobel Prize for Literature in 1932.

96.7–8   **(on goose's wings)** An allusion to the collection of nursery tales and rhymes known as *Mother Goose*, whose first literary appearance was in the poem 'La Mère Oye' in *La Muze historique* (1650). The figure was elaborated and made famous by Charles Perrault in his collection, *Histoires, ou Contes du temps passé* (1697), first published in an English translation by Robert Samber as *Histories, or Tales of Past Time*, in 1729.

96.18   **hewers of wood … water** A commonplace derived from the Bible – 'And the princes said unto them, Let them live; but let them be hewers of wood and drawers of water unto all the congregation; as the princes had promised them': Joshua ix.21.

96.34   **the sub-title** Galsworthy had contemplated supplying a subtitle, mooting as possible ones 'National Ethics I', 'Christian Ethics I' and 'Tales of a Christian People I' (Galsworthy to Edward Garnett, Tuesday [13? June 1905], responding to Garnett of 7 June 1905: H. V. Marrot, *The Life and Letters of John Galsworthy* (1935), p. 174). He did not in the end provide one, and the title-page features the following epigraph only – 'You will answer / "The slaves are ours"': Shakespeare, *The Merchant of Venice*, IV.i.97–8.

96.36–37   **not exactly of to-day** The novel opens in June 1886 and closes on a May day in the early 1890s.

97.6–7   **occasion … engagement** The allusion is to events in the novel's first chapter, '"At Home" at Old Jolyon's'.

98.4   **man and a woman … no Forsytes** Philip Bosinney, an artist and architect, engaged in a misalliance with June Forsyte, falls in love with Irene Heron, the wife of Soames Forsyte, involved in a loveless marriage. Their plans to run away together end in catastrophe and his death.

98.29 **hopeless portals** The reference to Part III, ch. 9 of *The Man of Property* may possibly allude to the motto written above the gates of hell in the *Inferno*, the first part of Dante's *The Divine Comedy* (1307–21): 'Abandon all hope, ye who enter here'. Conrad alludes specifically to it at the close of his short story 'To-morrow', *Typhoon and Other Stories*.

99.23–24 **mirror up to … nature** The phrase, a commonplace, is at least as old as Shakespeare – 'The purpose of playing … was and is to hold as 'twere the mirror up to nature': *Hamlet*, III.ii.17–19. The reference is to the Renaissance debate as to whether Art should be essentially imitative, reflecting life by presenting a kind of hyper-realism, or should indulge in fancy and fantasy, freed from realistic canons.

99.29 **this paper** The *Outlook*, a liberal weekly established in 1898. Conrad's review appeared in March 1906.

99.34–35 **reconciliation … son** Old Jolyon Forsyte and his son Jo become estranged when the latter divorces his wife in favour of a governess who bears his child. They are later reconciled.

99.36 **marital relations** Soames Forsyte unites with Irene in a loveless marriage, on the condition that Irene could leave if she were unhappy. The 'poignant comedy' leads to adultery, rape-within-marriage and death.

100.5 **Bosinney's tragedy** Distraught by the news that Soames Forsyte enforces the property rights of marriage on his estranged wife Irene, with whom Bosinney is in love, the latter is killed by a vehicle in a London street, with the possibility of his suicide mooted.

A GLANCE AT TWO BOOKS

101.15–16 **"This is genius!" ¶ Thackeray** This anecdote about the novelist and satirist William Makepeace Thackeray (1811–63) originates in an obituary appreciation, as follows – 'When we congratulated him, many years ago, on the touch in *Vanity Fair* in which Becky "*admires*" her husband when he is giving Lord Steyne the chastisement which ruins *her* for life, "Well," he said,—"when I wrote the sentence, I slapped my fist on the table, and said '*that* is a touch of genius!'"': James Hannay, *Edinburgh Evening Courant*, 5 January 1864, p. 3 (rpt as *A Brief Memoir of the late Mr Thackeray* (1864), pp. 20–21). A friend of Thackeray, Hannay (1827–73), a novelist and journalist, edited the *Edinburgh Evening Courant* from 1860 to 1864. This story has circulated in various forms; cf., for instance, 'When Thackeray struck his fist on the table as the story goes when he had finished the scene of Colonel Newcome's death, and, exclaimed, "By God, this is genius!"': Richard Le Gallienne, *Attitudes and Avowals with Some Retrospective Reviews* (1910), p. 163.

101.25–26 **denunciations … conventionalised society** The eighteenth-century English satirical novel culminated in Thackeray and Charles Dickens (1812–70). In this grouping, amongst others, are *Joseph Andrews* and *Tom Jones* by Henry Fielding (1707–54), *The Expedition of Humphry Clinker* by Tobias Smollett (1721–71), *The Life and Opinions of Tristram Shandy, Gentleman* by Laurence Sterne (93.22 *n.*) and, of course, the works of Jane Austen (1775–1817).

101.32–34   **Mr Osborne ... Captain Osborne ... Mr Pecksniff** In Thackeray's *Vanity Fair* (1848), Mr Osborne is a prosperous merchant in the City, without feeling but with social ambitions and a ruthless attachment to materialism; his favourite child, Captain George Osborne, a conceited profligate, is used as a vehicle for attaining his aims. Mr Pecksniff is a hypocrite who professes benevolence in Charles Dickens's novel *Martin Chuzzlewit* (serialized 1843–5; book form 1845).

102.1–2   **the brothers Cheeryble** In Charles Dickens's *Nicholas Nickleby* (serialized 1838–9; book form 1839), the kind-hearted and philanthropic twin brothers, Charles and Edwin ('Ned') Cheeryble are businessmen (based on real-life Scots named Grant) who befriend the title-character.

102.12   **Amelia Osborne** Amelia Sedley, who marries George Osborne (101.32–34n.), is the foil to Becky Sharp, the symbolically named 'heroine' of this 'novel without a hero', as its subtitle reads. Pale and passive, Amelia is devoted to her husband and son. Thackeray's list of characters for *Vanity Fair* describes her as 'an accomplished young lady, yet with more heart than brains'.

102.13   **Turgenieff ... Lisa** In *A House of Gentlefolk* (1859) by the Russian novelist Ivan Sergeyevich Turgenev (1818–83), 'Lisa' (Elisaveta Mihalovna Kalitina), considered by many to be Turgenev's greatest heroine, becomes the love interest of Lavretsky, unhappily married to her sister. The novel, although short, offers a portrait of Russian society, and became a favourite of early twentieth-century English readers. Conrad fervently admired Turgenev, and, although he is not known to have had much Russian, enthusiastically praised the translations of Turgenev and other Russian writers by Constance Garnett (1861–1946), the wife of his friend and early mentor Edward Garnett. Constance Garnett's translation of *A House of Gentlefolk*, with an introduction by Sergei Stepniak, appeared in 1895. For Conrad's views on the novelist, see 'Turgenev' (1917), *Notes on Life and Letters* (2004), pp. 40–42.

102.18–19   **her stupid mother ... Varvara** Marya Dmitrievna Kalitina, a widow of a provincial public prosecutor and man of business, who lives with her two daughters, the dutiful and serious 'Lisa' and the coquettish Varvara. The latter, Varvara Pavlovna Kalitina, a popular society hostess in Paris and the wife of Feodor Ivanitch Lavretsky, is unfaithful to her husband, deserted by him and later misreported as dead. Needing money and support, she suddenly returns to their loveless marriage, whilst Lavretsky has engaged his heart elsewhere, with 'Lisa' Kalitina.

102.24   **intelligent attention** The *Saturday Review* commented that Galsworthy was more satirist than iconoclast, with a sense of comedy that makes *The Island Pharisees* completely readable, but that perhaps he took his 'philosophy too seriously' (5 March 1904, p. 305); the *Athenæum* called it a subtle, sincere and occasionally humorous satire in light narrative form (26 March 1904, p. 394); the *Nation* (New York), however, dismissed it as a diatribe against morality characterized by 'cheap cynicism, labored epigram ... unconvincing psychology' and destructive criticism (23 June 1904, pp. 499–501); and the *Spectator* complained that Shelton's major fault is his lack of a sense of humour (16 April 1904, p. 608).

102.26   ***The Island Pharisees*** Conrad read the manuscript of *The Island Pharisees*, then titled *The Flying Goddess*, by 2 January 1903, a full year before its publication (*Letters*, III, 4–5). He later assisted his friend Galsworthy (18.20n.) in finding a publisher in Heinemann, which published the first edition on 28 January 1904. The firm remained Galsworthy's publisher throughout his career.

102.28 *Green Mansions ...* **Hudson** *Green Mansions: A Romance of the Tropical Forest* by the Argentine-born naturalist and ornithologist W(illiam) H(enry) Hudson (1841–1922) was published by Duckworth in 1904. The exotic novel focusses on a traveller to the Guyana jungle of south-eastern Venezuela, where he meets the forest-woman Rima. Hudson's descriptions of the 'green mansions' (the forests of South America) particularly intrigued Conrad, then writing *Nostromo*, set in the imaginary South American country of Costaguana. The two writers were personally acquainted, with Edward Garnett and R. B. Cunninghame Graham providing links. Twelve years after its publication in America, John Galsworthy persuaded Alfred A. Knopf to publish it with an introduction by himself.

102.36 **Shelton** As Galsworthy wrote in his preface to the revised 1908 edition of *The Island Pharisees*, the naïve Richard Shelton's journey through life, after he abandoned a career at the Bar, is away from his father's view of 'whatever is, is right' towards the contrary one of 'whatever is, is wrong'. The young Shelton evolves into a 'Pharisee', who recognizes that all institutions are 'half-truths', operating perhaps thirty years behind where life ought to have evolved. Galsworthy's formula is that perhaps 90 per cent of England's 'island Pharisees' remain in, or return to, the stability of the status quo, in contrast to the 10 per cent who, like Shelton, challenge it, with varying degrees of intensity and success. In September 1908, Conrad wrote to Galsworthy as follows:

Beware of *Sheltonism*. You understand me? I love Shelton with an exceeding love – but beware of him – I mean of that side of him which is purely and exclusively Sheltonian. No – don't abandon Shelton; he's your creation, your embodied conscience you[r] wistful spirit going about on the earth. Hold him. Stick to him – but don't let him write your novels. And if that would be like excising some part of your being – well you will suffer no doubt – but You can't pay too high a price for the greatness of inspiration for that voice which is in you. (*Letters*, IV, 121)

103.7 **Pharisaic** Heinemann publishers were concerned about the negative impact of calling the English 'Pharisees' (after the biblical hypocrites), and questioned the title. Conrad suggested to Galsworthy that if the publishers objected to the word, Galsworthy might substitute 'Phylacteries', or else the publishers should come up with an appropriate title (*Letters*, III, 84). Galsworthy's original title was *A Pagan*.

103.12 **Louis Ferrand** An outcast and vagabond 'educated by the Jesuits', Ferrand cries out against society's inequities and injustices while refusing to continue in gainful employment, despite Shelton's assistance. He eventually departs, leaving Shelton and Antonia aware of his basic dishonesty.

103.17 **tilting ... at windmills** An allusion to Miguel de Cervantes's *Don Quixote* (1605 and 1615) in which the title-character, of romantic temperament and at odds with the world's vision, madly mistakes windmills for giants in his quest for heroic adventure and knightly virtue.

103.19 **couch his lance** That is, to lower a lance into position for an attack; cf. 'A braver soldier never couched lance': Shakespeare, *1 Henry VI*, III.ii.134.

103.28 **Amadis de Gaul** The first published version of *Amadís de Gaula,* the chivalric thirteenth- or fourteenth-century prose romance that probably originated in Spain or Portugal, is that by Garci de Rodríguez de Montalvo dating from 1508.

The three-volume text apparently relied upon an earlier manuscript, fragments recently being found dating to about 1420. The work remained in vogue until mocked and superseded by Cervantes's *Don Quixote* (103.17*n*.).

103.35 **charming and limited Antonia** Shelton's betrothed, Antonia Dennant, accepts her parents' status quo existence and cannot understand her fiancé's increasing disenchantment with society. As Shelton is increasingly drawn to Louis Ferrand's view of life, Antonia becomes lukewarm about the prospect of marrying Shelton, and the possibility of her doing so ends after Ferrand leaves, Shelton laughing contemptuously at Antonia's comment: 'I thought at first we could do him [Ferrand] good.' The novel concludes with Shelton's sending Antonia a note, breaking off their engagement after realizing that she is 'ready without love to marry him, as a sacrifice to her ideal of what she ought to be!'

103.39 **best ... worlds** A phrase attributed to the German philosopher Gottfried Leibniz in his *Essais de Théodicée sur la bonté de Dieu, la liberté de l'homme et l'origine du mal* (1710). Leibniz's theodicy explores the origin of evil. 'The best of all possible worlds' ('le meilleur des mondes possibles') became the object of both philosophical certainty and satirical comment during the eighteenth century, most poignantly, perhaps, in the rejection of Leibniz's theodicy in Voltaire's philosophical romance *Candide, ou l'Optimisme* (1759), wherein the world consistently fails to live up to Dr Pangloss's expectations. Conrad sent a translation of Voltaire's book as a gift to his son Borys in May 1922 (*Letters*, IX, 241–2).

103.40 **shields ... tents** A reference to knights-errant issuing or accepting challenges in encampments wherever chivalry, at least in theory, was practised.

104.6 **beginning of Mr Galsworthy** *The Island Pharisees* was the first novel published under Galsworthy's own name, his previous books being published under the *nom de plume* 'John Sinjohn'. The first edition's title-page acknowledges Galsworthy's previous titles (*Man of Devon* and *Villa Rubein*) as published under a pseudonym.

104.27–31 **"Now ... eye."** This extract from ch. 5 (p. 62) introduces the novel's central scene, in which its protagonist, Abel, finally meets the bird-like Rima, who has drawn him into the forest. The spider, 'beautiful to the eye', attracts prey with its beauty, as Rima's bird-song draws him, and leads to his being bitten by a snake in an obvious allusion to the serpent in the Garden of Eden. In the original, the final sentence Conrad quotes continues, his text ending with 'eye' but Hudson's continuing thus: 'eye; and presently I discovered that this was no web-spinning, sedentary spider, but a wandering hunter, that captured its prey like a cat, by stealing on it concealed and making a rush or spring at last'.

PREFACE TO *THE SHORTER TALES OF JOSEPH CONRAD*

106.6–7 **hesitation on my part** S. A. Everitt of Doubleday, Page & Company had initially suggested that Conrad's friend the artist and engraver Muirhead Bone (1876–1953; knighted 1937) be invited to write the preface to this volume. Conrad resolved to write it himself in order to justify the principles of selection and, by adding a preface, to boost sales to collectors. (For more detail, see 'The Texts' pp. 249–50.)

106.12 the American public Not published in England, *The Shorter Tales* was designed to capitalize on Conrad's established reputation and wide popularity in America, partly the result of a concerted publicity campaign mounted by his publishers, Doubleday, Page & Company, and augmented by press coverage of his recent trip to New York and New England during May–June 1923.

106.22–23 philosophers ... "vain appearances" A commonplace, the idea that human life is transitory and meaningless has been expressed since Antiquity. Verses in the short story 'The Philosopher's Stone' (1859) by the Danish writer Hans Christian Andersen sum up a mid-nineteenth-century view: 'In the pretty turmoil here below, / All is a vain and paltry show.' The great nineteenth-century exponent of radically pessimistic attitudes towards human life was the German philosopher Arthur Schopenhauer (1788–1860), whose work Conrad appreciated. For a discussion of his influence on Conrad's outlook and writing, see Owen Knowles and Gene M. Moore, *Oxford Reader's Companion to Joseph Conrad* (2000), pp. 326, 328.

106.30–31 revelatory prefaces Conrad was commissioned to write 'Author's Notes' to preface the volumes of his collected editions (107.11–12*n*.) published during 1920–21. These, as well as occasional prefaces written before the specific commission for the collected edition, were brought together as *Notes on My Books* (1921).

106.33 here I am again By the time of writing, this phrase – used in both the first person plural and singular – had had a multiple life. Starting as the entrance catch-phrase of the great pantomime clown Joseph Grimaldi (1778–1837) (whose *Memoirs* Dickens edited), it was kept going in the music-halls by Dan Leno (né George Wild Galvin, 1860–1904) and revived during the war as the title of a song (1914) by Charles Knight and Kenneth Lyle, written for the comedian Mark Sheridan (né Fred Shaw, 1864–1918) and taken up by the troops. Conrad's context for its use is just right: the memory of danger, a hint of absurdity and the triumph of survival.

107.11–12 first collected edition The Heinemann and Doubleday collected editions were expensive sets got up for the collector's market, Heinemann's being numbered, signed and genuinely limited, with type distributed after setting, and Doubleday's designated the 'Sun-Dial' edition, first published in fine bindings and on quality paper. In 1923, Doubleday, Page & Company of New York issued its 'Concord' edition, featuring carefully selected frontispieces and a distinctive binding and rather fancier than its posthumous successors on cheaper paper (the 'Canterbury' edition, for instance, which uses the plates of the 'Sun-Dial' edition). In 1923, J. M. Dent & Sons of London issued its 'Uniform Edition', a collected edition priced and formatted in terms of the quality of its paper and bindings for the popular market. Hence, Conrad's adjective 'first' with respect to the Heinemann and Doubleday collected editions; originally to have been closely interdependent in production and to have been textually identical, these turned out, in fact, to be distinct.

107.12–13 my short-story volumes Conrad saw into print six collections of short stories: *Tales of Unrest*; *Youth, A Narrative, and Two Other Stories*; *Typhoon and Other Stories*; *A Set of Six*; *'Twixt Land and Sea: Tales*; and *Within the Tides*. Yet another collection, *Tales of Hearsay*, was posthumously published. (See 'Chronology' for years of publication.)

107.17   ***Tales of Unrest*** Published by Scribner's of New York in March 1898 and by T. Fisher Unwin of London in April 1898, the volume brought together five stories. Those set in the Malay world were 'Karain: A Memory' and 'The Lagoon'. 'The Idiots' was set in Brittany, 'An Outpost of Progress' in Africa and 'The Return' (not previously published) in London.

107.25   **one story** 'The Brute', a sea-tale, from the collection *A Set of Six* (1908).

107.29–30   **South America ... Italy** The settings of the stories are as follows – South America: 'The Anarchist' and 'Gaspar Ruiz'; England: 'The Informer'; Russia and France: 'The Duel'; Italy: 'Il Conde'.

107.35–36   **one of the reviewers** Alan Noble Monkhouse (1858–1936), who in his review of *Within the Tides* (1915) in the *Manchester Guardian* (4 March 1915, p. 5) wrote: 'Perhaps in this latest book the whole is greater than the parts.' Conrad also comments on this review in his 'Author's Note' to *Within the Tides*. A playwright, essayist and novelist, Monkhouse, long attached to the *Manchester Guardian*, was a sympathetic reviewer of Conrad's fiction, appraising, amongst other works, *The Secret Agent*, *Victory* and *Suspense*. (See also *Letters*, VIII, 303–05.)

108.28   **F. N. Doubleday** F(rank) N(elson) Doubleday (1862–1934). After working at Scribner's for nearly two decades, Doubleday established a partnership with S. S. McClure in 1897. It became the dominant American publishing firm of the early and mid twentieth century, and acquired a controlling interest in Heinemann in England as well in the early 1920s. Doubleday became friendly with several of his well-known authors, including Rudyard Kipling and J. M. Barrie. His friendship with Conrad was genuine, but Conrad found the American's business mentality sometimes irritating, and comments about Doubleday in his letters can be critical.

109.12   **writer of the sea** Early works such as 'Youth', *The Nigger of the 'Narcissus'*, *Typhoon* and *Lord Jim* led critics to classify Conrad as a spinner of sea-tales, a perception that lingered despite the later appearance of the political novels *Nostromo*, *The Secret Agent* and *Under Western Eyes*, not least because the publicity department of Conrad's American publishers, Doubleday, Page & Company, continued to encourage it.

109.18   **Calderón ... "Life is a Dream"** See 71.20–21 n.

110.2   **Eternal Shadow** Literally, encroaching death, the eternal presence, indebted to many biblical allusions. Cf. 'the valley of the shadow of death': Psalm xxiii.4.

110.5–6   **a thing ... patches** An echo of Gilbert and Sullivan's 'A Wandering Minstrel I – / A thing of threads and patches' from *The Mikado* (1885), Act I, which plays on 'A king of threads and patches': Shakespeare, *Hamlet*, III.4.102, itself a recollection of the fact that in the mystery plays Vice used to be dressed as a mimic king in a parti-coloured suit. See also 'Here is the thing of sheets and patches': Conrad to E. L. and Helen Sanderson, [mid or late April? 1921] (*Letters*, VII, 270).

110.8–9   **cast ... the waters** Cf. 'Cast thy bread upon the waters: for thou shalt find it after many days': Ecclesiastes xi.1.

111.9 **Part First** The stories in this section include 'Youth', 'The Secret Sharer', 'The Brute' and 'To-morrow'.

111.11 *esprit de corps* Literally, 'spirit of the body' (French), meaning a feeling of devotion to and pride in the group.

111.18 **Part Two** The stories in this section include 'Typhoon', 'Because of the Dollars', 'The Partner' and 'Falk'.

111.19–20 **Captain MacWhirr** The name is taken from Captain John McWhir (1858–95), of County Down, under whom Conrad served in 1887 in the *Highland Forest*, sailing from Amsterdam to Semarang, Java. An Ulsterman, he is recollected in *Lord Jim* as a 'Scotch captain' (ch. 2). His ancestors, however, would have come from Scotland to Ireland in the early seventeenth century during the Plantation of Ulster.

111.33 **said … in another preface** Cf. 'MacWhirr is not an acquaintance of a few hours, or a few weeks, or a few months. He is the product of twenty years of life. My own life': 'Author's Note' (1919), *Typhoon and Other Stories*, p. viii.

COOKERY
PREFACE TO JESSIE CONRAD'S *A HANDBOOK OF COOKERY FOR A SMALL HOUSE*

112.14–15 **the writer** Conrad's wife, Jessie (née George, 1873–1936), whom he had married on 24 March 1896. In addition to running the family kitchen, in time with the help of servants, she later wrote on cookery for several periodicals.

113.1 **A great authority** A specific source (if there was such) remains unlocated. Conrad may, however, have had in mind a passage such as this:

Notwithstanding the swiftness of their flight, one of the Indians had found an opportunity to strike a straggling fawn with an arrow, and had borne the more preferable fragments of the victim, patiently on his shoulders, to the stopping place. Without any aid from the science of cookery, he was immediately employed, in common with his fellows, in gorging himself with this digestible sustenance. (James Fenimore Cooper, *The Last of the Mohicans* (1826), ch. 11)

Conrad admired the American novelist, whose work he had read with enthusiasm in boyhood; he discusses Cooper in 'Tales of the Sea' (1898), *Notes on Life and Letters*.

The presumed relationship between diet and temperament was a general one; a popular nineteenth-century treatise by a physician takes up the question of the native American diet and 'savage' character as follows:

A man living solely on beef, as the Indians generally do, and full of freedom and fresh air, has blood very nearly approaching in chemical character to that of a lion, the fibrin and red globules being more abundant, in proportion to the *liquor sanguinis*, and the temper of his mind approximates to the indomitable savage. … Without exercise of a violent kind, this state of blood is apt to become intolerable, because it rouses the animal instincts to such an excessive degree, that reason becomes perplexed and confused by innumerable sensations, which she finds no means of subduing by demand on thought ... being disturbed, the animal is apt to prevail over the rational, and the man to behave like a brute. (George Moore, *The Use of the Body in Relation to the Mind* (1846), p. 366)

113.4   **Noble Red Man** A general reference to the concept of the 'noble savage' enunciated by the *philosophe* Jean Jacques Rousseau (1712–78), the phrase may also specifically echo the title of Mark Twain's essay 'The Noble Red Man' (1870), a biting satire on James Fenimore Cooper's idealized presentation of American native peoples in his series of novels known as the Leatherstocking Tales.

113.6–7   **Seven Nations ... Horse-tribes** The Seven Nations of Canada lived not in the area of the Great Lakes (the home territory of the Six Nations, mainly Iroquois), but in the St Lawrence and Richelieu river valleys. Primarily of Mohawk, Huron, Onondaga, Algonquian and Abenakis origin, their 'fires', or councils, consisted of seven settlements at Lorette, Wolinak, Odanak, Kahnawake, Kanesetake, Akwesasne and La Présentation in New France (now Québec). During the Seven Years War (1756–63), after the defeat of the French by the British at Quebec City in 1759, the Seven Nations negotiated the Treaty of Oswegatchie (August 1760), recognized by both the French and British. The equestrian and nomadic Plains Indians were primarily from the Sioux and Cheyenne nations.

113.18   **vendor of patent medicine** A possible source is George E. Ellis's *The Red Man and the White Man in North America from its Discovery to the Present Time* (1882), which makes the connection between white quacks and First Nations medicine. The book also gives a distinctly mixed review of native cuisines, emphasizing their unattractiveness to the European palate, although noting that New England's poor whites shared similar tastes.

THE FUTURE OF CONSTANTINOPLE

115.7   **Sultanate of Damascus ... Caliphate of Baghdad** Damascus (capital of present-day Syria) fell to the Ottoman Turks in 1516, their rule over the city extending for four centuries, while Baghdad (capital of present-day Iraq) became an integral part of the Ottoman Empire in 1638. It had been the capital of the Abbasid Caliphate from the mid eighth century, although its real influence had weakened within a century of its founding and its existence was nominal for some centuries, since the actual caliph was not resident after the mid thirteenth century. The caliph was the successor to Mohammed, the first being his brother-in-law Abu Bakr, appointed upon the Prophet's death in 632. The succession then passed, complexly, to other areas of the Islamic world.

115.8   **European chapter** The Treaty of Karlowitz (1699) was the first major treaty marking the beginning of the long decline of the Ottoman Empire's influence on the Balkan Peninsula, or, as some maps of the era labelled it, 'Turkey in Europe'.

115.9   **scramble for Constantinople** The prospect of the Turkish Army's defeat during the First Balkan War at Tchataldja (in greater Constantinople) in November 1912 occasioned this letter to *The Times*, the 'Imperial and Foreign Intelligence' section of which had for some while carried dispatches about the Ottoman Empire's anticipated defeat. Conrad's letter complements the newspaper's general coverage of the war on the day it appeared (7 November). For a detailed discussion of this topic, see Harold Ray Stevens, 'Conrad, Geopolitics, and "The Future of Constantinople"', *The Conradian*, 31, no. 2 (2006), 15–27.

Constantinople (present-day Istanbul) was originally the Greek port-city of Byzantium (115.14*n*.), on the Bosporus, re-named Constantinople, after the Emperor Constantine, in AD 330. It remained the residence of Roman and later Byzantine emperors until the Ottoman conquest of 1453. By 1890, the city's population was half Muslim, a quarter Greek and Armenian, an eighth Frank and an eighth Jewish, served by more than 300 mosques and a number of churches and synagogues. Conrad was in the city in May 1878, perhaps for as long as three weeks.

115.12 **Serbs and Bulgars ... historical claim** The Italo-Turkish War of 1911, fought over Tripoli, had led Serbia and Bulgaria to believe that they could defeat the Turks, and they consequently formed a secret alliance, with Russia as intermediary, agreeing to execute joint military action and divide the territory. The war began in October 1912, with Greece and Montenegro also joining in. The Balkan League of 1912–13 – Serbia, Bulgaria, Greece and Montenegro – was purportedly formed with Russian encouragement to limit Austrian power and influence in the Balkans. The historical claim referred to was an old one: Byzantium was built by Greeks from Megara in AD 667.

115.14 **Byzantium** An ancient city of Thrace, Byzantium was once the capital of the Byzantine Empire, important for its historic position as the guardian of the Bosporus Strait.

115.15 **most democratic of kingdoms** Greece had a monarchic form of government from the 1830s, its establishment following upon the defeat of the Ottoman Empire and the end of its hegemony over the country. Elected 'King of the Greeks', Otto I (1815–67; r. 1832–63), of Bavaria and a member of the House of Wittelsbach, was the modern nation's first monarch. Overthrown, he was succeeded by Prince William of the Danish Glücksburg dynasty as George I in 1863 (1845–1913; r. 1863–1913). From him, the Greek royal family was directly descended from the House of Schleswig-Holstein-Sonderburg-Glücksburg. (The Greek monarchy was abolished in 1973.)

115.19–20 **refuges of European civilization** The capital of the Empire of the East in Roman Antiquity, the city survived as a European centre until the Ottoman conquest of 1453. Even at the time of writing its European connections were sustained, the city being the seat of the Greek Patriarch of Constantinople, the head of the Greek Orthodox Church, and thus an outpost of Christian Europe in the Muslim East (although the centre of Orthodoxy shifted to Russia).

115.21 **the Powers** The term then current for the major European nation-states (Great Britain, France, Austria-Hungary and Germany).

115.26–27 **Burgomaster ... Patrician** A burgomaster (from the German *Burgomeister*) is a chief magistrate and usually chairman of an executive council at the sub-national administrative level, the equivalent of a town mayor. In explicitly rejecting this term for the new chief executive, Conrad hearkens back to the patrician class of Roman Constantinople, the city's noble ruling class.

115.29 **Slavonic influence** A specific reference to the members of the Balkan League (115.12*n*.), apart from Greece, Slavonic being an alternative term for the Slavic peoples occupying Central and Eastern Europe and speaking Slavonic languages, a sub-group of Indo-European, related to the Baltic group (notably, Bulgarian, Czech, Polish, Russian, Slovak, Serbian and Slovenian).

115.32   **Balkan Peninsula** The large land mass in south-eastern Europe bounded by the Black Sea, the Sea of Marmara and the Aegean, Mediterranean, Ionian and Adriatic Seas, including, at the time of writing, Greece, Bulgaria (including the annexed Eastern Roumelia), Bosnia, Herzegovina, Serbia and Montenegro.

116.5   **its geographical position** An allusion to the city's easy accessibility because of its proximity to the Mediterranean Sea.

116.7–8   **free Dardanelles … neutralized Bosporus** Important to settling the Balkan War was control of the Dardanelles, between Europe and Asia, providing Russia's access to the Mediterranean.

116.11   **you will allow** This commentary was not, in fact, published in *The Times*. For a discussion of its origins, see 'The Texts', pp. 257–8.

116.23–24   **"ideologue" … Napoleon I** Coined in 1796 by the French philosopher Antoine-Louis-Claude, comte Destutt de Tracy (1754–1836), the word *ideologue* originally signified 'a science of ideas', the study of ideas as entities derived from sense impressions and leading to the Revolutionary goal of a democratic, rational (that is, non-religious) and scientific society. Hostile to Revolutionary thought and jealous of his prerogatives, Napoleon Bonaparte detested this trend of thought as conducive to the subversion of morality, patriotism and civil authority, and heaped scorn upon 'ideologues' as irresponsible speculators.

116.29–30   **capital of a Bulgarian kingdom** Dispatches in *The Times* of 7 November mentioned that Bulgarian troops were rushing to claim Constantinople.

116.34   **Mussulman** Derived from Persian, this once usual term for Moslem or Muslim, already becoming rare in English at the time of writing, is now obsolete. (The spelling 'Musalman' also occurs; see *A Manual of Musalman Numismatics* (1904) by Oliver Codrington.) Conrad may also have been influenced by the French '*musulman*'. Cf. 'like that formula of Mohammedan faith the Mussulman father whispers into the ear of his new-born infant': *A Personal Record* (2008), p. 100.21–3.

117.4   **waned Crescent** The crescent moon is the symbol of Islam, the reference thus being to the Ottoman Empire's demise in Europe and with that the problem of what would happen to European Muslims, especially in relation to the Empire's historic claims. The crescent moon and star became a symbol for the religion with the rise of the Ottoman Empire in the fifteenth century.

117.7   **Balkan Children of the Cross** That is, in contrast to those of the Crescent, and thus the Orthodox Christian Serbs, Bulgarians and Roumanians (as they were then designated), but also possibly implying the Roman Catholic Croatians on the Balkan Peninsula in what was then part of Austria-Hungary.

117.16–17   **cut the crown** A reference to the probable political chaos that would ensue on dividing up Constantinople among the Powers of a victorious Balkan League.

117.26   **San Stefano** In spring 1878, Conrad, serving in the *Mavis*, himself witnessed the Russian Army stalled at the very gates of San Stefano (present-day

Yesilköy), a town of elegant summer houses about 15 miles (24 km) west of Constantinople, waiting to return to Russia, the Treaty of San Stefano having been signed on 3 March 1878, two months before his arrival in Constantinople (see 'Chronology').

118.14   *casus belli* Literally, 'occasion of war' (Latin), an event or political occurrence that brings about or is used to justify a declaration of war. The term came into wide usage in the seventeenth and eighteenth centuries with the rise of the political theory of the 'just war' (*jus ad bellum*).

118.36   **Caliph in Asia** From the sixteenth century until its abolition in 1924, the Caliphate of Constantinople was Islam's chief authority in Europe, Africa and Asia. From the mid thirteenth century on, the Sultan, the Supreme Caliph of Constantinople and the Defender of the Muslim faith, was invested with the sword of the Prophet, and other regalia, as the successor of Muhammad.

119.8   **Imperial City** A common epithet for Constantinople (as, for example, *La Serenissima* was for Venice), deriving from the city's position as the seat of the Roman Empire of the East and then of Byzantium.

THE CONGO NOTEBOOKS

THE CONGO DIARY

Some of the places, distances and times referred to in the notes below are drawn from an itinerary supplied to employees by the Société Anonyme Belge pour le Commerce du Haut-Congo titled 'Itinéraire de Matadi à Léopoldville', an inset on the 'Carte des routes de portage dans la région des chutes du Congo dressée par le lieutenant Louis chef de bureau à L'État du Congo' (1894?). The document is abbreviated 'Itinéraire'.

123.4   **Matadi** About 30 miles (48 km) upstream from Boma, Matadi was the administrative centre of the western Congo region at the mouth of the Congo, where Conrad had arrived from Europe in the *Ville de Maceio* the previous day, 12 June 1890. His base for the following fortnight, Matadi was at the time a hub for various Belgian enterprises in the Congo, including the Compagnie du Chemin de fer du Congo ('Congo Railway Company'), which was responsible for constructing the railway line that would eventually supersede the required overland passage from Matadi to Kinshasa at Stanley Pool (present-day Pool Malebo). The population included about 170 Europeans, mainly attached to trading companies established by English, Portuguese, Dutch and French businesses. For a detailed description of the river that Conrad paralleled, but seldom records in this notebook as having seen, see Henry M. Stanley's record of his down-river descent in 1877 from Stanley Pool to the Atlantic Ocean: *Through the Dark Continent* (1878), II, 309–467.

123.5   **Gosse** Formerly a sub-lieutenant in the Belgian Army, Joseph-Louis-Hubert Gosse (1860–91) was the manager of the Matadi trading post of the Société Anonyme Belge pour le Commerce du Haut-Congo. His reasons for detaining Conrad at the station for the period from 13 to 28 June are unknown, but he did have Conrad packing ivory, the 'idiotic employment' referred to in his entry for 24

June. Other reasons may have been the uncertainty about the fate of the *Florida*, the steamer he was to command, and Gosse's own lack of communication with the Central Station.

123.7   **Casement** Later a British government official, Roger Casement (1864–1916; knighted 1911) was at this time working for the Compagnie du Chemin de fer du Congo as a supervisor of railway construction. Conrad later recalled: 'For some three weeks he lived in the same room in the Matadi Station ... He knew the coast languages well. I went with him several times on short expeditions to hold "palavers" with neighbouring village-chiefs. The object of them was procuring porters for the Company's caravans from Matadi to Leopoldville' (24 May 1916, *Letters*, v, 596–7). In 1898, Casement became British Consul for the Congo Free State, and in 1903 prepared a widely publicized report on atrocities committed by Belgian colonists. After a distinguished diplomatic career, his involvement with the Irish National Volunteers and collusion with Germany during the First World War led to his arrest and execution for treason in 1916.

123.16–17   **Underwood ... Hatton & Cookson** The 'hearty and kind' Arthur J. Underwood headed the local branch of Hatton & Cookson, the only British commercial venture on the Congo river and one of the largest in the state. Their 'factory', a West African term for a trading centre, was a venue where 'natives can sell their produce for European goods, and of these latter cloth, rum, gin and gunpowder are mostly in demand' (FO 1896 10/667, National Archives). A long-serving administrator in Africa, Underwood, sometime British Vice-Consul and acting Vice-Consul in Boma in the late 1890s and later at Kinshasa, died during a trip to Europe in 1910. The Liverpool-based firm he worked for was founded in 1800 by James Hatton, a wholesale ironmonger and anchor-smith, the business being taken over in 1838 by his son Edward Hatton and son-in-law Thomas Worthington Cookson. Changing the firm's character, the two men established an extremely prosperous West African trading-house which, by 1854, owned some fifty sailing vessels that, apart from occasional voyages to America and India, were regularly engaged in trade with the Cameroons. The firm became part of the African and Eastern Trade Company in 1920.

123.21   **packing ivory** The last two pages of the notebook in which 'The Congo Diary' was composed include a list (dated 23 June 1890) of the number and weight of the pieces of ivory that Conrad packed. For a discussion of his involvement in this 'idiotic employment', see Ray Stevens, 'Conrad, Slavery, and the African Ivory Trade in the 1890s', *Approaches to Teaching 'Heart of Darkness' and 'The Secret Sharer'*, ed. Hunt Hawkins and Brian Schaffer (2002), pp. 22–30.

123.23   **Simpson** James L(iddon) Simpson (1844–99), who took over the Australian shipping firm of Henry Simpson & Sons of Adelaide, on his father's death in 1884. Conrad had captained one of its ships, the *Otago*, his only command, from January 1888 to March 1889.

123.23   **Gov. B** Possibly Tadeusz Bobrowski (1829–94), Conrad's maternal uncle and guardian, although why Conrad should qualify him as 'Gov.' is unclear.

123.23   **Purd** Identified by Richard Curle as 'Captain Purdy, an acquaintance of Conrad' (*Last Essays* (Dent, 1926), p. 239), this figure is possibly Robins Purdy (1844–1932), a master mariner originally from Great Yarmouth, but later London-based and returning to Norfolk in his retirement.

123.23   **Hope** Conrad's close friend George Fountaine Weare Hope (1854–1930) had been at sea, sailing in the *Duke of Sutherland* (not, however, at the same time as Conrad). A businessman in Stanford-le-Hope, Essex, he was the owner of the *Nellie*, which features prominently at the beginning of 'Heart of Darkness', a yawl on which he and Conrad made excursions on the Thames. For an account of Hope and certain aspects of the friendship, see G. F. W. Hope, 'Friend of Conrad', ed. Gene M. Moore, *Documents*, pp. 1–56.

123.23   **Froud** Captain A(lbert) G(eorge) Froud (1831–1901), secretary of the London Ship-Masters' Society, whose Fenchurch Street office Conrad frequented in the 1880s. A Somerset man by birth, he retired to Bristol. Conrad recalls him in *A Personal Record*, Froud having alerted him to a berth available in the *Adowa*.

123.24   **Mar** Marguerite Poradowska (née Marguerite-Blanche-Marie Gachet de la Fournière, 1848–1937), a Belgian-born novelist, was the widow of Conrad's distant cousin, Aleksandr Poradowski (1835–90). Well connected in Brussels, she had pulled strings to find Conrad employment in the Congo. Conrad and his 'aunt' shared an interest in serious music and in literature, and she translated 'An Outpost of Progress' for *Les Nouvelles Illustrées* (1903). For a discussion of the relationship and her family history, see Anne Arnold, 'Marguerite Poradowska, Conrad's Friend and Adviser', *The Conradian*, 34, no. 1 (2009), 68–83.

123.25   **speaking ill of each other** Cf. 'They beguiled the time by backbiting and intriguing against each other in a foolish kind of way. There was an air of plotting about that station ... It was as unreal as everything else': 'Heart of Darkness', *Youth*, (2010), p. 66.32–4.

123.27   **left Matadi** Cf. 'Next day I left that station at last! with a caravan of sixty men, for a two hundred mile tramp': 'Heart of Darkness', *Youth*, (2010), p. 61.17–18. Curle notes that 'On thirteen out of the nineteen travelling days taken by Conrad on this overland journey he kept a record of the distance covered, and it totals 197$^1/_2$ miles' (*Last Essays* (Dent, 1926), p. 240 n. 3).

123.27   **Harou** Prosper-Félix-Joseph Harou (1855–93), a 'sous-officier' (uncommissioned or minor officer) of the Société Anonyme Belge pour le Commerce du Haut-Congo, had arrived from Europe on the same ship as Conrad (*Mouvement Géographique*, 4 May 1890) and accompanied him on the overland journey from Matadi to Kinshasa. Harou's illness, often mentioned in the 'Diary', probably delayed Conrad's arrival at Stanley Pool. A Congo trader, Harou was the brother of Victor Harou, who collaborated with Stanley to establish Vivi, the first important post on the Congo river (*CWW*, p. 25).

123.30   **M'poso** The M'poso river, which would have been crossed by canoe, was approximately a one-and-a-half hour trek from Matadi.

123.30   **2 Danes** Not identified, the two Danes were probably among the large number of Scandinavians, mostly Swedes and Danes, who served as crew members in Congo river steamers (*CWW*, p. 39 n. 8). As a sea-faring nation, Denmark had a long history of involvement in Africa, active in the slave trade and the colonial power in the Gold Coast (later Ghana), which it sold to Britain in 1849.

124.1   **Palaballa** Listed in the 'Itinéraire' as 'Palaballa ou Kimpangala, vil [= village] Kimpunpu, Nlalu (marché journalier)', the village is situated in a range of hills bordering the Congo river.

124.2   **Nsoke-River** As recorded in the 'Itinéraire', the Nsoke was a two-hour trek from Palaballa.

124.2   **Mosquitos** Spelled in this form throughout the diary.

124.3   **Congo da Lemba** A trek of about six hours from Nsoke. Stanley's note about Congo da Lemba for 28 March 1887 is indicative of what Conrad might have witnessed three years later, as conditions deteriorated for the African population under the onslaught of European conquest:

We were in camp by noon of the 29th at Congo da Lemba, on the site of a place I knew some years ago as a flourishing village. The chief of it was then in his glory, an undisputed master of the district. Prosperity, however, spoiled him, and he began to exact tolls from the State caravans. The route being blocked by his insolence, the State sent a force of Bangalas, who captured and beheaded him. The village was burnt, and the people fled elsewhere. The village site is now covered with tall grass, and its guava, palm, and lemon-trees are choked with reeds. (*In Darkest Africa* (1890), I, 84)

124.8–9   **Lufu River** The Lufu river was spanned by a rope and bamboo bridge.

124.10   **market place** Probably in Mazamba, where Conrad presumably bought his '1st chicken'.

124.16   **andulating** Conrad's spelling reflects Polish pronunciation, the 'beginning "u" in "undulating" pronounced like the Polish "a"' (*CDP*, p. 16).

124.20   **Banza Manteka** Conrad's expedition on 2 July generally follows the time suggested in the 'Itinéraire', which estimates a 4½-hour trek. With a stop at the market to buy food, Conrad's journey was an hour longer.

124.21   **the missionary** Revd Charles E. Ingham (d. 1890s), of the Livingstone Inland Mission (American Baptist Mission Union) was one of the first missionaries to reach Stanley Pool, arriving in December 1881. He retired when the mission was transferred to the American Society, but returned to the Congo from 1887 to 1893, being killed near Lukunga by an elephant. He was at the Banza Manteka station when Conrad passed through. The author of *Congo Reading Book* (2 vols., 1890–91), he and his wife had translated hymns into Kikongo. For a history of Baptist missionary activity on the Congo, see Edmund F. Merriam, *The American Baptist Missionary Union and Its Missions* (1897), pp. 183–200.

124.29   **Backongo – Shot?** A Bantu-speaking people descended from the Congo people who gave the river its name, the Bakongo inhabit the area around Matadi. They were generally more given to agriculture (cultivating maize and manioc) and raising animals (goats, pigs, chickens) than their neighbours. Cf. Marlow's description of 'a middle-aged negro with a bullet-hole in the forehead': 'Heart of Darkness', *Youth* (2010), p. 62.3–4.

125.3   **Luinzono River** Perhaps the Unionzo river listed in the 'Itinéraire' as having both a ford and a 'pirogue' or dug-out canoe, to which Conrad refers; or he perhaps confused two rivers, the Unionzo and the nearby Luima river. Stanley, however, also refers to a Lunionzo river (*In Darkest Africa*, I, 85).

125.4   **Zanzibari** Belgian authorities relied on Zanzibaris for police and military duties, primarily because they were felt to demonstrate more discipline than other

Africans. Stanley comments on Zanzibaris in his 1887 expedition: 'the Zanzibaris carry 65 lbs. of ammunition, 9 pounds per rifle, four days' rations of rice, and their own kit, which may be from 4 to 10 lbs weight of cloth and bedding mats. After they have become acclimated this weight appears light to them ... ': *In Darkest Africa*, I, 84. In 'Heart of Darkness', Marlow speaks of 'an armed escort of lank Zanzibaris, very hospitable and festive', accompanied by sixty porters carrying 60-pound loads (*Youth* (2010), pp. 61.40–62.1).

125.10 **Palma Christi** The Latin name, meaning 'palm of Christ', for the castor oil plant.

125.13 **cal[a]bashes** Various species of gourd and pumpkin-like fruit.

125.13 **"malafu"** 'Palm wine' (Kikongo).

125.17 **ressembling** After the French *ressemblant*.

126.6 **Mpwe R.** According to the 'Itinéraire', this is the Mpete river, with a camping area, and an old and a new village. Conrad's trek of about four-and-a-half hours and 13 miles (21 km) is consistent with the estimated time in the 'Itinéraire'. The expected progress was for an early morning departure with a march of four to six hours, stopping before noon to assure proper accommodation for the night's camping, or, as Marlow comments: 'Camp, cook, sleep, strike camp, march': 'Heart of Darkness', *Youth* (2010), p. 61.32–33.

126.15–16 **shouts and drumming** Cf. 'Perhaps on some quiet night the tremor of far off drums, sinking, swelling, a tremor vast, faint; a sound weird, appealing, suggestive and wild': 'Heart of Darkness', *Youth* (2010), p. 61.36–38.

126.23 **hills ... ravines** Cf. 'a stamped in network of paths spreading over the empty land, through long grass, through burnt grass, through thickets, down and up chilly ravines, up and down stony hills ablaze with heat': 'Heart of Darkness', *Youth* (2010), p. 61.20–22.

127.1 **Nsona** More modern names for the village, which is at an altitude of 1,640 ft (499 m) along the Congo, are Sona-Bata, Nsona Bata and Nsona Mbata.

127.6 **Started at 5.40** Stanley provides an informative, if romanticized, comment on a day's trek, which for Conrad started at 5.40 a.m., and concluded at 11.00 a.m. 'There is nothing more agreeable than the feeling one possesses after a good journey briefly accomplished. We are assured of a good day's rest; the remainder of the day is our own to read, to eat, to sleep, and be luxuriously inactive, and to think calmly of the morrow.' Stanley then adds the rejoinder:

there can scarcely be anything more disagreeable than to know that, though the journey is but a short one, yet relaxation of severity [beatings of carriers, harassing laggards, etc., to prevent delays] permits that cruel dawdling on the road in the suffocating high grass, or scorched by a blistering sun ... water far when most needed ... the loads robbed and scattered about over ten miles of road; the carriers skulking among the reeds ... the officers in despair ... and hungry and vexed, and a near prospect of some such troubles to recur again to-morrow and the day after. (*In Darkest Africa*, I, 86–7)

127.24 **Inkandu** Nkandu is one of the four days of the Congo week, and the place-name here indicates the day on which a market operates. See 129.8–9*n*.

127.25 **Lukungu gov[ernmen]ᵗ station** Stanley comments (1887) that the Lukungu station was run by 'hospitable Belgians' who provided provisions for 800 members of his party (*In Darkest Africa*, I, 87). Conrad had no such luck. Lukungu had been the main half-way point for expeditions to Stanley Pool as late as 1888, where porters were often changed, because carriers recruited for the trip from Matadi often refused to continue up-river beyond Lukungu. Treks were further complicated by the looting of supplies and cargo (*CWW*, pp. 36–7).

127.26 **accidented** A Gallicism, from *accidenté* ('uneven' or 'hilly').

127.31 **manioc plantations** The 'stuff like half cooked cold dough' that Marlow sees the Bangala crew eating ('Heart of Darkness', *Youth* (2010), p. 85.24–25) is made from the tuberous roots of the manioc, or cassava, plant.

129.2 **Heyn & Jaeger** Lancashire-born Reginald Barwick Heyn (1860–1902) and the Paris-born Belgian Henri Jaeger (b. 1864) were employees of the Société Anonyme Belge pour le Commerce du Haut-Congo. Based at Manyanga, Heyn, the company's director of transport, was responsible for overseeing railway construction, hiring labour and organizing equipment. Jaeger's first posting with the company was as adjunct to Heyn at Manyanga; he later served as manager at the Equator and Upper Ubangi Stations.

129.4 **Stayed here till the 25** Conrad never fully explained the reason for this protracted stay at Manyanga, mid-point of the trek. For a discussion, see Najder, p. 153.

129.8–9 **Nkenghe ... Nsona** The Baptist missionary W(illiam) Holman Bentley (130.14–15 n.) provides the key to this list of the days of the marketing week: 'Markets in these parts are held once in every four days; the names of the days being *Nsona, Nkandu, Konzo, Nkenge*' (*Pioneering in the Congo* (1900) I, 358). He later elaborates: 'The Congo week consists of four days ... The markets are named after the day of the week and the town near which they are held' (I, 399). Here planning his itinerary to Stanley Pool for the next two weeks, Conrad converts the seven-day European week into the four-day Congo week in order to calculate when his journey would coincide with market-days.

130.5 **Mrs Comber** Annie Comber (née Smith), who had only recently arrived at the Sutili Baptist mission, would be dead before Conrad returned to Europe. She had come out from England in early 1890 and, at Matadi, married the Baptist missionary the Revd Percy E(benezer) Comber (1862–92), brother of the well-known missionary the Revd Thomas James Comber (1852–87). After repeated bouts of fever, she died at Banana on 19 December 1890 while waiting for a homeward-bound ship.

130.11 **Davis** The Revd Philip Davis, a Baptist missionary, had arrived in the Congo with Percy Comber (130.5 n.) in 1885. From October 1886 he was stationed at Wathen, where he died in December 1895.

130.14–15 **Rev. Bentley ... wife** The Suffolk-born Baptist missionary W(illiam) Holman Bentley (1855–1905) was the author of the two-volume *Pioneering in the Congo* (1900) and several other works on the cultures and languages of the Congo, as well as translations of the New Testament and some of the books of the Old Testament into Kikongo. He and his wife H(endrina) Margo Kloekers (1855–1938; m. 1885), who was actively engaged in his missionary work, had gone to Tungwa, near Makuta (Bentley, *Pioneering in the Congo*, II, 341). He died suddenly in Bristol after his return to Britain. His life is recounted by his wife in *W. Holman Bentley: The Life and Labours of a Congo Pioneer* (1907).

130.19 **Heche** According to G. Jean-Aubry, Conrad misnamed this individual, who is 'more probably Stache' (*Joseph Conrad in the Congo* (1926), p. 57). Antwerp-born Ernest-Albert-Louis-Adolphe Stache (1856–97), who had arrived in the Congo in March 1890, was a principal agent for the Société Anonyme Belge pour le Commerce du Haut-Congo, establishing some dozen factories for it on the banks of the Loulua river and engaged in exploration.

130.28 **much more trees** An ungrammatical phrase, influenced by the Polish *wiele wiecej drzew*.

131.8 **One wrecked** The ship Conrad had expected to command, the *Florida*, was wrecked on 18 July, but re-floated and returned to Kinshasa within five days (*CWW*, p. 41). Cf. 'One of them ... informed me with great volubility and many digressions ... that my steamer was at the bottom of the river': 'Heart of Darkness', *Youth* (2010), p. 62.35–38.

131.19 **shimbek** An African term for a temporary shelter, usually made of mud and wattle, occupied by people of the same employment (for example, railway builders).

131.31 **Ipeca** That is, ipecacuanha, a herbal antidote for dysentery.

132.1 **Row with carriers** Cf. 'Then he got fever and had to be carried in a hammock slung on a pole. As he weighed sixteen stone I had no end of rows with the carriers': 'Heart of Darkness', *Youth* (2010), p. 62.13–15.

132.13 **made a speech** Cf. 'one evening I made a speech in English, with gestures, not one of which was lost to the sixty pairs of eyes before me': 'Heart of Darkness', *Youth* (2010), p. 62.16–18.

133.13–15 **Mfumu Mbé ... Mfumu Koko** These were the lands of the tribal chief Makoko de Mbé, the King not only of Mbé and vicinity, including Kinshasa, but also of all the Tékés. The Kingdom of the Tékés (also called Anziku and Tyo) in the Stanley Pool area rivalled that of the Kongo (Bakongo) farther south-east.

133.22 **reached Nselemba** Conrad stopped recording his overland journey, which had occupied nineteen travelling days, on 1 August, when he reached Nselemba, about 15 miles (24 km) from Kinshasa on Stanley Pool. He travelled to Kinshasa on 2 August, and began both 'Up-river Book' and his voyage as supernumerary in the *Roi des Belges* the next day. Kinshasa was the base of the Upper Congo Flotilla, with a shipyard from which Stanley assisted in launching the hull of the *Florida* on 30 April 1887 (*In Darkest Africa*, I, 96). The hulls of the iron ships were made in Europe and were hauled in sections by porters along the overland route to Kinshasa. Once at Kinshasa, the sections were riveted together – thus the frustration in 'Heart of Darkness' about the absence of rivets.

135.9–18 **Naturalist ... Palmer** The full titles of these works are as follows:

C. M. Woodford, *A Naturalist among the Head-Hunters, being an account of Three Visits to the Solomon Islands in the years 1886, 1887, 1888* (1890)

Clements R. Markham, *John Davis: Arctic Explorer and Early India Navigator* (New York 1889 and London 1891)

James Grant, *The Newspaper Press: Its Origin, Progress and Present Position.* 3 vols. (1871–72)

Arthur V. Palmer, 'A Battle Described from the Ranks', *The Nineteenth Century*, March 1890, 397–407.

An explorer in the South Pacific and later Resident Commissioner of the British Solomon Islands, C(harles) M(orris) Woodford (1852–1927) was a member of several learned societies.

Clements R(obert) Markham (1830–1916; knighted 1871), geographer and explorer, wrote prolifically on topics related to exploration and was President of the Royal Geographical Society.

Of Scottish origin, James Grant (1802–79) was active in London as an editor, journalist and reporter. He wrote more than forty books on diverse topics, including theology, biography and travel.

Arthur V. Palmer served as sergeant in the 79th Highlanders and as a gunner in Royal Field Artillery during the Anglo-Egyptian War. He also wrote other articles for the *Nineteenth Century* (1890 and 1898) on military topics. The article that Conrad mentions discusses the 1882 battle of Tel-el-Kebir, fought between British and Egyptian armies about 68 miles (110 km) north-north-east of Cairo; other essays in that issue discuss the battle's context.

136.31–137.8   **Sam: ... nkenge** A list of the days of the week, sometimes abbreviated, in French, with their Kikongo counterparts.

137.11   **Eastman ... C°** This concern manufactured Kodak cameras and film and were suppliers of materials for developing photographs.

137.13   **Lukunga ... Hoste** See entry of 7 July 1890. Born in Hamilton, Ontario, the Revd T(heodore) H(amilton) Hoste (1863–1933), the son of Major-General Dixon Edward Hoste, studied at the Royal Naval College, Greenwich. He served as a missionary of the American Baptist Mission Union in the Congo from 1884 to 1896, returning to England because of ill-health. In 1888, he assisted Roger Casement in finding employment as a lay helper at the Union's mission at Wathen on the Upper Congo. Hoste, who translated parts of Genesis and Exodus and the first Epistle of St John into Kikongo, founded the Missionary Society of Lukunga in 1895.

137.16   **G. Stern** G. & G. Stern, at 62 Gray's Inn Road, were wholesale druggists.

137.17   **vepsalia salt** Probably Vestalia salt, after the Vestal Virgins who made ceremonial bread (*mola salsa* or holy cake), a cereal cake made of emmer wheat (sometimes called spelt) in June and two other times of the year, walking to a sacred spring to perform the ritual making. The salt used to make the cake was also prepared ritually, brine being pounded then baked in a jar until it formed a rock so hard that an iron saw had to be used to cut it.

138.1   **Up-river Book** This diary records observations made during Conrad's 28-day up-river passage on the river Congo, 3 August – 1 September 1890, in the *Roi des Belges* (138.6*n*.) from Kinshasa to Stanley Falls (present-day Boyoma Falls), its brevity setting a record (Miłobędzki, p. 9). Even though Conrad's expected ship the *Florida* was available, he was required to serve as a supernumerary in the ship to study the problems of navigation prior to assuming command.

Camille Delcommune (1859–92), deputy director of the Kinshasa Station of the Société Anonyme Belge pour le Commerce du Haut-Congo (hereafter SAB), reprimanded Conrad for his late arrival on 2 August. Although exhausted and ill from his overland trek from Matadi, Conrad had to depart the day after his arrival at Kinshasa, the *Roi des Belges* leaving hurriedly not only to assist in rescuing the steamer *Ville de Bruxelles*, which had struck a root near Upoto (Najder, p. 132), but also to rescue the dysentery-afflicted Georges-Antoine Klein, a French national recently appointed commercial agent at Stanley Falls. (He is considered by some to be one of the sources for Kurtz in 'Heart of Darkness'.) Klein died during the return leg, the ship having to stop at the village of Chumbiri (in French, Tchumbiri) to bury him (*CWW*, p. 378).

For a detailed description of the river, see George Grenfell, 'The Upper Congo as a Waterway', *Geographical Journal*, November 1902, 7–8; and for a study of general navigation conditions on it during the late nineteenth century, see Valérie Gelade, 'Les Débuts de la navigation à vapeur sur le Haut-Congo (1882–1898)', *Revue Belge d'Histoire Contemporaine / Belgisch Tijdschrift voor Nieuwe Geschiedenis*, 32, nos. 3–4 (2002), 383–418.

138.5   **3.Augst 1890** *Mouvement Géographique*, devoted to recording details of Belgian enterprises in the Congo, states on 21 December 1890 that the *Roi des Belges* left Kinshasa on 4 August (cited *CWW*, p. 50), a date Miłobędzki accepts (p. 25 n. 37). Two of the four dates in the notebook are 3 August (on its title-page) and 4 August. Because the date given in the *Mouvement Géographique* some four months later is retrospective, Conrad's date seems plausible.

138.6   **S. S. "Roi des Belges"** The SAB's stern-wheel, wood-burning steamer of 15 tonnes (metric tons) was commanded by a Dane, Ludvig Rasmus Koch (1865–1906). Built in Belgium in 1887, the ship, transported overland in sections and assembled in Kinshasa, was launched on 17 March 1888. Until the completion in 1898 of the railroad from Matadi to Kinshasa, river steamers were limited by the size of the sections of the hull that could be carried overland for assembly at Stanley Pool: thus the emphasis on the need for rivets to repair the steamer in 'Heart of Darkness' and Conrad's concerns about the condition of the *Florida*.

Employees of the SAB on board during Conrad's trip up-river were, in addition to Captain Koch, the manager Camille Delcommune, a mechanic named Goossens (not Gossens, according to Belgian records) and three company agents – Édouard-François-Léon Rollin (1866–1911), Georges van der Heyden and Alphonse Keyaerts (*CWW*, p. 56), the latter recalled in 'An Outpost of Progress'. The crew consisted of about twenty-five Africans, some 'cannibals', in fable if not in fact. On the return from Stanley Falls, Koch fell ill, with Conrad temporarily replacing him on 6 September, under conditions stated in Delcommune's letter of that date: 'Mr Conrad Korzeniowski, Captain. I have the honour to ask you to take over the command of the SS *Roi des Belges* as of today, until the recovery of Captain Koch' (Najder, p. 136).

Shallow-drafted rear-paddle-wheel steamers like the *Roi des Belges* and the *Florida* were necessary because of the Congo river's vagaries. Ranging in width from about 3–7 miles (4.8–11.2 km) upstream to a few hundred yards/metres in some of the cataracts of Livingstone Falls, the Congo had constantly shifting channels and sandbars, requiring daily soundings to locate channels deep enough to accommodate the steamers. Channel markings were non-existent, not only because channels throughout the Congo basin would shift frequently, but also because charting of the river was in its infancy. Traffic was possible only during daylight because no lights marked obstacles or river channels. In addition, constant attention had to be given to the locations of supplies of wood because of the need to replenish fuel at least every two or three days; the *Roi des Belges* had two canoes and two lighters in tow, the latter to haul wood.

Many points of identification and navigational records in this notebook refer to charts in the possession of Captain Koch, probably provided by the SAB. These charts, in turn, probably corresponded to the recently completed ten-panel map by George Grenfell (148.28*n*.), who worked closely with the Company. Conrad's progress can be followed by locating positions cited in the notebook on Grenfell's map (1884–9), beginning at the entrance to Livingstone Falls at Léopoldville, south of Kinshasa, and concluding 980 miles (1,568 km) up-river at Stanley Falls.

138.8   **On leaving – from A** The ship departed above the first of the thirty-two cataracts that constitute Livingstone Falls, entering Stanley Pool 3 miles (4.8 km) up-river where the 1.5-mile-wide (2.4 km) Congo river is bordered by cliffs ranging to 100 ft (30.48 m) high on the French Congo (north) side. The full force of the river rushes by Pointe de Kallina or Kallina Point (present-day Pointe de la Gombe) below Kinshasa, channelling its currents and counter-currents from Stanley Pool to Livingstone Falls.

Conrad does not mention Livingstone Falls in either 'The Congo Diary' or this notebook, but see 'Heart of Darkness': 'The rapids were near and an uninterrupted, uniform, headlong rushing noise filled the mournful stillness of the grove ... as though the tearing pace of the launched earth had suddenly become audible' (*Youth* (2010), p. 58.9–13). Passage through Stanley Pool was around rocks and detached reefs and between islands – the largest of which is the 70-square-mile (181.29 sq-km) marshy island of Bamu – and sandbanks ranging to several miles long. Stanley Pool is approximately 20 miles (32 km) long and 14 miles (22.4 km) wide. (See Map 3, adapted from Grenfell's charts of 1888–9.)

138.14–15   **East by the sun** Readings were taken by position of the sun in the absence of a compass. Conrad does, however, give evidence of compass readings, which would probably have been confirmed by the chart in Captain Koch's possession.

138.20–21   **H[igh] W[ater]** Grenfell records two such periods, May and November, with some locations also affected in June and December. At Stanley Falls, water may rise 8 ft (2.43 m); at Stanley Pool, the May high water can reach twice that. References later are to F. W. (full water), $\frac{1}{2}$ full water and the many soundings for depth (cited in terms of fathoms, most often as 'fth' and 'faths').

139.9   **1 $\frac{1}{2}$ foot (Capt Koch)** A reference to Captain Koch's map as well as instructions given by him en route. '1 $\frac{1}{2}$ foot' refers to the amount of water covering the sandbank, a highly dangerous condition for steamers, the larger of which drew a minimum of 3 ft (1 m) of water. A fathom (6 ft; 1.83 m) was considered minimal for safe passage.

139.19–20 **small island ... passage** The ship is leaving Stanley Pool, where a small island almost closes the channel into the 'bay' that leads from Stanley Pool to the river. Looking to 'port' (139.21) the 'high mountain' is probably Grenfell's 'One Tree Hill' that is several miles from Dover Cliffs, white cliffs approximately 100 ft (30.48 m) high near the north entrance named by Stanley during his first trip to Stanley Pool in 1877.

139.21 **bay 8** Such entries refer to positions near the upper end of Stanley Pool as depicted on the charts being used on the *Roi des Belges*.

139.32 **Entered.** Leaving Stanley Pool, the *Roi des Belges* entered the Congo at Ingu Point. Grenfell describes this entrance-point as follows:

Beyond the [Stanley] pool the channel for 125 miles is confined between steep-faced hills ... the distance ranges from 1 to 2 miles ... The hills rise to 800 feet above the river for some distance from the pool ... Irregular currents caused by rocks not charted in 1890 are hazardous. The Congo River has more than 4,000 islands and, with its estuaries, more than 20,000 miles [32,187 km] of overhanging wooded banks, with many trees falling annually into the river. These were dangerous for steamers drawing more than three feet [1 m] of water, especially in areas with many sand banks. ('The Upper Congo', *Geographical Journal*, pp. 9, 6–7)

140.2–6 **1st Reach ... 4th Reach** A reach is a section of a river between two bends. Beginning at Ingu Point on the French Congo (North) side of the river, the ship left Stanley Pool, passing the following locations to Sandstone Point, where the company spent its first night aboard: Lambert Rock, Reed Point, Shale Cliff, Big Tree Rock, Mpaai Point, Cedar Tree Point and Three Plantations. The many compass readings throughout the narrative indicate the Congo's winding turns.

140.11 **"2 sago-trees point"** A sago is a palm tree, whose starch is used for food, the point here being named for its most prominent feature – obviously, like others so cited, an informal or local name.

140.15–16 **bottom at 6 feet stones** A stony bottom covered by only a fathom of water is a hazard, shallow even for the *Ville de Bruxelles*, which drew 3 ft (1 m) of water, and which the *Roi des Belges* was steaming to rescue. 'Heart of Darkness' notes the potential danger as follows – 'The steamer was sunk ... in charge of some volunteer skipper, and before they had been out three hours they tore the bottom out of her on stones', and 'After all, for a seaman, to scrape the bottom of the thing that's supposed to float all the time under his care is the unpardonable sin. No one may know of it but you never forget the bump – eh?' *Youth* (2010), pp. 63.7–10, 78.9–10.

140.16 **Hauled out** That is, changed course.

140.21 **entrance – 5ʰ30** That is, the entrance to the Congo from the north point of Stanley Pool. The ship also travelled approximately 25 miles (40 km) across Stanley Pool, thus travelling about 50 miles (80 km) on the first day. Indicated is the time required to travel from point to point; this is as important to know as distance because of the need to find wooding-places (140.30n.) or other suitable stopping-points before nightfall.

140.30 **Wooding place** One of many stops along the route to replenish fuel; cf. 'Heart of Darkness': 'I had to keep a look-out for signs of dead wood we could cut up in the night for next day's steaming' (*Youth* (2010), p. 77.31–32). Stanley romanticizes such stops as follows: 'When darkness falls a great fire is lit ... [and] wood-choppers fall to and cut the logs into foot lengths for the boilers. The sound of smiting axes rings through the dark grove, to be re-echoed by the opposite forest ... It is varied by the woodman's chant': *The Congo and the Founding of Its Free State* (1885), II, 9.

140.33 **Covered at F[ull] W[ater]** Information provided by Captain Koch about the Congo at various times of the year, as part of Conrad's tutorial as supernumerary. Cf. also 'H[igh] W[ater]' (138.20–21 n.).

141.5–6 **entrance to Black River** Also called the Lufuna, a small river that flows into the Atlantic. A plantation was nearby. For a general contemporary (1883) account of this area from Stanley's perspective, see *The Congo and the Founding of Its Free State*, II, 1–74.

141.11 **point Licha** Also known as Lisa Point.

141.21–27 **Left. 6.15 ... 3 $\frac{1}{2}$ miles per $\underline{h}$** A notation of time-lapse required to navigate through Lisa Point. Compass bearings and the rate of travel, 3.5 miles (5.6 km) per hour, suggest a particularly tortuous section of the river.

142.9 **palms in the bight** A bight is a bend in the river. Grenfell identifies the 'many palms' here and in subsequent passages as 'Palm Plateau' and 'Palm Point'.

142.18–19 **long ... small island** Grenfell identifies the long island as Esika Malebo (Flamini Island). Many islands, some inhabited, impeded the progress of ships on this section of the river.

143.32–33 **12 hours steaming** Captain Koch instructs Conrad about the more rapid pace of a steamer running with the current. It took two days to reach this point travelling up-stream.

144.2 **Hills ... appearance** Bastion (or Red) Bluff, just south of Esika Malebo on the French Congo (left) side of the river.

144.5 **Point P at $5^h 50^m$ – moored** This concludes the second day, 4 August, of travel up-stream.

144.8 **Point P.$6^h 0^m$.** Presumably 5 August, the journey's third day. From this point dates are recorded inconsistently.

144.10 **Bankap bore** Technically, a bore is a large wave or billow, tidal flood or eagre – here the currents and turbulence of a stretch of water caused when the confluence of two rivers, the Kasai and the Congo, force the flow of the water into a narrower channel. (The spelling should be Bankab.) Reference is to currents, cross-currents and turbulence in the points, reaches and bights south of where the two rivers join – navigational challenges as the *Roi des Belges* passed 'Bankab Point'.

145.21 **rounding Bankab** The Kasai joins the Mbihé and Mfini rivers to form the Kwa river before it reaches the Congo. A government station, Kwamouth, was situated on the south bank and a Roman Catholic mission (146.23 n.) on the north bank. Names of rivers and villages vary, depending upon who cites them and when they are being cited; Stanley, for example, supplies Mbihé and Mfini (*The Congo and the Founding of Its Free State*, I, 410 n.).

145.25 **On coming down** The route downstream would differ at this bight from that taken upstream because of the current.

146.23 **the Cath[oli]^{c} mission** Berghe-Sainte-Marie, the mission of the Roman Catholic order of Scheut Fathers (the Congregation of the Immaculate Heart of Mary founded in Brussels in 1862), on the north bank. The Danish captain Johannes Freiesleben (1861?–90), whom Conrad expected to succeed on the *Florida*, was buried here.

147.16–17 **Stopped ... 7$^{\underline{h}}$ am.** Only four dates appear in the notebook, and this halt cannot be dated precisely. The third stop is mentioned (150.21), also without a date, and the next recorded overnight stop is given as 14 August (152.5), the trip's twelfth day. It can be assumed that other nights were spent at various wooding-places, given customary procedure: the African crew members went ashore to cut wood and to spend the night, while Europeans dined and spent the night aboard ship.

147.21–22 **cov[ere]^{d} at ... very full water** Another recording of Captain Koch's instructions, as likewise at 147.23–24.

147.27 **3f[a]th[oms] and 4f[a]th[oms]** Respectively, references to the depth of the river: 18–24 ft (5.48–7.31 m).

147.28 **Lawson river** The river was also called the Alima; its present-day name is the Mbali. A contemporary source notes it as 'a tortuous outlet – much blocked by sandbanks': H. H. Johnson, *The River Congo; from its Mouth to Bólóbó* (1884).

148.25–26 **marked A in sketch** The 'sketch' is described on 149.2–7.

148.28 **Eng[lish] Mission** The English missionary and explorer the Revd George Grenfell (1849–1906), who arrived in the Congo in 1878, founded the Baptist mission at Bolobo in 1888, witnessing almost daily killings for witchcraft on his arrival in post. His activities in the Congo, including tireless exploration, spanned nearly thirty years. Supervisor of Baptist missions, he often found himself in conflict with Belgian authorities and at times faced hostile natives.

150.23 **Remarkable. Islands.** Beginning at 'passing Mission P[oin]$^{\underline{t}}$' (148.20–21), Conrad charts the Congo through a widening of the river – to five or six miles (8 or 9.6 km) – and records his reaction after stopping for the night (147.16–17*n.*). The *Roi des Belges* passes through a broad expanse of the river with islands bearing such names as Esenga Bokaka, Papyrus and Hippopotamus. This section begins near the American Baptist Mission Union at Bwemba and passes Bolobo, the Ubangi river (in French, varyingly, Oubangi, Ou-bangi or Oubanghi) and the Roman Catholic French mission north of Bolobo. See 'Heart of Darkness':

On silvery sandbanks hippos and alligators sunned themselves side by side; the broadening waters flowed through a mob of wooded islands. You lost your way on that river as you would in a desert and butted all day long against shoals trying to find the channel till you thought yourself bewitched and cut off for ever from everything you had known once ... (*Youth* (2010), p. 77.11–16)

151.13–14 **F[ren]$^{\underline{ch}}$mission** The Roman Catholic mission located near Irebu, where the Ubangi joins the Congo.

151.25   **Irebu** The site of a government station, Irebu was in a highly populous area and a centre of trade. Stanley describes it as 'a Venice of the Congo, seated in the pride of its great numbers between the dark waters of the Lukanga and the deep brown channels of the parent stream': *The Congo and the Founding of Its Free State*, II, 21.

151.26–27   **R[iver Oubangi]** The Ubangi, which flows approximately 1,400 miles (2,240 km) when joined in its upper reaches to the Uele river, enters the Congo at Irebu.

151.28   **S[and]B[an]ks** Sandbanks are recalled in 'Heart of Darkness' as follows:

We had just floundered ... round a bend when I saw an islet, a mere grassy hummock of bright green in the middle of the stream ... I perceived it was the head of a long sand-bank or rather of a chain of shallow patches stretching down the middle of the river. They were discoloured, just awash, and the whole lot were seen just under the water exactly as a man's backbone is seen running down the middle of his back under the skin. (*Youth* (2010), p. 88.8–16)

152.3   **XXIII XXIII.A.** Points of reference on the chart Conrad was using jump from XVIII to XXIII, and two and a half leaves are blank, presumably a gap in note-taking. The last identifiable place before this gap is Irebu, situated on the mainland beside a narrow river channel that separates the mainland from a long island, the later of which obscures the major portion of the Congo river. The next identifiable place discernible on Grenfell's map is XXIII (152.14) – 'The river opens suddenly disclosing more islands –' – a group of islands in midstream after passing Ibata and Palm Islands and heading towards the very large island marked Bolia, in the middle of the river and not far from the equator.

152.5   **Thursday. 14th Augst** The third specific date. Two other passages (147.16–17 and 150.19) suggest that the recording of specific days has ended as the ship approaches the SAB's 'Equateur' station.

153.13   **V[i]ll[a]ge of Ikongo – Bad** Ikongo (also Ikengo and thus in its present-day spelling) lies just south of the equator.

153.14   **X[X]VII** Possibly an error for XXVII.

153.20–21   **your P[or]t hand** That is, the port (or left hand) side, the formula influenced by nautical terminology.

153.27   **the Am[erican] Mission** The American Baptist Missionary Union station at Bolengi (in French, Bolenge) near the equator. The ship's company probably spent the evening at the SAB's 'Equateur' Station. For details of the Mission and on missionary activity generally in this area of the Congo, see *The Encyclopædia of Missions: Descriptive, Historical, Biographical, Statistical, with a Full Assortment of Maps, a Complete Bibliography, and Lists of Bible Versions*, ed. Edwin Munsell Bliss (1891).

153.33   **Bangala** A station, also Nouvelle Anvers ('New Antwerp'), with a Roman Catholic Mission established by the Scheut Fathers (146.23*n*.), 150 miles (240 km) north of the equator about halfway to the destination at Stanley Falls.

154.2   **Charts in N[or]th Lat[itu]de** The ship crosses the equator, entering the northern hemisphere. Conrad's more frequent use of roman numerals north of the equator suggests that he had a more definitive chart for that area than the one available south of the equator.

154.3 **Saturday – 16th Augth** [*sic*]. **1890** – This is the last recorded date in 'Up-river Book', marking the beginning of Conrad's river journey in the northern hemisphere. It was entered three days before arriving at Bangala, where 'Up-river Book' ends.

154.6 **State Station** At Coquilhatville (present-day Mbandaka), a produce-collecting centre just north of the SAB station near the confluence of the Congo and Ruki (Rouki in French), named after the Belgian soldier and civil servant, Governor-General of the Congo Free State (1891–2), Camille-Aimé Coquilhat (1853–91), whose explorations are detailed in *Sur le Haut-Congo* (1888).

154.13 **Berouki R[iver]** Conrad may have misunderstood the name. Grenfell refers to the Berouki river as the 'Ruki or Juapa', the former name perhaps the most frequently used in contemporary accounts.

154.16 **I.N.** This is the first location on the chart in North latitude, that is, north of the equator.

156.19 **mentionned** This spelling error, influenced by the French *mentionné*, is characteristic. Cf., for example, 'I have mentionned in a short paper written two years ago': 'An Introduction to Thomas Beer's *Stephen Crane*' (MS leaf 2); 'Faculty to extend tenancy (on say, three months notice) might be mentionned': to J. B. Pinker, 26 February 1919 (*Letters*, VI, 372); 'in case of the two men mentionned above': to Eric S. Pinker, [January 1923] (*Letters*, VIII, 17).

156.20–23 **m[ai]ⁿ land ... M[ai]ⁿ L[an]^d** From this point until re-entering the 'Main River' (161.23), frequent references are made to 'Mainland' and 'main shore'. The river is broad here, often more than 5 miles (8 km) wide, and filled with many islands, some 15 miles (24 km) or more long.

157.18 [*A sketch ... reach of the river*] The Loulanga (also Lulanga and Lulonga) river passage. Charted here is a narrow channel between a long island at the mouth of the Loulanga and the main shore ('narrow appearance' (158.22) and 'The back island passage through <u>Lulanga</u>' (159.11)). Near the passage is a Congo Bolobo Mission. Accompanying the narrative are seven pages of charts detailing directions around obstacles such as sandbanks, snags, stones and small islands. The Loulanga passage extends north, weaving its way between two long islands and the shore to approximately 0° 51′ N latitude. Exploration of this section of the Congo and its estuaries was in its infancy. Grenfell records on his 1889 map that the Lulongo was first explored by cartographers on the steamer *Peace* in 1885.

158.5–6 **L^d elbow** The 'L' is a 90° angle with an arc drawn in it.

158.7 **there is 3 islands** The grammar is influenced by French: 'Il y a trois isles.'

158.32 **French Factory** Later abbreviated as 'F. F.' and 'F^{ch} F^{ry}'. (For this specifically West African term, see 123.16–17*n*.) The ship's company spent the night here, leaving after noon the next day. The French factory was particularly involved in obtaining rubber, a major export of the Congo Free State.

160.2 **Pass channel** This channel is charted on one of the six maps accompanying the narrative.

161.23   **Main River** Having navigated the narrow Loulanga passage – between the island and the main shore – the *Roi des Belges* re-entered the main river, halting for an overnight rest-stop. The direction of the 'Main River' is indicated by an arrow pointing NNE.

162.18   **shallow water (K[och])** Captain Koch's continuing instruction is noted.

163.18–20   **Excellent wooding ... Left 11.30** After moving upstream for almost eleven hours, the *Roi des Belges* stopped for the evening. Beyond the Loulanga passage, no more specific place-names are given, reference being made only to roman numerals on the chart used.

168.4–8   **Coming ... passage** This is the upper end of the northern bank passage, the final entry before reaching Bangala, where, according to *Mouvement Géographique* ('Le Port de Bangala Mouvement du 11 juillet au 13 octobre 1890', cited in *CWW*, p. 377), the *Roi des Belges* arrived on 19 August, departing for Stanley Falls the next day. The ship's company and passengers spent three nights on the river after leaving the French factory at Loulanga passage (162.10, 163.20, 166.10). The *Roi des Belges* averaged about 35 miles (56 km) daily on her up-river voyage (Miłobędzki, p. 53).

UNCOLLECTED ESSAYS

THE SILENCE OF THE SEA

171.3–5   **five years ... very page ... Daily Mail** Conrad's essay 'Overdue and Missing', collected in *The Mirror of the Sea* (1906), had appeared on the *Daily Mail*'s leader page under the title '"Missing!": The Passing of a Ship at Sea' on 8 March 1904 (p. 4).

171.6   **feelings remembered in tranquillity** Cf. 'Poetry is the spontaneous overflow of powerful feelings: it takes its origin from emotion recollected in tranquillity': William Wordsworth, 'Preface' to *Lyrical Ballads* (1802).

171.8   **narrow escape** An allusion to Conrad's sighting an ice-floe, 'a fragment, but still big enough to sink a ship', whilst serving in the *Highland Forest* (see 'Chronology'), not referred to by name in 'Overdue and Missing' but by the periphrasis 'a Clyde-built barque of 1,000 tons' (*The Mirror of the Sea*, p. 60).

171.19   **So ... beginning** A possible echo of the prayer of the Christian Church known as the Doxology: 'As it was in the beginning, is now and ever shall be, world without end'.

171.34   **anxiety ... Waratah** Sometimes referred to as 'Australia's *Titanic*', the 500-foot Lund's Blue Anchor Line twin-screw steamer of 9,000 tons disappeared at the end of July 1909, en route from Durban to Cape Town, with her 119 crew and 92 passengers, her fate remaining a mystery for some weeks.

172.14   **six weeks overdue** Having departed from Melbourne on 1 July 1909 on her homeward voyage (her second), the *Waratah* left Durban on 26 July in bad weather. Expected in Cape Town on the 29th, she never arrived. Cruisers were sent to look for her in August and September 1909. In December 1910, an official

Board of Trade inquiry was convened at Caxton Hall, London, to investigate her loss.

172.20–21 **water-tight bulkheads** Long used by Chinese shipwrights, water-tight bulkheads (internal partitions) did not, however, feature in European ship-design until the mid nineteenth century. In *Lord Jim*, the *Patna* has only one, and that dangerously weakened by rust. Isambard Brunel's *Great Eastern*, launched in 1857, had a system of transverse and longitudinal bulkheads creating twelve water-tight compartments. The *Mauretania*, launched in 1906, had 175 such compartments, designed to keep the ship afloat even in the event of drastic collision, and the *Titanic*, which sank three years after Conrad wrote this article, had sixteen.

172.26 **steamship *President*** The SS *President* made only two round trips between Liverpool and New York in 1840, and sailed from New York for Liverpool on 11 March 1841, never to be heard from again. Aboard her were 136 passengers and crew. It was assumed that she foundered in a storm or struck an iceberg.

172.32 **steamship *Arizona*** The Guion Line's *Arizona* bound for Liverpool from New York struck an iceberg head-on on 7 November 1879 off the Newfoundland Banks, about 300 miles (480 km) from St John's. Possibly the largest then afloat, the ship of 5,600 tons was travelling at 15 knots. Although damaged, she proved water-tight and made port unaided. Conrad also recalls this ship in 'Some Reflexions on the Loss of the *Titanic*', *Notes on Life and Letters* (2004), p. 172.24.

173.23 **Agulhas Bank** A broad and shallow part of the continental shelf at the very tip of Africa where the warm Indian Ocean and cold Atlantic Ocean meet, a convergence yielding treacherous sailing conditions. The bank extends for 160 miles (256 km) south of Cape Agulhas and then falls away steeply to the abyssal plain.

173.25–28 **August ... 1884 ... The vessel** Conrad was then second mate in the *Narcissus*. As she is on record as having passed St Helena on 19 August 1884, the incident, dramatized in *The Nigger of the 'Narcissus'*, would have occurred in early August.

174.1 **not deeply loaded** Some accounts suggest that the *Waratah* was, in fact, top heavy, and the official inquiry suggested that she may have capsized. On her first homeward voyage, the captain was sufficiently concerned about her stability to have her loaded under his direct supervision.

174.6 **another steamer overdue** Possibly the *Seestern*, a 539-ton steamer registered in the Bismarck Archipelago and owned by the German government. British and Australian ships joined in the search for her. See *The Times*, 27 July 1909, p. 17.

174.10 **lately ... Atlantic liner** Possibly an allusion to a recent incident involving the Cunard liner *Lucania*, which had caught fire in dock in Liverpool and was severely disabled, having taken on considerable water during the attempt to extinguish the fire. Her watertight bulkhead was credited with preventing further damage – 'Her second-class quarters ... together with the whole of the after part of the ship, including the engine-room, escaped injury. Indeed, the flames were checked from a sternwards course by her engine-room bulkhead': 'Fire on board the *Lucania*', *The Times*, 16 August 1909, p. 6.

AUTHOR'S NOTE TO *YOUTH* AND *GASPAR RUIZ*

175.4   **my first contribution ... "Maga."** 'Karain: A Memory' was published in the November 1897 issue of *Blackwood's Edinburgh Magazine*, familiarly known as 'Maga'. The story was collected in *Tales of Unrest* (1898).

175.5–6   **first appearance ... Marlow** This character is also the narrator of 'Heart of Darkness' (1899), *Lord Jim* (1900) and *Chance* (1914).

175.16   **dæmon** An inner or attendant spirit, often associated with the genius of creativity.

175.26–27   **occupation ... gone** See 45.12 *n.*

175.28–30   **Solomonian sense ... spirit** King Solomon delivered many aphorisms on the vanity of human wishes (see Proverbs 1–29). Also recalled here is 'I have seen all the works that are done under the sun; and, behold, all *is* vanity and vexation of spirit': Ecclesiastes i.14.

175.30   **discreet, understanding man** Perhaps once a commonplace phrase; cf. 'so deeming it unbecoming a discreet understanding man': *Winter-evening Amusement; being a Collection of Diverting Tales* (1815), Pt 1, p. 44; 'One of them has a preacher, ordained in the dissenting way, residing among them, a discreet, understanding man': Francis L. Hawks, *Documentary History of the Protestant Episcopal Church in the United States of America* (1864); 'I have found Sir Cyrill Wyche to be a very discreet understanding man': Royal Historical Society, *Camden Third Series* (1913), p. 132.

175.31–32   **very well received** Some three years before the publication of 'Youth' in book form, the critic and man of letters A. T. Quiller-Couch and the novelist Arnold Bennett, who had read the story in *Blackwood's Edinburgh Magazine*, praised it. Conrad probably mentioned these reviews to William Blackwood's literary editor, David S. Meldrum, who, in January 1899, wrote to his chief, 'It is wonderful to hear how generally Conrad's "Youth" is spoken of as one of the finest things recently published': *Joseph Conrad: Letters to William Blackwood and David S. Meldrum*, ed. William Blackburn (1958), pp. 43–4. For a detailed discussion of the story's reception, see 'Introduction', *Youth* (2010).

175.35   **Australia ... first command** Conrad's command of the *Otago*, which lasted from January 1888 to March 1889, began with a voyage from Bangkok to Singapore and from there to Australia. It provides significant material for *The Shadow-Line*.

176.9   **story "Gaspar Ruiz"** Originally published as 'Gaspar Ruiz: The Story of a Guerilla Chief' in the July–October 1906 issues of the *Pall Mall Magazine* and, in America, in the *Saturday Evening Post* from 28 July to 18 August 1906, the story was collected in *A Set of Six* (1908).

176.22–23   **book of travels ... 1830** *Extracts from a Journal, Written on the Coasts of Chili, Peru, and Mexico, in the Years 1820, 1821, 1822* by Captain Basil Hall, RN. The book was published in Edinburgh in two volumes in 1824. Conrad identifies his source (and also misdates the book's publication) in his 'Author's Note' to *A Set of Six*.

176.24   **real name** A Don Gaspar Ruiz is passingly referred to in Hall's *Extracts from a Journal* (I, 334) in his citing of the Chilean government's official gazette on Vicente Benavides (1785–1822). Conrad adopted these names for his own purposes.

176.29–31   **visited ... Englishmen** Cf. 'It was in consequence of their report of Benavides's proceedings made to Sir Thomas Hardy, the Commander-in-chief, that he deemed it proper to send a ship, to rescue, if possible, the remaining unfortunate captives at Arauco': Hall, *Extracts from a Journal*, II, 292.

176.32   **less than a full page** A lapse in memory: the adventures, fate and execution of Vicente Benavides are dealt with in several chapters, and the Chilean government's gazette on him is published in full.

177.2   **my boyhood's reading** This somewhat awkward formulation is characteristically Conradian. Cf. 'the childhood's recollections': 'Anatole France', *Notes on Life and Letters* (2004), p. 36.8; 'my boyhood's dreams': The *Torrens*: A Personal Tribute' (22.37); 'a childhood's friend', *Suspense*, Pt II, ch. 3 (p. 112).

INTRODUCTORY NOTE TO *A HUGH WALPOLE ANTHOLOGY*

178.5   **Hugh Walpole's work** A novelist of popular 'middle-brow' fiction, Hugh Seymour Walpole (1884–1941; knighted 1937), born in New Zealand and educated at Cambridge, was widely and well connected in the literary scene of his day, counting not only Conrad but also Arnold Bennett, Henry James, H. G. Wells and Virginia Woolf among his friends and acquaintances. Walpole had produced a short critical book on Conrad in 1916, and he and Conrad became acquainted in 1918. Highly popular in its day, particularly the Rogue Herries series, Walpole's writing fell into rapid eclipse after his death. For a detailed treatment of the personal side of the Conrad–Walpole relationship, see J. H. Stape, 'Sketches from the Life: The Conrads in the Diaries of Hugh Walpole', *The Conradian*, 34, no. 1 (2009), 163–84.

178.8   **Sophistication** Not used in its modern sense of the quality or fact of being sophisticated but corresponding at least approximately to the *OED*'s second definition: 'the use or employment of sophistry; the process of investing with specious fallacies or of misleading by means of these; falsification'.

FOREWORD TO *LANDSCAPES OF CORSICA AND IRELAND* BY A. S. KINKEAD

179.5   **exhibition** The exhibition of fifty-three pictures by the Irish artist A. S. Kinkead (179.6*n.*) was held at the United Arts Gallery, 23a Old Bond Street, London, during November and December 1921.

179.6   **the artist** Alice Sarah Kinkead (1871–1926), born in Tuam, County Galway, trained in London and Paris in various media, including drawing and metal work, and settled in London. She and the Conrads met in Corsica (see 179.14*n.*), where she was on a painting trip. For a detailed account of her life and career, see Susan Jones, 'Alice Kinkead and the Conrads', *The Conradian*, 33, no. 1 (2008), 103–18.

179.13–14   **visit ... boyhood** The visit occurred some time during Conrad's years of residence in Marseilles. Arriving in September 1874, he left in April 1878, and was absent mainly on voyages to the Caribbean (December 1874 to May 1875, June to December 1875 and July 1876 to February 1877). More precise dating is impossible, as this is the only reference to the visit in his writings.

179.14   **revisiting it ... this year** Conrad and his wife Jessie arrived in Corsica from Marseilles on 1 February 1921, staying at the Grand Hôtel d'Ajaccio in the capital. They made various excursions both locally and somewhat farther afield on the island. They left again for Marseilles on 1 April, and arrived home on the 10th.

179.19   **envelope of the soul** See 31.26*n*.

179.32   *suavità de aiere* Literally, 'gentle air' (Italian). The phrase, which became conventional, alludes to a description of the talents of Leonardo da Vinci, originating in a letter to him of 14 May 1504 from the Marchesa Isabella d'Este (1474–1539), who, on asking him to paint Christ as a boy of about twelve, refers to his skill as follows: 'facto cum quella dolcezza et suavità de aiere che haveti per arte pexuliare in excellentia' ('done with that air of sweetness and suavity that your art shows so abundantly'). See Adolfo Venturi, 'Nuovi documenti su Leonardo da Vinci', *Archivio storico dell'arte* (1888), I, 45–6.

FOREWORD TO
BRITAIN'S LIFE-BOATS: THE STORY OF A CENTURY OF HEROIC SERVICE BY A. J. DAWSON

181.1–4   *Britain's Life-boats ... Service* The volume, with an introduction by the Prince of Wales, was published in early November 1923 in anticipation of the institution's centenary. Formal celebrations began at the Mansion House on 4 March 1924, exactly a century after the institution's founding, and included, in London, a Centenary Life-boat Day in May, a Life-boat Ball in June and a Life-boat Centenary Dinner in July. Various festivities were held in other cities and county towns, particularly those on the coast.

181.5   **A. J. Dawson** Major A(lec) J(ohn) Dawson (1872–1951), a novelist and traveller, was a noted authority on Empire and colonial matters. He served throughout the First World War, was active in recruiting and intelligence, and was awarded the Croix de Guerre and an MBE. He was briefly Director of Information in Bombay. Conrad was personally acquainted with him, but friendlier with his brother, Major Ernest Dawson.

181.8–9   **Royal National Life-boat Institution** Founded on 4 March 1824 as the Royal National Institution for the Preservation of Life from Shipwreck at a public meeting at the City of London Tavern, the charity (renamed in 1854) has as its aim the preservation of life at sea through the establishment of life-boat stations maintained by volunteers and supported by public subscription. The Archbishop of Canterbury, the Bishop of London and William Wilberforce were among those who, under royal patronage, took a leading part in the charity's formation.

181.14   **twenty years' service** Conrad's service in British ships began in 1878 and formally ended in 1894 (see 'Chronology' for details).

181.23   **boats of characteristic shape** That is, small life-boat-shaped money-boxes designed to hold contributions made by the public. These were displayed in venues such as shops and post offices, so as to encourage and facilitate donations.

181.24–25   **drop ... paying-off days** Conrad is on record as having enthusiastically supported the institution. His son John recalled:

My father had the greatest admiration for the lifeboat service, and whenever he came ashore after a voyage put money in a lifeboat box. There is a story – I don't know whether or not it is true – that when he first landed in England at Lowestoft he put all he had in one. Certainly, he always made me put my coppers in. When we used to go on holiday, he used to spend a great amount of time at the lifeboat station. (*The Times*, 16 October 1968, p. 10)

Under the terms of the Merchant Shipping Act, payment was not immediately made upon the cessation of a voyage and the landing of a ship's crew at dock, the paying-off of the crew being, at times, a ceremonial and public occasion. Conrad fictionalizes this event at the end of *The Nigger of the 'Narcissus'*.

181.29   **obscure lives** Conrad declares his aim in *The Nigger of the 'Narcissus'* to be 'to present an unrestful episode in the obscure lives of a few individuals': Preface, p. viii.

GLOSSARY OF NAUTICAL TERMS

This glossary briefly explains nautical terms as well as the vocabulary related to shipping used in *Last Essays*. Definitions are provided in the context of the time-period of the late nineteenth and early twentieth century. Terms in general currency (for example, 'deck' and 'rudder') are not glossed, but an attempt has been made to address the needs of various readers, including those approaching Conrad from language backgrounds other than English.

Readers needing greater detail than that provided below may usefully consult the following: on Merchant Service terms, C. W. T. Layton's *Dictionary of Nautical Words and Terms* (1955), and on naval vocabulary, Admiral W. H. Smyth's *The Sailor's Word-Book: An Alphabetical Digest of Nautical Terms, including some more especially military and scientific, but useful to seamen; as well as archaisms of early voyages, etc.*, revised by Vice-Admiral Sir E. Belcher (1867; rpt 1991).

A. B.s	able-bodied seamen: men who can perform all duties of seamen, a rating ranking above ordinary seaman
abaft	in the rear of, or behind
aloft	above, overhead; also, anywhere about the upper yards, masts and rigging
approaches	the area of a harbour or bay near a port or landing-place, lying outside the destination proper
astern	behind; towards the stern, or rear, part of a ship
barks	formerly, small ships, but, in modern use, applied poetically or rhetorically to any sailing vessel
beam	horizontal transverse timber or an iron or steel girder that supports the deck and holds the vessel together; the breadth of a ship; thus, a ship 'on her beam ends' is one that has heeled over to such an extent that her deck beams are nearly vertical
blue-jacket	enlisted person in the navy, so designated for the colour of the dress uniform
boatswain	(pronounced 'bo'sun') a trustworthy and experienced petty officer, the foreman of the deck seamen, and in some ships a day worker (that is, not participating in watches); the seaman in charge of caring for the ship's boats, sailing and rigging, and responsible for calling the crew to duty
bow	foremost end of a ship, the opposite of stern
bowers	anchors, usually two ('best-bower' and 'small-bower') carried on the bow of a ship; also, the bower anchor's cable

braces	ropes or lines attached to the end of a yard, to swing or to trim the sail
brought to the wind	to have put the helm to leeward
bunt	central or hanging portion of a square sail when furled; hence, buntlines used to gather in the sail
capstan	upright mechanical device turned by bars or levers for winding in heavy ropes or cables
caravel	generally, a large masted ship of the sixteenth and seventeenth centuries, varying according to time period and country as to its specific configuration
catting	securing the anchor to the cathead (the timber attached to the ship's bow to keep the anchor from hitting the ship when it is raised)
chocks	cradles in which a ship's boats are secured on deck
clew-garnet	tackle for hauling the clew or corner of a course, or lowest square sail, to the yard when furling
clew-lines	ropes attached to the lower corner of a sail
clipper	generic name used to describe types of fast sailing ships, so named, according to popular legend, because they could 'clip' the time taken by regular packet ships
coaming	raised border around a hatchway or other opening on deck to prevent water from running below
coasters	ships engaged in carrying cargo or passengers from port to port along a coast
companion-way	ladder or stairway connecting two decks, or a covering over the entrance to a ship's stairway
courses	sails that hang from the lower yards of a square-rigged ship, usually the foresail, mainsail and mizzen (crossjack) sail
coxswain	(pronounced 'coxsun') the sailor who steers a ship's boat or life-boat
cross-jack course	(pronounced 'cro'jack' course) sail on the mizzen mast of a square-rigged ship
cross-jack yard	(pronounced 'cro'jack' yard) lower yard of the mizzenmast
davits	small cranes usually paired, either hand-driven or mechanical, for lowering a ship's boat(s) into the water
dead reckoning	method of finding a ship's position without celestial reckoning; that is, based on distance covered (using estimated speed) and courses steered by a compass, with corrections for estimated currents
dead weight capacity	total weight (also dwt: dead weight tonnage) of a ship's crew, passengers, cargo, fuel and other items
deck-house	house, room or box on the deck
dinghy	small rowing-boat, often carried or towed by a larger vessel
drifters	small fishing vessels that operate in home waters, originally fitted with sails but today more commonly using

diesel engines; unlike trawlers, which drag their nets or lines along with them, drifters let their nets go with the tides

dug-out canoe made from a hollowed-out log

ensign flag carried by a ship to indicate her nationality

falls the entire length of rope in a tackle (one or more ropes in a pulley block to assist in lifting heavy loads); the rope in the block is called the 'standing part', the opposite end is the 'hauling part'

fishing drawing up the flukes (triangular plates on each arm of the anchor) to the gunwale (the upper edge of a ship's side) to secure the anchor

fore area of the ship near the bow and the fore (forwardmost) mast

forecastle-head forward part of the forecastle (pronounced 'foksul' and sometimes spelt fo'c's'le), which in merchant vessels is the forward part of the vessel

forecastlemen men stationed on the forecastle, the forward part of a merchant vessel where sailors live, either below the deck or in a compartment above it; later, crew were accommodated elsewhere in merchant ships, and in steamers at the stern, the space retaining the name 'forecastle'

fore-deck the portion of the deck in a ship's bow; generally applied in wooden ships to that part of the deck where the planks begin to arch inward and extend to the prow

fore-end fore part or front of a vessel

forerigging a ship's lines in the forward, or bow, section; rigging in general refers to the lines used on a ship to support masts, yards and the bowsprit (standing rigging); and to move and control sail (running rigging); the term 'her lines' refers to the plans of the hull and hence the shape of the hull

foresail (pronounced 'forsul') the course, or lowest sail, on the foremast

fore upper topsail the second sail above the course (or bottom) sail on the foremast; 'upper topsail' (pronounced 'topsul') because, as ships were enlarged in the last days of sail to carry more canvas, the topsail came to have both a 'lower' and 'upper' sail to expedite handling

fore-yard-arm either end of the lowest long wooden or metal spar on the foremast

harbour watch spell of duty whilst the ship is inactive and in port, and thus less demanding than the usual watch

hawsers ropes or cables used in towing

headsails (pronounced 'headsuls') sails set between the foremast and bowsprit

heavy sea	a storm-tossed sea, or nearly so, consisting of large swells and turbulent or gusty winds
helmsman	seaman assigned to steering the ship, usually by a wheel that controls the rudder
hove up	moved (or move) to a certain position; 'hove' is the past tense of 'heave'
Indiamen	sailing ships engaged in trade with the Indian subcontinent, usually of large tonnage and robust appearance
jib boom	spar that extends from the bowsprit (a large spar running out from the vessel's stem – the curved upright bow timber into which the bow's planks are joined) to which the tack (the lower forward corner of a fore-and-aft sail) of the jib (a triangular head sail) is attached
kedge	small anchor used in mooring to keep a ship steady and free from the bower anchor as the ship rides in a harbour, especially when the tide changes
keelson	structure or timbers parallel with and above the keel and fastened to it by long bolts passing through the floor timbers
King's ships	vessels belonging to a small, select group of Royal Naval commands flying the sovereign's colours and thus carrying the monarch's personal authority; formerly employed on missions of national importance, but today a looser term and referring to ships used on ceremonial occasions
lanyard	line or short rope
lee helm	lee is the sheltered side of a ship facing away from the wind, and the helm, the tiller or wheel controlling the rudder; thus, the sheltered side of the wheel; also refers to the rudder angle away from the fore and aft line of the vessel needed to keep her on a particular heading
log book	official record of a ship's activities, kept by the first mate and recording the events, distances travelled and Notices to Mariners in a succinct, unadorned style and with precision as regards fact; the estimated runs recorded in the deck log book gave each watch the basis for the dead reckoning position at noon or any other chosen time
lower fore-topsail	first sail above the lower yard of the foremast
lower main-topsail	first sail above the lower yard of the mainmast
luffed up	sailing or steering towards the direction from which the wind is blowing
lying off	standing at some distance from the shore or from another ship
main	principal mast and the area immediately surrounding it; in a three-masted ship, the central mast

main upper topsail	second sail above the course (or bottom) sail on the main, or centre, mast of a three-masted ship
main yard	wooden spar slung at its centre from the mainmast
mean draft	half the sum of the forward and after drafts or depth of water at which a vessel is at any time
midshipman	in merchant ships, a title for trainee officers or a socially superior kind of boy officer whose parents paid large premiums; in the navy, an officer above a cadet and below a sub-lieutenant (since 1794 new midshipmen have been candidates for commission as officers)
mizzen-mast	sternmost mast in a three-masted ship, or the third mast of a four- or five-masted ship
mizzen-topmen	a ship's most agile and talented seamen stationed in the tops (the platform surrounding the head of the lower mast) to work the upper sails
mizzen-topsail	in a three-masted ship, the sail above the lower yard on the aftermost mast
petty officer	in the Merchant Service, one of the ratings under the category of mate and typically the bo'sun, carpenter and sailmaker; in the navy, a non-commissioned officer
poop	from Latin *puppis* ('stern'), the short, aftermost deck raised above the quarterdeck, or the open deck behind the mizzen-mast – such decks being usually found only in very large vessels
poop ladder	stairway leading to the poop deck
promenade-decks	upper decks of a passenger ship, allowing for leisurely walking, relaxation and socializing
quarter-boats	boats stored on the upper parts of a ship's side between the stern and main chains (hardware used to secure the rigging of the main mast to the outside of a ship)
rail	narrow ornamental plank(s) on the upper works of a ship
rigged fore and aft	sails set lengthwise (the jib, staysail and gaff sails), in contrast to square-rigged sails (set athwartship or across the hull, possibly at right angles to lengthwise)
rigging	all ropes, wires or chains used to support the masts and yards, and for hoisting or lowering sails, or trimming them to the wind
royals	small sails above the topgallant sail, used in light and favourable winds
saloon	in a passenger ship, a large cabin for the common use of passengers, but occasionally only for first-class (or 'saloon') passengers

second officer	the third in command (also called second mate) in a Merchant Service ship
sheets	ropes or chains attached to the lower part of the sail, which regulate the angle the sail is set in relation to the wind
short canvas	minimal sails unfurled as ships move slowly through the water
skids	beams or reserve spars kept in a ship and used as a support for the ship's boats
spar	stout wooden pole used for a mast, gaff or boom
square-rigged masts	masts with square sails placed at right angles to the length of a ship
staysails	(pronounced 'staysuls') triangular fore-and-aft sails hoisted on a stay (a rope bracing a mast); thus, the sails set between masts
steam winches	steam-powered machines having one or more barrels or drums on which to coil a rope or chain for hauling or hoisting; a winch is a more elaborate windlass
stern cabins	housing (utility) units at a ship's rear
stock anchor	anchor with a horizontal cross-bar at the top set at right angles to the arms and flukes at the bottom
stream	anchor at the ship's stern, used along with bower anchors when moored in areas where there is insufficient room for the ship to swing freely with the tide
tackles	pulleys or other arrangements consisting of one or more ropes and pulley-blocks to increase the power of a rope to raise or lower heavy items
tacks	ropes used to hold in place the forward lower corner of a course; a tack can also be the lower forward corner of a fore-and-aft-sail or, on square sails, the lower weather (windward) corner of the sail and the rope holding it down
timber	one of the curved pieces of wood springing upward and outward from the keel; a rib
toggled in	a toggle is a short, wooden pin used to connect two ropes so that they can be disconnected quickly, especially the topsails in case of emergency
tonnage	a ship's cargo capacity; according to the Merchant Shipping Act of 1854, the ship's entire internal cubic capacity in tons of 100 cubic feet each, determined by a formula established in the Act (hence, net tonnage, gross tonnage, etc.)
top-gallantsails	third sails above the deck, above the topsails
topsails	(pronounced 'topsuls') the second sail above the deck, set above the course; at one time, the uppermost sail in a square-rigged vessel
trim	the act of setting the sails; also the fore-and-aft angle of a floating ship to the horizontal, by the stern or by the head

truck	small wooden cap at the top of a flagstaff or masthead, usually having holes in it for reeving flag or signal halyards
upper main-topsail	second sail above the lower yard of the mainmast
waist-cadets	seamen who work in the middle part of the upper deck of a ship, between the quarterdeck and the forecastle; their labour for the most part is unskilled, such as hauling on ropes
ward-room	in a warship, the common recreation area and dining-room for commissioned officers
watch	spell of duty typically lasting four hours, beginning at midnight and again at noon; the officers and crew on duty during such a four-hour spell
water-breakers	casks or small barrels for storing drinking water
water-tight bulkhead	partition, perpendicular to a ship's fore-and-aft centre-line, usually near the bow, for preventing water from entering in the event of a collision
wearing ship	bringing a ship around by turning its head away from the wind; the opposite of tacking
windlass	machine for hoisting, usually consisting of a barrel (a revolving cylinder) to hold the rope or chain with whelps (teeth in a sprocket wheel) turned by hand spikes inserted in radial holes near each end
wool-clippers	swift sailing ships, with raking bows and three-masted square rigs, carrying wool as their main cargo
yard	long spar, usually cylindrical and tapering to the ends, designed to support and extend a square, lug or lateen sail
yard-arm	either end of a yard; square-rigged ships flew signal flags from them

MAPS

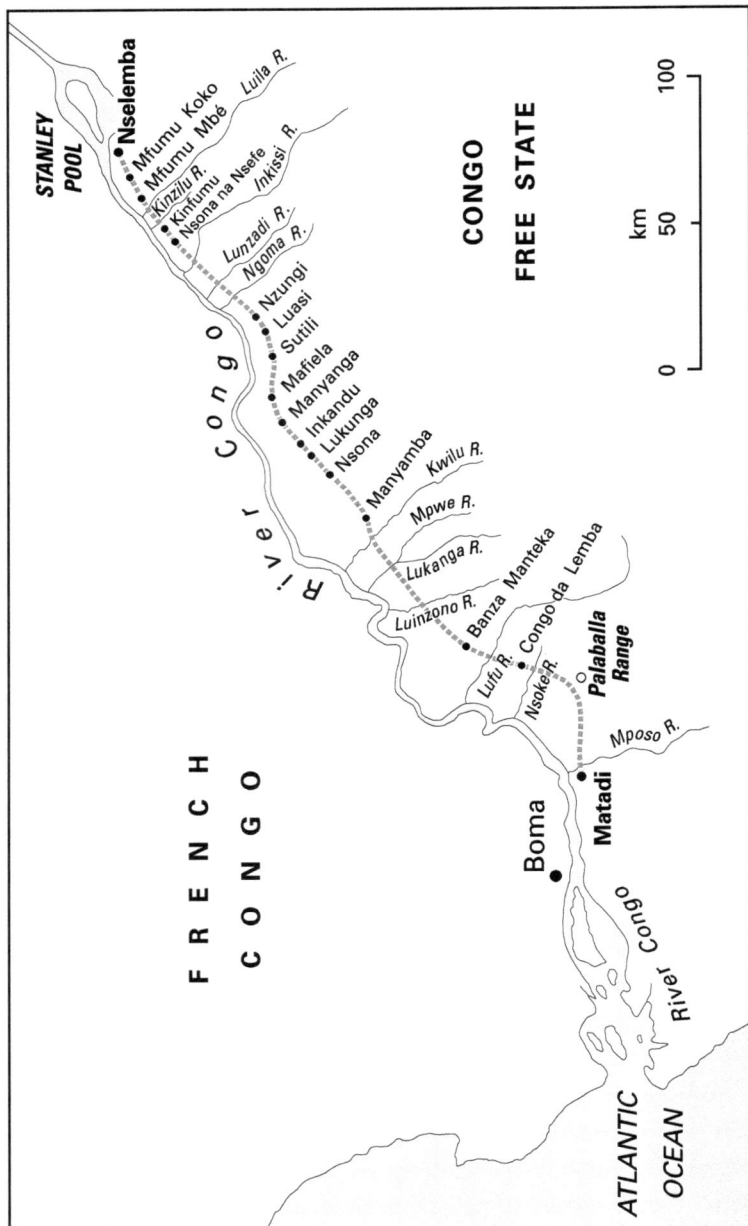

[1] Conrad's overland journey in the Congo from Matadi to Nselemba, June–August 1890

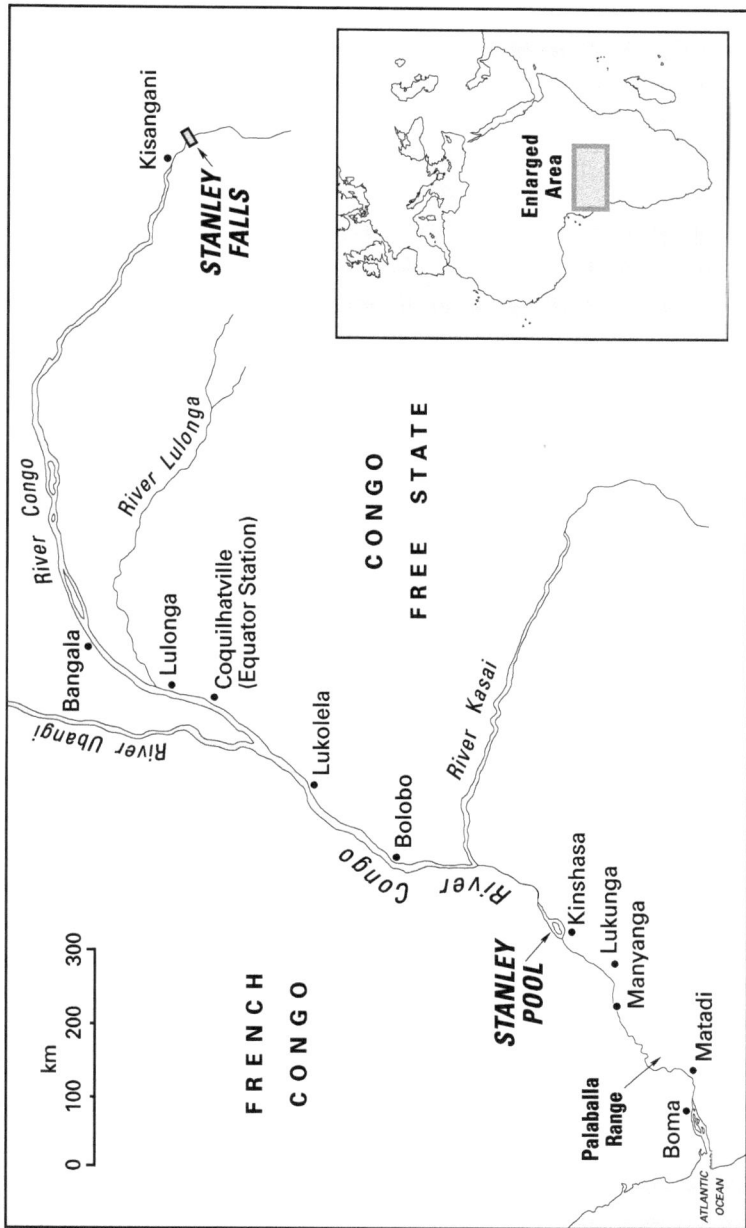

[2] Route of the *Roi des Belges*, August–September 1890

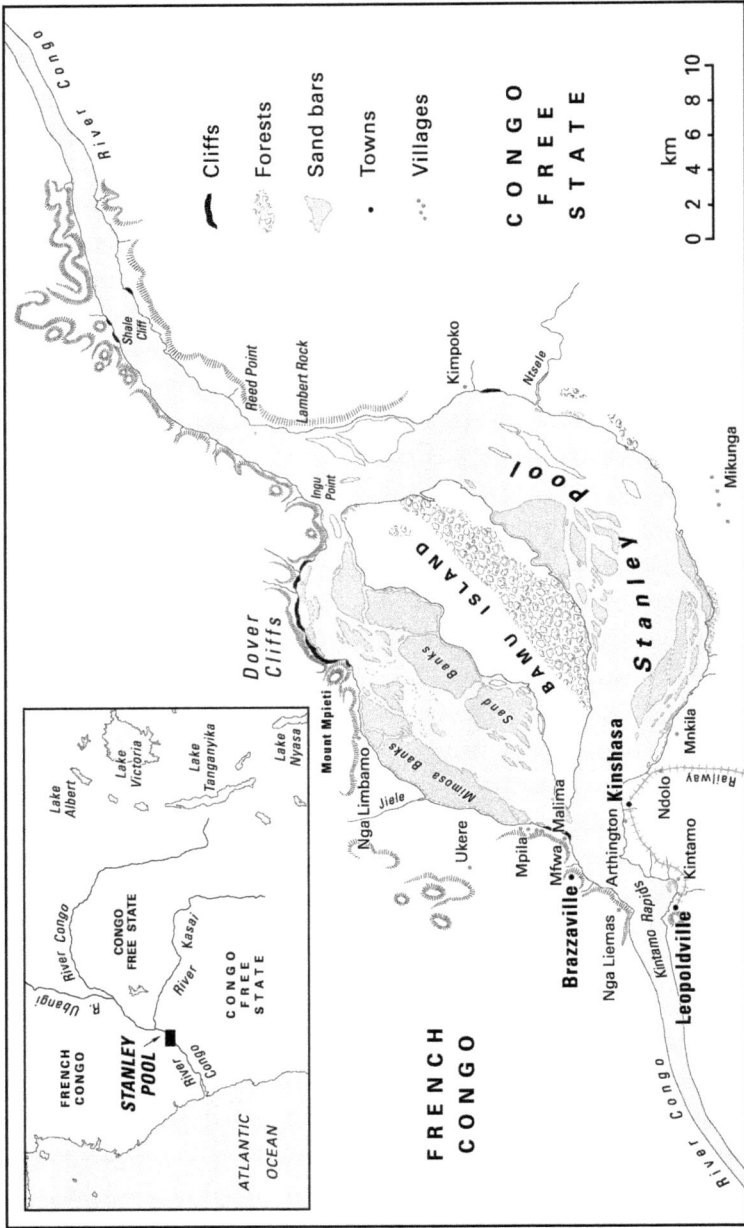

[3] Stanley Pool

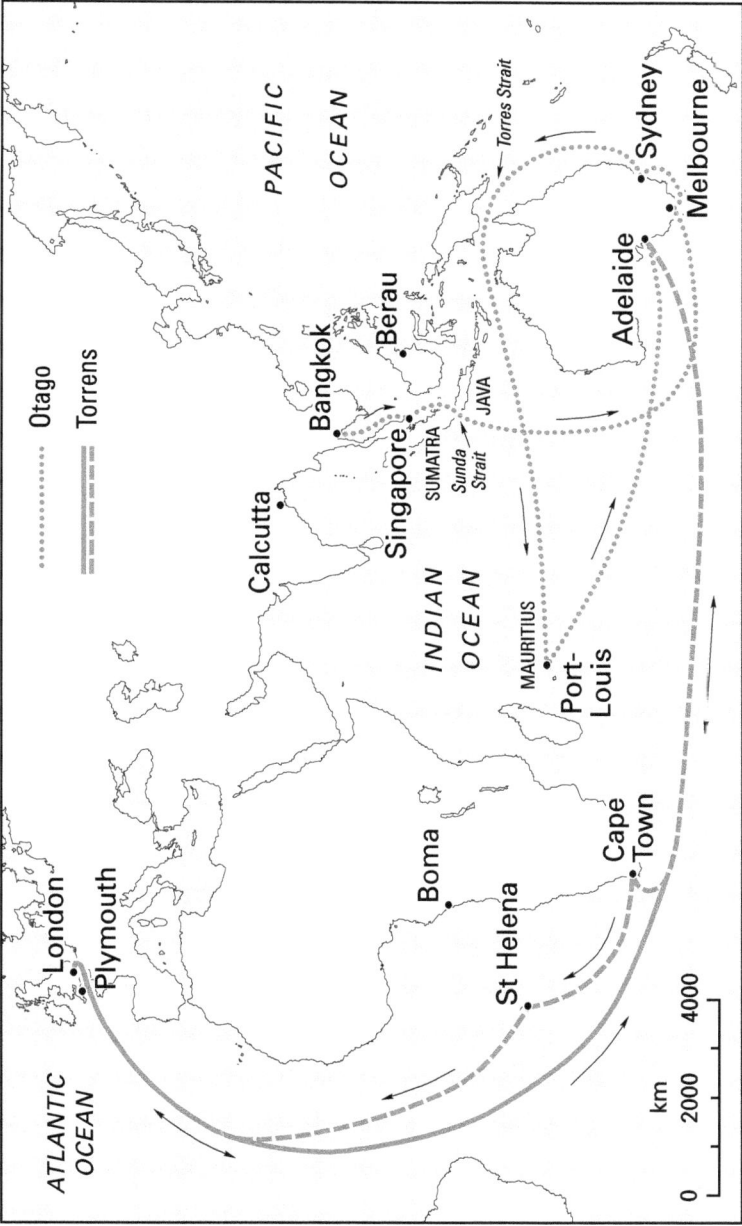

[4] Routes of the *Torrens* and the *Otago*

9 780521 190596